OPEN
10

The COMPLETE ILLUSTRATED ENCYCLOPEDIA OF THE WORLD'S MOTORCYCLES

A QUARTO BOOK

The COMPLETE ILLUSTRATED ENCYCLOPEDIA OF THE WORLD'S MOTORCYCLES

Edited by Erwin Tragatsch

Holt, Rinehart and Winston
NEW YORK

A QUARTO BOOK

Copyright © 1977 Quarto Limited

All rights reserved, including the right to
reproduce this book or portions thereof in
any form.

Published simultaneously in Canada by Holt,
Rinehart and Winston of Canada, Limited.

Library of Congress Catalog Card Number:
77-71370
ISBN: 0-03-019296-X

First Edition

Printed in Britain

10 9 8 7 6 5 4 3 2 1

I am most grateful for the assistance given to me,
especially in the matter of illustrations, by many
friends in the motorcycle industry. My particular
thanks to: Rudi Albert, Alan Blackwood, Helmut
Werner Bönsch, Curt Borgenstam, Walter Brand-
stetter, Henri Cochard, Christian Christophe, Peter
Clare, Bob Currie, Jaroslav Divišek, H. H. von
Fersen, Michael Heise, Rudolf Hiller, Ted Hodgdon,
Bob Holliday, Helmut Hütten, Basil Jones, Helmut
Krackowizer, Abramo Giovanni Luraschi, Ghislain
Mahy, Emmett Moore, Václav Petřik, Siegfried
Rauch, Karl Reese, Bernhard Reichert, Cyril J.
Scott, Peter Schneider, Dr Rolf Schrödter, Robert
Sexé, Phil Smith, Martin Stolle, Alfred Winkler,
Kurt Wörner, August Wurring and Ludwig
Zemene. Others, including Fritz Hintermüller,
Ferdinand Eichler, John Griffith and G. L. Hartner
are unfortunately no longer with us. Among
motorcycle factories which kindly assisted me are:
Ancilotti, Aspes, Benelli, Beta, BMW, Bultaco,
Can-Am (Rotax), ČZ (Motokov), DKW, Dot,
Ducati, Dunstall, Gori, Greeves, Harley-Davidson,
Hercules, Honda, Jawa (Motokov), Kawasaki,
KTM, Maico, Monark, Montesa, Motobécane,
Moto Guzzi, MV Agusta, MZ, Norton-Triumph,
Puch, SWM, Suzuki, Windhoff, Yamaha and
Zündapp. Additional illustrations came from
the magazines *Das Motorrad*, *Motociclismo*,
Radmarkt and from the archive of the author. My
thanks also to the Zweirad Museum at Neckarsulm,
West Germany, and the Zweitakt Museum in the
Augustusburg.

CONTENTS

INTRODUCTION

Triumphant moment . . . the author worked for the British firm in the 1950s

THIS ENCYCLOPEDIA lists in alphabetical sequence more than 2,500 makes of motorcycle, produced in at least 30 countries, from 1894 to the present day. The companies' commercial and sporting histories and their ranges of models, whether great or small, are discussed. Facts, figures, dates and technical details are provided. Many of the entries are illustrated, sometimes with hitherto-unpublished photographs.

Some of the early firms listed were very small, and assembled their machines entirely from bought-in parts, but all of them made production motorcycles. Companies which produced only 'one-offs', or which were merely workshops or dealers, are not included. The principal engines used by each manufacturer are detailed, and there are additional lists of important proprietary engines. There are also separate lists showing the major models of motorcycle produced throughout the world during interesting periods in the history of the industry.

I believe this to be the most comprehensive book of its kind, and I hope that it will be interesting not only to the motorcycle technician, dealer and sportsman but also to the collector, owner (past or present) or simply the enthusiast. When I began to compile my previous book *The World's Motorcycles, 1894–1963,* some of my friends in the industry suggested that I had engaged myself in an impossible task. When the book was published, it became a best-seller, filling a gap in the bookshelves of many a motorcycle enthusiast. That success led to the compilation of this much bigger book, with its extensive illustration and up-to-date information.

My involvement with motorcycles has been life-long. I have worked within the industry itself, in the motorcycle trade, in motor-sport, and in the motoring Press. My own experience, and widespread international research over a long period, have helped me fill the pages which follow. I have been helped by veteran riders, designers, manufacturers and their employees, many of them personal friends. Some of them have provided from memory details of machines which were built many decades ago.

Acquaintanceships have been renewed, and pleasant times recalled. It may have been 'impossible', but it was thoroughly enjoyable. I hope you enjoy it, too.

Erwin Tragatsch

THE STORY OF AN INDUSTRY

THE HISTORY of the motorcycle also offers a short course in design philosophy and industrial economics, with some politics thrown in.

Great pioneers like Hildebrand and Wolfmüller were clever inventors, but their design went into production without any development work. The result was that the factory went broke in a very few years. The same fate befell Colonel H. C. L. Holden's 'moto-bicycle', which had four horizontal watercooled cylinders directly driving the rear wheel. This, too, was an ingenious design, but was already obsolete before it would have gone into quantity production in 1900. In France, the Russian-born Werner brothers, Michael and Eugene, built a motorcycle to a design using De Dion proprietary engines from 52 to 70mm bore and always a 70mm stroke. The 70/70 model built in 1899 had 2·25 hp (269cc). These were smaller and lighter engines than had been used before. After 1902, they used strengthened bicycle frames, mounting the engine above the pedalling gear, and this machine became the ancestor of motorcycles as we know them today.

A practical basic design had been established, but the story of the motorcycle continued to be a story of designers and technicians who sometimes had no commercial sense. There were also designs which worked briefly but which look strange to modern eyes: the German Megola, designed by Fritz Cockerell, was clutchless and gearless, and had to be started by being pushed. It would be hope-lessly impractical, and even dangerous, in modern traffic, but more than 2000 of them were sold in the 1920s.

The founders of the great motorcycle factories had to be visionary men of great technical ability and with no small amount of idealism. The profit margin in this developing competitive business was usually lower than that in other industries. It often happened that when the founder died or retired, the factory went into decline, being managed by industrialists rather than motorcycle men: a good example of this was the Indian factory at Springfield, Massachusetts. In 1912, Indian was one of the largest motorcycle factories in the world, employing about 3,000 people on three shifts. When founder George M. Hendee retired in the mid-1920s, the factory began a long, slow decline. When it was finally bought in 1959 by Associated Motor Cycles Ltd., of London, the only thing left was the Indian name on motorcycles produced for the American market.

Designers were often people who wanted to sell their designs to others, and get on with something new. They were often less interested in the continuous development of a machine once it was in production. So it was that William Henderson created his big four-cylinder aircooled Henderson, sold it and went on to design the not dissimilar Ace. After Henderson's death in an accident in 1922, it was Arthur Lemon who continued development work on the Henderson for Ignaz Schwinn's Chicago-based bicycle company. On the other hand, sometimes a good design has been develop-ed but basically unchanged for many years because of its intrinsic excellence: the best example of this is the famous BMW twin. Since the machine was first shown in Paris in 1923, BMW has never built a twin which was not horizontally opposed, mounted transversely in the frame and which did not drive a shaft rather than a chain. The original designer was Max Friz.

The motorcycle industry, like any other, is also subject to factors outside its control. A great many factories went under during the Great Depression of the 1930s, to say nothing of the German hyper-inflation of 1923. After each of the two world wars, motorcycles were in such short supply that small companies sprang up in every country, doing well for a short time with designs which in many cases were essentially undistinguished. When Hitler gobbled up Central Europe in the late 1930s, some small producers of motorcycles disappeared because they could not be fitted into the Nazis' industrial plans.

By contrast, the Italian motorcycle industry has broken nearly every rule in the book: before the Second World War, the Italians built good machines, but did not try very hard to export them; since the war, while the Italian economy may have experienced its vicissitudes, a surprising number of relatively small producers, as well as a few big ones, have managed to stay in business. They have also continued to uphold the traditional Italian reputation for good design. There has been no lack of great designers in the Italian industry: Carlo Guzzi's designs in developed form

9

The 1920s was the boom period for the small manufacturer, though producers like BMW (left, top) had already adopted a methodical approach. Half a century later, the masters of the production line are the Japanese, with Kawasaki (bottom picture) among the leaders.

became the famous Albatross racers. Angelo Parodi, Giulo Carcano and Lino Tonti also helped to design the Moto Guzzi machines; in the mid-1950s, Carcano was designing four-cylinder and V-8 double-ohc racing machines. In the late 1950s, very fine Bianchi double-ohc vertical twins were designed by Tonti, who then went on to create transverse-mounted V-twins with shaft drive for Moto Guzzi. The six Benelli brothers and many others have contributed to the excellence of Italian machines; yet today, even the Italian industry is falling victim to the post-war trend towards industrial conglomeration.

The saddest story of all is the decline of the British motorcycle industry, for decades the world's leader. The incompetence of management, and of various governments, has seen the British motorcycle industry lose its leadership by default. For one thing, it is not possible to stay in the motorcycle business on any sizable scale unless a wide range of models is offered. In the face of Japanese competition, British factories gave up the mass-production of small machines; for some years thereafter, British superbikes were still very popular, but it was no longer economically feasible to build them.

The Japanese deserve their success, there can be no doubt about that. The Honda factory has stayed on top because it has been ready to re-invest its profits in up-to-date plant and equipment, and because Soichiro Honda does not need weeks or months of consultation with banks, Boards of Directors and numerous unions before making a decision. The character of designing has also changed: if Mike Mizumachi is responsible for the

brilliant success of the Kawasaki factory, it is also true that he has not done it single-handedly, but is the head of a brilliant team of younger men who will no doubt become famous in their own right. Times have changed. The motorcycle business is no different from any other; only people who can change with the times can stay on top.

The motorcycle factories which survived the Great Depression were those which were large and strong, and which already had networks of dealers and customers dependent on a good name for service, spare parts and so forth. The day of the committed idealist who could start his own factory on a shoe-string was past. Designers became less freelance geniuses and more valued employees of established manufacturers. Even before the Second World War, the process of combination began in which, for example, Matchless swallowed AJS to become Associated Motor Cycles which in turn took over Francis Barnett, James, Norton – and even the American Indian factory after WWII.

In the post-war years this process accelerated, until it actually became uneconomic to build motorcycles in countries with high per-capita incomes. In the 1920s, there were perhaps fifteen different companies building very good machines in the USA; eventually only Harley-Davidson was left. Even Harley had to buy the Italian Aermacchi works in order to produce comparatively small machines at competitive prices. Small countries such as The Netherlands, Belgium, Denmark and Switzerland once had notable indigenous producers; today motorcycle production in these countries is virtually nil. Nations such as Italy and Spain, which have the

design and engineering skill but which are relatively undeveloped, have thriving motorcycle industries because they are economically competitive.

The special cases are Socialist countries, such as Czechoslovakia and East Germany. Whatever else one might say about nationalized industry, these countries produce their own two-wheeled transport and they have no unemployment to speak of. Another special case is Britain, the world's leader for decades; during the 1950s, British imports spelled the end of much American competition in the industry. Yet today Britain's industry is almost finished. It is perhaps not too much to say that part of Britain's problem is that it can't decide what kind of economics it wants; certainly the measures it has taken in the motorcycle industry are half-measures. Britain has the skills, and with the fall of the Pound it should be economically competitive; one can only hope that it will have a Renaissance of spirit.

The overwhelming factor in the post-war motorcycle industry has been Japan. In 1970, Britain built about 64,500 machines; Germany built about 70,000, and Japan built nearly three million. The fact that Japan has beaten the Western countries at their own game, and in a very short time, is a tribute to her industry and her single-mindedness, but she has also brought Western-style problems upon herself. In the electronics industry, even the Japanese are farming out work to places like Taiwan. What the world's industry will look like when there are no poor people left to exploit is anybody's guess: at any rate, motorcycles as transport and for racing are as popular today as they have ever been.

MOTORCYCLE PRODUCTION IN MAIN MANUFACTURING NATIONS

Country:	1969	1970	1971	1972	1973	1974	1975
Austria	4,278	7,044	7,643	11,768	12,253	14,244	10,746
Britain	71,010	64,521	86,650	48,832	48,439	40,000	
Czechoslovakia				270,000			118,566
France	3,375	4,292	6,508	6,627	8,686	9,038	8,513
Germany	52,568	70,123	66,462	69,099	84,357	66,901	74,660
Italy	580,000	560,000	617,000	682,500	694,500	795,500	833,000
Japan	2,576,873	2,947,672	3,400,502	3,565,246	3,767,327	4,509,420	3,802,547
Spain	32,514	30,437	36,661	49,465	54,176	59,747	58,351

THE PIONEER YEARS

IT IS IMPOSSIBLE to bestow on any individual the credit for having 'invented' the motorcycle. There was much preliminary development to be accomplished before any kind of motor vehicle could be practical.

In 1876, Nikolaus August Otto built a four-stroke internal combustion engine. Dugald Clerk, in 1877-78, developed a two-stroke compression machine with a charging pump. In 1883, Gottlieb Daimler and Wilhelm Maybach invented surface ignition, which made possible a fast-running lightweight engine. Otto invented a low-tension make-and-break (coil) ignition in 1884, and the next year Daimler and Maybach built a two-wheeled vehicle with a wooden frame and belt drive. Finally, in 1894 Heinrich Hildebrand and Alois Wolfmüller designed the first commercially-built two-wheeler to be called a motorcycle.

In 1895 there were French three-wheelers using the De Dion engines, such as the Gladiator, and in England the Beeston. The year 1896 saw the quantity manufacture of these engines, and in 1897 the Werner

machine appeared in Paris with the engine above the front wheel. Soon, the Werners also had a factory in London. The Coventry Motor Company was building machines in the city of the same name, in the industrial Midlands of England. In the same city, Humber and Beeston were in production. In the same year, Italy's Edoardo Bianchi commenced production. In 1898, the factory of Georges Bouton and Count De Dion began production of a three-wheeler, using their own 239cc engine.

De Dion engines were extremely successful. By 1899, they had overtaken the Hildebrand and Wolfmüller design; in that year, Laurin and Klement began motorcycle production in what was then the Austro-Hungarian Empire, using the 239cc De Dion engine until they developed their own. Engines were also being made by Sarolea in Belgium, and a clever Frenchman called André Boudeville began manufacture of high-tension magnetos in Paris. 1899 also saw the first 211cc Minerva engine, the first engine-assisted Raleigh bicycles, the first Matchless motorcycles

Early days in France and Germany . . . Above: the first Daimler and Maybach two-wheeler (left) and the 1894 Hildebrand & Wolfmüller. Bottom: the Parisian Werner Motorcyclette, and the De Dion-Bouton three-wheeler. T. Tessier broke a speed record on an English BAT (right) in 1903.

THOSE MAGNIFICENT MEN ON THEIR CYCLING MACHINES

A steam engine, fired by petrol, powered this von Sauerbronn-Davis velocipede, 1883

The 1887 Millet prototype had a radial engine similar to those later used in aircraft

Propellor power . . . a chitty, chitty, bang bike by Anzani had its test flight in 1906

Look, no pedals! An ordinary bicycle gets a shove from an auxiliary engine . . . Italy, 1893

'Luxurious, high-powered, all-weather car-ette' . . . twin engined Quadrant, made in Britain, 1905

Where to put the engine? Above the front wheel, perhaps? That (1) was Werner's solution, in 1899. Enfield placed the engine in the same place, but to drive the rear wheel

Strange layouts abounded at the turn of the century . . . Singer positioned the engine in the hub of the front wheel (2). Further variations came from British Excelsior (3), Phelon and Moore (4), Hildebrand and Wolfmüller (5), Beeston (6), Ormonde (7), Singer again (8) and Humber (9).

In Czechoslovakia, Laurin & Klement
produced the elegant single-cylinder
B–D in 1903 (top), and more
sporting versions such as the V-twin
CCR (below). Bottom: Ludwig Opel
with a 2¾ hp Opel motorcycle
on army manoeuvres in 1905.

and the first motorcycle races: at the Friedenauer Cycle Track in Germany and the Exelberg in Austria.

The first year of the new century brought the introduction of the Perks & Birch (later Singer) motor wheel, Joah Phelon's first P&M motorcycle, the first Excelsiors built by Bayliss-Thomas, and in America, the Orient motorcycle designed by Charles H. Metz. In 1901, Swedish-American Oscar Hedström built the first Indian motorcycle, and the Werners experimented with vertical engines mounted in the centre of the frame. Puch and NSU built their first motorcycles, the latter using the Swiss Zedel engine. In England, Yorkshire's Alfred Angas Scott began the development of his unorthodox two-stroke engines, which are still famous today. Also in 1901, Orient became the first American company to export a machine to Europe. Emil Hafelfinger, also an American, created the first two-speed gear, and Condor, a Swiss factory, began producing motorized bicycles.

Also in Switzerland, the Dufaux brothers began producing bicycle attachment engines, calling their product Motosacoche (engine in the pocket). The same factory later produced the MAG engine, playing the same part on the Continent as JAP (J. A. Prestwich & Co. Ltd.) in England, who began producing proprietary engines in 1902. (The Swiss factory always made complete machines as well, but the London factory after 1908 made engines only.) The year also saw the manufacture of ohv engines by the French Clément works, Strickland's design of vertical twins, and Ariel's first motorcycles, built in Birmingham with Belgian Kerry engines. Wicker sidecars were being made by Mills & Fulford in Coventry.

The aircooled four-cylinder FN, with shaft drive, came into quantity production in 1903. Another four was built by Charles Binks, and Buchet in France was supplying a vertical twin with no less than 4245cc capacity. Shaft-driven singles were built by FN and by William Starley. White & Poppe began building 3 hp single-cylinder proprietary engines. America saw the first Harley-Davidson motorcycle, made in Milwaukee, Wisconsin. Triumph, in Britain, began making their own engines; with the help of Bettmann and Schulte, the two Germans who had come to Coventry to found Triumph, the German

company of the same name began to build motorcycles in Nuremberg. The British BAT machine had a spring frame; the factory at Penge was owned by the Tessier family. It was widely thought that BAT stood for 'best after test', but the designer's name was Batson.

In France the Bichrone two-stroke was installed in Griffon frames. In 1904 the International Coupé Race in France became the first international motorcycle event. Demester of France won it riding a Griffon; number two was Toman riding a Laurin & Klement. Automatic inlet valves became common on engines and Peugeot of France now used Truffault's swinging arm forks. Dürkopp and Laurin & Klement built four-in-line engines. While England had 21,521 machines registered, only 776 were exported. Hercules and Victoria of Germany entered the market, and a Peugeot rider reached 76·5 mph on a machine weighing 110 pounds.

The following year, 1905, saw the introduction in England of quantity production of Scott's, not yet at the famous works in Shipley, Yorkshire, but at the Jowett works in nearby Bradford. Another new make was the Fairy, with a horizontally opposed twin designed by J. Barter. This was the forerunner of the Douglas. There were more vertical twins, too; the Belgian Bercley designed by Gustave Kindermann and Eugene Werner's own Werner, built in Paris. Both the Werner brothers, great pioneers of motorcycling, died the same year.

There was a switch to magneto ignition by most factories in 1906. In that year the

The start of the first T.T. race in 1908 (inset, far left), and the twin-cylinder class winner Harry Reed astride his D.O.T. Big picture: the circuit's notorious Devil's Elbow. Bottom: winner of the 1905 International Coupe, Václav Vondřich, on a CCR.

British firm of JAP built the first ohv V-twin engines. A JAP engine powered the first three-cylinder Dennell, from Yorkshire. The same county produced the P&M, which had a two-speed gear, with clutch. The year 1906 also saw the first Druid spring forks. The year before, Václav Vondřich, riding a Laurin & Klement V-twin, had won the Coupé International, but in 1906 it was the Austrian Edward Nikodem, on a Puch.

After this race, British riders complained about the bad organisation, and mainly about the interpretation of the rules by certain Continental teams. After their return they decided to start their own event, and the result was the first Tourist Trophy race in the Isle of Man. This was in 1907, the same year that a trade slump caused the disappearance of some motorcycle producers. Glenn Curtis, an American manufacturer of aircraft engines, allegedly reached an unofficial 130 mph using a modified transverse-mounted V-8. Douglas had started quantity production of their machines with the Barter-designed flat-twin engine, and Eysink in Holland introduced their own vertical twins. 1908 saw the opening of Brooklands, the famous racetrack at Weybridge, south of London. It also saw the first Italian entrant in the TT race, riding an English Rex. A new design by the Dufaux brothers had a seven-cylinder rotary engine built into the rear wheel. This was the first and last seven ever built.

Triumphs in England got hub clutches in their rear wheels in 1909, a very good design by Maurice Schulte. That year also saw the P. G. Tacchi-designed Wilkinson TAC (Touring Auto Cycle, with a steering wheel) which soon became the TMC (Touring Motor Cycle, with handlebars). Both had aircooled (or optionally watercooled) four-in-line engines, and both were built by the Wilkinson Sword Company, later famous for razor blades. The Stevens brothers began manufacture of complete motorcycles called AJS. Renouf's James design was interesting, with its chassis-type frame and a spring seat pillar. Giuseppe Gilera's was a new make. At Brooklands, an NLG (North London Garages) reached 90 mph with an ohv V-twin of 2713cc built by JAP. The rider was W. E. Cook. F. A. McNab broke the one-hour record riding a Trump, which also had a JAP engine. McNab was one of the owners of the Trump factory.

A motorcycle boom started in 1910, but didn't help the new Renouf-designed James, a horizontally-opposed two-stroke twin with overheating problems. Britain had exported £24,202 worth of motorcycles in 1909, and more than doubled it in 1910 to £53,661. The boom in the USA resulted in 86,414 registrations. In Britain, Zenith's Fred Barnes designed the famous Gradua gear and a spring frame.

In 1911 the American Indian machines scored a 1-2-3 victory in the Senior TT, the biggest shock for the British industry until the Japanese invasion of the 1960s. The Indians were ridden by O. C. Godfrey, C. B. Franklin and A. J. Moorhouse. Rudge (Rudge Whitworth) came onto the scene that year with a 499cc single which had overhead-inlet and side-exhaust valves and which afterwards got the well-known Multi gear. Britain's motorcycle exports rose to the value of £120,289 and Charlie Collier — one of the three brothers of Matchless fame — broke the official world record with 91·37 mph. In France, Meuriot rode a Rene-Gillet at the Gomez-le-Chatel hill climb. The machine had a cross-shaped four-cylinder 20 hp engine which was really a radial. John Wooler built his first machine: a 346cc two-stroke with a horizontal cylinder and an additional pumping piston in the crankcase. (The same John Wooler was designing four-cylinder machines 40 years later, after the Second World War.) 1911 was also a busy year in America, with Bill Henderson creating his aircooled four-in-line, Pope building 498cc singles and 996cc ohv V-twins, and Jack Prince building a famous racetrack at Los Angeles.

Sunbeam machines entered the market in 1912. Designed by J. E. Greenwood and built at Wolverhampton in the West Midlands of England, they were of outstanding design and quality, among the finest machines ever built. Also from Wolverhampton came the Villiers proprietary engines, which in those far-off days were four-strokes, not the two-strokes we knew so well later. During this period, the Indian factory was a busy, thriving place, and the Italian Bianchi factory was the same. In 1912, founder Edoardo Bianchi

at the age of 45 was made a *Cavaliere del Lavoro*. Alas, Sunbeam, Indian and Bianchi are all gone today.

C. B. Redrup designed his first three-cylinder radial engine in 1912; Rex in Coventry and others built two-speed countershafts in front of the engines; ASL, a spring factory, built motorcycles with spring frames. In races, Charlie and Harry Collier of Matchless fame used new six-speed gearboxes. At Brooklands, they got more American competition in the form of H. A. Shaw on a 7 hp Thor and J. E. Hogge on a 4 hp Indian. A boost for two-strokes came in the Isle of Man, when Frank Applebee won the Senior TT on a 3·5 hp Scott with an average speed of 48·70 mph, and the fastest lap with 49·44 mph. G. E.

Stanley's hour record at Brooklands stood until 1920.

The Americans went on and on. Harley-Davidsons got chain drive to replace the belt drive; Indian supplied some models with full electrical equipment, a rarity in those days. In 1913 Andrew Strand designed with John McNeill the first commercially-built 996cc ohc V-twin, the Cyclone, and many were sold to private sportsmen in the USA.

Technically, the most outstanding motorcycle of 1913 was the 494cc vertical twin Peugeot racing machine, designed by Antoinescu, but based on the Peugeot racing car engine design of 1912. This double-ohc engine was re-designed many times and was still winning races in 1927; it was never sold to private entrants. Triumph in England experimented with a vertical twin, and Humber with a three-cylinder model, but they never went into quantity production. A new English sporting event, the International Sixdays Trial, was introduced and is still with us. Russia was in the news when a rider from that country participated in the Senior TT; his name was Kremleff. He rode a Rudge and retired after a crash.

Britain had by this time 179,926 registered motorcycles, the Americans produced 70,000 machines in 1913 and Carl Goudy, riding an American Schwinn-built Excelsior, won the 100 mile race at Columbus. A new Indian was the 2·25 hp two-stroke 211cc machine.

THE FIRST WORLD WAR

As the 1914 war broke out in Europe, the Chicago-based Schwinn-owned Excelsior Company moved to new works at 3700 Cortland Street. Glen Boyd won on an Indian the first race at Dodge City. In Britain, Cyril Pullin on a Rudge and Eric Williams on an sv AJS won the last pre-first-war Senior and Junior TT races. Jack Emerson took an ABC with a Bradshaw-designed 496cc flat-twin engine to Brooklands and got a speed of 80·47 mph. Despite the world political situation, the British motorcycle industry exported 20,877 motorcycles. Puch, the Austrian factory, built machines with horizontally opposed cylinders. Burman in England, famous for gears and gearboxes, entered the manufacture of proprietary engines, but the war prevented their mass production.

Motorcycles played an important part in the war. The British used mainly Triumph, Douglas, P&M, Clyno and Sunbeams: the Germans NSU and Wanderer machines; the French René Gillets, the Austrians Puchs and the Italians Bianchis and a variety of other makes. Britain supplied machines to the Czar of Russia, including Rovers and Premiers. A cargo of 250 Premier machines was sunk in the North Sea on its way to Russia.

Premier built in 1915 the prototype of a new 322cc two-stroke vertical twin. For two years they developed it, but never began quantity production. It was in fact the last Premier ever made in Coventry; soon after the war, the factory was bought by Singer. Also new was a 90-degree V-twin, made by Phelon & Moore at Cleckheaton, in Yorkshire, the works which supplied many singles to the British Air Force during the war. Like the Premier, it

During the First World War, the American Forces ordered 70,000 Harleys, some rigged as armed outfits (above). Britain had a Clyno-Vickers machine-gun outfit (below).

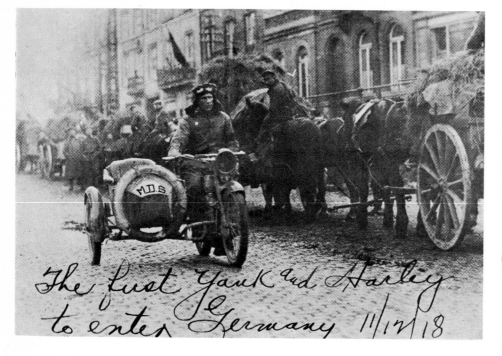

The first Yank and Harley to enter Germany 11/17/18

was never built in quantities. The same applied to a new watercooled 746cc flat-twin made by Humber. Britain registered 147,904 motorcycles and exported 10,979.

America was still having big races. Otto Walker, riding a Harley-Davidson with a 996cc V-twin won at Dodge City; watching was Bill Ottoway, who had just created a new 8-valve ohv V-twin for racing on America's long tracks. He was at that time chief designer and head of the racing department at the famous Milwaukee factory. On this 8-valve Harley-Davidson

Historic border-crossing (left) by Harley-Davidson on Armistice Day, 1918. British dispatch-riders used machines by Phelan and Moore, Douglas, BSA, Triumph and others.

German dispatch-rider (below, left), in Düsseldorf. German Triumph motorcycles were used by the Kaiser's Forces, along with Neckarsulm (NSU) and Ardie machines. Below, right: British rider photographed in 1917 during the German East Africa campaign.

Jack Janke was the winner at Dodge City in 1916. In the same year, William Hendee —the founder of Indian at Springfield— sold most of his shares in the factory; Roy Artley, riding a four-cylinder Henderson, broke the Los Angeles to San Francisco record with 10 hours and 4 minutes and Britain's number of motorcycles stood, despite the war, at 153,000.

Motorcycle prices increased during the war; even in the USA one had to pay the equivalent of £170 for a 269cc two-stroke Cleveland. That was in 1917, when Indian built the first 996cc Powerplus V-twins, the 15 hp Thor V-twin got a reverse gear, Excelsior in Chicago bought the Henderson design and Harley-Davidson got a big Army order for their machines. In 1918, nearly all factories in the world worked for the war. Some prepared for peace; others were anxious because when the war was over they would lose valuable government contracts.

THE 1920's...THE GOLDEN AGE

THE FIRST YEAR OF PEACE saw much activity in the motorcycle industry. There was such a demand for machines that many factories switched over to the assembly or manufacture of motorcycles, without having the necessary experience or suitable equipment. Second-class machines, and even really bad ones, found customers, until the market was quite satisfied and buyers of motorcycles could tell good designs from bad ones. It was a technically interesting, but commercially unstable period. There were many producers which arrived from nowhere and soon disappeared, leaving behind unhappy customers and problems.

The year 1919 saw the introduction of a good two-stroke single, the 497cc Dunelt with the double-diameter piston, which created a certain amount of forced induction. In the USA appeared the first Bill Henderson-designed four-in-line ACE, which eventually became in 1927 the first Indian four. In Germany a new make, DKW, became famous for good two-strokes. The first one was designed by the very experienced Hugo Ruppe, who was also the creator of Bekamo two-strokes, which had wooden frames and a pumping piston in the crankcase for forced induction. Bekamos were to win many races in the early 1920s. Another new creation was the Bradshaw-designed 398cc ABC with the transverse-mounted flat-twin ohv engine, produced by the Sopwith Engineering Co. It was a modern conception, but was not fully developed when it was put on the market. Sunbeam became part of the Nobel (ICI) group.

In Italy, the 346cc Garelli with the double-piston two-stroke single-cylinder engine was another make which soon after the war gained popularity and successes in sporting events. Adalberto Garelli created this unorthodox design. A short-lived scooter boom swamped England. Alfred Angus Scott had sold his interests in the now Shipley-based Scott Motorcycle Company. The new make Francis Barnett bought the Bayliss-Thomas works at Coventry, after Bayliss-Thomas — manufacturers of English Excelsior motorcycles — had moved to Birmingham. The other Excelsior factory — owned by Ignaz Schwinn at Chicago — built new John McNeill-designed motorcycles with ohc racing engines (498cc and 996cc) for the works team, while Charles Franklin crea-

ted the famous 596cc sv V-twin Scout for Indian, one of the finest machines ever made in the USA. Franklin, an Irishman, had been one of the winners in the 1911 Senior TT.

A very interesting machine, the German Mars, was designed in 1920 by Franzenberg. It had a frame made from pressed steel plates which were welded and rivetted together.

The Mars' power unit was the only motorcycle engine ever built by the famous Maybach car and aero-engine works at Friedrichshafen. It had two horizontally-opposed cylinders, a capacity of 956cc and side valves. Starting was by a crank. This design was produced for nearly ten years in slightly developed form. And there was a motorcycle boom in nearly all countries; Britain had 280,000 registered machines, produced by nearly 200 different assemblers and manufacturers. A new design was a 248cc V-twin made by Diamond, but it never went into quantity production. The first official world speed record for motorcycles was established on April 14, 1920 by Ernie Walker at Daytona on a 994cc V-twin Indian with more than 101 mph. Racing in America was again in full swing and the leading factories such as

Indian, Harley-Davidson, Excelsior (including Henderson) and Reading-Standard competed in most events. Dodge City was won by Jim Davis on a Harley-Davidson, where there was a new flat-twin of 584cc with side-valves designed by Bill Ottoway.

Many new makes and models appeared in 1921. It was the year of the first Carlo Guzzi-designed 497cc Moto-Guzzi, with a horizontal single-cylinder ioe engine, and the first George Brough-designed 974cc Brough-Superior V-twin with a JAP engine. At Munich, the first Megola — the Fritz Cockerell-designed machine with a 5-cylinder radial engine of 640cc built directly into the front wheel — appeared on the scene. It had neither clutch nor gearbox. Around 2000 were built when after four years the factory closed down. It was also 1921 when Hugo Ruppe, who had created the first DKW, began manufacture of his own 129cc Bekamos. The same year, Sun in England used 269cc and afterwards 247cc Vitesse engines, two-strokes with a rotary valve on the induction side. Harry Ricardo, later Sir Harry Ricardo, was busy at Triumph in Coventry, developing his excellent 498cc ohv four-valve single-cylinder 'Riccy' model. Barr & Stroud of Glasgow began manufacture of 347cc sleeve-valve proprietary engines. Scotts got saddle-tanks. Scooters began to disappear, but motorcycles sold like hot cakes, despite the very high prices. Some examples: 247cc Levis two-stroke, £65; 799cc V-twin AJS with sidecar, £210; 748cc four-cylinder FN with shaft drive, £160; 490cc Norton with sv engine, £132.

Belgium had its first Grand Prix motorcycle race in 1921 and Ernst Neumann-Neander, the well-known German designer, created a prototype with an Adler-built 123cc engine. Italy had a TT race in 1921 at the Circuito del Lario and Amedeo Ruggeri — in the 1930s a Maserati racing-car driver — won it on a 998cc Harley-Davidson. The year's registration figure in the UK: 373,200; in the USA: 154,000. New in 1921 also was a 596cc V-twin Bianchi from Italy and a similar 494cc version made by Galloni; Benelli entered the market with a 98cc two-stroke. The V-twin 477cc Borgo racing machine had 8 valves and ohc, as well as a partly oil-cooled unit-design engine.

The many flat-twins built in 1921 mainly in Britain and Italy included the Fongri,

The post-war years saw a short-lived craze for the scooter (left). The unorthodox 5-cylinder Megola was raced by Toni Bauhofer and reached speeds up to 140 km/h.

Maxima, SAR, Raleigh, Humber, Wooler, Zenith, Dalton, Slaney, Brough, Douglas, Williamson, ABC and also the American Harley-Davidson and Czechoslovakian Itar, as well as the German Victoria, Aristos, SBD, Mars, Astra and more.

The year 1922 saw the last Tourist Trophy success by a British two-stroke, when Geoff Davison on a Levis won the Lightweight race. It saw also the first double-piston 122cc single-cylinder Puch two-stroke, designed by Giovanni Marcel-lino. Blackburne motorcycle production was taken over by Osborne Engineering Company (OEC), but manufacture of proprietary motorcycle engines continued at Burney & Blackburne. The year also saw the introduction of the first Norton with an ohv engine; Rex Judd rode it at Brooklands. New were Val Page-designed 248cc and 348cc ohc racing engines made by JAP while Hubert Hagens, the British Anzani designer, created the successful 998cc V-twin ohc racing engine, which— ridden by Claude Temple— broke many records.

DKW in Germany built the scooter-like Lomos machine, Walter Handley in 1922 rode his first race on an OK Supreme, Dolf in Germany built an eight-port two-stroke and FN of Belgium entered the market with a 347cc ohv single-cylinder machine. Sheffield-Henderson and Coventry-Victors got saddle-tanks and there was for the first time not only a separate Lightweight TT race, but also the first Ulster GP and

'Lawrence of Arabia' (big picture) owned no less than eight Brough-Superior machines. In the bottom picture, designer and manufacturer George Brough is shown on the left, with business associates and staff, outside his factory in 1927.

at Monza the first Italian Grand Prix. A shaft-driven 498cc Krieger-Gnädig (KG) won the first Avus race at Berlin and a Della Ferrera broke the Italian km record. Interesting, because this works 498cc V-twin had an ohc engine, with chain-driven camshafts; the chains were uncovered and if one takes account of the poor quality of chains in the period, there was a real danger for the rider. This unique design was still seen in 1927 in Italian hill-climbs.

The year 1923 saw the introduction of the first complete 493cc BMW with the transverse-mounted horizontally opposed sv engine, which was already of unit design. This led to the end of proprietary engine production by the Munich factory. Max Friz created the BMW. Less successful than the German factory was Matchless with a new 348cc ohc single, which was never a good racing machine and never really a touring motorcycle either. More interesting was a banking sidecar, used by Freddy Dixon on his Douglas, when winning the 1923 (first ever) sidecar TT race. The same year also saw the first TT race of Amateurs, which eventually became the Manx Grand Prix.

New creations were the A. A. Sidney-designed 348cc ohc Dart and a 398cc BSA prototype, which with its transverse-mounted flat-twin had much in common with the then also new R32 made by BMW. Extremely fast were 144cc and 244cc Hirth two-stroke racers, designed by Helmuth Hirth in Germany. The light-alloy engines were watercooled and of the double-piston variety. Rudge built in 1923 their first ohv models and there was the German Ermag two-stroke, which had a 246cc rotary inlet valve engine, designed by Albert Roder, who created earlier the not unsimilar Ziro. In America, Arthur Lemon took over Henderson design and development from C. Gustafson, while Indian competed for the last time in the Isle of Man TT races. And there was another new TT race; this time in Austria.

The year 1923 was another boom period for motorcycle factories and for manufacturers of proprietary engines as well. The last included the makes JAP, Blackburne, Villiers, Bradshaw, Precision, Coventry-Victor, Broler, Liberty, Dart and on the Continent MAG (Motosacoche), Train, Moser, Zurcher, Chaise, Bekamo, Kühne, Küchen, Baumi, Gruhn, Alba, DKW, Grade etc. A new event in the sporting calendar was the 1000 Mile Stock Trial organised in 1924 by the Auto Cycle Union in England. The year saw also some new designs, including the first ohv BMW model, designed by Rudolf Schleicher, and the new Roconova ohc machines, the first commercially built 248cc and 348cc ohc motorcycles in Germany. Unfortunately Roconova, a design by Johannes Rössig, lasted only three years. In Britain, Connaught bought JES and Brough-Superior introduced Castle forks on the SS100 models, their newest design. Marchant on a Blackburne-engined 348cc Chater-Lea was the first man officially to break the magic 100 mph limit on a 350cc machine. On April 1, he reached 100·81 mph on a modified 350cc ohc machine. He was a superb designer-tuner as well. Also his friend and opponent Bert le Vack broke records in 1924 and with his 996cc Brough-Superior (ohv JAP) he reached in France over the flying kilometre 119·05 mph, with a one-way run of 122·24 mph. The Americans were fast too and a four-cylinder ACE ridden by Rod Wolverton reached 134 mph. It did not become a world record, as it was not observed officially by the FIM (then still the FICM). The number of registered motorcycles was half a million in England, and British motorcycle exports reached a value of £2,000,000; it was still a period of British supremacy. For Garelli 1924 was a very successful year and the double-piston two-strokes of 348cc won many races against strong opposition. Scott in England was now headed by R. A. Vinter.

Among new machines in 1925 were the 497cc Sunbeam works racers with ohc engines, which never went into quantity production. More successful were the new Italian 348cc Bianchis with double ohc engines, which were nearly unbeatable in Italy until 1931. Velocette in England had a new 348cc ohc single, which was designed by Percy Goodmann and which eventually won races all over the world. New makes were HRD and McEvoy, among others. DKW in Germany produced new water-cooled 173cc racing two-strokes with a charging cylinder at the bottom of the crankcase. The first Dutch TT was run at Assen. A team of very fast 124cc two-stroke singles from Italy won many events. Wal Handley won three 1925 TT races in the Isle of Man in one year. All his machines were made by Rex Acme and had Blackburne ohv engines. In London an unknown young designer named Edward Turner created a 348cc ohc machine; he joined Ariels in 1927 and 10 years later was head of Triumph. George Brough, who built at Nottingham the most expensive machines in England, introduced spring frames. Stefan and Nikolaus v. Horthy, sons of the Hungarian head of state, rode in many races.

Among the most enthusiastic motorcyclists was King Albert of Belgium, who got his fifth machine in 1925, a Belgian built Jeecy-Vea with a British engine.

Old William Brough built his last flat-twins in 1926, but his son continued producing the famous Brough-Superiors, including a new 996cc ohv V-twin with the 45 hp JAP engine, for which he guaranteed a top speed of 100 mph (160 km/h). Therefore the name for this model: SS100. Out went the German 5-cylinder Megola, and Paul Kelecom, the famous Belgian designer, left the FN works. Garelli machines broke not less than 48 world records and Chater-Lea built the first 347cc ohc singles with face cams. In Germany, Adolf Brudes broke the German 1 km record with 104 mph on a supercharged 498cc Victoria, designed by Gustav Steinlein. Sepp Stelzer won the big Avus race on a BMW. A new TT race in Czechoslovakia was won by Rupert Karner of Austria on a 497cc ohv double-port Sunbeam, made in England.

Richard Küchen created new 348cc and 498cc face cam ohc proprietary engines, while DKW—then the biggest motorcycle factory in the world—also supplied 124cc, 127cc, 173cc and 206cc two-stroke deflector-type three-port engines to many motorcycle assemblers. Indian and Harley-Davidson still headed motorcycle sales in the USA; Indian with the 596cc Scout, 997cc Chief and 1234cc Big Chief, all side-valve V-twins, and the 348cc single-cylinder Prince. All models were also popular in Europe and Australia. Harley-Davidson built a 348cc sv and ohv single cylinder model in 1926.

The 144cc Austro-Motorette, from the drawing-board of Karl Schüber, was a technically-interesting vertical twin two-stroke machine, made in Austria. Puch added to the 123cc model a 174cc double-piston two-stroke and DSH built a whole range with Villiers and JAP engines. Dunelt now had a 248cc version of the double-diameter piston engine, while FN added a 497cc ohv single to the already existing 347cc ohv single and the big 748cc air-cooled four-in-line. Husqvarna built 548cc and 992cc V-twins with their own sv engines. James had small V-twins with 496cc sv and ohv engines in its wide range.

Equipped with ioe engines, NSU of Germany also had V-twins from 498cc to 996cc and Jock Porter, manufacturer and rider from Edinburgh, still supplied his Blackburne-engined New Gerrards, which brought him many racing successes. A one-model range was introduced by Rudge-Whitworth Ltd. in Coventry. It was a

THE ENGINES OF THE TWENTIES				
Make	Bore:	Stroke:	Cubic Capacity:	Cyl
Alcyon	62	56	174	TS 1
Blackburne	53	79	174	sv 1
	56.2	79	196	sv 1
	63	79	246	sv 1
	69	79	295	sv 1
	69	92	345	sv 1
	81	96.8	498	sv 1
	85	105	598	sv 1
	50	88	173	ohv 1
	56.2	79	196	ohv 1
	60	88	248	ohv 1
	71	88	348	ohv 1
	71	88	348	ohv 1
	71	88	348	ohv 1
	81	96.8	496	ohv 1
	81	96.8	496	ohv 1
	81	96.8	496	ohv 1
	85	105	598	ohv 1
BMW	68	68	493	sv 2
Bradshaw	68	96	349	ohv 1
Coventry-Victor	63	78	499	ohv 2
	69	78	596	sv 2
	75	78	688	sv 2
	78	78	749	ohv 2
DKW	64	64	206	TS 1
	68	68	246	TS 1
Hanfland JAP	55	65	149	TS 1
	60	62	174	sv 1
	55	83	197	sv 1
	64.5	76	248	sv 1
	70	78	299	sv 1
	70	90	345	sv 1
	85.7	85	490	sv 1
	85.7	104	599	sv 1
	70	88	674	sv 2
	70	97	746	sv 2
	85.7	85	976	sv 2
	85.7	85	976	sv 2
	85.7	85	976	sv 2
	53	78	174	ohv 1
	62.5	80	248	ohv 1
	70	90	348	ohv 1
	85.7	85	490	ohv 1
	85.7	104	599	ohv 1
JAP	70	88	674	ohv 2
	74	85	731	ohv 2
	85.7	85	981	ohv 2
Küchen ('K')	70	90	346	sv 1
	79	100	490	sv 1
	70	90	346	ohc 1
	79	100	490	ohc 1
Kühne (Bark)	72	84	342	ohv 1
	84	90	498	sv 1
	84	90	498	ohv 1
MAG (Motosacoche)	64	77	248	ioe 1
	72	85	346	ioe 1
	82	94	496	ioe 1
	64	77	496	ioe 2
	72	91	741	ioe 2
	82	94	996	ioe 2
	82	103.5	1094	ioe 2
	64	77	248	ohv 1
	72	85	346	ohv 1
	82	94	496	ohv 1
Moser	56	50	124	ohv 1
	60	61	172	ohv 1
Norman Villiers	60	60	170	ohv 1
	50	62	122	TS 1
	55	62	147	TS 1
	57.15	67	172	TS 1
	57.15	67	172	TS 1
	61	67	196	TS 1
	67	70	247	TS 1
	79	70	342	TS 1
Vulpine	78	104	498	ohv 1
	78	104	996	ohv 2

498cc four-valve, four-speed ohv single with coupled brakes. Wanderer in Germany had four-valve cylinders too; one model used a V-twin of 708cc and had therefore a total of 8 valves. They also built a flat 196cc single with 4 valves.

A 498cc ohv AJS single, the Douglas sv models—horizontal twins—and a heavy 496cc single-cylinder unit-design D-Rad were among the new creations of 1926. Another was the 498cc V-twin Blackburne ohv racing engine, used in the Senior TT, by Wal Handley and Jock Porter. It was quite fast, but had a tendency to overheat and never went into quantity production. A similar fate befell the MAG ohv V-twins of 498cc and 598cc, as well as works racing V-twins with 748cc. They could be used in short distance events, but overheated in long road races.

Many designers devoted much time and expense to new two-stroke machines. Among them was the Austrian Anton Gazda, who built 248cc motorcycles but became well-known for his Gazda handlebars, consisting of a bundle of leaf springs. An interesting design was the Paramount-Duo, because of its long wheelbase, two very low bucket seats and an enclosed engine supplied by JAP. It was shown at Olympia in London, but was never built in quantity. The Czechoslovakian Böhmerland also had a very long wheelbase and many other interesting technical details. The engine in this case was a 598cc ohv single, designed by Böhmerland boss Albin

Liebisch. Villiers built a 344cc vertical-twin proprietary two-stroke for the first time, but after a short period it was dropped. A few machines using it were made by Francis-Barnett in England, NSH in Germany, MT in Austria, La Mondiale in Belgium and Monet-Goyon in France.

1927 brought the opening of the Nürburgring, the first 'Cammy' AJS and also the first ohc 490cc Norton, designed by Walter Moore. Indian bought the ACE four, Dougal Marchant joined Motosacoche as designer, and Granville Bradshaw, creator of the ABC, designed the similarly unlucky 247cc Panthette with a transverse-mounted V-twin. Europe's only production version of a 996cc ohc V-twin was a French Koehler-Escoffier, while Windhoff in Germany—where they already built 122cc and 172cc watercooled two-strokes—entered the market with a unique oilcooled 748cc four-cylinder machine with shaft drive. George Brough

tried a prototype of a 996cc transverse-mounted V-4 with aircooling, while many German towns saw motorcycle taxis, mainly supplied by Mabeco, D-Rad and NSU. Austrian designer Adalbert Freyler created a 347cc ohc single with a rotary valve in the cylinder head, while Karl Schüber built the 347cc Titan with a blade arrangement for steering the incoming mixture. Humber built 348cc sv and ohv singles and also introduced an ohc version, Francis-Barnett still used screwed triangular frames with Villiers engines up to 344cc, and Sunbeam fascinated many sportsmen with beautiful 347cc and 493cc double-port ohv models 80 and 90, which won many races.

BSA had a 174cc two-stroke in 1927, Douglas a new 347cc ohv horizontally-opposed twin and there was also a Villiers-engined 172cc NUT, while AKD (Abingdon King Dick) now built 173cc singles with their own ohv engines. There were many factories which switched to saddle tanks, including Ariel, the English Excelsior, Raleigh, New Hudson, James, P&M-Panther, Sun, Coventry-Eagle, Dunelt, Royal-Enfield, Zenith and others. New was the DKW-like 490cc W&G with a nearly vertical twin-cylinder two-stroke engine, but while DKW built this type of machine until the Second World War, the British make soon disappeared.

'Lawrence of Arabia' acquired his fifth Brough-Superior in 1928, FN in Belgium now built 497cc ohv singles, while another Belgian make, Gillet Herstal, had the 348cc Tour de Monde two-stroke single, as well as 498cc ohv singles with their own unit-design engines, and 998cc V-twins with MAG-built ioe engines. In America, the combination of ACE and Indian led to the aircooled 1265cc four-in-line Indian ACE. AJS added a 498cc ohc model to the existing 347cc version of the chain-driven Cammy and Rush, the Belgian make, now built 345cc and 495cc sv and ohv models with their own engines. Moto-Guzzi showed at Milan a spring frame with a 497cc ohv engine and Della Ferrera (not to be confused with Frera) had a new 173cc unit-design ohv model. There was a beautiful production version of the 348cc ohc Bianchi with double ports. And while many experts regarded the English Sunbeam as the nonplus-ultra in motorcycling, it was the Swiss Motosacoche which had this dis-

A rocket-powered motorcycle was tested by Fritz von Opel in 1928. The machine was basically a 496cc Opel Motoclub ohv production model with rockets strapped to the rear end. Soon after this short-lived experiment, Opel stopped making motorcycles.

tinction on the Continent. A new German make, Standard, came very near to Motosacoche as far as quality and finish were concerned.

America had in contrast to Europe only few makes left in 1928: Harley-Davidson, Indian, Super-X, Henderson and Cleveland. DKW was the leading make in Europe. Japan imported machines from England and the USA; their own production was on a very limited scale. The French DFR had a car-type ball gearchange in its four-speed box. The German Neander had a frame made from Duralumin, the BMW new 739cc sv and ohv flat twins, as well as new frames made from pressed steel. BMW works racers got supercharged twins for the 500cc and 750cc classes and Puch of Austria had a new 248cc double-piston two-stroke designed by Giovanni Marcellino. Sturmey-Archer, famous for gearboxes, entered the field with proprietary four-stroke engines from 173cc to 597cc, including a 248cc face-cam ohc version, fitted by Dunelt. Italian factories now built 174cc ohv and ohc models; these included Benelli, Miller, Augusta, Ladetto & Blatto, FVL, Gazzi, Giacomasso, Piana and others.

George William Patchett, ex-McEvoy designer, joined FN and two years later Jawa. Dougal Marchant created very fast 348cc and 498cc ohc racing machines for Motosacoche, with which Walter Handley won the GP of Europe in both classes. England saw the unorthodox Cyril Pullin-designed Ascot-Pullin with a horizontal 497cc ohv single-cylinder engine and OEC introduced duplex steering.

A Rocket-driven Opel motorcycle was tested by Fritz von Opel in Germany, and with Speedway racing coming from Australia to Britain, many factories there — including Douglas, Rudge, Sunbeam, Norton, BSA, James, Calthorpe, Zenith, etc. — built special machines for the sport. Even Scott had such a model. Harley-Davidson came to Europe with such machines, which became known as 'peashooters'.

A new motorcycle factory entered the market in 1929: Jawa of Czechoslovakia. The first model was built under German Wanderer licence. It had a 497cc single-cylinder unit-design ohv engine, a pressed-steel frame and shaft drive. Puch built the first watercooled 248cc works racing two-strokes with double-piston engines and a piston-pump in the crankcase.

Among works machines at Brooklands, Bert Denly rode a 743cc single-cylinder ohc AJS and Bert le Vack a 665cc ohv New Hudson. Germany produced in 1929 195,686 motorcycles, England 164,000. Spanish makes did not appear abroad until after WWII. There was quite a big production in Belgium, with FN, Saroléa, Gillet-Herstal, Rush, La Mondiale, Lady, Ready and a few smaller producers. New in 1929 was a 497cc Harley-Davidson sv single, a 996cc René-Gillet sv V-twin from France and Gillet-Herstal broke 32 world records with the Van Oirbeck-designed 498cc ohc machine. The factory never sold ohc machines and tried everything to hide them from photographers. Even when they had a model called the Record in the catalogue, it had an ohv engine.

We had overhead camshaft engines — like the Velocette, Norton, Chater Lea, AJS — mainly for racing, but other factories including Praga, Chaise, Matchless, Soyer, Dollar etc. also built such power-units in sports models or even touring machines. And when Bert Le Vack broke the world record on August 25, 1929 with 129 mph (208 km/h), his JAP racing V-twin 55 hp engine in its Brough-Superior frame also had overhead valves. New was the five-country Trial in the centre of Europe, but there was a debacle at the International Six-Day Trial, because of the very bad organisation.

Motosacoche's chief designer Dougal Marchant created a new 248cc single-cylinder ohc racing machine with 27 hp running on alcohol, which was then permitted in road races. 27 hp was for 1929 a superb output by a two-fifty. Interesting also were the four-port 498cc ohv NUT, the 247cc six-port Levis two-stroke, the 494cc watercooled vertical-twin DKW two-strokes, Terrot's square cylinders on the 173cc two-strokes, Sunbeams new saddle tanks, the 493cc ohv Slopers made by BSA and the big 998cc JAP and partly Anzani-engined ohv V-twins produced by Brough-Superior, AJW, Delta-Gnom, Tornax, Ardie, Bücker, Standard, Zenith, OEC and others.

1929 was the year when a 498cc ohv Sunbeam (ridden by Charlie Dodson) won for the last time a Senior TT race and when a 172cc Villiers engine of the Brooklands type in a James frame won the 175cc class in the Belgian Grand Prix, with Bert Kershaw riding. Harley-Davidson introduced a new 746cc sv V-twin, Premier in Czechoslovakia a 498cc long-stroke ohv single and Motobécane of France built a 498cc air-cooled four-in-line.

With the dawn of a new decade, so the era of the entrepreneur-engineer was ending. It had been a golden age.

THE SECOND WORLD WAR

THE MOTORCYCLE saw considerable service in both of the two world wars, but its duties on each occasion were rather different. In the First World War, it had been frequently used by the infantry; in World War Two, it was seen first and foremost as a vehicle of communications, particularly by the Allies. Thus the dispatch rider became one of the war's heroic figures.

About 300,000 American motorcycles were built for World War Two. The bikes were all V-twins. One model, the 500cc Indian, was especially designed for the European war, but this bike was low in power and high in weight. The 750cc Harley 45, on the other hand, was a considerable success. With a top speed of more than 85mph from its racing-trained engine, and the ability to cruise for long distances at high speeds, it out-performed its European contemporaries in road work. It was also successful in the North African campaigns.

The Harley-Davidson company had produced bikes in Japan under the name of Rikuo before the war, then the plant was taken over by the state. Although the Eastern theatres of war rarely had the right terrain for motorcycles, the Japanese Army was equipped with these 'Rikuo' Harleys and they were even used by the Emperor's escort.

The British military motorcycles were mainly medium-weight, 350 singles, with top speeds of little more than 70 mph, capable of good performances both on the road and across country. The Matchless G3L was one of the most popular, with the Ariel NH and the Triumph HRW close behind. Then came the AJS R7, the forerunner of the marque's post-war Grand Prix machine.

The Willys-Ford Jeep did much of the general purpose work which the Axis powers consigned to motorcycle variations. One of the more bizarre among such variations was the tracked motorcycle. This creature was exemplified by the excessively heavy German 'Kettenkrad', made by NSU and powered by a 1·5 litre Opel engine.

A simpler and more effective approach was found in the development of motorcycle combinations with sidecar-wheel drive. The Belgian FN factory launched a 1,000cc flat-twin series, the M12, in 1934 for Service use. This was essentially a tricycle, driving on the two rear wheels, which could be fitted with a differential gear. FN chose to drop the tricycle layout in favour of a conventional combination when they produced a heavily-armoured version, the M86, in which the sidecar wheel was driven but had no differential. The usefulness of this machine was destroyed by its great and badly distributed weight.

The Germans took over the FN factory once they occupied Belgium. In France, they were also impressed by the Gnome-Rhône combination, which had sidecar-wheel drive but no differential. When the German Forces needed a new outfit to replace the BMW R12 motorcycle combination, the FN and Gnome & Rhône combinations were available for study and the project was given to BMW and Zündapp. The resulting BMW R75 with an overhead-valve engine could reach 55 mph with a three-man crew and full loading, and had remarkable off-road performance, only exceeded by the new Zündapp KS.

Zündapp then introduced the differential gear, which was unique on a conventional combination. The gear did not split power equally between the two driving wheels, but shared torque according to the centre of gravity between them. BMW shared this system, along with numerous other components, such as electrical and carburation equipment. These outfits were very effective, though they were costly and complicated to build and could not be manufactured quickly enough.

The Italians placed their faith in the solo machine with a classic Moto-Guzzi, the Alce, the forerunner of today's uprated Falconi. The Alce was a beautifully designed bike: its top speed was 80 mph, and the forward facing horizontal layout of its 500cc engine contributed to a weight distribution which helped stability and manoeuvrability. An Alce was produced with a machine-gun mounted on the handlebars, and an additional pair of dummy handlebars for the pillion passenger to support the bike while the driver used the gun. Alternatively the pillion passenger could lean over and fire the gun while the driver supported the bike. Predictably neither of these methods proved very

Military requirements led to a variety of special design. The U.S. Army used Harley-Davidson 45 WLAs (facing page) with a holster for a submachine gun. The British experimented with attachments for a mortar and a submachine gun (big picture) on Norton motorcycles. The Germans tried a scooter for paratroops, and a tracked vehicle, the NSU HK101 Kettenkrad.

practicable for safe and effective use.

Gilera manufactured a 500cc single, which was notable for the use of both side and over-head valves within the same engine, and Bianchi and Sertim produced more conventional side-valve 500cc models. All three were frequently fitted with side-cars.

As the portability, reliability and range of radio improved, and other means of communication developed, the military usefulness of the motorcycle faded from immediate view. Nor in the post-war period would motorcycling ever quite recover its former colour, though the British Corgi and American Cushman 'parascooters' briefly brought a minuscule new dimension to two-wheel riding, and the Piaggi aircraft company developed the Vespa scooter.

Many different manufacturers supplied machines for military use. American M.P.s used the Harley-Davidson; BMW supplied their R35 (below) and R75 (right). Bottom: BSA were one of the major British suppliers, making both 350 and 500cc models. The Indian soldier is reclining on a Matchless G3/L, a 350cc ohv machine.

THE GREAT DESIGNERS

The most famous and successful motorcycles have been designs so good that they have been produced for many years with a minimum of modernization and development.

Adalberto Garelli designed his first double-piston two-strokes before 1914; they continued to be developed until 1935. J. L. Norton designed the Norton sv singles which won so many races; as a normal production version, the 16H was in the catalogue for many years and was made in thousands for the military during the Second World War. The Austrian Puch machines had a very long run; designed by Giovanni Marcellino in 1923, they were made until the 1960s. Marcellino's masterpieces were works racing machines having 248cc watercooled engines with pumping pistons in the crankcase. At the German Grand Prix in 1931, they beat everything in sight. Not all designers stayed with one

company. Edward Turner had joined Ariel in 1927; his 1930 Ariel square four was a big success. In 1936 he took over Triumph on behalf of its new owner, Jack Sangster; the next year he built Triumph's first 498cc vertical twin, the Speed Twin, by fitting the engine into an existing frame from a single-cylinder model. It was an instant success. There had been two previous Triumph vertical twins: a 448cc prototype in 1913, and a 649cc ohv unit-design model designed by Val Page in 1933, which was marketed at a time when few buyers could afford such a big machine. Page was a very good designer who had worked for years on JAP proprietary engines, but the 1937 Triumph vertical twin was a perfect example of the right design at the right time; it was the first commercially successful vertical twin, and inspired a great many others.

Famous designer George William Pat-

chett joined Jawa in Prague, after being with George Brough, Michael McEvoy and the FN works. His designs for Jawa included two machines — a 173cc and a 246cc two-stroke with pressed steel frames, and 346cc sv and ohv singles. There were also 247cc two-strokes with Auto-Union (Schnürle patent) flat-top engines.

Harold Willis designed the Roarer for Velocette in 1939; this was a supercharged vertical twin ohc with 498cc and shaft drive. The war and Willis's death prevented racing of the machine. After the war, Charles Udall was responsible for the silent watercooled Velocette LE, with a 198cc transverse-mounted flat twin, in connection with Percy and Bertie Goodmann.

In the 1920s Richard Küchen designed the famous 3-valve 'K' series of proprietary engines; in the 1930s, he was responsible

The famous British designer Bradshaw began his career with the ABC in 1913

The designs created by Marcellino (centre) for Puch lasted from the 1920s to the 1960s

D. R. O'Donovan (on bike) . . . Norton genius

Creator of the Speed Twin . . . Edward Turner (standing directly behind the fuel tank)

W. W. Moore (left), of Norton and NSU . . . and George William Patchett, of Jawa

for sv and ohv engines as well. In 1933, he created the Zündapp range, with pressed steel frames and two and four-stroke engines from 198 to 798cc. The biggest was a transverse-mounted flat four, and many models had shaft drive. After the Second World War, Küchen designed Opti vertical twin ohc proprietary engines, double-piston two-strokes and even racing car engines. His engines were always of clean design, but their finesse was often the work of his lesser-known brother, Xaver.

Between the wars, George Brough continued to construct the most expensive motorcycles in the world, but he never built his own engines, using MAG, JAP and Matchless units. In 1932 he built 796cc models with two rear wheels, and they had watercooled Austin car engines. Some prototypes had engine parts made by Motosacoche; among these was the Dream, with a 996cc transverse-mounted flat-four.

An outstanding design of 1935 was the AJS 499cc double-ohc V-four, which was the work of Bert Collier. It was afterwards modified to watercooling and also supercharged in 1939, and was the fastest prewar British road racer of its size.

W. W. Moore had designed the first Norton ohc machine in 1927. In 1930 he joined the German NSU works and created the not dissimilar 490cc single. His work at Norton was taken over by Arthur Carroll, while Irishman Joe Craig took over development and team management. Carroll redesigned the camshaft arrangement and made the Nortons faster and more reliable before his death in an accident in 1935. (From 1950 onwards, Norton machines had the superb featherbed frame, the Irish invention of Rex and Crommie McCandless and Artie Bell.)

After World War II, German Victoria had the 198cc 'Swing', a swinging arm two-

stroke designed by Norbert Riedel. In 1948 Riedel designed the very unorthodox Imme, a 98cc two-stroke with a one-sided fork and the engine on the swinging arm. Sunbeams designed after the war by Ealing Poppe were entirely different machines from the pre-war models, with 498cc vertical-twin ohc in-line engines and shaft drive. Vincenz Sklenar designed 348 and 498cc double-ohc racing twins right after the war; Jaroslav Walter created 248 and 348cc ohc singles for CZ after 1949. When MV-Agusta entered racing in the early 1950s, the 498cc four was designed by Piero Remor.

Among today's designers, Mario Sucher is responsible for Austrian Puch machines, Walter Kaaden for MZ two-strokes, and Jörg Möller of West Germany designed the very fast Italian Morbidellis. Alan Clough's CCM moto-cross four-strokes are still among the leaders in their class.

Crommie McCandless . . . of featherbed fame

Remor (left) with Gilera

Val Page . . . of JAP and Triumph renown

Fabio Taglioni (above) designed the Ducati desmodromic valve gear in the early 1960s. The system is still in use. Right: Giulio Carcano with Moto-Guzzi Junior TT winner in 1956.

Jack Williams, chief development engineer on the AJS 7R, with son-in-law Tom Herron, of Yamaha

Pioneer Max Friz . . . he made aircraft engines, then the first BMW motorcycle

THE CLASSIC BIKES THROUGH THE DECADES

NO FOUR-CYLINDER MOTORCYCLE has achieved such pre-eminence in its own time as the Henderson. It provided riders in the early years of motorcycling with simple starting, smoothness, silence, oil tightness, reliability and generous power to a degree unmatched elsewhere. The model shown here is that of 1912, the first year of production. The original 7 hp model was soon further developed, with a multi-speed gearbox, improved power, and more robust construction. Sales rose accordingly, and the model achieved greater popularity than any comparable machine in the United States. Finally Ignaz Schwinn's Excelsior Company bought the firm in 1917, initially retaining the services of founders William and Tom

Henderson. After that, the Henderson big four also incorporated the name Excelsior on the tank. Two years later, William and Tom Henderson left Excelsior, unhappy with the new business arrangement. William founded his own motorcycle company, under the name of Ace. He was soon manufacturing an Ace four, and challenging the Henderson's reputation for quality. After many successful years Ace ran into financial troubles, and was bought by Indian.

THE NAME SCOTT is central to the history of the motorcycle. Alfred Scott was an inventor and engine-designer who played a leading part in the development of the two-stroke machine. Scott built his first motorised bicycle in Yorkshire as early as 1898, using a twin-cylinder two-stroke. The engine was fitted to a heavy pedal-cycle, and transmission was by friction roller. By 1903, he had built a machine with rear-wheel power, and a year later Scott was granted British patent rights on a two-stroke vertical-twin engine. Scott's first true production motorcycle was manufactured in 1908. Its engine was built to the Scott design by the nearby Jowett car factory, another Yorkshire concern famous in automotive history. This 333cc engine had a bore and stroke of 58 × 63mm, and the entire unit weighed only 371 lbs. The cylinder heads were water-cooled through a thermosiphon system, but the barrels were air-cooled. By 1914, Scott had settled the design of his machines, and was using a wholly water-cooled engine. The two-speed machine had standard gear-ratios of 3:1 and 4:1, and the unusual "open" frame design which characterised the marque. This frame design was popular with women motorcyclists, whose dignity it helped preserve. Telescopic front forks were used from the very first, and a disc-valve induction and exhaust system was introduced at an early stage. Other machines could match the Scott's 55 mph top speed, but none of its contemporaries offered the same handling qualities. It was this characteristic in particular which afforded Scott such great racing success. Like most unconventional machines, the Scott was the creature of its designer. Alfred Scott himself left the company after the First World War, and died in 1923; within four or five years, the marque had lost much of its shine. Production since a takeover in 1950 has been limited to small-scale revivals. The Scott shown here is a 486cc model specially reconstructed for vintage racing.

INDIAN WAS WITHOUT DOUBT one of the foremost names in the development of the modern motorcycle. In 1905, the factory became one of the first to put a V-twin into commercial manufacture. The first V engine was little more than a doubling up of two Indian 1·75 hp singles, but improved and enlarged versions soon followed. These ultimately provided the basis for the very advanced motorcycles produced under the aegis of the factory's founder, George Hendee, and the great designer Oskar Hedström. After they had left the company, Charlie Gustafson became Indian's chief designer in 1915. He established the side-valve style which became a tradition of the factory and of the American motorcycle industry. His great machine was the 7 hp 998 cc Power Plus shown here. This sophisticated and speedy motorcycle included such advanced equipment as leaf-spring suspended pivoted fork rear suspension, all chain drive, electric lighting, electric starting and a proper kick-start.

Indian

AS THE ORIGINAL William Brough motorcycle company entered the last year of its life, the son's rival firm launched the most famous machine to bear the family name. The Brough Superior SS100, introduced in 1926, was more popular than any other prestige sports roadster before or since. The SS100, shown here, was an overhead-valve V-twin. It became one of the two mainstays of Brough Superior's 16-year production period, along with its predecessor, the SS80 side-valve V-twin. As with all engines of its type, the side-valve twin was less durable at speed than the ohv. The '100' and '80' model designations referred to the machines' guaranteed top speed. Brough Superior was also known for a proliferation of multi-cylindered exotica.

The machines were largely assembled from proprietary components—the engines were principally JAP or Matchless units, and even the famous Castle forks were originally a Harley Davidson design. This philosophy was the Achilles' heel of Brough Superior.

The company tried unsuccessfully to develop its own power-units, and the cost of buying-in specially-manufactured engines in small quantities eventually proved to be crippling. The company went out of business in 1938.

Brough Superior

SUNBEAM

THE SUNBEAM MODEL 90, shown on the right in its traditional black-and-gold livery, is probably the finest example of British single-cylinder engineering. It used simple, proven designs, with meticulous finish. The machine was conceived in 1923 as a sports roadster, and successfully adapted as a works racer. It was produced in both 350 and 500cc ohv versions. Production standards dropped after the factory was bought in 1930 by ICI (Imperial Chemical Industries). Sunbeam was later owned by Associated Motorcycles and BSA.

Douglas

ALTHOUGH DOUGLAS did sometimes use other engine layouts, the marque was always known for its horizontally-opposed twins. Today, Douglas is usually remembered for its post-war series of transverse-engined 350cc machines, but these were only made in the company's last seven years. In its earlier days, and for more than three decades, Douglas found its fame and fortune in exceptionally well-planned twins with a fore-and-aft arrangement. The success of these machines owed much to the work of the company's chief development rider, Freddie Dixon, during the middle and late 1920s. Fate also played a part. When the Douglas EW series of 350sv racers began to find the competition tough, Douglas had planned a new ohc model, but a fire at the works destroyed the blueprints and set back the company's work. The new engine was abandoned, and the company chose instead to give a new life to its old ohv twins, with considerable development work by Dixon. By happy chance, these machines proved most successful in the newly-arrived sport of speedway. Some of their success was due to a freak of design which led the frame to flex during broadsliding, but their achievements on the cinder track boosted all aspects of the Douglas reputation. During this period, the classic Douglas machine was the model FW, which was produced in 500cc and 600cc versions. The road-racing version is shown here. The road-racing models were capable of 90 mph and 95 mph respectively. In 1929 alone, 1300 machines were sold.

Rudge

SOME OF THE BEST British production bikes were replicas of their makers' works racing models. A fine example was the 1929 Rudge-Whitworth Ulster, which came from a factory famous for its advanced approach. The machine was introduced to celebrate Graham Walker's win in the Ulster Grand Prix, and it proved to be exceptionally fast and reliable. It had a four-speed positive-stop, foot-change gearbox, dry sump lubrication with a mechanical pump, and a four-valve cylinder head in a penthouse combustion chamber.

THE BRITISH EXCELSIOR company is remembered with affection for a 250cc single which was popularly known as the "Mechanical Marvel," but this four-valve ohv machine suffered from its own complexity. Undaunted, Excelsior continued along the same development path with an improved four-valver, the famous Manxman, shown here. This machine had a single overhead camshaft, and each inlet valve was fed by its own Amal RN carburettor. The bronze head, as shown, improved thermal efficiency in the days before aluminium had come into common use. The Manxman shown is a 250, but a 350 was also produced. Valve gear and carburettor tune still proved "very pernickerty" according to Excelsior's managing director Eric Walker, and in 1938 the firm introduced two-valve engines. These were equally fast, but wholly reliable. They had sprung frames, and proved so successful that they continued to be raced in private hands into the early 1950s.

Velocette

OTHER SINGLE-CYLINDER machines may have exemplified a particular aspect of engineering or of performance, but those produced by Velocette demonstrated the full range of attributes. This was best accomplished by the KTT (left), a racing replica of the works' own grand prix machinery, which was also notable as the first model to sport the Velocette-perfected foot gear-change system. This was an ohc single of 350cc, sold with a guaranteed top speed of 85 mph. As an option, Velocette offered a 100 mph dope-tuned model sporting a 9:1 compression ratio. The range ran from the 1929 Mk 1 illustrated here to the 1949 Mk VIII. In 1956, Velocette demonstrated its skills with a quite different range of well-remembered singles. These were ohv sports roadsters. First came the 499cc Venom, shown above, with a "square" (86 × 86mm) engine, then the smaller 349cc Viper. The Venom engine developed 36 bhp at 6,200 rpm, giving the machine a top speed of 95 mph. After 12 and 24-hour records had been set at Montlhéry, a highly-tuned version was produced as a clubman racer. This was the Thruxton (right), which had a top speed of approximately 120 mph.

BSA

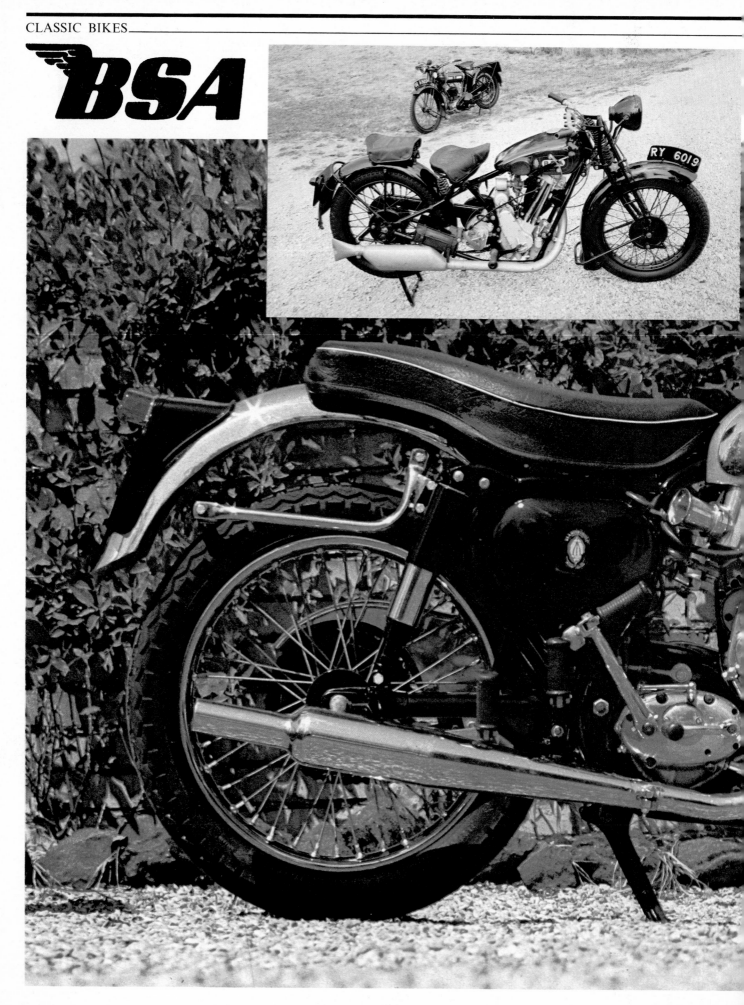

OR MOST OF ITS LIFE, the BSA marque was known primarily for singles of simple and inexpensive design, made for everyday transport. The motorcycles in the small picture are examples: a 250cc machine from 1925 (background) and the 1928 "Sloper". In later years, the same qualities of durability and reliability were showcased in a much more exotic motorcycle, the Gold Star. No clubman racer has ever enjoyed the success or reputation of the "Goldie". The range was produced in trial, scramble, touring and racing versions, and a 1959 model of the latter is shown here. The 500cc engine developed up to 40 bhp at just over 7,000 rpm, through a close ratio gearbox. Top speed was around 120 mph in full clubman trim.

HARLEY-DAVIDSON

THE HARLEY-DAVIDSON Electra-Glide has its origins in the SV 74 twin of 1922, although its more recent and direct ancestor is the first ohv 1200 of 1941. These early machines displayed the familiar styling features of most American motorcycles: leading link front forks, solid rear wheel mounting, pan saddles, footboards, high, wide handle-bars, and a V-twin engine, all of which produce comfort at low cruising speeds. Over the years, the range has been modernised and renamed, but the essential concept has remained the same. In 1949, the Hydra-Glide was introduced with a telescopic front fork. The next model, with pivoted-fork rear suspension, produced in 1959, was the Duo-Glide. With the addition of a starter motor in 1965 came the name Electra-Glide. Since then, little has changed except the adoption of cast alloy wheels, although numerous Japanese components, such as forks and carburettor, have been adopted. The Electra-Glide is the heaviest mass-produced motorcycle ever built, weighing 800 lbs fully equipped. The 45°, 1207cc V-twin has hydraulically-activated push-rods and produces 62 bhp at 5,200 rpm, and 70ft/lbs of torque at 4,000 rpm. For all its cumbrous luxury, the Harley has a speedy history. In the 1920s, when the marque was locked in competition with Indian, sporting feats were constantly being publicised. In 1920, several new times were set over a kilometre at Daytona. Harley, which was already well known in Britain, also made several celebrated runs at Brooklands. The 1,200cc machine shown below broke the Flying Kilometre record in 1923, at 108·6 mph, in the hands of the famous British rider Freddie Dixon.

THERE ARE MANY REASONS for celebrating the famous marque founded by Howard R. Davies (hence its original name, HRD) and bought shortly afterwards by Philip Vincent. Modern motorcycle manufacturers have still barely caught up with the progressive chassis-group designs produced by Vincent 35 years ago, though the marque is more commonly remembered for its spree of speedy achievement during the 1950s. Perhaps these sporting feats were the inspiration for the unusually-large and ambitious speedo which was fitted to Vincent motorcycles. Factory and private riders captured national and world speed and sprint records by the

VINCENT

handful on the competition model of the period, the Black Lightning. The word "Black" featured in the names of several famous Vincent machines. One unsupercharged Black Lightning achieved a speed of 185·15 mph in the hands of Russell Wright, a New Zealander, in 1955. Sadly, this was also the last year of full production.

The firm went out in a blaze of glory, with the announcement of the semi-streamlined Series D models, but few were actually made. In design, these machines were the natural successors to the Series C Rapides, which had been launched in 1949, with 50-degree 998cc V-twin engines. The Series C standard touring machine provided a top speed of approximately 105/110 mph, and its sporting counterpart the Black Shadow (shown here) went to 110/120 mph, reaching 56 mph in only six seconds. These machines were in turn developed from the Series A Rapides, which were launched in 1937, had 47-degree engines, and had a web of external pipes.

ARIEL was in every sense an historic British marque. Established since 1898, the firm exhibited all the characteristics of British motorcycle manufacture. The products were well made, even sporty, but initially of conventional design. In 1929, a much more sophisticated machine made a considerable break with tradition. This was a 500cc four with a highly-unusual "square" cylinder configuration and single overhead camshaft. This distinctive engine layout became so identifiable with the marque that the nickname "Squariel" passed into the language of motorcycling. Like the later Triumph Speed Twin, another pace-setting machine, the Square

Four was designed by Edward Turner. It had an all ball-and-roller bearing engine and horizontally-split crankcase. In 1931, the engine was bored out from 51 to 56 mm, thus increasing capacity to 600cc. Although some modest success was achieved in competition, such as the Bickel

brothers' supercharged 111·42 lap at Brooklands in 1934, the machine was really a sporting tourer. In 1936, Ariel launched a 1,000cc Square Four of quite new engine design. This model had a pushrod power-unit, with plain bearings, and it also utilised a unique trailing-link rear-suspension system. It remained in production in various roadster forms until the late 1950s, by which time it boasted four individual exhaust-pipes ports and an all-aluminium engine. The 1956 luxury roadster shown here develops 42 bhp at 5,800 rpm, providing a top speed of 105 mph. It has a bore and stroke of 65 × 75 mm. The machine's kerb-weight is 495 lbs.

TRIUMPH

TRIUMPH WILL ALWAYS be associated with the vertical-twin engine-layout. This classic design was introduced in 1938, in the 498cc Speed Twin, which was the fore-runner of many famous motorcycles. A memorable example was the larger Thunderbird (above), introduced in 1949. This 649cc tourer produced 34 bhp at 6,000 rpm on a compression ratio of 7:1. Three standard models averaged 101·06 mph between them for 500 miles at Montlhéry. A total break with the vertical-twin layout came in the 1960s with the transverse three-cylinder Trident (left), which had an ohv 740cc engine of 67 × 70 mm bore and stroke, developing 58 bhp at 7,500–8,000 rpm. This machine had a top speed of more than 125 mph.

Norton

IT WAS THE GREAT racing success of the Norton marque which created the need for an improved frame in the 1940s. The need was met by the McCandless brothers' Featherbed frame, which in turn influenced motorcycle design almost everywhere. After being introduced on the Manx racers, the Featherbed frame was modified for road use in the existing 497cc tourer, which became the Dominator in 1952. The example shown above was made a year later. Ten years after its launch, the Dominator had grown to 647cc, with a maximum road speed of 112 mph. In 1965, Norton launched the 745cc Atlas, but a more significant development came two years later. The same engine was fitted, with rubber mountings, into a new duplex frame. This new model, the Commando, was subsequently increased in size to 828cc. With a top speed of 120 mph, the Commando (left) is the most powerful road-going Norton ever produced.

LIKE THE LAMBORGHINI CAR, the equally exotic Laverda motorcycle is the product of an Italian agricultural engineering group. With a speed of 150 mph, verified in independent tests, the Laverda "Jota" is by far the fastest production roadster ever made. The Jota was developed in a collaboration between the factory and the British concessionaire. The standard 981cc dohc Laverda shown here still manages a tidy 130 mph, and develops 80 bhp at 8,000 rpm.

THE MV AGUSTA AMERICA is arguably the finest sports roadster in production, and without doubt a classic among the multi-cylindered big bikes. The entire power-unit is a development of the company's racing 500cc four of the 1950s. MV was the last European marque to dominate the Grand Prix circuits, and retired solely for commercial reasons, but it took several attempts before the factory's sporting experience could be translated into a successful roadster. The 788cc dohc America develops 75 bhp at 8,500 rpm, and its top speed is approximately 135 mph.

MOTO GUZZI

WHILE JAPANESE motorcycles have become increasingly sophisticated, the largest of the Italian manufacturers has responded by offering machines of comparable performance but robust simplicity. The V 850 GT of 1972 typifies Moto Guzzi's approach. The transverse twin turns out 64·5 bhp at a mere 6,500 rpm, providing a top speed of 115 mph. In 1975, the entire range was expanded to include the revolutionary V 1,000, with hydraulic torque converter.

DUCATI

IT WAS BUILT for its high-speed handling, apparently with no other priority in mind, and in this respect the Ducati Desmo 864cc of 1975 has no serious rival. Its top speed is 135 mph, its kerb weight a mere 428 lbs, and it is a remarkably stable motorcycle. The machine also benefits from the efficiency and reliability of the desmodromic valve system. Only Ducati has used this system with total success. The technique was employed to great effect in the 1972 750 SS clubman racer, after being first introduced by the factory's chief engineer, Fabioni Taglioni, in the successful Grand Prix period which was during the late 1950s.

THERE HAS NEVER BEEN a more aerodynamically advanced motorcycle than the BMW R100/RS. Nor has there been a simpler, more practical machine within this class of motorcycle. The horizontally-opposed 980cc ohv twin produces 70 bhp at 7,250 rpm (DIN), and a top speed of more than 125 mph. This performance can be achieved without any special effort or skill on the part of the rider. Furthermore, the rider is protected from the weather by a pocket of still air, thanks to a fairing developed in the Pinin Farina wind tunnel in Milan. The fairing also improves penetration by 5·4 per cent, negates front wheel lift, and increases downward pressure by 17·4 per cent. Lateral stability in particular is improved by 60 per cent.

These benefits were brought about by designer Hans Muth, whose background in car styling taught him how to utilise the wind, rather than fighting it. The dimensions and shape of the seat were also evolved with aerodynamic requirements in mind. The cockpit layout is in the sports car idiom, and the rider is even equipped with voltmeter and electric clock. The R100 weighs 530 lbs equipped for the road, and will cover a quarter-mile sprint in 13·5 seconds.

IT WAS WITH the racing success of machines like the 1960 Honda 250 four (small picture) that the Japanese motorcycle industry first claimed the attention of the Western world. When the sophisticated Gold Wing was launched in 1974, it met with some scepticism, but its elaborate design soon proved itself. The horizontally-opposed transverse four-cylinder layout makes for smooth running; the water-cooling improves the mechanical silencing and temperature control; shaft-drive affords longevity in the transmission; a low centre of gravity is achieved by the positions of the gearbox (beneath the engine) and the 4·2-gallon tank (beneath the seat nose); the dummy tank above the engine neatly and accessibly contains the coolant header tank, the majority of ancillary electrical components, tools, and emergency crank. Unusually, in a shaft driven motorcycle, the countershaft-mounted clutch is of the wet, multi-plate type. A contra-rotating generator along-side it successfully counteracts the lateral torque effect inherent in "flat"-engined machinery. At 6,500 rpm, torque amounts to 60ft/lbs, and at 7,500 rpm, the engine develops a DIN-rated 84 bhp. Top speed is more than 120 mph.

⚡ SUZUKI

WHEN SUZUKI LAUNCHED the first mass-produced rotary-engine motorcycle in 1975, the company took a calculated risk The success or failure of the Suzuki RE5 hinged on a paradox: the well-known selling-point of the rotary engine was its fundamental simplicity, yet precisely this advantage was seriously challenged by the complexity of the ancillary parts which it required. The engine of the RE5 demands two separate cooling systems, one using water and the other oil, and each with its own radiator. While the unusually-hot combustion area of the unit needs cooling, the induction side needs warming, for which purpose the same water is circulated. Such convoluted engineering has to be monitored with an instrument panel which contains a total of ten warning systems. Although it is rated as a 500cc engine, the power-unit has three chambers of this size, thus making for a large motorcycle. At 550 lbs, it is equal in weight to a conventional 750cc machine. Top speed is approximately 112 mph; there is no vibration; and the power-band is broader than that of any conventional motorcycle. Maximum torque of 54·9 ft/lbs is developed at 3,600 rpm, and 62 bhp at 7,000 rpm. Ignition is by transistorised capacitator discharge, incorporating carburettor sensors for advance and retard operation. The engineering and constructional skills used in the development of the RE5 were quite exceptional, and for them the machine wins a place in the history of the motorcycle, whatever the future of the rotary engine.

⊛ YAMAHA

IF ANTI-POLLUTION LAWS and the cost of fuel prevent the further development of the two-stroke engine in full-size roadsters, the Yamaha twins will be remembered as the last of the line. These machines have probably the most efficient two-stroke roadster engines ever made. The 398cc RD400 shown here develops 40 bhp at 7,000 rpm, and its powerful mid-range torque development provides impressive acceleration, with a top speed of more than 100 mph. The combustion efficiency is attributable to reed-valve controlled carburation and an extra, seventh-port induction system. It had a six-speed gearbox and very powerful brakes.

K Kawasaki

THREE-CYLINDER TWO STROKES had been made before, but none so deliberately aimed at massive power and speed as the 1969 Kawasaki H1 Mach III, a 498cc transverse three. From an unusually weak torque development below 6,000 rpm, the engine roused itself at 7,000 to produce 42·3ft/lbs, and at 7,500 a DIN-rated 60 bhp. Top speed was approximately 120 mph, and a quarter-mile sprint resulted in a time of little more than 12 seconds. Unfortunately, the design of the cycle parts was less successful, and the machine's mighty performance proved difficult to handle. The engine was progressively de-tuned in later years until it faded out in 1974.

THE A-Z
OF THE WORLD'S
MOTORCYCLES

Key to abbreviations:

TS = Two-stroke

sv = Side-valve

ohv = Overhead-valve

hc = High camshafts

ohc = Overhead camshafts

dohc = Double overhead camshafts

ioe = Inlet over exhaust

DEFINITIONS:

Horsepower = bhp
33,000 ft-lb per min or 550 ft-lb per second = 1·01387 cv (764·08 watts).

Kilogramme (kg) =
Metric standard unit of mass = 2·20462 lb.

Litre (1) =
The volume occupied by 1 kg of distilled water at 4°C and 760mm of mercury pressure.

Mile =
1760 yards (5280 ft) = 1609·344 m.

Millimetre (mm) =
1/1000 metre = 0·0393701 ins.

TABLE OF RAC HORSEPOWER RATINGS:

Cylinder-Diameter in mm:	1 Cyl:	2 Cyl:	Cylinder-Diameter in mm:	1 Cyl:	2 Cyl:
50	1·54	3·1	67	2·78	5·6
51	1·61	3·2	68	2·87	5·7
52	1·67	3·34	69	2·95	5·9
53	1·74	3·48	70	2·04	6·1
54	1·80	3·6	71	3·12	6·2
55	1·87	3·7	72	3·21	6·4
56	1·94	3·98	73	3·30	6·6
57	2·01	4·0	74	3·39	6·8
58	2·08	4·16	75	3·49	6·98
59	2·15	4·3	76	3·58	7·2
60	2·23	4·5	77	3·67	7·3
61	2·30	4·6	78	3·77	7·5
62	2·38	4·8	79	3·87	7·7
63	2·46	4·9	80	3·97	7·9
64	2·54	5·1	85	4·48	8·96
65	2·61	5·2	90	5·02	10·0
66	2·70	5·4			

RAC RATING FORMULAE:

$$\frac{\text{Bore (squared} \times \text{No of cylinders)}}{2\cdot5} = \text{Power at flywheel}$$

For power at road wheels divide by 3 (cylinder dimensions in inches). If taken in mm, divide by 1613 instead of 2·5 for power at flywheel.

This formula used mainly before WWII

CYLINDER DISPLACEMENT

Multiply the bore with the bore
Multiply the result with the stroke
Multiply this result with 0·785 and
Multiply with number of cylinders.

Sample: Moto Guzzi V 1000:
88mm × 88mm = 7744
7744 × 78mm = 60,4032
6040 × 0·785 = 47,4140
474 × 2 = 948cc

MILES = KILOMETRES:

10	=	16
15	=	24
20	=	32
30	=	48
40	=	64
50	=	80
100	=	160
200	=	320
300	=	480

CONVERSION FACTORS:

Multiply:	By:	To obtain:	Multiply:	By:	To obtain:
Centimetres	0·0328084	Feet	Kilometres per hour	0·621371	Miles per hour
Centimetres	0·393701	Inches	Kilometres per litre	2·82473	Miles per Imp. gal.
Centimetres per second	0·036	Kilometres per hour	Litres	1000·028	Cubic centimetres
Cubic centimetres	0·0610237	Cubic inches	Litres	61·0255	Cubic inches
Cubic inches	16·3871	Cubic centimetres	Litres	0·264178	Gallons (US)
Feet	30·48	Centimetres	Litres	0·219976	Gallons (Imperial)
Feet	12	Inches	Litres	1·7598	Pints (Imperial)
Gallons (Imperial)	4·54596	Litres	Litres per kilometre	0·354016	Gal. (Imp.) per mile
Gallons (United States)	0·832680	Gallons (Imperial)	Litres per kilometre	0·425153	Gal. (US) per mile
Gallons (United States)	3·78533	Litres	Miles (also mph)	1·609344	Kilometres (also kph)
Horsepower (British)	745·7	Watts	Millimetres	0·0393701	Inches
Horsepower (Metric)	0·986320	Horsepower (British)	Pounds	0·45359237	Kilogrammes
Inches	2·54	Centimetres	Square centimetres	0·15500	Square inches
Inches	25·4	Millimetres	Square inches	6·4516	Square centimetres
Kilogrammes	35·274	Ounces	Square inches	645·16	Square millimetres
Kilogrammes	2·20462	Pounds	United States gallons	0·83268	Imperial gallons
Kilometres	0·621371	Miles	United States gallons	3·78533	Litres
Kilometres	1093·61	Yards	Yards	0·9144	Metres

ABAKO/*Germany 1923–1925*
Small 129cc single-cylinder machines with own two-stroke deflector-type three-port engines, two and three-speed Sturmey-Archer gearboxes and chain drive to the rear wheel.

ABBOTSFORD/*England 1919–1920*
Scooter-like lightweights with 1·5 hp ohv power units. Limited production.

ABC/*England 1913–1914*

Designed by Granville Bradshaw for the All British (Engine) Company, this 496cc ioe flat twin was the first motorcycle created by Bradshaw. Some of these engines were supplied to W. Brough.
1914–1919 The reorganised ABC Motors Ltd,

originally at Brooklands, Byfleet, moved to Walton-on-Thames and produced mainly war material and motorcycle engines for the military.
1920–1922 Another reorganisation, which took place at Walton-on-Thames. Production centred around spare parts and the development of new designs, but there were no new motorcycles put on the market. Bradshaw's policy was to sell his designs to a manufacturing concern.
1919–1922 This was the *real* ABC, built by The Sopwith Aviation & Engineering Co. Ltd at Kingston-on-Thames, a company which built aircraft during the war and which afterwards took over Bradshaw's newest creation. This was a transverse-mounted 398cc flat twin with ohv, 4-speed gearbox, all chain drive, spring frame and forks, automatic lubrication etc. Often regarded as the predecessor of the first BMW, the Sopwith-ABC was an advanced but under-developed design when Sopwith put it on the market. The valve gear was unreliable, the lubrication bad and although they could sell more than they were able to produce, the ABC failed and by 1921 Sopwith were in liquidation, mainly because failures of the design led to too many

guarantee claims. The price for the Standard Model was £98, the Lucas Dynamo Model was offered at £118.
France 1920–1924 Made under licence from Sopwith by a branch factory of the French Gnome & Rhone aero-engine and motorcycle company, the French ABC lasted longer than the English original. Cpt. Bartlett, who headed the production in France, used modified cylinder heads for his machines and supplied in addition to the 348cc ABC a 493cc machine. Together with Naas, he competed in races and other sporting events with great success.

ABC Scootamota/*England 1919–1922*
Another design by Granville Bradshaw, the Scootamota was a quite popular scooter with 147cc ioe and later 110cc ohv engines. It was the most widely sold scooter in England after WWI, but after 1922 it faded out.

ABC/*England 1920–1924*
Built by J. Barwell at Birmingham, this ABC had no connection with Bradshaw's ABC designs. It was an assembled machine with 296cc and afterwards 247cc Villiers two-stroke proprietary engines.

ABC/*Germany 1922–1925*
Another, but little known ABC built in Berlin. The engine was a deflector-type 149cc two-stroke of the company's own design and manufacture.

ABENDSONNE/*Germany 1933–1934*
Designed by Georg Weissbinder, who coupled two 98cc Villiers engines together. Few of these machines were actually made.

ABERDALE/*England 1946–1959*
London-built 48cc autocycles and lightweight motorcycles with 98cc and 123cc Villiers and Sachs two-stroke power units. Bown, another

398cc ABC (ohv flat-twin) 1921

manufacturer of such machines, took over Aberdale production in 1959.

ABE-STAR / *Japan 1951–1959*
One of the many Japanese motorcycle factories of the 1950s. Top model was a 148cc four-stroke with the company's own ohv engine.

ABINGDON / *England 1903–1925*
Early models had MMC, Minerva Kerry and Fafnir engines; later ones used Abingdon's own 3·5 hp singles and 5–6 hp V-twins. After 1918 the range consisted of 348cc singles, 496cc and 796cc V-twins with Abingdon sv engines. A 624cc single was built for a short period. The producer, Abingdon-King-Dick, a well-known tool factory at Birmingham, after 1925 renamed the machines AKD and concentrated on singles up to 346cc. Abingdon motorcycles were of sturdy design and many were sold in the colonies.

ABJ / *England 1950–1954*
Lightweights with 48cc, 98cc and 123cc Villiers two-stroke engines, made by a bicycle factory. The 48cc Auto-Minor was sold for £41 15s.

ABRA / *Italy 1923–1927*
Assembled motorcycles with German 146cc DKW two-stroke engines. From 1924 onwards also used their own 132cc engines. Small production.

ACE / *America 1919–1929*
William 'Bill' Henderson sold his famous four-cylinder Henderson design in 1917 to the Chicago-based Schwinn company and in 1919 founded the ACE Motor Corporation in Philadelphia. There he once more built four-cylinder air-cooled

in-line unit-design motorcycles with 1168cc, later 1229cc and 1266cc engines. He was killed in 1922 in an accident while testing a new model and another famous designer, Arthur Lemon, took over design and development. All engines had ioe valves, light-alloy pistons and Schebler carburettors. The engines developed between 20 and 25 bhp. In 1927 Indian took over the ACE, which ran into commercial difficulties, and moved production to Springfield, Massachusetts. After 1929 the machine was renamed Indian 4.

ACHILLES / *Czechoslovakia 1906–1912*
Built by a bicycle factory in what is now Czechoslovakia, Achilles motorcycles had 3·5 hp single-cylinder and 5 hp V-twin proprietary engines made by Fafnir and Zeus.

ACHILLES / *Germany 1953–1957*
Scooter-like machines with 98cc and 123cc Sachs engines and also sporting 48cc mopeds. The same company built motorcycles in the Austro-Hungarian Empire before WWI. When they closed down in 1957 in Germany, the English Norman motorcycle factory bought the production equipment.

ACMA / *France 1948–early 1960s*
Licensed production of Italian 123cc, 147cc and 173cc Vespa scooters. The factory was at Fourchambault.

ACME / *England 1902–1922*
Built motorcycles with 2 hp Minerva and 2·5 hp Automoto engines. After 1918, 293cc JAP, their own 348cc sv singles and 997cc sv V-twins came into production. In 1922 Acme amalgamated with Rex at Coventry. The result was Rex-Acme motorcycles, which became famous when Walter Handley won races on Blackburne-engined racing models. *See also* Rex-Acme.

293cc Acme (sv-JAP) 1922

ADER / *France 1901–1906*
Pioneer manufacturer, who also built cars. Motorcycles built by Clément Ader had 2 hp single-cylinder and transverse-mounted V-twin 4 hp engines.

246cc Adler (TS twin) 1953

ADLER / *Germany 1900–1957*
Famous manufacturer whose early motorcycles had their own 3 hp, 3·5 hp and 5 hp engines. From 1907 to 1939 the Frankfurt-based works concentrated on cars, typewriters and bicycles. They re-entered motorcycle production in 1949 with two-strokes of 98cc and afterwards also built first-class 123cc, 147cc, and 198cc and 246cc two-strokes of their own design. The last ones were vertical twins, well-tuned watercooled racing engines producing 38 to 39 bhp. Ridden by Luttenberger, Beer, Vogel, Lohmann, Falk and others, these Adler racing two-strokes won many races. There were also trials and moto-cross models. All Adler machines were of sound design and excellent finish.

1229cc ACE (ioe four-in-line) 1923

ADONIS / *France 1949–1952*
Small Vap-engined 48cc and 75cc scooters of simple design.

ADRIA / *Germany 1912–1928*
Sturdy sv singles of 276cc, 282cc, 294cc and 346cc capacity. Adria also built proprietary engines for cars and boats, but motorcycle manufacture was on a limited scale only.

ADS / *Belgium 1949–1954*
Small assembler of 98cc machines with Sachs and Ilo two-stroke engines.

ADVANCE / *England 1906–1912*
Once a well-known make with own 3 hp, 3·5 hp and V-twin 6 hp power units. Compared to other makes of that period, Advance motorcycles had very low frames.

AEL / *England 1919–1924*
A motorcycle and accessories dealer in Coventry who fitted various 147cc to 348cc proprietary engines made by Villiers, JAP and Blackburne. The frames were probably built by Hobart in Coventry.

AEOLUS / *England 1903–1905*
Interesting 492cc single-cylinder design with shaft drive to the rear wheel. Production was on a limited scale.

AEOLUS / *England 1914–1916*
Had no connection with the first London-made Aeolus. This Aeolus was fitted with its own 269cc two-stroke engines. The company — Bowns Ltd. — produced Bown lightweight machines after 1945.

AER / *England 1938–1940*
Scott motorcycle specialist A. E. Reynolds produced from 1927 onwards modified 498cc and 598cc Scott machines, called Reynolds Special. In the late 1930s, modern 246cc single-cylinder and 346cc vertical twin two-strokes of his own design and manufacture came into being. WWII stopped production.

AERO-CAPRONI / *Italy 1948–1964*
Once a famous aircraft factory at Trento, Aero-Caproni built after the war motorcycles of their own design with 73cc, 124cc and 148cc ohv and partly face-cam ohc engines. Some had tubular, others pressed steel frames, 48cc machines were also built and there was a 149cc model with a transverse-mounted ohv flat-twin unit-design

engine in a pressed steel frame. This model had 7·5 bhp at 6000 rpm and a 60 mph top speed. Small two-stroke models assembled by Aero Caproni (Capriolo) had NSU engines.

AER MACCHI / *Italy 1948–*
Now belonging to AMF Harley-Davidson, Aer Macchi was originally a well-known aircraft factory at Varese. The first models had unorthodox frames and flat single-cylinder 123cc two-stroke engines. They looked like a hybrid between motorcycle and scooter. Later versions employed more conventional frames and 172cc, 246cc as well as 346cc single-cylinder ohv power units. The range also included the fully-enclosed 172cc Chimera and very fast ohv racing singles, including the Ala D'Oro production racing versions. There was also the 123cc Zeffiro two-stroke scooter and a 248cc model with a flat twin engine. Alberto Pagani and Gilberto Milani were among the many successful riders in races, where they rode mainly 248cc single-cylinder ohv models. When the factory ran into difficulties in 1960, AMF Harley-Davidson of Milwaukee, Wisconsin bought it and now produces models from 49cc to 248cc there. In later years the famous two-stroke racing machines, especially with Walter Villa in the saddle, won numerous championships in the 250cc and 350cc class.

AEROPLAN / *Germany 1922–1925*
Assembled on a limited scale 123cc and 173cc DKW two-stroke engines into their own open frames.

AEROS / *Czechoslovakia 1927–1929*
Designed by Franz Brezina, the Aeros had a BMW-like frame with a leaf spring fork and German 347cc and 497cc Küchen three-valve ohc proprietary single-cylinder engines.

AETOS / *Italy 1912–1914*
Produced one model only, a 492cc V-twin 3·5 hp machine.

AFW / *Germany 1923–1925*
Limited manufacture of 246cc ohv machines with engines supplied by the Bielefeld-based Hansa factory.

AGF / *France 1948–1956*
Well-known as producer of scooters and motorcycles with 123cc and 173cc Ydral proprietary engines.

AGON / *Germany 1924–1928*
The Benninger-designed machines had different engines, including the 197cc Paqué, 346cc Bradshaw, 498cc Küchen and JAP units from 173cc to 996cc. 746cc and 996cc JAP-engined Agons were V-twins.

AGRATI / *Italy 1958–*
Commenced scooter production in 1958 and merged in 1961 with the famous Garelli factory. Large-scale production of 49cc two-stroke mofas, mopeds and other vehicles with such engines. *See also* Garelli.

AGS / *The Netherlands 1971–*
Moto-cross machines with 123cc two-stroke engines supplied by Sachs, Puch, Zündapp and other makers.

AIGLON / *France 1908–1953*
Zurcher, Minerva, Mirus, Peugeot, AMC, FMC and others supplied engines for many years to Aiglon. Debarelle's last models had 123cc and

346cc AER (TS twin) 1953

174cc ohv AMC engines and FMC-built 248cc two-strokes.

AIM / Italy 1974–

Producer of sports machines, especially motocross versions with 49cc and 124cc Franco-Morini two-stroke engines.

AIROLITE / England 1921–1923

Lightweight machines with 110cc Simplex two-stroke engines.

AJAX / England 1923–1924

Cheaply assembled machines with open frames. These housed 147cc, 247cc and 269cc Villiers two-stroke and 346cc Blackburne sv engines.

AJR / Scotland 1925–1926

One of the few Scottish makes, A. J. Robertson of Edinburgh built machines which housed 346cc and 490cc single-cylinder ohv engines made by JAP in London. Robertson rode them in many sporting events.

AJS / England 1909–

Joe Stevens built engines at Wolverhampton in 1897; his sons Harry, George, Jack and Joe built at their father's Stevens Screw Co. Ltd. the first AJS motorcycle in 1909. It had a 298cc sv engine of their own design and manufacture. 346cc and 498cc sv and ohv versions followed and during the following years there were also models with V-twin sv engines from 550cc to 990cc. The 348cc (74mm × 81mm bore/stroke) ohv single was one of the first English machines with ohv while the 498cc ohv (84mm × 90mm bore/stroke) came along in 1925, five years after the smaller model. Two years later, AJS introduced racing engines with chain-driven ohc and three-speed gearboxes. They too were 348cc and 498cc designs; a special engine for Brooklands races had 743cc, and a V-twin built for attacks on the world record had 996cc and two chain-driven camshafts. For the TT two 248cc ohc singles were built and among prototypes they had 498cc models with transverse-mounted sv and ohv V-twin engines. There was even a 498cc model with an aircooled four-in-line sv engine. In 1931 the Stevens brothers had to sell AJS. The London-based Collier brothers, manufac-

turers of Matchless motorcycles at Plumstead, bought the make and moved it to London. In the following years, Matchless and AJS had many parts in common.

Most AJS models built during the 1930s had 248cc, 348cc and 498cc sv and ohv engines and also 996cc sv V-twins. There were trials and racing models and even — at the Olympia Show in London — an aircooled 495cc ohc V-four. A racing version of it competed in the 1936 Senior TT. Improved 4-cylinder AJS racing models with watercooled and supercharged 495cc engines came into being in 1939. They proved to be the fastest British road racing machines built until war broke out. Associated Motor Cycles Ltd., as the company was called, bought Sunbeam in 1937 from I.C.I. in Wolverhampton, transferred it to London and sold it in 1940 to the Birmingham-based BSA Group. After the war, James in Birmingham, Francis-Barnett in Coventry and in 1952 even Norton in Birmingham joined Associated Motor Cycles Ltd.

Soon after the war a new 498cc AJS racing machine, the twin-cylinder Porcupine with gear-

996cc AJS (sv V-twin) 1930

498cc AJS (H10) 1927

496cc AJS (ohc V-four Prototype) 1935

495cc AJS (supercharged ohc V-four) 1936

driven ohc, was ridden by the works team. For private riders a new 348cc ohc single, the 7-R 'Boy's Racer', came into production in 1949, and was also used by the works team. H. J. Hatch, who created many Blackburne engines and in the thirties the Mechanical Marvel for Excelsior, also developed several new 348cc ohc singles

498cc AJS (ohc twin Porcupine) 1947

348cc AJS (ohc 'Boy's Racer') 1948

348cc AJS (3 ohc 3-valve works racer) 1953

with bevel-driven triple camshafts, and other new AJS racing models. In 1954 the factory withdrew from racing with special machinery. From then onwards, development was on a limited scale. In the meantime Norton lost the Bracebridge Street home in Birmingham and was transferred to Plumstead too. With three makes—Matchless, AJS and Norton—under one roof, Associated Motor Cycles Ltd. left the old home at Plumstead Road, London in 1969 and moved to a new factory at Andover. Now owned by Manganese Bronze Holdings and headed by ex-racing-car driver Dennis Poore, AJS came into the sphere of Norton-Villiers Limited of Wolverhampton, founded in 1966, where they built engines. All AJS four-strokes were dropped and only 247cc two-stroke single-cylinder trials and moto-cross machines were built in the new works. Some frames were even made by Cotton in Gloucester.

Matchless, Francis-Barnett and James had already disappeared from the scene and after a few successful years with the 247cc moto-cross model, AJS also faded out. Gone was the once great and famous make, a machine which during the years gained much success, with such great riders as Jimmy Simpson, George Rowley, Jimmy Guthrie, Freddy Hicks, Eric Williams, Cyril Williams, Howard Davies, Frank Longmann, Walter Handley, Bert Denly, Pat Driscoll, Harold Daniell, Walter Rusk, Bob Foster, Jock West, Les Graham, Bill Doran, Leo Davenport, Tommy Spann, Bob McIntyre, Rod Coleman, Reg. Armstrong, Hugh Viney, Bob Manns, Gordon Jackson, Frank Giles, Derek Ennett, Mike Duff, Phil Read, Michael Gayer, Hans Baltisberger, H. G. Tyrell Smith, Ted Frend, Ernie Thomas and many others.

For all its troubled history, AJS is not entirely dead. A new company, headed by Fluff Brown, is producing at Andover 248cc and 358cc two-stroke moto-cross machines.

AJW / England 1926–

Designed by A. J. Wheaton as a machine to oppose George Brough's Brough-Superior motorcycles, the AJW had at first big V-twin sv and ohv JAP and British-Anzani engines with 678cc and 996cc capacity. Beautifully made with

678cc AJW (ohv JAP) 1929

saddle tanks and a very low saddle position, Sturmey-Archer gearboxes. Pilgrim oil-pumps, Binks and Amal carburetters etc. they were expensive. This led to smaller models with 172cc

490cc AJW (ohv JAP) 1952

and 247cc Villiers engines. During the 1930s, most AJW machines had 496cc single-cylinder ohv power units made by Python (Rudge), JAP and Stevens (the Stevens brothers, former owners of the AJS factory). After 1945 the reorganised AJW factory, now owned by J. O. Ball, built beautiful 498cc vertical twins with JAP sv engines. Limited production of these engines forced AJW to stop manufacture of these machines. Assisted now by Ball's son Alan, manufacture concentrates on 49cc mopeds with Sachs and Franco-Morini engines and other—mainly Italian—components.

AKD / England 1926–1933

Successor to Abingdon motorcycles. The factory still exists as manufacturer of tools. The range of

173cc AKD (ohv Sport) 1929

models included 147cc, 173cc and 198cc ohv singles and 298cc and 346cc sv singles of AKD's own design and manufacture. 173cc supersports models were successful around 1930 at races.

346cc AKD (sv) 1929

AKKENS / *England 1919–1922*
Made by a small company, Akkens motorcycles had 292cc Union two-stroke engines with deflector-type pistons.

ALATO / *Italy 1923–1925*
Made by the Gosio brothers at Turin, Alato machines had their own 131cc two-stroke power units.

ALBA / *Germany 1919–1924*
A good four-stroke machine with 198cc and 247cc sv engines. The last model was a unit-design 249cc ohv version. Alba at Stettin (now Poland), owned by Alfred Baruch, also built delivery three-wheelers and supplied motorcycle engines to other factories including Huy and Teco. Although they stopped motorcycle manufacture in the mid-1920s, a company headed by Alfred Baruch's son Manfred supplied spares until the mid-1930s.

249cc Alba (ohv) 1924

ALBERT / *Germany 1922–1924*
Built during the inflation period in Germany 183cc two-strokes with own engines in limited quantities.

ALBERTUS / *Germany 1922–1924*
Was the original manufacturer of motorcycles with the Julius Löwy-designed crude-oil two-

142cc Albertus (TS crude-oil engine) 1922

stroke engines of 113cc, 142cc and 176cc. While the engines were made at the Königsberg works, complete Albertus motorcycles came from Achern in Badonia.

ALCYON / *France 1902–late 1960s*
Once a leading motorcycle producer. Bought during the years other French makes including Labor, Thomann, Amor and Olympique. Already built in pre-1914 days potent V-twins and vertical twins, and when Alcyon competed in 1912 in the Isle of Man TT races, they had 348cc ohv singles with two inlet valves and two exhaust valves. These engines were designed by Zurcher. Between the wars, most Alcyon models had 98cc to 248cc two-stroke and 173cc to 498cc four-stroke sv and ohv engines. Some bigger versions already had shaft drive around 1930, and some had pressed-steel frames. 173cc Alcyon racing models, ridden by Joly and Lemasson, won many races in the late 1920s and early 1930s. After 1945 Alcyon produced two- and four-strokes up to 248cc with AMC, Zurcher, Vap and other engines and concentrated on 48cc mopeds and similar designs.

ALDBERT / *Italy 1953–1959*
Well-designed typical Italian machines with 49cc to 173cc two-stroke and 173cc to 246cc four-stroke ohv engines. The Razzo model had a 174cc 60mm × 61mm bore/stroke ohv unit-design 4-speed engine and a 93 mph top speed.

ALECTO / *England 1919–1924*
Had own 295cc and 345cc two-stroke deflector-type three-port engines and belt drive to the rear wheel. An all-chain 345cc model was made 1923–1924. It had 76mm bore and 76mm stroke.

ALERT / *England 1903–1906*
Made by Smith & Molesworth at Coventry, these machines had 2·35 hp, 2·75 hp and 3·25 hp Sarolea engines.

ALEU / *Spain 1953–1956*
Conventional design with 198cc and 247cc two-stroke engines of Spanish manufacture.

ALFA / *Germany 1925–1928*
Designed by former BMW chief development engineer Alexander von Falkenhausen the Alfa had 172cc Villiers engines; some later models had bigger ones including a 344cc vertical twin.

ALFA / *Italy 1923–1926*
Assembled machines with English 170cc ohv Norman and 346cc ohv Bradshaw and Black-burne engines. Limited production.

ALFA-GNOM / *Austria 1926–1928*
Made by Franz & Anton Rumpler, manufacturers of FAR motorcycles, the 598cc Alfa-Gnom had a single-cylinder ohc engine.

ALGE / *Germany 1923–1931*
Produced 173cc to 498cc single-cylinder sv and ohv machines of conventional design and also transport three-wheelers with motorcycle engines. Owned by Alfred Geissler, Alge also fitted from 1928 onwards 173cc and 347cc Villiers engines and 497cc sv Blackburne engines.

ALIPRANDI / *Italy 1925–1930*
Beautiful 123cc and 173cc machines with Swiss

Moser ohv engines. Other models made by the Aliprandi brothers had 173cc to 498cc sv and ohv power units by JAP and Sturmey-Archer.

ALLDAYS / *England 1903–1915*
Built as early as 1898 De Dion-engined three wheelers, later cars and motorcycles. These had their own 499cc single-cylinder and 539cc V-twin sv engines. Concentrated afterwards on Allon motorcycles.

ALLEGRO / *Switzerland 1925–early 1960s*
Well-known make which won many races in the 175cc class with Marcel Bourquin and the manufacturer Arnold Grandjean in the saddle. These machines had 172cc Villiers Brooklands two-stroke racing engines. In 1929 Grandjean built a 344cc racer for his own use in races, which had two such engines coupled together in tandem. Production versions had engines up to 348cc, supplied by Villiers, MAG and Sturmey-Archer. Allegro supplied mopeds in later years.

ALLON / *England 1915–1924*
Already mentioned with Alldays, the Allon housed its own 292cc deflector-type two-stroke engine. The second model, supplied 1923–1924, had a 346cc sv engine made by JAP.

ALLRIGHT / *Germany 1901–1927*
Known in England as Vindec-Special and VS, the Allright was also sold in other countries under the Tiger and Roland trademark. Early models had Belgian Kelecom, Minerva and FN, from 1905 onwards German Fafnir engines and Belgian Truffault forks (swinging arms). The German Cito works amalgamated in 1922 with Allright with the result that Allright also produced the famous KG (Krieger-Gnädig) motorcycle. This was a 503cc, later 498cc ohv unit-design single with shaft-drive to the rear wheel. The range also included 149cc two-strokes of the company's design and 248cc to 996cc sv and ohv JAP engines. Some models had MAG and Blackburne engines. All were of orthodox 'English design' and also had many English components. Chief designer Rudi Albert in the mid-1920s modified the 1919 KG design, which now received a horizontal shaft to the rear wheel and also the improved ohv engine. Allright motorcycle production stopped when they decided to concentrate on the manufacture of Tiger forks, hubs and other accessories. Paul Henkel, a former KG technician, took over the production of these machines until his death in 1932. Among successful Allright and Allright-KG riders were Zündorf, Soenius, Ehrlenbruch, Kniebecke, Roggenbuck, Fast, and Karsch.

ALLSTATE / *Austria 1953–1963*
This is the name of Austrian Puch machines sold in the USA since about 1953 by Sears-Roebuck of Chicago through their nationwide branches. Allstate is a Sears trademark, also applied to car parts, insurance etc.

ALMA / *France 1949–1959*
Producers of mopeds, scooters and lightweight machines from 49cc to 149cc with their own engines and also proprietary engines made by Le Paulin and Ydral.

ALMORA / *Germany 1924–1925*
Interesting but not very successful design. Used Julius Löwy-developed 113cc, 138cc and 176cc two-stroke engines which ran on crude oil after they had been 'hotted up' on petrol. They failed because they didn't develop enough power and proved unreliable.

ALP / *English 1912–1917*
Was originally an English branch of the Swiss Moto-Rêve motorcycle factory. Produced models with 3 hp and 3·5 hp V-twins, with vertical twin-cylinder engines and as a bread-and-butter model a 199cc machine with an English Precision proprietary engine. The last Alp had a 348cc two-stroke engine.

ALPHONSE THOMANN / *France 1908–1923*
Once a well-known make, which was not the same as Thomann. Main production concentrated around 98cc to 173cc two-strokes.

ALPINO / *Italy 1948–1962*
Typical Italian post-war machines from 48cc to 174cc with two- and four-stroke ohv engines. 48cc models broke world records with Tamarozzi, Pennati, Pasini and Sozzani.

ALTA / *Wales 1968–1971*
Not connected with the former Alta car factory, this Swansea company produced trials and moto-cross machines with Japanese Suzuki engines of 49cc to 130cc.

ALTEA / *Italy 1939–1941*
Designed by former MAS boss Alberico Seilig for the famous Max Türkheimer motorcycle company at Milan, the modern Altea had a 198cc unit-design engine with vertical overhead valves among its interesting features. Türkheimer, since 1897 Ariel importer and once even shareholder of the English Ariel works, also built Astra motorcycles.

ALTER / *France 1955–1956*
Small French manufacturer of 49cc machines with various two-stroke engines.

AMAG / *Germany 1924–1925*
Another small producer of lightweight machines. These had 149cc Bekamo two-stroke engines which used a pumping cylinder in the crankcase.

AMBAG / *Germany 1923*
Fitted 155cc Gruhn sv single-cylinder engines into their own frames.

AMBASSADOR / *England 1947–1964*
Owned by ex-motorcycle, car and motor-boat racing driver Kaye Don, the Ascot-based company was also importer of German Zündapp motorcycles and American Pontiac cars. All Ambassador motorcycles housed 147cc to 248cc two-stroke Villiers engines. When he retired in

346cc Allright (ohv JAP) 1924

1964, everything connected with Ambassador manufacture was sold to the DMW factory.

AMC / *America 1912–1915*
There was no connection between this American Allied Motor Corporation at Chicago and Associated Motor Cycles Ltd. of London or the French AMC proprietary engine company. The AMC was a big V-twin with a 980cc ioe engine and was equipped with a very unusual front suspension.

AMERICAN / *America 1911–1914*
It is possible that this make was identical with the above AMC, although the address reads American Motorcycle Co. of Chicago. Manufacture consisted of a 4 hp single with 550cc.

AMERICAN-X / *America 1910–1930*
Made by Ignaz Schwinn's Excelsior Company at Chicago, this was really a 996cc Excelsior ioe V-twin, exported to England. As there was already an English Excelsior factory, the American product was renamed American-X.

AMI / *Germany 1921–1925*
A 49cc ohv engine for bicycles designed by Heinrich Hillebrand, late of Hillebrand & Wolfmüller motorcycle-pioneering fame. A similar engine was made by the Columbus engine factory (later Horex) and called Gnom. Both had to be fitted in front of the pedalling gear. This started a fight between Ami and Gnom which lasted a long time in the courts.

AMI / *Switzerland 1950–1954*
Designed by Jaroslav Frei, former boss of the Czech Jawa factory, the Ami was a scooter with 98cc and later 123cc two-stroke engines.

AMMON / *Germany 1923–1925*
Interesting frame design, which consisted partly of tubes and partly of pressed steel. Used various proprietary engines which included DKW, Baumi and Bekamo two-strokes and the 123cc Paqué ohv engine.

AMO / *Germany 1921–1924*
Simple design of 146cc two-stroke lightweight machines.

AMO / *Germany 1950–1954*
Mopeds with own 48cc two-stroke engines made by Westendarp & Pieper, a company which built TX motorcycles in the mid-1920s. The factory was at Berlin.

AMS / *Spain 1954–1965*
Assembled two-stroke motorcycles with 124cc, 198cc and 247cc Hispano-Villiers engines. They also built 248cc vertical twins.

ANCILOTTI / *Italy 1967–*
One of the newer makes which concentrates on superb 49cc and 123cc machines. The production includes special trials and moto-cross versions of up-to-date design. The machines are also known under the Scarab trade mark.

124cc Ancilotti (TS Sachs Trial) 1974

ANCORA / *Italy 1923–1939*
Fitted for many years 147cc to 347cc Villiers engines and won many races during the late 1920s when the late Raffaele Alberti rode a 172cc Brooklands Villiers-engined Ancora in competitions. Umberto Dei bought the factory in the early 1930s and built 60cc, 74cc and 98 cc models; after 1945 Dei supplied more lightweights, this time with the Garelli-built 39cc Mosquito bicycle engine.

ANDREES / *Germany 1923–1929*
Assembled good machines with oilcooled 346cc and 496cc flat twin Bradshaw engines and also

used after 1925 proprietary units made by MAG and Blackburne. These included 346cc single-cylinder and 498cc and 598cc V-twin MAG motors with ioe valves. Among successful Andrees riders were Heinz Kürten and Franz Sieder. The end came in 1929, when H. W. Andrees built a new factory for the mass-production of 198cc single-cylinder two-stroke motorcycles and engines. The commercial depression at that period wrote the finish to his ambitions.

ANGLIAN / *England 1903–1912*
Built at Beccles in Suffolk, the Anglian was in its time a well-known make. Many models were fitted with 269cc De Dion Bouton, others with engines supplied by MMC, Sarolea and Fafnir.

ANGLO-DANE / *Denmark 1912–1914*
Built in Copenhagen by Fredricksen Motors, the Anglo-Dane was made from English components and with different engines of JAP and Villiers manufacture. The production was on a limited scale.

ANKER / *Germany 1949–1958*
A once famous German bicycle factory which built Ilo and Sachs-engined two-stroke mopeds and motorcycles from 48cc to 244cc. Afterwards they concentrated on business machines including cash registers, but closed down early in 1976. The actual motorcycle production was transferred in 1952 to a branch factory at Paderborn. The main works were at Bielefeld.

496cc Andrees (ohv Bradshaw oilcooled) 1924

ANTOINE/*Belgium 1900–1910*
A pioneer company which first fitted Kelecom engines and afterward produced 3, 3·5 and 4 hp singles and 4·5 and 5 hp V-twins. They also supplied engines to other motorcycle manufacturers. Other Antoine products included car and aero engines.

APACHE/*America 1907–1911*
Made by Brown & Beck at Denver, Colorado, the Apache had a rearward-facing 597cc single-cylinder ioe engine of their own manufacture.

APEX/*Germany 1925–1926*
Assembled sporting machines at Cologne with 247cc and 347cc ohv Blackburne single-cylinder engines. The production was on a small scale.

APOLLO/*Sweden 1951–*
Now part of the Volvo-controlled MCB group, Apollo motorcycles had among others 123cc Villiers and 198cc Zündapp engines. Production now concentrates on 49cc mopeds.

APRILIA/*Italy 1968–*
Produces good 123cc Sachs and Hiro-engined two-strokes for trials and moto-cross as well as numerous 49cc machines. Some versions have 6-speed engines of Minarelli manufacture. Aprilia machines are also known under the Scarabeo trade mark. There are also models with Franco-Morini engines.

AQUILA/*Italy 1927–1935*
The Turin-built Aquila was originally a 174cc two-stroke and later ohv machine. Made by a small company, during the 1930s they used English Rudge-built Python 248cc, 348cc and 498cc four-valve, single-cylinder ohv engines.

Other models had the 497cc Küchen sv single-cylinder and the Italian OBM engine.

AQUILA/*Italy 1953–1958*
The Rome-built Aquila had no connection with the older machine of the same name. The range of models included 48cc, 123cc and 158cc two-strokes and 98cc and 174cc ohv four-strokes of sound design and finish.

ARAB/*England 1923–1926*
Simple lightweight machines with 147cc Villiers engines.

ARBINET/*France 1927–1934*
Used exclusively their own two-stroke engines of 98cc, 173cc, 198cc, 347cc and 497cc capacity in conventional frames.

ARC/*Spain 1954–1956*
Hispano-Villiers-engined 123cc two-strokes of simple design.

ARCO/*Germany 1922–1931*
Watercooled 248cc and 348cc ohv single-cylinder machines and from 1929 onwards also a water-

499cc Arco (ohc watercooled) 1929

cooled 498cc ohc single formed the range of Speyer/Rhine-built Arco models. From 1927 onwards, the make was owned by an Amsterdam finance group.

ARDEA/*Italy 1928–1933*
A Moto-Guzzi-like design with a flat single-cylinder 173cc and later also 248cc ioe and ohv engine. Competed successfully in trials with Silvio Vailati, Virginio Fieschi and Bruno Martelli.

ARDEN/*England 1912–1920*
Small but versatile company which built small cars and also motorcycles with 269cc two-stroke Villiers as well as their own engines. These were supplied also to other producers, including Priory.

ARDENT/*France 1950–1957*
Mini-scooters and motorcycles with 49cc and 64cc Vap and Le Paulin engines.

ARDIE/*Germany 1919–1958*
Founded by ex-Premier technician Arno Dietrich, the first Ardie machines had their own 305cc and 348cc two-stroke deflector-type engines. After 1925 Ardie— since Dietrich's fatal

305cc Ardie (TS) 1924

accident in 1922 owned by the Bendit family— used exclusively JAP engines from 246cc to 996cc. Bestseller was the 490cc single-cylinder sv machine, but there were even V-twins with the 45 hp and 55 hp ohv JAP racing engines. Frames made from Duralumin were used in the early 1930s. Bark, Küchen, Sturmey-Archer and Sachs afterwards supplied to Ardie proprietary engines up to 598cc. Tubular frames were used again and in 1938 Richard Küchen designed an interesting 348cc V-twin ohv machine with the engine transversely mounted. It never went into quantity production. After the war, Noack created new crossflow two-strokes with flat pistons from 124cc to 346cc. The last ones were

346cc Arco (ohv watercooled) 1927

vertical twins. The Nuremberg factory was at that time owned by the Barthel-controlled Dürkopp works at Bielefeld. Ardie was a successful make in races during the 1920s and early 1930s. Besides the Thumshirn team — Hans, Konrad and Georg — they had excellent riders in Franz Islinger, Karl Dobberkau, Gerd in der Elst, Josef Schörg and Karl Dobler and won many events, including TT races in Austria and Hungary.

490cc Ardie (sv JAP) 1928

246cc Ardie (TS twin) 1954

ARDITO / *Italy 1951–1954*
A small producer with a big production programme of various two-strokes from 48cc to 98cc and ohv four-strokes from 123cc to 173cc.

ARGENTRE / *France 1927–1932*
Assembled machines with many English components. Built 247cc and 347cc two-strokes with their own engines and also 348cc sv and ohv models with JAP engines.

ARGEO / *Germany 1924–1927*
Berlin-built two-strokes with own 198cc and 246cc deflector-type engines.

ARGUL / *Germany 1923–1926*
Limited production of two-strokes from 146cc to 198cc with engines supplied by DKW and Bubi and of four-stroke machines with Alba power units.

ARI / *Germany 1924–1925*
Another small producer of 146cc two-stroke motorcycles with DKW engines.

ARIEL / *England 1902–1970*
Built De Dion-engined three-wheelers at Birmingham in 1898 and four years later began the manufacture of motorcycles with 3·5 hp single-cylinder White & Poppe engines. In later

years, Ariel built them under licence. When the 1914 war broke out, the Ariel range consisted of 498cc sv singles and 998cc ioe V-twins. Other models had 348cc and 669cc V-twin power units, which were superseded by 794cc V-twins. In 1921 a 586cc single with 86·4mm bore and 100mm stroke came on the market, followed in 1922 by a 664cc single with 92mm bore and 100mm stroke. Another new model was a MAG-engined 992cc V-twin which was sold for £125 solo and £160 with sidecar. The price for the 499cc sv single was then £95. By 1924 the Ariel range consisted of a 247cc sv Blackburne-engined machine, 498cc sv and ohv models and a 993cc ioe V-twin.

Ariel, then owned by Jack Sangster, was joined in 1927 by the young technician Edward Turner. Chief designer was Val Page, who designed new 498cc ohv and 557cc sv singles, which proved to be bestsellers. In charge of publicity was Vic Mole, and of competitions the famous Harold Perrey. New 248cc and 348cc machines appeared

557cc Ariel (sv) 1929

497cc Ariel (ohv) 1930

498cc Ariel (ohc Square Four) 1931

596cc Ariel (ohc Square Four) from a 1934 brochure

997cc Ariel (ohv 4-cylinder) 1959. Right: The famous Square Four engine.

248cc Ariel (ohv Red Hunter) 1936

198cc Ariel (TS-twin 'Arrow') 1962

soon afterwards and 1931 saw the introduction of the well-known 498cc Square-Four, with the four aircooled cylinders set in a square formation and the ohv gear operated by a chain-driven camshaft. This machine was designed by Edward Turner. Redesigned Square-Fours with 596cc and 996cc followed during the 1930s, and also models with forward inclined engines (slopers) and some very nice sports models, the 248cc, 348cc and 498cc ohv Red Hunter range. The big sv single now had 598cc and on the big Square Fours the ohc valve gear was superseded by pushrods.

In 1936 Edward Turner left to become boss of Triumph in Coventry, after Jack Sangster bought that factory. During the war, many 347cc ohv Ariel machines were used by the Forces. Main Ariel production after the war concentrated around 347cc and 497cc ohv Red Hunter singles including competition models, 498cc ohv vertical twins, a 598cc sv single and the 997cc Square Four. This machine sold in 1952 for £287 10s. On the other end of the scale, the 197cc Colt, an ohv single selling for £134, came into production and also the twin-cylinder Huntmaster range, including 646cc ohv versions. Jack Sangster, also head of BSA at Birmingham since the early fifties, moved Ariel nearer to Armoury Road. Many BSA and Ariel parts were identical. Edward Turner moved from Meriden (Triumph) to Armoury Road (BSA). He was also responsible for Ariel—which eventually moved from Selly Oak (Birmingham) into the BSA factory— and created in the early 1960s the 49cc Pixie, an ohv single, which did not gain much fame. In contrast, the famous 247cc vertical twin two-strokes, the Leader and the Arrow which were designed once more by Val Page, proved to be excellent machines. A 197cc version was the last real Ariel machine to be built. By 1970 the name Ariel was unfortunately no more on a two-wheel machine. All that are left are memories of success in trials and of famous trials riders, including Harold Perrey, Fred Povey, Ted Ray, Ron Langston and the famous Sammy Miller.

614cc Aristos (sv flat-twin watercooled) 1923

ARISTOS / *Germany 1923–1924*
Designed by Johannes Pässler, the 614cc Aristos was a very unorthodox machine with a water-cooled flat twin sv engine. The Mars-like frame was made of welded steel plates and allowed a low seat position. The Berlin-based company never developed this machine to the full. This led to more reorganisations and also to two more trade names for the Aristos inside of three years: Menos and Sterna. The differences between the three makes were small; they included, besides different tank transfers, the colour and the fork design.

ARLIGUE / *France 1950–1953*
Small assembler of motorcycles with AMC and Ydral proprietary engines from 98cc to 248cc.

ARMAC / *America 1911–1913*
Produced 14 different models with their own 4 hp single-cylinder and 7 hp V-twin engines.

ARMIS / *English 1920–1923*
Well-made machines with 269cc Precision two-stroke, 293cc and 348cc JAP, 346cc and 538cc Blackburne and 654cc V-twin ioe MAG engines.

ARMOR / *France 1910–1934*
Once a popular make and since the 1920s part of Alcyon. Produced two-strokes from 98cc and four-strokes from 173cc upwards. These included 498cc ohv and ohc unit-design singles, some with shaft-drive to the rear wheel.

ARMSTRONG / *England 1902–1905*
Assembled machines with 211cc Minerva engines and frames supplied by Chater-Lea.

ARMSTRONG / *England 1913–1914*
Only a single model with a 269cc Villiers engine was made before WWI stopped manufacture.

ARNO / *England 1906–1914*
Coventry-made machines with 249cc, 348cc and 498cc sv engines. Limited production.

ARROW / *England 1913–1917*
Birmingham-built 211cc two-stroke machines with engines supplied by Levis and Precision.

ARROW / *America 1909–1914*
Lightweight motorcycles with 1 hp engines of own manufacture.

ASAHI / *Japan 1953–1965*
Old arms factory which already built in 1909 prototypes of motorcycles. When they went into quantity production in 1953, most models had 123cc and 173cc two-stroke engines of own design and manufacture.

ASCOT / *England 1905–1906*
Assembler of motorcycles with Minerva and Antoine engines.

ASCOT-PULLIN / *England 1928–1930*
Cyril Pullin's most advanced motorcycle design, the 498cc Ascot-Pullin, was built at Letchworth. It had 82mm bore, 94mm stroke, a flat single-cylinder ohv engine with alu-pistons, dry-sump lubrication, 3-speed gearbox, fully enclosed chains, hydraulically operated brakes, quickly detachable and interchangeable wheels, handle-bars of pressed steel with a range of built-in

instruments, leg-shields, windscreen etc. Despite the comparatively low price of £75, the Ascot-Pullin failed to gain much popularity.

492cc Ascot-Pullin (ohv single) 1928

ASHFORD / *England 1905*
Assembled machines with 3·5 hp engines supplied by Minerva and Fafnir.

ASL / *England 1907–1915*
The name came from the first letters of Associated Springs Limited. Used 3·5 hp and 5 hp proprietary engines made by Simms, Precision, Fafnir and JAP and interesting frames with pneumatic buffers for the front and rear suspension. From 1913 onwards, the saddle was sprung, the front suspension remaining as before.

496cc ASL (sv JAP) 1909

ASPES / *Italy 1967–*
Up-coming manufacturer of excellent 49cc and 123cc trials and moto-cross machines with engines made by Franco-Morini, Minarelli and their own engine department. Uses mainly 5 and 6-speed gearboxes. The weight of the complete 123cc Aspes RGC with the 54mm bore/stroke square engine with its 22 bhp at 9500 rpm and 6-speed gearbox is only 96 kg (192 lbs).

ASSO / *Italy 1927–1931*
Sporting lightweights with own 174cc unit-design ohv engines.

ASTER / *French 1898–1910*
Originally a producer of proprietary engines during the pioneering period, Aster also built

492cc Astra (ohv) 1939 (I)

three-wheelers, cars and motorcycles. Most Aster engines had horizontally-split crankcases made of bronze. One of the most popular models was a 355cc single, which was also supplied to the Orient motorcycle factory in the USA.

ASTON / *England 1923–1924*
Was a 142cc two-stroke machine not unlike the Atlas. It had a deflector-type three-port engine with outside flywheel and was supplied with one, two and three-speed gearboxes and belt drive. Only the last versions could be supplied with belt-cum-chain drive.

ASTORIA / *Germany 1923–1925*
Built 289cc two-stroke machines on a limited scale. Nestoria, another Nuremberg factory, took over Astoria when they ran into difficulties.

ASTRA / *Germany 1923–1925*
The first Astra had 293cc Bosch-Douglas flat twin engines; from 1924 onwards they fitted also 348cc and 490cc (496cc) sv and ohv JAP and Blackburne single-cylinder engines into low frames. Ernst Henne, who later broke world records for BMW, in 1924–1925 rode an Astra machine with a 348cc ohv Blackburne engine. SMW at Munich built the Bosch-Douglas flat twins under licence.

ASTRA / *Italy 1931–1951*
A famous former Italian motorcycle importer, Max Türkheimer & Co. at Milan was since 1898 closely connected with Components Ltd. (Ariel) at Birmingham and shareholder of Charles Sangster's company. This arrangement continued when Jack Sangster took over from his father. Türkheimer used many Ariel-made parts, especially frames, for his Astra machines; many

248cc and 498cc Astra sv and ohv singles used Ariel engine parts. Other models had 123cc, 174cc and 220cc. In pre-1914 days, Otav and other motorcycles were also made by the Türkheimer group.

ASTRAL / *France 1919–1923*
Concentrated on 98cc and 122cc two-strokes and was part of the Austral group which was again part of the Alcyon combine.

ATALA / *Italy 1925–1934*
An assembled machine which used mainly English components. Among them were the 174cc to 496cc sv and ohv engines made by JAP and Blackburne.

ATALA / *Italy 1954–*
Producer of spares and accessories, who built during the years also a large number of lightweight machines, mopeds, scooters etc. with two-stroke engines of 49cc, 69cc, 98cc and 124cc.

ATLANTA-DUO / *England 1935–1937*
Made by OEC at Portsmouth, Hants., these machines had duplex steering, rear springing, foot boards, leg-shields and a low position (19 inches from ground) and Dunloppilo seats for two. The JAP engines used were 248cc and 490cc ohv singles and 746cc sv V-twins.

ATLANTIC / *France 1929–1932*
Limited manufacture of 98cc two-strokes and 347cc and 497cc ohv and ohc engines made by Chaise, Blackburne and other suppliers of proprietary engines. At a Paris show, Atlantic exhibited a motorcycle equipped with a fully enclosed engine.

ATLANTIC / *Germany 1923–1925*
Small producer of 193cc sv single-cylinder motorcycles with engines supplied by the former Hansa factory at Bielefeld.

ATLANTIK / *Germany 1925–1926*
Built on a limited scale 173cc two-stroke machines.

ATLANTIS / *Germany 1926–1932*
Made by a small company, the first models had own 348cc and 398cc single-cylinder two-stroke engines. From 1927 onwards, 497cc ohc Küchen, 498cc sv JAP, 598cc sv Blackburne and 498cc, 746cc and 990cc ioe MAG engines came into production. All MAG engines were V-twins.

ATLAS / *England 1913–1914*
Also a small company. Used 492cc JAP and 496cc sv single-cylinder Blumfield proprietary engines.

ATLAS / *England 1922–1925*
Birmingham-built 142cc two-stroke of simple design with forward-facing carburettor and belt drive to the rear wheel. Used one and two-speed gearboxes. Price with 2-speed gearbox: £30/9.

142cc Atlas (TS) 1924 (GB)

ATLAS / *Germany 1924–1929*
Fitted own 248cc and 348cc single-cylinder two-stroke engines. Designer/manufacturer Schleif rode these machines with success in hill-climbs.

248cc Atlas (TS) 1925 (D)

ATTOLINI / *Italy 1920–1923*
Equipped with rear suspension, the Attolini housed a 269cc Villiers two-stroke engine.

AUGUSTA / *Italy 1924–1931*

This machine had no connection with MV-Agusta machines. Designed by the famous Angelo Blatto, the first Augustas had 348cc ohc, later ones 123cc and 174cc ohc single-cylinder engines. They were fast, but lacked reliability. The small company probably had insufficient resources for a proper development of these nice designs.

AURORA / *England 1902–1907*

Used a variety of proprietary engines from 2·25 hp to 3·25 hp. Engine suppliers included MMC, Coronet, Whitley, Coventry-built Condor and other makes.

AURORA / *Isle of Man 1919–1921*

Built in Douglas—the Aurora was a machine with a 318cc two-stroke engine made by Dalm. The other Isle of Man-built motorcycle was the Peters.

AUSTEN / *England 1903–1906*

Small assembler who fitted 2·25 hp Kelecom engines, among others.

AUSTRAL / *France 1908–1932*

Old established factory. Produced for many years 211cc two-strokes, after 1918 ones with 246cc capacity. The range also included machines with 246cc and 346cc sv and ohv JAP and Zurcher engines. Austral was also part of the Alcyon group of companies.

AUSTRIA / *Austria 1903–1907*

Was one of the first producers of bicycle attachments. The engine, designed by Josef Mezera, had 0·8 hp. His son Rudolf Mezera was with the Austro-Motorette factory during the 1920s and also raced in the Austrian TT of 1926.

AUSTRIA / *Austria 1930–1933*

The Lamperts-owned Austria motorcycle factory—housed in the former DSH works at Trautmannsdorf—built 246cc and 347cc machines with frames made from Duralumin and actually built by Ardie in Nuremberg. The range of engines included watercooled Villiers and aircooled Villiers, as well as the 347cc sv single made by Sturmey-Archer in Nottingham. Designer at the Austria factory was Hauler.

AUSTRIA-ALPHA / *Austria 1933–1952*

Formerly with the Werner-MAG factory and a successful racing motorcyclist, Josef V. Illichmann designed first various racing machines including a 248cc narrow-angle ohc V-twin and a 498cc ohv single. After the war he built mainly models with 248cc double-piston Puch two-stroke engines and 244cc Ilo vertical twin two-strokes. Afterwards he concentrated on the manufacture of foot gear-changes, rear suspensions, full-width hubs, forks and other parts. Now he owns one of the largest foundries in Austria.

AUSTRO-ILO / *Austria 1938*

Only a few of these 120cc Ilo-engined two-strokes had been built when Hitler occupied Austria and stopped this company from further manufacture of motorcycles.

AUSTRO-MOTORETTE / *Austria 1924–1927*

Built first 82cc two-stroke bicycle engines, afterwards Karl Schüber-designed 144cc vertical-twin two-stroke motorcycles. Interesting were the 173cc Austro-Motorette racing machines of 1926 with vertical-twin double-ohc engines, raced in the Austrian TT by Rudolf Mezera and Ladislaus Hajos-Hihalom. They proved very fast, but did not finish.

144cc Austro-Motorette (TS twin) 1927

AUSTRO-OMEGA / *Austria 1932–1939*

Superbly finished and well made 348cc, 490cc and 746cc machines with sv and ohv JAP engines and other English components. A few racing models had 348cc Sturmey-Archer ohv power units. Ridden by Hermann Deimel, Rudi Hunger and Franz Behrendt, they won many races. Martin Schneeweiss used in 1934–1935 a JAP-engined 498cc Austro-Omega ohv racing single.

490cc Austro Omega (ohv JAP) 1932

198cc Autinag (TS) 1925

AUTINAG / *Germany 1924–1925*

Limited production of 127cc and 198cc two-strokes and of a MAG-engined 496cc single-cylinder machine with ioe valves.

AUTO-BI / *America 1902–1912*

Produced motorcycles and scooter-like machines with enclosed engines. Supplier of engines with 1·5 hp and 2·5 hp was E. R. Thomas.

347cc Austria (TS Villiers) 1931

UTO-BIT / *Japan 1952–1962*
Produced 249cc single-cylinder machines on typical English lines.

UTO-ELL / *Germany 1924–1926*
Designed by racing motorcyclist Max Ell, these lightweight machines had 142cc Grade two-stroke power units.

UTOFLUG / *Germany 1921–1923*
Scooter-like machines with a long wheelbase and small wheels, designed by Egon Weitzel for a former aircraft manufacturer. The normal Auto-flug motorcycle had identical 129cc and 146cc Bekamo engines to the scooter-like machines. The Ruppe-designed Bekamo engine was a two-stroke with a pumping cylinder in the bottom of the crankcase.

122cc Autoflug (TS Bekamo) 1922

AUTOGLIDER / *England 1919–1922*
Another scooter-like machine with a 269cc Union two-stroke engine above the small front wheel.

AUTOMOTO / *France 1901–1962*
A pioneer make which built for many years very sturdy — and quite heavy — motor cycles with engines up to 499cc. Used engines made by Zurcher, Chaise, JAP, Villiers; after 1945 mainly AMC ohv engines up to 248cc. Never regarded as a very sporty machine, the Automoto of pre-1939 days was a typical 'farmers machine' of great durability. During the concentration of the French motorcycle industry, Automoto joined the Peugeot group, which already included the Terrot-Magnat Debon combine.

490cc Automoto (ohv Chaise) 1929

AUTOPED / *America 1915–1921*
Once a well-known scooter with a 155cc four-stroke engine above the small front wheel. Krupp in Germany and CAS in Czechoslovakia built the Autoped under licence.

AUTOSCO / *England 1920–1921*
Another early scooter, which failed to become popular. The engine had 180cc.

AVADA / *The Netherlands 1953–late 1950s*
Small moped manufacturer who used 49cc two-stroke engines.

AVENIR / *Belgium 1956–*
Another mofa and moped manufacturer who built two-strokes of 49cc capacity.

AVIS-CELER / *Germany 1925–1931*
Hanover-based Avis-Celer built machines with Villiers engines from 172cc to 346cc and — from 1928 onwards — also bigger models with 347cc and 497cc ioe and ohv single-cylinder MAG engines. Leading rider was Hermann Wiede-mann, whose 248cc, 348cc and 498cc racing versions housed engines made by JAP.

AVON / *England 1919–1920*
Limited production of motorcycles with 347cc Villiers single-cylinder two-stroke engines.

AWD / *Germany 1921–*
August Wurring, the designer-manufacturer, used during the years a variety of proprietary engines in his excellent frames. These included DKW, Kühne, Küchen, JAP, Blackburne, Villiers and Sachs. In addition, Wurring built many special racing frames for leading riders. After 1945, most AWD machines housed Sachs and Ilo two-stroke engines up to 248cc, including 244cc twin-cylinder Ilos. *See also* WURRING.

248cc AWO (ohv shaft-driven racer) 1953

AWO / *East Germany 1949–*
Built at the former Simson-Supra car factory at Suhl in Thuringia, the AWO was a 246cc single-cylinder ohv machine with unit-design engine and shaft drive to the rear wheel. Special works racing models had 248cc vertical twin-cylinder single and double ohc power units with chain, bevel and gear-driven ohc and also single-cylinder engines with overhead camshafts. During the 1950s, the name changed to Simson.

AYRES-HAYMAN / *England 1920*
A 688cc machine built at Manchester. The engine was an SV flat twin, made by Coventry-Victor.

AZA / *Czechoslovakia 1924–1926*
Light-weight machines with 147cc engines. The same Prague factory also built the big 996cc JAP-engined MC V-twin machines.

AZZARITI / *Italy 1933–1934*
Designed by Vincenzo Azzariti, these 173cc and 348cc ohc machines had twin-cylinder engines, some of which had desmodromic valve gear, in which the valve is opened by a cam and then closed by another cam, rather than by a spring.

496cc AWD (sv Columbus) 1936

B

BAC/*England 1951–1953*
The Gazelle, made by this Blackpool-based aircraft company, was one of the first British scooters after WWII. It was supplied with 98cc and 123cc Villiers engines. The BAC lightweight motorcycle also had the 98cc Villiers engine.

BADGER/*America 1920–1921*
Unconventional design with the 163cc four-stroke engine built into the rear wheel.

BAF/*Czechoslovakia 1927–1930*
Designed by B. A. Frisek, the Prague-built BAF motorcycles had Bekamo two-stroke 173cc and 246cc 'pumping-piston', 346cc ohv Kühne and 496cc Chaise unit-design ohc single-cylinder engines.

BAIER/*Germany 1924–1930*
One of the many two-stroke motorcycle factories which existed during the 1920s in Berlin, then the German capital. The first models were 173cc, 198cc and 248cc singles with some unit-design engines. From 1927 onwards, the only model in production—a design by Willy and Karl Baier—was a 492cc double-piston single-cylinder machine with a BMW-like triangular frame.

487cc Baier (TS double-piston single) 1928

BAILEUL/*France 1904–1910*
Small producer who fitted Peugeot and Buchet engines into his machines.

BAKER/*England 1927–1930*
Designed by F. A. Baker, who was once with Cleveland in the USA and who afterwards produced Precision proprietary engines in England.

249cc Baier (TS) 1925

After leaving the Beardmore-Precision company he created Villiers-engined two-strokes of 147cc, 173cc, 198cc and 246cc with modern and sturdy frames. In 1930 he sold out to James.

BALALUWA/*Germany 1924–1925*
The Balaluwa was a nice 346cc ohv single-cylinder machine of very advanced design. Like other German factories of that period, it probably had insufficient finances to carry on.

BALKAN/*Bulgaria 1958–1975*
Built Jawa-like 246cc single-cylinder two-stroke and concentrated afterward on various models—including mopeds—with 49cc and 73cc two-stroke engines of own manufacture.

BAM/*Germany 1933–1937*
The 'Germany' in this case refers mainly to the transfer, i.e. the 'BAM', on the tank. Reason for BAM 'production' was Adolf Hitler, who made import of foreign motorcycles nearly impossible. The Belgian FN works had an assembly plant at Aachen and a sales office at Berlin; as they were not able to send their own motorcycles via Aachen to Germany, they created a new name which stood for 'Berlin Aachener-Motorradwerke'. Apart from the name everything was original FN. The range included 198cc two-stroke singles, 346cc sv and 497cc sv and ohv models. This arrangement satisfied the Hitler Government.

BAMAR/*Germany 1923–1925*
Assembler of lightweight motorcycles with 149cc and 198cc engines made by DKW, Gruhn, Baumi, Alba and other engine suppliers. Limited production.

BAMO/*Germany 1923–1925*
Another small German make. Used 148cc and 173cc DKW proprietary engines.

BANSHEE / *England 1921–1924*
Produced machines with 269cc Villiers engines and was among the first to fit the 347cc Barr & Stroud sleeve-valve engine. Other models had oilcooled 346cc Bradshaw and 347cc and 497cc Blackburne sv and ohv engines.

BARDONE / *Italy 1938–1939*
Once a well-known producer of delivery three-wheelers, Bardone also built heavy 499cc motorcycles with their own unit-design ohv single-cylinder engines.

BARNES / *England 1904*
A little-known make which fitted various proprietary engines, including the MMC and 211cc Minerva.

BARON / *England 1920–1921*
Concentrated on assembling motorcycles with 269cc Villiers and 348cc Blackburne sv engines.

BARRY / *Czechoslovakia 1932–1939*
The first models were 248cc ohv racing singles, designed by Friedrich Drkosch. A 98cc two-stroke of up-to-date design was ready for production when WWII broke out.

BARTALI / *Italy 1953–1961*
Named after a famous bicycle racer, Gino Bartali, these good-looking motorcycles had 48cc, 124cc and 158cc two-stroke and 123cc, 174cc and 198cc ohv engines. The 158cc Marziano was a super-sport model.

BARTER / *England 1902–1905*
Unusual single-cylinder machines with rear-wheel drive taken directly from the camshafts.

The designer W. J. Barter afterwards created the Fairy (Fee) motorcycles with flat-twin engines which were the forerunners of Douglas machines.

BARTISCH / *Austria 1925–1929*
Franz Bartisch designed in 1925 a 348cc single-cylinder machine with chain-driven ohc and added in 1928 a 498cc model with bevel-driven ohc. This machine had no outside oil pipes and was of very clean design. Lack of finance prevented the manufacture of large numbers of these excellent machines.

BASTERT / *Germany 1949–1955*
Still well-known company which produced Sachs and Ilo-engined motorcycles from 49cc to 247cc and also various mopeds and scooters.

BAT / *England 1902–1926*
Owned by the Tessier family and designed by T. H. Tessier, BAT (Best after Test) produced many sporting machines. These included 492cc ohv singles and 654cc, 770cc, 964cc and 980cc V-twins. Some had rear suspension and most were fast. A BAT ridden by W. A. Bashall was second in the 1908 TT. When Martinsyde in 1923 stopped motorcycle production the Tessiers took over that make.

BATAVUS / *Holland 1911–*
Factory known for 49cc mofas, mopeds and lightweight motorcycles which also produced in earlier years motorcycles up to 198cc with Ilo, Villiers and Sachs engines.

BAUDO / *Italy 1920–1928*
Produced at Turin JAP-engined V-twins with 474cc, 668cc and 972cc. After 1924 the range included models with 248cc Train engines (two-

strokes), 348cc Barr & Stroud sleeve-valve singles, 173cc Moser ohv motors and also JAP-engined versions of 173cc, 246cc and 346cc.

BAUER / *Germany 1936–1954*
Well-known bicycle factory. Produced in pre-1939 days mopeds with 74cc and 98cc Sachs engines, after 1945 motorcycles with 123cc, 147cc and 173cc Sachs and Ilo two-strokes. A new 247cc machine, introduced in 1952, led to technical and resulting commercial difficulties. This machine had an ohv single-cylinder engine with the carburettor in front and the exhaust valve on the rear of the engine. This arrangement led to overheating and a comparatively low output. Bauer carried on bicycle production, but withdrew completely from the manufacture of motorcycles in 1954.

BAUGHAN / *England 1930–1936*
Built by an experienced trials man who later as ACU official was in charge of big trials including the International. Most Baughan machines were made for cross-country events and his sidecars had their own drive. The engines used were 247cc 347cc and 497cc sv and ohv Blackburne.

BAYERLAND / *Germany 1924–1930*
A 996cc V-twin with a JAP ohv racing engine, ridden by Sepp Giggenbach, won the Grand Prix of Europe in 1927 in the 1000cc class. Bayerland machines had 248cc, 348cc and 490cc sv and ohv JAP engines. Designer of Bayerland motorcycles was Anton Bayerlein.

BAYERN / *Germany 1923–1926*
The first models had 293cc Bosch-Douglas flat twin engines, built under licence by SMW of Stockdorf, near Munich. After 1924 new versions with 498cc, 746cc and 988cc V-twin MAG engines came into being. The production of these machines was not large.

746cc Bayern (ioe MAG V-twin) 1926

BAYLEY-FLYER / *America 1914–1917*
Very unorthodox design with a flat 3·5 hp twin-cylinder engine, shaft drive, automatic gear change and hand starter. Despite these features, not many Bayley-Flyers reached the market.

8½ hp BAT single, 1903

BB/*Germany 1923–1925*
Assembled machines with 197cc Alba sv single-cylinder engines.

BB/*Italy 1925–1927*
Small 123cc two-strokes with a horizontal cylinder. Designer-manufacturer of these nice lightweights was Ugo Bocchi.

BCR/*France 1923–1930*
Raynal's motorcycles were among the first to use rear springing. He was also manufacturer of Poinard machines. Most models had 98cc and 174cc two-stroke engines, others were fitted with sv and ohv JAP engines of 248cc, 348cc and 498cc.

BD/*Czechoslovakia 1927–1929*
Superb J. F. Koch-designed 490cc unit-design ohc touring-sport single-cylinder machines, made by the Breitfeld-Danêk machine factory at Prague. When Praga, the well-known car makers, took over this factory, they continued the manufacture of motorcycles under the Praga trade-mark. Koch also joined Praga.

490cc BD (dohc) 1928

BEARDMORE-PRECISION/*England 1921–1924*
Once a large group of companies, Beardmore built not only F. E. Baker's Precision motorcycles, but also cars, aircraft, ships, airships, locomotives and so forth. The motorcycles had 247cc, 347cc, 498cc and 596cc Precision engines; there was also a model with the 348cc Barr & Stroud sleeve-valve engine. Some special racing models had 248cc and 348cc ohv engines with four-valve heads, some with leaf springs for the

346cc Beardmore-Precision (sleeve-valve B&S) 1923

1¾ hp Beeston (De Dion engine) 1897

valves. At the Glasgow Beardmore branch factory A. Francis created a 248cc ohc engine which never became fully developed.

BEAUFORT/*England 1923–1926*
Producer of Argson invalid threewheelers, Beaufort also produced a 170cc single-cylinder two-stroke motorcycle.

BEAU-IDEAL/*England 1905–1906*
Assembled motorcycles with Clement, Minerva and JAP engines.

BEAUMONT/*England 1921–1922*
Designed by Monty Beaumont, these machines had 269cc Wall two-stroke engines and also 348cc Blackburne sv motors. Beaumont became better known in the 1940s when he designed the ill-fated Kendall 'people-car' with a three-cylinder radial engine.

BE-BE/*Germany 1923–1927*
Small 117cc two-stroke made by a small iron-producing company.

BECCARIA/*Italy 1925–1928*
Motorcycles assembled from mainly English components. These included 346cc Villiers and 348cc sv and ohv Blackburne engines.

BECKER/*Germany 1903–1906*
Limited production of machines with their own and with Fafnir single-cylinder and V-twin engines.

BEESTON/*England 1898–1910*
Owned by the motor pioneer Harry John Lawson, Beeston was one of the oldest makes in the trade. They produced at and around Coventry in different factories three-wheelers, motorcycles and cars. Beeston motorcycles had strengthened bicycle frames and the 1·75 hp engine housed between the pedalling gear and the rear wheel. The engine was of De Dion design, of which H. J. Lawson had all patent and production rights for England. The capacity of the engine used in Beeston motorcycles was 346cc.

BEFAG/*Germany 1922–1924*
Used the Julius Löwy-designed 113cc and 176cc crude-oil engines in conventional frames.

BEHAG/*Germany 1924–1926*
Simple design with open frames. Fitted own 218cc two-stroke and JAP engines of 348cc and 490cc with side-valves.

BEKAMO/*Germany 1922–1925*
Famous two-stroke machines with a pumping piston at the bottom of the crankcase. Designed by Hugo Ruppe, the first models had wooden frames, from 1923 onwards they had orthodox tubular frames. The powerful 129cc engines won many races and were also sold to other motorcycle producers as proprietary power units. Other factories produced Bekamo engines under licence. Among them were Windhoff, MFZ,

129cc Bekamo (TS) 1924 (D)

Eichler, TX and Böhme. Leading Bekamo riders were Sepp Thevis, Max Hucke, Paul Lüdtke, Karl Jurisch, Kurt Pohle, Gerhard Ahrens, Otto Heller and others.

173cc Bekamo (TS) 1927 (CS)

BEKAMO / *Czechoslovakia 1923–1930*

The first Czechoslovakian Bekamo machines were made at the Berlin Bekamo works. For tax reasons they had the two-stroke pumping-piston engines reduced to 124cc and while the German factory still used wooden frames, the Czechoslovakian Bekamo works at Rumburk fitted these power units into equally unorthodox TX frames. These had a top tube of 8-inch diameter which acted as the petrol/oil tank. The Rumburk factory was until 1925 an assembly plant for Bekamo machines supplied to Czechoslovakia, but when the German factory at Berlin closed down, everything was transferred to Rumburk. A 174cc model was added in 1927 and in 1929 a 248cc Bekamo with an orthodox tubular frame, made at the Aeros factory, came into being. Leading riders on Czechoslovakian Bekamos were Heller, Franz Olbrich and Josef Kosinka.

BENELLI / *Italy 1911–*

Founded by the six Benelli brothers — Mimmo, Filippo, Giuseppe, Francesco, Giovanni and Tonino — the Pesaro factory built 98cc, 148cc and 173cc two-strokes and from 1927 onwards a superb 173cc racing model with a gear-driven ohc. Tonino Benelli, Carlo Baschieri and Ricardo Brusi won many races with it. In production were also 124cc two-strokes and from 1926 onwards a 174cc ohv sports machine. A 174cc double-ohc racing machine was built in 1934, and a 498cc version in 1935. The quarter-litre machine was more successful than the bigger version. Production also included 498cc sv and ohv singles. In racing, Benelli concentrated on the 250cc class and with Ted Mellors riding won the 1939 Lightweight TT in the Isle of Man.

248cc Benelli (ohc) 1939

They also built supercharged versions and even a watercooled and supercharged 'Four' in 1939, but these were never fully developed. After the war it was mainly Dario Ambrosini who won

248cc Benelli (dohc works-racer) 1952

races on single-cylinder double-ohc Benellis in the 250cc class.

Quantity production at Pesaro re-commenced in 1949, as the Pesaro factory had been destroyed during the war. New models had 98cc and 123cc two-stroke engines and in 1952 a 247cc ohv vertical twin was added. Meanwhile, Giuseppe Benelli left and founded the 'B' (Motobi) factory, also at Pesaro, which after some years returned to the family fold. Tonino was killed in pre-war days in a road accident.

In the next years, various two and four-strokes — mainly from 49cc to 174cc — left the Pesaro factory, which also built 249cc and 349cc double-ohc four-cylinder and other racing models during the 1950s and 1960s. In the early 1970s Alessandro de Tomaso, who already headed Moto Guzzi and other factories, took over Benelli. The result was a close co-operation between both famous Italian makes and later also with Motobécane

748cc Benelli (ohc 750 Sei) 1975

231cc Benelli (ohc four) 1977

of Pantin in France. The latest Benelli range includes 120cc single-cylinder and 232cc twin-cylinder two-strokes, four-cylinder in-line engines transverse mounted with a single ohc, 231cc and 498cc models and the highly individualistic '750 Sei' with its unusual transverse-mounted 748cc 6-cylinder ohc engine configuration.

231cc Benelli (TS twin) 1977

BENOTTO / *Italy 1953–1957*
One of the many small factories of the 1950s Benotto fitted German Ilo two-strokes from 48cc to 198cc and also ohv engines to 198cc.

BERCLEY / *Belgium 1905–1909*
Designed by Gustave Kindermann, the Bercley was one of the first vertical twins in quantity production. The sv engine had 616cc and was of advanced design.

BERESA / *Germany 1923–1925*
Produced motorcycles with 198cc sv engines on a limited scale.

BERGFEX / *Germany 1904–1909*
Berlin-built single and V-twin machines with

their own and also with Aachen-built Fafnir proprietary engines.

BERGO / *Germany 1924*
Assembled machines with 145cc DKW two-stroke power units.

BERINI / *The Netherlands late 1950s*
Well-known manufacturer of mopeds etc. with 49cc two-stroke rotary-valve engines.

BERLIN / *East Germany 1958–1965*
Scooter, equipped with 148cc MZ two-stroke engines.

BERNARDET / *France 1930–1934*
Chaise and Train proprietary engines from 98cc to 498cc drove these machines, which were in limited production.

BERNARDET / *France 1949–1957*
Another business founded and owned by the three Bernardet brothers — René, Robert and Roger — produced exclusively scooters, which in the 1950s were among the leaders in France.

616cc Bercley (sv twin) 1905

They had 123cc and 246cc Ydral two-stroke engines.

BERNEG / *Italy 1954–1961*
Beautiful small 159cc and 174cc vertical-twin machines, designed by Alfonso Drusiani. They had their own ohc engines and were built to the highest standards.

BERO / *Germany 1924–1925*
Light-weight machines with 145cc DKW two-stroke engines. Limited production.

BERTIN / *France 1955–1958*
Manufacturer of small machines with 49cc engines.

BERWICK / *England 1929–1930*
The only English make which fitted shaft drive to the rear wheel at that time. The engines used were 246cc and 346cc single-cylinder Villiers.

BETA / *Italy 1950–*
Designed by Giuseppe Bianchi, Beta produced during the years a wide range of machines from 48cc to 249cc. These included two and four-strokes with special versions for trials, enduro and moto-cross. In the USA they became known under the Premier trade mark. The latest range of Beta models includes 123cc, 248cc and 362cc versions with 5 and 6-speed gearboxes and also a great variety of 49cc machines with many competition versions. During the late 1950s, Beta also produced very fast 173cc super-sports machines with single-camshaft power units.

BEUKER / *Germany 1921–1929*
Two-stroke machines with 145cc, 173cc, 198cc, 231cc and 246cc engines of own design and manufacture. The Beuker engines were of the deflector-type and had three ports.

BEZDĚZ / *Czechoslovakia 1923–1926*
Produced bicycle engines and also complete machines with these 145cc sv power units.

BH / *Spain 1956–1960*
Small moped manufacturer, who used 49cc two-stroke engines.

B & H / *England 1923*
Engine producer who also built 996cc V-twin sv machines on a limited scale and for a limited period. These machines were made at the once-famous Napier Works.

BIANCHI / *Italy 1897–1967*

Edoardo Bianchi was one of the great pioneers in Italy. His first motorised bicycle was made in 1897, his first car in 1900. By 1903 he fitted engines in the centres of strengthened bicycle frames; by 1905 he used Truffault leading-link forks and by 1910 a superb 498cc single made Bianchi a very successful make. A 650cc V-twin was built in 1916 and in 1920 enlarged to 741cc. A smaller, 598cc V-twin came into production in 1921 and there was also a new all chain-drive 498cc single. It was followed in 1923 by a 348cc sv single and two V-twin models with 498cc and 598cc; in 1924 by 173cc ohv single-cylinder machines. 1925 saw the introduction of the 348cc ohv single and of the famous 348cc double ohc works racing machines designed by Bianchi chief engineer Albino Baldi. Ridden by Tazio Nuvolari, Amilcare Moretti, Mario Ghersi, Karl Kodric, Gino Zanchetta, Luigi Arcangeli and others, these Bianchi 'doubleknockers' were until 1931 the most successful Italian racing 350s. In addition, they were probably the fastest of their kind in the world. Bianchi also built during the 1930s Baldi-designed 498cc single-cylinder ohc racing machines. Ridden by Giordano Aldrighetti, Aldo Pigorini, Terzo Bandini, Dorino Serafini, Guido Cerato, Alberto Ascari and others, they too were successful. A new 1938-built 498cc four-cylinder double-ohc machine with supercharger was never fully developed. After 1945 Bianchi returned to racing with 123cc and 248cc single-cylinder ohc machines, and—during the late 1950s—with new 248cc and 348cc twin-cylinder double-ohc models, designed by Colombo and Tonti. Among the riders was

348cc Bianchi (dohc works-racer) 1925

500cc Bianchi dohc early 1950s

205cc Bianchi Sprint 1953

Ernesto Brambilla and there were also a few bored-out models for the 500cc class. Production versions of Bianchi machines included many 49cc, 122cc and 173cc two-strokes and also the Tonale, with its own 173cc ohc engine, which had the camshaft driven by chain. Some 49cc two-strokes had engines built under Puch licence. Bianchi had given up car manufacture many years ago and it was a sad day in 1967 when this once great company also stopped the production of motorcycles.

BICHRONE / *France 1902–1907*

One of the first producers of motorcycles with two-stroke engines of 2·25 hp, 2·50 hp and 2·75 hp, also supplied to other factories.

BIM / *Japan 1956–1961*

Was one of the small Japanese factories which built BMW-like sv twin machines without great commercial or sporting successes. Models included 248cc, 348cc, 498cc and 598cc machines.

BIMA / *France 1952–*

Two-stroke mofas and similar products, made by the famous Peugeot factory. The flat single-cylinder engines are of 49cc capacity.

BIMM / *Italy 1972–*

Younger Italian producer of trials and motocross machines with 49cc and 123cc Minarelli two-stroke engines.

BIMOFA / *Germany 1922–1925*

Designed by Gustav Kunstmann, German Bimofa 1·8 hp and 2·5 hp machines had sv engines made by Hansa.

BINKS / *England 1903–1906*

Charles Binks, who later became famous as a producer of carburettors, was one of the pioneers

173cc ohc Bianchi Sportster 1962

of four-cylinder motorcycle manufacture. His 'fours' had aircooled in-line engines of 385cc. Some models had them transverse mounted.

385cc Binks (sv four) 1905

BINZ / *Germany 1954–1958*
Simple scooter with 49cc Sachs and Ilo engines.

BIRCH / *England 1902–1905*
The first Birch was already made in 1901. The designer J. J. Birch of Nuneaton near Coventry, had the single cylinder built into the rear wheel. This design was sold to the Coventry Singer Company. The conventional Birch motorcycles had a triangular frame, which included a built-in crankcase and bottom bracket casting. Bradbury built such machines under Birch licence. Birch engines were of 2, 2·5 and 3·5 hp. All had direct belt drive to the rear wheel.

BIRMA / *France 1949–late 1950s*
Lightweight machines of 98cc with Aubier-Dunne two-stroke engines.

BISMARCK / *Germany 1904–1956*
Produced big V-twins up to 1300cc with engines

supplied by Minerva, Anzani and Fafnir. Around 1908 they stopped motorcycle manufacture and resumed in 1931 with motorised bicycles of 75cc and 98cc. Emil Fischer designed after 1945 well-made two-stroke motorcycles of 98cc, 147cc and 173cc capacity. Sachs and Ilo supplied the engines.

BISON / *Austria 1924–1926*
Designed by Oskar Hacker, who later became chief designer of the Austro-Daimler car factory, Bison motorcycles always had flat twin-cylinder engines. Among them were the 293cc Bosch-Douglas, the 493cc BMW and the Coventry-built 678cc Coventry-Victor. Production was on a limited scale.

493cc Bison (sv BMW flat-twin) 1925

BITRI / *The Netherlands 1955–1957*
Small producer of scooters with 147cc engines.

BJR / *Spain 1953–early 1960s*
Produced 123cc and 174cc machines with two-stroke engines.

BLACKBURNE / *England 1908–1921*
Cecil and Alick Burney were pioneers of the British motorcycle industry. Originally con-

448cc Blackburne (sv) 1921

nected with Geoffrey De Havilland, they designed engines, later complete motorcycles of 3·5 and 4 hp (singles) and 8 hp (twins). They eventually left the company and concentrated on the manufacture of proprietary power units. In 1921 Osborn Engineering Company (OEC) took over the manufacture of Blackburne motorcycles.

BLACKFORD / *England 1902–1904*
Designed by Frank Blackford, these machines had 211cc Minerva engines.

BLACK-PRINCE / *England 1919–1920*
E. W. Cameron's design was more a black sheep than a prince. It had a 497cc flat-twin two-stroke engine with one plug only and a pressed steel frame with rear suspension. It is unlikely that this engine was ever fully developed. When Cameron closed down, the production concentrated on a more orthodox model with a tubular frame and 348cc Union two-stroke engine.

174cc Bleha (TS) 1924

BLEHA / *Germany 1923–1926*
Not a big factory, which fitted 247cc DKW two-stroke and 247cc sv engines of own design and manufacture.

BLÉRIOT / *France 1920–1923*
There was a certain similarity between Sopwith in England and Blériot. Both aircraft factories turned to motorcycle production after WWI, Sopwith with the ABC, Blériot with 498cc vertical twins. Blériot's were built with sv and

123cc Bismarck (TS Ilo) 1953

498cc Blériot (sv twin) 1920

with ohv, but proved to be a failure, like the ABC, because they were not fully developed.

BLOTTO / *France 1951–1955*
Limited production of two-stroke machines with proprietary engines from 123cc to 348cc.

BLUMFIELD / *England 1908–1914*
T. W. Blumfield, who assisted in producing the unsuccessful Pennington motorcycle, eventually became the creator of Blumfield motorcycles and engines. Some versions had watercooled engines and competed in TT races.

48cc BM (dohc) 1956

BM / *Italy 1950–*
During the early years, Mario Bonvincini produced Ilo-engined 123cc and 173cc machines; later models had Italian-made two-strokes, especially Franco-Morini engines. The most interesting BMs were beautifully made 49cc ohv and ohc models with their own unit design engines, 83cc ohv machines and 123cc as well as 174cc ohc versions. There was also a 73cc scooter with a two-stroke power unit.

BM / *Italy 1928–1931*
Meldi's BM motorcycles, built in limited numbers, had 490cc single-cylinder sv and ohv JAP engines.

BMG / *Hungary 1939–1944*
Lightweight machines with their own 98cc two-stroke engines.

BMP / *Italy 1920–1925*
Two-stroke machines with their own 240cc engines and four-speed gearboxes.

BMW / *Germany 1923–*
This famous make was originally built at Munich; the main production lines are now at Spandau. Founded in 1916 as an aircraft engine factory, the Bayerische Moteren Werke entered the motorcycle trade in 1921 with a proprietary engine, a 493cc flat-twin-cylinder sv model with 68mm bore/stroke designed by Max Friz and developed by Martin Stolle. Designated M2B15, it was supplied to Victoria, SMW, Bison, SBD and other small companies. It also powered the Helios motorcycle, which in 1922 was built at the BMW factory. The design was not of the highest standard, so it was decided to build a complete BMW motorcycle. Friz created it, with shaft drive, a triangular duplex frame and a leaf-spring fork. It had the 493cc engine, now in a unit with the gearbox and transverse-mounted. It was first shown in Paris in 1923. BMW have never built a machine without shaft drive, with a separate gearbox or with a twin-cylinder engine not transversely mounted; the integrity of the 1923 design is proved by the fact that it is still the basis of one of the world's most prestigious and best selling makes, more than half a century later.

That first machine was designated the R32. In 1924 Rudolf Schleicher developed the R37, with an ohv engine. The R32 had 8·5 bhp; the new model had 16 bhp at 4000 rpm and won many

races. In 1925 the first BMW single was built; this was the R39, with an ohv engine having 248cc and 6·5 bhp at 4000 rpm.

While maintaining the basic design conception, development led to more sophisticated and faster machines. All BMWs built to 1929—except the R39 which was dropped in 1927—had half-litre sv and ohv engines. The first 733cc model, the R62, came into production in 1929. It was identical with the smaller models except for the bigger engine; a bigger ohv model was the R63. Soon BMW also introduced the 733cc sv and ohv engines in pressed steel frames. A new single-cylinder ohv with 198cc in a pressed steel frame was built in 1931. 248, 298, 348 and 398cc singles followed; the last BMW single was the R27, built from 1960 to 1967. From 1935 BMW dropped pressed frames on most models and reverted to tubular frames.

By 1935 BMW had dropped leaf spring forks; new models had telescoping forks. The first

493cc BMW (sv R-32) 1923

733cc BMW (ohv supercharged works-racer) 1929

198cc BMW (ohv R-2) 1931

BMW with telescopic rear suspension was the R51 of 1938, a sporty model with a 496cc ohv twin. The similar R61 had a new 598cc sv with 18 bhp at 4800 rpm; an ohv version, the R66, had 30 bhp at 5700 rpm. From 1941 the R75, with a 746cc ohv engine, had a side-car drive and no

246cc BMW (ohv R-25) 1950

fewer than ten gears: four road-going, four cross-country and two reverse. It was built for the armed forces. After the war, the first new model was the R24, a single ohv with 12 bhp at 5600 rpm introduced in 1949. The first new twin appeared in 1950; the R51/2 had a 496cc ohv with 24 bhp at 5800 rpm. A similar 598cc came into production in 1951; this was the R67, mainly a side-car machine with 26 bhp.

All BMWs to 1954 had telescopic forks, tubular frames and plunger rear suspension. Then the R50 and R60, with 498 and 598cc ohv twins, used swinging arms front and rear. A new

496cc BMW (ohc Racer) 1954

range was introduced in 1969: the R50/5, R60/5 and R75/5 had new frames, improved telescopic forks and ohv engines of 498, 598 and 746cc with 32, 40 and 50 bhp. A new 898cc with 60 bhp at 6500 rpm was first sold in 1974; this was the R90/6. A sports version with 67 bhp at 7000 rpm was called R90S, but after only two years in production all 898cc models were superseded in late 1976 by new 980cc ohv models with slightly 'colder' twins. The R100/7 with 94mm bore and 70·6mm stroke (60 bhp at 6500 rpm) and the R100S with 65 bhp at 6600 rpm are the flagships of the BMW fleet. Other models now being built are the R60/7 (599cc ohv; 40 bhp at 6400 rpm) and the R75/7 (745cc with 50 bhp at 6200 rpm).

BMW produced from 1928 supercharged machines for the works riders which won races in all parts of the world, as well as breaking the

496cc BMW (ohv R-51) 1938

746cc BMW (ohv R-75 Army model) 1941

596cc BMW (ohv R168) 1955

world speed record several times between 1929 and 1937 with Ernst Henne in the saddle. Other successful riders included Toni Bauhofer, Karl Stegmann, Georg Meier, Jock West, Otto Ley, Josef Stelzer, Ludwig Kraus, Walter Zeller, Willi Noll, Willi Faust, Helmuth Fath, Dickie Dale, Fritz Scheidegger, Florian Camathias, and Gerold Klinger. Schleicher designed 498 and 748cc supercharged twins and in 1935 a new 498cc ohc racing model. When Germany again became an FIM member in 1950, superchargers were no longer allowed; BMW no longer competes officially in races, but BMW riders are still gaining successes in long-distance events. Un-supercharged 498cc ohc machines have been built in limited numbers and sold to good private riders.

599cc BMW (ohv R60/6) 1974

980cc BMW (ohv R-100 RS) 1977

BNF / *Germany 1903–1907*
Bielefeld based, the company produced mainly machines with 2·75 hp single and 3·5 hp V-twin Fafnir engines.

BOCK & HOLLÄNDER / *Austria 1905–1911*
Produced in 1898 four-wheeled vehicles with engines, afterwards a real car, the Regent. On the motorcycle side, 3·5 hp and 6 hp machines with V-twin engines came into being. When WAF—a car factory—took over Bock & Holländer at Vienna, no more motorcycles were built.

BODO / *Germany 1924–1925*
Small assembler who used 147cc DKW two-stroke engines.

246cc Boge (sv) 1924

BOGE / *Germany 1923–1927*
The well-known manufacturer of shock-absorbers built 246cc and 346cc sv machines with their own engines; a very successful 246cc Boge had an ohv Blackburne single-cylinder engine and was ridden in races by Curt Wemhöner.

BÖHME / *Germany 1925–1930*
Designed by two-stroke expert Martin Böhme, these watercooled 123cc, 129cc, 173cc and 246cc

129cc Böhme (TS watercooled) 1925

single-cylinder machines had also Dunelt-like double-diameter pistons and horizontal cylinders.

598cc Böhmerland (ohv 'Touring') 1927

BÖHMERLAND / *Czechoslovakia 1925–1939*
Very unconventional motorcycles which were also supplied with the name Čechie instead of Böhmerland on the tank. Designed by Albin Liebisch, they had a very long wheelbase, a very strong frame and fork and disc wheels made of cast light alloy. Some extra-long models had

three 'officially permitted' seats and two petrol tanks, mounted on each side of the rear wheel. There was also a racing-model with a shorter wheelbase, which was used in hill climbs. All models had the ohv single-cylinder 598cc Liebisch engine and even the last machines made just before WWII had engines with open pushrods and valve-gears—not dissimilar to the ones designed in 1925 by Liebisch. A new 348cc two-stroke single-cylinder Böhmerland with a lighter but still unconventional frame was built in 1938. As a result of the war, only a few were made.

BOLIDE / *France 1902–1910*
Made at Pantin, these machines had own 1·5 hp power units.

BOND / *England 1949–1955*
The first Bond product was a 98cc Minibike with a pressed steel frame. More orthodox motorcycles with tubular frames had 98cc and 123cc Villiers and 123cc JAP two-stroke engines.

BOOTH / *England 1901–1903*
London-built motorcycles with 2·75 hp, 3·50 hp and 4 hp engines made by De Dion and Minerva.

BORD / *England 1902–1906*
Another London-built machine with a 1·5 hp engine.

BORGHI / *Italy 1951–1963*
Assembler of lightweight machines with 38cc Mosquito and 49cc Cucciolo engines. The 123cc Olympia had a BSA Bantam two-stroke engine.

598cc Böhmerland (ohv 'Long-Touring') 1935

BORGO/*Italy 1906–1926*
Once a famous factory, founded by A. B. Borgo and his brother Carlo. Built fast 497cc singles with ioe valves, and afterwards singles with 453cc, 493cc, 693cc and even 827cc. Another Borgo—Edmondo Michele—designed bicycle engines and built at his Turin factory in 1915 a 996cc V-twin with belt drive to the rear wheel. A 477cc ohv V-twin was built in 1921. It reached up to 6000 rpm. With four-valve heads, these machines won many events. The last Moto-Borgo was a 496cc V-twin with ohv and a two-speed gearbox in unit with the engine. It had chain drive and a very low saddle position. The top speed was around 80 mph. After 1926 Borgo concentrated mainly on making pistons.

BORHAM/*England 1902–1905*
Minerva 2 hp and 2·5 hp engines were fitted to these primitive machines.

BOUCHET/*France 1902–1905*
Not much is known about these machines, which used acetylene instead of petrol.

BOUGERY/*France 1896–1902*
One of the first French makes. The engine was mounted between the pedalling gear and the rear wheel.

BOUNDS-JAP/*England 1909–1912*
Assembled motorcycles with 345cc single-cylinder and 492cc V-twin JAP proprietary engines.

BOVY/*Belgium c1906–1932*
Albert Bovy built transport vehicles in 1902 and also cars in limited numbers. His motorcycles were of typical English design and sturdy appearance. They had 98cc to 996cc proprietary engines made by JAP, MAG, Python, Blackburne, Aubier-Dunne and others.

BOWDEN/*England 1902–1905*
Frank Bowden, who eventually became Sir Frank, fitted 2 hp and 2·5 hp engines made by FN and also by his own works into his motorcycles. He was also the founder of the Raleigh-Sturmey-Archer Company at Nottingham.

BOWN/*England 1922–1924*
Small assembler of machines with 147cc Villiers and 248cc and 348cc JAP and Blackburne engines.

BOWN/*England 1950–1958*
Originally known under the Aberdale trade

123cc Brand (TS Bekamo) 1923

mark, Bown autocycles were built in different versions with 98cc Villiers engines. Motorcycles made by this company had 98cc and 123cc Villiers engines, but from 1955 onward manufacture concentrated around 49cc Sachs-engined mopeds.

BPR/*Switzerland 1929–1932*
Founded by former Moto-Rêve and Moto-sacoche employees—Buratti, Ponti and Roch—BPR fitted 347cc and 497cc single-cylinder Moser and Motosacoche engines into well-made frames. They had also a branch in France.

BPS/*France 1973–*
Young French producer of trials and motocross machines with engines of 49cc to 123cc supplied by Franco-Morini, Sachs, Aspes and Minarelli. Good and successful design.

BRAAK/*Germany 1923–1925*
Assembled machines with 129cc and 198cc Heilo and Namapo engines with frames, which were supplied by Gruhn of Berlin.

BRADBURY/*England 1901–1925*
Once a leading British motorcycle factory at Oldham. Built under Birch patent, the first single-

554cc sv Bradbury 1914

cylinder models had 2 hp and 2·5 hp. When WWI broke out, the range of models included 554cc singles, 749cc V-twins and 499cc flat twin versions. Improved machines followed after the war and before Bradbury stopped cycle production, there was a 349cc sv single.

788cc Bradbury (sv V-twin) 1921

BRAND/*Germany 1925–1930*
Small factory which built two-stroke machines with flat single-cylinder Bekamo licence engines of 123cc, 147cc and 173cc. These Hugo Ruppe designed engines had a pumping cylinder at the bottom of the crankcase.

BRAVIS/*Germany 1924–1926*
A famous German rider, Franz Seelos of Munich, rode these 148cc two-strokes and 293cc flat-twins with Bosch-Douglas licence engines successfully in many events, mainly in the Bavarian part of Germany.

BREDA/*Italy 1946–1951*
Like Macchi and Caproni, Breda was originally a leading aircraft factory. After the war the firm built motorised bicycles with their own 65cc two-stroke engine.

BRÉE/*Austria 1902–1904*
Of French origin, Théodor Brée built at Vienna lightweight machines with 1·5 hp single-cylinder,

two-stroke engines of his own design and manufacture.

BRENNABOR / *Germany 1902–1940*
There were two periods when the firm built motorcycles. The first was until 1912, when they fitted 3·5 hp, 4 hp and 6 hp engines of Zedel, Fafnir and of their own manufacture into sturdy frames. Afterwards they concentrated on bicycles and cars, but when they stopped car manufacture in 1933, production at the Brandenburg/Havel factory included motorised bicycles with 73cc and 98cc Sachs and Ilo engines.

BREUIL / *France 1903–1908*
Fitted different proprietary engines from 4 hp to 6 hp into their own frames. The engines were mainly Peugeot, Aster and Zurcher.

BRIDGESTONE / *Japan 1952–early 1970s*
Was part of the famous Bridgestone tyre factory and commenced manufacture of motorised two-wheelers with 49cc two-stroke mopeds. Later they built first class motorcycles, mainly 98cc singles and 173cc, 247cc and 348cc vertical twins; all two strokes with rotary-disc engines of their own manufacture. Among the models were many special versions for the USA market, which was of great importance for Bridgestone as they were not interested in the home market, because of the opposition of Honda, Yamaha, Suzuki and Kawasaki, which were among the best customers of Bridgestone tyres. To keep such big tyre customers, Bridgestone decided eventually to pull out of the manufacture of motorcycles.

BRILANT-ALCYON / *Czechoslovakia 1932*
Built by a well-known bicycle factory — Fuchs & Co. at Zuckmantel — the Brilant-Alcyon (Alcyon licence) had a 98cc two-stroke engine and was intended to become a 'people's motorcycle'. Only few of these machines were made.

BRILLANT / *France 1903–1904*
Small assembler of motorcycles which used Peugeot and Zurcher engines.

BRITAX / *England 1954–1956*
Produced mini-scooters with 48cc Ducati ohv engines and were also the first in England to build 49cc racing machines, called Hurricane. They were powered by Cucciolo ohv engines. Britax is still a leading producer of accessories.

BRITISH-RADIAL / *England 1920–1922*
Interesting and unorthodox motorcycles with 369cc three-cylinder radial sv engines, designed

497cc Brondoit (ohv MAG) 1928

by J. E. Manes. The engines were made by C. B. Redrup; Chater-Lea supplied the frames. The 120 degree three had a vaned outside flywheel, detachable heads, enclosed valves etc. Production was on a limited scale.

BRITISH-STANDARD / *England 1919–1923*
A wide range of 147cc to 548cc engines made by Villiers, TDC, JAP, Bradshaw, Blackburne and Barr & Stroud, powered these 'perfectly standard' motorcycles.

BRM / *Italy 1955–1957*
Produced small 48cc two-stroke machines and had no connection with the once famous British BRM racing car firm at Bourne.

BROCKHOUSE / *England 1948–1955*
Famous engineering company and one time producer of 98cc Corgi Mini-scooters which could be folded up. Eventually bought the Indian motorcycle factory at Springfield, Massachusetts in the USA and produced for them at the English factory the 248cc Indian Brave, which had its own sv single-cylinder unit-design engine.

Some other firms, including OEC and DOT, fitted it also into their frames. Brockhouse afterwards sold Indian to Associated Motor Cycles Ltd. in London.

BRONDOIT / *Belgium 1924–1929*
Paul de Bussy's Brondoit (Brondoit-Herstal) factory produced 248cc and 348cc two-stroke machines with outside flywheel engines and also from 1928 onward a sporting 498cc model with the Swiss single-cylinder double-port ohv engine, made by MAG (Motosacoche).

BROUGH / *England 1908–1926*
This was the machine designed and built by W. E. Brough, George Brough's father. The range consisted first of singles and V-twins, but soon William Brough became a flat-twin devotee. With Granville Bradshaw on friendly terms, he used first Bradshaw's 496cc ABC engines, afterwards his own 496cc ohv and 692cc as well as 810cc sv engines. All were flat twins, a design which was not favoured by his son George Brough, who eventually left his father's works and founded his own motorcycle factory at Haydn Road, Nottingham in 1921.

497cc Brough (ohv flat-twin) 1919

BROUGH-SUPERIOR / England 1921–1940

Known as the 'Rolls-Royce among motorcycles', Brough-Superior motorcycles were built regardless of costs by George Brough, son of W. E. Brough. He was a famous technician and since his youth a very successful competitor in sporting events, first with his father's Brough machines, then with his own Brough-Superiors, which were mainly built with V-twin engines. These included

models with 678cc, 746cc, 980cc, 996cc and 1150cc engines, made by JAP, MAG and Matchless; in some cases especially for Brough-Superior, in other cases with special parts for this make. There was also a 498cc ohv V-twin with a JAP engine in 1930 and in 1932 a 796cc four-in-line with a watercooled and modified Austin car engine. This model, destined for sidecar work, had two rear wheels, which were only a few inches apart and fitted in the centre. Most famous were George Brough's SS100 ohv and SS80 sv V-twins and there were also many interesting one-off prototypes, ie machines which never came into quantity production. These included aircooled 996cc V-fours, aircooled 990cc fours-

998cc Brough-Superior (sv JAP SS80) 1930

in-line and also the famous Dream of 1938, which had a transverse-mounted flat four-cylinder 996cc engine and shaft drive. It was not yet fully developed when the war broke out. Brough intended to produce motorcycles again after 1945, but as there were no suitable engines available, he eventually had to give up. Famous Brough-Superior personalities included Harold 'Oily' Karslake, works manager Icke Webb and T. E. Lawrence of Arabia, who owned seven BS machines during the years. Among the leading racing men were Brough himself, Eric Fernihough, Freddy Dixon, E. C. E. Baragwanath, Bert le Vack, Joe Wright, Eddy Meyer, Kpt. Vladimir Kučka, Ernst Zündorf, Otokar Weinhara, Bob Berry and Lucky Schmied.

998cc Brough-Superior (ohv Matchless SS100) 1938

1150cc Brough-Superior (sv BS 1150) 1938

BROWN / England 1902–1919

Brown motorcycles had 348cc and 498cc single-cylinder and 498cc V-twin sv engines. After 1919 they used the name Vindec, but had no connection with the former German Allright motorcycles of the same name, Vindec-Special (VS). These names were used by Allright only for machines exported to England.

BROWN-BICAR / England (USA) 1907–1913

Equipped with 3 hp single-cylinder and 5 hp V-twin engines, the Brown-Bicar was an unusual motorcycle design with enclosed engines. It was also built in the USA under licence, but was not a commercial success.

BRUNEAU / France 1903–1910

The first versions had Zedel proprietary engines, but around 1905 Bruneau built 498cc vertical-twin machines of his own design. They were among the first vertical-twins ever made.

996cc Brough-Superior (ohv four-cylinder 'Dream') 1938

BSA / *England 1906–1971*

Years before BSA (Birmingham Small Arms) produced complete motorcycles, they supplied most British and foreign factories with cycle parts of the highest calibre. The first complete machines were motorized bicycles. Afterwards, single-cylinder sv models with their own engines were built. These were 498cc (85mm × 88mm bore/stroke, 3·5 hp) and 555cc (85mm × 98mm bore/stroke, 4·5 hp) designs. The first sv V-twin had 770cc and was built in 1921. The following year another V-twin with 986cc made its first appearance. Other models built during the 1920s and early 1930s included the famous round-tank 249cc version, 349cc sv and ohv singles and similar 498cc models. There were also 174cc two-strokes, and in the late 1920s 493cc singles including the famous Slopers with sv and especially ohv engines. The 1930 range included 249cc sv and 249cc double-port ohv singles, 349cc sv and ohv singles and also 493cc versions with (as always) BSA's own sv and ohv power units. Most models were supplied with vertical or inclined engines, the ohv versions with one or, if required, two exhaust pipes. The V-twins had 770cc and 986cc engines. The 174cc two-stroke was superseded by a 149cc ohv single during the 1930s. Other models in these pre-war days had 249cc sv and ohv and similar 348cc and 499cc single-cylinder engines. Then came 498cc and 748cc ohv V-twins and a 595cc sv single. The prices in

246cc BSA (sv 'Roundtank') 1924 **497cc BSA (ohv 'Sloper') 1928**

493cc ohv BSA Empire Star 1938

497cc BSA (ohv 'Gold Star') 1960

493cc BSA (sv) 1929

1936: 149cc ohv £31/7s./6d., 499cc sv £56/10s., 748cc ohv V-twin £75 and the same for the 986cc sv V-twin. Although BSA never competed officially in races, in the late 1930s they produced very sporting singles. Walter Handley won a Gold Star in June 1937 at Brooklands (riding a tuned 493cc ohv Empire Star), an award made to all riders who lapped the track at over 100 mph. This led in 1938 to the first 'Gold Star' BSA model, which — also with 348cc engine — was built for many years and after WWII was one of the most popular sports machines ever built in England, especially among clubmen, as these machines were not only fast and reliable, but also comparatively cheap and of simple design. Among many other events, they won clubman's TT races and also showed great reliability and high speeds in the 'pure' TT events. New 123cc, 148cc and 174cc two-stroke singles, the Bantam models, were introduced after the war, in which 493cc sv singles were among the leading machines of the Forces.

Among the post-war BSA models were the single-cylinder 249cc and 343cc ohv Star versions new 497cc and 646cc vertical ohv twins and also different single-cylinder trials and scrambles models. During the late 1960s they had 441cc single-cylinder Victor and twin-cylinder Royal Star versions with 499cc (65·5mm × 74mm bore/stroke) engines as well as 654cc (75mm × 74mm bore/stroke) twins, which included the Thunderbolt, Lightning, Hornet and Spitfire models. In the early 1970s BSA produced 173cc Bantam two-strokes, 247cc and 441cc Starfires and Shooting Stars with ohv single-cylinder engines, 654cc Thunderbolt ohv twins, the very popular 654cc Lightning ohv twin and the Firebird, a 654cc twin-cylinder 55 bhp scrambler. New was the 740cc Rocket, a three-cylinder ohv machine with a transverse mounted engine. This machine had 58 bhp at 7250 rpm and a top speed of over 120 mph. Later models had 64 bhp at 7500 rpm. In addition, there was also a new Gold Star, the 500SS, with a 499cc single-cylinder ohv engine. BSA, once England's leading motorcycle factory, went out of motorcycle production in the early 1970s. Left are memories of successful machines and of many great riders: Bert Perrigo, Fred Powey, Howard Uzzell, Len Crisp, Marjorie Cottle, Fred Rist, Donald Munro, Jeff Smith, Arthur Lampkin, Scott Ellis, Vic Eastwood etc.

646cc BSA (ohv 'Lightning Clubman' twin) 1965

249cc BSA (ohv 'Star') 1967

173cc BSA (TS 'Bantam Sports') 1967

B & S / *Germany 1925–1930*
Identical to Brand two-stroke machines with 123cc, 147cc and 173cc pumping cylinder Bekamo engines. The B&S stood for Brand & Söhne of Berlin.

BUBI / *Germany 1921–1924*
Small bicycle producer who built 1·5 hp two-stroke engines into strengthened bicycle frames.

BUCHER / *Italy 1911–1920*
Known also as Bucher-Zeda, the once prominent factory built singles and V-twin cylinder machines of 342cc, 499cc and 568cc with their own ohv engines.

BUCHET / *France 1900–1911*
Better known as producer of proprietary engines and cars, Buchet also built motorcycles in limited numbers and even some unusual three-wheelers; one—a racing version in 1903—had a vertical twin-cylinder engine of 4245cc.

BÜCKER / *Germany 1922–1958*
Was a leading assembler of motorcycles from 98cc to 996cc in Germany. The proprietary engines used included the makes Cockerell, Rinne, Columbus, MAG, JAP, Blackburne and Bark. After 1945 all Bücker machines had Ilo or Sachs two-stroke engines, including 244cc twin-cylinder versions. In the late 1940s, a pre-war 248cc Bücker with an ohv JAP engine, ridden by Friedl Schön, won the 250cc road-championship of Germany.

BULLDOG / *England 1920*
Small assembler of orthodox lightweight machines. Used 269cc Villiers two-stroke engines.

BULLO / *Germany 1924–1926*
Unconventional electric motorcycle made at Bremen. The power unit was mounted in the steering centre and supplied via a 120-Ah-Battery 0·7 hp. Only a limited number were built.

BÜLOW / *Germany 1923–1925*
Produced 2, 2·5 and 3 hp machines with own two-stroke engines.

BULTACO / *Spain 1958–*
Founded by Francesco Bulto, who was previously with Montesa, Bultaco is among the

244cc Bultaco (TS 'Metralla') 1971

leading European motorcycle factories. The range of models includes two-strokes of their own design with capacities from 74cc to 352cc. The Barcelona factory built many moto-cross, trials and road-racing machines. There are now also special versions for youngsters, off road models etc. Well-known Bultaco models include the 244cc Metralla GT, the 124cc Lobito trials model, the Sherpa 244cc and 326cc trials versions and the three 124cc, 244cc and 352cc Pursang moto-cross machines. Many road races were won in the 1960s on 124cc Bultaco two-strokes. Afterwards the factory 'retired', but came back in 1976 with new 49cc and 124cc versions. Angel Nieto soon came into the lead of the 50cc championship and proved the ability of Bultacos to produce fast and reliable racing machines.

BURFORD / *England 1914–1915*
The war prevented any larger production of these 496cc single-cylinder sv and 269cc two-stroke Villiers-engined machines.

BURGERS-ENR / *The Netherlands 1897–1961*
Once a leading Dutch make which for a long period fitted engines of their own design; afterwards 497cc Blackburne single-cylinder and 676cc JAP V-twin engines. There was also a 246cc two-stroke with the Vitesse engine.

BURKHARDTIA / *Germany 1904–1908*
Early two-stroke machines with 165cc single-cylinder and 244cc twin-cylinder engines, made by the famous Grade works at Magdeburg. The twin-cylinder versions had vertical cylinders.

BURNEY / *England 1923–1925*
Designed by Cecil Burney, formerly of Burney & Blackburne fame, these 497cc machines had their own sv engines with an outside flywheel. Cpt. Baldwin, the well-known rider, was commercially connected with this make. Burney also built a very limited number of 679cc sv V-twins.

BUSI / *Italy 1950–1953*
Sporting two-stroke machines of typical Italian design. The range included 123cc, 160cc, 173cc and 198cc versions.

244cc Bücker (TS Ilo twin) 1953

BUSSE/*Germany 1922–1926*
Well-designed and sturdy machines with 143cc Grade and 147cc and 173cc DKW two-stroke proprietary engines. There was also a 198cc model with the ohv Paqué engine and other versions with power units of their own design and manufacture.

BUYDENS/*Belgium 1950–1955*
Produced two-stroke machines with Ydral and

198cc Busse (ohv Paqué) 1925

Sachs engines from 123cc to 248cc. The production was on a limited scale.

BV/*Czechoslovakia 1923–1930*
Made by a small factory, the BV—Balzer & Vemola—were fitted with the company's own engines. These included 173cc two-strokes, 346cc and 746cc sv, as well as 496cc ohv versions. The biggest model was a V-twin. Julius Vemola himself raced a 496cc single with ohc in 1925.

C

CABTON/*Japan 1954–1961*
Was a leading manufacturer. The machines, built much on typical English lines were 123cc to 246cc two-strokes and — mainly — ohv vertical-twins from 248cc to 648cc.

CAESAR/*England 1922–1923*
Small assembler of lightweights with 269cc Villiers two-stroke engines.

CALCOTT/*England 1910–1915*
Built by a well-known car-factory at Coventry. White & Poppe proprietary engines of 292cc and also their own 249cc and 292cc singles powered these machines.

CALTHORPE/*England 1911–1939*
Founded by George Hands, Calthorpe had a very mixed story with many ups and even more downs, but they built some very nice machines at reasonable prices. The first machines had 211cc two-stroke engines, others four-stroke Precision and JAP power units. During the 1920s, various 147cc to 498cc single-cylinder Villiers, JAP and Blackburne engines powered Calthorpes. From 1925 onward, new 348cc ohv and 498cc ohc single-cylinder models of their own manufacture

came into being. From 1929, the Ivory range of new 348cc ohv machines, later also 248cc and 498cc versions—all with ohv double-port engines—headed Calthorpe production. Prices were comparatively low and just before the Birmingham factory closed down in 1938, official prices for the fully equipped machines were as follows: 248cc £47, 348cc £52 10s. and 498cc £54 10s. When the receiver sold the works, Bruce Douglas of Bristol, who was a

496cc Calthorpe (ohv Matchless) 1939

493cc Calthorpe (ohc) 1926

99

nephew of the founder of the Douglas motorcycle factory and who owned a firm producing parts for aircraft engines, bought the Calthorpe production equipment and moved it to Bristol. There he built new models with 347cc and 497cc ohv Matchless single-cylinder engines. Only a few were finished when the war broke out. After 1945 he did not return to motorcycle manufacture and eventually sold the equipment to the DMW factory. Calthorpe was never a leading producer of successful racing machines, but had some successes with Stanley Gill and the Austrian Rudi Hunger.

CALVERT / *England 1899–1904*
Motorcycle pioneer, who used Minerva engines as well as their own 2·25, 2·75 and 3·25 hp motors.

CAMBER / *England 1920–1921*
Built by a motorcycle dealer, these machines had 492cc sv Precision engines.

CAMBRA / *Germany 1921–1926*
The Berlin-built Cambra was (unlike most other Berlin-made motorcycles of that period) a four-stroke, with 180cc and 198cc and had their own sv engines.

CAMILLE-FAUCEAUX / *France 1952–1954*
Producer of mini-scooters with 65cc engines.

CAMPION / *England 1901–1926*
Was a well-known bicycle factory at Nottingham, which used a variety of proprietary engines when they produced motorcycles. These had capacities from 147cc to 996cc. Engine suppliers were Minerva, MMC, Fafnir, Precision, Villiers, Blackburne and JAP. The big models with the

173cc Can-Am (TS Rotax) 1973

V-twin JAP engines had Brough-Superior-like petrol tanks. Campion also supplied frames to other firms and when Jock Porter's New Gerrard factory at Edinburgh could not cope with production, from 1924 to 1926 they had New Gerrards built at the Campion works.

CAN-AM / *Austria 1973–*
At the former Rotax factory, once owned by Sachs and Lohner, the Can-Am production includes 124cc, 175cc and 248cc two-stroke engines and complete machines, mainly motocross versions. The Austrian factory is part of the Canadian Bombardier Group, well-known for their snowmobiles. Jeff Smith, for many

years with BSA at Birmingham, is now one of the leading men at the Bombardier works, where they produce successful trials machines too. Can-Am two-strokes have rotary-disc inlet ports.

CAPPONI / *Italy 1924–1926*
Two-stroke machines with own 173cc three-port engines. Limited production.

CAPRIOLO / *Italy 1948–1963*
Former aircraft factory, which produced 73cc ohv machines with pressed steel frames and unit-design engines. Later models also included 123cc ohv versions with tubular frames. There were also NSU-engined two-strokes and some interesting face-cam ohc machines with capacities up to 123cc. Another interesting Trento-built Capriolo design was a 149cc flat twin with a transverse-mounted unit-design ohv engine and a pressed steel frame. Capriolo also built transport three-wheelers with 75cc and 150cc engines.

CAPRONI-VIZZOLA / *Italy 1953–1959*
Sturdily built machines with — mainly — engines supplied by NSU of Germany. The range included the 198cc Cavilux, as well as the 173cc and 248cc ohv singles. The last one was based on the NSU Max and was called Cavimax. This engine developed 17 bhp at 6500 rpm.

CARABELA / *Mexico 1971–*
Mainly built for the USA market, the Mexican Carabela shows typical Italian lines. The range

198cc Cambra (sv) 1925

149cc Capriolo (ohv flat-twin) 1955

includes two-strokes of 102, 123, 173, 193 and 245cc for moto-cross, trials (enduro) and also use on normal roads. Earlier models used European engines, partly even Jawa and Villa.

CARDAN / *France 1902–1908*
Motorcycles with De Dion engines and shaft drive ('Cardan-drive') to the rear wheel.

CARFIELD / *England 1919–1924*
Equipped with spring frames, Carfield motor-cycles had 247cc and 269cc Villiers two-stroke and 347cc Blackburne sv single-cylinder engines. Another model used the Coventry-Victor 688cc sv flat twin engine.

CARLEY / *France 1950–1953*
Mini-scooter with a flat 49cc two-stroke engine.

CARLTON / *England 1913–1940*
Bicycle factory, which is now part of the Raleigh group. Owned in the 1930s by former tuning wizard and racing motorcyclist Don R. O'Dono-van who was also motorcycle designer at Raleigh (Sturmey-Archer), Carlton produced 123cc two-strokes with Villiers engines and also supplied similar machines under a different name to a leading motorcycle dealer at London.

CARLTON / *Scotland 1922*
Orthodox lightweight machines with 269cc Villiers engines, built in limited numbers.

CARNIELLI / *Italy 1951–*
Producer of the well-known 48cc Graziella folding mofa, Carnielli built during the years many different lightweights. These included 73cc two-strokes and also models with 98cc ohv NSU engines. There was also a co-operation with the German Victoria factory which supplied 48cc two-stroke and other engines.

CARPATI / *Rumania 1960–*
Leading moped producer in Rumania. Builds its own 65cc two-stroke engines.

CARPIO / *France 1930–1935*
Lightweight machines with 98cc and 124cc Aubier-Dunne and Stainless two-stroke engines.

CARREAU – *France c1903*
Produced motorcycles with 1·5 hp engines.

CAS / *Czechoslovakia 1921–1924*
Autoped-like scooters with flat twin engines of 129cc and 147cc. Motorcycles made by this Prague-based factory had 173cc and 225cc two-stroke engines; and both scooters and motor-cycles used disc wheels. The designer was J. Reichziegel.

CASAL / *Portugal 1966–*
The first Casal machines had Zündapp engines and also a Zündapp-like appearance. After-wards they fitted their own two-stroke engines

from 49cc to 248cc and also produced a water-cooled 49cc machine. Other versions included 74cc machines and various trials and moto-cross models. A 248cc trials model has a 27 bhp motor.

CASALINI / *Italy 1958–*
Mini-scooter producer who switched to the manufacture of a wide range of 48cc mopeds.

CASOLI / *Italy 1928–1933*
Sporting 172cc machines with Villiers and own two-stroke engines. Limited production.

CASTADOT / *Belgium 1900–1901*
Only few of these machines — which had 1·5 hp Zedel engines — were built.

CASTELL / *England 1903*
Assembler who fitted Minerva and Sarolea engines into their own frames.

CASWELL / *England 1904–1905*
Strengthened bicycle frames with 2·5, 2·75 and 3·5 hp Minerva engines.

CAYENNE / *England 1912–1913*
Interesting design with 497cc ohv V-twin water-cooled engines. A possibility exists that they were of French Buchet manufacture.

CAZALEX / *France 1951–1955*
Lightweight machines with two-stroke engines from 49cc to 124cc.

CAZANAVE / *France 1955–1957*
Producer of 49cc mopeds and lightweight ma-chines.

CBR / *Italy 1912–1914*
Turin-built machines. The range included two-strokes, a 225cc sv machine and also bigger models with 3, 5 and 8 hp engines.

248cc CAS (sv flat-twin) 1922

746cc CEMEC (sv flat-twin) 1954

CC / *England 1921–1924*
The initials 'CC' were those of Charles Chamberlain, a small producer in Bispham, Blackpool, Lancashire. CC machines were offered in capacities ranging from 147cc to 996cc, but it is not certain what went into production. Engines included a 269cc Villiers, and Blackburnes of 347 and 497cc.

CCM / *England 1971–*
The first Alan Clews-designed CCM moto-cross machines had many BSA parts, later models had most parts designed and made by his own company. The range includes 499cc, 545cc and 580cc single-cylinder ohv machines. Successful CCM riders: Vic Allan, John Banks and Vic Eastwood.

CECCATO / *Italy 1950–1963*
Produced a wide range of two-strokes from 49cc to 173cc and also ohv — partly even ohc — models from 73cc to 123cc. The 73cc ohc Super Sport had 8 bhp at 11,000 rpm, the 98cc version 11 bhp at 10,500 rpm. The single ohc was driven by a train of gears; the top speed of these machines was 71·5 and 77·5 mph respectively.

CEDOS / *England 1919–1929*
Well-made 211cc and 249cc two-strokes which were also delivered with open frames for use by ladies. From 1924 onwards, the range included also 348cc ohv models with Bradshaw and Blackburne engines, a 348cc sv Blackburne-engined version and a 990cc V-twin with an sv JAP engine and Brough-Superior-like petrol tank.

CEMEC / *France 1948–1955*
Predecessor of Ratier and successor to CMR, CEMEC built mainly BMW-like 746cc transverse-mounted flat twins with sv engines, and a limited number of 746cc and 493cc ohv models

on similar lines. All had plunger rear suspension and telescopic forks.

CENTAUR / *Germany 1924–1925*
Small assembler of lightweight machines with 1·5 hp sv engines supplied by Gruhn of Berlin.

CENTAUR / *England 1901–1915*
Once a well-known make and also a technically interesting design. Among the models were 348cc V-twins and a 492cc sv single, which originally had the silencer inside the front downtube. Later Centaur models used square cylinder cooling fins.

CENTER / *Japan 1950–1962*
Sporting 149cc ohv singles with own unit-design engines.

CENTURY / *England 1902–1905*
A long forgotten make which used Minerva and MMC engines.

CF / *Italy 1928–1971*
Designed by Catelli and Fiorani, these were potent 173cc and 248cc ohc singles, which won many Italian races. Fusi, closely connected with Belgian FN, bought the CF factory in 1937. After an interruption, a reorganised company built 49cc two-stroke machines from the late 1960s onwards.

CFC / *France 1903–1906*
Strengthened bicycle frames with 1·5 hp engines.

CHAMPION / *America 1911–1913*
Made by Peerless at St. Louis, the aircooled 1261cc four-in-line Champion had a car-like frame built under Militaire licence and idler wheels on both sides. The ioe engine had ball gear-change and shaft drive to the rear wheel. Both wheels had wooden spokes. Production of these unconventional motorcycles was on a limited basis.

CHAMPION / *Japan 1960–1967*
These machines, made by Bridgestone Tyre Co., had two-stroke engines from 49cc to 123cc.

1306cc Champion (ioe Militaire-Patents four-cylinder) 1917

CHARLETT/*Germany 1921–1924*
Lightweight machines with their own 195cc sv single-cylinder engines.

CHARLKRON/*Germany 1925*
Small producer of 348cc and 498cc single-cylinder machines with 3-valve ohc 'K' (Küchen) proprietary engines.

CHARLTON/*England 1904–1908*
These motorcycles were equipped with 402cc Buchet engines, which were originally made in France.

CHASE/*England 1902–1906*
Made by the Chase brothers, of London, then leading bicycle racers. Chase motorcycles had various engines made by Minerva, MMC and Precision.

CHATER and CHATER LEA/*England 1900–1937*
Produced many different motorcycles with Kelecom, Fafnir, Brown, Trent, MMC, Antoine, De Dion, Minerva, Peugeot, Sarolea, Precision, JAP, Blackburne and Villiers engines, before they fitted their own engines. The most famous Chater Lea models were the sv 990cc V-twin, the 545cc sv single and the Woodmann-designed 348cc face-cam ohc single, which was based on a very fast ohv Blackburne engine. This machine, developed and ridden by Dougal Marchant, won the world's flying kilometre record with a speed of 102·99 mph in 1926 in the 350cc and 500cc classes. The 'Camshaft' model won many Continental TT and GP races with Michael Gayer of Austria, in the saddle. Other successful

riders were the Italian Carlo Barsan, England's George Tucker, Dougal Marchant and Czechoslovakia's Josef Hajek. Chater-Lea is a manufacturer of parts and accessories.

CHELL/*England 1939*
Lightweight machines with 123cc Villiers engines, made in limited numbers only.

CHIORDA/*Italy 1954*
Produced 48cc ohv machines; afterwards mainly 49cc two-strokes with Franco Morini engines, including moto-cross versions.

CHRISTOPHE/*France 1920s*
Identical production to Automoto with two-strokes up to 248cc and sv models up to 498cc. The range also included 498cc double-port ohc models with unit-design engines.

$8\frac{1}{4}$ hp Blackburne-engined Chater Lea outfit, 1906–1914

CIE / *Belgium 1900–1905*
Pioneer in the motorcycle game with 3 hp and 4 hp machines designed by M. Coutourier and the famous Paul Kelecom, who also built proprietary engines and became technical director at the FN works at Herstal.

CIMA / *Italy 1924–1927*
Assembler of sporting motorcycles with 247cc and 347cc sv and ohv Blackburne engines. Limited production.

CIMATTI / *Italy 1949–*
Produces a variety of lightweight machines from 49cc to 173cc, some with Minarelli and Franco-Morini two-stroke engines. There have also been HMW and Demm-engined two-strokes and 173cc FBM-engined ohv four-strokes. Present production includes Kaiman trials and moto-cross 49cc models.

CITA / *Belgium 1922–1925*
Motorcycles with triangular frames and own 173cc, 198cc and 348cc ohv engines.

CITO / *Germany 1905–1927*
Old established bicycle factory. Produced first singles and V-twins with Fafnir engines and in the early 1920s a 346cc two-stroke with its own three-port engine. These machines were made at the branch factory of Cito-Cologne, at Suhl in Thuringia, now part of the DDR. At Suhl was also the Krieger-Gnädig (KG) motorcycle factory, which built 503cc and later 499cc singles of advanced design with shaft drive to the rear wheel. As the demand rose for these machines Cito took over the KG production, but in 1923

Cito became part of the Cologne-based Allright works. Allright was a motorcycle producer in its own right, but they continued with the manufacture of KG motorcycles until 1927 at the Suhl works, partly also at Cologne. And even when Allright ceased building motorcycles to concentrate on bicycles, forks, brake-hubs and other parts, the KG was not dead; production moved to the Paul Henkel bicycle factory at Mäbendorf near Suhl and continued until 1932.

CITYFIX / *Germany 1949–1953*
Produced mini-scooters and lightweight machines with 58cc Lutz and 98cc Sachs two-stroke engines.

CL / *Germany 1951*
Offered mini-scooters with 34cc engines. Production was very small.

CLAES / *Germany 1904–1908*
Made by a once well-known bicycle factory, Claes motorcycles with 3·5 hp and 5 hp Fafnir engines were also known with the Pfeil badge on the tank.

CLARENDON / *England 1901–1911*
Coventry-based bicycle and car producer, whose motorcycles had not only own 3 hp engines, but also proprietary engines made by Scout, Birch, Hamilton, Whitley and Coronet. Clarendon machines were of sturdy design and had an excellent finish.

CLAUDE DELAGE / *France 1925*
Small company which produced motorcycles

and cars on a limited scale, but had no connection with the famous Delage car factory.

CLEMENT / *France 1897–1905*
Famous French motorcycle and car pioneer. Built singles and V-twins, in 1920 even a 998cc ohc racing V-twin. The last model built by the Louis Clement works — which still had the name Adolphe Clement on the door and which were at Levallo, Mézières — was a 63cc machine with an ohv unit-design engine.

142cc Clement-Garrard 1902

CLEMENT-GARRARD / *England 1902–1911*
Clement-Garrard was connected with the French factory of Adolphe Clement. Their English importer was Charles Garrard who called the imported motorcycles Clement-Garrard. He was also connected with James Lansdowne Norton, who produced frames for him until Norton founded his own motorcycle factory and used these Clement-Gerrard 1·5 hp and 2 hp single and 3 hp V-twins which had very large outside flywheels and very small crankcases.

CLEMENT-GLADIATOR / *France 1901–1935*
Produced large cars until they built motorcycles too. Became successful in the 1920s when some potent 248cc JAP-engined ohv machines left the old works on the Seine. Clement-Gladiator was also a pioneer of good rear suspensions, which they used with triangular frames during the late 1920s and Andreino won many races on these machines. The range of models included machines from 98cc to 498cc with two-stroke sv and ohv engines.

CLESS & PLESSING / *Austria 1903–1906*
This Graz-built motorcycle had its own 2·75 hp and 3·5 hp single-cylinder and 5 hp V-twin engines. In the Czech parts of the old Austro-Hungarian Empire, the Cless & Plessing was known as the Noricum.

CLEVELAND / *America 1915–1929*
Made by the once famous Cleveland car factory, the Cleveland motorcycle was of very sound design. The first machine was a 269cc two-stroke;

346cc Cito (TS) 1922

269cc Cleveland (TS) 1918

346cc Cleveland (ohv) 1925

996cc Cleveland (ioe four-in-line) 1929

in 1924 came a 347cc single with an ioe engine and soon afterwards a 746cc four-in-line with air-cooling was built. The last Cleveland, built from 1928 onward, was an improved and modernised version of the 746cc Four with a 996cc capacity.

CLEVELAND / *England 1911–1914*
Freddie Dixon, the famous rider, was closely connected with this Middlesbrough-based producer. The models included 2·75 hp and 3·5 hp singles with Precision engines.

CLUA / *Spain 1952–1964*
Connected with the Italian Alpino factory, Clua built two-strokes with 74cc, 98cc, 123cc and 173cc engines.

CLYDE / *England 1898–1912*
G. H. Wait of Leicester, designer and manufacturer of these superb machines, died in the 1950s. He was a pioneer who also built cars and three-wheelers. His machines had 2·75, 6·5 and 8 hp engines of JAP and also of his own manufacture. Some models already had watercooled engines in 1903.

CLYNO / *England 1911–1924*
Another factory which built motorcycles and cars. Motorcycles had 5, 6 and 8 hp engines made partly by the Stevens brothers, who owned the AJS works at Wolverhampton, where the Clyno was built too. A reorganisation after WWI led to new 269cc two-strokes and 925cc V-twin sv models. When in 1924 demand for Clyno cars

increased, it was decided to drop motorcycle manufacture.

744cc Clyno machine gun outfit, 1915

CM / *Italy 1930–1957*
Created by two famous riders and technicians Oreste Drusiani and Mario Cavedagna, the first CM was a 173cc ohc machine. Other models included 248cc, 348cc and 496cc ohc and also 496cc ohv singles. Headed now by Salvia, CM also built in the mid-1930s very fast 348cc ohc racing machines which were ridden by Guglielmo Sandri. After the war, all CM machines had 123cc, 158cc and 173cc single-cylinder and 248cc twin-cylinder two-stroke engines. In addition, there was the Francolino, a very sporting 173cc ohc machine built in the mid-1950s. This engine had 9·5 bhp at 6500 rpm.

CM / *Germany 1921–1923*
The Munich-built CM had a 110cc Cockerell two-stroke engine and was in limited production only.

CMM / *England 1919–1921*
Small producer who fitted 269cc Union two-stroke engines into their own frames.

CMP / *Italy 1953–1956*
Fitted 48cc, 73cc, 98cc and 123cc Ceccato two-stroke engines and also 48cc Sachs two-strokes into modern frames of their own manufacture. Another model had the 123cc Ceccato ohv engine.

CMR / *France 1945–1948*
Produced after the war from existing and partly new parts BMW models R12 and R71 in France. These flat twins had 745cc and were, of course, transverse mounted.

110cc Cockerell (TS) 1922

COCKERELL/*Germany 1919–1924*
Designed by Fritz Cockerell, who also created the 5-cylinder Megola, these lightweight machines had his own flat single-cylinder two-stroke engines of 110cc, 145cc and 169·5cc capacity. Sporting versions had watercooled power units. Cockerell also designed 38cc bicycle attachments and created many other engines in the late 1920s including a watercooled four-cylinder motorcycle and Diesel and two-stroke engines. In addition, he created four and six-cylinder two-stroke cars and other power units. Cockerell motorcycles were fast, economical and reliable and in 1924 his riders on watercooled 145cc racing machines—Karl Adam and Hans Letnar—won the Championship of Germany in the 150cc class.

CODRIDEX/*France 1952–1956*
Manufacturers of mopeds with 49cc and 65cc engines.

COFERSA/*Spain 1953–1960*
Assembler of two-stroke machines with engines from 98cc to 198cc.

COLIBRI/*Austria 1952–1954*
Scooters with 123cc two-stroke Auto-Union (DKW) engines. Limited production.

COLOMB/*France 1950–1954*
Small assembler of scooters and lightweight motorcycles.

COLONIAL/*England 1911–1913*
The Carter-designed single-cylinder machine had its own 450cc two-stroke engine.

COLUMBIA/*America 1900–1905*
Built at the Pope works, the Columbia had Pope-built single-cylinder and V-twin engines.

COLUMBIA/*France 1922–1926*
Sv singles of 197cc and 247cc capacity in simple and open frames.

745cc Cockerell (TS 4-cylinder Prototype w/c) 1927

COLUMBUS/*Germany 1923–1924*
Built good bicycle attachment engines and a 248cc ohv machine, which became the first Horex motorcycle when the Kleemann family bought the Columbus engine factory.

COM/*Italy 1926–1928*
One of the many small Italian producers of 123cc and 173cc machines.

COMERY/*England 1919–1922*
A factory owned by racing motorcyclist Archie Cook. Produced motorcycles with 269cc Villiers two-stroke engines.

COMET/*England 1902–1907*
Fitted Minerva engines of 2·75 and 3·5 hp into own frames made from BSA cycle parts.

COMET/*Italy 1953–1957*
Superb, but quite expensive 173cc ohv and 173cc as well as 246cc vertical twin ohc machines designed by Alfonso Drusiani and built in his own works.

COMMANDER/*England 1952–1953*
Made at the last pre-war Rudge factory at Hayes, the R. W. Dennis-designed Commander was an unorthodox design. It had a frame made from

123cc Commander (TS Villiers Prototype) 1952

...quare tubes and a partly enclosed engine. This was a 98cc or 197cc Villiers two-stroke. The factory belonging to the General Steel group never went into quantity production.

CONDOR / *England 1907–1914*
Built proprietary engines and complete motorcycles. Unique was a single-cylinder model with 96mm bore and 122mm stroke. At 810cc this was probably the biggest single in commercial production.

CONDOR / *Switzerland 1901–*
Next to Motosacoche, Switzerland's leading motorcycle manufacturer. Fitted in early years Zedel, afterwards mainly MAG (Motosacoche) engines from 246cc to 746cc with ioe and partly ohv engines. Small models had 147cc to 198cc Villiers motors. After 1945, a 346cc two-stroke

497cc Condor (ohv MAG) 1931

twin was built but main production concentrated on 678cc flat twins with their own transverse-mounted sv engines and shaft drive to the rear wheel. Another Condor had its own 247cc ohv engine as well as shaft drive. Together with the twin, these machines were built mainly for the Swiss forces. There was also a 248cc machine which had an ohc engine, supplied by Ducati. Condor was a very active competitor in races and during the late 1920s and early 1930s when they used 248cc, 348cc and 498cc Marchant-designed

678cc Condor (sv flat-twin) 1955

ohc Motosacoche racing engines they were very successful. Among leading Condor riders were Georges Cordey, Ernst Hänny, Léon Divorne, Paul Wuillemin, Armin Bättig and Paul Dinkel.

CONDOR / *Germany 1953–1954*
Scooter-like motorcycles with 48cc two-stroke engines.

346cc Connaught (sv JAP) 1927

CONNAUGHT / *England 1910–1927*
Producer of excellent 293cc and 347cc two-stroke singles with belt and chain drive to the rear wheel. The range of models became larger when Connaught introduced 1925 models with 348cc sv and ohv Blackburne and ohv Bradshaw (oil-cooled) engines. Bert Perrigo, who afterwards went to BSA, and Jack Sprosen were among leading Connaught riders. The Birmingham-based factory bought in 1924 the JES motorcycle production which was at Gloucester.

CONSUL / *England 1916–1922*
Small assembler, who produced Villiers-engined 269cc and 247cc models with orthodox frames.

COOPER / *America 1972–*
Made in Mexico by Islo at Salfillol for the American importer, Cooper machines are equip-

ped with 246cc single-cylinder two-stroke engines. There are different models for trials (enduro) and moto-cross.

CORAH / *England 1905–1914*
Superbly made 498cc single-cylinder sv machines and 746cc ohv V-twin JAP engined models. The small factory fitted upon request other proprietary engines as well.

CORGI / *England 1942–1948*
Originally made for the British Air Force during the war, Corgi folding scooters had 98cc Sprite two-stroke engines and 12·5 inch wheels. Manufacturer was Brookhouse Engineering of Southport, who afterwards owned the American Indian factory and produced the 246cc Brave single-cylinder sv model.

CORONA / *England 1901–1904*
Small producer of machines with 1·5 hp Minerva, 2 hp Clement and British 2·5 hp proprietary engines.

CORONA / *Germany 1902–1924*
The first Corona motorcycles had single-cylinder and V-twin engines mounted between the saddle

2½ hp Corona (sv) 1904

tube and the rear wheel. Zedel and Fafnir supplied the engines. Afterwards they had a more orthodox design. Motorcycle production stopped in 1907, but was taken up again in 1922, when Corona announced 346cc sv singles and 493cc flat twins. The later ones had BMW sv engines.

CORONA-JUNIOR / *England 1919–1923*
Concentrated manufacture on a 447cc single-cylinder sv machine which in 1919 was sold for £85 and in 1923 for £75.

CORRE / *France 1901–1910*
Better known as a car manufacturer which eventually was bought by La Licorne, Corre built also a range of motorcycles with Zurcher, Peugeot and Zedel engines.

CORYDON / *England 1904–1908*
Produced 2·5 hp single-cylinder and 3 hp as well as 4·5 hp V-twin machines of good quality.

COSMOS / *Switzerland 1904–1907*
Fitted 3 hp and 4 hp Zedel and Fafnir engines into strengthened bicycle frames.

COSSACK / *Russia 1973–*
Name for Russian-built motorcycles in some foreign countries. The Russian state-owned factories produce the 174cc Voskhod and 346cc Ish-Planeta single cylinder two-strokes, the 347cc Ish-Jupiter two-stroke twin, the BMW-like 650cc Ural flat twin with a transverse-mounted ohv engine and the Dneipr, which is a modernised version of the Ural, although both models have 32 bhp only.

650cc Cossack (D model) 1977

COTTEREAU / *France 1903–1909*
One of the first car producers in France. Cottereau motorcycles had Minerva, Peugeot and also their own engines from 2 hp to 6 hp. From 1911 onward, Cottereau cars became known as CID cars.

COTTON / *England 1920–*
Triangulated frames and superb road-holding qualities made Cotton motorcycles, designed by F. Willoughby Cotton, famous and successful. Most models had 173cc to 597cc sv and ohv Blackburne engines, later ones 147cc to 246cc Villiers two-strokes and also single-cylinder sv and ohv engines built by JAP. There were also Cottons with four-valve 248cc to 498cc Python engines. After 1945, the reorganised factory used Villiers two-strokes, later also 123cc Minarelli and 248cc DMW power units. The range included besides road-going models also trials and moto-cross versions. There was also a 248cc two-stroke racing version with the Villiers Starmaker power-unit. Interesting is a 1936 price comparison for 147cc Cotton models: Villiers-engined £36/15, ohv JAP-engined £31/15 and ohv Blackburne-engined £32/10. 498cc ohv-singles with JAP and Blackburne engines were sold for £62/10. Soon afterwards Blackburne stopped manufacture of proprietary engines, but most Cotton successes—including the 1923 Junior TT—were achieved with Blackburne-engined

machines. Famous Cotton riders included Stanley Woods, Paddy Johnston, Frank Morgan, Len Hieatt, Bill Colgan, Wal Phillips and Bill Lacey.

Late in 1976, Cotton moved to a new factory, and after a long period of stagnation have introduced a new 247cc two-stroke machine with an Austrian Rotax engine for the police, as well as a watercooled version for clubman racing. These engines are rotary valve singles; the police version achieves 27 bhp at 8000 rpm.

COULSON / *England 1919–1924*
Built 347cc and 497cc sv singles and also 497cc ohv V-twins with JAP engines. The last Coulson-

B had a 346cc ohv Bradshaw engine with oil cooling. Most models used a spring frame and Eric Longden gained many successes with F. Aslett Coulson-designed machines. Originally made at Kings Cross, London, the factory was afterwards bought by A. W. Wall and eventually H. R. Backhouse & Co. Ltd. of Birmingham.

COVENTRY-B&D / *England 1923–1925*
Barbary and Downes were ex-employees of the defunct Hobart motorcycle factory and founders of this make. They also built 170cc Wee-McGregor two-stroke machines. The Coventry-B&D was built with JAP engines from 346cc to 996cc and with the 346cc Barr & Stroud sleeve-valve engine. The production was on a limited scale.

COVENTRY-CHALLENGE / *England 1903–1911*
A bicycle dealer who fitted into strengthened frames engines made by Fafnir, Minerva and other makes. Designer-manufacturer was Edward O'Brien.

346cc Cotton (ohv Blackburne) 1923

490cc Cotton (ohv JAP) 1938

248cc Coventry-Eagle (ohv Blackburne) 1936

497cc Coventry-Eagle (ohv Sturmey-Archer) 1929

172cc Coventry-Eagle (TS Villiers) 1931

497cc Coventry-Eagle (ohv Matchless) 1937

COVENTRY-EAGLE/ *England 1901–1939*
Well-known assembler of superb machines. Owned by the Moxo family, Coventry-Eagle was originally a bicycle factory which built over the years motorcycles with engines from 98cc to 996cc They used Villiers, JAP, Sturmey-Archer, Blackburne and Matchless engines. During the 1920s they had Brough-Superior-like petrol tanks and the Flying 8 was a popular model with the big 996cc V-twin sv JAP engine. Among the racing versions, the JAP-engined 248cc single, ridden by Mita Vychodil of Czechoslovakia and Martin Schneeweiss of Austria, won many events. At Brooklands a 996cc ohv JAP-engined V-twin broke records and when Bert Le Vack in 1922–1924 raced new ohc JAP engines, he used Coventry-Eagle frames too. An interesting frame was introduced in 1928. It was a pressed steel, channel section frame, which over the years housed various Villiers engines. Mammut of Germany built this frame under licence. Another sensation was the Pullmann, introduced in 1935 with a chassis-like pressed steel frame and rear suspension. The rear wheel was enclosed by deeply valanced mudguards. Engines for the Pullmann were the 247cc Villiers deflector-type, the 247cc Villiers flat-top and the 246cc ohv Blackburne. The last Coventry-Eagle motorcycles had tubular frames with 123cc Villiers engines and 247cc, 347cc and 497cc ohv single-cylinder power-units made by Matchless in London. Production ceased with the outbreak of World War II.

COVENTRY-MASCOT/ *England 1922–1924*
Produced exclusively motorcycles with 348cc engines. Blackburne supplied sv versions, Bradshaw the oilcooled ohv motor and Barr & Stroud delivered their sleeve-valve power units to this small factory.

COVENTRY-MOTETTE/ *England 1899–1903*
Improved Bollée design with a 2·5 hp engine, designed by Turrell.

COVENTRY-STAR/ *England 1919–1921*
Assembled machines with 269cc Liberty and Villiers engines.

COVENTRY-VICTOR/ *England 1919–1936*
England's leading producer of opposed twin-cylinder engines of 499cc, 688cc and 749cc capacity and of complete motorcycles with these engines. From 1926 onwards there was also a three-wheeler in production; in 1929 Coventry-Victor also produced Speedway machines with 499cc ohv flat twins. McKechnie, Bison, Jeecy-Vea, Socovel and others used C-V power units.

CP-ROLEO/ *France 1924–1939*
Interesting design, which used frames made from pressed steel and partly cast iron. These frames included the petrol and oil reservoir. Some

models had normal tubular frames. Engines used were 247cc to 498cc sv and ohv JAP, Voisin, LMC and Chaise.

CR / *Germany 1926–1930*
Assembled machines with 172cc Villiers two-stroke engines.

CRESCENT / *Sweden 1954–*
Famous also for outboard engines, Crescent at Varberg now belongs to the MCB group, ie to Volvo. Monark is also part of this combine. Present production concentrates on two-stroke machines with 49cc and 123cc Sachs and Franco-Morini engines. Some versions are special trials and moto-cross machines with engines modified by Crescent. Ove Lunden, former moto-cross champion, is responsible for many competition machines made by this large Swedish factory.

CREST / *England 1923*
Assembled machines with 346cc Barr & Stroud sleeve-valve and 347cc Villiers two-stroke engines.

CROCKER / *America 1936–1941*
Built a 3 bhp scooter and afterwards 998cc ohv V-twin machines with Harley-Davidson, Indian and their own parts. Albert G. Crocker's machines gained popularity among sporting motorcyclists.

CROFT / *England 1923–1926*
Known also as Croft-Anzani, as most Croft machines housed 996cc four and eight-valve V-twin Anzani ohv engines, designed by the famous Hubert Hagens. A few Croft machines had the 1078cc Anzani engine and all had the Brough-Superior-like petrol tank. The production was on a limited scale.

CROWNFIELD / *England 1903–1904*
These Jack Perkins-designed machines had open frames. Engines fitted were the 1·75 hp and 2·25 hp Kerry and Givaudan.

CRT / *Italy 1925–1929*
Designed and built at Treviso by Cavasini and Romin, the CRT was a sporting 248cc and 348cc machine with Blackburne ohv engines.

CRYPTO / *England 1902–1908*
Leading make during the period. Designed by W. G. James, most Crypto machines had 2·5 hp and 3 hp Peugeot and Coronet proprietary engines.

CSEPEL / *Hungary 1932–1951*
Once the leading Hungarian motorcycle factory, which was part of the great Manfred Weiss steel works at Budapest. The Laszlo Sagi-designed two-strokes had 98cc, 123cc and 146cc engines. During a reorganisation, the state-owned factory dropped the Czepel transfer in 1952 and the new models got the Pannonia and Danuvia transfers on the petrol tank.

CUDELL / *Germany 1898–1905*
Pioneer which first built three-wheelers and afterwards 402cc and 510cc motorcycles with De Dion engines.

CUSHMANN / *America 1944–1957*
Made by the Johnson-Evinrude outboard motor branch factory at Lincoln, Nebraska, the Cushmann was an early scooter with 4·8 hp and 7·95 hp ohv engines.

CURTISS / *America 1903–1912*
Glenn Curtiss, the famous pilot and aircraft engine producer, built single and V-twin motorcycles and also supplied his engines to other motorcycle producers, including Marvel. Riding a motorcycle with one of his aircooled V-8 aircraft engines, he broke many records.

CURWY (CURSY) / *Germany 1923–1931*
Produced mainly 348cc and 498cc sv and ohv machines with own power-units; a few 348cc ohc machines were also built. Curt Szymanski, the designer-manufacturer, changed in 1927 the name Curwy to Cursy, probably because th word 'curwe' means 'prostitute' in German.

CYC-AUTO / *England 1934–1956*
This was the predecessor of modern mopeds. had a strengthened bicycle frame and a 98cc five port Scott two-stroke engine mounted in fron of the pedalling gear.

CYCLE-SCOOT / *America 1953–1955*
Scooter with a 2·5 bhp ohv engine, which was no successful.

CYCLON / *Germany 1901–1905*
Leading producer during the early years of motorcycle manufacture. Used De Dion, Werner and Zedel engines and concentrated eventually on the production of the three-wheeled Cyclonette.

996cc Cyclone (ohc V-twin) 1913

CYCLONE / *America 1913–1917*
For many years the only commercially built 996cc V-twin with an ohc engine. Designed by Andrew Strand, the Cyclone won many races but became outclassed when big factories including

348cc Curwy (ohv) 1924

Harley-Davidson entered the market with 8-valve 996cc V-twins and entered racing with such machines. Only one other make — Koehler Escoffier in France — built big V-twin ohc machines before 1939.

CYCLOP/*Germany 1922–1925*
Assembled motorcycles with 127cc to 198cc two and four-stroke engines made by Kurier, Bubi, Teco, Namapo and others.

CYKELAID/*England 1919–1926*
Attachment engines of 1·25hp and 1·50hp (133cc) for bicycles and also complete lightweight machines with these power units.

CYRUS/*The Netherlands 1931–1971*
Producer of bicycles and mopeds and motorcycles with 49cc to 148cc Villiers, Sachs, and Ilo two-stroke engines.

ČZ/*Czechoslovakia 1932–*
Started production with 73cc and 98cc lightweights and soon became a leading motorcycle factory in the country. Originally belonged to the big Skoda works. ČZ stands for Česká Zbrojovka', ie Czech arms factory. Other pre-

246cc C.Z. (TS twin) 1977

173cc C.Z. (TS) 1935

war models were good-looking 173cc and 248cc unit-design two-strokes with pressed steel frames. The factory also built 348cc two-strokes and even ohv prototypes, which never went into quantity production; a 496cc aircooled vertical twin-cylinder, two-stroke machine had the same fate. After 1945, ČZ became part of the nationalised Czechoslovakian motorcycle industry and also became commercially and technically connected with Jawa. This co-operation increased during the years. Among the first post-war ČZ

machines were 123cc models, and other versions with tubular frames up to 348cc twins. The big Strakonice works had over the years many superb technicians and designers, including Václav Pavliček, Ignaz Uhl, J. F. Koch, Jaroslav Walter and Jaroslav Pudil; among successful riders in trials and races were Cyril Němec, Čeněk Kohlicek, Eman Marha, Josef Paštika, Milada Bayerová, Ján Bedrna, Bickers, Friedrichs, De Coster, Ján Lucák, František Bartoš, Václav Parus, Ján Koštíř, Franta Boček, Sammy Miller, Geoff Mayes, Jiří Churavy, Zdenek Velky, Vladimír Khudiakov, Pawel Rulev, Jaroslav Janis, Vilem Toman, Jaroslav Falta, Antonin Babarovsky and others. Many among these are moto-cross specialists and while Jawa concentrated more on trials and road races it was up to ČZ to succeed in moto-cross with excellent machines. Since 1949 the Strakonice factory has built superb 123cc, 248cc and 348cc road racing machines with ohc engines, of which most were designed by the late Jaroslav Walter.

248cc C.Z. (dohc single works-racer) 1957

173cc C.Z. (TS 'American Version') 1976

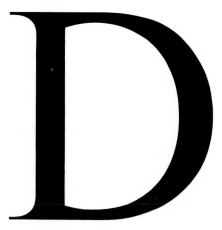

D

DAK/*Germany 1923–1925*
Association of some German car manufacturers, which also sold 117cc and 147cc deflector-type two-strokes, assembled by Ilo of Pinneberg. When demand for Ilo proprietary engines increased, the factory stopped manufacture of complete machines.

DALESMAN/*England 1969–1974*
Financed mainly by US dollars, Dalesman built good competition machines with 98cc and 123cc Puch as well as 123cc Sachs engines.

DALTON/*England 1920–1922*
Some versions of Dalton motorcycles had disc wheels. The small factory fitted 347cc and 497cc sv Blackburne singles and 688 flat-twin cylinder Coventry-Victor engines into sturdy frames.

DANE/*England 1919–1920*
Limited production using 348cc two and four-stroke Precision engines and 990cc sv V-twin JAP engines.

DANUBIUS/*German 1923–1924*
Made by the big Ratibor machine factory Ganz & Co., the Danubius was a 198cc sv machine of conventional design.

DANUVIA/*Hungary 1955–1963*
Of Czepel design, the Danuvia was a mass-produced 123cc two-stroke machine.

DARDO/*Italy 1924–1929*
Well-made lightweights with flat 132cc and 174cc two-stroke engines.

DARLAN/*Spain 1958–1960*
Limited production of machines with own 94cc two-stroke engines.

DARLING/*Switzerland 1924–1926*
Open-framed machines with 246cc three-port two-stroke engines of own manufacture.

DART/*England 1923–1924*
Built up-to-date 348cc single-cylinder ohc machines with 74mm bore and 81mm stroke. Designer was A. A. Sidney. Few machines were built.

DART/*England 1901–1906*
Designed by Frank Baker — not the Baker of Precision engine manufacture and of Baker motorcycles — the old Dart had 2·5 hp engines made by Minerva and MMC.

DAVENTRY/*Belgium 1951–1955*
Assembled 123cc and 175cc two-strokes with Puch, Sachs, Ilo and other proprietary engines.

DAVISON/*England 1902–1908*
Good early motorcycles with English Simms and Belgian 2 hp and 2·5 hp Minerva engines.

DAW/*England 1902–1905*
Motorcycles with 2·75 hp and 3 hp engines made in their own factory under licence by Minerva.

DAW/*Germany 1924–1925*
Unconventional fully enclosed motorcycle. Designed by Ernst Köhler, it had a single-cylinder 405cc two-stroke engine.

DAX/*France 1932–1939*
Excellently designed machines with two-stroke engines from 98cc to 174cc and four-stroke ohv unit-design engines from 123cc to 498cc.

DAY-LEEDS/*England 1912–1914*
Big machine factory which built three wheelers before entering motorcycle manufacture. The only model was a 496cc single with its own ioe engine. WWI stopped manufacture.

DAYTON/*America 1911–1917*
Built by the Huffman Manufacturing Co. at

492cc Dax (ohv) 1932

998cc Della Ferrera (sv V-twin with sidecar) 1924

Elkhart, Indiana, Dayton motorcycles had 7 hp, later 9–10 hp V-twin Spake engines.

DAYTON/*England 1913–1920*
The first product was a 162cc bicycle attachment engine; later Dayton designs had 269cc Villiers two-stroke engines.

DAYTON/*England 1954–1960*
Was among the first producers of modern scooters after WWII. They were nice scooters with 173cc, 198cc and 246cc Villiers engines.

DE-CA/*Italy 1954–1957*
Built interesting 48cc and 98cc ohv singles and also a 123cc vertical ohv twin in limited numbers and for a not very low price. The smallest model had 39mm bore and 40mm stroke. It had 2·4 bhp at 6000 rpm and a 44 mph top speed. The DE-CA range included also a 48cc ohv bicycle engine.

DE-DE/*France 1923–1929*
Limited production of a wide range of models. These included two-strokes from 98cc to 174cc and sv and ohv versions with JAP engines from 248cc to 498cc.

DE DION BOUTON/*France 1926–1930*
There was no real connection between the once famous engine and car factory of the same name and these motorcycles. These had 173cc and 247cc two-stroke, deflector-type engines; a bigger model a 348cc ohv engine.

DEFA/*Germany 1921–1924*
Built not only complete 198cc sv machines, but supplied other builders of motorcycles frames.

DEFY-ALL/*England 1921–1922*
Motorcycles with quite unusual spring frames. The engines fitted were the 269cc Villiers and the 348cc and 545cc sv single-cylinder made by Blackburne.

DEI/*Italy 1932–1966*
When Umberto Dei took over the Ancora motorcycle factory, he produced lightweights with 49cc, 60cc, 73cc and 98cc two-stroke engines, supplied partly by Sachs. Others had Mosquito power units.

DELAPLACE/*France 1951–1953*
Simple machine with 173cc and 247cc Ydral two-stroke engines of good design.

DELIN/*Belgium 1899–1901*
No details are available about this pioneer who, according to some sources, fitted 1·5 hp and 2·5 hp De Dion engines.

246cc Delta Gnom (TS) 1929

996cc Delta Gnom (sv JAP V-twin) 1930

DE LUXE/*America 1912–1915*
Made by Excelsior, ie the Schwinn company of Chicago, De Luxe motorcycles had mainly V-twin proprietary engines made by F. W. Spake of Indianapolis.

DE LUXE/*England 1920–1924*
Everyone who bought a De Luxe with the 346cc Barr & Stroud sleeve-valve engine got a free side-car frame. Earlier models had 269cc Villiers engines.

DELLA FERRERA/*Italy 1909–1948*
The Della Ferrera brothers built not very good-looking but interesting machines. Among them were the 498cc V-twin ohc racing machines of 1922, which had the overhead camshafts driven

496cc Della Ferrera (ohv) 1927

by chains. They won many hill-climbs and short-distance races despite the very high saddle position and chains which were not enclosed at all. Production versions included 498cc, 598cc, 746cc and 996cc sv V-twins as well as 498cc ohv and 637cc sv singles. So the models had — even in the 1920s — a rear suspension. The last model built was a unit-design 499cc sv single.

DELOMA/*Germany 1924*
Lightweight built at Magdeburg (now DDR) with Julius Löwy's crude-oil 142cc two-stroke engine.

DELTA/*Germany 1924*
Very unorthodox fully enclosed motorcycle with a dual-seat and rear suspension by semi-elliptic leaf springs. The 499cc single-cylinder two-stroke engine with 75mm bore and 113mm stroke was a three-port deflector-type. Limited production.

DELTA-GNOM/*Austria 1925–1955*
Was a well-known make in Austria. The first machines had their own 246cc two-stroke engines, later versions — with one exception — sv and ohv JAP engines from 346cc to 996cc. The exception was the Hans Pitzek-designed 498cc ohv single, built from 1928 onwards. After 1945 the reorganised factory built only two-stroke

machines with 98cc, 123cc and 173cc. The engines came from Rotax, Puch, Ilo and HMW. Many leading Austrian racing men, including Leopold Killmeyer, Karl Bohmann, Hans Walz, F. J. Meyer, Ladislaus Möslacher and Franz Behrendt rode Delta-Gnom machines in pre-war days.

DEMM / Italy 1953–

Produced a wide range of two-strokes from 49cc and also sold the engines to other manufacturers. Four-strokes with own ohv engines included 123cc and 173cc versions. Built in the late 1950s the 173cc Formula 3 with a 60mm × 61mm bore/stroke ohc engine developed 10·5 bhp and had a top speed of 90·6 mph. Demm still builds 49cc mofas and mopeds in a great variety of models.

174cc Demm (TS) 1955

DENE / England 1903–1922

Old motorcycle assembler. Dene machines had 2·5 hp and 3·5 hp Fafnir engines, 2·25 hp to 8 hp Precision engines, 3·75 hp watercooled Green-Precision engines, the 3·75 hp Abingdon and also the 6–8 hp JAP V-twin sv engine. Despite the wide range of models, Dene production was on a limited scale.

DENNELL / England 1903–1908

Designed by Herbert Dennell of Leeds, these machines had Minerva, NSU and JAP engines, but among the JAP-engined models was also the

494cc Delta Gnom (ohv) 1929

660cc three-cylinder, which made headlines. The three single-cylinders were aircooled and set in line on a common crankcase. Rear drive was by belt. Dennell also fitted a few four-cylinder in-line Franklin & Isaacsson engines.

DERBI / Spain 1951–

Built mainly 49cc two-stroke machines including very fast racing versions, which were successfully ridden by Angel Nieto. They also had 123cc racing versions with watercooled two-stroke engines. Among Derbi's latest models is a vertical twin 187cc road version with 51·5mm bore, 45mm stroke and 26 bhp at 8000 rpm.

DERNY / France 1949–1957

Quite unorthodox 123cc and 173cc two-stroke motorcycles in a range which also included 173cc scooters.

DERONZIERE / France 1903–1914

Built 282cc singles with their own engines and other models with power units made by Zedel and Peugeot.

DESPATCH-RIDER / England 1915–1917

The name more or less states the purpose of these machines. They were powered by 210cc Peco and 269cc Villiers two-stroke engines.

DEVIL / Italy 1953–1957

Made at Bergamo, the Devil was a good motorcycle. Production included 48cc and 158cc two-strokes and 123cc and 173cc ohv singles with inclined cylinders on the beautiful Soncini-designed engines. The 173cc version had a five-speed gearbox in unit with the motor, and top speed was 81·2 mph.

DFB / Germany 1922–1925

Producer of 159cc two-stroke bicycle engines and of complete machines with the same power units.

DFR / France 1921–1933

Ambitious factory. The first models had their own 346cc two-stroke engines, afterwards they also built sv and ohv versions. There was also a

660cc Dennell (sv three-cylinder JAP) 1906

348cc D.F.R. (ohv) 1927

248cc Bradshaw-engined single, probably a sleeved-down oilcooled 346cc engine. The factory raced this machine with a supercharger and with Pierre in the saddle during 1925–1927. There were also MAG-engined 348cc and 498cc ohv singles and soon after 1932 DFR introduced a new model with a pressed steel frame and a 498cc vertical-twin ohv Dresch engine. They were later taken over by Dresch.

DGW / *Germany 1927–1928*
London's 1927 Olympia motorcycle exhibition saw DKW machines with DGW on the petrol tank. The reason was a dispute with another German factory which already used the DKW trade mark.

DIAG / *Germany 1921–1928*
Machine factory, which produced 83cc and 101cc bicycle attachment engines, afterwards also complete 173cc, 246cc and 346cc sv and ohv motorcycles. The frame design had the tubes above the crankcases; the engines virtually hung in the tubular frames. The Diag was never a widely known motorcycle.

DIAMANT/*Germany 1903–1940*
The first Diamant vehicles were three-wheelers and the first motorcycles made had Fafnir power units, afterwards their own single and

498cc Diamant (ohv Kühne) 1929

V-twin engines. From 1907 or 1908 until 1926 there were no motorcycles made, but new models built from 1926 onward were designed by the famous Franz Gnädig and also had Gnädig-designed 346cc Kühne ohv engines, followed by 496cc sv and ohv versions. On special order, JAP engines could be fitted too. During the late 1920s, Diamant and the Elite car factory joined forces and while Elite faded out as a car manufacturer, part of the Diamant factory was taken over by Opel for producing 496cc Opel motorcycles with Duralumin frames, a design by Ernst Neumann-Neander. When this production stopped in the early 1930s, a limited number of new 348cc and 498cc EO (Elite-Opel) machines — with Küchen instead of the original Opel engines — were built before the factory closed forever as a motorcycle and car producer. The frames of the EO were nearly identical to the ones used in the late 1920s and early 1930s by Opel. From 1933 onward, production concentrated on 73cc and 98cc mopeds with Sachs two-stroke engines.

DIAMOND / *England 1910–1938 (1969)*
This bicycle factory assembled motorcycles of good quality. They fitted Villiers two-strokes from 147cc to 346cc, 346cc Barr & Stroud sleeve-valve engines and also JAP, Bradshaw and Blackburne engines. In the late 1920s Sunbeam bought Diamond but kept it independent. Vic Brittain, the Sunbeam works rider, rode Diamond machines in 1931 in three TT classes. During the 1930s the factory built mainly frames for other factories, but supplied also Villiers-engined machines. Not much was heard after 1945 from this factory, but in 1969 a new Birmingham-based Diamond Company offered Sachs-engined 123cc five-speed motorcycles.

DIETERLE-DESSAU / *Germany 1921–1925*
Known also by the Dreipunkt trade-mark, Dieterle's factory built bicycles and lightweights. The last ones had 'exhaust-injected' 198cc and 248cc sv engines of patented design.

198cc Dieterle-Dessau (sv) 1923

DIFRA / *Germany 1923–1925*
Assembler who fitted mainly 198cc sv Namapo engines into their own frames.

DIHL / *Germany 1923–1924*
Berlin-built 269cc single-cylinder two-stroke machines. Limited production.

4 HP Diamant (sx Forecar) 1905

DILECTA / *France 1920–1939*
Producer of machines with engines from 98cc to 498cc. Engine suppliers were Villiers, Aubier-Dunne, Soyer, Chaise, JAP and others.

DJOUNN / *Germany 1925*
Designed by Alexander von Djounkowski, a former Russian pilot, the Djounn was built in Berlin. Its 499cc single-cylinder engine was full of new and undeveloped innovations which soon caused its commercial demise.

DKF / *Germany 1923–1924*
Assembler of lightweights with 148cc and 198cc sv engines.

DKR / *England 1957–1966*
Manufacturer of Villiers-engined scooters with 148cc, 173cc, 197cc and 247cc single-cylinder and 244cc vertical-twin power units.

DKW / *Germany 1919–*
Famous make, founded by Danish-born Joerge Skafte Rasmussen at Zschopau, near Chemnitz. This city is now called Karl-Marx-Stadt, and is in East Germany. DKW built exclusively two-stroke machines. The first was a Hugo Ruppe-designed 1 hp bicycle engine. It was followed by

122cc D.K.W. (TS 'Golem' scooter) 1921

scooter-like 122cc Golem and 142cc Lomos models. The first complete DKW motorcycles had 142cc, 173cc and 206cc single-cylinder deflector-type three-port engines of own design and manufacture. They were also supplied to many assemblers of motorcycles which included Hulla, Elfa, Aeroplan, Bamar, Freital, Defa, EMA, AWD, Falke, Eichler, Maco and others. Ait and watercooled vertical twins came into being in 1927. They also had their own 498cc two-stroke engines. A 598cc version was added later. From 1929 onward, the range of models included many 198cc versions with belt and chain drive to the rear wheel, 246cc, 346cc, 498cc twin-cylinder models and also a 123cc and a 173cc machine. In the mid-1920s, DKW became the largest motorcycle factory in the world. The Zschopau factory also built many watercooled 173cc, 248cc, 348cc, 498cc and 598cc racing machines with different kinds of forced induction. These included Hugo Ruppe-designed pumping pistons in the crankcase

123cc D.K.W. (TS Model RT-125) 1952

and Roots-type superchargers. In 1932 DKW became part of the then newly-founded Auto Union, which included also the DKW, Audi, Horch and Wanderer car factories. Chief designer of the very successful racing motorcycles was Hermann Weber, chief of the racing department, and August Prüssing. Germany's most famous riders rode DKW machines. These included Walfried Winkler, Ewald Kluge, Siegfried Wünsche, Toni Bauhofer, Xaver Gmelch, Bernd Rosemeyer, Otto Ley, H. P. Müller, Kurt Mansfeld, Ernst Zündorf, Josef Klein, Hans Kahrmann, Kurt Hamelehle, Oskar Steinbach, Karl Bodmer, Wilhelm Herz, Heiner Fleisch-

206cc D.K.W. (TS 206) 1925

174cc D.K.W. (TS watercooled racer) 1926

mann, Hans Schumann and many others. Ewald Kluge, riding a 248cc DKW, won in 1938 the lightweight TT at the Isle of Man and in 1939 finished in second place. DKW machines also won many championships and trials.

After the war the Zschopau factory, now in the DDR, became nationalised and the name changed to Ifa, later to MZ (Motorradwerke Zschopau). DKW (Auto-Union) resumed production of motorcycles in 1949 at the newly founded West German factory at Ingolstadt and later at Düsseldorf. They again built two-strokes from 98cc to 246cc, as well as new vertical-twins with 346cc. All were aircooled as were racing machines developed by H. P. Müller and later by Erich Wolf and Helmut Görg. New works racing singles of 123cc, twins of 248cc and three-cylinder versions of 348cc—designed by Wolf—came into being in 1952. After 1954 Görg developed them and they were raced until 1957 with great success by pre-war DKW riders Siegfried Wünsche and Ewald Kluge and by such new men as Len Parry, Karl Hoffmann, Cecil Sandford, August Hobl and others. After a reorganisation in 1957, DKW became part of

346cc D.K.W. (TS 2-Cylinder RT-350) 1955

124cc D.K.W. (TS model RT-125) 1972

the newly founded Zweirad-Union, which included also the Victoria and Express factories. Proprietary two-stroke engine manufacturer Fichtel & Sachs—once the greatest competitor of DKW—in 1966 bought the Zweirad-Union and added their own Nuremberg-based Hercules motorcycle factory. Since then they have slowly dropped the DKW trade mark, as well as others, with the aim of concentrating on the Hercules

brand. Still, the name DKW has such a great reputation in many countries that they use it when exporting to Italy and other parts of the world. Hercules (DKW) also produces various models with 49cc two-stroke engines. In addition, Hercules is a leading bicycle manufacturer in Germany.

DKW also produced cars from 1929 to the late 1960s.

DMF / *The Netherlands 1940–1957*
Owned by former racing driver Joop Verkerke, this assembler used proprietary engines made by Villiers, Ilo and Puch. They were of 123cc, 148cc and 173cc capacity. The last model made by DMF, which stood for Driebergsche Motorrijwielen Fabriek N.V., was an Ilo-engined 244cc two-stroke twin.

DMG / *Germany 1921–1924*
Limited production of 147cc sv single-cylinder bicycle engines and later of complete motorcycles with their own 198cc sv power units.

DMW / *England 1945–1971*
Founded at Wolverhampton by 'Smoky' Dawson for the production of JAP-engined 348cc and 398cc grass-track machines, DMW—which stood for Dawson Motor Works—later moved to Sedgley, Dudley, Worcs. and manufactured motorcycles and scooters with 98cc to 247cc Villiers engines. There were also models with Velocette ohv flat twins of 248cc, prototypes with their own 498cc twin-cylinder two-stroke engines and also machines using French-made 123cc and 173cc AMC proprietary engines. When in 1962 Kaye Don finished production of his Ambassador machines, Arthur Frost, then DMW boss, bought the remains.

DNB / *Japan 1957–1961*
Produced single-cylinder two-stroke machines with 123cc, 197cc and 247cc.

DOBRO-MOTORIST / *Germany 1923–1925*
Made by a branch of Mercur Aircraft of Berlin, this company built 145cc DKW two-stroke and 346cc sv and ohv JAP engines into triangular frames.

492cc Dollar (ohv) 1931

DOGLIOLI & CIVARDI / *Italy 1929–1935*
Designed by Cesare Doglioli, these sporting machines had 170cc Norman ohv engines, later versions 173cc, 247cc, 347cc and 498cc JAP and four-valve ohv Python engines. Production was on a limited scale.

198cc Dolf (TS 8-port) 1925

DOLF / *Germany 1922–1925*
Good, but very unorthodox 198cc two-stroke machines with unit-design engines of their own manufacture. The Dolf engines had no less than eight transfer and exhaust ports. In addition, they used a conic inlet rotary sleeve in the crankcase. The 62mm × 66mm bore/stroke engine developed 3 hp.

DOLLAR / *France 1925–1939*
Once a leading French make, Dollar built many different models from 98cc to 748cc. Among them were two-strokes from 98cc to 246cc and 746cc models with four-cylinder unit-design air-cooled ohv engines. There were also Dollar machines with shaft drive and versions with power units made by Chaise.

DOMINISSIMI / *Italy 1924–1928*
Small producer of sporting 172cc and 248cc ohv single-cylinder machines.

DONISELLI / *Italy 1951–*
Once a producer of motorcycles with Ilo and Alpino engines from 63cc to 174cc, Doniselli has concentrated lately on different lightweights with engines of 49cc capacity.

DOPPER / *The Netherlands 1904*
Early ohv design of a 269cc single cylinder machine, which had a long wheelbase and belt drive.

DORION / *France 1932–1936*
Lightweights with 98cc and 123cc Aubier-Dunne two-stroke engines.

DORMAN / *Hungary 1920–1937*
Assembled machines from 172cc to 499 cc with Villiers, MAG and JAP proprietary engines. Limited production.

148cc Dobro-Motorist (TS D.K.W. engine) 1925

346cc DOT (ohv JAP) 1929

976cc DOT (sv JAP v-twin) 1923

DOT / *England 1903–*
Old established factory, founded by racing motorcyclist Harry Reed, who won the twin-cylinder class in the 1908 TT with a 680cc Peugeot-engined machine. He rode in 1924 in the sidecar TT and finished second on a Bradshaw-engined 348cc machine. DOT's heyday was during the 1920s, when they fitted not only Bradshaw engines, but mainly JAP motors from 246cc to 986cc V-twins. There were also Blackburne-engined 347cc versions and in the late 1920s and early 1930s machines with 173cc and 247cc Villiers two-stroke engines. The Manchester-based company gained further successes in TT races, when Syd Ollerhead was second in the 1924 Junior and Jack Cooke third in the Lightweight of the same year. Two third TT places were won in 1928, with Kenneth Twemlow in the Junior and his brother Eddy in the Lightweight. Kenneth was also second in the 1929 Lightweight. The engines were ohv racing singles, made by JAP. Some experimental racing

248cc DOT (TS Villiers) 1957

DOTs had flat cylinders, but these failed to gain success. Motorcycle production stopped in 1932, but a reorganised company re-entered the market after 1948 and built a range of Villiers-engined two-strokes of 123cc to 246cc, of which many were moto-cross and trials machines.

Later, there were also Sachs and Minarelli-engined two-stroke models.

DOTTA / *Italy 1924–1926*
Small assembler who fitted 173cc Piazza two-stroke engines.

DOUE / *France c1903*
Long forgotten make. Fitted 1·5 hp engines into bicycle frames.

DOUGLAS / *England 1907–1956*

Famous for motorcycles with flat-twin engines, the first Douglas was designed by J. F. Barter and had 2·5 hp. It was identical with Barter's previously built Fairy (Fee) machines. For many years Douglas exclusively built opposed twin-cylinder machines of 348cc (60·8mm × 60mm bore/stroke), 498cc (68mm × 68mm) and 596cc (68mm × 82mm) with sv and partly ohv engines. During WWI many 348cc sv models were supplied to the forces and soon after the war, two Douglas engines of 293cc and 348cc were made in Germany by Bosch under licence. Douglas was also in 1928 the first British factory which built special dirt-track (speedway) racing machines of 496cc and 596cc, which became very successful. During the 1930s 248cc sv flat twins, 496cc transverse-mounted shaft-driven ohv flat twins and even a 148cc two-stroke single were built. This was after the Douglas family, which until then controlled this make, left in 1932. Their aim was to produce high-quality machines and only after a reorganisation was it decided to build cheap models in larger quantities. The result can be seen in the 1936 prices: 248cc = £27.10s., 348cc = £31.10s., 498cc = £37.10s., 598cc = £39. All models had sv flat twin engines. There was also the Endeavour with a transverse-mounted flat twin unit-design engine with shaft drive and 498cc for £59.10s., but it never found

350cc Douglas (sv flat twin) 1911

346cc Douglas (ohv transverse flat-twin) 1949

349cc Douglas (sv flat-twin) 1927

346cc Douglas (ohv transverse flat-twin 'Dragonfly') 1957

596cc Douglas (sv flat-twin 'Wessex') 1934

many customers. The same was true of the 148cc two-stroke. After the war, Douglas concentrated on 348cc flat twins with transverse-mounted ohv engines, including the beautiful Dragonfly. In addition to motorcycles, Douglas (Sales & Service), then already part of Westinghouse at Bristol, handled Vespa scooters, with which they are still connected. Manufacture of Douglas motorcycles stopped in 1956. Left are memories of leading Douglas technicians and successful riders, who included Sid Bailey, Cyril Pullin, William 'Bill' Douglas, Rex Judd, C. T. Atkins, Freddy Dixon, Bill Bashall, Tom Sheard, the Alexander brothers, Len Parker, J. W. Whalley, Alec Bennett, Rudolf Runtsch, Toni Babl, Max Reheis and Juan Santos.

D-RAD / *Germany 1921–1933*
Built at a state-owned former arms factory at Berlin-Spandau, the first machine was a 393cc flat twin, designed by Günther. Originally called the Star, it was renamed D-Rad and built until 1926. In the meantime chief designer Christian-

398cc D-Rad (sv flat-twin) 1923

sen created the first true D-Rad, a heavy 496cc single-cylinder sv unit-design machine with a leaf spring fork. The famous Martin Stolle, formerly with BMW and Victoria, joined the Spandau factory in 1927 and developed this design. In 1929 he created an ohv model (R10) with a new fork, coil springs and a separate gearbox, and in 1930 a similar machine, the R11, with an sv engine. The D-Rad motorcycles were always of sturdy design and often ridden with sidecars. Some regarded them as 'farmer's machines', but many big trials and long-distance events were won by these excellent machines, which also competed in races. Stolle was not only

497cc D-Rad (sv Model R-11) 1931

in charge of D-Rad design, but also of the very active competition department. Among leading riders in it were Curt Weichelt, Erich Tennigkeit, Franz Seelos, Max Polster, Hans Przybilski, Franz Ischinger, Paul Bütow, Franz Heck and others. The last models built by D-Rad were 198cc and 246cc two-stroke singles with German Bark engines. Not many were made when NSU at Neckarsulm took over and stopped D-Rad motorcycle production.

DREADNOUGHT / *England 1915–1925*
Made by William Lloyds Cycle Ltd. at Birmingham, where they built Quadrant and LMC motorcycles too. The Dreadnought had an impressive name, but was only an assembled 269cc two-stroke machine with a Villiers engine.

DRESCH / *France 1923–1939*
Built many models over the years. These included 98cc to 246cc two-strokes and sv, ohv and ohc machines with Chaise, Aubier-Dunne,

Stainless, Train, JAP, MAG and other proprietary engines up to 748cc. Among them were models with shaft drive, pressed steel frames and 498cc and 748cc four-cylinder in-line versions. Also a 496cc vertical twin with pressed steel frame and shaft drive was built 1930–1932.

DREVON / *France 1946–1953*
Machines with engines from 98cc to 173cc.

DS / *Sweden 1924–1928*
Made mainly for the Swedish armed forces, the DS had Swiss MAG ioe engines of 746cc.

DSH / *Austria 1924–1932*
The name came from the owners Döller, Seidl and Hauler. The first machines had 172cc and 246cc Villiers engines, later ones also 346cc, 490cc and 746cc sv and ohv JAP and MAG engines. The famous Rupert Karner, many times Austrian Champion, joined DSH in 1927

498cc Dresch (sv two-cylinder, shaft-drive) 1930

746cc DSH (sv V-twin JAP) 1929

as a rider and with commercial interests. His death at the 1928 Hungarian TT when the fork on his 348cc machine broke during the race led to a hiatus for DSH until it was revived in 1929 by Franz Döller. He built new JAP-engined models with 246cc, 497cc and 746cc engines, among them a very sporting 246cc ohv double-port version. Among successful DSH riders were Anton Hunek, Josef Opawsky, Rudolf Runtsch and Friedrich Schwarz.

DS-MALTERRE / *France 1920–1958*
During the 1920s, production concentrated around a not very modern 496cc single-cylinder sv machine. After the war, DS—it stood for Deblades & Sigran—built Ydral-engined 123cc to 247cc two-stroke and 124cc to 248cc ohv versions with French-made AMC proprietary engines.

248cc DS-Malterre (ohv AMC) 1954

173cc DS-Malterre (ohv AMC) 1955

DSK / *Japan 1954–1962*
Built many two-strokes from 172cc upwards and also 497cc ohv machines with transverse-mounted flat-twin power units.

DUCATI / *Italy 1950–*
The first Ducati machines had 48cc and 65cc ohv engines. Ducati's scooter the Cruiser had a 173cc ohv power unit. Chief designer Fabio Taglioli created afterwards a range of 85, 98, 123, 174 and 199cc ohv and 174cc and 248cc ohc single-cylinder models. Among them were very fast 124cc and 248cc ohc racing versions with desmodromic valve gear (see note under AZZARITI), which won many races. Luigi Taveri, Bruno Spaggiari, Mike Hailwood, Francesco Villa, Gianni Degli Antoni and others were Ducati riders. Partly State-owned Ducati concentrated for a long time on production machines with ohc engines from 124cc to 436cc. These were made in slightly different form at Mototrans, the Spanish subsidiary of the Bologna-based Ducati works.

The programme included also single-cylinder moto-cross versions and production versions with desmodromic valve gear. In 1971 the first 748cc V-twin ohc machine appeared with 80mm bore and 74·4mm stroke and a 115 mph top speed. The 750S which followed had desmodromic valve gear and 72 bhp at 9500 rpm with a top speed of over 124 mph. A 862cc V-twin appeared in 1974, and even more potent 144 mph Ducati 900 Super Sport in 1976. Other new Ducatis were the 123cc, 22 bhp enduro two-stroke, the 349cc and 496cc vertical ohc twins with chain-driven camshafts and the 500 Sport Desmo with a 50 hp 496cc vertical-twin engine and desmodromic valve gear, which, with new frames and a new 864cc V-twin, reaches 144 mph, and accelerates from 0 to 63 mph in 3·6 sec.

198cc Ducati (ohc) 1958

158cc Ducati (ohc) 1965

864cc Ducati (ohc V-twin) 1976

496cc Ducati (ohc two-cylinder) 1976

DUCATI (MOTOTRANS) / *Spain 1959*

Produced for many years nearly identical models to the Bologna Ducati factory. Mototrans-Ducati of Barcelona is still closely connected with Italian Ducati, which also supplies the licences for the Spanish machines. They are still producing various 340cc ohc singles with touring and sporting specifications and also a 72cc trials two-stroke machine with 6 bhp at 6100 rpm. The latest Spanish-built Ducati (Mototrans) models are improved and developed 246 and 346cc ohc singles, called Forza and Vento.

DUCSON / *Spain late 1950s–early 1960s*

Small producer of 49cc two-stroke machines.

DÜMO / *Germany 1924–1925*

Sporting version of the 198cc Autinag, designed by Frankowski.

DUNELT / *England 1919–1956*

Equipped with double-diameter pistons, the first Dunelt two-strokes had single-cylinder engines with 499cc. A similar version with 248cc was built from the 1920s onwards. From 1929 the factory also fitted 346cc, 498cc and 598cc sv and ohv engines made by Sturmey-Archer, as well as a 246cc version with the Sturmey-Archer face-cam ohc engine. During the following years, the main range consisted of Villiers-engined machines up to 344cc and of sv and ohv models up to 498cc with engines made by Python (Rudge) and JAP. After a reorganization, the Birmingham factory moved in 1931 to Sheffield and discontinued the manufacture of motorcycles in 1935. They re-entered the trade in 1955 with a 49cc moped with its own ohv engine, but had not

246cc Dunelt (TS) 1924

much success. The greatest sporting success gained by Dunelt was winning the 1930 Maudes Trophy in the Isle of Man for the most meritorious performance of the year. Despite severe conditions, a 498cc Dunelt with an ohv engine covered 13,119 miles in 16 days at an average speed of 34·8 mph.

DUNKLEY / *England 1913*

Produced a variety of machines for a very few years with 199, 499, 746 and 988cc Precision engines, 342cc Peco two-strokes and also JAP-engined models from 293cc to 748cc.

DUNKLEY / *England 1957–1959*

Modern mopeds with own 61cc, 64cc and eventually 49cc ohv engines. These were of unit design. 'Whippet' was the trade name of these products.

DUNSTALL / *England 1967–*

Producer of sporting and luxurious frames for multi-cylinder engines including four-cylinder Hondas, twin-cylinder Nortons, three-cylinder Suzukis and others, including modified 1098cc Kawasaki ohc engines with 86 bhp at 7800 rpm. The idea is to produce frames for modified power units which as a result of additional bhp need improved road-holding qualities.

DURAND / *France 1920–1923*

Assembled motorcycles with Zurcher engines. Limited manufacture.

DURANDAL / *France 1925–1932*

Some models had pressed steel frames and most used JAP, Zurcher and Chaise proprietary engines from 246cc to 490cc. There was also a successful works racing machine with a 348cc KTT Velocette ohc engine.

DÜRKOPP / *Germany 1901–1959*

Pioneer of the German motorcycle industry. In 1905, they already produced single and V-twin machines and a four-in-line with aircooled cylinders. Also a leading bicycle and car producer — now a leading manufacturer of needle-

7 hp Dürkopp (sv V-twin) 1903

148cc Dürkopp (TS) 1952

bearings—Dürkopp stopped motorcycle production before WWI, built in the 1930s motorized bicycles and in 1949 resumed motorcycle manufacture with Sachs-engined 98cc and 123cc two-strokes. They also fitted Ilo engines of the same size and built after 1951 their own 147cc,

174cc and 198cc two-stroke engines designed by Goslau. A beautiful scooter, the 198cc Dürkopp Diana, came out in 1953 and was made until the famous factory stopped producing two-wheelers.

DUVAL / *Belgium 1950–1955*
Limited production of small 123cc two-stroke machines with engines supplied mainly by Royal Enfield.

DUX / *England 1904–1906*
Small assembler who used frames made by Rex at Coventry and engines supplied by Minerva, MMC, Sarolea and others. They were singles and V-twins.

DUZMO / *England 1919–1923*
A 496cc single-cylinder ohv machine designed by John Wallace and partly developed by the famous Bert le Vack, who was for a short period with Duzmo.

DWB / *Germany 1924–1926*
After Juhö closed down, Dorko Werke Bamberg took over manufacture of the 195cc sv machines and added in 1925 a 269cc two-stroke model to the range.

DYSON-MOTORETTE / *England 1920–1922*
Scooter-like lightweight with a 1·5 hp engine on the left side and the petrol tank above the rear wheel.

EADIE / *England 1898–1903*
Pioneer make, which first built three-wheelers and then motorcycles with engines made by De Dion, Minerva, MMC and other factories. Eadie was also closely connected with the foundation of the Royal Enfield factory.

EAGLE / *America 1910–1915*
Well-made Spake-engined 4 hp singles and 7 hp and 9 hp V-twins. According to the late Floyd Clymer, the Eagle was one of the best machines ever made in the USA.

EAGLE-TANDEM / *England 1903–1905*
Limited production of De Dion-engined machines, which were fitted with a chairlike seat.

EBE / *Sweden 1919–1930*
After manufacturing 173cc bicycle engines, EBE produced motorcycles with own 172cc ohv and 598cc sv engines.

EBER / *Germany 1924–1928*
Motorcycles of typical English design with 347cc and 497cc sv and ohv Blackburne, then also 348cc and 498cc ohv Kühne and ohc Küchen engines.

EBO / *England 1910–WWI*
Assembler who fitted Precision engines and also single and V-twin JAP engines.

EBS / *Germany 1924–1930*
Berlin-based manufacturer who fitted engines of own manufacture with 198, 246, 348, 398, 496cc and a V-twin with 796cc. After 1928 a Villiers-engined 198cc two-stroke was added. The factory produced also three-wheeled transport vehicles with motorcycle engines.

EBU-STAR / *Japan 1952–1955*
Interesting 248cc twin-cylinder ohv machine with a vertical and a horizontal cylinder.

198cc EBS (sv) 1924

246cc EBS (ohv) 1925

EBW / *Germany 1923–1924*
Assembled 139cc machine with engines made by Bekamo.

ECA / *Germany 1923–1924*
Simple 142cc two-stroke machines made in limited numbers.

ECEKA / *Germany 1924–1925*
Another small make which fitted 145cc and 173cc engines.

ECHO / *Japan late 1950s–early 1960s*
Producer of 123cc and 148cc two-stroke machines and the Pandra scooter.

ECKL / *Germany 1923–1926*
Hugo Eckl first produced bicycle attachment engines, afterwards also a 198cc single with its own ohv engine.

ECONOMIC / *England 1921–1923*
Unusual 165cc twin-cylinder two-stroke machines with friction drive of a design which came from the USA. The first models had the horizontally opposed twin fitted in orthodox fashion – in line. Afterwards it was transverse-mounted in a low duplex frame. Although its price was only £28.10s., it failed to make the grade.

165cc Economic (TS transverse flat-twin) 1923

EDETA / *Spain 1951–1960*
Two-stroke machines with 147cc and 173cc engines.

EDMONTON / *England 1903–c1910*
Was a small assembler of motorcycles who fitted Minerva and Fafnir engines.

EDMUND / *England 1907–1924*
Well-designed and sturdy machines, some with spring frames using leaf springs. Charles Edmund fitted various proprietary engines of 269cc to 546cc which included the makes Fafnir, MAG, JAP, Barr & Stroud and Blackburne. There was also an early model with the sv Villiers engine.

149cc Eichler (TS DKW) 1922

EGA / *Germany 1922–1926*
Made by the Gaggenau iron works, the EGA machines had own 246cc and 346cc three-port, deflector-type two-stroke engines.

EICHELSDÖRFER / *Germany 1929–1931*
Builder of 198cc machines with ohv engines made by JAP.

EICHLER / *Germany 1920–1925*
Well-known assembler of lightweight motorcycles with 119, 145 and 173cc DKW and 129cc to 149cc Bekamo two-stroke engines. Produced also DKW-designed 123cc Golem and 145cc Lomos scooters, then in Germany called Sesselräder. Ernst Eichler, founder of the factory, left in the mid-1920s and built machines with pressed-steel frames. After less than a year he returned to his old Berlin-based factory where he continued producing these red motorcycles.

EISENHAMMER / *Germany 1923–1926*
Two-stroke machines of heavy design with 206cc DKW and 225cc engines of own manufacture.

206cc Eisenhammer (TS) 1925

EISLER / *Czechoslovakia 1920–1926*
Agriculture-machine factory which produced not only 148cc two-stroke bicycle attachment engines, but also complete lightweight motorcycles with these power units.

ELAND / *The Netherlands 1955–1959*
Small assembler, who fitted 123cc to 158cc two-stroke engines, mainly supplied by Sachs, into own frames.

ELECT / *Italy 1920–1923*
Interesting design by Ladetto — later of Ladetto & Blatto fame — Ubertalli and Cavalchini. It was a horizontal twin with 492cc and three valves for each cylinder.

ELFA / *Germany 1926–1932*
Built during the years a variety of models with 73, 98, 123, 198, 298, 346 and 497cc proprietary engines made by DKW, Kühne, Küchen, Windhoff, Sachs, Bark and also JAP. Mofa production continued until 1940.

ELFE / *Germany 1923–1925*
Unorthodox frames with own 196cc three-port deflector-type engines built in small numbers.

ELF-KING / *England 1907–1909*
Equipped with hand-starters like cars, these machines had V-twin Minerva engines.

ELFSON / *England 1923–1925*
Well-designed machines with their own 294cc

three-port two-stroke power units. Another model had 170cc Norman ohv engines.

ELI / *England 1911–1912*
Accessory factory which produced motorcycles with 3·5 hp Precision engines.

ELIE HUIN / *France early 1950s–early 1960s*
The post-war Elie Huin machines had Ydral, AMC and other French proprietary engines from 123cc to 248cc.

ELIG / *Spain 1956–1959*
Small producer who used Hispano Villiers engines from 123cc to 198cc.

ELITE / *Germany 1903–1940*
Founded by Diamant, where motorcycles were built in 1903. Elite started car production in 1914 and the manufacture of a 1 hp engine for bicycles in 1923. Elite and Diamant joined forces in 1927 and produced Diamant motorcycles until 1928–1929, when Opel took over the factory for the manufacture of their own 498cc motorcycles with Duralumin frames. In 1932 these models were succeeded by similar machines called EO (Elite-Opel). These had 348cc and 498cc ohc engines made by Küchen, while the 'real' Opel motorcycles of that period had their own sv and ohv single cylinder power units. Few EOs were actually built.

ELLEHAM / *Denmark 1904–1909*
One of the few Danish producers. The design included an open frame, a larger front wheel and a 2·75 hp Peugeot engine.

ELMDON / *England 1915–1921*
Limited manufacture of 269cc two-strokes with Villiers engines.

ELRING / *Germany 1924–1925*
This was just another name for the 196cc Elfe two-strokes.

ELSINORE / *Japan 1973–*
This is not an independent make, but a Honda moto-cross version. It is made with 123cc and 248cc two-stroke high-efficiency engines. The smaller model has 24 bhp at 10,000 rpm, the bigger 33 bhp at 7500 rpm. Most Elsinores are exported to the USA.

ELSTAR / *England 1968–1971*
Produced mainly frames for competition machines, including moto-cross, grass track and speedway. Fitted Jawa, Bultaco and other mainly two-stroke engines. Production stopped when Ellis, the founder, was killed in a road accident.

ELSTER / *Germany 1924–1926*
A comparatively small factory which produced 197cc sv machines with engines of own design and manufacture.

ELSWICK / *England 1903–1920*
Well-known bicycle manufacturer who fitted into 348cc and 498cc single-cylinder motorcycles the proprietary engines made by Precision.

ELVE / *Belgium 1958–early 1960s*
Moped producer who fitted 49cc Sachs engines.

EM / *Austria 1928–1930*
Produced one model only in limited numbers. It was a 497cc single-cylinder ohv machine with the MAG double-port engine.

497cc EM (ohv MAG) 1929

EMA / *Germany 1922–1926*
Designed by Eduard Molitor, these low-built machines had 145cc DKW engines with horizontal cylinder.

206cc EMA (TS DKW) 1925

EMBLEM / *America 1909–1925*
Big 996cc V-twin machines of sound design, which competed with success in sporting events.

EMC / *England 1947–1952*
The first machines had their own 348cc double-piston two-stroke engines. Afterwards the Ehrlich Motor Company fitted 123cc and 248cc Puch engines. A 123cc JAP-engined two-stroke exhibited at Earls Court in 1952 never went into quantity production. Joe Ehrlich built from 1960 to 1964 the 124cc De Havilland rotary disc two-stroke racing machines, which were ridden in races by such famous men as Mike Hailwood, Derek Minter, Phil Read, Rex Avery and Paddy Driver.

EMH / *Germany 1927–1929*
Limited manufacture of 348cc and 498cc machines with open frames and Küchen ohc engines.

EMMAG / *Hungary 1924–1927*
Built unorthodox watercooled 670cc two-stroke twins and also aircooled 495cc two-stroke singles. Production was on a limited scale.

196cc Elster (sv) 1925

340cc EMW (ohv shaft-drive) 1953

EMURO / *Japan 1953–late 1950s*
Produced two-stroke machines with own engines from 98cc to 248cc.

EMW / *East Germany 1945–1956*
Produced in the former Dixi-BMW car and motorcycle factory at Eisenach a 348cc single-cylinder ohv machine with shaft drive and pressed steel frame which was similar to a 1934 BMW model.

EMWE / *Germany 1924–1925*
Using a welded box frame, EMWE fitted a 293cc two-stroke engine of their own design.

ENAG / *Germany 1924–1925*
The Theo Steininger-designed two-stroke machines had 248cc and 348cc capacity, watercooled barrels and aircooled cylinder heads.

ENDRICK / *England 1911–1915*
Built different machines with Fafnir, Peugeot and JAP engines, until the Olton (Birmingham) factory concentrated on models with 346cc Peco two-stroke and 496cc Precision sv engines.

ENDURANCE / *England 1909–1924*
Among the C. B. Harrison-designed models were those with 269cc Villiers engines and versions with their own 259cc and 297cc two-stroke three-port motors.

ENERGETTE / *England 1907–1911*
Designed by the famous J. L. Norton—founder of the Norton factory—the Energette had a British-built Moto-Rêve engine of 274cc. It was a V-twin with 50mm bore and 70mm stroke.

ENGEE / *Germany 1925*
Single-cylinder ohv machines with Kühne proprietary power units. Apparently only a 348cc model was marketed.

EO / *Germany 1930–1931*
Mentioned already under Elite, the EO had an Opel-like frame made from Duralumin and 348cc and 498cc ohc Küchen engines. Designer of the frame was Ernst Neumann-Neander, of the engine Richard Küchen. Only few EO machines were actually built.

EOLE / *Belgium c1900*
Built in the pioneer period, the Eole had Kelecom and Fafnir engines.

EPA / *Germany 1924–1925*
Small assembler, who fitted 293cc JAP sv engines into own frames.

ERCOLI-CAVALLONE / *Italy 1922–1923*
One of the few makes in the world which produced 496cc V-twin machines with two-stroke engines. Others were the British Stanger and WAG. None had much success and soon all disappeared from the market.

ERIE / *America 1905–1911*
The Hammondsport factory fitted Minerva, Spake and Curtiss engines and was commercially connected with the Glenn Curtiss factory.

ERIOL / *France 1932–1939*
Lightweight motorcycles with 98cc two-stroke engines.

ERKA / *Germany 1924–1925*
Simple 269cc two-stroke machines made by a small factory.

ERKÖ / *Germany 1922–1924*
Another small producer of lightweights with 145cc DKW motors.

ERMAG / *Germany 1923–1930*
Good machines designed by ex-Ziro designer Albert Roder. The first 246cc Ermag had a

497cc EO (ohc Küchen Prototype) 1930

498cc Ermag (sv) 1927

246cc Ermag (ohv) 1927

Dunelt-like double diameter piston and a rotary inlet valve for the single-cylinder two-stroke engine. From 1925 Ermag produced a fast 246cc ohv machine and sv singles with 497cc and 547cc capacity. Successful Ermag riders: Hans Hieronymus, Karl Perl, Paul Bittorf. Roder was with Victoria in the 1930s and before the war joined the NSU works at Neckarsulm.

ERNST EICHLER / *Germany 1924–1925*
Originally the founder of the Berlin-based Eichler motorcycle factory, Ernst Eichler left the works after differences and set up a new factory. There he created some interesting 142cc two-stroke and 172cc two and four-stroke sv machines with frames made from pressed steel. After a comparatively short period he returned.

ERNST-MAG / *Germany 1926–1930*
The first machines had 348cc and 498cc ohc engines made by Küchen, but from 1928 onwards the Silesian factory relied exclusively on

Swiss MAG engines of 348, 498, 598, 746 and 996cc capacity. Among them were fast 348cc ohv double-port singles and 498cc and 598cc ohv V-twins. Factory riders even had some 498cc ohc V-twins. These included Landolph Rhode, Edgar Kittner and Orlindo Geissler.

ERR-ZETT / *Austria 1938*
Lightweights with 98cc Sachs and Ilo engines.

347cc Ernst-MAG (ohv MAG) 1927

As result of political circumstances at that period in Austria, only few of these machines were actually built.

ESCHAG / *Germany 1923–1925*
Simple 298cc two-stroke machines with belt drive to the rear wheel.

ESCH-REKORD / *Germany 1927–1930*
Designed and built by racing motorcyclist Adolf Esch, these racing machines used 248cc, 348cc and 498cc engines made by Blackburne, MAG and JAP. Among the riders were Joseph Wenzel and Wilhelm Etzbach. The design resembled that of leading English machines.

ESCOL / *Belgium 1925–1938*
Built on English lines in limited numbers, Escol used Villiers engines from 147cc to 247cc. Larger models had 248cc to 596cc JAP and Python engines. The last Escol had its own 348cc two-stroke engine.

ESO / *Czechoslovakia 1949–*
Now part of the Jawa factory, Eso was founded by ex-racing rider Jaroslav Simandl for the purpose of producing 498cc speedway ohv single-cylinder engines. Afterwards they built at the Divišov factory not only complete speedway machines but also models with modified 348cc and 498cc engines for road races and moto-cross events. Now they produce track engines and complete motorcycles including long-track and ice-racing versions. The latest Jawa (née Eso) speedway engines have four-valve cylinder-heads and are very successful.

198cc Europa (TS Schliha) 1933

ETA / *England 1921*
Interesting 870cc three-cylinder machine with a radial engine, unit-design and shaft drive. The Eta never went into quantity production.

ETOILE / *France 1933–1939*
Aubier-Dunne-engined two-strokes from 98cc to 198cc.

EUROPA / *Germany 1931–1933*
Officially made at Munich with 98cc and 146cc Villiers engines as well as with Berlin-built 147cc and 198cc Schliha two-strokes.

EVANS / *America 1919–1924*
One of the finest American lightweights ever built, the Evans had a 119cc two-stroke engine and also gained popularity in Germany. The Berlin-based Stock factory, then part of the Kuhn industrial empire, eventually took the Evans licence and built these machines in improved form as the first models made by Stock.

EVANS-PONDORF / *Germany 1924–1925*
Built also the 119cc Evans, but ran into licence problems with Stock and tried to enter the market with a beautiful 496cc single of advanced design, which included foot gear change. Unfortunately lack of money prevented quantity production of this Pondorf design.

119cc Evans (TS) 1922

EVART-HALL / *England 1903–1905*
The first machines had single-cylinder engines fitted into strengthened bicycle frames and mounted near-horizontally above the pedalling gear. The 2·5 hp engines had sight-feed lubrication, spray or surface carburetters and back-pedalling hub brakes. From 1904 onwards, Evart-Hall produced also the aircooled in-line four-cylinder 385cc machine designed by Binks.

EVEREST / *Germany 1925–1926*
Offered by a Berlin-based company, the Everest was actually built by the G. A. Rempp factory at Münster. It was a heavy 496cc single with its own ohv engine.

EVO / *Germany 1923–1925*
Designed by well-known motorcycle journalist Eduard Voigt, 146cc Evo machines had Ilo as well as their own two-stroke engines.

EVYCSA / *Spain c1956*
Well-designed 173cc machines with four-speed gearboxes made in limited numbers.

EWABRA / *Germany 1921–1924*
Heavy 550cc single-cylinder sv machines, designed and built by Ewald Brackelsberg, a cousin of the late Bugatti driver Karl Brackelsberg.

EXCELSIOR / *England 1896–1964*

Four motorcycle factories used the Excelsior trade mark. The oldest was—surprisingly—one of the German Excelsior factories. Birmingham-built Excelsiors when sold or even raced in Germany, had to be renamed Bayliss Thomas. This was their original trade mark, while the

name Excelsior was used after the Germans had it secured. Owned by the Walker family in Coventry, Excelsior produced during the years motorcycles up to 996cc with Minerva, De Dion, MMC and other engines, among them an 850cc single, which probably was made by the British company Condor of Coventry for Excelsior. Most models built during the 1920s and 1930s had Blackburne, JAP and Villiers engines, of which 248cc JAP-engined ohv racing models gained many successes with such riders as Syd

and Leslie Crabtree, Chris Staniland, Eric Fernihough, Jack Worters, Rudi Hunger, Josef Schörg and Otto Kühar. There were also potent 173cc racing machines with JAP engines and in 1933 Syd Gleave won the lightweight TT on the Mechanical Marvel, a very interesting and complicated four-valve 248cc ohv racing machine designed by H. J. Hatch. It never went into quantity production and was superseded in the following years by 248cc, 348cc and 498cc ohc Manxman models. The first versions also had four valves, but later ones only two. In 1938 they got spring frames. The development in that

period was in the hands of Alan Bruce; the rider included H. G. Tyrell Smith and S. 'Ginger Wood. The 248cc Manxman, most highl developed of these ohc machines, was especiall successful and won many races even after 1945 It was a bit on the heavy side, but very reliabl and had a good road-holding quality. In 193 the Villiers-engined 98cc Excelsior Autobyk appeared a forerunner of many mopeds. Th engine with the horizontal cylinder was in fron of the pedalling gear. After 1945, all Excelsior had two-stroke engines. During the war the factory produced 98cc Sprite two-strokes fo

248cc Excelsior (ohc 'Manxman') 1936 GB

490cc Excelsior (ohv JAP) 1930 GB

Corgi; afterwards they built singles and vertical twins with Villiers and their own engines up to 328cc. Among them were models with fully enclosed engines, and scooter-like machines. The last racing machines were built in 1938 and after the war the successful racing department at Excelsior in Birmingham was a thing of the past.

EXCELSIOR / Germany 1923–1924

This company was evidently not considered a problem for the older German Excelsior factory at Brandenburg, for they apparently never fought the use of the Excelsior trade mark. The short-lived Munich firm built only a simple 245cc two-stroke machine.

EXCELSIOR / Germany 1901–1939

This was originally a bicycle factory at Brandenburg, now in East Germany. After using Minerva, Zedel and Fafnir engines, during the 1920s the factory used English 198cc, 298cc and 346cc sv and ohv JAP engines too. Their motorcycles, of typical English design, were not unsimilar to English Excelsiors, although there was no direct connection between Excelsior-Birmingham and

269cc Excelsior (TS) 1914 USA

992cc Excelsior (ioe V-twin) 1922 USA

192cc Excelsior (TS Bark) 1936 D

Excelsior-Brandenburg. Never as famous as the English make, the German factory fitted in the 1930s 198cc two-stroke and 196cc to 496cc sv engines made by Bark of Dresden, and while Walker built successful racing machines, Conrad & Patz — owners of the German factory — never showed any interest in sporting events.

EXCELSIOR / America 1908–1931

This was the biggest factory producing Excelsior motorcycles. It was the Excelsior Supply & Mfg. Co at Chicago, part of the still-existing Schwinn bicycle empire. The range consisted of 269cc two-strokes built along the lines of the English Triumph Baby and of 499cc singles and 746cc to 996cc V-twins with their own ioe engines. Only a few 499cc and 996cc works racing models had ohc power units. There was a problem when the Chicago-based factory sold machines to England. These had the name American-X and in the mid-1920s all V-twins built by Schwinn were renamed Super-X. In addition, the factory produced since 1919 the famous Bill Henderson-designed four-in-line machines, of which the last version had 1301cc with ioe valves, separate cylinder barrels and a common cylinder head. Super-X and Henderson had next to Indian and Harley-Davidson the largest motorcycle production in the USA when Ignaz Schwinn decided in 1931 to stop manufacture of motorcycles.

EXPRESS / Germany 1903–late 1950s

Produced Fafnir-engined motorcycles in the early years of motorcycling. Resumed manufacture of mofas in the 1930s with 74cc and 98cc two-stroke engines and re-entered the market in 1949 with two-stroke motorcycles up to 248cc. An old bicycle factory, Express also supplied mofas and mopeds again. These now had 47cc engines. Experiments in the mid-1950s with the Küchen-designed 248cc twin-cylinder ohe engine proved not very successful. In 1957 Express became part of the then newly-founded Zweirad-Union at Nuremberg, together with Victoria and DKW, but the name Express was soon dropped.

247cc Express (TS ILO 'Radex') 1952

EYSINK / *The Netherlands 1899–1956*
Leading Dutch motorcycle factory. Fitted first Minerva, Fafnir and other engines into own frames, built in 1905 vertical twins with Kindermann-designed Bercley engines and also entered car production. The most famous pre-1914 models were the 365cc and 425cc singles, used also by the Dutch forces during the war. There were also 366cc and 409cc singles and 774cc V-twins with own engines. During the early 1920s, a flat twin came into being. It had 702cc and its engine was unsimilar to the British Raleigh of that period. The first Villiers-engined two-strokes were built in 1926. Eysink built 147cc,

172cc and 198cc versions. The Dutch factory was also closely connected with foreign factories including New Hudson and Sunbeam in England and Dollar in France, which supplied certain parts to the Dutch. They also fitted the English Rudge-built 348cc and 498cc four-valve Python ohv engines and some JAP engines, including racing versions. In the mid-1930s bread-and-butter versions with Sachs and Ilo two-stroke engines up to 198cc came into production at the Amersfoort factory, then headed by Dick Eysink. After 1945 most Eysink machines had Villiers engines. During the late 1940s and early 1950s, very fast 172cc machines were developed.

123cc Eysink (TS Villiers) 1939

F

FABULA / *Germany 1922–1924*
Designed by ex-Dürkopp designer Nikolaus Henzel, the Fabula was of very advanced design. It had its own 246cc unit-design two-stroke

246cc Fabula (TS shaft-drive) 1923

deflector-type engine and shaft drive to the rear wheel. Many parts of it were made for Fabula by the superbly equipped Dürkopp factory at Bielefeld.

492cc Fadag (ohv) 1926

FADAG / *Germany 1921–1925*
Made by a car factory, Fadag's first product in the sphere of two-wheelers was a 118cc bicycle attachment engine. Motorcycles, built from 1923 onward, had 'own' 497cc single cylinder sv and ohv engines which — according to unconfirmed sources — were supplied by Sarolea of Belgium to the Düsseldorf-based factory.

FAFNIR / *Germany 1900–1914*
Pioneer producer of proprietary engines and from 1903 onward of complete motorcycles, Fafnir supplied in the early years most German-made motorcycle power units. The Aachen-based factory had the Werner brothers licence for the manufacture of proprietary engines and produced many versions up to 8 hp V-twins.

FAGAN / *Ireland 1935–1937*
Only one model, a Villiers-engined 123cc single, was made by the Irish factory.

FAGARD / *Germany 1923–1925*
Limited production of 145cc two-stroke machines with DKW engines, also known as FG.

FAGGI/*Italy 1950–1953*
Lightweight machines with Villiers engines from 123cc to 147cc. Good design, small production.

FAINI/*Italy 1923–1927*
Manufacturer of 108cc bicycle engines and of 198cc motorcycles with own sv engines.

FAIRFIELD/*England 1914–1915*
Only one model, a 269cc two-stroke, was built by this Warrington factory. WWI prevented a large output.

FAKA/*Germany 1952–1957*
A scooter with 8 inch and later 10 inch wheels and Ilo engines of 147cc, 174cc and 197cc capacity.

FALCO/*Italy 1950–1953*
Built at Vercelli, the Falco was powered by German 98cc and 147cc Sachs engines.

FALKE/*Germany 1923–1925*
Assembled machines with 142cc Grade and 145cc DKW three-port, deflector-type two-stroke engines.

FALTER/*Germany 1952–*
Moped and mofa producer, whose products were also known as Stoewer Greif. The still-existing Bielefeld-based factory used mainly 49cc engines.

FAM/*Italy 1951–1969*
Founded by Giovanni Benelli—one of the five brothers of Benelli motorcycle fame of Pesaro—the FAM produced 115cc singles and 195cc flat-twins which had the B trade mark. The egg-shaped engines were of modern design.

FAMA/*Germany 1923–1925*
Limited manufacture of 190cc ohv and 420cc sv single-cylinder machines with own engines.

FAMO/*Germany 1923–1926*
Triangular frames and 127cc two-stroke three-port engines formed the basis of all Famo models.

127cc Famo (TS) 1925

49cc TS Fantic GT Super, 1976

123cc TS Fantic Caballero 125 RC, 1976

49cc TS Fantic Super Rocket, 1976

FANTIC/*Italy 1968–*
Sporting 49cc and 124cc two-strokes built with an eye on the American market. Produces many models, including choppers, trials and moto-cross versions. Some belong to the Caballero range with 124cc 21 bhp at 9500 rpm engines and six-speed gearboxes, while moto-cross versions have 26 bhp at 10,000 rpm. Fantic belongs among the younger but active Italian factories.

FAR/*Austria 1924–1927*
Assembled machines with 346cc and 490cc single-cylinder sv and ohv JAP engines. The name stood for Franz and Anton Rumpler.

FARNELL/*England c1901*
Long forgotten make which had 2·75 hp Minerva engines fitted into bicycle frames.

FAVOR/*France 1919–1959*
Was a well-known make in France. Built two-strokes from 98cc to 248cc and JAP-engined sv and ohv models with 346cc single-cylinder power units. After the war the Favor range included Aubier-Dunne-engined two-strokes and AMC-engined ohv singles up to 248cc.

FAVORIT/*Germany 1933–1938*
The first machines had 996cc V-twin JAP engines, afterwards the small manufacturer concentrated on 98cc and 123cc lightweights with Sachs engines. Favorit's main product was sidecars.

FB/*Germany 1923–1925*
The first machines were 269cc two-strokes, afterwards JAP and Blackburne-engined 348cc and 498cc sv and ohv models came into being. Designed by Friedrich Benz, these machines were also known with the Meteor transfer on the petrol tank.

FB/*England 1913–1922*
Fowler and Bingham built proprietary two-stroke engines of 206cc, 269cc and 411cc and also complete motorcycles.

FB-MONDIAL (Mondial)/*Italy 1948–*
Not to be confused with the Belgian La Mondiale, the Fratelli Boselli-built Mondial appeared soon after WWII. In pre-war days, the Milan factory concentrated on delivery three-wheelers. The first motorcycles had 123cc and 159cc two-stroke and 198cc ohc engines. Among FB-Mondial

designers were such men as Alfonso Drusiani and Lino Tonti. They created superb 123cc, 173cc and 248cc ohc—partly double-ohc—racing machines which won many races. Among the riders were Tarquinio Provini, Mike Hailwood, Crommie McCandless, Carlo Ubbiali, Gianni Leoni, Cecil Sandford and many others. There were also twin-cylinder 248cc works racers while the range of production machines included 49cc and 73cc two-strokes and 88cc, 123cc, 173cc, 198cc and 248cc ohv and partly ohc versions. Lately Mondial has concentrated on 123cc two-strokes and 49cc machines for road, off-road and moto-cross.

FBM / *Italy 1950–1955*
Interesting design with partly pressed steel frames and the flat single-cylinder engines mounted directly on the swinging arm of the rear suspension. The range included 48cc and 74cc two-strokes and ohv engines with 158cc and 198cc capacity.

269cc Federal (TS Villiers) 1921

FECHTEL / *Germany 1924–1926*
Small assembler who fitted Hansa-built 198cc ohv engines into their own frames.

FEDERATION / *England 1919–1937*
The Co-op machine, built at Birmingham, was also known with the Federal trade mark. Most models had the 269cc Villiers engine, later ones 147cc Villiers and 246cc ohv JAP engines. The price for the smaller model in 1936 was £25, for the bigger £44.

FEE / *England 1905–1908*
The Barter-designed sv flat twins had 198cc, 346cc and 676cc engines. Also known as the Fairy, the Fee was really the forerunner of the Douglas machines.

FEILBACH LIMITED / *America 1912–1915*
Like the Harley-Davidson, the Feilbach Limited was built at Milwaukee, Wisconsin, but unfortunately for a short period only. The range consisted of 548cc singles and 990cc to 1130cc V-twins with their own ioe engines. Most models could be obtained with either chain or shaft drive.

FEMINIA / *France 1933–1936*
Assembled lightweights with 98cc and 123cc Aubier-Dunne and Stainless two-stroke engines.

FERBEDO / *Germany 1954*
Very simple but unsuccessful mini-scooter with 49cc Zündapp engines.

FERRARI / *Italy 1951–1954*
A big name, but a small factory. There was no connection with Enzo Ferrari and his cars. Still, Ferrari motorcycles were of sound design and the range included two-stroke and ohv machines from 123cc to 248cc. The last model was a beautiful 173cc vertical-twin ohc machine.

FERRARIS / *Italy 1903*
Short-lived make which had 2 hp Peugeot engines in bicycle frames.

FERT / *Italy 1926–1929*
Calamidas Fert machines had no connection with the then well-known Italian plug of the same name. The motorcycles used 173cc ohv engines of Fert's own design and manufacture. Ridden by Passera and Aldi in races, they were not successful.

FEW-PARAMOUNT / *England 1920–1927*
Waller's long wheelbase design with two bucket seats and a fully enclosed engine was not the dream of many customers. Offered with 498cc JAP and Blackburne as well as with 996cc V-twin

JAP engines, only few of these unorthodox machines were actually built.

490cc FEW-Paramount (sv JAP) 1927

FEX / *Germany 1923–1924*
Fitted DKW and Bekamo engines, after his own 170cc two-stroke proved to be a technical failure.

FG / *Germany 1923–1925*
Identical with Fagard.

FHG / *Germany 1927–1929*
Offered by the German AJS importer Pleus & Co., the FHG was probably a French Grimpeur 173cc two-stroke built to the Pleus specification.

FIAM / *Italy 1923–1925*
A 110cc bicycle attachment engine designed by Lelio Antonioli and built in limited numbers.

FIAMC / *Germany 1951–1953*
Producer of 123cc two-stroke motorcycles and of scooters with identical engines.

1196cc Feilbach (ioe V-twin) 1914

FIDUCIA / *Switzerland 1902–1905*
Made by the Weber foundry at Zürich-Uster, these machines had own 450cc single-cylinder engines.

FIFI / *Germany 1923–1924*
Another name for the 145cc and 173cc Eichler motorcycles.

FIGINI / *Italy 1898–1910*
Luigi Figini together with Lazzati were pioneers in the motorcycle field. They produced their first machine in 1899 and entered commercial manufacture of motorcycles in 1902.

FINZI / *Italy 1923–1925*
Built actually at the Maxima factory, the Finzi was a machine of advanced design with the 598cc ohv V-twin unit-design engine transverse-mounted. It had a saddle sprung by leaf springs and a fully enclosed rear chain. Despite the modern conception, the Finzi was not a commercial success.

FIORELLI / *Italy 1951–*
Assembled machines with 123cc and 173cc Ilo engines and concentrated afterwards on the production of components for other factories and on bicycles and mopeds.

FIT / *Italy 1950–1954*
Another assembler, who fitted Ilo engines of 123cc and 147cc into own frames.

FIX / *Germany 1922–1926*
A branch of the Hansa-Lloyd car factory, Fix produced two-strokes with own 3 hp engines.

FKS / *Germany 1921–1926*
Produced a range of machines with 149cc two-stroke engines. These were mounted originally above the front wheel, afterwards above the pedalling gear. Another model was a 298cc flat-twin two-stroke, not unsimilar to the KC.

FLANDERS / *America 1911–1914*
Made by the Michigan car factory of the same name, the Flanders was a 499cc sv single with the exhaust valve on the rear side of the cylinder.

496cc Finzi (ohv transverse V-twin) 1924

298cc FKS (TS flat-twin) 1923

497cc Flanders (sv) 1913

FLANDRIA / *Belgium late 1950s–*
Well-known manufacturer of bicycles, mofas, mopeds and lightweight machines with 49cc two-stroke engines. Showed in 1976 a very sporting motorcycle with a six-speed gearbox and 17 inch alloy wheels. All engines are made by the A. Claeys-Flandria N.V. at Zedelgem.

FLINK / *Germany 1920–1922*
Built by a company which is now part of BMW at Munich, the Flink was a 148cc two-stroke machine with a Kurier deflector-type proprietary engine. Not a very successful design.

FLM / *England 1951–1953*
Designed by former P&M Panther designer Frank Leach, the little lightweight had 123cc

198cc Flottweg (ohv Bark) 1936

119cc Flottweg (TS) 1922

980cc Flying Merkel (sv twin) 1913

Villiers and JAP two-stroke engines and also 198cc Villiers power units.

FLOTTWEG / *Germany 1921–1937*
The first products were good 119cc bicycle attachment engines over the front wheel. They were followed by 183cc and 246cc ohv machines with their own engines. JAP-built 198cc and 346cc ohv engines powered Flatwegg machines from 1928 to 1931. After an interruption, new models again with their own 198cc ohv engines came into being but did not make headlines. The factory — not far from BMW at Munich — was eventually sold to that maker.

FLUX / *Germany 1923–1924*
Assembled motorcycles in limited numbers with 198cc two-stroke engines.

FLYING MERKEL / *America 1909–1915*
The yellow Merkels were machines of modern and advanced design. The Middletown factory built 545cc singles and 980cc ioe V-twins and in 1913 built models which had not only two-speed gearboxes, but spring frames and some electric starters.

FM / *Italy 1925–1927*
Very unorthodox frame, designed by the Molteni brothers. (Fratelli Molteni means Molteni Brothers in Italian.) The frame was made from cast alu-alloy and allowed a low saddle position; it was also nice looking. Engines fitted were the 346cc MAG single and afterwards the 346cc ohv Bradshaw with oilcooling.

FN / *Belgium 1901–1957*
Pioneer in the motorcycle field and for many years the leading make in Belgium. Became famous for using shaft drive from 1903 to 1923, for great successes in races and long distance events and after 1945 in moto-cross. Great

designers, including Paul Kelecom, Van Hout, Dougal Marchant, George-William Patchett and others have been connected with this big factory of arms, motorcycles and cars. There were also famous racing men like Kicken, Flintermann, Lovinfosse, Lempereur, Sbaiz, De Grady, Milhoux, Charlier, Demuiter, Noir, Van Gent, Renier, S. 'Ginger' Wood, Handley Mellors, Abarth and others, who — like Mingels, Leloup and R. Beaten in moto-cross — won many races. The first FN machines had 225cc and 286cc

283cc FN (sv shaft-drive) 1921

748cc FN (sv four-cylinder shaft-drive) 1922

single-cylinder and 496cc and 748cc four-cylinder in-line engines. All models from 1924 onwards had chain-drive to the rear-wheel, as shaft drive production was then too expensive. Afterwards mainly 348cc and 498cc sv and ohv models were built. All had unit-design engines. There were also 596cc ohv versions, and in 1937 a BMW-like 992cc four-cylinder machine with a tranverse-mounted, aircooled sv engine was made for the Army. Already in 1931 there was a 198cc Villiers-

493cc FN (sv four-cylinder shaft-drive) 1908

498cc FN (ohv 'Super-Sport') 1936

engined two-stroke in the FN range and when Marchant joined the Belgian factory in 1930, he created very fast 348cc and 498cc racing ohc singles. Van Hout developed these during the following years and designed in 1937 a super-charged 498cc vertical twin-cylinder ohc racing machine, which was ridden in 1938 by 'Ginger' Wood. The war prevented more successes by this fast machine. After the war, FN built a range of sv and ohv unit-design models with 249cc, 344cc, 444cc and 498cc and also two-strokes from 49cc to 248cc, mainly with their own Ilo engines. With mainly Belgian riders, they competed successfully with 498cc machines in moto-cross events, but withdrew in the mid-1950s. FN car production stopped before WWII.

446cc FN (ohv) 1954

FOCESI / *Italy 1952–1956*
Well-designed 49cc two-stroke machines with the flat unit-design engine mounted directly on the swinging arm of the rear wheel. The machines became known under the Gloria trade mark.

FOCHJ / *Italy 1954–1957*
Assembler who used German NSU two and four-stroke engines from 49cc to 246cc. They included the famous Max single-cam engine.

FOLLIS / *France 1903–1960*
Fitted in pre-1939 days different proprietary engines made by JAP, Python and Blackburne; after 1945 machines from 124cc to 248cc with Ydral two-stroke and AMC ohv engines. The factory was at Lyon.

FONGRI / *Italy 1919–1925*
Designed by Eugenio Grignani, Fongri—the name came from Fontana and Fratelli Grignani—concentrated on machines with sv opposing twins having capacities of 579cc, 575cc and 499cc.

FORCE / *Austria 1925–1926*
Small producer of 346cc single-cylinder, two-stroke machines with their own three-port, deflector-type engines.

349cc Force (TS) 1925

FORELLE / *Germany 1955–1958*
Bicycle factory, which built 49cc mopeds with Sachs and Ilo engines.

FORSTER / *Switzerland 1921–1932*
Producer of two-stroke machines with 140cc, 198cc and 246cc. Designer was Karl Kirschbaum.

FORTONIA / *Germany 1924–1925*
Motorcycles with 2·5 hp and 3·8 hp single-cylinder engines.

FORTUNA / *Germany 1921–1928*
Two-strokes with 247cc and 297cc three-port engines and big outside flywheels.

FORWARD / *England 1909–1915*
Produced by a leading bicycle, accessory and parts manufacturer, the Forward was really a comparatively backward motorcycle design with a strengthened bicycle frame and its own V-twin engines of 339cc and 479cc.

FP / *Hungary 1924–1925*
Single-cylinder machines with own 346cc sv engines.

FRANCE / *France 1931–1935*
Two-stroke machines with own engines from 98cc to 245cc. The frames were of simple design.

FRANCIS-BARNETT / *England 1919–1964*
The first models had 293cc and 346cc sv JAP engines. From 1924 onwards, the Coventry-based factory concentrated on screwed triangular frames, in which Villiers engines from 147cc to 344cc and JAP sv engines of 174cc and 346cc

were fitted. Among them also—from 1927 onwards—the vertical-twin two-stroke of 344cc, made by Villiers. During the 1930s they built Villiers-engined machines from 148cc to 248cc with the exception of the Stag, which had a Blackburne-built 248cc ohv engine with entirely enclosed valve mechanism and crossed push-rods. Once more Villiers-engined two-strokes formed the backbone of the Francis-Barnett programme after the war; they were 98cc to 248cc. In the late 1950s AMC (Associated Motor Cycles Ltd.) took over the Coventry factory and built Piatti-designed 248cc two-stroke engines. It was not a successful venture and soon they

346cc Francis-Barnett (sv JAP) 1927

246cc Francis-Barnett (TS Villiers 'Cruiser') 1936

248cc Francis-Barnett (TS Model M/C 82) 1960

reverted to Villiers power units. They also moved FB production to the James Works at Birmingham, another factory which belonged to AMC Ltd. Afterwards both makes ceased to exist.

FRANCHI / *Italy 1950–late 1950s*
Assembler, who fitted Sachs two-stroke engines of 98, 123, 147 and 174cc and also called his machines Franchi-Sachs.

FRANKONIA / *Germany 1923–1925*
Another assembled machine. Used 145cc DKW engines with horizontal cylinders.

FRANZANI / *Germany 1923–1932*
Small factory. First used their own 283cc two-stroke engines, afterwards 198cc to 490cc JAP engines and the German 497cc Küchen ohc proprietary power unit.

FRECO / *Germany 1923–1925*
Fitted 145cc and 173cc DKW two-strokes, 197cc Runge sv engines and for racing purposes 173cc and 247cc ohv Blackburne engines. Production was on a limited scale.

FREITAL / *Germany 1925–1926*
For commercial reasons, the DKW factory at Zschopau used this name for a short period on 173cc machines.

FREJUS / *Italy 1960–1968*
Turin-built machines, including mofas, mopeds etc, from 48cc to 198cc.

FRERA / *Italy 1906–1956*
For many years a leading make. Built 320cc and 570cc singles and 795cc V-twins, afterwards also a big 1140cc sv V-twin. During the 1920s, Frera machines had a very Sunbeam-like black and gold appearance and were designed on English

123cc Frera (TS) 1958

lines. A 269cc two-stroke was made for a short period, but 346cc and 496cc sv and ohv singles formed the main range in the period between the wars. Leading riders: Felice Macchi, Virginio Fieschi, Mario Acerboni, Edoardo Self, Mario Ventura, F. J. Meyer. Reorganisation after 1945 resulted in 73cc and 124cc two-strokes and a 147cc ohv machine. The founder, Corrardo Frera, died before the last war.

346cc Freyler (ohc sleeve-valve engine) 1929

FREYLER / *Austria 1928–1929*
This was a 'valveless' ohc machine of 348cc capacity. It used a rotary valve—driven by a vertical shaft—in the cylinder head. The interesting design by Adalbert Freyler was not fully developed when the Vienna-based factory closed.

139

FREYER & MILLER / *America c1902*
Had the engine behind the saddle and the petrol
tank was mounted above the rear wheel. The
Freyer & Miller was one of the first machines
using a rotation magneto.

FRIMO / *Germany 1923–1925*
Made by the Vis AG., producer of Vis-Simplex
and Vis-Duplex machines, the Frimo was a conventional 246cc two-stroke machine with a three
port engine.

FRISCHAUF / *Germany 1928–1933*
Assembled 198cc sv singles with JAP and Black-
burne engines and 497cc ohc machines with the
Küchen proprietary engine.

198cc Frischauf (TS Villiers) 1932

FRISONI / *Italy 1951–1957*
Produced 123cc Villiers-engined two-strokes
and 160cc scooters in limited numbers.

FUBO / *Germany 1923–1925*
Two-strokes of 170cc and 269cc with their own
engines, but also supplied 247cc and 347cc
models with sv and ohv Blackburne engines.

FUCHS / *Italy 1953–1957*
Produced bicycle engines and 124cc to 159cc
motorcycles with two-stroke and ohv engines.

FUJI / *Japan early 1950s–early 1960s*
Producer of the Gasuden scooter and of two-
stroke machines from 49cc to 249cc. This
factory was not the same as the Fuji Heavy
Industries Ltd.

FULGOR / *Italy 1922–1926*
Lightweight two-strokes of 143cc, made by a
small factory at Milan.

FUSI / *Italy 1932–1957*
For many years Italian FN importer, Fusi
bought the CF motorcycle factory in 1937 and
produced first a 248cc ohc machine. They fitted
174cc, 246cc and 490cc JAP engines into own
frames, which had also many FN parts; according to some sources, FN even built the frames for
Fusi machines. The JAP engines were made in
Italy under licence. After 1945, Fusi built an
improved 248cc machine with the old but
developed CF ohc engine.

173cc FVL (ohv Moser) 1929

FVL / *Italy 1926–1935*
Designed by former racing motorcyclist Francesco Vincenzo Lanfranchi, the first FVL lightweight machines had 124cc and 174cc ohv Moser
engines. Bonamore and Forlani, designers of the
now defunct Fert factory, joined the Lanfranchi
works in 1929 and created beautiful ohv machines with 174cc and in 1932 a 248cc. Another
version had a 174cc ohc power unit.

248cc Fusi (ohc Ex-CF) 1939

496cc Fusi (ohv) 1939

G

GA / *Italy 1925–1927*
Assembler of sporting V-twin machines, Franco Azzara fitted 678cc ohv engines made by Blackburne in England.

GABBIANO / *Italy 1954–1956*
Lightweight machine with flat 123cc two-stroke engine.

GABY / *England 1914–1915*
Well-made 269cc machines with Metro three-port, deflector-type engines.

GADABOUT / *England 1948–1951*
Made by the Swallow sidecar factory, the Villiers-engined Gadabout was a 123cc scooter, which for various reasons could not beat the leading foreign scooters in England.

GAIA / *Italy 1922–1932*
The Turin-based factory always built machines of sound design. The first products were bicycles fitted with Rubinelli engines; the next were motorcycles with the then popular Swiss 123cc and 173cc ohv Moser engines. After 1927, most models had Ladetto & Blatto-built 173cc ohv power units.

GALBAI / *1921–1925*
Producer of 276cc, 301cc and 348cc two-stroke machines with own engines. Other models had 492cc V-twin MAG and oilcooled 346cc single-cylinder Bradshaw ohv engines.

GALBUSERA / *Italy 1934–1955*
Gained popularity with a transverse-mounted supercharged 498cc two-stroke V-8 cylinder prototype at the 1938 Milan show. There was also a V-4 version of 248cc, built on identical lines. Plinio Galbusera's bread-and-butter models had

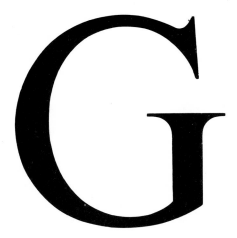

346cc Galloni (sv Sport) 1924

173, 246, 348 and 498cc Rudge-built (Python) four-valve ohv engines, the smallest version supplied by Miller, which had exclusive rights for this engine. Technical head of Galbusera was Egyptian-born Adolf Marama, who rode Rudge-engined machines in all kinds of races. He was also responsible for the design of the speedway frames made by this Brescia factory, which after

496cc Galbusera (TS V-8 cylinder Prototype) 1938

1945 concentrated on lightweight machines with Sachs engines from 98cc to 173cc. The sensational two-strokes of the immediate pre-war period never went into production.

GALLONI / *Italy 1920–1931*
Was a leading make and also successful in many races with Alfredo Panella, Nino Bianchi and Augusto Rava. The early models had 494cc and 746cc V-twin sv engines; later ones 249cc, 349cc and 499cc sv and ohv single-cylinder engines of their own design and manufacture. From 1927 the red Galloni was overshadowed by the Bianchi, Frera and Moto-Guzzi. The last Galloni was a 173cc ohv machine with a Blackburne engine.

GAMAGE / *England c1905–1924*
The motorcycles sold by the Gamage stores were made mainly in England by factories which in-

Advertisement from Gamage's 1913 catalogue

cluded Wolfruna, Omega, Radco and others. The models included 269cc two-strokes and 293cc, 347cc and 497cc single-cylinder sv machines.

290cc Gamage (sv) 1903

GANNA / *Italy 1923–late 1960s*
Varese-built, the Ganna was a good machine with many different engines fitted during the years. Among the first were 347cc sv and ohv Blackburnes, afterwards 173, 248, 348 and 498cc JAP engines, partly built under licence in Italy.

There was in 1936 an interesting 499cc four-valve ohc model with a Ganna-designed and built engine. After the war and a reorganisation of the company, most Gannas had two-stroke engines made by Puch, Sachs and Minarelli. They were from 48cc to 248cc. In addition, a 174cc ohv model was in the range too. Although Ganna never belonged to the leading makes in races, all models had a very sporting appearance and a superb finish.

GAR / *Germany 1924–1926*
The Rempp-designed 499cc ohv machines had their own single-cylinder engines and were built in limited numbers only.

GARABELLO / *Italy 1906–1929*
Francesco Garabello was one of the pioneers of the Italian motorcycle industry. He produced 240cc and 480cc singles and from 1922 onward a big, watercooled 984cc four-cylinder in-line model with shaft drive. Although a clever techni-

996cc Garabello (sv watercooled four-cylinder) 1926

cian, he never achieved financial success. When Luigi Comini took over the Alba factory, he transferred it to Turin. Garabello's last (and unorthodox) design was a 173cc single with watercooling and a rotary valve in the head. The drive to this valve as well as the rear wheel drive was by shaft. The radiator was mounted directly in front of the petrol tank, the carburettor in front of the vertically mounted cylinder. The design was unsuccessful.

GARANZINI / *Italy 1921–1931*
Made by a racing motorcyclist Oreste Garanzini
—who imported the English Verus machines
which were renamed Veros in Italy—the design
was on typical English lines. Also from England
came the 346cc sv JAP engines and on later
models 147cc to 248cc Villiers and 248cc to 490cc
sv and ohv power units made by JAP and Blackburne. Garanzini rode his machines in many
races during the mid-1920s.

346cc Garanzini (sv JAP) 1926

GARELLI / *Italy 1913–*
Still a well-known lightweight machine with
49cc two-stroke engines. The big factory at
Monticelli Brianza, now connected with Agrati,
produces such machines in a large number of
models, including mopeds and moto-cross versions. The original Alberto Garelli design was a
double-piston two-stroke of 346cc and was
developed in stages from 1913 to 1935. It won

**346cc Garelli (TS double-piston single racer)
1924**

many races during the early 1920s and broke
many records. Famous riders: Ernesto Gnesa,
Achille Varzi, Isacco Mariani, Enrico Manetti
and Erminio Visioli. The first post-war design
was the 38cc Mosquito bicycle engine; afterwards Garelli built motorcycles from 70cc to
123cc and eventually the present 49cc machines.

GARIN / *France 1950–1953*
Small producer of 49cc mopeds and 98cc two-
stroke motorcycles.

GARLASCHELLI / *Italy 1922–1927*
Produced 65cc and 123cc two-strokes, from 1925
onwards also 173cc machines with two-stroke
ohv engines.

346cc Garelli (TS double-piston single racer) 1926

346cc Garelli (TS double-piston single) 1935

GASUDEN / *Japan late 1950s–late 1960s*
Identical range of models to Fuji.

GATTI / *Italy 1904–1906*
Pioneer who fitted 1·75 hp De Dion engines into
strengthened bicycle frames.

GAZDA / *Austria 1926–1927*
Created by the inventor of the Gazda leaf-spring
handlebars Anton Gazda, the 246cc two-stroke
machines—built in small numbers only—were
of unorthodox design. They had a pumping
cylinder and three ports.

GAZELLE / *The Netherlands 1903*
Famous bicycle factory which fitted Sarolea

engines into the first motorcycles made at the
Dieren works. Resumed production of motorised
two-wheelers in 1932 with Ilo-engined 60cc and
75cc machines. Motorcycles with Ilo and Villiers engines followed in the mid-1930s. They had
98cc, 123cc and 148cc. The range was similar

246cc Gazda (TS Prototype) 1926

after the war, until the Dutch factory concentrated on various models with 49cc engines, many of which had Minarelli engines.

GAZZI / *Italy 1929–1932*
A small factory which produced well-made 173cc ohv machines of modern design.

GB / *England 1905–1907*
Motorcycles with different Minerva engines from 3·5 hp to 5 hp and a very long wheelbase.

GD / *Italy 1923–1938*
Very fast 122cc two-strokes with a great racing history, ridden by such famous riders as Alfonso Drusiani, Frederico Castellani, Guglielmo Sandri, and Amilcare Rosetti. The GD stood for Ghirardi and Dall'-Oglio. From 1928, the factory built besides these flat singles also 248cc vertical twin two-strokes, 173cc ohc singles and 98cc two-stroke machines.

GÉCO-HERSTAL / *France 1924–1928*
Gérkinet's factory was closely connected with the Belgian Gillet works at Herstal, and also built part of the Gillet model range. In addition, they had their own 173cc to 346cc sv models.

GEER / *America 1905–1909*
Early producer of single and V-twin machines. Fitted their own engines into strengthened bicycle frames.

GEHA / *Germany 1920–1924*
Lightweight machines with their own 1·5 hp two-stroke engines.

148cc Geha (TS) 1922

GEIER / *Germany 1934–early 1960s*
Built mofas and motorcycles with 73cc, 98cc and after 1945 also 123cc, 147cc and 173cc Ilo and Sachs two-stroke engines.

GEKA / *Germany 1924–1925*
Fitted 173cc DKW engines into lightweights. Limited production.

GE-MA-HI / *Germany 1924–1927*
Built a wide range of machines with tubular and also with wide-tube petrol tank frames. The last ones were partly made from welded steel, not unlike the big Mars. Among the engines fitted were the 131cc Esbe, 149cc Bekamo, 149cc Grade and also the 147cc and 173cc DKW.

GEMINI / *Taiwan 1970–*
Partly Suzuki-licence machines, including many having the 'off-the-road' look. Among them 49cc versions with 8 inch wheels and more orthodox 78cc, 123cc and 173cc models, of which many are exported to the USA.

GEMS / *Italy 1921–1923*
Lightweight machines with 269cc two-stroke power units.

GENIAL-LUCIFER / *France 1928–1956*
Assembler of two-stroke machines with 98cc to 246cc Aubier Dunne, Train and Sabb engines.

GENTIL / *France 1903–1904*
With the horizontal single-cylinder engine in front of the pedalling gear, the Gentil had the look of a modern moped. Produced also V-twin machines and 98cc mopeds.

GEORGES RICHARD / *France c1899*
Assembled motorcycles with Minerva, Buchet, Zedel, Peugeot and other engines and later became part of the Unic car factory.

GEPPERT / *Germany 1925–1926*
Small factory which assembled two-stroke machines with 147cc Grade and DKW engines.

GERALD / *France 1927–1932*
Designed by Charles Gerald, these machines had 98cc and 173cc Aubier-Dunne two-stroke engines. Other models were powered by 248cc ohv JAP and 348cc and 498cc ohc Chaise power units.

GERARD / *England 1913–1915*
Of simple design, the 269cc Gerard had a Villiers engine and was built at Birmingham.

GERBI / *Italy 1952–1953*
Sachs-engined 98cc, 123cc and 173cc motorcycles.

GERMAAN / *The Netherlands 1935–1966*
Another Dutch bicycle factory, which assembled good lightweight machines with 98cc Sachs and Ilo, as well as 123cc Ilo and 147cc Villiers engines. After the war, Germaan also used Hungarian 123cc Czepel engines and Ilo engines which included the 244cc vertical twin two-stroke. Germaan is now part of the Batavus group.

GERMANIA / *Germany 1901–1908*
These were actually Czechoslovakian Laurin & Klement motorcycles, built by the once famous Seidel & Naumann typewriter factory at Dresden under licence. The range of models included 3·5

148cc Geier (TS Sachs) 1954

GERMANIA-MOTORRAD
mit 2 Cylindern, 3½ HP (System Laurin & Klement)

615cc Germania (sv V-twin) 1904

hp and 4·5 hp V-twins. Laurin & Klement was the forerunner of the present Skoda car factory.

GEROSA / *Italy 1953–*
One of the younger makes, which produces at Brescia a variety of 49cc models and also 123cc two-strokes of sound design. Earlier, there were also 124cc and 174cc ohv machines in the range.

GERVO / *Germany 1924–1925*
Limited production of 198cc sv and 173cc DKW-engined two-stroke machines.

GH / *Czechoslovakia 1924–1925*
Gustav Heinz designed 172cc machines with Villiers power units. Heinz also produced

Sirocco and Velamos motorcycles. Now nation-alised, Velamos is one of the leading bicycle factories in the country.

GIACOMASSO / *Italy 1926–1935*
Superbly designed machines with 174cc Moser ohv engines, but from 1927 onward Felice Giaco-masso designed his own power units with ohv and even ohc. New 489cc and 595cc ohv vertical twins appeared in 1933.

GIGANT / *Austria 1936–1938*
Designed by the former Delta-Gnom technician Johann Teichert, the light-green Gigant mach-ines had 498cc and 598cc ohv and 746cc V-twin sv engines. All were of JAP manufacture. Also produced successful racing machines with 498cc

ohv JAP and Husqvarna single-cylinder engines, which were ridden by the Austrian champion Martin Schneeweiss, Josef Lukeš and others.

490cc Gigant (ohv JAP) 1936

GIGUET / *France 1903*
Equipped with strong frames, Giguet motor-cycles had De Dion and Minerva engines.

GILERA/*Italy 1909–*

Designed by Giuseppe Gilera, the first Arcore-built machine had a 317cc sv engine with 2·5 hp. Bigger versions with 3·5 hp and a V-twin with 5 hp followed. Also singles with 499cc, 508cc and 569cc, which proved their speed and reliability in many events. With Rosolino Grana, Luigi Gilera (the designer's brother), Miro Maffeis and others, Gilera represented Italy during the 1930s in the International Six Day Trials. They also built the 498cc Saturno ohv singles; when in 1936 the Rondine design was available, Gilera bought everything connected with these water-cooled and supercharged 499cc double-ohc four-cylinder racing machines, designed by Carlo Gianini, Pietro Remor and Piero Taruffi, who also acted as team manager. Gilera rode these fast machines himself and broke many records with them. Fully developed, this four-cylinder was one of the fastest pre-war road-racing machines in the world. Ridden by Dorino Serafini, Giordano Aldrighetti, Silvio Vailati etc., the Gilera 4 gained many successes. Production models during the 1930s included 174cc, 220cc, 248cc, 348cc, 498cc singles with sv and ohv. Some already had since 1934 frames with rear suspension. The ban on forced induction (super-chargers) forced Gileras to build new 498cc racing machines after the war; Remor then created new aircooled four-cylinder machines, which in developed form won many races until the late 1950s. There were also 348cc versions with transverse-mounted four-cylinder double-ohc racing engines. The best riders available, including Geoff Duke, Bob McIntyre, Reg Armstrong, Carlo Bandirola, Arcisio Artesiani, Giuseppe Colnago, Alfredo and Albino Milani, Libero Liberati, Umberto Masetti, Bob Brown, Dick Dale and others gained great successes for Gilera with the four-cylinder racing models. After the war, Gilera concentrated mainly on

498cc Gilera (dohc 4-cylinder racer) 1939

496cc Gilera (ohv 'Saturno') 1939

496cc Gilera (sv) 1921

250cc Gilera ohv 'Nettuno' (Neptune) sports, 1946

498cc Gilera (dohc aircooled 4-cylinder racer) 1952

498cc Gilera (dohc aircooled 4-cylinder racer) 1953

123cc Gilera (ohv 'Sei Giorni') 1965

machines from 48cc two-strokes to 300cc vertical-twins, of which many models were of 123cc and 173cc with ohv engines. The 498cc single-cylinder Saturno was built in limited numbers. After the untimely death of young Feruccio Gilera and later the deaths of his uncle Luigi and his father Giuseppe, the Gilera factory was taken over by the Piaggio group, who produce Vespa scooters. Soon afterwards, Gilera withdrew from competition in trials, where they had scored many successes in the early 1970s.

GILLET-HERSTAL / *Belgium 1919–early 1960s*
Together with FN and Sarolea, among the leading Belgian makes. Became famous with the rotary-valve 346cc two-stroke, which Robert Sexé rode around the world. This was in the mid-1920s. Other models included 348cc and 498cc unit-design sv and ohv machines and a 996cc

V-twin with the ioe engine, made by MAG in Switzerland. The factory also showed great interest in racing and had such riders as Kicken, Debay, Bentley, Milhoux, Jackl, Deimel, Uvira and others. Chief designer Van Oirbeck created in 1929 works machines with single-cylinder ohc engines and René Milhoux broke many records with them. Two-strokes from 98cc to 248cc were

built after the war and there were also vertical-twins up to 720cc.

GIMA / *France 1947–1956*
The machines were beautiful lightweights with Ydral, AMC and other proprietary engines from 123cc to 248cc.

GIMSON / *Spain 1956–1964*
Bicycle factory which built 49cc and 65cc mopeds.

GIRARDENGO / *Italy 1951–1954*
Another Italian assembler who produced 123cc, 147cc and 173cc two-stroke engines.

GITAN / *Italy 1951*
Old established producer of 49cc two-strokes, including moto-cross versions. In the early years

of the company, motorcycles with up to 198cc two and four-stroke Minarelli engines were also built.

GITANE / *France 1953–early 1960s*
Well-known bicycle manufacturer, whose motorcycles had 49cc to 173cc and engines made by Ydral, VAP and Mistral.

GIULIETTA / *Italy 1959–*
Leading manufacturer of 47–49cc mofas, mopeds and a wide range of other such small machines with a variety of engines, including Sachs and Morini. These Peripoli-built lightweights are of sound design and have gained great popularity.

GIVAUDAN / *England 1908–1914*
Small assembler, whose motorcycles had single and V-twin engines made by Villiers, Precision and other companies.

GL / *France 1919–1921*
Mainly built from English components, this French design by Georges Lévy, had a 990cc V-twin JAP sv engine, Sturmey-Archer gearbox and Binks carburettor.

GLENDALE / *England 1920–1921*
Simple assembled machines with 269cc Villiers and 346cc Blackburne engines.

GLOBE / *England 1901–1911*
Produced different models with Minerva, MMC and Sarolea engines.

GLORIA / *England 1924–1925*
With frames built by Campion in Nottingham, the Gloria also had strong ties with France. In

498cc Gillet-Herstal (ohv) 1929

both countries it was sold with the 173cc Train two-stroke engine.

GLORIA/*England 1931–1933*
Made by Triumph at Coventry, this Gloria had a 98cc Villiers two-stroke engine.

GLORIA/*Italy 1948–1955*
Designed by Alfredo Focesi, the little Gloria had the 48cc two-stroke engine mounted directly on the swinging arm of the rear wheel.

GN/*Italy 1920–1925*
Assembled mainly from English components, Giuseppe Navone's motorcycles had 346cc two-stroke single-cylinder engines. Navone was also closely connected with the Italian branch of the French Train engine works.

GNÄDIG/*Germany 1925–1926*
When KG at Suhl was sold to Allright, Franz Gnädig—one of the designers—left for Berlin and built there his own 348cc ohv machines. Afterwards he took the design to Kühne at Dresden and this was the first engine built by this proprietary engine factory.

GNOM/*Germany 1921–1923*
Bicycle attachment engine of 63cc, built by the Columbus engine factory, which was eventually taken over by Horex of Bad Homburg.

GNOME & RHONE/*France 1919–1959*
Famous for their aircraft engines in the First World War, Gnome & Rhône built first the English Bradshaw-designed 398cc, afterwards also a 498cc ABC with the flat-twin ohv engine transverse-mounted under licence. Cpt. Bartlett headed the manufacture at the big Paris factory. Together with Naas he also won many races. From 1923 onwards, single-cylinder machines of own designs came into being. They consisted of 306cc sv, 344cc ohv and 498cc sv and ohv versions and again Naas, together with Georges Bernard, gained many successes. During the late 1920s, BMW-like sv and ohv flat twins, transverse-mounted in pressed steel frames, came into

492cc Gnome-Rhône (ohv Super-Sport) 1927

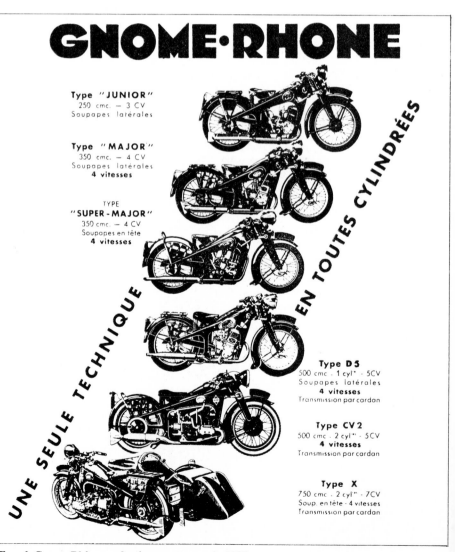

The French Gnome-Rhône production programme in 1938

496cc Gnome-Rhône (sv) 1926

production. They had 495cc and 745cc capacity. After 1945, Gnome & Rhône concentrated on small two-stroke machines, of which most had 124cc and 174cc.

GOEBEL / *Germany 1951–*
Still a producer of mofas and mopeds, Goebel uses 49cc Sachs engines for his product.

GOETZ / *Germany 1925–1935*
Built in 10 years a total of 79 machines, most individually at the request of customers. They had 246cc Villiers, 346cc, 498cc and 676cc JAP, 498cc Küchen and even 796cc vertical twin Columbus (ohc) engines.

GOGGO / *Germany 1951–1954*
Now part of BMW, the Glas factory at Dingolfing built a range of nice scooters with 123cc, 147cc and 173cc Ilo engines. Afterwards they created the 248cc Goggomobil and scooter sales went down.

GOLD-RAD / *Germany 1952–*
Producer of mofas, mopeds etc. with 49cc Sachs and Ilo engines; now mainly importer of Italian Motograziela products, which also have 49cc power units.

GOLEM / *Germany 1921–1923*
Called Sesselrad (chair-wheel), the DKW-built Golem was a scooter-like vehicle with a 122cc two-stroke engine which had a horizontal cylinder. The improved successor was the 144cc Lomos. When DKW dropped the production, Eichler at Berlin bought the production equipment and all rights for both designs.

GOLO / *Austria 1923–1925*
Limited manufacture of machines with 346cc and 490cc JAP and 347cc Bradshaw engines.

GORI / *Italy 1969–*
Younger and very efficient factory which produces Sachs-engined 49cc, 123cc and 245cc

124cc Gori (TS Sachs Racing) 1974

490cc Goetz (ohv JAP) 1933

machines, mainly moto-cross and trials versions. The 123cc machine has 24 bhp at 9800 rpm and the 245cc version has 33 bhp at 8000 rpm. There are also Franco-Morini-powered Gori two-strokes of excellent design.

GÖRICKE / Germany 1903–
Once well-known for racing bicycles, Göricke was one of the pioneer motorcycle producers in Germany. Built in the early days single and V-twin machines and during the 1920s assembled models with 172cc to 247cc Villiers as well as 346cc and 496cc MAG engines. Touring versions had ioe and sporting machines ohv engines. There were also Blackburne-engined Göricke machines, but the motorcycle production was never very big. Designer was Alfred Ostertag. Still building mofas etc., Göricke also produced until the mid-1950s Sachs and Ilo-engined two-strokes from 98cc to 198cc.

GORRION / Spain 1952–1955
Sachs-engined mopeds and motorcycles. The range also included 124cc and 174cc machines.

4½ hp Göricke (sv V-twin) 1905

4½ hp Göricke (sv V-twin Forecar) 1905

348cc Göricke (ioe MAG) 1927

49cc Göricke (TS Sachs) 1956

GOUGH / England 1920–1923
Assembled machines with 293cc sv JAP and 548cc sv Blackburne engines.

GOUVERNEUR / Germany 1903–1907
Long forgotten make which used 3·5 hp GN engines.

GR / Italy 1925–1926
After Count Mario Revelli won the 500cc class of the Grand Prix des Nations at Monza in 1925 on an Antonio Boudo-designed 490cc JAP-engined ohv single-cylinder machine, his brother Count Gino Revelli built these machines with the GR trade mark in limited numbers.

GRADE / Germany 1903–1925
Designed by Hans Grade, a leading aircraft pioneer, all the products (airplanes, cars and motorcycles) had two-stroke engines. He also supplied engines to other producers. His 118cc and 132cc motorcycles were very successful and were really a creation of his designer-in-chief, Hans Plog. Leading Grade riders: Hans Przybilski and the Hartmann brothers.

132cc Grade (TS) 1924

GRANDEX-PRECISION (GRANDEX) / England 1917
As the factory first fitted Precision engines from 2·5 hp to 6 hp, the early machines used the Grandex-Precision trade mark. The Precision was dropped when the factory also fitted 225, 293, 490, 597 and 746cc JAP engines. Most of them were sv models.

GRAPHIC / England 1903–1906
Small producer who fitted De Dion, Minerva and MMC engines.

GRASETTI / Italy 1952–1965
Produced 123cc and 148cc machines with their own two-stroke power units.

GRATIEUX / France 1919–1921
Aircraft engine producer who tried building motorcycles with two-stroke radial engines.

247cc Greeves (TS Villiers) 1963

GRAVES/ *England 1914–1915*
This was a supermarket of that period which sold
Speed King motorcycles with 293cc JAP sv
engines and a simple specification. Producer was
Omega at Wolverhampton on behalf of Graves.

GREEN/ *England 1919–1923*
In pre-WWI days closely connected with Green-
Precision and Regal-Green. Charles Green was
mainly an engine producer and a strong sup-
porter of watercooled power units. He produced
mainly 3·33 hp and 4 hp singles. After the war he
tried again to join the ranks of motorcycle manufacturers, but was not very successful. In his last
years he offered to rebuild aircooled Precision
engines to watercooled versions.

GREEVES/ *England 1952–*
Very successful Villiers-engined two-stroke
machines, which for a long period dominated the
250cc class in moto-cross events with riders who
included Dave Bickers and the late Brian Stone-
bridge. Designed by Bert Greeves, the first
versions had an unorthodox fork and other unusual features, but during the years the Greeves
became a popular sporting machine. They built
models from 169cc to 380cc for moto-cross,
trials, road racing and also touring. In 1973,
Bert Greeves retired and handed over the factory

248cc Greeves (TS Villiers racer) 1963

to Brian Gilroy of Tiepolas Ltd., where they also
fitted other engines, including Puch and QUB.
Moto-cross models are now built with 246cc
engines which develop 28·5 bhp at 7500 rpm and
also 380cc QUB motors with 44 bhp at 6750
rpm. The weight of the machines is 105 kg and
110 kg respectively.

GREYHOUND/ *England 1905–1907*
Small assembler, who fitted proprietary engines
made by Minerva, MMC and Fafnir.

GREYHOUND/ *America 1907–1914*
Once a well-known make. The 4·5 hp single-
cylinder was developed and built at the Thor
factory.

197cc Greeves (TS Villiers) 1963

GRG/ *Italy 1926–1927*
Technically interesting design with two coupled
174cc Della Ferrera single-cylinder ohv engines
and rear suspension.

GRI/ *England 1921–1922*
The name came from the designer G. R. Inshaw,
who offered these machines with 348cc and
496cc. The engines had one valve only, probably the main reason they failed.

GRIFFON/ *France 1902–late 1920s*
Old established and once very successful make
at races. Built singles and V-twins, but the last
model was a nice 348cc single with sv and ohv
engines. In the 1920's Peugeot took over Griffon.

343cc Grigg (TS Villiers) 1923

GRIGG / *England 1920–1925*
A 1·75 hp scooter was the first Grigg product. It was followed by a 161cc two-stroke and a 181cc ohv machine with their own engines. Other models had Villiers and Blackburne single and V-twin engines up to 680cc. The biggest model had the rare 990cc V-twin sv B&H engine.

GRINDLAY-PEERLESS / *England 1923–1934*
Originally a factory for sidecars, the first motorcycle models had 490cc JAP single-cylinder and 996cc Barr & Stroud sleeve-valve V-twin engines. Machines with 346cc and 496cc single-cylinder Barr & Stroud motors followed. Many models had sv and ohv JAP engines from 248cc to 996cc and Brough-Superior-like petrol tanks and there was a 490cc JAP-engined version with a Castle-type fork. Small models from 147cc to 247cc were powered by Villiers two-stroke engines and there were also Grindlay-Peerless

346cc Grindlay-Peerless (sleeve-valve Barr & Stroud) 1924

49cc Gritzner (TS Sachs) 1962

machines with Rudge-built Python four-valve ohv engines from 248cc to 498cc. Bill Lacey, famous tuner and rider, broke many records on JAP engined machines while Karl Abarth of Austria and Jan Mocchari of Czechoslovakia gained many successes in road-races and hill-climbs with various grand prix machines. The Grindlay-Peerless factory was only a few hundred yards from the former Rudge works.

GRINGO / *America 1973–*
Newer make which concentrates on 248cc and 358cc single-cylinder two-stroke machines for moto-cross and flat tracks. The frames are made from chrome light alloy.

GRITZNER / *Germany 1903–1962*
A famous sewing-machine factory, which during the early years built Fafnir-engined singles and V-twins. After WWII, motorcycle manufacture was resumed and Sachs engines of 98cc, 147cc, and 174cc fitted. The last Gritzner was a 49cc motorcycle of very sporting appearance and originally known as the Mars-built Monza. Gritzner-Kaiser AG is the factory name and the Kaiser part built three-wheelers in 1901.

GRIZZLY / *Czechoslovakia 1925–1932*
Designed by Josef Matyaš, the Grizzly was a modern 246cc two-stroke machine with deflector-type three-port engine. The range included after 1929 348cc MAG-engined ioe and ohv models. Works rider Zdenek Hermann had a 348cc ohc MAG engine in his machine. Other riders: Trnka, Adamek, Korbel.

246cc Grizzly (TS) 1929

GROSE-SPUR / *England 1934–1939*
Lightweight machines with 123cc Villiers engines built by Carlton for the London-based dealer Grose.

GROTE / *Germany 1924–1925*
Very unorthodox 305cc two-stroke singles, which — by adding one or two more engines! — could be brought to 614cc or 921cc.

490cc Grindlay-Peerless (ohv JAP) 1929

148cc Guazzoni (TS) 1966

GRÜCO / *Germany 1924–1925*
Assembler who fitted 346cc Kühne ohv engines into simpler frames.

GRUHN / *Germany 1909–1932*
Old established Berlin-based manufacturer of sv machines and proprietary engines with 148cc, 196cc and 246cc. A new 198cc single-cylinder ohv machine came into production in 1928. It had shaft drive to the rear wheel and was of up-to-date design. The last Gruhn was a 123cc two-stroke. Richard Gruhn's machines never had any kind of sporting image.

198cc Gruhn (sv) 1922

GRUHN / *Germany 1920–1926*
Another Berlin-based Gruhn, owned by Hugo Gruhn. He was Richard Gruhn's brother and concentrated mainly on the production of frames for others. His own machines housed the 198cc Alba single-cylinder sv engine.

GRUTZENA / *Germany 1925–1926*
Sturdy but not very modern 348cc singles with Kühne ohv engines. Production was on a limited scale.

GS / *Germany 1920–1924*
Lightweight machines with 129cc two-stroke engines. These could be bought also as bicycle attachments. This was the Gustav Schulze GS.

GS / *Germany 1923–1925*
This, the Georg Schroff — Berlin built — GS was a 145cc machine with Gruhn sv engines as well as many other Gruhn parts.

GSD / *England 1921–1923*
R. E. D. Grant's interesting design had a transverse-mounted 496cc flat-twin engine, four speeds and shaft drive to the rear wheel. A second model housed the 342cc White & Poppe single-cylinder two-stroke and also had shaft drive.

GUARALDI / *Italy 1905–1916*
The first machines had German Fafnir, later ones Belgian Sarolea engines with capacities up to 550cc.

348cc Grutzena (ohv Kühne) 1925

GUAZZONI / *Italy 1949–*
After Aldo Guazzoni left Moto Morini, he created many interesting two-strokes and ohv models up to 248cc. Among them were some very fast 49cc versions. Lately Guazzoni has concentrated on 49cc mini-machines and 123cc models — two-strokes — for trials and moto-cross.

GUIA / *Italy 1950–1954*
Small assembler of 98cc, 123cc and 147cc two-stroke machines.

GUIGNARD / *France 1933–1938*
Jéan Guignard produced mainly 98cc and 123cc two-stroke machines.

GUILLER / *France 1950–late 1950s*
One of the leading French factories after WWII. Built two and four-stroke ohv machines from 49cc to 248cc with engines supplied by Ydral, AMC, VAP, Aubier-Dunne and others.

GUIZZARDI / *Italy 1926–1932*
Produced 124cc and 174cc ohv and also 174cc ohc singles with their own power units. They were modern machines of sound design.

GUIZZO / *Italy 1955–1962*
Built 48cc mopeds and a well-designed 149cc scooter in a period when others had dropped scooter manufacture.

490cc Güldner (ohv) 1925

GÜLDNER / *Germany 1925*
A short-lived but superb Norton-like 490cc ohv single-cylinder machine, built by a well-known agriculture machine factory. Dr. Güldner's design was so Norton-like that it was possible to use Norton spare parts after Güldner dropped motorcycle production. Top rider was Josef Klein, who later rode for DKW and Horex.

GUSTLOFF / *Germany 1934–1940*
Mopeds with 98cc Sachs engines, designed by Martin Stolle of D-Rad fame.

G&W / *England 1902–1906*
Long forgotten assembler who used Minerva, Peugeot and Fafnir proprietary engines.

H

HACK / *England 1920–1923*
Mini-scooter with 103cc and 110cc Simplex two-stroke engines built in limited numbers.

HADEN / *England 1920–1924*
Built a single model only. It had a 347cc Precision two-stroke engine.

HAGEL / *Germany 1925*
Two-stroke machines with their own 247cc three-port engines.

HÄGGLUND / *Sweden 1973–*
Developed for the Swedish Army, this machine had a single-cylinder 345cc Rotax two-stroke engine with 76mm bore and stroke. It developed 24 bhp at 5300 rpm. The monocoque frame included the petrol tank; drive was by shaft, and the wheels were made from pressed steel. The weight was 135 kg. Late in 1976, Husqvarna got the army order and the fate of the Hägglund was in the balance.

HAI / *Austria 1938*
The cast Hai frame included the petrol tank; the engine was a 108cc two-stroke. Only few were actually built as this machine was not in the production programme sanctioned by the Hitler Government.

HAJA / *Germany 1924–1925*
Simple 198cc sv machines with Hansa-built single-cylinder engines.

HAKO / *Germany 1924–1925*
Copies of HRD machines. Even the 348cc and 490cc ohv JAP engines used were identical.

HALUMO / *Germany 1923–1926*
Produced 147cc two-strokes, afterwards 146cc

248cc Hansa (ohv) 1926

and 198cc ohv machines with their own engines.

HAM / *The Netherlands 1902–1906*
Single-cylinder machines with 2 hp (at 2000 rpm) Altena engines.

HAMILTON / *England 1901–1907*
Built 2·25, 3·25 and 4 hp singles as well as 4·5 hp V-twins and sold power units to other producers.

HAMPTON / *England 1912–1914*
Well-made 492cc sv machines with single-cylinder power units made by T. D. Cross.

HANFLAND / *Germany 1920–1925*
Built Hanfland and Kurier motorcycles with own 147cc two-stroke engines. Curt Hanfland also supplied these engines to Flink, a branch of the famous BMW factory.

HANSA / *Germany 1922–1926*
Once a well-known factory at Bielefeld, Hansa produced two and four-stroke singles from 148cc to 246cc. The last models had 198cc and 246cc ohv engines with horizontally-mounted valves and low triangular duplex frames.

HANSAN / *England 1920–1922*
Assembler who fitted 269cc Arden two-stroke and 346cc Blackburne sv engines.

148cc Hanfland (TS Model Sport) 1922

HAPAMEE / *Germany 1925–1926*
Meinke-designed 198cc and 246cc two-strokes with own deflector-type motors.

HARDING-JAP / *France 1912–1914*
Built from English components, the Harding motorcycle had a 496cc V-twin JAP engine. H. J. Harding was an Englishman living in St. Cyr.

HAREWOOD / *England 1920*
Assembled machines with 269cc Villiers two-stroke and 346cc Precision sv engines.

HARLETTE / *Austria 1925–1928*
This was the name for Austrian Puch 123cc and 173cc double-piston two-strokes in some countries including Italy, France and Belgium. In France they were called Harlette-Géco because of their assembly at the factory of Gerkinet & Co. at Jeumont. Top rider of Harlettes in Italy was the champion Umberto Faraglia.

HARLEY-DAVIDSON / *America 1903–*
Founded by William A. Davidson, Walter Davidson Sr., Arthur Davidson and William S. Harley in a small shed at Milwaukee, Wisconsin, Harley-Davidson is now the leading motorcycle

factory in the USA. Indian was the great opponent for many years, but faded out in the mid-1950s. The first Harley-Davidson was a belt-driven model with a 3 hp single-cylinder engine. 1906 production numbered 50 machines; in 1907 the company was incorporated and produced 150 units. Ten years later the number was 18,000. Today the Milwaukee factory has over 500,000 square feet of space; the Capitol Drive plant at Wauwatosa, a suburb of Milwaukee,

has nearly 400,000 square feet of space. Harley-Davidson operation increased in 1960 when they bought the Aermacchi factory at Varese in Italy, where they could produce smaller machines at competitive prices, a thing not possible at home because of high costs.

The first Harley-Davidson motorcycles had 3 hp, afterwards 4 hp single-cylinder engines. A 5 hp 573cc single with a good clutch came next. The first V-twin was built in 1911. There were models offered with optional chain or belt drive and with a single-speed transmission. The

61 Twin . . . from 1915 brochure

three-speed transmission was introduced in 1915. The 1920 electric sport model was powered by a longitudinally-opposed twin cylinder engine. It had 584cc and a fully enclosed chain. New V-twins with 986cc and 1208cc were introduced in 1922. They had ioe valves and became very popular machines. A 348cc single with sv and ohv was introduced in 1926. It had 73mm bore and 82·5mm stroke. A special ohv speedway model, the Peashooter, became famous with one of these engines. A few similar 498cc versions were also built, but it was not until 1929 that the Milwaukee factory introduced a 493cc single-cylinder pro-

3 hp Harley-Davidson (sv) 1903

584cc Harley Davidson (sv flat-twin) 1921

346cc Harley-Davidson (ohv 'Peashooter' racer) 1930

duction model with a sv engine. It had 78·5mm bore and 101·6mm stroke. New also was a 748cc sv V-twin with 69·8mm bore and 96·8mm stroke.

A bigger sv V-twin was the famous 80, which had 1311cc and was introduced in 1936. Shortly after, the spectacular and completely new 61, a 999cc ohv V-twin came into being. From 1923 Harley-Davidson also built the servi-car, a three-wheeled commercial vehicle with a motorcycle engine. During the war the ohv type 71 V-twin

998cc Harley-Davidson (ohv V-twin) 1936

883cc Harley-Davidson (ohv V-twin 'Sportster CH') 1958

901cc Harley-Davidson (ohv V-twin 'Sportster CH') 1965

1215cc Harley-Davidson (ohv V-twin 'Duo Glide') 1963

347cc Harley-Davidson (ohv) 1974

(1157cc) came into production. In addition a model was destined for the US Army with a transverse-mounted flat-twin sv engine and shaft drive to the rear wheel was built. After the war, the 74 and 80 were replaced by the new 74 with the 1206cc ohv engine, which eventually had hydraulic valve lifters and aluminium heads. Entirely new was a 173cc single-cylinder two-stroke, built since 1947. Improved versions with 165cc and 173cc engines replaced it during the following years. In 1949 the Hydra-Glide fork was introduced and the new 45 model K came as replacement for the WL V-twin. From the 45

version the famous 55 Harley-Davidsons were made. These 883cc 45-degree ohv V-twins had 76mm bore and 96mm stroke, light-alloy barrels and heads, duplex cradle-frames and in-unit four-speed gearboxes. The 1960 range consisted also of a new scooter, the Topper, with a 163cc reed-valve two-stroke engine. Soon afterwards, Harley-Davidson bought the Italian Aermacchi factory, where new models—including 49cc mopeds—came into production.

Interesting also are the 45 sv V-twin models, of which the KR was also made as a racer for tracks and the KR TT as a racer for road events. They were the last production racing machines ever made with sv engines. The reason was American race regulations, which gave them—theoretically—a certain advantage against

smaller ohv racing machines. The K models had 733cc engines and were quite fast. Still, production concentrated more and more on 883cc and 1207cc ohv V-twins, especially 997cc ohv models. The last range consists of XLH and XLCH models with 80mm bore, 97mm stroke and 67 bhp at 6000 rpm; the FX and FXE models with 87·3 bore and 100·8mm stroke and 66 bhp at 5200 rpm and the well-known FLH 1200 (Electra Glide) with a near-identical 1207cc ohv V-twin power unit. This big and luxurious model weighs 325 kg (660 lbs), reaches 107 mph, has an Electro-starter and hydraulically operated brakes on both sides. In addition to this Milwaukee range, the Varese-built range includes 123cc, 175cc and 243cc two-stroke singles; mainly off-road models. The 246cc and 346cc ohv singles with the flat

123cc Harley-Davidson SX-125 (TS) 1974

976cc Harley-Davidson XL (ohv V-twin) 1977

1200cc Electra Glides for New York Police 1975

1208cc Harley Davidson FLH (ohv V-twin) 1977

cylinders faded out during the early 1970s. Varese-built Harley-Davidson two-stroke racing machines, ridden by Walter Villa, won the 1974, 1975 and 1976 World Championship in the 250cc class and in 1976 also in the 350cc class, beating very strong Japanese opposition. Another leading rider on these machines is Gianfranco Bonera.

Harley-Davidson, always very keen on racing, had already built in 1915 special racing machines with 996cc 8-valve ohv engines. They also supplied 348cc, 498cc and 996cc ohv racing models with ioe and ohv engines and during the 1950s and 1960s the already-mentioned very fast 733cc sv V-twins. Around 1930 special hill-climb machines were also built and the Peashooters were for some time nearly unbeatable at speedway races. Numerous were the leading riders using Harley-Davidsons during the years: Ralph Hepburn, Sam Arena, Billy Huber, Everett Brashear, Babe Tancrede, Roger Soderstrom, Cal Rayborn, Eddie Brinck, Floyd Clymer, Ben Campanale, Paul Goldsmith and Joe Leonard, to mention only a few. Also in Europe, famous men rode and won on these superb American machines. In England Freddy Dixon, D. H. Davidson, Frank Longmann, Claude Temple; in Germany Paul Rüttchen, Franz Heck, Alois Drax, Paul Weyres, Kurt Stoll; in Italy Amedeo Ruggeri, Alfredo Winkler, Biaggio Nazzaro; in Switzerland Claude Ceresole and Alfredo Carmine; in Czechoslovakia Bohumil Turek, Jaroslav Kaiser, Victor Rindler; in Austria Martin Schneeweiss, Lucky Schmid, Max Grumbier, Franz Suchy and others.

HARPER / *England 1954–1955*
Scooter with 198cc Villiers two-stroke engine. The production was on a limited scale.

HARRAS / *Germany 1922–1925*
Fitted Ruppe's Bekamo two-stroke engines—built under licence—into own frames. They had 139cc and 145cc and a pumping cylinder, housed at the bottom of the crankcase.

HASCHO / *Germany 1923–1926*
Fitted first 143cc and 173cc DKW engines, superseded by English Villiers two-strokes.

HASCHÜT / *Germany 1929–1931*
Limited production of machines with 172cc Villiers deflector-type engines.

HASTY / *France 1930–1934*
Lightweights with 98cc Aubier-Dunne two-stroke power units.

HAVERFORD / *America 1909–1914*
Small American factory. Built 4 hp single-cylinder machines with automatic inlet valves.

346cc Haweka (sv) 1926

HAWEKA / *Germany 1923–1926*
Very English-looking motorcycles with 348cc, 490cc and 678cc sv and ohv JAP engines. Another model had the 497cc ioe MAG single-cylinder engine. Leading riders: Bremer and Schulz.

HAWKER / *England 1920–1923*
Made by the eccentric but famous aircraft pioneer Harry Hawker, the motorcycles had their own 293cc two-stroke and also 347cc and 548cc Blackburne sv engines. Hawker was also a good racer. He arrived in his Rolls-Royce at the start and switched over to his motorcycle already prepared and warmed up by his mechanics.

HAXEL-JAP / *England 1911–1913*
Assembler who fitted the 293cc JAP sv engine into a limited number of frames.

HAZEL / *England 1906–1911*
This was another assembler which fitted first V-twin Peugeot and from 1909 also 393cc JAP engines.

HAZLEWOOD / *England 1905–1923*
Once a big motorcycle factory, but never a well-known one at home. The Hazlewood production included V-twin sv machines of 499cc to 998cc and JAP-engined models from 245cc to 548cc and V-twins to 996cc in strong duplex frames. These were exported to the British Colonies: few reached the home market. A make which built exclusively road-going models.

HB / *England 1919–1924*
Simple well-made machines with 346cc and 498cc sv and ohv Blackburne engines.

HEC / *England 1922–1923*
The Hewin-built machine had 247cc Villiers two-stroke engines.

HEC / *England 1939–1955*
One of the first Autocycles ever built. It had its own 80cc two-stroke engine made at the Levis works. When Levis stopped motorcycle production after WWII, HEC took over the factory at Stetchford near Birmingham.

HECKER / *Germany 1921–1956*
Was a leading factory. Built 245cc two-stroke machines with their own engines, afterwards 346cc ohv models, with power units not unsimilar to the AJS of that period. They were followed by JAP-engined machines from 198cc to 548cc and a 746cc V-twin with the ioe MAG

490cc Hecker (sv JAP) 1928

199cc Hecker (ohv JAP) 1931

247cc Hecker (TS Ilo) 1954

493cc Helios (sv flat-twin BMW-engine) 1922

engine. The range also included from 1931 onward Sachs-engined 73cc and 98cc two-strokes, some with frames made from square tubes. After 1945 Hecker machines housed Sachs and Ilo engines from 98cc to 248cc.

HEIDEMANN / *Germany 1949–1952*
Well-known bicycle factory which built lightweights with 98cc and 123cc Sachs engines.

HEILO / *Germany 1924–1925*
Well-designed 348cc deflector-type, three-port, two-stroke single with own engine. Experimented also with super-charged two-strokes.

HEINKEL / *Germany 1952–1962*
Built 49cc mopeds and scooters with own 149cc ohv engines in a former aircraft factory. The range was extended by 123cc two-stroke and 174cc ohv scooters, which gained commercial success.

HELI / *Germany 1923–1925*
Watercooled 246cc two-stroke, unit-design engine in tubular duplex frame, with belt drive and leaf-spring fork.

HELIOS / *Germany 1921–1922*
Although not designed by BMW, the machine was actually BMW built. Its engine was a 493cc BMW-made M2B15 proprietary sv flat-twin. The Helios had many faults and so BMW decided to produce completely new motorcycles with transverse-mounted flat-twin engines.

147cc Hella (TS) 1922

HELLA / *Germany 1921–1924*
Built at Munich, the Hella was a two-stroke with a flat cylinder. The range consisted of 147cc and 183cc models.

HELLER / *Germany 1923–1926*
Used, like the Helios, the 493cc flat-twin BMW

M2B15 engine; from 1924 onwards also the similarly-built 746cc MJ (Mehne) sv flat-twin power unit.

746cc Heller (ohv flat-twin MJ engine) 1924

HELO / *Germany 1923–1925*
Fitted with 149cc Bekamo-type two-stroke, which had an additional piston in the crankcase. Production was on a small scale.

HELYETT / *France 1926–1955*
Produced motorcycles with 98cc to 996cc V-twins. Among them were transverse-mounted JAP-engined 746cc V-twins with shaft drive, which had the gearbox in unit with the engine. Also built some fast 996cc racing machines with 45 bhp and 55 bhp ohv JAP engines. After 1945 only two-strokes from 48cc to 123cc were made.

HENDERSON / *America 1911–1931*

A famous four-cylinder design by William 'Bill' Henderson, whose father built Henderson cars. The motorcycles had aircooled in-line unit-design engines with 1068cc and 1301cc; for a short period also 1168cc. The designer sold his creation to the Chicago-based Schwinn factory in 1917 and created afterwards the not unsimilar ACE. He was killed in 1922 in a road accident. Henderson motorcycles had three-speed gearboxes with a reverse gear.

Another famous American designer, Arthur Lemon, continued after Henderson's death in developing the big four-cylinder until 1931, when Ignaz Schwinn decided to withdraw from the manufacture of motorcycles. According to

experts who knew most American fours, which included the Militaire, the Champion, the Cleveland, the ACE and Indian-ACE and others, the big Henderson was the finest of them all. Red Wolverton, who rode Hendersons in the mid-1920s' won many races on them.

1301cc Henderson De Luxe 1925

HENKEL / *Germany 1927–1932*

Was the last in the line who built the once-famous 503cc and 497cc Krieger Gnädig (KG) motorcycles. This unit-design single with shaft drive was originally designed by the Kreiger brothers and Franz Gnädig. They handed production over to the Cito works, which eventually became part of the Allright factory. When Allright decided in 1927 to drop motorcycle production in favour of the manufacture of forks, hubs etc., it was Paul Henkel who built these machines. Rudi Albert had them redesigned and developed in the mid-1920s, but by 1932 they were outmoded. Henkel made after 1929 a 198cc sv single with a Blackburne engine.

HENLEY / *England 1920–1929*

Assembled machines with modern tubular frames. The first models had 269cc Villiers two-stroke and 497cc Blackburne sv engines. Other models with 248cc, 293cc and 346cc sv and ohv JAP and Blackburne engines followed. After a reorganisation in 1927, the name became New Henley. Afterwards the make was bought by Arthur Greenwood and Jack Crump, and was transferred to Oldham from Birmingham. Among new models were 678cc and 748cc sv V-twins. Henley would fit MAG engines if required, mainly the 497cc double-port ohv model.

HERBI / *Germany 1928–1932*

Two models of sound design formed the Herbi production. One was a 198cc sv machine with Blackburne engine, the other a 498cc model with the ohc three-valve Küchen motor.

7 hp Henderson (sv 4-cylinder) 1913

HERCULES / *Germany 1903–*

Now a leading factory, Hercules is part of the Fichtel & Sachs empire. During the years many proprietary engines were used by this Nuremberg-based factory. Among them Fafnir, JAP, Moser, Villiers, Sachs, Ilo, Bark, Küchen and Columbus. Carl Marschütz, the founder of Hercules, emigrated later to the USA. The works always showed great interest in smaller machines and they built in the 1930s models from 73cc to

98cc, after the 1939–1945 war mainly two-strokes from 48cc to 248cc. The present production includes bicycles, mofas, mokicks and mopeds in many different shapes. The smallest motorcycles are the 49cc K50 Sprint, K50RL and K50 Ultra with 6·25 bhp at 8000 rpm. The 122cc military model has 12·5 bhp at 7000 rpm, the 122cc K 125S an engine which develops 17 bhp at 7500 rpm. This is a sporting road model with wheels cast from light alloy and with a disc-brake

498cc Hercules (sv JAP) 1930

497cc Hercules (ohv Moser) 1931

at the front. The trials models are of 122cc, 173cc and 245cc with 22 bhp, 26 bhp and 32 bhp engines. Similar 122cc and 245cc moto-cross models have—like the trials versions—gearboxes with 7 speeds. All engines are made by Fichtel & Sachs. The W2000, a Wankel-engined three-chamber single-disc machine with 294cc and 27 bhp at 6500 rpm—top speed 87·5 mph—is the first commercially-built Wankel-engined motorcycle. JAP-engined 248cc and 498cc Hercules ohv racing machines—mainly ridden by Hans Kahrmann—won many races in the early 1930s, while Charlie Geffers was for a long period the leading Hercules trials rider.

198cc Hercules (TS ILO) 1951

49cc Hercules (TS Sachs K50RX) 1971

294cc Hercules (Wankel-engine) 1975

49cc Hercules (TS Sachs K50RL) 1977

HERCULES / *England 1902*
Assembler who used engines made by MMC, Minerva and White & Poppe.

HERDTLE-BRUNEAU / *France 1902–1914*
Produced a range of unorthodox motorcycles including a watercooled 264cc (48mm bore × 73mm stroke) vertical twin. Other models had V-twin Bichrone two-stroke engines. Herdtle-Bruneau was also among the first motorcycle manufacturers using ohv engines.

HERKO / *Germany 1922–1925*
Built lightweight machines with 122cc and 158cc two-stroke engines and also 198cc sv engines. Engines as well as frames were also supplied to other makes.

159cc Herko (TS) 1925

HERKRA / *Germany 1922–1923*
Another small manufacturer of motorcycles with their own 141cc two-stroke engines.

HERMA / *Germany 1921–1924*
Bicycle attachment engines which could be fitted on either front wheel or the rear. They were of Herma design and had 148cc.

HERMES / *Germany 1922–1925*
Designed by Berwald, the Cockerell-like machines with a flat single-cylinder two-stroke engine had 124cc.

HERMES / *Germany 1924–1925*
JAP-engined 348cc, 490cc and 678cc motorcycles with sv engines and open frames. Production was on a limited scale.

HEROS / *Germany 1921–1929*
Built in the Saxonian part of the country, Heros machines had own 155cc, 185cc and 247cc engines with outside flywheels and used also two and three-speed gearboxes of own manufacture. The engines were two-strokes as well as four-strokes. The last ones had sv, in some cases also overhead-inlet and side-exhaust valves.

HEROS / *Germany 1923–1924*
Another Heros, made by a Berlin-based factory, which used 142cc DKW two-stroke engines.

HERTHA / *Germany 1924–1925*
Lightweights, made on the line of the Eichler. Also the Hertha had a 142cc DKW engine.

799cc Hess (ioe four-cylinder) 1925

HESS / *Germany 1925*
Made by a Darmstadt machine factory, the Hess was a 799cc aircooled four-cylinder in-line motorcycle; the only such design ever made in Germany. Production was on a limited scale only.

HEXE / *Germany 1923–1925*
Producer of bicycle attachment engines and of 142cc and 269cc two-stroke motorcycles. The last model was a 346cc sv single with belt drive.

HIEKEL / *Germany 1925–1932*
Only a single model was ever made by Hiekel. It was a sturdily built 348cc single-cylinder three-port two-stroke with a strong triangular frame, which provided a low saddle position.

346cc Hiekel (TS) 1925

HILAMAN / *America 1906–late 1910s*
Produced ioe single-cylinder and in 1912 also V-twin models with strong frames. Good machines.

HILDEBRAND & WOLFMÜLLER / *Germany 1894–1897*
This was the first motorcycle built in the world on commercial lines. It was also the first two-wheeled machine called a *Motorrad* (motor-

cycle). Heinrich Hildebrand and Alois Wolfmüller created it together with Hans Geisenhof, a clever mechanic. The Munich-based factory soon had five branch factories also at Munich, but luck was not with them. After less than four years, the production of the Hildebrand & Wolfmüller had to be stopped forever. While the factory stopped development and became uncompetitive, other factories — especially Werner in France — went on developing motorcycles. The number of machines made by Hildebrand & Wolfmüller is not known exactly. Some sources

1488cc Hildebrand & Wolfmüller, 1894
The world's first production motorcycle

claim there were 2000 made; others say there were no more than 800 produced.

The Hildebrand & Wolfmüller had a low frame made from steel tubes and a flat four-stroke twin-cylinder engine, which developed 2·5 hp at 240 rpm. With a 90mm bore and 117mm stroke it had a capacity of 1488cc. The connecting rods of both cylinders were connected directly with the rear wheel, which acted also as flywheel. Rubber bands assisted the rods in returning, while the rear mudguard housed the radiator for watercooling the engine. Total loss lubrication

1488cc Hildebrand & Wolfmüller (Twin-cylinder 2.5 hp at 240 rpm) 1894

low combustion and a surface carburettor were other features of this design.

Mr. Moritz Schulte bought such a machine in 1895 and took it to England, where it created great interest. A few years afterwards, Schulte became a director of Triumph at Coventry, but by then the original Hildebrand & Wolfmüller design was a thing of the past. Heinrich Hildebrand designed more engines in later years, but never regained the fame which he had with his original motorcycle.

HINDE / *The Netherlands c1900–1938*
Pioneer who used 2 hp De Dion engines in his first motorcycles. After an interruption of many years, the reorganised factory built in the second part of the 1930s 98cc and 118cc two-stroke machines with Ilo engines.

HIRANO / *Japan 1952–1961*
Mini-scooter producer, who used 49cc and 78cc two-stroke engines. The motorcycle production included models with 123cc and 173cc two-stroke engines.

HIRONDELLE / *France 1921–1926*
Former arms factory which built motorcycles with 198cc sv and also other engines.

HIRSCH / *Germany 1923–1924*
Two-stroke machines with own 128cc and DKW 142cc engines. Small production. This was one of the many Berlin-based companies which built two-stroke motorcycles during the 1920s.

HIRTH / *Germany 1923–1926*
Racing two-strokes with watercooled double-piston engines, designed for experimental purposes by the famous WWI pilot and racing car driver Helmut Hirth. The experiments concerned the material 'Electron', used on these comparatively very powerful 144cc singles and 244cc vertical twins. Ridden by Hirth's famous brother Wolf Hirth, by Erwin Gehrung, Karl Fischer and others, these machines won many races. After they ceased racing, the Stuttgart Bosch factory used them for plug-testing purposes.

HJ / *England 1920–1921*
Assembled machines which housed 269cc Liberty and Villiers engines.

HJH / *Wales 1954–1956*
Built in Neath in Wales, the Hulsman motorcycles were of orthodox design and housed 147cc, 197cc and 247cc Villiers two-stroke engines.

HKR / *Germany 1925–1926*
After a reorganisation at Hako, these HRD-like machines became known as HKR, which stood for Hans Korn, Rothenburg. The range of these sporting machines included 348cc and 498cc models with sv and ohv engines made by JAP in London.

HMK / *Austria 1937–1938*
Built in limited numbers, also the HMK was a JAP-engined motorcycle built on typical English lines. Production included sv, but mainly ohv models from 248cc to 594cc with single-cylinder engines.

490cc HMK (ohv JAP) 1938

HMW / *Germany 1923–1928*
Heavy single-cylinder 3 hp machines with their own sv engines.

HMW / *Austria 1949–1964*
The first product was the 49cc Fuchs bicycle engine. Afterwards a wide range of nice 49cc two-stroke mopeds and lightweight machines were built. The factory also supplied engines to other manufacturers.

HOBART / *England 1901–1923*
A big, Coventry-based factory which also supplied engines, frames and other parts to motorcycle assemblers. Built own machines with single-cylinder and V-twin engines, but used also own two-strokes as well as proprietary engines made by Morris, JAP, Villiers and Blackburne. 170cc Hobart two-strokes were popular. The last model built was a 246cc two-stroke with internal flywheel. McKenzie motorcycles also came from the Hobart works.

2¾ hp Hobart (sv) 1904

HOCHLAND / *Germany 1926–1927*
Limited in production numbers, the Hochland, designed by Emslander, was a well-made 496cc flat-twin ohv machine.

HOCKLEY / *England 1914–1916*
As a result of WWI only a limited number of Hockley machines with 269cc two-stroke Liberty and Villiers engines came into being.

HOCO / *Germany 1924–1928*
Interesting design with a wooden frame and on some models a fully enclosed engine. Nabob

498cc Hochland (ohv flat-twin) 1926

supplied 146cc and 246cc two-stroke engines; JAP sv engines of 293cc and 346cc capacity were also fitted.

HODAKA / *Japan 1964–*

When Yamaguchi, once a well-known motor-cycle factory, closed down, the American Henry Koepke resumed work in this Negoya-based Japanese factory and called his new machines Hodaka. Main production went to the USA, although he also tried to gain part of European markets. Main production concentrates around moto-cross and enduro machines with 98cc, 123cc and 246cc two-stroke engines of modern design. The American base of Hodaka is the Pacific Basin Trading Co. at Athena, Oregon.

HOENSON / *The Netherlands 1953–1955*

Bicycle factory, which built good-looking motor-cycles with 147cc Sachs and 198cc Ilo single-cylinder two-stroke engines. The last model had the 244cc Ilo twin two-stroke motor.

HOFFMANN / *Germany 1949–1954*

Produced the Italian Vespa scooter under licence for Germany, and in addition two-stroke motorcycles with Sachs and Ilo engines from 98cc to 247cc. Richard Küchen, one of the leading German motorcycles designers, created in the early 1950s beautiful BMW-like 246cc and 298cc machines with transverse-mounted horizontally-opposed twin-cylinder ohv unit design engines and shaft drive to the rear wheel. Called Gouverneur, these Hoffmann machines were of clean and up-to-date design with telescopic forks and plunger-type rear suspension. They were quite expensive in production and the motorcycle market was not good in those days.

HOLDEN / *England 1898–1903*

Designed by Colonel H. Capel Holden, this machine had a watercooled 3 hp four-cylinder engine with direct drive to the small rear wheel. Some of these interesting machines are still in existence. Colonel Holden afterwards went to Australia.

HOLLEY / *America 1902–late 1910s*

One of the first companies in the USA building motorcycles on a commercial basis. The machines had a rearward facing single-cylinder engine of about 2 hp which was mounted in a strengthened bicycle frame.

HOLROYD / *England 1922*

Racing motorcyclist Jack Holroyd built a number of sporting machines with 246cc and 346cc ohv JAP engines, without much success.

123cc Hodaka (TS) 1974

246cc Hoffman (ohv flat-twin transverse mounted) 1953

3 hp Holden (First four-cylinder built) 1897

HONDA/*Japan 1948–*

Soichiro Honda, founder of the largest motorcycle factory in the world, was born in a small rural village near the city of Hamamatsu, Japan, in 1906. Soon after WWII the genial engineer first designed a motorised bicycle and in September 1948 the Honda Motor Company Limited was incorporated. In 1946 the output of Japanese motorcycle factories was a total of 270 machines. Honda's 98cc D-type, a two-stroke single, appeared on the market after the previous A, B and C types did not find the approval of Honda and his staff. Production in 1950 was 300 machines a month. After the D followed the

98cc TS Honda D-Type single 1947

146cc Honda (ohv single 3E-Type) 1953

98cc Honda (TS) 1951

Honda E with a 148cc ohv engine. Like the D it had a pressed steel frame and 5·5 bhp. Top speed was 50 mph and in 1953 32,000 were built. It was a great success. In 1952 Honda built the Bike Cub, a bicycle attachment engine, mounted outside the axle of the rear wheel. It had 49cc, 1·5 bhp and around 6500 were built monthly. Another bestseller was the 89cc Benly with a 3·8 bhp engine with ohv and a three-speed gearbox. Other models of the early 1950s were the J and E models and the Juno KB-type scooter of 1955.

During 1953 and 1954 Soichiro Honda bought new machinery for his factories, spending more than a million dollars on it in America, Germany and Switzerland, so that he stayed competitive in the following years, when other factories had to close down. Steadily increasing the number of new designs, Honda soon supplied markets in all parts of the world. By 1960, over 50 countries imported 168,554 machines. These numbers grew and many overseas subsidiaries came into action. New factories had to be erected in Japan, where Honda built cars and trucks. Racing played a big part during the 1950s and especially 1960s when riders like Mike Hailwood, Jim Redmann, Tom Phillis, Luigi Taveri, Derek Minter, Tommy Robb, Bill Smith, Bob Bryans and many others gained wins and broke records for Honda. Many single, twin, four and even six-cylinder double-ohc racing machines were built during the years, including the famous 248cc Six. Over 600 scientists and technicians are working in Honda's design and development department. The big factory supplies not only a variety of production models from 49cc upwards, but too many new development projects to mention

246cc Honda (ohc 'Dream') 1960

161cc Honda (ohc Model CB 160) 1965

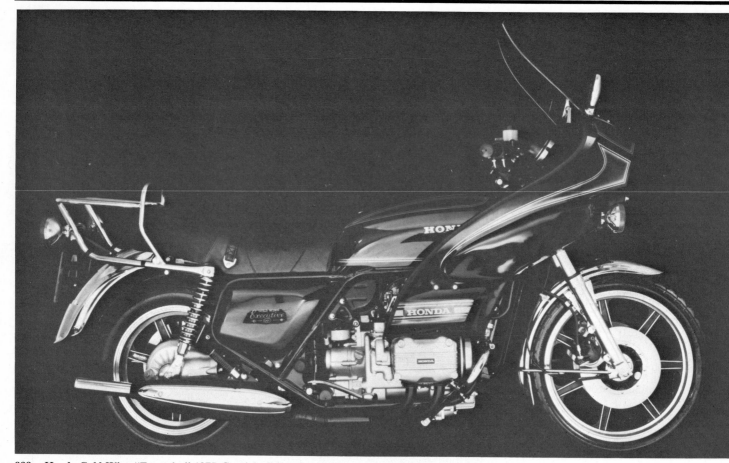

999cc Honda Gold Wing "Executive" 1975. Special edition of standard model for limited production

here. Around 1970 Honda supplied 49cc City Bikes and mopeds and 89cc ohc singles with chain drive to the camshafts, as well as 99cc singles and 124cc vertical twins. These were also available with 174cc, 249cc, 325cc and there was also a 444cc double-ohc two-cylinder version. The largest Honda had a 735cc ohc four-cylinder engine, aircooled and transverse-mounted. Its top speed was 112 mph and there were 65 bhp at 8000 rpm. A smaller 499cc vertical four came into production in 1971. It had 48 bhp at 9000 rpm and a top speed of 110 mph. 1972 saw the introduction of a 347cc four-cylinder version with 34 bhp at 9500 rpm. The range included also moto-cross and trials models. In 1974 a new two-stroke Honda, the 248cc Elsinore moto-cross model came into production. New models included 49cc and 69cc lightweights with near-flat single-cylinder chain-driven ohc engines, a 356cc ohc twin, Citybikes with 72cc ohc engines, a new 198cc ohc twin and a 498cc double-ohc twin version developing 40 bhp at 8000 rpm. New also was a 408cc aircooled four and a 539cc four with 50 bhp at 8500 rpm.

The sensation of 1975/76 was a 999cc water-cooled Honda. The transverse-mounted double-ohc engine had four horizontal cylinders, two on

408cc Honda (ohc four-cylinder) 1977

166

124cc Honda (ohc twin) 1977

748cc Honda (ohc four) 1974

each side. With a 72mm bore and 61·4mm stroke, this Honda flagship, the Golden Wing, has an Electro-starter, a five-speed gearbox and shaft drive to the rear wheel. Despite the heavy weight it reaches 125 mph and became a comparatively good seller. The power output is 82 bhp at 7500 rpm. Hundreds of Honda models have been built since 1948 and even the present range consists of about four dozen different machines, of which many are now off-road versions.

Thanks to modern production machinery, sound design and a very large production figure, Honda is very competitive in most countries.

HOOCK / *Germany 1926–1928*
Hoock & Co. of Cologne were importers of English Villiers engines and built the 342cc single-cylinder three-port version into their own frames. Not many were actually made.

HOREX / *Germany 1923–1959*
Built at Bad Homburg, the Horex was for many years a leading make in Germany. Fritz Kleemann, a well-known racing motorist, founded the factory together with his father, whose factory produced glassware under the Rex trade mark. From this name and from the first two letters of Homburg emerged the Horex trade mark. Closely connected with it was the Columbus proprietary engine factory; nearly all Horex motorcycles used these power units, although around 1930 some engines were made under Sturmey-Archer licence. In addition, Columbus engines were used by other motorcycle factories including Victoria, AWD, Tornax etc. The first design was the Gnom, a 63cc bicycle attachment, which was fitted in front of the pedalling gear. The first Horex was a good-looking 246cc ohv single, which — ridden by Fritz Kleemann Junior and Phillip Karrer — won many sporting events.

498cc Horex (SV Columbus) 1928

Bigger 498cc and 598cc sv and ohv singles and also 198cc, 298cc and 346cc ohv models followed. Hermann Reeb, then chief designer at Bad Homburg, created in 1932 sensational 598cc and 796cc vertical twins with chain drive to the ohc. This was a technically very advanced design. Some of the bigger versions had their capacity increased to 980cc and competed successfully in the 1000cc

792cc Horex (ohc twin Columbus) 1934

sidecar racing class. Karl Braun used a supercharger on such an engine and won many races. Other models, especially 248cc and 498cc versions, ridden by Josef Klein, Franz Islinger and others were successful too and when Tom Bullus rode a 498cc Horex in the 1929 Grand Prix at the Nürburgring, he was leading the race until he had to retire. In the mid-1930s Horex also built 498cc four-valve ohv singles. After 1945, Horex was the first German motorcycle factory to get permission to build a motorcycle with more than 250cc. Some claimed it was because the Kleemanns had close connections with the Americans.

498cc Horex (dohc twin works racer) 1952

346cc Horex (ohv 'Regina' Columbus) 1950

At any rate the 349cc Horex Regina, an ohv single, was an excellent machine. There were also 248cc and 398cc versions of it, but none could outsell the 349cc version. It was, after many years, replaced by 248cc and 348cc Resident singles and 398cc, 448cc and 498cc Imperator vertical twins. All these new models had modern ohv engines. In addition, Horex also produced 348cc and 498cc twin-cylinder double ohc machines for the works team, which included such famous riders as Kurt Mansfeld, Hugo Schmitz, Friedl Schön, Werner Gerber and Englishman Bill Petch. The last Horex racing twin, a 348cc double-ohc machine, was designed by the well-known Austrian Ludwig Apfelbeck and ridden by Hans Bartl and Fritz Kläger among others. In addition to these twins, Horex built in the early 1950s together with German racing motorcyclist/designer Roland Schnell new 248cc, 348cc and 498cc single-cylinder Schnell-Horex ohc racing machines, which were ridden not only by Kläger, but also by the late H. P. Müller and by Schnell as well as by Hermann Gablenz, Georg Braun, Robert Zeller, Erwin Aldinger, and others. Horex also produced a scooter and eventually a small 98cc two-stroke machine. During the 1950s they made parts for Mercedes.

HORSY / *France 1952–1953*
Scooter with a 83cc two-stroke engine, made by a small factory.

HOSK / *Japan 1953–early 1960s*
Produced 123cc two-strokes, 248cc and 348cc ohv singles as well as 498cc vertical twins, which were not unlike the German Horex motorcycles.

HOSKISON / *England 1919–1922*
Assembler whose range consisted of three basic models: 269cc Villiers, 292cc Union and 497cc sv Blackburne-engined. Small output and orthodox open frames. Like the Villiers, the Union was also a three-port two-stroke.

HOWARD / *England 1905–1907*
Interesting 2·5 hp single, because the designer used fuel injection instead of a carburettor.

H&R (R&H) / *England 1922–1925*
A simple 147cc Villiers-engined two-stroke, hailing from Coventry. The H&R stood for Hailstone and Ravenhall, which occasionally became Ravenhall and Hailstone.

H&R / *Germany 1921–1925*
This H&R stood for Hartmann and Richter, the original name for Heros motorcycles which had their own 155cc, 185cc and 249cc sv engines.

HRD / *England 1924–1950*
Founded by famous racing motorcyclist Howard R. Davis, the company built Massey-designed machines of advanced design. They had 348cc and 490cc sv and mainly ohv JAP engines, a low saddle position and a very sporting appearance. H. R. Davis himself won the 1925 Senior TT and Freddy Dixon the 1927 Junior TT on these

490cc HRD (ohv JAP Racer) 1925

498cc HRD (hc Vincent-engine Racer) 1934

998cc HRD (hc V-twin Vincent-engine) 1946

machines. In 1928 Bill Humphries of OK-Supreme fame bought HRD but soon sold it again to Phil Vincent, who continued production at Stevenage. In addition to JAP engines, he also used in the following years Villiers, Blackburne and four-valve ohv Python engines from 248cc to 498cc and fitted on all frames his unusual rear suspension. From 1934 onwards, his own high-camshaft 496cc ohv singles and from 1937 his 996cc high-camshaft V-twins came into modern frames. (See also Vincent-HRD.) The original HRD design was copied by many other producers, including Hako.

HT / *England 1920–1922*
Scooter-like design with two seats and with leaf rear suspension. Used first 292cc Union two-stroke, afterwards 346cc Barr & Stroud sleeve-valve engines. The engines were fully enclosed. The production was on a limited scale.

HUC / *Germany 1924–1925*
Designed by Max Hecker of Berlin, the HUC was fitted with 145cc and 172cc DKW two-stroke proprietary engines.

HUCKE-RINNE / *Germany 1924–1926*
Racing motorcyclist Max Hucke was building frames for 124cc, 174cc and 247cc Rinne engines, which had evaporation cooling. They were fast two-strokes and — ridden by Hucke, Rannacher, Lücke, Michael, Köhler etc. — won many races.

HÜFFER / *Germany 1923–1925*
Assembler of lightweights, who fitted 150cc to 198cc engines made by DKW, Rapid, Baumi etc.

HULBERT-BRAMLEY / *England 1903–1906*
Successor to the Booth Motor Company. Produced three-wheelers, lightweights and the Binks-designed 385cc four-cylinder in-line machine.

293cc Hulla (sv JAP) 1931

HULLA / *Germany 1925–1932*
Fitted mainly DKW two-stroke engines of 173cc, 198cc, 206cc and 298cc into own frames. There was another model which housed the 293cc JAP sv engine. Hulla sales were concentrated in the northern parts of Germany.

HULSMANN / *The Netherlands 1939–1955*
Bicycle factory which fitted for a long period 123cc Villiers engines. During the 1950s, Villiers-engined 198cc and 225cc machines were added.

498cc Humber (sv flat-twin) 1924

346cc Humber (ohc single) 1929

HUMBER / *England 1900–1930*
Famous manufacturer of De Dion-engined three-wheelers and of cars, whose first motorcycles were built under Phelon & Moore licence with a forward inclined single-cylinder engine. Models of own design had 496cc, 596cc and

746cc sv flat twin engines, of which the 596cc version was built until 1923. Afterwards Humber concentrated on 347cc singles with sv, ohv and ohc. A Humber ridden by P. J. Evans won the 1911 Junior TT.

HUMMEL / *Germany 1951–1954*
Became known as producer of the Sitta scooter, which had 120cc, 123cc and 149cc Ilo engines. Motorcycles also had 49cc to 248cc Ilo two-stroke engines.

HURIKAN / *Czechoslovakia 1947–1949*
Designed by Jaroslav Vlk, the Hurikan was a luxurious 247cc ohc sports machine of advanced design. Only a few were made.

HURRICANE / *Japan late 1950s–1961*
Producer of the 90cc and 123cc Rabbit scooters and of motorcycles with two-stroke engines up to 248cc. The biggest model was a 348cc ohv single.

HURTU / *France 1903–late 1950s*
Once a well-known car factory which built lightweight motorcycles and after WWII also 49cc attachment engines for bicycles.

HUSAR / *Germany 1923–1925*
A rear suspension by means of leaf-springs was common to all Husar machines. Engines fitted were side-valve singles of 296cc capacity.

198cc Hulla (TS DKW engine) 1929

HUSQVARNA / *Sweden 1903–*
Famous arms factory and also famous for superb and successful motorcycles. The first machines had FN and Moto-Rêve proprietary engines. For many years built 546cc and 992cc V-twins with own sv engines, also fitted single-cylinder JAP ohv power units. In 1926 Husqvarna chief

designer Harold Toller created new ohv 730cc V-twins. These had 71mm bore and 92mm stroke. Production concentrated on these sv V-twins, of which the model 180 had 65mm bore and 83mm stroke, 546cc and 14 bhp at 4000 rpm, while the model 600 with the 992cc V-twin engine had 79·5mm bore, 100mm stroke and 22 hp. Production increased around 1928 and there were many models in the early 1930s; including 248cc sv singles, 248cc JAP-engined ohv models, 348cc sv machines with HVA motors, 496cc JAP-engined ohv models and also 496cc singles with sv and ohv engines made by Sturmey-Archer. Folke Mannerstedt, formerly with FN, and Calle Heimdahl, a superb technician, created in 1929/1930 new 498cc ohv V-twin racing machines, which became world famous in the following years. In addition the Swedish factory also built 248cc, 348cc and 498cc racing singles with modified ohv JAP and also their own ohv engines. But the leading model was the 498cc V-twin ohv racer. There was also a 348cc version of it, while a 249cc racing model had one cylinder of the 498cc machine 'cut off'. Mannerstedt experimented with many racing machines and there was also a 248cc single-cylinder ohc Husqvarna. The first 498cc ohv V-twins had 65mm bore, 75mm stroke and 24 bhp at 6200 rpm. During the 1930s they were developed and also lightened: from 177 kg to 125 kg. Four-speed gearboxes superseded three-speeds; the compression rose to 8·5, the power to 36 bhp at 6400 rpm. Top speed of the twin-carburettor racer running on 50% petrol, 25% benzol and 25% methanol was 115 mph. The 349cc V-twin ohv racing machine had 56mm bore, 71mm stroke, a 10:1 compression and developed on 50/50 petrol/benzol 32·5 bhp at 7200 rpm. The last versions of the 499cc Husqvarna ohv twin racing machines had 44 bhp at 6700 rpm and a top speed of 121 mph.

Famous works and semi-works riders of that period were Stanley Woods, Ragnar Sunnqvist, Yngve Ericsson, Gunnar Kalen, Ernie Nott, Sten Edlund, Martin Strömberg, Arthur Olsson, Ove Lambert-Meuller, Helge Karlsson, Michael Gayer, Hugo Roigh, Arie van der Pluym, Rolf Gülich, Karl Kihlskog and others. More successes came after WWII when Husqvarna built sporting two-strokes from 124cc to 456cc with an eye on moto-cross and trials. With Heikki Mikkola in the saddle, Husqvarna proved a winner

498cc Husqvarna (ohv V-twin Racer) 1934

354cc Husqvarna Automatic, single-cylinder, two stroke. 1976

in moto-cross. The present range consists of 124cc, 245cc and 354cc singles with their own two-stroke engines.

HUY / *Germany 1923–1926*
The first model made by this firm was a 198cc sv single which gained some popularity, although it had a very high saddle position and a hard front suspension.

The Huy, whose name was Thiele, had the engine built by Alba at Stettin. In addition there was a 347cc single with an ioe MAG engine which was built in limited numbers.

124cc Husqvarna MC 125 CR-76. 1976

I

IBIS / *Italy 1925–1928*
Piazza-engined 173cc sports machines with ohv and an open frame built on English lines.

IDEAL / *Germany 1924–1925*
Two-strokes with 173cc deflector-type three-port engines of own manufacture.

IDRA / *Italy 1923–1926*
Designed by O. Idra, this 123cc ohv engine could be fitted into bicycles and was obtainable also as a complete lightweight with a strengthened bicycle frame.

IDROFLEX / *Italy 1949–1954*
With the 105cc two-stroke engine fitted directly to the swinging arm of the rear wheel, the Idro-flex was a complicated and quite unusual design.

IFA / *East Germany 1945–1960*
Successor to the pre-war DKW motorcycles and made at the former DKW factory at Zschopau, the name IFA disappeared when it became superseded by the name MZ, which stands for Motor-radwerke Zschopau. A nationalised factory, the production concentrated around two-stroke singles from 98cc to 298cc, built in large numbers. Most interesting was a twin-cylinder two-stroke of 346cc, which had the flat twin mounted transverse. It had also shaft drive to the rear wheel. The unique engine had 58mm bore, 65mm

342cc Ifa (TS transverse flat-twin) 1955

stroke and 15bhp at 5000rpm. Not a big output, but everyone was at that period glad to get a motorcycle at all. In addition, the 346cc IFA was comparatively cheap. When IFA disappeared and MZ took over, the only difference on the single-cylinder two-strokes up to 298cc was the different badge on the petrol tank. IFA also built aircooled 123cc and 248cc racing two-strokes. Among riders were such famous names as Petruschke, Brehm, Krumpholz, Fügner, Degner, etc. Racing manager was the well known Walter Kaaden who was also responsible for part of the development.

147cc Ilo (TS) 1923

ILO / *Germany 1923–1925*
Famous manufacturer of two-stroke proprietary engines, who also built complete 117cc, 132cc, 147cc and 170cc motorcycles until the demand for engines forced the Pinneberg factory to give up manufacture of frames and other parts.

IMHOLZ / *Switzerland 1924–1927*
Built 123cc two-strokes, afterwards also 173cc versions with their own two-strokes and 173cc Moser ohv engines. Limited production.

IMME / *Germany 1948–1951*
Unorthodox 98cc two-stroke with a pressed steel frame. The Imme had the power-egg swung together with the rear wheel, which was connected via the exhaust pipe—which acted as

one side of the frame—to the centre of the machine. Similarly unorthodox was the one-sided front fork. Before Imme closed down forever Norbert Riedl, the creator of this design, produced a similar 148cc twin-cylinder model, which was made in small numbers only.

98cc Imme (TS) 1949

IMN / *Italy 1950–1958*
Concentrated first on 49cc to 248cc two-strokes, also built ohv machines and failed. They then created a sensational 198cc flat-twin ohv of unit design with shaft drive. This design was not fully developed when it was put on the market, and that was the end of the IMN Rocket, made at Naples.

IMPERIA / *Germany 1923–1925*
Assembler who fitted 346cc and 496cc JAP engines into open frames. No connection with the other German Imperia.

IMPERIA / *Germany 1924–1935*
Becker's Imperia factory at Cologne was building 247cc and 347cc ohv Blackburne-engined machines and also versions with the 490cc single-cylinder ohv JAP, but most had Swiss MAG power units of 346cc, 496cc, 596cc, 746cc and 996cc. With the exception of the smallest, all were V-twins with ioe and ohv. Becker went broke in 1926 and the Schrödter family of Bad Godesberg bought Imperia. New models with

498cc single-cylinder double-port MAG ohv engines and 678cc V-twin ohv JAP engines came into being. During the 1930s there were also other models with MAG and Bark engines, but mainly 248cc, 348cc and 498cc four-valve ohv singles with Rudge-built Python proprietary power units. Racing versions ridden by Ernst Loof, A. F. Dom, Wilhelm Schminke, Sebastian Roth, Gerd in der Elst, Otto Kohfink etc. won many races and championships. Dom, born in the Dutch East Indies and formerly with Moto-sacoche and Standard, was a famous designer-rider. The same was the case with Ernst Loof, the top Imperia rider. In the mid-1930s import of foreign engines into Germany became nearly impossible. As a result, Imperia boss Rolf Schrödter designed a range of new and very unconventional two-strokes. The first was a 348cc double-piston single with the pistons running in opposite directions and the single plug in the centre. There were really two crank-cases, one on each side of the cylinder. They were connected by a chain and on top was a supercharger. This aircooled engine was not fully developed when Imperia ran out of money;

the reason for this was too many unconventional designs to produce with limited means. These included a 498cc transverse-mounted flat-twin two-stroke with Trilok gearbox and shaft drive as well as 746cc sports and racing cars.

IMPERIAL / *England 1901–c1910*
Fitted with 3·5 hp Coronet engines, these machines had a kind of disc brake.

IMPERIAL / *America 1903–c1910*
This was a 444cc single-cylinder machine, of which nothing else is known.

497cc Imperia (ohv MAG) 1928

678cc Imperia (ohv JAP V-twin) 1929

346cc Imperia (ohv Bark engine) 1934

INDIAN / *America 1901– (England 1951–1963)*
Once the biggest motorcycle factory in the world, Indian is now only a memory. The famous Springfield factory stopped producing motor-cycles in the mid-1950s; afterwards they put the Indian badge on other makes. Then owned by

the Brockhouse Group of Southport in England, they also built a 246cc sv single under the Indian trade mark, which was already a long way from the once famous red V-twins. This make was founded by George W. Hendee and had great designers such as Oskar Hedström and C. B. Franklin on the staff. Indians already became famous before WWI even in Europe, where they had much success in races. At the Brooklands track in south London G. L. Evans on an Indian

998cc Indian (sv V-twin 'Electric Spec.') 1914

finished second in 1909, and in 1911 the first three riders—O. C. Godfrey, C. B. Franklin and A. Moorhouse—rode Indians in the Senior TT. Jake de Rosier, another American works rider, competed successfully in Europe. After WWI in the 1920s, Indian machines had more success with such riders as Freddy Dixon, Bert Le Vack, Harry Herkuleyns, Domenico Malvesi, Zdenek Pohl, Hugo Tichy, Michael Gayer, Alfredo Car-mine, Franta Chlad, Georg Retienne, Johnny Seymour, Gene Walker, Otto Pechar, Jim Davis, Charles Spencer, Floyd Dreyer, Ralph Hepburn, Erminio Visioli, Paul Anderson and others.

Technically speaking, Indian built during the years a variety of racing machines but only few were sold. The Indian riders were either employed by the works or rode for dealers, who—in many

346cc Indian (sv 'Prince') 1926

countries — got racing machines from the factory for publicity purposes. There were 348cc, 498cc, 746cc and 998cc ohv racers, singles and V-twins for track races. When Freddy Dixon won the Belgian Grand Prix in 1923, his Indian was a 498cc sv single. In other events he rode 998cc sv V-twins, and also 998cc 8-valve ohv V-twins. Some racing singles had ioe and ohv cylinders leaning to the rear, some forwards. C. B. Franklin, the Irish Indian designer, was a very busy creator during the early 1920s of fast racing motorcycles.

Indians were of very advanced design for many years and already in 1914 there were 998cc production V-twins with rear suspension and an electric starter. The most famous models during the 1920s were the 347cc sv and ohv single-cylinder Prince, the 596cc and 746cc sv V-twin Scout and Police Scout and the 998cc and 1206cc sv V-twin Chief and Big Chief. The latter gave 24 bhp at 3000 rpm, an 83mm bore and a 113mm stroke. From 1927 onwards, Indian also built the W. Henderson/Arthur Lemon-designed 1265 cc ACE, which eventually became the Indian-4. This was an aircooled in-line four-cylinder machine with ioe valves, 70mm bore and 83mm stroke.

596cc Indian (sv V-twin 'Scout') 1926

1200cc Indian Big Chief 74 (four-in-line) 1928

1200cc Indian-4 1931

All Indian machines were of sturdy design with duplex frames and the twins and fours had leaf-spring forks. Like other American machines, they had big petrol tanks, pan saddles, twist-grips etc. Soon after WWII Indian designers created new 220cc ohv singles and 440cc and 498cc vertical ohv twins. Although of up-to-date design, they were not successful because they were never fully developed. After Indian founder William Hendee left in the 1920s, permanent changes on the Indian board led to the end of this great factory. When during the late 1950s the London based AMC (Associated Motor Cycles Ltd.—producers of Matchless, AJS, Norton etc.) bought the Indian, nothing was left at Springfield. Another attempt to bring Indian back was made by publisher and ex-racing motorist, Floyd Clymer. His aim was to produce new models at the German Mammut-Münch factory, but it ended with another failure. The present Indian two-strokes are also made outside America, but the official address is Beverly Hills in California. There remain memories of some great designs, with the Scouts and Police Scouts of the late 1920s as the most outstanding.

INDUS / *Germany 1924–1927*
Fitted with 346cc ohv Kühne engines, 346cc and 490cc ohv JAP engines and the 497cc ohc three-valve Küchen single-cylinder engine, Indus machines were built in limited numbers only. They had front and rear leaf-spring suspension.

746cc Indian (sv V-twin 'Police Scout') 1931

218cc Indian (ohv) 1949

246cc Indian (sv Brockhouse-made 'Brave') 1955

INTRAMOTOR / *Italy 1971–*
Produces a variety of 49cc models with Minarelli two-stroke engines and also 122cc trials and moto-cross machines.

INVICTA / *England 1902–1906*
Assembled machines with Minerva and Kelecom engines.

INVICTA / *England 1913–1923*
Built at the Francis-Barnett factory at Coventry, the Arthur Barnett-designed machines had 269cc Villiers two-stroke engines, other models 499cc sv Abingdon and 346cc and 678cc sv JAP engines.

293cc Invicta (sv JAP) 1921

INVICTA / *Italy 1951–1954*
Two-strokes with engines from 74cc to 123cc of typical Italian design.

IRESA / *Spain 1956–1959*
Small assembler who fitted Spanish-built Villiers engines up to 198cc into own frames.

IRIS / *England 1902–1906*
Quite unorthodox machines with 5 hp V-twin watercooled engines. There was also a hand starter and a friction clutch.

IRIS / *Italy 1952–1953*
Two-stroke machines with German 123cc Ilo engines. Limited production.

IRUNA / *Spain 1953–late 1950s*
Produced 123cc scooters with their own two-stroke engines.

ISH – *Russia 1928–*
The oldest Russian factory at Izevsk. Early models had 1200cc V-twin sv and 746cc ohv engines. They were followed by 198cc two-strokes and a Neander-like 498cc ohc machine. From 1938 onwards, the 348cc single-cylinder two-stroke Ish came into being and was built in large numbers. Early models had 18 bhp, later ones 25 bhp. Successor to this model is the 347cc Jupiter-3 with a twin-cylinder, two-stroke engine, designed on German lines. This engine has

25 bhp at 4600 rpm. Another version is the single-cylinder Jupiter Planeta Sport, whose 348cc two-stroke engine has 76mm bore, 75mm stroke and 32 bhp at 6500 rpm. Top speed is 87·5 mph.

ISLO / *Mexico 1960–*
With two-stroke engines built under Sachs licence from 48cc to 248cc. Supplies also the Cooper-Islo machines for America.

ISO / *Italy 1949–1964*
Once a famous producer of luxury cars and also of scooters and motorcycles with their own double-piston two-stroke engines of up to 248cc. Fitted also 123cc and 173cc ohv engines, but a BMW-like 499cc machine with transverse-mounted ohv flat twin never went into quantity production.

ITALA / *Italy 1933–1939*
Giuseppe Navone's motorcycles were of sound design, but built in limited quantities. As he was importer of French Train proprietary engines, his first models used the 98cc Train two-stroke. Afterwards he used 173cc, 246cc and 346cc Chaise, as well as English 248cc, 348cc and 498cc Python four-valve ohv engines. The Super-Itala had an aircooled 498cc Chaise four-cylinder engine.

ITALEMMEZETA / *Italy 1958–1966*
Designed by Leopoldo Tartarini, this machine was really an MZ built on Italian lines with MZ two-stroke engines from 98cc to 248cc.

ITALJET / *Italy 1966–*
Known lately for small 49cc schoolboy-motorcycles, but produces also 123cc and 124cc two-stroke trials, moto-cross and similar off-road machines. In earlier years, Italjet fitted different Minarelli, CZ, MZ and Yamaha as well as 646cc Triumph vertical-twin ohv engines into their own frames. Italjet's 124cc Buccaneer is a road-going two-stroke twin with 18 bhp at 9500 rpm and an 81·2 mph top speed.

ITAR / *Czechoslovakia 1921–1929*
Produced the Zubatý-designed 746cc sv flat-twin for the Czechoslovakian army, but sold also civilian versions. A 346cc single, designed in

746cc Itar (sv flat-twin) 1929

746cc Itar (sv flat-twin) 1922

1923, never came into quantity production. In 1928 they built new 346cc and 490cc singles with sv and ohv engines made by JAP. They had—like the flat twin—modern frames with saddle tanks.

ITOM / *Italy 1948–late 1960s*
Produced a variety of two-strokes, partly with Franco-Morini engines, from 48cc to 98cc.

IVEL / *England 1902–c1905*
Used De Dion and MMC engines in strengthened bicycle frames.

IVER-JOHNSON / *America 1907–1915*
Superbly designed singles and V-twins with capacities up to 1090cc. Some models had rear suspension.

IVO LOLA RIBAR / *Yugoslavia 1956–*
Produced Italian 123cc Vespa scooters under licence.

IVY / *England 1908–1932*
Newman's first machines had Precision, water-cooled Green-Precision and JAP proprietary

1090cc Iver-Johnson (sv V-twin) 1914

engines. Own two-stroke engines had 225cc and 296cc; after 1919 there were also 246cc and 346cc versions with outside flywheels. After an interruption of some years, Ivy returned to motorcycle production with 248cc two-strokes and 293cc JAP-engined sv singles.

IXION / *England 1901–1903*
Bicycle producer who fitted De Dion, MMC and —according to unconfirmed sources—also French 1·5 hp Bichrone two-stroke engines.

IXION / *England c1900s–1923*
The green machines had a variety of engines. Among them were the 670cc Abingdon V-twin, the 499cc and 597cc Precision sv singles and 349cc Precision and 293cc Peco two-strokes. When Ixion closed New Hudson bought the trade mark.

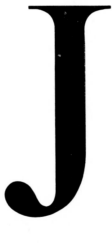

JAC / *Czechoslovakia 1929–1932*
Interesting 498cc single-cylinder sleeve-valve unit-design machine with shaft drive and a welded frame of triangular design, made from pressed steel. Designed by J. A. Cvach, the machine had a leaf-spring fork, a low saddle position and the triangular fuel tank between saddle and gearbox.

JACKSON-ROTRAX / *England 1949–1966*
Speedway machines with 499cc JAP single-cylinder ohv Speedway engines, designed and built by former rider Alec Jackson.

JACK SPORT / *France 1927–1931*
Assembler of motorcycles with 348cc and 498cc sv and ohv engines.

JAK / *Germany 1922–1925*
Lightweight machines, fitted with 119cc, 142cc

498cc JAC (Sleeve valve, shaft drive) 1930

nd 173cc DKW and 129cc Bekamo engines, which had a charge-pump in the crankcase.

ALE/*Germany 1923–1925*
Produced air and watercooled 170cc two-strokes with deflector-type, three-port engines in limited numbers.

AMATHI/*The Netherlands 1973–*
Limited manufacture of sporting 49cc two-strokes.

JAMES/*England 1902–1964*
Made in Birmingham, this well-known make initially fitted FN engines, but also their own 297cc two-strokes. Other models had 496cc and 596cc single and V-twin sv engines of own manufacture. The small 496cc sv and ohv V-twins were famous. Unorthodox machines, designed in 1910 by Renouf, failed to gain popularity and so Kimberley, then James chief, continued manufacturing more orthodox designs. Among them were Villiers-engined versions from 98cc to 248cc and also models with the 499cc four-valve Python ohv engine. Most James machines had their own sv and ohv engines, including 246cc, 346cc and 496cc versions. The Baker motorcycle factory was bought in 1931. After 1945 only Villiers-engined James machines were built, until Associated Motor-Cycles Ltd. of London — then producer of Matchless and AJS machines — bought James and fitted their own Piatti-designed two-strokes. They also bought the Coventry-based Francis-Barnett factory and moved it to the James home at Greet (Birmingham). Around 1961 production of their own two-strokes was discontinued and Villiers engines were once more fitted. These had been successful in competition: Bert Kershaw won in 1929 the 175cc class in the Belgian GP on a James with the 172cc Villiers Brooklands engine running on alcohol. At that time, the factory produced also 496cc Speedway machines with their own V-twin ohv engine. Among riders who rode James machines on the Continent was Karl Abarth, the famous car designer.

2¾ hp James (sv) 1911

346cc James (sv) 1923

498cc James (ohv V-twin) 1929

198cc James (TS 'Captain') 1957

248cc James (TS 'Cotswold M/C') 1965

JAP/*England 1904–1908*
Famous as manufacturer of proprietary engines from 123cc to 1098cc, JAP also built complete motorcycles until 1908, when J. A. Prestwich of Tottenham (London) decided to concentrate on building power units only. After 1945 the engine factory was taken over by Villiers.

JAVON/*Germany 1929–1932*
Small assembler of JAP-engined motorcycles with 198cc and 498cc single-cylinder sv engines.

JAWA/*Czechoslovakia 1929–*

In 1929 the manufacturer of arms František Janeček of Prague decided on the production of motorcycles. He got the licence of the German Wanderer design, bought eventually the production equipment for this model and thus entered the motorcycle market with a 498cc single-cylinder unit-design ohv machine with shaft drive and a pressed steel frame. The leaf-sprung fork was also made from pressed steel. The whole design was expensive to produce and not fully developed when it was bought. There were many teething troubles with the lubrication system, the valve gear and the frame. The name Jawa was a combination of the first two letters of the names Janeček and Wanderer. This model despite its faults was quite successful in big trials, including the Sixdays, with riders who included Jaroslav Kaiser, Antonin Vitvar, Franta Brand, Richard Dusil, Zdenek Houška, Robert Uvira and others.

George-William Patchett, the famous English designer, joined the Jawa factory in 1930 and soon created new racing machines with 498cc unit-design ohv engines and chain drive to the rear wheel. In later years they got separate gearboxes and were followed by 348cc, eventually 248cc and 173cc models, used exclusively by works riders such as Franta Juhan, Fritz Bardas,

246cc Jawa (TS A.-U. Patent engine) 1936

Leopold Killmayer, Václav Stanislav, Lada Nerad, Josef Paštika, Jiři Bayer, Hermann Gunzenhauser and others. Patchett himself was also a good rider, besides being designer-in-chief. The big 498cc production (ex-Wanderer) model was not a commercial success, but when Jawa in 1932 introduced a very nice-looking 173cc two-stroke with Villiers deflector-type engine and a triangular frame also made from pressed steel, it was immediately a bestseller. These red-yellow machines became very popular; they were comparatively cheap as well as good-looking. Many riders who afterwards became famous started their careers on tuned versions of this little machine. Jawa afterwards built the Villiers engines under licence, while a 246cc two-stroke version of 1934 introduced the Schnürle patent flat-top two-stroke engine as then used by DKW in Germany, also under licence.

Patchett-designed 346cc sv and afterwards ohv models completed the Jawa range in the mid-1930s. The last pre-war version was the

Robot, designed by the famous Czech designer Josef Jozif. This was a 98cc two-stroke model. When the war broke out, Patchett returned to England and concentrated on the design of arms for Enfields and other firms, a job which brought him fame and financial rewards. Jawa at the Prague-Nusle and Tynec factories repaired motorcycles during the war for the German occupants, but Czech designers and other technicians secretly developed new machines for the immediate post-war period under the noses of the Germans. Among them was a highly sophisticated 248cc two-stroke single with unit design, automatic clutch, telescopic fork and plunger-type rear suspension. In 1947 Jawa took over the Ogar factory and added a new 346cc two-stroke

twin in a frame identical to the 248cc machine to the range. Václav Sklenář, another Czech designer, created in the same period new 348cc and 498cc supercharged and unsupercharged vertical-twin double ohc racing machines for the works riders. These included again Antonin Vitvar, Richard Dusil, Jan Novotny, Karel

497cc Jawa (ohv shaft-drive) 1929

98cc Jawa (TS 'Robot') 1938

174cc Jawa (TS) 1966

348cc Jawa (TS two-cylinder) 1977

498cc Jawa (dohc twin-cylinder works racer) 1955

Rykr, Ladia Stainer and others. During the 1950s and 1960s, new racing twins came into being. Designers have been Josef Jozif, Jan Křivka and others. These new double-ohc models had 248cc, 348cc and 498cc and in the mid-1950s there was a 498cc production model with a single ohc vertical twin engine. With František Stastny and Gustav Havel in the saddle, the 348cc racing twins won many road races in the late 1950s and early 1960s. Afterwards Jawa — since 1945 a nationalised factory — built two-stroke machines — including 248cc and 348cc racing versions — only. They also produced very successful trials and moto-cross versions and, after taking over the Eso factory, very successful 498cc ohv singles for speedway, ice racing and so forth. Many of these machines are exported to nearly every country in the world but especially to Russia, Poland, East Germany, etc. Even Barry Briggs and Ivan Mauger ride Jawa speedway machines. Jawa riders won many trials and they form — since 1931 — the Trophy Team at the Sixdays. The present Jawa range (with the exception of the speedway models) consists of two-strokes from 49cc to 362cc; the machines are of sound design and developed from the early 248cc model of 1946. The smallest model currently in production is a 49cc machine with a flat single-cylinder 4 bhp (at 6500 rpm) engine, the largest road-going version the 343cc vertical-twin with 26 bhp at 5250 rpm. Among trials Jawas, the 174cc has 22·5 bhp at 7000, the 246cc 28·5 bhp at 7000, the 344cc 35 bhp at 6400 and the 362cc 36 bhp at 6500 rpm. These machines are excellent in performance, reliability

and road-holding. There is a close technical and commercial connection between Jawa and the other leading Czechoslovakian motorcycle factory CZ.

JB-LOUVET / *France 1926–1930*
Fitted 173cc and 246cc Aubier-Dunne two-strokes and 348cc and 498cc sv and ohv JAP engines and French-made gearboxes, which formed a unit with the engines.

JD – *England 1920–1926*
Made by Bowden, the JD was a 116cc bicycle attachment engine. It was also supplied with a strengthened bicycle frame.

116cc JD (TS) 1923

JE-BE / *America late 1950s to late 1960s*
For the US market, built in Germany 98cc and

123cc two-stroke machines with engines made by Fichtel & Sachs. The name stood for Joe Berliner, the importer.

JEAN THOMANN / *France 1920–1930*
Was part of the Alcyon Group and produced two-strokes from 98cc to 248cc. There was also a 499cc ohv single with a big outside flywheel.

JEECY-VEA / *Belgium 1923–1927*
Concentrated on producing motorcycles with opposing flat-twin engines. These power units were 498cc ohv and 688cc sv Coventry-Victor as well as 746cc sv Watelet engines. The late King Albert of Belgium rode such a machine in the mid-1920s.

998cc Jefferson (ohv V-twin) 1914

JEFFERSON / *America 1911–1914*
The superb Jefferson was a development of the Perry E. Mack-designed PEM machines. It had its own ohv engines of 499cc (singles) and 998cc (V-twins), a swinging arm fork and rear suspension.

JEHU / *England 1901–c1910*
Was in the pioneering years a well-known factory. The engines fitted were Minerva, MMC and also of the company's own design and manufacture. They had 2·25 hp, 2·5 hp and 3 hp.

2 hp Jehu (sv) 1903

JELINEK / *Czechoslovakia 1904–1907*
Produced motorcycles with engines made by Minerva, Orion and Fafnir. These had from 2·5 hp to 5 hp.

JES / *England 1910–1924*
In pre-1914 days was already building 116cc and 189cc ohv machines. In the 1920s, models with 169cc and 247cc two-strokes came into production. There were also 246cc and 498cc sv and ohv singles with Blackburne engines when JES was taken over by Connaught.

JESMOND / *England 1899–1907*
One of the pioneers in the motorcycle trade. Fitted De Dion, MMC and Sarolea engines into the strengthened bicycle frames.

JFK / *Czechoslovakia 1923–1926*
Designed by J. F. Koch, this 348cc ohc single was of modern design. Koch was also the creator of BD, Praga, Koch and some CZ designs.

JH / *England 1913–1915*
Assembled machines with various JAP and 269cc Villiers engines. There was also a model with the 6 hp V-twin MAG engine.

JHC / *Germany 1922–1924*
Simple 183cc machines with their own three-port, two-stroke engines.

JNU / *England 1920–1922*
The only model made had a 312cc two-stroke Dalm engine. The production was limited.

JNZ / *New Zealand 1960–*
The JNZ stands for Jawa New Zealand; the machine is built under Jawa licence.

JOERNS / *America 1910–1915*
Once a well-known motorcycle factory. Built singles and V-twins and fitted two-speed gearboxes. Produced also the 996cc Cyclone, probably the first V-twin ohc machine built in large numbers.

JONGHI / *France 1931–1956*
Concentrated first on 348cc sv singles, designed by the Italian Giuseppe Remondini, who came to Jonghi from Negas & Ray. His first 348cc ohc machines were made in 1933 and were successful in races. Afterwards he built also 248cc and 173cc ohc versions. Famous Jonghi riders were Jeanin, Perrin, Renier (Sen.) and the great Georges Monneret. The factory also built small two-strokes with Aubier-Dunne engines. In the mid-1930s, Jonghi amalgamated with Prester. Most models built after 1945 had two-stroke engines from 98cc to 248cc. Jonghi machines also broke many long-distance records at the Montlhéry race track.

123cc Jonghi (ohv) 1952

JOOS / *Germany 1900–1907*
Machine factory which built engines, later also motorcycles, with horizontal twin-cylinder engines. Later models were orthodox singles and V-twins with Fafnir engines.

JOUCLARD / *France 1903–1907*
Was a machine equipped with 1·5 hp and 2·25 hp single-cylinder engines.

JOYBIKE / *England 1959–1960*
This was a cross between a lightweight and a scooter. It was powered by 70cc JAP and 49cc Trojan two-stroke engines.

JSL / *Germany 1923–1925*
Lightweights with own 132cc and 180cc as well as 206cc DKW two-stroke three-port deflector-type engines.

JUCKES / *England 1910–1926*
Very underrated machines, made by a well-known engineering company at Wolverhampton. Produced well-made two-strokes of 269cc, 274cc and 399cc and a 348cc ohv single. All had their

346cc Juckes (ohv) 1925

346cc Juckes (ohv) 1926

own engines and gearboxes; the last version of the four-stroke also had an additional tube on both sides, leading from the bottom of the steering head directly to the hub of the rear wheel.

JUERGENSEN / *Denmark 1904–WWI*
One of the first Danish motorcycle factories. Built English Humber machines under licence, which is interesting because these early Humber machines, with the cylinder inclined to the front and forming part of the front down-tube, were themselves made under Phelon & Moore licence.

JUERY / *France 1931–1939*
Paris-built 346cc and 498cc sv and ohv singles with Chaise as well as own engines.

198cc Juhö (sv) 1923

JUHÖ / *Germany 1922–1924*
The name came from the manufacturer Julius Höflich. Designed by Leo Falk with own 148cc sv and 195cc two-stroke engines.

JULES / *Czechoslovakia 1929–1934*
These were 120cc two-stroke bicycle engines and were sold also complete with the Leopold

škřivanek-designed Praga bicycles. They had a single leaf spring below the saddle as suspension for the rear wheel. There was no connection between Praga motorcycles and the Jules.

JUNAK / *Poland 1956–1964*
Made at the former German town of Stettin, the Junak was the only four-stroke machine made after 1945 in Poland. Of sound design, it had its own 247cc and 347cc ohv single-cylinder engine.

JUNCKER / *The Netherlands 1932–1935*
Basically a bicycle factory, the Dutch firm built a range of two-strokes from 98cc to 198cc with Ilo and Villiers proprietary engines. They used triangular frames on some models, which were so similar to German Europa motorcycle frames that the impression was created that Juncker built them for the Munich company. There was after the war a merger with Gazelle.

JUNCKER / *France 1935–1937*
Stainless and Aubier-Dunne two-stroke engines propelled these French-built 98cc, 123cc and 147cc lightweight machines.

JUNIOR / *Italy 1924–1935*
This Italian machine was made by Edoardo Mascagni, son of the opera composer Pietro Mascagni. Equipped with triangular duplex frames, the Junior housed its own 174cc and 346cc two-stroke engines, later models also 173cc to 499cc sv and ohv JAP and 248cc and 348cc ohv Blackburne engines. The end came when Edoardo Mascagni lost his life with Italian forces in Abyssinia.

JUNO / *England 1911–1923*
Small assembler. When demand rose, it was the Birmingham-based Sun motorcycle factory which supplied the London-based Juno works with frames. Among the engines used were the 269cc Villiers, 597cc Precision and 770cc V-twin JAP. There was also a 147cc Villiers-engined model. If required Juno were also prepared to supply motorcycles equipped with other proprietary engines.

JUPP / *England 1921–1924*
The Baker-designed Jupp was a cross between a scooter and a motorcycle. It had an open frame, rear suspension and a 269cc Liberty two-stroke engine.

246cc Jurisch (TS four-cylinder w/c racer Prototype) 1926

JURISCH / *Germany 1926–1930*
The designer/producer of this very unorthodox two-stroke was Carl Jurisch, a well-known technician and racing motorist. His own 248cc double-piston twin-cylinder racing machine was watercooled and supercharged. Jurisch was a two-stroke specialist, who rode many such machines including Bekamo, Puch and DKW.

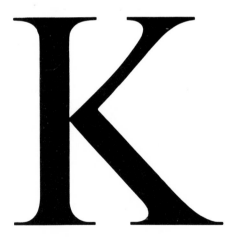

K

KADI / *Germany 1924–1930*
Small producer of good 198cc sv machines and of 498cc versions with the three-valve ohc Küchen proprietary single-cylinder engine.

KANTO / *Japan 1957–1960*
Was one of the many Japanese factories which produced two-strokes, in this case a 124cc model only.

KAPTEIN / *The Netherlands 1938–1951*
Was closely connected with the French Motobecane factory and fitted 123cc sv and 173cc ohv Motobecane engines into his machines, which had many other parts from that source.

KARÜ / *Germany 1922–1924*
Designed by Dr. Karl Rühmer, who was also behind SMW motorcycles, these machines had opposing flat-twin engines. One was the 398cc

398cc Karü (sv flat-twin Bosch-Douglas) 1923

Bosch-Douglas, built by SMW under licence, the other the 492cc BMW flat-twin.

KATAKURA / *Japan late 1950s to late 1960s*
Built a variety of two-strokes, including mofas, mopeds etc., from 48cc to 248cc.

KATHO / *Germany 1923–1925*
Assembler of 198cc sv machines with engines supplied by Alba.

KAUBA / *Austria 1953–1955*
Scooters with 98cc and 124cc Rotax-Sachs engines, built in limited numbers.

KAWASAKI/*Japan 1949–*

Famous group of factories, existing since 1878 when the Kawasaki Dockyard was established at Tokyo. Produced since 1907 locomotives, coaches, freight cars, bridge trusses, marine transportation etc. In 1937 the Kawasaki Aircraft Company was established and it was at the former aircraft plant at Akashi where in 1949/1950 the first motorcycle, the 148cc KE with an ohv engine, was built. In 1954 Kawasaki engineers built 58cc two-stroke engines for a subsidiary company, Kawasaki Meihatsu Industry. Late in 1960, Kawasaki Aircraft Co., Ltd. established an assembly plant in Kobe to develop and mass-produce motorcycles. The first machine made was a 123cc two-stroke with 8 bhp at 6500 rpm, built in 1961. Soon afterwards, a technical and sales agreement was made with the old Meguro motorcycle factory, where they produced among others a very BSA-like 498cc vertical ohv twin. Various 123cc models also left the works,

among them moto-cross and racing versions. New 85cc and 246cc two-strokes were introduced in 1964 and the following year the first 49cc Kawasaki was introduced. An improved 246cc machine with disc-valves and two cylinders which produced 31 bhp came into production in 1966. The range included new 89cc, 98cc, 118cc and 123cc two-strokes. The first four-stroke was the 646cc Meguro-based ohv vertical twin, built in 1967. A Kawasaki group reorganisation in 1969 led to new models. These included a 497cc 3-cylinder two-stroke with 60 bhp and CDI ignition and a 348cc off-road machine. It was at that period that a 123cc Kawasaki, ridden by Dave Simmonds, became World Champion in road races. New 498cc racing models as well as the 123cc F6, 175cc F7 and 248cc F8 off-the-road machines came into production in 1970. After the success of the 498cc H1R racer, Kawasaki developed in 1971 the 746cc 3-cylinder series with the Mach IV model

H2, the 348cc model S2 and 248cc model S1.

A racing version of the 746cc H2, called the H2R, was developed and became the most successful of all Kawasaki road racers. In 1972 Kawasaki range consisted of 89cc, 124cc, 174cc and 247cc singles; 247cc and 338cc vertical inclined twins and 346cc and 498cc three-cylinder (also vertical and inclined to the front) in-line and transverse-mounted engines. The bigger was the 746cc Mach IV with 74 bhp at 6800 rpm and 125 mph top speed. Many different models followed. There were new 99cc two-strokes and in 1972 the first Kawasaki four-stroke, not counting earlier Meguro models. This 903cc ohc four-cylinder model had the aircooled in-line engine — like the three-cylinder two-strokes — transverse-mounted in the frame. It had 66mm bore and stroke, four Mikuni carburettors and 82 bhp at 8500 rpm. All two-stroke versions had until 1972 rotary disc inlet ports; new versions became piston-port two-stroke power units. The

85cc Kawasaki (TS) 1965   123cc Kawasaki (TS racer) 1966

652cc Kawasaki (dohc four-cylinder 'Z 650') 1977

498cc Kawasaki (TS three-cylinder 'KH 500') 1977   748cc Kawasaki Mach IV Model H2 1972

1015cc Kawasaki (dohc four-cylinder 'Z 1000') 1977

124cc Kawasaki (TS 'Enduro') 1977

398cc Kawasaki (ohc two-cylinder 'Z 400') 1977

main 1974 Kawasaki production programme included a 73cc Mini-bike, 99cc road and off-the-road models, 124cc off-road versions, 246cc moto-cross singles and also enduro models, which were available with 346cc single-cylinder two-stroke engines. Others included 249cc, 346cc, 498cc and 748cc three-cylinder two-strokes. The four-stroke range was increased by a 746cc ohc four-cylinder model with 69 bhp at 9000 rpm; mainly because in Japan motorcycles with more than 750cc capacity are not permitted. Main destination for the 903cc Four was always America.

From Japanese factories one can expect many changes and many new models in a comparatively short period. Kawasaki Heavy Industries Ltd. Motorcycle Division in Tokyo lately increased the range of four-strokes. The biggest is the Z1000 with a 1015cc four-cylinder engine, developing 85 bhp at 8000 rpm. A 652cc version has 67 bhp at 8500 rpm. Both use double ohc, while vertical twin 398cc and 745cc Kawasakis with 36 bhp and 51 bhp respectively have only one ohc. The newest model is a 198cc (chain-driven ohc) single. Three-cylinder two-strokes include

249cc, 398cc and 498cc models, while the biggest single-cylinder two-stroke is a 401cc moto-cross model with 82mm bore, 76mm stroke and 42 bhp at 7000 rpm. Together with Honda, Yamaha and Suzuki, Kawasaki is one of the leading motorcycle factories in Japan.

KC / *Germany 1921–1924*
Designed by the motoring pioneer Fritz Kirchheim, the first KC product was a 105cc rotary-valve two-stroke bicycle engine with 1·2 hp at

257cc KC (TS flat-twin) 1923

2100 rpm. Another product by KC—which stood for Kirchheim & Co.—was an opposing flat-twin motorcycle with 257cc. This was also a two-stroke. Most parts including even the carburettor were made by KC.

KELLER / *Switzerland 1930–1932*
Equipped with a triangular duplex frame of strong design, the 347cc Keller had its own sv single-cylinder unit-design engine of very clean lines. It could be taken very easily out of the frame and dismantled using very few tools. Still, the Keller was not very successful.

KEMPTON / *England 1921–1922*
Lightweight machines and scooters with 124cc ohv engines supplied by ABC.

KENI / *Germany 1921–1923*
Yet another Berlin-based producer of two-stroke machines. The Kempff-designed machines had 145cc and 158cc deflector-type, three-port engines.

145cc Keni (TS) 1923

KENZLER-WAVERLEY / *America 1910–1914*
Closely connected with Jefferson, Kenzler-Waverley also produced singles and V-twins with their own ohv engines.

KENILWORTH / *England 1919–1924*
Produced orthodox motorcycles with 293cc single-cylinder sv JAP engines. Another product was a scooter, supplied with various engines including the 143cc ohv Norman, 269cc Villiers and 293cc JAP. They had front and rear suspension and a hand starter. Despite the advanced design, sales figures did not show any scooter boom.

KERRY / *England 1902–early 1960s*
Various sources claim that the first Kerry machines—equipped with Kelecom and FN engines—were made in Belgium for the London-based East London Rubber Co., who sold these machines in England. From 1910 onward Kerrys were made at the Abingdon factory with 499cc

347cc Keller (sv) 1932

sv single-cylinder and 670cc V-twin sv engines. Production finished when WWI broke out, but entirely different Kerry machines—49cc mopeds—appeared in the late 1950s.

KESTREL / *England 1903*
Assembled machines with 211cc Minerva and MMC engines.

KG / *Germany 1919–1932*
Very advanced single-cylinder design by the Krieger brothers and Franz Gnädig. The first models had 503cc ioe, later ones 499cc ohv unit-design engines with shaft drive to the rear wheel. Early models had leaf-spring forks; from 1922 onwards, girder forks were used. At that date, the KG was being built by the Cito works of Suhl in Thuringia, which in 1923 became part of the Allright factory at Cologne. When they stopped building motorcycles, Paul Henkel—formerly with Cito—bought in 1927 the whole design including the production equipment and moved it to his works at Mäbendorf near Suhl. So the original KG became the Cito-KG, the Allright-KG and eventually the Henkel-KG, but was after 1927 only a shadow of the big make of the early 1920s. Rudi Albert had it redesigned in 1924 and fitted with a horizontal shaft, but it could not compete with the latest BMW and other designs. Until the mid-1920s these machines

498cc KG (ohv shaft-drive) 1924

gained many successes in sporting events. Leading riders were Max and Oskar Krieger, Hemming, Kniebecke, Faust, Ehrlenbruch, Greifzu, Roggebuck and others. When Allright took over, the Krieger brothers and Gnädig left the factory. The Kriegers afterwards built 'Original Krieger' motorcycles with Blackburne engines, and Gnädig created new 348cc ohv singles, bearing his name and eventually built by the Diamant works.

KIEFT / *England 1955–1957*
Produced small sports and racing cars and sold Hercules (Nuremberg-built) 147cc and 198cc scooters and 197cc two-stroke Sachs-engined motorcycles in England under the Kieft trade mark.

KILEAR / *Czechoslovakia 1924–1926*
Brno-based machine factory which built 247cc two-stroke machines with three-port, deflector-type engines.

KING / *England 1901–1907*
Pioneer who built three-wheelers and afterwards motorcycles. Both had De Dion Bouton engines, the motorcycles also Minerva, MMC, DAW, Antoine, Sarolea and other power units.

KING-JAP / *Germany 1928–1931*
Although built in Germany, most parts—including the 198cc, 346cc, 490cc and 545cc sv and ohv JAP engines—came from England.

KINGSBURY / *England 1919–1923*
Aircraft engine factory, which produced after WWI small cars, scooters not unlike the Autoped and Krupp and also 261cc motorcycles with their own engines.

KINGSWAY / *England 1921–1923*
Motorcycles of simple design with 293cc sv JAP engines.

K&K / *Germany 1924–1925*
Two-stroke machines with own 170cc and 289cc three-port engines.

KLOTZ / *Germany 1923–1926*
Excellent 246cc two-stroke three-port deflector-type engines of their own manufacture in modern frames (for that period) of good design. Ridden by Gebhardt and others, Klotz machines gained many successes in trials and races. Connected with Klotz was Wilhelm Gutbrod, who after the demise of the Klotz make founded the Standard motorcycle factory.

246cc Klotz (TS) 1925

KM / *Germany 1924–1926*
Produced 142cc and 159cc two-stroke machines with own three-port engines in limited numbers.

KMB / *Germany 1923–1926*
Built single-cylinder machines with 4·2 hp two-valve and 6 hp four-valve engines of own design and manufacture.

4.2 hp KMB (sv) 1923

KMS / *Germany 1922–1924*
Interesting 196cc ohv singles with the valves in a sloping position. These engines were of own design and manufacture. A smaller model had the 142cc Grade two-stroke power unit.

KÖBO / *Germany 1923–1926*
Köhler & Bovenkamp at Barmen-Hatzfeld was a well-known factory for chains. Motorcycles made by this company had own 276cc two-stroke

engines and never gained the reputation of the chains made by Köbo.

KOCH / *Czechoslovakia 1934–1935*
When the Praga factory decided to give up manufacture of motorcycles, chief designer J. F. Koch founded his own factory. There he built very advanced 348cc unit-design ohc singles with four-speed gear-boxes. Production was on a limited scale.

KOEHLER-ESCOFFIER / *France 1912–1957*
Designed by Roger Guignet, Koehler-Escoffier machines became famous during the 1920s with

347cc Koehler-Escoffier (ohv) 1929

497cc Koehler-Escoffier (ohc) 1929

a 996cc V-twin which had — as the only machine of this capacity and configuration in the world — an ohc engine of their own design and manufacture. There was also a 498cc ohc single with a sloping cylinder. Other versions had 347cc and

497cc MAG and Chaise single-cylinder ohv engines. There was a great similarity with Monet-Goyon motorcycles, after the MG factory at Macon took over the Guignet works in 1929. After 1945 Monet Goyon and Koehler-Escoffier motorcycles were near-identical. Most models had 98cc to 248cc Villiers two-stroke engines with J. A. Gregoire rear suspension. Among successful Koehler-Escoffier riders were the famous George Monneret and Jean Eddoura.

KOFA / *Germany 1923–1925*
Assembled machines with 283cc two-stroke engines.

KOHOUT / *Czechoslovakia 1904–1906*
Minerva and Fafnir-engined 2·5 hp and 2·75 hp single-cylinder machines.

KOLIBRI / *Germany 1923–1930*
A good 110cc two-stroke attachment engine supplied for existing bicycles and also with the firm's own bicycle.

KOMÁR / *Poland late 1950s to late 1960s*
Nationalised producer of various 48cc two-stroke mopeds.

KOMET / *Germany 1902–1905*
Originally a bicycle factory, Komet was among the first producers of two-stroke motorcycles in Germany. These engines were made under French Ixion licence and had from 1 hp to 4 hp.

KONDOR / *Germany 1924–1925*
A two-model range which consisted of a 3 hp version with an Ideal sv engine and a 3·5 hp

3 hp Komet (TS) 1905

model, which had a Simplex single-cylinder two-stroke power unit.

KOSTER (KS) / *Germany 1923–1925*
Unorthodox lightweight with a frame made partly from pressed steel, partly from tubes. It was supplied with 123cc Bekamo or with 144cc Cockerell engines. The wheels were disc wheels, the drives (chain and belt) fully enclosed while the petrol tank formed the top part of the frame.

KOVROVETZ / *early 1960s*
Was for a few years the leading 123cc and 174cc two-stroke single in Russia. Eventually superseded by the Voskhod.

KR / *Germany 1924–1925*
Successor to the Karü, the KR had also the old 492cc sv flat-twin BMW proprietary engines; another model was the big 998cc V-twin MAG with ioe valves and a duplex cradle frame.

KR / *Germany 1930–1933*
Although both KR machines were made at Munich, they had nothing in common. This one was an assembled machine with 198cc sv and ohv as well as 298cc sv engines made by JAP.

KRAMMER / *Austria 1926–1929*
Vienna-based Rudolf Krammer's first machines had 172cc Villiers two-stroke engines. His 496cc ohv models had the rare single-cylinder Anzani or the MAG engine; the 996cc V-twin versions housed 8-valve Anzani ohv engines. The production was on a limited scale.

497cc Krammer (ohv Anzani engine) 1928

KRASNY-OKTOBR / *Russia 1930–1934*
These were the first motorcycles made in large numbers in Russia. They were not unlike the German DKW machines of that period and had 296cc two-stroke engines.

KREIDLER / *Germany 1951–*
Concentrated on the production of 50cc machines, including mofas, mopeds etc. As a result of steady development, the motorcycles — equipped with flat two-stroke engines of 40mm bore, 39·7mm

129cc Koster (KS) (TS Bekamo engine) 1925

49cc Kreidler (TS 'Florett Sport') 1977

49cc Kreidler (TS 'Super TS') 1966

49cc Kreidler (TS 'Florett Touring') 1974

stroke and 6·25 hp at 8500 rpm — are among the leaders in this class. The Kreidler frames are made from pressed steel, the wheels on some models from light alloy. Top speed of the Florett is around 53 mph. Designed by chief engineer Hilber, Kreidler machines include some very fast 49cc racing machines which have broken world records. Among leading riders were Anscheidt, Kunz, Rittenberger, Blatter, Zeebroeck, Lazzarini and many others.

KRIEGER (ORIGINAL KRIEGER) / Germany 1925–1926
After the Krieger brothers left the KG factory (taken over by Allright), they founded at Suhl in Thuringia another motorcycle factory, this time with the Original Krieger trade mark. With frames very similar to the KG, this new machine had a 347cc sv Blackburne engine, but failed to gain much popularity. Interesting is the fact that the Kriegers also offered their old 499cc ohv single with its shaft drive until 1926, although the machine was made by then at the Allright-owned Cito factory at Suhl. They also produced frames for other companies and a Hamburg company supplied KG frames with various JAP engines.

KROBOTH / Germany 1951–1954
Produced scooters of sound design with 98cc, 147cc and 173cc Sachs two-stroke engines. Was already during the 1920s connected with motorcycles, when he not only raced on Roconova and Gillet-Herstal machines, but when the K&R (Kroboth & Richter) motorcycle was made. In the 1930s he was also behind the design of Favorit and Kroboth light cars.

KRS / Germany 1921–1926
Assembler, who fitted 148cc and 198cc ohv Paqué proprietary engines and also the 293cc Bosch-Douglas flat twin, made under licence by SMW.

KRUPP / Germany 1919–1921
The autoped-like scooters — called at that time Motorläufer in Germany — had 185cc and 198cc engines fitted outside the small front wheel. Producing scooters was not a good proposition then and even the financially strong Krupp group was not in the trade for long.

KSB / Germany 1924–1929
Small, but very active make. Fitted a variety of engines into own frames. These included the 142cc and 173cc DKW, 348cc ohv Kühne, 248cc Blackburne and eventually the 248cc and 490cc sv and ohv JAP single-cylinder.

KTM / Austria 1953–
Became in a comparatively short time one of Europe's leading factories. Produced 98cc Rotax-engined two-strokes, afterwards also models with 123cc and 147cc as well as scooters and eventually also 49cc mofas, mopeds, mokicks.

49cc KTM (TS Sachs 'Comet GP 50RS) 1977

49cc KTM (TS Sachs 'Comet') 1971

246cc KTM (TS Own eng. '250 GS') 1977

Moiseev, Vladimir Kavinov, Jaak van Velthven, Alessandro Gritti, Heino Buse, Walter Luft, Erwin Lechner, etc. In the USA, KTM machines are known as Penton after the importer Jack Penton who, like his sons, rides them successfully in sporting events. Over the years KTM has won many trials and moto-cross events.

KULI / *Germany 1922–1924*
Yet another Berlin-based producer of two-stroke machines with 145cc and 198cc. Limited output.

KUMFURT / *England 1914–1916*
With frames made under Waigh patents, these machines housed 269cc Villiers and 496cc Precision V-twin engines.

KURIER / *Germany 1921–1924*
Designed by Curt Hanfland, these 147cc two-stroke engines had square-finned barrels. Hanfland supplied such engines also to other manufacturers, including the Bavarian Flink.

KURRAS / *Germany 1925–1927*
The Kurras sport machines had triangular frames with watercooled 173cc Bekamo two-stroke engines, which had an additional pumping piston at the bottom of the crankcase. Not many were actually made.

KV / *Germany 1924–1927*
Simple ohv machines with own 197cc and 246cc single-cylinder engines.

KYNOCH / *England 1912–1913*
Now an unknown make, but Kynoch was once a famous arms factory at Birmingham. Produced mainly 488cc single-cylinder and 770cc V-twin sv machines with own engines of first class design and quality. Kynoch's Perry Barr factory housed afterwards the Amal carburettor works.

346cc KZ (ohv Kühne engine) 1925

KZ / *Germany 1924–1925*
Assembler, who fitted besides 198cc sv Alba engines, also 348cc ohv engines, made by Kühne at Dresden. They were designed by Franz Gnädig, formerly of KG (Krieger-Gnädig) fame.

Rotax, originally a Sachs branch factory, produced two-strokes only and is now part of the Canadian Bombardier group. Puch also supplied some engines to KTM, where they built Apfelbeck-designed 124cc ohc racing machines. Afterwards the up-coming factory concentrated more on trials and moto-cross machines and gained great fame in events. The present range includes different automatic mofas and mopeds, 49cc motorcycles of sporting appearance, 123cc Sachs-engined models and the successful 123cc, 246cc, and 352cc moto-cross machines. Trials models are available with 98cc and 123cc Sachs six-speed engines and with KTM's own 173cc, 246cc, 346cc and 355cc two-stroke engines. The Sachs-engined models have 16 and 19 bhp at 8200 rpm, the others 24 bhp at 8300 rpm, 32 bhp at 7200 rpm and 36 and 39 bhp at 6800 rpm. And there is also a 124cc trials model with a 23 bhp at 9200 rpm KTM engine. Also the moto-cross machines are powered by own KTM engines of 24 bhp, 36 bhp and 44 bhp. Leading riders: Gennadij

L

L-300/*Russia 1932–*
Produced DKW-like 294cc and 346cc two-strokes and — in 1940 — also a 348cc single-cylinder machine. The two-strokes were built in large numbers for the Russian forces.

LABOR/*France 1908–1960*
One of the many motorcycle factories belonging to the Alcyon group of companies. Labor produced 98cc to 248cc two-strokes and mainly ohv models from 174cc to 498cc.

LADETTO (LADETTO & BLATTO)/*Italy 1923–1932*
Like other Italian factories, Ladetto's first machines were 123cc and 173cc two-strokes. After Emilio and Giovanni Ladetto were joined by Angelo Blatto they built potent 173cc sv and ohv models and a 247cc sv machine with own engines. Alfredo Panella won his class in the 1928 Grand Prix of Europe at the Meyrin Circuit in Switzerland, where the 173cc Ladetto & Blatto was extremely fast. Blatto left the Turin-based factory in 1930.

LADIES PACER/*England 1914*
Built in Guernsey, this open-framed machine housed a 110cc two-stroke engine, made by JES at Gloucester.

LADY/*Belgium 1925–1938*
Designed by Lambert van Ouwerkerk, these well-made machines had 172cc to 498cc proprietary engines made by Villiers, MAG, Blackburne, JAP and Python (Rudge) and — on some models — already in 1932 a good rear suspension.

LAFOUR & NOUGIER/*France 1927–1936*
A variety of engines made by Aubier-Dunne, Chaise, Stainless, Train, Villiers and JAP powered these machines, from 98cc to 498cc capacity.

LAG/*Austria 1921–1929*
The first products were 118cc and 148cc two-stroke bicycle engines. Afterwards a few JAP engines with 346cc and 490cc were fitted into LAG frames. A 246cc two-stroke came into production in 1925, but from 1927 until the demise of motorcycle manufacture, only a single model with a 346cc two-stroke engine was made by the Liesing (near Vienna) factory. They fitted these engines also to Draisines. A 348cc model with an ohc engine, designed by LAG designer Ludwig Stein, never came into quantity production. The two-strokes had 70mm bore, 90mm stroke, Tiger forks, Sturmey-Archer 3-speed gearboxes and — in the last models — modern saddle tanks.

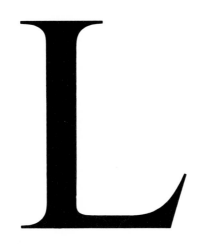
346cc LAG (TS) 1928

LA GALBAI/*Italy 1921–1925*
Equipped with own 276cc, 301 and 347cc single-cylinder and 492cc V-twin two-stroke engines of own design and manufacture, these machines were not well-known internationally.

LAGONDA/*England 1902–1905*
The Lagonda factory owner was an American, W. 'Bill' Gunn, who came to England to build motor vehicles. His first products were three wheelers, followed by cars and motorcycles. Most had De Dion, MMC or Minerva engines.

L'ALBA/*Italy 1924–1926*
Slightly modified German 198cc Alba sv machines, assembled at Milan by Valeri.

LA LORRAINE/*France 1922–1925*
Lightweight machines with own two-stroke engines from 98cc to 248cc.

LAMAUDIÈRE/*France 1901–1907*
Used big engines and there was even a single-cylinder engine with a capacity of 942cc.

LAMBRETTA/*Italy (Spain) 1946–*
The Innocenti-built Lambretta was one of the first and most successful scooters on the international market. It had engines from 123cc to 198cc and there were also 49cc mopeds and for a short period also 123cc motorcycles. A special racing machine bearing the name Lambretta and designed by the famous Salmaggi was a 248cc transverse-mounted double ohc V-twin. Pagani rode it in a few races during the early 1950s.

LA MONDIALE/*Belgium 1924–1933*
These machines had nothing in common with the Italian-built Mondial. Blavier's La Mondiale, built at Brussels, was one of the first machines using a pressed steel frame and fork. The two-stroke engines had 308cc (75mm × 68mm bore/stroke) and 349cc (75mm × 79mm bore/stroke); bigger versions used 346cc and 498cc Chaise ohc engines. There was also a 347cc Villiers-engined model and there were JAP-engined 346cc (70mm × 90mm bore/stroke) and 490cc (85·7mm × 85mm bore/stroke) sv and ohv singles. Thanks to triangular frames, La

496cc La Mondiale (ohc Chaise engine) 1928

Mondiale machines had a very low saddle position. Among the works riders were Fondu and Schuoppe, who rode 248cc ohv racing machines with JAP engines.

LAMPO / *Italy 1925–1927*
Well-designed lightweight machines with 123cc, 173cc, 198cc and 247cc two-stroke and 173cc ohv engines. The last came from Piazza.

LANCER / *England c1904*
Minerva, MMC and their own engines powered these 2 hp, 2·75 hp and 3·5 hp machines.

LANCER / *Japan 1957–early 1960s*
Produced two-stroke machines up to 248cc and built eventually a Lilac-like 248cc V-twin, which was transverse-mounted in the frame and had shaft drive to the rear wheel.

LANCO / *Austria 1922–1926*
The best-known model built by Lanco was the Josef Wild-designed 496cc machine with its own ohv single-cylinder engine. There was also an sv

496cc Lanco (ohv) 1924

version and earlier models had 492cc, 746cc and 986cc ioe MAG engines.

LANDI / *Italy 1923–1926*
Built 122cc and 172cc machines with own two-stroke three-port deflector-type engines.

LA PANTHERRE / *France 1928–1932*
Chiefly assembled orthodox machines with 346cc and 490cc sv and ohv JAP engines.

LAPIZE / *France 1930–1937*
Another small but active factory. Fitted different engines, including Aubier-Dunne, LMP, JAP and others into machines from 98cc to 498cc.

LATSCHA / *France 1948–1953*
Assembler, who fitted 98cc and 123cc Aubier-Dunne two-stroke engines into own frames.

LAURIN & KLEMENT / *Austria (Czechoslovakia) 1899–1908*
One of the leading motorcycle factories in the early years, Laurin & Klement produced singles, V-twins and even four-cylinder in-line machines. Some models were watercooled. The first models had the engine above the front wheel; thereafter a wide variety of engine placements were designed. Famous were the single-cylinder models BZ with 2·5 hp, L with 2·75–3 hp and BZP with 2·5 hp. The model CC was a V-twin with 3 hp and front suspension, the CCD a stronger version

4 hp Laurin & Klement (sv Type 'CCD' V-twin) 1904

3 hp Laurin & Klement (sv Type 'B') 1903

5 hp Laurin & Klement (sv Type 'CCCC II') 1905

75cc Laverda (ohv) 1951

98cc Laverda (ohv) 1956

with 3·5 to 4 hp and the CCRW was a water-cooled 4·5 to 5 hp machine. The first four-in-line was built in 1905. Motorcycle production stopped when Laurin & Klement concentrated in 1908 on car production. The L&K motorcycles—then an Austrian make—were built in Germany with the Germania trade mark under licence. In the mid-1920s, Laurin & Klement was bought by the Skoda works. While producing motorcycles, the factory won many big races with riders who included Vondřich, Podsedníček, Toman, Count Kolowrat, Merfeit etc.

L'AVENIR/ *Belgium 1959–*
Producer of 49cc mofas, mopeds etc. with HMW and Sachs engines.

LAVERDA/ *Italy 1950–*
Was originally a factory for agricultural machinery. The first motorcycles were 74cc ohv singles; afterwards there were 49cc and 99cc ohv singles. During the late 1960s, Francesco Laverda built a 744cc vertical-twin, which had a chain-driven overhead camshaft and 52 bhp at 6900 rpm. A sporting version, the 750S, had an engine which developed 60 bhp at 6600 rpm and reached 120 mph. Further development brought the 750 SFC—again with 80mm bore and 74mm stroke

124cc Laverda (ohv 'Trail') 1969

744cc Laverda (ohc twin Model 750 S) 1969

191

—with 70 bhp at 7300 rpm and in 1972 also a 980cc double-ohc three-cylinder, the Laverda 1000, with 75mm bore, 74mm stroke and 80 bhp at 7200 rpm. The top speed: 127·5 mph. Two new 744cc twins came into production in 1974; the SF with 61 bhp at 7000 rpm and the SFC with 75 bhp at 8000 rpm. They were followed by the GTL, with 52 bhp at 6900 rpm. Completely new was a 247cc two-stroke single, built for moto-cross and trials. It had 68mm bore and stroke and 26 bhp at 7000 rpm. Another new Laverda came in 1975, the four-valve 496cc twin ohc model, more or less a smaller version of the 744cc twin. This new twin had 72mm bore, 61mm stroke and 44 bhp. It was built in a new up-to-date Laverda factory at Breganze (Vicenza). A new 124cc two-stroke single, with 55mm bore and 52mm stroke, like the 247cc single is intended for moto-cross and trials.

LAZZATI / Italy 1899–1904
The Milan factory was among the first in Italy producing motorcycles. The De Dion engines were mounted into strengthened bicycle frames.

L&C / London c1904
Small assembler, who fitted De Dion, Minerva and Antoine engines.

LDR / Germany 1922–1925
Designed by Josef Herz, the 548cc sv single was a primitive design, although it had a low saddle position. The engine had an outside flywheel and neither chain was sufficiently enclosed. Early machines had belt drive to the rear wheel.

LEA FRANCIS / England 1911–1926
George Bernard Shaw was one of the Lea Francis customers. He rode a MAG-engined 592cc ioe V-twin. Other models had 496cc versions of the same make of engine. Until 1920, the Coventry-based car and motorcycle factory also fitted V-twin sv JAP engines — including 746cc power units — into their own frames.

744cc Laverda (ohc twin Model 750 SF2) 1974

980cc Laverda (ohc) 1972

497cc Laverda two-cylinder 1977

592cc Lea-Francis (ioe V-twin MAG) 1923

LEBELT / Germany 1924–1925
Small producer of machines with own 3·8 hp two-stroke and 4·6 hp sv engines.

LECCE / Italy 1930–1932
Built 173cc ohv machines with modified Swiss-made Moser engines. Otello Albanese, the Lecce boss, modified the cylinder-heads to V-valves.

LE FRANCAISE-DIAMANT / France 1912–1959
Another Alcyon-owned motorcycle producer, who built machines from 98cc to 498cc. After the war, only two-strokes up to 248cc were made.

LEGNANO / Italy 1954–
Concentrated on mopeds, mofas and other lightweights with 49cc engines, made mainly by Sachs and Minarelli.

LE GRIMPEUR / France c1900–1932
Produced a variety of machines from 98cc two-strokes to big V-twins with engines made by MAG, JAP, Aubier-Dunne, Stainless, Chaise etc. Another French factory, Dresch bought Le Grimpeur in the late 1920s.

LEIFA / Germany 1924–1925
Lightweights with 148cc sv engines, built by a former shipyard.

LELIOR / *France 1922–1924*
Built an Evans-like 246cc two-stroke machine and also a 174cc two-stroke flat-twin.

LEM / *Italy 1974–*
Young factory which produced a wide range of 47cc and 49cc mofas, mopeds and lightweight motorcycles.

LEONARD / *England 1903–1906*
Small assembler of motorcycles with Minerva, MMC and Fafnir engines.

LEONARDO FRERA / *Italy 1930–1934*
When Frera founder Corrado Frera retired in 1929 and Emilio Fossio took over the famous factory, young Leonard Frera became technical director. Two years later he left and founded his own motorcycle works at Tradate. He built there 173cc to 346cc sv and ohv machines with JAP single-cylinder engines.

LEOPARD / *Germany 1921–1926*
Produced 248cc and 346cc two-strokes with their own engines, afterwards also 248cc and 348cc ohv models.

LEPROTTO / *Italy 1951–1954*
Well-made two and four-stroke (ohv) models of 123cc, 158cc and 198cc capacity.

LETHBRIDGE / *England 1922–1923*
Small assembler of machines with 247cc and 269cc Villiers two-stroke three-port engines.

LETO / *Germany 1926–1928*
Interesting design with a frame made of pressed steel, which was welded together and included the petrol tank. Lehmann, the designer, fitted 173cc and 198cc Rinne two-stroke engines into his unusual frames.

LE VACK / *England 1923*
Famous designer-rider Herbert Le Vack — who was also with JAP, Duzmo, New Hudson, Indian, Motosacoche — built for a short period his own 346cc ohv single-cylinder machines, using JAP engines.

LEVIS / *England 1911–1940*
For many years one of England's leading manufacturers of two-stroke machines. Built well-made 211cc and 246cc three-port single-cylinder

246cc Levis (TS Model 'K') 1926

machines, including sporting versions. Most had 67mm bore and 70mm stroke. There was also a six-port model and from 1928 onward Levis produced 247cc (67mm × 70mm bore/stroke) and 346cc (70mm × 90mm bore/stroke) four-stroke ohv machines and eventually also 498cc ohv four-strokes. There was for a short period a 346cc sv single and a 247cc ohc single with chain drive to the overhead camshafts. Levis two-strokes, ridden by Geoff Davison, R. O. Clark,

246cc Levis (TS Model 'O') 1927

247cc Levis (ohv Model 'B') 1930

Phil Pike and others, won many races including the 1922 Lightweight TT, while four-strokes excelled as a result of the excellent torque and the wide power band. Percy Hunt rode 346cc versions successfully in races, while Bob Foster gained just before WWII many wins with a 598cc ohv Levis in trials and moto-cross. The factory also built many prototypes, including flat-twin two-strokes, 173cc single-cylinder racing versions, 247cc machines with additional pumping cylinders and others. Responsible for

346cc Levis (ohv Model 'A2') 1930

Percy Hunt, successful rider for Levis, on his 346cc machine

the Levis design department for many years was Bob Newey, brother-in-law of the Butterfield brothers, who owned the factory.

LFG / *Germany 1921–1925*
The first product of this former airship producer was a separate small wheel with a 163·5cc sv engine, which could be attached to any bicycle. More unorthodox was a 305cc single-cylinder two-stroke motorcycle, which had an airship-like body.

LGC / *England 1926–1932*
Made at Birmingham by the Leonard Gundle Motor Co., a manufacturer of delivery three-wheelers, the machine had a very sporting appearance, but was never built in large quantities. Engines fitted were the 247cc Villiers, 293cc sv JAP and both 346cc sv and ohv JAP single-cylinder versions.

LIAUDOIS / *France 1923–1927*
Assembled machines with Train two-stroke engines from 98cc to 173cc.

LIBERATOR / *France 1902–late 1920s*
Old producer who fitted mainly Antoine, Saro lea and JAP proprietary engines.

LIBERIA / *France 1920–1965*
Bicycle factory which produced motorcycles with mainly Aubier-Dunne two-stroke engines from 98cc to 248cc.

LILAC / *Japan 1952–1961*
Was a leading make and built many expensive and luxurious models. Among them were shaft-driven 246cc flat and transverse-mounted ohv V-twins, 173cc ohv singles with shaft drive, etc. Lilac produced also 49cc mopeds, mofas, etc.

246cc Lilac (ohv transverse V-twin) 1960

LILIPUT / *Germany 1923–1926*
Assembled in a modest way motorcycles with proprietary engines made by Namapo, DKW, Baumi, Gruhn and others.

LILLIPUT / *Italy 1899–c1906*
Pioneer who fitted into bicycle frames 285cc engines with 1 hp.

LILY / *England 1906–1914*
Another assembler of motorcycles with 269cc, 293cc and 499cc engines, made by Minerva, Villiers and TDC (Cross).

LINCOLN-ELK / *England 1902–1924*
Was a well-known make. Designed by James Kirby, pre-WWI models had his own 402cc and 499cc single-cylinder sv engines. After the war, production concentrated around 349cc and 596cc sv singles and 770cc sv V-twins.

LINER – *Japan 1961*
Like Lilac, Liner also built quite expensive motorcycles. Among them were 148cc ohv

singles and a 246cc vertical twin, which had — like the Sunbeam S7 and 8 models — one cylinder behind the other. It had an ohc unit-design engine and also shaft-drive to the rear wheel.

LINSER / *Austria (Czechoslovakia) 1904–1910*
Linser motorcycles were also known under the Zeus trade mark. The range consisted of 492cc singles and 618cc V-twins with their own power units.

LINSNER / *Germany 1922–1924*
Assembled flat-twin machines with 293cc Bosch Douglas and 492cc BMW sv proprietary engines.

LINTO / *Italy 1965–1968*
Designed by the famous Lino Tonti, these 498cc vertical twins were double-ohc road racing machines, built in very limited numbers. The

5 hp Linser (sv V-twin) 1905

3½ hp Linser (sv) 1905

490cc Lloyd (ohv JAP) 1925

riders included Alberto Pagani, Jack Findlay, John Dodds and Marszowsky.

LINX / *Italy 1929–1941*
Made by a small factory, Linx motorcycles were of modern design. The engines were 173cc to 598cc sv and ohv singles, made by Blackburne, Piazza, and JAP, and the four-valve Rudge-built Python.

LION-RAPIDE / *Belgium 1936–1953*
Assembled machines with 98cc to 247cc Villiers and Ilo two-stroke engines and there were also models with the 347cc FN engine.

LITO / *Sweden 1959–1965*
Produced 498cc ohv motocross machines with modified single-cylinder BSA and Husqvarna engines. An engine, designed by Folke Manner-stedt, had 87mm bore, 83·5mm stroke, 496cc and a semi-desmodromic valve gear for the ohv. The clutch and the declutching mechanism was built into the graduated flywheel.

LITTLE GIANT / *England 1913–1915*
Assembled machines with 225cc two-stroke and 199cc sv single-cylinder Precision engines.

LLOYD / *England 1903–1923*
Heavy machines, built mainly for use in the former British Colonies. The range included 499cc and 497cc singles and 842cc V-twins, all with their own sv engines.

LLOYD / *Germany 1922–1926*
Produced a single model, a 144cc two-stroke version, only.

LLOYD / *Germany 1923–1926*
The first product was an Ottmar Cramer-designed 137cc bicycle engine. Bigger machines included 293cc, 346cc and 490cc JAP-engined sv and ohv models of typical English design and with many parts made in England.

LLOYD / *The Netherlands 1930–1931*
Was closely connected with the German DKW and Hulla factories, which supplied the 198cc two-stroke engine and (Hulla) most of the parts for the frames. The frame was made from pressed steel.

LMP / *France 1921–1931*
Was really an engine factory which built also JAP engines under licence in France. The range of LMP motorcycles included 173cc and 248cc two-strokes and sv and ohv single-cylinder models from 247cc to 497cc. Marc and CP Roleo fitted LMP engines.

LMS / *Germany 1923*
Another builder of airships, which tried to produce unorthodox motorcycles with airship-like bodies. Only very few machines, which had 142cc DKW engines, were built.

LOCOMOTIEF / *The Netherlands 1957–early 1960s*
Mopeds with 49cc Pluvier and Sachs engines.

LOHNER / *Austria 1950–1958*
Produced first class car bodies etc. and also Porsche-designed electro-motor vehicles. The scooters had 98cc and 123cc Rotax-Sachs and 198cc Ilo engines.

98cc Lohner (TS ILO Model 'Sissy') 1957

LOMOS / *Germany 1922–1924*
Early scooter with a pressed steel frame, made by DKW and afterwards by Eichler of Berlin. A 142cc DKW two-stroke engine was used.

LONDON / *England c1903*
Forgotten producer, whose machines housed De Dion, Minerva and MMC engines.

LORD / *Germany 1929–1931*
Despite the English name, a German machine with a 198cc JAP sv engine.

LORENZ / *Germany 1921–1922*
Another early scooter with a 211cc two-stroke engine which soon disappeared from the market.

LORENZ / *Germany 1921–1925*
Known also as the Rapid bicycle attachment engine, the interesting Lorenz was a 126cc two-stroke flat-twin with the cylinders set opposite. It was supplied also as a complete machine with a strengthened bicycle frame.

LORIOT / *France 1927–1930*
Bredier & Charon, a French gearbox factory, supplied units which could be attached to existing JAP proprietary engines for the use of shaft drive to the rear wheel.

LOT / *Poland 1937*
Unit-design machine with a 346cc single-cylinder two-stroke engine and shaft drive, built in limited numbers.

LOUIS CLEMENT / *France 1920–1932*
Limited production of 598cc and 996cc V-twins with own ohc engines. From 1928 onwards, manufacture concentrated around 98cc two-stroke machines.

LOUIS JANIOR / *France 1921–1924*
Heavy machines with 499cc flat-twin sv engines.

LUBE / *Spain 1949–1965*
For many years closely connected with NSU of Germany, Louis Bojarano, the head of this Spanish factory, built NSU-engined two and four-strokes from 49cc to 246cc into his own frames. Only after NSU gave up motorcycle production did Lube build their own two-strokes.

LUCAS / *Germany 1923–1924*
The first models had the 129cc Bekamo two-

126cc Lorenz (TS flat-twin bicycle engine) 1923

stroke engine with pumping cylinder; later ones their own 148cc ohv engines.

LUCER / *France 1953–1956*
Most models had 173cc AMC ohv engines, others the Aubier-Dunne two-strokes from 98cc to 173cc.

LUCIFER / *France 1928–1956*
Used a variety of the proprietary engines. These included the 98cc to 246cc two-stroke Train, 248cc to 496cc ohv MAG and Chaise and also the 498cc unit-design ohc Chaise.

LUDOLPH / *Germany 1924–1926*
Fitted own two-strokes of 247cc and 299cc into simple frames.

LUGTON / *England 1912–1914*
Limited production of 498cc machines with Precision and JAP engines.

LUPUS / *Germany 1923–1926*
The Stuttgart-based factory concentrated production on a single model with its own 148cc two-stroke engine.

LUTÈCE / *France 1921–1926*
Heavy and luxurious 997cc and 1016cc vertical twins with strong duplex frames, built much on American lines. They had shaft drive to the rear wheel. The last model was a 98cc two-stroke with belt drive.

LUTRAU / *Germany 1924–1933*
A producer of car accessories, whose two-stroke singles had 198cc, 246cc and 346cc engines of own design and manufacture. There was also a 497cc sv single-cylinder model. Designer: Ludwig Traunspurger.

348cc Latrau 1928

LUTZ / *Germany 1949–1954*
Produced 48cc and 49cc two-strokes, mainly scooters and mopeds. The last Lutz scooter had a 173cc two-stroke engine.

LUWE / *Germany 1924–1928*
Designed by Ludwig Weber, the first models had 148cc and 198cc Paqué ohv engines. There was also a version with the 198cc ohc engine made by Paqué. Other models used the 348cc ohv Kühne engine and 348cc to 746cc singles and V-twins made by JAP, MAG and Blackburne.

LWD / *Germany 1923–1926*
A small factory, which produced 197cc and 247cc sv engines and fitted them into simple tubular frames.

M

MABECO / *Germany 1923–1927*
This design was a perfect copy of the American Indian Scout. Built by Max Bernhardt & Co. at Berlin, the engines were really made by Siemens & Halske. They were 596cc and 749cc sv V-twins and in 1925 a 749cc ohv version which in racing trim had four exhaust pipes, was added. Originally green in colour, Mabecos became eventually red like the Indians of that period. This led to difficulties, as the Springfield company went to court. Mabeco was liquidated, but after a change of name from Max Bernhardt & Co. to Mabeco-Werke GmbH, they re-entered motorcyle production, still with the big Siemens & Halske Group as the main shareholder. A few 996cc ohv racing-machines and 346cc double-piston single-cylinder two-strokes built under Garelli licence were made too. Mabeco gained many racing successes with such riders as Hermann Rossner, Erich Tennigkeit, Gustav Gubela, Peter Birnholz, Rudi Arnat, Paul Kozal, Gustav Dierks, Karl Reisdorf, Hans Friedrich, Franz Heck, Konrad Leimer, André Klein and others.

749cc Mabeco (sv V-twin Model 'Luxus') 1927

749cc Mabeco (ohv V-twin Model 'Sport') 1927

MABON / *England c1905*
Strengthened bicycle frames with MMC, Fafnir and own engines. Limited production.

MABRET / *Germany 1927–1928*
Small assembler, whose machines had 346cc sv and ohv Kühne engines; a few also the 496cc Kühne sv single.

MACKLUM / *England 1920–1922*
Scooter-like machines with 2·5 hp Peco two-stroke engines. Production was on a limited scale.

MACO / *Germany 1921–1926*
Produced a variety of DKW-engined two-strokes and also 198cc sv machines with own engines.

MACQUET / *France 1951–1954*
Two-strokes with 123cc and 174cc, built into modern frames.

MADC / *Switzerland 1901–1905*
This was the original name for the 215cc Moto-sacoche bicycle-attachment engines, built by the Dufaux brothers.

MAFA / *Germany 1923–1927*
Bicycle factory which used 119cc to 246cc DKW two-stroke engines as well as the 348cc ohv and 496cc sv single-cylinder Kühne power units.

MAFALDA / *Italy 1923–1928*
Sporting two-stroke machines with own 123cc and 173cc three-port, deflector-type engines.

MAFFEIS / *Italy 1903–1935*
Like the Maserati brothers in the racing car field, the Maffeis brothers built and raced their their own product. The first Maffeis machines had Belgian 2·25 hp Sarolea engines. Maffeis chief Bernardo Maffeis later designed 348cc single-cylinder and also V-twin models, but concentrated during the 1920s on producing machines with 248cc, 348cc and 496cc sv and ohv Blackburne engines.

MAGATY/ *France 1931–1937*
Small assembler of 98cc two-stroke machines with Train and Stainless engines.

MAGDA/ *France 1933–1936*
Small production of 98cc and 123cc two-stroke machines.

MAGNAT-DEBON/ *France 1906–late 1950s*
Was among the leading French makes. Built different V-twins partly with Moto-Rêve engines in pre-1914 days. After WWI new two-strokes and single-cylinder sv and ohv models to 498cc capacity were built. Became part of Terrot in Dijon during the 1930s and had more or less identical models to the Terrot, among them, after 1945, mopeds, scooters and ohv singles up to 499cc with their own single-cylinder power units. Top rider in pre-war days was Paul Boetsch, who joined Terrot together with others when Magnat-Debon was taken over.

MAGNAT-MOSER/ *France 1906–1914*
A Magnat-Debon branch factory—also at Grenoble—which fitted Swiss Moser engines up to 746cc.

MAGNEET/*The Netherlands 1950s to early 1960s*
Moped and mofa producer. Used mainly 48cc Sachs two-stroke engines.

MAGNET/ *Germany 1901–1924*
Leading motorcycle producer in pre-1914 days, who also built own ioe and sv engines. Most famous was the 4·5 hp V-twin model.

4½ hp Magnet (sv V-twin) 1906

MAGNI/*Italy 1928–1930*
The most interesting model which appeared under this name was a 348cc ohc twin-cylinder machine with the two cylinders facing forward. Another model had a vertical 498cc single-cylinder. Both models were put into limited production by the designer Luigi Magni.

MAICO/ *Germany 1926–*
Was originally an assembler of motorcycles, mainly with 98cc and 123cc Ilo two-stroke engines. After 1945, Maico expanded and although the factory had very difficult periods in the late 1950s, they now included own engines in production. Most of them were road-going models, but also many trials and moto-cross engines, as well as complete machines. There were, besides 123cc and 149cc models, also 174cc versions with 9·5 bhp at 5600 rpm, 197cc engines with 11 bhp at 5000 rpm and there were also the 348cc and 394cc vertical twin-cylinder Taifun two-stroke models with 19 bhp and 22 bhp respectively at 5300 rpm. These streamlined twins had integral gearboxes, bores of 61mm and 65mm and a 59·5mm stroke. They had fully sprung frames with a swinging arm in front. The Maico range includes now the following rotary-disc two-stroke models: 49cc with 6·3 bhp at 8200 rpm, 245cc with 27 bhp at 780 rpm and moto-cross versions with 124cc, 247cc, 386cc, 438cc and 501cc. The last one has 48 bhp at 7300 rpm and is, like the others, a single-cylinder with a 5-speed gearbox. Only 124cc models have 6-speed gearboxes. The trials models are obtainable in identical sizes as the moto-cross versions. Maico also produces a 247cc military machine and 124cc road-racing singles with air and watercooled engines. The aircooled has 27 bhp at 11,500 rpm, the watercooled 29 bhp at the same revs. The aircooled Maico racing engines are also very popular among go-kart drivers. Maico moto-cross machines are world-famous and have won numerous championships with such riders as Weil, Bauer, Maisch Jun., Jonsson, Noyce, Sigmans, Seel, Pohl, Bender and others. Maico was always a factory which produced first-class machines in smaller numbers, hence its reputation as a manufacturer of good motorcycles.

174cc Maico (TS Model 175 SS) 1960

123cc Maico (TS Model 'MD 125' Racer) 1969

386cc Maico (TS Model 'MC 400 Moto-Cross') 1977

MAINO/ *Italy 1902–1956*
A small factory which built motorcycles in limited numbers and with interruption. In early years they fitted Swiss 2·25 hp Souverain engines; after a long period of abstaining from building motorcycles, Giovanni Maino produced after 1945 lightweights with 38cc Mosquito and Sachs and NSU engines from 98cc to 147cc.

MAJESTIC/ *England 1931–1935*
When the London-based Collier brothers of Matchless fame bought AJS in Wolverhampton, existing AJS parts were bought by Ernie Humphries, the boss of OK Supremes at Birmingham. He built the AJS machines (slightly modified) and called them Majestic. Most versions had 348cc and 498cc ohv engines.

MAJESTIC/ *Belgium 1928–1931*
Made from English components, this machine was fitted with 346cc and 490cc single-cylinder sv and ohv JAP engines, Burman gearboxes, Amal carburettors and other proprietary parts.

MAJESTIC/ *France 1927–1934*
Another assembled machine, using Train, Chaise and JAP engines up to 498cc. A sensational 498cc four-in-line model with an aircooled Train engine and a car-like bonnet over the power unit, with duplex steering, a car-like frame and rear suspension, never went into quantity production.

MAJOR/ *Italy 1947–1948*
Yet another motorcycle with a fully enclosed engine and with shaft-drive to the rear wheel. Designed by Salvatore Majorca, this machine had a 347cc engine of his own design.

MALAGUTI/ *Italy 1958–*
One of the newer Italian makes. Builds mainly a wide range of 49cc mofas, mopeds, mokicks and lightweights. Also a 123cc two-stroke with a 54mm × 54mm bore/stroke Franco-Morini engine, a modern design with optional electric starters, automatic gearchange etc.

MALANCA/ *Italy 1957–*
Produces like Malaguti a wide range of 49cc mopeds etc. and also 124cc and 149cc two-stroke machines with twin-cylinder engines. Malanca's 123cc watercooled two-stroke racer built in the mid-1970s was a very successful vertical twin.

MAMMUT/ *Germany 1925–1933*
The first models had 198cc Baumi, afterwards

346cc Mammut (sv JAP) 1925

197cc and 246cc own two-stroke engines. From 1928 onwards, Mammut used 198cc Villiers and 198cc to 497cc Blackburne engines. Mammut also built Coventry-Eagle frames under licence. They were made from pressed and rivetted steel.

198cc Mammut (sv JAP) 1931

MAMMUT/ *Germany 1953–1956*
Had nothing in common with the other Mammut. Production concentrated on 49cc mopeds and lightweights of 123cc, 147cc, 173cc and 198cc two-stroke machines with Sachs and Ilo proprietary engines. Identical to these Bielefeld-built machines were also Meister and Phänomen motorcycles, also Doppler products.

MAMOF/ *Germany 1922–1924*
Assembled machines with 145cc DKW and Grade two-stroke engines. Also small production of machines with own 155cc sv motors.

MANET/ *Czechoslovakia 1948–1967*
This factory in Slovakia is part of the nationalised Czechoslovakian motorcycle industry. The only motorcycle built under this name was an 89cc double-piston two-stroke single, designed by Vincenz Sklenař; afterwards the factory produced scooters with 123cc engines and is still working closely together with Jawa and CZ.

MANON/ *France 1903–c1906*
Strengthened bicycle frames with their own 1·5 hp engines.

MANTOVANI/ *Italy 1902–1910*
Produced 1·5 hp, 2·75 hp and 4 hp machines, of which some had watercooled engines of own manufacture.

124cc Malanca (TS Model 'Sport') 1976

199

MANURHIN/*France 1955–1962*
After DKW (Auto Union) stopped manufacture of the Hobby scooter in 1955, Manurhin took over production and supplied it with a 75cc two-stroke engine.

MANUFRANCE/*France 1951–1955*
Lightweight machines and scooters with 124cc and 174cc engines.

MARATHON/*America 1910*
A two-stroke twin with shaft drive. It has been impossible to find out if this design was marketed.

MARC/*France 1926–1951*
Well-known make which built machines of typical English design. The range included models with 247cc Staub-JAP and 347cc and 490cc sv and ohv engines made by JAP and LMP.

MARCK/*Belgium 1904–1908*
Produced single-cylinder machines with own 499cc ioe engines.

MARIANI/*Italy 1930–1934*
Interesting 496cc single-cylinder sv machines, supplied with two valves for the use of petrol and with three valves for running on naphta. They never became a world-sensation.

MARINI/*Italy 1924–1928*
Not to be confounded with Morini, Emilio Marini's machines — built in limited numbers — had 124cc two-stroke engines.

MARLOE/*England 1920–1922*
Small assembler, who fitted 346cc Precision and 348cc and 498cc sv Blackburne engines into open frames.

MARLOW/*England 1920–1922*
There have been discussions in the motorcycle press about whether this make was identical with the Marloe, which was made at Birmingham. There was really no connection with the War-wick-built Marlow, where the main production concentrated on 269cc Villiers-engined machines. Models with 346cc and 490cc JAP engines were built to order.

MARMONNIER/*France 1947–1951*
Produced mainly 124cc and 174cc machines with Aubier-Dunne engines.

MARS (MA)/*Germany 1903–1957*
Swiss Zedel and German Fafnir engines powered Mars motorcycles built in Nuremberg before WWI. Fame came in 1920 when Franzenberg designed the famous white Mars with a box frame made from welded and rivetted pressed steel. The engine was exclusively made by the Maybach car and aircraft engine factory for Mars. It was a 956cc sv flat twin with opposing cylinders. The first models had a two-speed gearbox with two chains to the rear wheel; from 1927 onwards, a three-speed gearbox was used. There was a hand starter below the low saddle; the gear change was inside the petrol tank and so was the tool kit. Early models had a swinging arm on the front, later ones a Druid-like Tiger fork. Half of the rear wheel was enclosed and leg shields were standard. For a couple of years, this Mars — which was delivered in white, afterwards also in green, violet and dark red — was a good seller. During the inflation in Germany the factory ran into difficulties, and production stopped between late 1924 and 1926, when Johann and Karl Müller,

two leading technicians of the Mars works, started up again with improved models. As they could not use the Mars trade mark, the machines were known for a while as 'MA'. In 1929 they added new models with MAG, later also with Sturmey-Archer, JAP and Villiers engines from 198cc to 596cc. During the 1930s, manufacture concentrated on bicycles and mopeds with 75cc and 98cc Sachs engines. There was a 60cc two-stroke lightweight with 57mm bore × 68mm stroke. Typical for all Mars and MA products was the excellent workmanship and finish. This was still true after 1945, when Rudi Albert — formerly designer with Allright and Phänomen — created the unorthodox Mars Stella, with a low frame, small-diameter wheels and rubber suspension for the fork and the saddle. Sachs supplied the 147cc, 174cc and 198cc two-stroke engines. Albert also designed the last Mars model, the sporty Monza with a Sachs 49cc engine. When the factory closed down, Gritzner took over manufacture of this lightweight. Chief designer Albert left and joined the Fichtel & Sachs proprietary engine factory.

956cc Mars (sv flat-twin Maybach engine) 1923 (D)

497cc Mars (ioe MAG) 1929 (D)

147cc Mars (TS Sachs Model 'Stella') 1952 (D)

MARS / *England 1905–1908*
Small factory which—like the German Mars—also fitted Fafnir engines into strengthened bicycle frames. It is not known if there was a connection with the German factory. The London-based firm also used the 211cc Minerva engine, which was not used by Mars in Germany.

MARS / *England 1923–1926*
A variety of engines powered these well-made machines, built in Coventry. Among them were the 247cc Villiers two-stroke, 293cc and 346cc JAP sv models, the 348cc sleeve-valve Barr & Stroud and the 348cc oilcooled Bradshaw. Production was on a small scale, but workmanship was excellent. Mars already used modern saddle tanks in late 1923.

346cc Mars (sleeve valve Barr & Stroud engine) 1923 (GB)

MARSH / *America 1901–late 1910s*
Pioneer of the American motorcycle industry. Produced singles and V-twins with their own engines. After they bought the Metz motorcycle factory, Marsh's machines became known as MM, which stood for Marsh-Metz.

MARSEEL / *England 1920–1921*
Designed by racing-driver D. M. K. Marendaz, the Marseel was a 232cc scooter which failed to make the grade.

MARTIN / *England 1911–1922*
Assembled standard-looking machines with 198cc Precision and 293cc, 347cc and 490cc sv JAP engines. There was also a V-twin with the 64·5mm × 76mm bore/stroke 498cc JAP engine.

MARTIN / *Japan 1956–1961*
Assembled two-stroke singles with 124cc, 198cc and 246cc engines.

MARTINA / *Italy 1924–1927*
Small producer of 173cc two-stroke machines.

MARTIN-JAP / *England 1929–1957*
Specialist in the manufacture of JAP-engined 348cc and 498cc speedway machines. Was known all over the world and supplied such machines to many famous riders.

MARTINSHAW / *England 1923–1924*
Fitted the 346cc Bradshaw 'oilboiler' (oilcooled) engine into their own frames. Production of this ohv single was limited.

MARTINSYDE / *England 1919–1925*
A former aircraft factory which built 346cc singles and 498cc to 676cc V-twins with their own eoi (exhaust over inlet) engines. Of good design and quality, the biggest version had 70mm bore and 88mm stroke, drip lubrication, an AJS three-speed gearbox and Amac carburettor. When this factory closed down, BAT in London bought the remains and the name.

346cc Martinsyde (ioe) 1923

676cc Martinsyde (ioe V-twin) 1923

MARUSHO / *Japan 1966–c1970*
Was a very BMW-like 498cc transverse-mounted ohv flat-twin with unit-design engine, four-speed gearbox and shaft drive to the rear wheel. The Marusho was built in the former Lilac factory and destined mainly for the USA market.

MARVEL / *America 1910–1913*
Closely connected with Glenn Curtiss, Marvel used Curtiss single-cylinder and V-twin engines.

MAS / *Italy 1920–1956*
Founded by Alberico Seilig, one of Italy's leading designers of motorcycles, the first machines were strengthened bicycles with their own 123cc ohv engines. The first motorcycles made by MAS had 148cc and 173cc ohv engines with big outside flywheels and pedalling gears. 173cc sv and 244cc ohv singles followed. During the 1930s the range included 248cc and 348cc sv machines and a 568cc sv single. There were also 348cc and 498cc ohv models, which—like the sv versions—had inclined cylinders. Although main production concentrated for a long time on 173cc ohv models in different shapes, Seilig had already designed in 1929 a modern 492cc vertical-twin with an sv engine, and later, very good rear suspensions for nearly the whole range. He left the MAS factory in 1938 and founded the Altea. After the war he was in Argentina for many years, but eventually returned to Italy, where he died. MAS during the war supplied 498cc ohv singles to the Italian forces and also produced the 173cc Lupatta two-stroke, followed by a 340cc sv and a new version of the 598cc ohv model. The 122cc Stella Alpina, with cooling by forced air, was interesting but not a success. That was soon after the war, and in 1950 a new 492cc vertical-twin with a single

498cc Marusho (ohv transverse flat-twin Model 'Magnum') 1965

496cc MAS (ohv) 1938 (I)

ohc engine also failed to make the grade. Better was the 173cc Zenith of 1951, a very modern ohv single with telescopic fork and swinging-arm rear suspension. Another model had a 173cc ohc engine and was exhibited in 1954 at the Milan show. Other models included a range of 124cc two-strokes and a Sachs-engined 49cc mini-scooter.

MAS/*Germany 1923–1924*
Built 183cc two-strokes in small numbers.

MASCOTTE/*France 1923–1924*
Lightweight machines with own 174cc sv engines.

MASERATI/*Italy 1953–1961*
Famous factory which entered motorcycle production with modern 123cc two-strokes and 158cc ohv models. There were also 248cc ohv and 173cc ohc singles, a 158cc two-stroke and eventually a 248cc vertical-twin with an ohc engine, built in small numbers only. Although of excellent design and finish. Maserati motorcycles never became as famous as the cars.

248cc Maserati (ohv) 1955

MASON & BROWN/*England 1904–c1908*
Assembled machines with De Dion, Antoine and mainly the 2 hp Minerva engine.

MASSEY (MASSEY-ARRAN)/*England 1920–1931*
Designed by E. J. Massey, these machines had a hectic life, as the company moved nearly every year. They built good, light motorcycles with 172cc to 490cc engines made by Villiers, Jap, Blackburne and Bradshaw. Massey also designed the first HRD motorcycles.

MAT/*Czechoslovakia 1929–1930*
Not unlike the Ariel Square Four, the 498cc Votroubek-designed MAT had a square four-cylinder engine, but Votroubek used an sv design with shaft drive to the rear wheel. The factory, owned by Bugatti racing driver Miloš Bondy, built only few of these machines.

MATADOR/*Germany 1925–1926*
Limited production of lightweights with their own 269cc two-stroke engines.

MATADOR/*England 1922–1927*
Concentrated on 348cc machines with Blackburne sv and ohv engines and with the oilcooled Bradshaw ohv engine. Bert Houlding, the designer, also built Toreador motorcycles. Successful riders: B. Houlding, A. Tinkler.

159cc Maserati (ohv) 1953

MATCHLESS/*England 1899–1969*
Famous make, which in the pioneering period fitted De Dion, MMC, JAP and MAG engines. Harry and Charlie Collier, riding mainly JAP-engined models, won in 1907 the very first TT race on a 432cc ohv model. In 1908 Charlie came in second. Brother Harry won in 1909 and was second in 1910 when Charles once more was first. Charles's average speed in 1907 was 38·22 mph; in 1910 he reached 50·63 mph. Many successes were gained with 994cc ohv V-twins (85mm bore/stroke), on other occasions they used 580cc V-twins (76mm × 64mm bore/stroke) or 297cc singles with 76mm bore and 65·5mm stroke. In 1910 Charlie Collier reached 91·37 mph over a flying mile with a JAP-engined 998cc V-twin with 90mm bore and 78·4mm stroke. Other Matchless racing machines had 496cc V-twin ohv engines with 70mm bore and 64·5mm stroke; some had MAG engines with 64mm bore and 77mm stroke. A third brother, Bert Collier, raced in the 1920s, but there were really no special racing machines built by the London-based Matchless factory. All Matchless 'racing' models between the wars were really only modified sports models, for example a 347cc ohc single with 69mm bore and 93mm stroke, which had the vertical shaft for the camshaft mounted behind the cylinder and both ports—inlet and exhaust—facing forward. This machine was ridden by such famous riders as Jimmy Guthrie and Gus Grose, and in Austria by Botric, but never had great success.

Production models for a long period had khaki-enamelled tanks, afterwards Brough-Superior-like round-shaped tanks and also white enamelled reservoirs. They were now equipped with their own engines: 246cc sv, 347cc sv and ohv as well as 498cc sv, 495cc and 591cc ohv singles and 990cc sv V-twins. The last one superseded the 996cc MAG-engined V-twin with ioe valves and spring frame, which was a popular sidecar machine. H. H. Collier, father of the three Collier brothers, died in 1926 and two years later the factory at Plumstead Rd, in Woolwich became a limited company. In 1931, when AJS in Wolverhampton—owned

986cc Matchless (sv flat-twin) 1916

976cc Matchless (sv V-twin JAP) 1923

347cc Matchless (sv Model 'Comfort') 1925

398cc Matchless (sv V-twin 'Silver Arrow') 1930

346cc Matchless (ohv) 1947

646cc Matchless (ohv twin Model G12 CSR) 1961

248cc Matchless G2 (ohv single) 1960

347cc Matchless G3 (ohv single) 1960

496cc Matchless G6 (ohc single) 1960

497cc Matchless (ohv Model G80CS Trails) 1961

498cc Matchless G9 (vertical twin) 1960

models included machines from the 246cc sv single to the modernised 990cc V-twin with the square 85·5mm bore/stroke sv engine. For a couple of years, the singles had inclined cylinders. Responsible for design until the war was Bert Collier, youngest of the three brothers. Matchless supplied engines during the 1930s to other makes, including Brough-Superior, OEC, Morgan, Coventry-Eagle, Calthorpe and their own AJS. Very popular at that period was the Clubman range with ohv single-cylinder engines. Some prices in 1938: 246cc = £45.10s, 347cc = £58.10s, and 498cc = £61.10s.

During WWII, Matchless supplied large numbers of 347cc ohv G3 and G3L singles to the forces. The G3L had telescopic forks. After 1945 the factory continued the manufacture of singles up to 498cc and also produced vertical ohv twins up to 745cc in different shapes. Among them was the G45 racing twin with 498cc and afterwards the G50 racing version, which had a single-cylinder 498cc ohc engine and was an enlarged 348cc AJS 7R 'Boys Racer'. Both these racing models became very popular and were also ridden by a works team which was headed by former racer C. J. Williams, who was also responsible for development. Among Matchless designers were Philip Walker, H. J. Hatch and Charles Udall. Famous Matchless riders were Bob McIntyre, Fred Stevens, Bob Anderson, Colin Seeley, Derek Ennett, Frank Perris, Gavin Dunlop, Ernie Rigg, Ernst Hiller, Bob Brown, Mike Duff, Peter Murphy, Derek Farrant, Bill Lomas, Ken Toistevin and others. Also in trials, Matchless machines gained many successes. Hugh Viney, Ron Langston, Arthur Rathcliffe were among the leading trials men.

After the death of the Colliers and the bad years of the mid-1950s, many changes occurred. Earlier — 1937 — the Colliers bought Sunbeam, but sold it early in the war to the BSA group. Then Associated Motorcycles Ltd. took over Francis-Barnett, James, Norton and even Indian in Springfield, Massachusetts. They also went into production of Piatti-designed two-stroke engines, but none of these ventures proved to be a lasting commercial success. The end came in the late 1960s and was only temporarily prevented when Dennis Poore — ex-racing-car driver and head of a big industrial finance group — took over Associated Motor Cycles Ltd. As the Plumstead Rd. factory had to be broken up he transferred production to Andover, where new buildings were erected, but only for Norton and partly AJS. The once great Matchless faded out. Engine production was taken over by the Wolverhampton factory of Villiers, who had already bought the JAP engine factory years before, and were part of the Poore-controlled Manganese Bronze group of companies. And Villiers, once England's leading producer of two-strokes, stopped supplying them to other motorcycle producers.

by the Stevens brothers — ran into trouble, the Colliers bought it and took everything down to London. For some years AJS kept its identity, but finally there was — with the exception of a few models — not much difference between this make and Matchless. Among exceptions were two unusual Matchless models. One was the 394cc Silver Arrow, with a 54mm bore × 86mm stroke V-twin sv engine, which had the cylinders in one block, enclosed valves and a common camshaft. The other the Silver Hawk was even more unusual, by having what amounted to two V-twins in one block. This 593cc ohc four with 50·8mm bore and 73mm stroke had a common cylinder head and only one carburettor. Both models had rear suspension by means of coil springs below the saddle. Other Matchless

496cc Maxima (sv flat-twin) 1922

MATRA / *Hungary 1938–1947*
Designed by former racing motorcyclist Laszlo Urbach, these machines had 98cc and 198cc Sachs and Ardie two-stroke engines.

MAURER / *Germany 1922–1926*
Was originally a car factory at Nuremberg. Produced afterwards 1·5 hp bicycle attachments with rotary-disc-valve two-stroke engines. Maurer motorcycles had watercooled vertical 247cc and horizontal watercooled 494cc twin-cylinder two-stroke motors. With its opposing cylinders in line with the duplex frame, this model was probably the only watercooled two-stroke flat-twin built as a production model. Production was not large-scale. Interesting was the big outside flywheel and the position of the forward-facing carburettor, which was connected with the rearward-facing cylinder via a long inlet pipe and had a shorter pipe to the forward-facing cylinder. It is unlikely that this unusual system worked satisfactorily. Unusual also was the position of the radiator. The single-cylinder Maurer had it below the saddle, where four-strokes usually have the oil tank. The flat-twin had the radiator directly below the full length of the petrol tank.

MAUSER / *Germany 1924–1927 (1932)*
Extremely unorthodox two-wheeler with a car-like body and with outrigger wheels on both sides. The chassis comprised two pressed steel channel members, while steering was by a huge D-shaped handlebar. The watercooled single-cylinder 510cc sv engine had 10 bhp at 3400 rpm. It was mounted in front of the rear wheel and had the cylinder mounted horizontally. Chains drove the gearbox and rear wheel. At 638 lb it was a heavy vehicle and business for the producer, the Mauser arms factory, was not brisk. The Mauser did not look very safe. When Mauser in 1927 abandoned manufacture of this 'Einspurauto' (single-track car), another company at Oberndorf/Neckar — Gustav Winkler — continued production until 1932. During the second half of the 1920s, the French firm Mono-trace built the Mauser under licence.

MAVISA / *Spain 1957–c1960*
Luxurious lightweight with a horizontal 248cc two-stroke, twin-cylinder engine of unit design and with shaft drive to the rear wheel.

490cc Mawi (sv JAP) 1930

MAWI / *Germany 1923–1930*
Assembled machines with 142cc and 173cc DKW two-stroke and 198cc to 546cc sv and ohv single-cylinder four-stroke JAP engines. Good orthodox design, small production.

MAX / *Germany 1924–1925*
Produced 180cc two-stroke and 446cc sv machines with their own power units.

MAX / *France 1927–1930*
French and English proprietary engines from 98cc to 496cc were fitted into motorcycles made by this small company.

MAXIM / *England 1919–1921*
One of the many assemblers. Fitted 318cc Dalm single-cylinder two-stroke engines.

MAXIMA / *Italy 1920–1925*
Well-designed 690cc and 747cc horizontal twins with opposing cylinders. The sv engines were of their own design and manufacture.

MAY BROS / *England 1903–1906*
Motorcycles with Minerva, MMC, Sarolea and other engines made to order.

MAZZUCHELLI / *Italy 1925–1928*
A long name, a small factory and a German 198cc Alba single-cylinder sv engine in a simple frame.

MB / *Czechoslovakia 1927–1928*
Built, like the Mat, in the Avia factory of racing car driver Miloš Bondy, the Šlechta-designed 498cc single-cylinder MB machine was quite unusual, because it had a rotary valve in the cylinder head, which steered the incoming and outgoing fuel mixtures and gases respectively. The design was never fully developed and became superseded by the Mat.

MB / *America 1916–1920*
Modern machines with 746cc parallel-twin engines and shaft drive to the rear wheel. The Buffalo-based factory never built large numbers of machines.

MBM / *Italy 1974–*
Concentrates on 49cc mopeds and similar small transport.

MBR / *Italy 1924–1926*
This firm was a small producer of 124cc two-stroke machines.

MC / *Czechoslovakia 1924–1927*
Concentrated on the manufacture of a 996cc V-twin sv machine for use with a sidecar. The design by Vladimir Guth was on English lines.

MCB / *Sweden 1902–*
Famous factory which now includes former motorcycle producers as Hermes, Monark (Esse), Nordstjernan, NV-Bohlin, Apollo and others. The main range of models includes two-strokes from 48cc to 123cc with mainly Sachs and Franco-Morini engines.

MCC / *England 1903–c1910*
Fitted De Dion, Minerva and other engines. Produced also their own engines using Minerva patents.

McEVOY / England 1926–1929

Michael McEvoy, the founder of this Derby-based factory, was earlier with Rolls-Royce; Cecil Allerhead Birkin, who financed the enterprise, was a brother of famous racing-car driver Tim Birkin; and George Patchett, the leading technician, came from George Brough's Brough-Superior works at Nottingham. McEvoy soon offered machines from the Villiers-engined 172cc two-stroke and 248cc, 348cc and 498cc sv and ohv singles with Blackburne and JAP engines, to 998cc JAP and Anzani-engined sv and ohv V-twins, including 8-valve versions and racing engines. George Patchett—who eventually became FN and Jawa designer—also rode in 1926–1927 a supercharged 996cc McEvoy with the big JAP racing engine. McEvoy and Cecil Birkin also competed in sporting events and when Birkin was killed in a TT practice accident in 1927, the factory got into difficulties. Before McEvoy closed down, he built prototypes of a 346cc three-valve ohc single and of an aircooled 498cc four-in-line, which was also an ohc design. He was an expert on supercharging, represented afterwards German Zoller superchargers in England and also built some supercharged cars.

McKECHNIE / England 1922

Luxurious twin-cylinder with a 688cc Coventry-Victor flat-twin engine. The McKechnie had rear suspension and a very strong duplex frame. The production was on a limited scale.

McKENZIE / England 1921–1925

Lightweight machine with 169cc two-stroke engine, which was also supplied in open frames for ladies. McKenzie machines were made for this London-based company by the Hobart works at Coventry.

MDS / Italy 1955–1960

Produced modern lightweights with own unit-design, single-cylinder ohv engines of 65cc, 70cc, 75cc and 80cc. There was also a miniscooter with a 65cc engine. Some versions of the motorcycle had separate gearboxes.

MEAD / England 1911–1916

According to some sources, Premier in Coventry was the actual producer of the machines for the Liverpool-based Mead Cycle Co. The range included Precision-engined 198cc, 492cc and 592cc models, 293cc JAP-engined singles and 746cc and 980cc versions with V-twin Premier engines.

MEAD / England 1922–1924

Assembler, who used 1·75, 2·75 and 3·75 hp Precision, Wall and Villiers engines.

MEGOLA / Germany 1921–1925

This was probably the most unorthodox motorcycle ever made on a commercial basis. Designed by Fritz Cockerell, the 640cc Megola had an aircooled 5-cylinder radial engine with the side-valves built directly into the front wheel. It had no clutch or gearbox, but a lot of power at the low end. Starting was by pushing or by 'kicking with the heel into the spokes of the front wheel' while the machine was on the stand. The petrol tank was in the normal position, but petrol first had to be pumped into a smaller tank, mounted on the right side of the leaf-sprung fork. Below it, outside the front axle, was the carburettor, on the opposite side the magneto. Some models also had rear suspension by means of half-elliptic springs. Changing ratios was by using bigger front wheels. Racing models had top speeds of around 85 mph, production versions of 68 to 70 mph. Thanks to the low centre of gravity, Megolas had first class road-holding quality. They won many races and trials with a works team which consisted of Toni Bauhofer,

Sepp Stelzer and Albin Tommasi. The name Megola came from the first two letters of the three men who founded this Munich-based factory: Meixner, Cockerell and Landgraf. Interesting, because Cockerell in this case wrote his name with G instead of the usual C as with his second motorcycle enterprise, the Cockerell lightweight motorcycles. He was quite clever, although it would now not be possible to use a gear and clutchless motorcycle in modern traffic conditions. The design of the spokes of the front wheel enabled the dismantling of the cylinders without taking a spoke out of the wheel. There was also a specially designed tube in the tyres. It could be changed without dismantling the wheel, ie it was an open tube, which could be 'pushed' together. The five small cylinders had 52mm bore and 60mm stroke; the frame consisted of a welded and rivetted box. Touring models had mostly bucket-seats; sports versions had saddles. Today, the Megola—of which nearly 2000 were made—is one of the most valued collector's items.

540cc Megola (sv 5-cylinder radial engine) 1921

540cc Megola (sv 5-cylinder radial engine model 'Sport') 1923

MEGURO / *Japan 1937–1964*
Once a leading Japanese factory, which eventually was taken over by Kawasaki. Produced mainly singles with capacities from 124cc to 498cc and also a 498cc vertical-twin ohv model. All were designed on typical English lines.

MEIHATSU / *Japan 1953–1961*
Was also part of the Kawasaki group and concentrated on two-strokes up to 248cc capacity. There were also twin-cylinder models.

MEISTER / *Germany 1949–early 1960s*
The Alfred Ostertag-designed machines were of standard design and good finish. Production included 49cc Zündapp-engined mopeds and motorcycles with 98cc, 123cc, 147cc, 173cc and 198cc Sachs as well as Ilo two-stroke power units.

MELDI / *Italy 1927–1937*
Concentrated on the production of racing machines with 248cc, 348cc and 498cc ohv JAP and Python (Rudge product) engines.

MEMINI / *Italy 1946–1947*
Concentrated on a limited manufacture of 173cc two-strokes with own engines.

MENON / *Italy 1930–1932*
Touring machines with inclined 174cc and 198cc single-cylinder sv engines.

MENOS / *Germany 1922–1923*
This was nothing else but a slightly redesigned and renamed Aristos. Identical was the water-cooled 614cc flat-twin sv engine, the rivetted and welded box frame made from pressed steel and the position of the radiators on both sides

498cc Meguro (ohv twin-cylinder) 1959

of the rear wheel. Only differences were a new fork design and a Zebra-like enamelling of the whole machine.

MERAY / *Hungary 1921–1944*
Was once the leading Hungarian make over the years produced machines from 172cc to 996cc with Villiers, Moto-Rêve, Puch, Blackburne

346cc Méray (ohv JAP) 1929

and JAP engines. After 1936 also had their own 346cc and 496cc single-cylinder engines. Ferencz Meray, Laszlo Erdély, Bertalan Szoter, Josef Weber etc. won many races on these machines.

MERCIER / *France 1950–1962*
Built 49cc machines, mainly mofas, with Lafalette engines. Also miniscooters and afterwards motorcycles with from 98cc to 173cc Villiers and Ydral engines.

MERCO / *Germany 1922–1924*
Very simple design of 148cc two-stroke machines with deflector-type three-port engines of their own manufacture.

MERCURY / *England 1956–1958*
Offered a wide range of 49cc and 98cc motorcycles and miniscooters, but actual production was limited. Among the models were the Dolphin, Hermes and Whippet scooters.

614cc Menos (sv flat-twin watercooled) 1923

MERKEL / *America 1902–1922*
For many years a leading make, Merkel built well-designed singles and V-twins up to 986cc. Some models already had rear suspension before WWI. The end came when Indian bought the Milwaukee factory.

MERLI / *Italy 1929–1931*
Small production of 173cc two-stroke machines with French Train engines.

MERLONGHI / *Italy 1927–1930*
Another small producer of small 132cc two-stroke two-speed machines.

MESSNER / *Austria 1928–1933*
Racing motorcyclist who produced 248cc racing machines with ohv JAP and his own ohc engines.

METEOR / *Czechoslovakia 1909–1926*
The first products were 211cc bicycle attachment engines. The motorcycles had 147cc and 169cc two-stroke deflector-type three-port engines.

METEOR / *Germany 1925–1926*
Simple machines with 185cc sv engines. Limited production.

METEOR / *Germany 1924–1926*
Lightweights with 172cc two-stroke engines which came probably from Thumann in France.

METEORA / *Italy 1955–*
Produced 49cc NSU-engined and 123cc FBM-engined two-strokes and also a 148cc ohv model. Later models had 49cc Franco-Morini engines and included moto-cross versions.

METISSE (RICKMANN) / *England 1959–*
The Rickmann brothers, who were among England's leading moto-cross riders, produce a wide range of superb frames for a variety of engines; mainly big ones, including 650cc and 750cc Triumph twins, 736cc Honda fours, 903cc Kawasaki fours, Nortons and others. Also frames for two-strokes like 123cc Zündapps, Montesas and for moto-cross and trials models.

METRO / *England 1912–1919*
Well-made machines with own 269cc two-stroke engines. *See also* next entry.

METRO-TYLER / *England 1919–1923*
The Metro became the Metro-Tyler when the London-based Tyler Apparatus Co., Ltd. bought the remains of the Birmingham-based Metro Manufacturing and Engineering Co. The price in 1921 for the 269cc two-speed model was £80, for the three-speed version £85.

MEYBEIN / *Germany 1922–1926*
Fitted 119cc and 142cc DKW two-stroke engines into their own very low and very simple frames. Some versions had a horizontal cylinder.

269cc Meybein (TS) 1924

MEYBRA / *Germany 1923–1925*
Another simple machine with its own 168cc two-stroke engine.

MEZO / *Austria 1923–1926*
Designed by Medinger, who was a racing motorcyclist and also importer of English engines into Austria, the Mezo range included 172cc and 247cc two-strokes with Villiers engines and 293cc, 346cc and 490cc sv and ohv singles with JAP engines. Actual production was on a limited scale, partly because of Medinger's injuries, sustained in 1924 in the Austrian Tourist Trophy race.

MF / *Germany 1922–1925*
The Nuremberg-built, Max Fischer-designed machine first had 492cc flat-twin sv engines made by BMW, afterwards 347cc and 497cc sv engines made by Blackburne in England.

MFB / *Germany 1923–1924*
The frames were made of wood. Engines fitted were the German 198cc Nabob and the English 293cc sv JAP. When this Hamburg factory went bust, Hoco in Minden took over.

MFB / *Italy 1957–1964*
Bologna-built 48cc, 74cc and 124cc two-strokes and 174cc ohv singles.

MFZ / *Germany 1921–1928*
Produced always 'farmer's' motorcycles and never any kind of 'hot' design. Nearly all models had their own ohv engines with 198cc, 247cc and

346cc MFZ (ohv) 1927

347cc capacity. The biggest version had in 1926 chain-drive and three instead of two speeds.

MGC / *France 1927–1929*
Interesting design with a light-alloy frame which included the petrol tank. Most engines fitted were JAP or Chaise of 248cc, 348cc and 498cc with ohv heads.

MGF / *Italy 1921–1925*
Designed by a well-known racing motorcyclist, the MGF — Motocicli Garanzini Francesco — machines had Blackburne ohv engines from 248cc to 498cc and also their own 142cc two-stroke engines.

MGF / *Germany 1923–1931*
Produced quite a large number of 122cc, 140cc, 173cc and 198cc two-stroke three-port and also Bekamo-licence pumping-cylinder two-stroke machines. Also made engines for other assemblers of lightweights.

MG-TAURUS / *Italy 1933–late 1950s*
Vittorio Guerzoni's first machines had 173cc two-stroke Train engines. Afterwards he built own 248cc ohv and 496cc ohv and eventually ohc models. There were also Sachs-engined mofas and after 1945 two-strokes and ohv models from 75cc to 198cc.

MIAMI / *America 1905–1923*
Was closely connected for some time with the manufacture of the Flying Merkel and produced also their own 298cc sv singles with pedalling gears and a rearward facing cylinder.

246cc Miami (sv) 1916

MICHAELSON / *America 1910–1915*
A well-made machine with 492cc single-cylinder and 992cc V-twin engines. They had oh inlet and side exhaust valves, duplex frames, leaf-sprung forks and chain drive to the rear wheel, when most other factories used belt drive.

13 hp Michaelson (ioe V-twin) 1913

MIDGET-BICAR / *America 1908–1909*
This was an English design by J. F. Brown, who sold the licence to the American Walton Motor Company. The unusual frame was made from welded and rivetted steel, while the engines used in the American version were their own V-twins. The machine never gained much popularity.

MIELE / *Germany 1953–1962*
Big and still famous factory which before WWII built bicycles with 73cc and 98cc Sachs two-stroke engines. After the war, the same make of proprietary engine powered machines from 48cc to 147cc. Miele products were known for their high quality.

MIGNON / *Italy 1923–1932*
After producing 123cc bicycle attachment engines, Vittorio Guerzoni designed the modern Mignon with a vertical 246cc twin-cylinder sv engine and a crank case made of Electron. That was in 1925 and in 1932 his next design appeared.

246cc Mignon (TS twin) 1926

This was a 498cc single with ohv and chain-driven ohc. Other models were 173cc versions with ioe and also ohv.

MILANI / *Italy 1970–*
Produces a wide range of Minarelli-engined 49cc models and also 124cc models for trials and moto-cross. Most of the production goes to the USA.

98cc Miele (TS) 1952

4 hp Militaire single 1912

MILITAIRE (MILITOR)/*America 1911–1917*
Heavy four-cylinder in-line car-type aircooled 1306cc ohv unit-design engine fitted into unusual frames with shaft drive. The frames consisted of a one piece stamping while the front suspension embodied coil springs in the front fork tubes. There was also a rear suspension which included quarter-elliptic cantilever springs mounted on a patented axle suspension. The gearbox had three speeds and a reverse gear; lubrication was full force feed by gear pump. The whole design was unorthodox and very expensive in production. In the seven years of limited production, these machines were made by not less than eight companies in Cleveland, Buffalo, New Jersey, Springfield and Bridgeport. The total output was probably less than 100 units. A single-cylinder version, built in the early years, never reached even this figure. This single had 480cc, a steering wheel instead of handlebars, a bucket seat instead of a saddle and, like the four, wheels with wooden spokes.

MILLER-BALSAMO/*Italy 1921–1959*
Was a leading make in Italy, first with 123cc two-strokes, afterwards with very fast 174cc ohv machines, which had Swiss Moser and afterwards also Miller-built English Rudge (Python) four-valve single-cylinder engines. In addition, there were also Miller models with 248cc, 348cc and 498cc four-valve Pythons. Carlo Fumagalli, Aldo Pigorini, Silvio Vailati, Gino Zanchetta and others won many races and on 174cc Python-engined racing machines broke

1306cc Militaire (ioe four-in-line) 1915

173cc Miller (ohv Moser engine) 1926

world records. The range of models included after 1934 98cc Sachs-engined two-strokes and a 246cc ohv model with its own single-cylinder

engine. A completely enclosed version, built just before the war, had a 198cc two-stroke engine. After 1945, production concentrated around two-strokes from 123cc to 246cc and the 246cc ohv model, but Ernest Balsamo's machines never regained the popularity they had in the late 1920s and early 1930s. The big 499cc ohv singles, built after the war, were basically pre-war models slightly modernised. They were soon dropped, while a new 169cc ohc single made its appearance in the 1950s. The last model was a 49cc two-stroke.

MILLIONMOBILE / *England c1902*
Motorised bicycle with a 1·5 hp engine.

MIMOA / *Germany 1924*
Used a 142cc Albertus two-stroke engine, designed by Julius Löwy. This power unit could be run also on crude oil, but lacked power and reliability.

MINERVA / *Belgium 1901–1914*
A famous name in the motoring world, Minerva not only built complete motorcycles with their own engines from 2 hp to 8 hp, but supplied these engines to other producers, as well as licences for manufacture in other countries.

MINETTI / *Italy 1924–1927*
One of the many small Italian producers of 124cc two-strokes with three-port engines.

MINEUR / *Belgium 1924–1928*
Liège was once the centre of the motorcycle industry in Belgium. Paul Mineur produced there his 348cc and 496cc sv and ohv singles with a variety of proprietary engines. These included JAP, Bradshaw, MAG and Liége-built Sarolea motors.

MINISCOOT / *France 1960–1962*
This was a folding miniscooter with a 74cc two-stroke engine.

MINNEAPOLIS / *America c1900–1915*
Well-designed singles and V-twins with two-speed gearboxes in unit. The Minneapolis-based factory used telescopic forks and produced also three-wheelers.

MINSK / *Russia 1954–early 1960s*
Produced inside the Russian motorcycle industry two-strokes up to 246cc vertical-twins, but was also closely connected with other Russian works via the CKEB, the common design centre.

MIRANDA / *Germany 1951–1954*
Originally known as Schweppe scooter, the design was renamed Miranda when the Dortmund-based Pirol works took over its manufacture. It was offered with 173cc Sachs and 198cc Küchen two-stroke engines.

MISTRAL / *France 1902–early 1960s*
Produced lightweights with 1·75 hp engines and after WWII modern lightweights from 49cc to 247cc until they specialised in various 49cc models and also supplied the power units to other mofa and moped manufacturers.

MITCHELL / *America 1901–c1906*
Was a famous car factory which also built 345cc single-cylinder motorcycles with rearward-facing cylinders.

MIVAL / *Italy 1950–1966*
Produced 123cc two-strokes and in 1954 took over the licence for the German Messerschmitt cabin-scooter. They fitted a 172cc two-stroke engine into this three-wheeled vehicle and used a four-speed gearbox with it. New motorcycles included 123cc, 174cc and 199cc ohv versions. There was also a racy-looking 174cc single-cylinder double-ohc machine and a similar moto-cross version with a single-ohc engine. The production included 49cc bicycle attachment engines and also 248cc ohc moto-cross models, of which some had five and even six-speed gearboxes. Mival also built trials versions.

MIYATA / *Japan 1909–1964*
Old factory which produced Asahi motorcycles after WWII. Among the models were 249cc sv and ohv singles, 344cc ohv singles and 496cc vertical twins with ohv engines. Other models included 123cc two-strokes. Based on English lines, Asahi's were never imported into Europe.

MJ / *Germany 1925*
Produced experimental 249cc two-stroke machines which never went into quantity production. Concentrated on the manufacture of air and watercooled flat twin engines with opposing cylinders of 596cc and 746cc, supplied to motorcycle producers such as Heller. Mehne, another machine factory, took over MJ when they ran into financial difficulties.

MJS / *Germany 1924–1925*
Motorcycles of simple design with their own 245cc three-port deflector-type two-stroke engines.

MM / *America 1906–WWI*
The MM had, like other early American motorcycles, single-cylinder rearward facing sv engines, supplied by Thomas. Afterwards they used single-cylinder and V-twin power units made by Marsh, Royal, Holley and Pope.

MM / *Italy 1924–1964*
This MM was founded by Angelo Mattei, Mario Mazzetti, Alfonso Morini (who became founder of the Morini works) and Giuseppe Massi. Afterwards Massi and Mattei left and Antonio Salvia joined the MM factory, where they built superb 123cc and later 173cc two-strokes with a forward-facing horizontal cylinder. In 1927 Alfonso Morini and Amedeo Tigli, riding 123cc two-strokes which had the gearbox in unit with the engine, broke world records and reached speeds of over 66 mph. A 173cc ohv machine and 348cc sv and ohv singles as well as 248cc ohv and 496cc sv models followed. New racing singles with 173cc and 348cc chain-driven ohc engines came into production in 1932 and 1936 respectively. Both proved to be very successful. Luigi Bonazzi broke the world record for the flying kilometre with the 348cc version and reached 116·6 mph, while Guglielmo Sandri won many races with this machine. He also ran it under the CM trade mark. Michaele Mangione became Champion of Italy in 1938 on an im-

122cc MM (TS racing machine) 1927

246cc MM (ohv) 1936

248cc MM (ohv 'Super-Sports') 1956

proved version of this 348cc single with the chain-drive single ohc engine; Salvia was responsible for the design. All MM machines were superbly made and had an excellent finish; this was the case with a new 248cc ohc single built in 1947, and with 346cc and 492cc sv singles made in the same period. MM afterwards dropped the big model and concentrated on 247cc and 347cc ohc singles. Unfortunately they never built racing machines after the war, but only 247cc moto-cross versions. The last MM design was a 173cc ohc single, although they also built 123cc two-strokes of excellent design. A 247cc production racer was the 1956-built Sport SS, with a single ohc unit-design engine.

M&M / *England 1914*
Assembled machine with open frame and 269cc Villiers two-stroke engine.

MMM / *Germany 1925–1927*
Small producer of 148cc two-stroke machines.

MOCHET / *France 1950–1955*
Lightweights with 149cc Ydral two-stroke engines.

MOFA / *Germany 1920–1925*
Produced 70cc and 148cc bicycle attachment engines and also complete lightweight machines.

MOHAWK / *England 1903–1925*
The first models had 2·5 hp and 3 hp engines. After an interruption of some years, the bicycle factory re-entered the motorcycle market in the 1920s. The wide range of assembled machines included models with 269cc Villiers, 293cc JAP and 492cc Abingdon engines. Other models used a 154cc two-stroke flat-twin Economic power unit and a 346cc sv JAP engine.

MOLARONI / *Italy 1921–1927*
Made by the Molaroni brothers at Pesaro, early models were 296cc two-stroke singles of their own design and manufacture. Others housed a 596cc flat twin two-stroke with opposing cylinders and automatic lubrication. Designed by Alfredo Sgrignani, a new range of models included the improved 296cc model with 70mm bore and 78mm stroke, a 344cc version with 75mm bore and 78mm stroke and a 348cc ohv single with 74mm bore and 81mm stroke which had a Blackburne engine.

MOLTENI / *Italy 1925–1927*
Very ambitious design of a frame and fork, chain cases etc. made from aluminium alloy. The good-looking Molteni, fitted with 348cc oilcooled Bradshaw and with 492cc MAG single-cylinder engines, was not a commercial success.

MONACO-BAUDO / *Italy 1926–1928*
After Augusto Monaco produced an experimental 246cc vertical twin engine at the Della Ferrera factory, he built a 496cc single-cylinder sv model with a unit-design engine and a big outside flywheel. Co-designer was Antonio Baudo, whose earlier V-twin engines had 474cc, 686cc and 996cc capacity. Other models housed 346cc and 490cc single-cylinder JAP and Blackburne sv and ohv engines.

MONARCH / *America 1912–1915*
Another USA factory which produced 496cc singles and 990cc V-twins with their own ioe engines and spring frames.

10 hp Monarch (ioe V-twin) 1913

MONARCH / *England 1919–1921*
Actually made by Excelsior of Birmingham, the Monarch was a cheaper version. It had 296cc Villiers and 293cc JAP sv engines.

MONARCH / *Japan 1955–1962*
Produced Norton-like 346cc and 496cc ohv single-cylinder machines.

MONARK / *Sweden 1920–*

Famous make belonging to the MCB group. Monark now includes not only the early Esse trade mark, but also other factories including Crescent, NV, Bohlin, Apollo, Hermes, Nordstjernan etc. Models built had engines from 98cc to 596cc, but during the war there was also a 998cc V-twin ohv model. Two-strokes used included Sachs, Villiers and Ilo, after 1945 also Franco-Morini and others. The factory also built machines with ohv engines and there were even 499cc singles in the late 1950s which proved very successful in moto-cross events, trials and road racers. Among leading riders were Sten Lundin, Ove Lundell, L. Persson etc. Monark products, which include bicycles, boats etc., have a good reputation. The present range of two-strokes includes 49cc and 123cc models and also 49cc schoolboy moto-cross versions. MCB 123cc moto-cross and trials models have 21 bhp (at 9000 rpm) engines with six-speed gearboxes.

244cc Monark (TS Ilo twin) 1952

498cc Monark (ohv moto-cross works-machine) 1959

MONET GOYON / *France 1917–1957*

Was for many years a leading make successful in races. The first product was a wheel with a small engine, which could be attached to any bicycle. It had 114cc and ioe valves. Motorcycles made by the Macon works used for many years 147cc, 172cc, 247cc and 342cc Villiers two-stroke and 347cc and 497cc ioe and ohv single-cylinder MAG power units. With Sourdot, Hommaire, Goussorgues and Debaisieux many races were

342cc Monet-Goyon (TS Villiers) 1930

won, partly with Brooklands-Villiers 172cc two-stroke engines, partly with ohv and ohc MAG 347cc and 497cc singles. The ohc versions were works engines; Monet Goyon as one of the biggest MAG engine customers was the only French factory to get them from the Swiss engine works. The only engine built by Monet Goyon around the early 1930s was a 344cc sv single of unit design and with a slightly inclined cylinder. After the war, new 98cc, 124cc, 198cc

346cc Monet-Goyon (sv) 1931

and 232cc two-strokes and 345cc sv and ohv singles came into production. There was also—from 1953 onwards—the Starlet, a nice 98cc two-stroke scooter. Many of these machines had J. A. Grégoire rear suspension. The same was the case with similar Koehler Escoffier models, which were also built by Monet Goyon. Both makes used Villiers engines made under licence. They were fitted also to the Lemardelé-designed fully enclosed motorcycles and scooters.

498cc Monet-Goyon (ohv MAG) 1931

MONFORT / *Spain late 1950s*

Assembled machines with 124cc and 198cc two-stroke engines in limited numbers.

MONOPOLE / *England 1911–1924*

One of the best assembled machines. Fitted 247cc and 269cc Villiers engines, 293cc and 680cc sv JAP motors and also the 499cc Abingdon single-cylinder sv engine.

MONOTRACE / *France 1926–1928*

Licence-built German Mauser one-track car. Had a watercooled 520cc engine, a car-like open body and on each side an outrigger wheel.

MONTEROSA / *Italy 1954–1958*

Producer of 49cc mopeds. Small factory and limited output.

MONTESA / *Spain 1945–*

The first big motorcycle factory in Spain, concentrated first on 124cc two-strokes. Among them were also fast racing machines which gained many successes in the 1950s. Top riders: Grace, Cama, Gonzalez etc. During the years the range of models was extended to machines with 48cc, 147cc, 172cc, 247cc, 305cc and 351cc. Many versions are destined for trials and moto-cross; all engines are two-strokes of their own design and manufacture. The 48cc engines now have 38mm × 43mm bore/stroke; 123cc models 54mm × 54mm bore/stroke and 13 bhp at 7000 rpm; 172cc versions 60·9mm × 54mm bore/stroke and 16 bhp at 7000 rpm; 247cc models 70mm × 64mm bore/stroke and 25 to 36 bhp at 7000 to 8500 rpm. Among Montesa Directors in early years was Francesco Bulto; he left in 1958 and founded his own Bultaco motorcycle factory.

247cc Montesa (TS 'King Scorpion') 1973

247cc Montesa (TS 'Cota') 1974

247cc Montesa (TS 'Cappra') 1974

MONTGOMERY / *England 1902–1939*

Before WWI William Montgomery built motorcycles with proprietary engines at Bury St. Edmunds. Afterwards he moved to Coventry, where his products included not only a model with a 688cc flat twin sv engine but also sidecars. After the war his son Jack Montgomery resumed motorcycle production and built a wide range of machines from 147cc Villiers-engined two-strokes to 996cc V-twins with ohv Anzani and JAP engines. There were also models with 348cc Bradshaw engines, but from the mid-1930s onwards, only 246cc, 346cc and 496cc ohv JAP engines were fitted. The sporting Greyhound models with JAP special engines were

490cc Montgomery (ohv JAP engine) 1939

996cc Montgomery (ohv Anzani V-twin) 1923

MOSER

famous; successful also were some JAP-engined racing models. Riders included Sid Jackson, Erich Hiller, Otto Kohfink and Mita Vychodil. Montgomery built the first Brough-Superior frames in 1920/1922 and afterwards produced the P&P motorcycle frames. In 1925 a fire destroyed the Montgomery works; P&P also had to interrupt production until new Montgomery factories were built.

MONTLHERY / *Austria 1926–1928*
Limited production of 346cc sv and ohv machines with JAP engines.

MONVISO / *Italy 1951–1956*
Sachs-engined 98cc, 123cc, 147cc and 173cc two-strokes of typical Italian design.

MOONBEAM / *England 1920–1921*
Utility machines with 296cc Villiers two-stroke engines built by a small producer.

MORBIDELLI (BENELLI) / *Italy 1975–*
Made at a new Benelli branch factory, the Jörg Müller-designed 123cc and 348cc Morbidelli racing machines are built in limited numbers. Giancarlo Morbidelli was the initiator of these successful machines, which with Pier Paolo Bianchi and Paolo Pileri gained many championships in a short period. The 124cc twin-cylinder racing engine has forward-facing, watercooled cylinders with 43·9mm bore and 41mm stroke and a 15·5:1 compression ratio. The machine has a 6-speed gearbox in unit, Kröber igignition, two Mikuni carburettors and a Hoeckle crankshaft. There are around 42 bhp in the latest version of this 123cc racer. Morbidelli's first machine, a 49cc racer with 10 bhp at 14,500 rpm, was made in 1969 and ridden by Eugenio Lazzarini; a 1970 123cc twin had 32 bhp at 14,500 rpm and in 1973 came the first 349cc four-cylinder with 95 bhp at 14,500 rpm. An improved version was ridden in 1976 by Dieter Braun.

MORETTI / *Italy 1934–1952*
Known as producer of small sports cars, Giovanni Moretti began producing machines with Ladetto, DKW and JAP engines, mainly lightweights up to 248cc. After 1945 the range included 123cc and 248cc ohc machines and also a 246cc vertical twin with shaft drive. Production was on a limited scale.

MORINI / *Italy 1937–*
Co-founder and racing rider of MM, Alfonso Morini left it just before the war and entered the market in 1946 with his first 123cc Morini

174cc Morini (dohc 'Rebello' racer) 1957

two-strokes. They were followed by 123cc ohc versions with 12 bhp at 10,000 rpm and a Jawa-like 246cc two-stroke with a four-speed gearbox in unit with the engine. Other models included very fast 173cc ohc versions, including the Rebello, a production racer. There were also various 173cc ohv machines and 98cc Sbarazzino models. Much development went also into the 123cc ohc racing machines, which in 1954 had 16 bhp and a 100 mph top speed. They had double-ohc engines and there were also 173cc and 246cc Rebello models with double-ohc in production, the smaller with 22 bhp at 9000 rpm, the bigger with 29 bhp at 10,000 rpm. This new engine had 72mm bore and 61mm stroke. After some development power went up to 32 bhp at 10,500, the speed up to 131 mph, then to 35 bhp at 11,000 rpm and 137·5 mph. Tarquinio Provini, for many years leading rider for Morini and others, won many races on these very fast and reliable ohc versions. New 48cc and 148cc two-stroke and ohv models were added to already existing types after 1963. Alfonso Morini, the great designer, died in 1969 and his daughter Gabriella took over the Morini factory. The range of models consists of 49cc, 98cc, 124cc and 153cc ohv singles with partly trials specifications; a very modern 123cc (125 T) road-going ohv machine with 14 bhp at 8500 rpm, of which a 246cc version is due to be produced; and the now famous 344cc V-twin with 35 bhp at 8200 rpm or 39 bhp at 8500 rpm, to which a 496cc version is to be added soon.

MORRIS / *England 1902–1905*
Founder of this factory was William Morris, who later became Lord Nuffield of what is now the Leyland car group. His motorcycles had 2·75 hp single-cylinder engines made by De Dion and MMC.

MORRIS / *England 1913–1922*
Had no connection to the above factory. Produced a single model, a 247cc two-stroke with its own three-port, deflector-type engine.

MORRIS-WARNE / *England 1922*
A 248cc two-stroke single, which was offered with a vertical as well as with a horizontal cylinder. They were built in limited numbers.

MORS (SPEED) / *France 1951–1956*
Cars bearing this name were among the finest products in the pioneer period. In the 1950s a branch of the original Mors factory produced scooters with 60cc, 115cc and 124cc two-stroke engines.

MORSE-BEAUREGARD / *America 1912–1917*
Very advanced 492cc vertical-twin unit-design machines, which had the cylinders mounted in line with the frame. Drive to the rear wheel was by shaft.

MORTON-ADAM / *England 1923–1924*
Produced 292cc three-port, deflector-type two-strokes in small numbers and also Harry Sidney-designed 248cc and 348cc ohc models with chain-driven camshafts.

MOSER / *Switzerland 1905–1935*
Was—like Motosacoche—not only producing complete motorcycles from 123cc to 598cc, but also a leading supplier of proprietary engines to factories like Miller-Balsamo, FVL, Lecco, Dollar and others. Most were ohv singles and the 123cc and 173cc versions gained great popularity, especially in Italy. Both models also won many big races and during the 1920s in a Grand Prix in Switzerland, Lehman and Brehm riding 123cc ohv Moser machines gained first and second place with the great Italian rider Omobono Tenni on a GD in third position. Another quite popular Moser model was the 198cc ohv version fitted also by Hercules of Germany in the early 1930s. These engines had 60mm bore and 70mm stroke, the 173cc version 60mm bore and 61mm stroke. The biggest Moser engine, the 598cc single, had 85mm bore and 106mm stroke, double-port and a JAP-like appearance.

123cc Moser (ohv) 1927

496cc Moser (ohv) 1932

215

MOSER / *Austria 1953–*
This make, which produced 98cc and 123cc two-stroke machines with Rotax engines has been defunct for many years. Actually it was the make from which the present KTM motorcycles were developed.

MOSKVA / *Russia 1940–early 1960s*
Produced during the war, heavy V-twins, called M-72, for the Russian forces. Peace-time production consisted of 123cc and 173cc DKW-like two-strokes, which are now superseded by the 174cc Voskhod. Other models connected with this factory were the shaft-driven M-31 with a 346cc ohv engine and the BMW-like M-61, a 592cc ohv flat-twin, transverse-mounted, which eventually became the 649cc Dneipr M-10, with 34 bhp at 5200 rpm.

MOTAG / *Germany 1923–1924*
Advanced design by Josef Schneeweiss. The Motag had a cast alloy-frame made from Electron and was offered with three variants of vertical twin-cylinder ohv engines and also— as required—with air or watercooling. The engines had 514cc, 642cc and 804cc. The production must have been very small, as only very few of these machines actually reached the market.

652cc Motag (ohv watercooled twin-cylinder) 1923

MOTA-WIESEL / *Germany 1948–1952*
The original name was Motra-Wiesel. It was a cross between moped and scooter with small wheels and 74cc and 98cc two-stroke engines.

MOTEURCYCLE / *France 1921–1924*
Unusual 206cc two-stroke machine with friction drive to the rear wheel.

MOTOBECANE (MOTOCONFORT) /
France 1922–
Famous for mofas, mopeds etc., the Pantin-based factory is also the leading producer of motorcycles in France. Produced during the 1920s and 1930s a range of 99cc, 172cc, 249cc and 308cc two-strokes as well as sv singles of 172cc, 249cc, 346cc and 498cc. Sensational 499cc and 749cc aircooled four-cylinder in-line ohc models were built in the early 1930s. They had $54 \times 54 \cdot 5$mm and 54mm $\times$ $81 \cdot 7$mm bore/stroke unit-design engines with three-speed gearboxes

346cc Motobécane (ohv) 1939

and with shaft drive to the rear wheel. Motoconfort, part of the Motobecane group of companies, produced identical machines. Some early models had Blackburne engines, including some with ohv, but during the 1930s all the engines were made in the factory, among them very sporty 173cc and 348cc ohv singles. Motobecane, since 1974 in close connection with the De Tomaso group which owns Moto-Guzzi,

Benelli and other Italian factories, produced after the war two and four-strokes and also a very nice 348cc V-twin, but concentrated largely on 48cc machines, mainly mopeds, mofas and similar machines. The only motorcycle now in quantity production is a 123cc two-stroke twin with 16 bhp at 7500 rpm and a five-speed gearbox. An aircooled 349cc two-stroke three-cylinder, transverse-mounted, with 38 bhp at 7500 rpm is now on the verge of quantity production. This is a sporting machine with 103 mph top speed. An interesting recent Motobecane

348cc Motobécane (ohv twin) 1952

development is building sporting 123cc twins with 22 bhp for production races and the possibility of tuning these machines to higher outputs of around 38 bhp. Equipped with rotary discs, watercooled versions should do even better.

MOTOBI / *Italy 1951–*
Designed by Giovanni Benelli, who had left his brothers in the Pesaro factory but later returned —now with the Motobi—to the old Benelli home, the first Motobi machines had 98cc, 114cc and 123cc flat single-cylinder egg-shaped two-stroke engines and also 198cc twin-cylinder versions. Afterwards he also built ohv models of similar design with capacities up to 248cc. That was in 1956, when the B on the petrol tanks was superseded by the Motobi transfer. Bestsellers were the 173cc Catria single with ohv, and 198cc and 248cc Spring Lasting two-stroke twins. A

123cc Motobi (TS) 1955

scooter with a 74cc two-stroke engine failed to succeed. After the return of Motobi to Benelli, some models stayed in production and there were others sold with both names, according to the demand. There are still 123cc and 245cc ohv singles with Benelli transfers in 1976 catalogues which are equipped with developed and improved Motobi-based egg-shaped power units, installed in pressed steel frames with telescopic forks.

MOTOBIC / *Spain 1949–early 1960s*
This firm initially produced 49cc mopeds, afterwards also 123cc motorcycles with two-stroke engines.

MOTOBIMM / *Italy 1969–1971*
Was a small factory which built 49cc moto-cross and trials machines with FB-Minarelli two-stroke engines.

MOTOBLOC / *France 1948–late 1950s*
Made at Vichy, the Motobloc products included 44cc mopeds, 65cc Sulky scooters and motorcycles from 124cc to 248cc with Villiers and Aubier-Dunn two-strokes and French AMC 123cc and 248cc ohv engines.

MOTO-BORGO / *Italy 1906–1926*
Designed by Carlo and Alberto Borgo—and also successfully raced by them—the early single-cylinder models had 493cc, 693cc and even 827cc. During WWI V-twins with 990cc and afterwards 746cc came into being. Most of these machines had overhead-inlet and side-

exhaust valves and there was at that period a co-operation with the English Rudge-Whitworth works at Coventry too; therefore a certain similarity between Borgo and Rudge machines. New 477cc V-twins with unit-design ohv engines came into production in 1921. Improved versions for sporting purposes had four-valve heads. The last Moto-Borgo, built from 1925 onwards, was of clean design and had a two-speed gearbox built into the engine unit; it was one of the few 492cc ohv V-twins ever made on a commercial basis. The Borgos gave up motor-cycle production soon afterwards and subsequently concentrated their efforts on the manufacture of pistons.

Moto-Borgo

496cc Moto-Borgo (ohv V-twin) 1926

MOTOCLETTE / *Switzerland 1904–1915*
Small producer who fitted Zedel and afterwards Moser single-cylinder proprietary engines.

MOTO GELIS / *Argentina 1963–*
Two-stroke machines up to 246cc with engines and other parts imported from Italy.

MOTO GUZZI / *Italy 1921–*
For many years not only a leading make in Italy, but also one of the very few Italian machines which became known abroad. Founded at Mandello del Lavio by Carlo Guzzi and Giorgio Parodi, all pre-war models had a horizontal single-cylinder engine with forward-facing cylin-

der. The first models were 493cc single-cylinder ioe versions, followed by ohv and ohc singles and from 1925 onwards also 246cc ohc machines. Other models were 173cc ohv and eventually 246cc ohv. Many prototypes and racing machines were designed, but only few went into quantity production. There were already in 1932 three and four-cylinder prototypes and in 1933 the famous 120-degree 498cc V-twin ohc racing model came into being. This machine was developed during the years and competed

499cc Moto Guzzi (ioe) 1921

499cc Moto Guzzi (ohc racing machine) 1926

498cc Moto Guzzi (ohc V-twin racer) 1935

successfully in races until the early 1950s. The first races were won on machines with ioe 493cc machines, from 1924 onward with ohc versions. The first 246cc ohc racers were built in 1926. In developed form—including the Albatross and Gambalunghino—this single-cylinder model was also raced successfully until the mid-1950s, while the bigger four-valve ohc single became obsolete in races after 1927. There were supercharged 246cc racing models in 1939, and soon afterwards a supercharged 498cc three-cylinder double-ohc racer. The many successful Moto Guzzi racing men in that period before the war included Guido Mentasti, Erminio Visioli, Ricardo Brusi, Alfredo Panella, Pietro and Mario Ghersi, Achille Varzi, Amedeo Ruggeri, Siro Casali, Luigi Arcangeli, Primo Moretti, Ugo Prini, Mario Saetti, Arrigo Cimatti, Orlindo Geissler, Carlo Fumagalli,

246cc Moto Guzzi (ohc Model 'Albatros') 1947

499cc Moto Guzzi (dohc watercooled 4-cylinder works racer) 1953

499cc Moto Guzzi (dohc 3-cylinder works supercharger racer) 1940

98cc Moto Guzzi (TS Model 'Zigolo') 1958

498cc Moto Guzzi (dohc 8-cylinder watercooled works racer) 1955

Nello Pagani, Rafaele Alberti, Guglielmo Sandri, Amilcare Moretti, Omobono Tenni, Stanley Woods, Terzo Bandini, Aldo Pigorini, Wal Handley, Gordon Burney, Maurice Cann and many others.

Among leading designers of these machines were Carlo Guzzi and Angelo Parodi, a relative of Giorgio Parodi. Unfortunately Parodi, who designed the supercharged 246cc single in 1939 and also the supercharged 498cc Three, died during the war. After the war it was mainly Giulo Carcano who designed Moto Guzzi's machines. Among them were 248cc double-ohc twins, 320 and 348 as well as 498cc double-ohc singles and also the 498cc Gambalunga and Dondolino with push-rod single-cylinder power units. Built on Gambalunga-lines, the 248cc Gambalunghino was really a cross between a Gambalunga and a developed Albatross. Built from 1938 onwards, the Albatross, with a single-ohc 248cc engine was the last production racer of that period. Most other racing machines were for works riders and only very few were sold to leading private competitors, who included Enrico Lorenzetti, Fergus Anderson, Tommy

231cc Moto Guzzi (TS twin Model 250 TS) 1977

Wood, Manliff Barrington, Maurice Cann, Franta Juhan, Benoit Musy, Hein Thorn-Prikker, Alex Meyer, Rupert Hollaus, Alano Montanari etc., but some of them got works support, occasionally also the loan of works machines. Moto Guzzi works riders in the post-war period included Fernando Balzarotti, Omoboni Tenni, Bill Lomas, Dickie Dale, Fergus Anderson (who also became team manager), Cecil Sandford, Keith Campbell, Bruno Bertacchini, Gianni Leoni, Guido Leoni, Bruno Ruffo, Dulio Agostini, Ken Kavanagh, Manliff Barrington etc. Works riders in 1953 got also watercooled 498cc four-cylinder in-line double-ohc machines with shaft drive and in 1956 a more complicated model, the 498cc 90 degree V-8, which also had a double-ohc engine, but chain drive instead of shaft drive. Dickie Dale was among the few riders who rode this, the last Moto Guzzi works racing machine. Soon afterwards the racing department was closed.

Moto Guzzi changed manufacturing policy after 1945 and while they continued with improved 246cc and 498cc ohv singles, they added during the years 44, 48, 65, 73, 98, 123 and 153cc motorcycles and scooter-like designs such as the Galetto, with two-stroke ohv engines. The death of Giorgio Parodi in the 1950s was a big loss for the Mandello del Lario factory, which in the early seventies fell into the Alessandro de Tomaso group, which also controlled Benelli at Pesaro and which afterwards became closely connected with Motobecane in France. New

Lino Tonti-designed transverse-mounted 748cc ohv V-twins came into the range in 1969. They had unit-design engines with four and later five-speed gearboxes and shaft drive. Bigger and also more sporting versions followed. At the time of writing, the range includes the 748cc model S3 with 82·5mm bore, 70mm stroke and 72 bhp at 7000 rpm; the 844cc model T3 with 83mm bore, 78mm stroke and 68·5 bhp at 7000 rpm, a more luxurious California-version of this machine and the 949cc model V1000 Convert, whose engine with 88mm bore and 78mm stroke

supplies 71 bhp at 6500 rpm. In production are also 122cc single-cylinder and 232cc twin-cylinder two-strokes, a 123cc ohv single, transverse-mounted aircooled 231cc and 397cc ohc four-cylinder models and the single-cylinder 499cc Sahara model with 25 bhp at 4800 rpm, which is with its horizontal ohv engine not only a successor of the Falcone, but really a successor of the very first 1921-built Moto Guzzi. The newest models are Tonti-designed smaller transverse-mounted ohv V-twins with 490cc and 348cc, which are scheduled for 1977.

490cc Moto Guzzi (ohv transverse V-twin Model V 50) 1977

748cc Moto Guzzi (ohv transverse V-twin Model 750-S3) 1976

MOTOM / *Italy 1947–early 1960s*

Produced a variety of lightweight-machines with pressed steel frames. Most engines used were ohv units; the first a 48cc bicycle engine with pedalling gear. The next design was the 147cc Delfino, which eventually got a 163cc ohv engine. In this form it had 8 bhp at 6000 rpm. Very popular was a 98cc ohv model with a horizontal fully-enclosed engine. There were also versions with 92cc and 98cc, models with tubular frames and also — in 1964 — a 48cc version with a Peugeot two-stroke engine. There were many versions with automatic gearboxes, moto-cross models and machines with partly foreign engines, including the 49cc Zündapp two-stroke, which had a four-speed gearbox.

48cc Motom (ohv) 1958

MOTO MONTE / *France 1932–WWII*

Small manufacturer of 98cc two-stroke machines.

MOTOPEDALE / *France 1933–1939*

Two-strokes with 98cc and 123cc Aubier-Dunne engines. Other models included 248cc, 348cc and 498cc JAP and Python single cylinder engines. Limited production.

MOTOPIANA / *Italy 1923–1931*

Assembled for years 147cc to 247cc Villiers-engines and also 246cc to 490cc JAP sv and ohv motors into their own very sporty frames. Late in 1927, Gualtiero Piana produced his first 248cc sv engine, afterwards also an ohv version.

MOTO RÊVE / *Switzerland (England) 1904–1925*

Once a leading motorcycle and proprietary engine manufacturer. Built 298cc, 403cc and 497cc V-twins and already in 1909 a vertical twin. They had a branch factory in England which produced Alp motorcycles. Their last model, in 1925, had a modern 346cc ohv engine.

MOTORMEYER / *The Netherlands 1949–1951*

Built a limited number of 346cc two-stroke, double-piston, single-cylinder machines.

MOTOSACOCHE (MAG) / *Switzerland 1899–1957*

Founders Armand and Henry Dufaux gained fame with 241cc and 290cc bicycle attachments. Afterwards they built a seven-cylinder radial engine, but production models had 247cc to 996cc ioe and partly ohv single-cylinder and V-twin engines. From 1930 onward new sv versions superseded the ioe engines. In addition to motorcycles, the Swiss factory also supplied proprietary power units to motorcycle factories in many countries. There were also branch factories in Lyon and Milan; other firms including Royal-Enfield in England and Triumph in Germany built Motosacoche engines under licence. Among factories which fitted these superb engines in England were Brough-Superior, Matchless, Ariel, Rex Acme, New Henley, Lea Francis, Morgan and New Hudson. Motosacoche proprietary engines were also known as MAG. Other factories included the German Standard, OD, Triumph (Orial), Imperia, Spiegler, MA, Bayern, Neander, Luwe, Hecker, Bücker; the Austrian DSH, Werner-MAG, EM; the French Monet Goyon; the Hungarian Meray, the Swiss Condor and Allegro. Very prominent were the 347cc and 498cc ohv singles, also 497cc and 597cc ioe and ohv V-twins.

Dougal Marchant and Bert Le Vack were among leading Motosacoche designers and it was Marchant who produced between 1927 and 1929 extremely fast 248cc, 348cc and 498cc ohc single-cylinder works racing engines. Only a few good MAG engine customers, including Standard, Triumph, Monet-Goyon etc., got such engines for their works riders. Wal Handley won in 1928 the 350cc and 500cc class in the Grand Prix of Europe on them. For their own works riders, Motosacoche also had in the years up to 1927 a few 498cc and 748cc V-twins with ohc engines, but these were suitable only for the many hill-climbs of that period. Among leading Motosacoche works riders were Francesco Franconi, Luigi and Bruno Martinelli, Paul Oilter, Artur Bizzozero, Ernst Haenny, Jean Gex, Augsburger, Rossi and among foreign works riders besides Handley, Luigi Arcangeli, Carlo Barsanti, Charly Dodson, Artur Simcock, Ignaco Faura, Hans Soenius and Anton Uroič. There were also other riders such as Otto Ley, Toni Fleischmann (both Triumph); Artur Dom, Karl Gall, Paul Rüttchen, Rudi Ecker and Hermann

498cc Motosacoche (ioe V-twin) 1924

598cc Motosacoche (ohv V-twin) 1926

Lang (all Standard); Jean Goussorgues and Pierre Debasieux (all Monet Goyon) etc. who won races on MAG-engined machines.

Privateers got from 1931 onward a 498cc ohv racer, the D50, with a special engine which had both push-rods in a centre-tube and looked like an ohc design. These engines were catalogued not only in Motosacoche's own motorcycles, but also at Standard, OD, Triumph and other factories. Among riders of such 'private' racers were Count von Alvensleben, Fritz Köhler, Franz Hecker and others. Production engines of the 1930s included besides 347cc and 497cc sv singles and 497cc ohv singles also a superb 846cc sv V-twin touring model, the last Le Vack design before he was killed when testing a model. A few new 498cc ohc singles were built in the mid-1930s for the works team, but no new designs appeared from that time until after the war, when Dougal Marchant created a very unorthodox 235cc single-cylinder sv model, which never went into quantity production. The only post-war versions built were a 248cc ohv single with unit-design engine and shaft-drive and a 246cc vertical twin with the Richard Küchen-designed Opti ohc motor.

496cc Motosacoche (ohv) 1929

498cc Motosacoche (ohv) 1931

746cc Motosacoche (ioe V-twin) 1931

496cc Motosacoche (sv) 1933

498cc Motosacoche (sv) 1931

MOTOTRANS (DUCATI) / *Spain 1957–*
This is a Ducati branch factory which produces its own 48cc mofas, mopeds etc. and also a range of Ducati single-cylinder ohc machines with capacities of 157cc, 204cc, 247cc and now mainly 340cc. This Vento has 76mm bore, 75cc stroke and 28 bhp at 7500 rpm. The machine has a 100 mph top speed and looks like other ohc models, very much like the Italian Ducati singles.

MOUNTAINEER / *England 1902–1926*
Early machines had Minerva, Fafnir and MMC engines. After the war, only one model, a 269cc two-stroke with a three-port engine, was built in small numbers. It had an Albion two-speed gearbox and belt drive.

MOVESA / *Spain 1952–early 1960s*
Closely connected with Peugeot of France, the Movesa had a 173cc Peugeot two-stroke engine.

MOVEO / *England c1907*
Assembled machines with 3·5 hp single-cylinder and 5 hp V-twin JAP engines.

MÖWE / *Germany 1903–1908*
Produced by the same factory which in later years built Walter motorcycles, the Möwe was

246cc Motosacoche (ohc twin-cylinder Opti) 1955

equipped with 3·25 hp and 3·50 hp single-cylinder and 5 hp V-twin Fafnir engines.

MOY / *Poland 1937–1940*
Small factory which produced lightweights with own 172cc two-stroke engines.

M&P / *France late 1920s to late 1930s*
Producer of lightweight-machines with 98cc and 123cc Aubier-Dunne engines.

MP / *Italy 1934–1935*
Built by Mario Penazio at Turin, the MP had a modern pressed steel frame and English Sturmey-Archer proprietary engines, ie ohv singles with 347cc and 497cc.

MPH / *England 1920–1924*
Like the Mountaineer a very simple machine. The 269cc Wall two-stroke engine was fitted. The gearbox was a two-speed Roc.

MR / *France 1924–1926*
Equipped with various Train engines, the Italian MR was made by the Officine Mecchaniche Romeo Raimondi at Turin. Most versions had 174cc two-stroke engines; earlier ones 98cc.

MR / France 1926

This MR also concentrated on lightweights. 98cc and 123cc Aubier-Dunne, Ydral and Sachs engines played a major part. Special versions made by the factory competed successfully at long-distance events.

MT / Italy 1949–1953

Teresio Muratore designed modern 248cc vertical ohc twins, but was unable to produce larger numbers of these interesting touring and sports machines.

MT / Austria 1925–1937

The Austrian MT was designed by Count Matthias Thun on typical English lines with mainly English parts. Among them were 147cc to 344cc Villiers engines as well as 346cc, 490cc and 746cc JAP sv and ohv engines. The last ones were V-twins. Special models, mainly racing machines, had also 248cc ohv Blackburne and 497cc ohv MAG motors. Thun, who also imported Villiers engines into Austria, used the 344cc Villiers vertical-twin and the watercooled 247cc single-cylinder engine. Among leading MT riders were Count Phillip Boos-Waldeck, Josef Opawsky, Friedrich Schwarz, Robert Wolf, F. J. Meyer and Lorenz Hubbauer.

MÜCO / Germany 1921–1924

Bicycle attachment engines of 118cc, which had to be fitted outside of the rear wheels.

MUFI (IMPERATOR) / Germany 1925–1926

Built one model only. This was a simple 348cc two-stroke machine with a three-port, deflector-type engine.

MÜLLER / Italy 1950–

Designed by Bruno Müller, these machines had for a long period German NSU two and four-stroke engines from 49cc to 248cc. There were also versions with Franco-Morini and Sachs power units. Good design and workmanship.

MÜLLER / Austria 1924–1926

Another two-stroke and yet another simple design, the Austrian Müller was a 183cc machine with a strengthened bicycle frame and a unit-design engine, which had a two-speed gearbox and a big outside flywheel.

MÜNCH-4 / Germany 1966–

Originally known under the Mammut trade mark and equipped with a 996cc NSU four-cylinder car engine, the Friedl Münch-designed big and expensive motorcycle got in later years a similar 1177cc power unit with 88 bhp at 6500 rpm. Another version with fuel-injection had 100 bhp at 7500 rpm. The latest version, the 1200 TTS-E, has the aircooled, transverse-mounted four-in-line NSU engine brought up to 1278cc. In this form it develops 104 bhp at 7500 rpm with its chain-driven ohc and a Kugelfischer suction-line injection. The bore is 78·5mm, the stroke 66·5mm, while the four-speed gearbox drives the rear wheel by a fully-enclosed chain. The telefork is an oildamped Marzocchi while Ronal light-alloy wheels can be supplied instead of wire wheels. In front is a hydraulically-operated Brembo dual disc brake and starting is by a Bosch Electrostart. The weight is 590 lb, the top speed is over 125 mph and 62·5 mph (100 km) is reached in 4·3 seconds. All Münch-4 machines are hand made. A 1973 three-cylinder two-stroke prototype of 700cc capacity never reached the production stage. The late Floyd Clymer of Los Angeles was for some time connected with the Münch-4 factory, which in 1973 was acquired by the present owner, Heinz W. Henke.

MUSTANG / America 1946–1964

Destined mainly for town-riding, the primitively built Mustang had a 314cc sv single-cylinder engine.

MV AGUSTA / Italy 1946–

Famous helicopter factory which—owned by the Count Agusta family—entered motorcycle production with 98cc two-stroke motorcycles. Afterwards 123cc two-strokes came into production: touring, sporting and also racing versions. Other models, two-strokes as well as four-strokes up to 348cc, followed. A 497cc in-line four-cylinder aircooled transverse-mounted unit design model with shaft drive to the rear wheel was offered, but never actually built in quantity. Its square engine had double-ohc, 54mm bore/stroke and 45 bhp at 7500 rpm. This was to be a production version of the Pietro Remor-designed 497cc MV road racing machines, which since 1950 appeared with great success in the big races. MV Agusta also produced a range of scooters and very fast single-cylinder ohc and double ohc racing motorcycles of 123cc, 173cc, 204cc and 248cc. Most double ohc models were for works riders only. These included Carlo Ubbiali, Tarquinio Provini, Luigi Taveri, Bill Lomas, Cecil Sandford and Gary Hocking who—like others—also rode the 497cc and in later years also 347cc four-cylinder racing models. These others included Les Graham, Umberto Masetti, Carlo Bandirola, Mike Hailwood, John Surtees, Nello Pagani, John Hartle, Giacomo Agostini, Phil Read, Gilberto Milani etc. There were also three and even six-cylinder works racing machines; all aircooled, transverse mounted in the frame and with double ohc heads. The racing department, for many years headed by Arturo Magni, built also a variety of frames, forks etc. for the works racers. Privateers could buy mainly 123cc and 173cc single ohc machines; occasionally also an ex-factory model, but never a multi-cylinder racing version. The first fours in production form were sold in the late 1960s. They had 492cc and 62 bhp at 8200 rpm; the next version, a 743cc four had 78 bhp at 7900 rpm. This model had an Electrostart and a top speed of 140 mph. Further development led to a variety of 743cc versions. The very first MV Agusta fours of the late 1940s and early 1950s had shaft drive, yet racing models soon got chain drive and even the later 347cc and 497cc works machines used chain drive. In contrast, the new production fours again have shaft drive. Among them are 790cc and 893cc versions with 67mm × 56mm bore/stroke and 70mm × 58mm bore/stroke. Both have gear-driven double-ohc four-cylinder engines with 90 bhp and 105 bhp respectively. Both have five speeds and Electrostarters. These superbly designed machines are in the luxury class; they show the experience gained in the production of successful racing machines. The range of MV Agusta machines now includes a 123cc ohv single; two vertical-twin models with 349cc and 472cc push-rod engines and 32 bhp at 8800 rpm and 35 bhp at 8900 rpm respectively and—built only by special order—a 497cc

1197cc Münch 4 (ohc four-cylinder NSU engine) 1971

498cc MV Agusta (dohc four-cylinder works racing machine) 1952

147cc MV Agusta (TS) 1957

743cc MV Agusta (dohc four-cylinder Model 750 S) 1975

349cc MV Agusta (ohv two-cylinder Model 350 GT EL) 1975

743cc MV Agusta (dohc four-cylinder Model 750 GT) 1975

double-ohc twin with 66 bhp at 11,000 rpm. For many years, Count Domenico Agusta was leading the motorcycle side of the factory. After his death Count Corrado Agusta took charge.

Big orders for helicopters and other factors forced a rundown of motorcycle production at Verghera. Lack of racing success by three and four-cylinder works racing machines added to a pessimistic atmosphere at the works. First the factory withdrew from racing; then it was decided to build motorcycles at the Bologna Ducati works. But this factory, despite good sales, has suffered financial losses, and a possibility exists that, like Moto Guzzi and Benelli, it will be taken over by the Alessandro de Tomaso group, which will affect MV Agusta.

MVB / *Italy 1954–1956*
Produced 49cc mopeds and motorcycles with 123cc and 147cc two-stroke engines in limited numbers.

MW / *Germany 1923–1926*
The MW, designed by Paul Paffrath, was an unorthodox design with a frame part of which was cast from light alloy and part made from pressed steel, welded and rivetted. The first version had a 249cc ohv single-cylinder engine and three-speed gearbox; the second model a 144cc two-stroke vertical-twin of own design and manufacture. Both machines had rear suspension. After WWII, Paffrath — whose original home was in East Germany — lived in West Germany and produced from 1949 to 1953 a bicycle attachment engine, called Eilenriede.

MYMSA / *Spain 1953–1962*
Produced a wide range of small two-strokes of 75cc, 99cc, 123cc and 175cc in limited numbers.

MZ/*East Germany (DDR) 1946 –*
Made in the pre-war DKW works at Zschopau, the MZ also succeeds the Ifa, but until the late 1950s in this factory. MZ (Motorradwerke Zschopau) became during the years one of the leading motorcycle producers in eastern Europe and also one of the most successful in trials and road races. The factory concentrates on quantity production of good two-stroke singles of 123cc, 143cc, 173cc and 243cc capacity. The range includes also trials models with identical capacities. In addition, there is also a 344cc single-cylinder version. So far these trials versions are not obtainable in western countries. Production 123cc models have 52mm × 58mm bore/stroke and 10 bhp at 6000 rpm; 147cc versions 56mm × 58mm bore/stroke and 11·5 bhp at 6300 rpm, while the latest 243cc single with 69mm bore and 65mm stroke, delivers 17 bhp at 5200 rpm. Not very high outputs in bhp figures, but well-developed machines of comparatively simple design. The smaller models have four, the quarter-litre machine five speeds in unit. Primary drive is by gears, drive to the rear wheel by fully enclosed chain. The very active racing department, headed by Walter Kaaden, produced many good 123cc and 248cc racing singles and vertical twins with air and afterwards also watercooling. They competed in many international races with Mike Hailwood, Luigi Taveri, Garry Hosking, Ernst Degner, Horst Fügner, Alan Shepherd, Derek Woodman, Heinz Rosner, Klaus Enderlein, Dieter Braun and other fine riders. MZ machines also play a leading part in the International Sixday Trials and are always included in the national team of the DDR. For some years they also competed successfully in moto-cross events.

248cc MZ (TS aircooled twin-cylinder works-racer) 1959

248cc MZ (TS watercooled twin-cylinder works racer) 1972

248cc MZ (TS Model Trophy 250/2) 1971

123cc MZ (TS Model 125/G) 1966

248cc MZ (TS Model 250/1 G) 1967

N

NAMAPO / *Germany 1921–1924*
Designed by Bernhard Nagl, the Namapo was built in the northern part of Germany — at Stettin which belongs now to Poland — and was nearly unknown in the south. It was made with own 147cc and 197cc sv single-cylinder engines. The smaller version was sold also as a bicycle attachment engine.

NARCISSE / *France 1950–1953*
Assembler of two-stroke machines with 48cc and 98cc Aubier-Dunne and partly also Sachs engines.

NARCLA / *Spain 1955–late 1960s*
Small assembler who concentrated on 123cc two-strokes.

NASSETTI / *Italy 1951–1957*
Manufacturer of accessories, whose lightweight motorcycles — which included the 49cc Pellegrino with a horizontal cylinder and friction drive — had two-stroke engines and modern frames with telescopic forks. Ettore Nassetti, the designer-manufacturer, used tubular and pressed steel frames for his motorcycles.

NASSOVIA / *Germany 1925*
Small producer, whose motorcycles had the rare 2·75 hp Anzani engine.

NAZZARO / *Italy 1926–1928*
Made by Eugenio Nazzaro of Turin, brother of the famous racing-car driver Felice Nazzaro (Fiat), the machine had a 173cc ohv engine and was built in limited numbers only.

NEALL / *England 1910–1914*
Fitted with 2·5 hp and 3 hp Precision proprietary engines, the Neall was an assembled machine.

NEANDER / *Germany 1924–1929*
Designed by the famous Ernst Neumann-Neander, who was known for his unorthodox creations, the Neander had a frame made from Duralumin covered with cadmium, so that enamelling of the frame was not necessary. The frame included the petrol tank. A fork with small leaf springs and a bucket seat were other features of the Neander, which was also built under licence by the famous Opel car factory. While Opel fitted own 498cc engines, all Neander machines had proprietary power units from 122cc to 996cc. These were Villiers two-strokes, Küchen single-cylinder ohc engines of 347cc and 497cc, MAG engines with ioe valves of 497cc, 746cc and 996cc, JAP sv and ohv engines from 490cc to 996cc and if required other power units could also be fitted. Racing successes were gained by 172cc models with Villiers Brooklands engines ridden by Gohr and Goretzki.

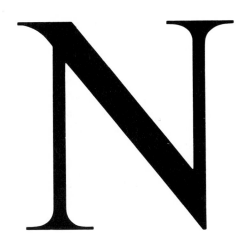

172cc Neander (TS Villiers) 1925

996cc Neander (ioe MAG V-twin) 1929

NECCHI / *Italy 1951–1953*
Assembled motorcycles with 98cc and 123cc Villiers two-stroke engines.

NECO / *Czechoslovakia 1923–1927*
Limited production of 346cc and 490cc sv and ohv machines with JAP engines.

NEGAS & RAY / *Italy 1925–1928*
Milan motorcycle importers which ventured into motorcycle production with 348cc unit-design sv singles which had big outside flywheels. Giuseppe Remondini, the designer, also built an ohv version in 1927 and in the 1930s joined the French Jonghi factory.

NEGRINI / *Italy 1954–*
Concentrates on the quantity production of 48cc and 49cc two-stroke machines, some with three and even four speeds. Also moto-cross versions are in the Negrini range. Earlier models had 110cc and 123cc two-stroke engines.

NEMALETTE / *Germany 1924–1925*
Unorthodox design with two rear wheels, a car-like body and a 173cc DKW two-stroke engine. It is not known if this machine was produced in any large quantities.

NERA / *Germany 1949–1950*
Designed by W. Neuscheler, the Nera was among the first post-war scooters in the country. Engines used were the 120cc Ilo and the 149cc Sachs.

NERACAR / *America (England) 1921–1926*
Designed by J. Neracher, the American-built machine had a low, channel-steel car-like frame. The engine used was a 283cc two-stroke with friction drive to the rear wheel. Built under

licence in England, developed versions of this unorthodox machine had 347cc Blackburne sv and ohv engines. Some models built in 1925 and 1926 also had bucket seats and deeply valanced mudguards. The Neracar was a comfortable machine with excellent road-holding. The machines built in England had chain drive and also an improved fork design.

348cc Neracar (sv Blackburne) 1924

285cc Neracar (TS Simplex engine) 1923

348cc Neracar (sv Blackburne 'De Luxe') 1924

NERVOR / *France 1947–*
Closely connected with Radior, Nervor produced well-finished machines with engines from 48cc to 248cc. Among them were their own power units, but also proprietary engines made by NSU and the French AMC. Nervor's top model was a 248cc vertical two-stroke twin with aircooling.

NESTOR / *England 1913–1914*
Produced in limited numbers Villiers-engined 269cc two-strokes and Precision-engined 296cc and 347cc sv machines.

NESTORIA / *Germany 1923–1931*
Produced 289cc and 346cc two-strokes with their own engines; took over the Astoria factory in 1925 and built afterwards Küchen-engined 348cc and 498cc three-valve, single-cylinder ohc machines. Other versions had 496cc and 596cc MAG engines with ioe valves and eventually 198cc ohv Sturmey-Archer and 497cc sv Sturmey-Archer single-cylinder engines.

346cc Nestoria (TS) 1925

NETTUNIA / *Italy 1950–1953*
Equipped with Busi-designed 123cc and 158cc two-stroke engines, all Nettunia machines were equipped with four-speed gearboxes and were of sound design.

NEVA / *France 1926–1927*
Made by a small factory, these machines had 347cc ohv Anzani single-cylinder engines.

NEVE-ILO / *Germany 1924–1926*
Was among the first factories which fitted the then new 132cc and 170cc Ilo two-stroke proprietary engines into their own frames. Ilo became eventually one of the leading producers of two-stroke proprietary engines in the world.

NEW COMET / *England 1905–1932*
Built motorcycles with interruptions. Haden, the designer-manufacturer, used Villiers, Peco, JAP and Precision engines for his frames and there was also a Climax-engined 293cc two-stroke version. An interruption was from 1924 to 1931, when the last New Comet machines were built. They were equipped with 198cc Villiers engines.

NEW COULSON / *England 1922–1924*
Originally the Coulson-B, the New Coulson had long leaf springs on either side of the rear wheel and a double leaf-sprung front fork. Otherwise it was a normal motorcycle with 269cc two-stroke and 346cc and 498cc sv and ohv engines made by Bradshaw and by Blackburne. Eric Longden won many races on Blackburne-engined machines. Some racing models had also JAP engines, including a V-twin ohv version of 496cc.

496cc Nestoria (sv Sturmey-Archer engine) 1930

NEW ERA / *America c1908–1913*

Open-framed unorthodox design with a 546cc sv engine below the bucket seat and the petrol tank above the rear wheel.

NEW ERA / *England 1920–1922*

Used mainly the 311cc Dalm two-stroke engine, but also other power units made by Precision and JAP.

NEW GERRARD / *England 1922–1940*

To be exact, this machine was really a Scottish product, made by famous racing motorcyclist Jock Porter. For a period when demand was bigger than production at Edinburgh, Campion in Nottingham produced frames on behalf of the Scottish factory. For years Porter fitted Blackburne engines from 173cc to 498cc into good and comparatively light frames, but concentrated from the late 1920s onward on 348cc models with ohv engines. When Blackburne stopped supplying such engines, Porter switched to JAP. He won TT and Grand Prix races on his machines. Other successful riders were the Austrians Georg Gartner, Karl Gall, Willi Melichar and Franz Putzker. Scottish patriots could get Scottish proprietary engines fitted; around 1922–1923 346cc sleeve-valve Barr & Stroud engines were available.

348cc New Gerrard (ohv JAP) 1928

NEW HENLEY / *England 1920–1929*

This make already mentioned under Henley, as there was not much difference between the Henley and the New Henley. The Clarke brothers, original owners of the Birmingham-based factory, had to sell it when their own father, who put up the money, withdrew his support.

348cc New Henley (ohv JAP) 1929

NEW HUDSON / *England 1909–1957*

Was a well-known motorcycle factory, which had with Fred Hutton and Bert Le Vack two leading designers and riders. Other famous racing men with this make were Jimmy Guthrie and Tom Bullus. Most models built were sv and ohv singles with own 346cc, 496cc and 598cc engines, although a 211cc two-stroke was also made around WWI. This nice little machine had 62mm × 70mm bore/stroke, a two-speed gearbox, and according to the model, belt or chain drive. Le Vack broke many records at Brooklands in the late 1920s; soon afterwards further development led to models with sheetmetal panels over engines and gearboxes. Vic Mole, a motorcycle sales expert, was the man behind this idea, which was not too successful. Motor-

346cc New Hudson (ohv) 1927

496cc New Hudson (ohv) 1929

496cc New Hudson (ohv) 1930

cycle production was stopped in 1933 and the name revived by BSA after 1945, when they produced mopeds with 98cc Villiers engines, in contrast to the big V-twins also made by New Hudson in pre-WWI days. There were also MAG-engined three-wheelers built between the wars; via Bert Le Vack, the English factory had good connections with the Swiss make.

NEW IMPERIAL / *England 1903–1939*

Engines made by Precision (Baker) and JAP were fitted until 1925 to all models made by this Birmingham-based factory. They had capacities from 246 to 996cc and were ohv or sv singles. From 1926 onwards, their own power units came into production. Among them were 146cc ohv models as well as 248cc, 346cc and 498cc sv and ohv engines. Unit-design racing engines of 248cc came in 1936, rear suspension in 1938. The factory ran into difficulties in 1939, was bought by Jack Sangster of Ariel and Triumph and should have been moved from Birmingham to Coventry. This was prevented by WWII and production switched to war material after Jack Sangster had once more sold the factory. Racing successes were gained by the Twemlows (Kenneth and Eddie), Leo Davenport, Les Archer, Ted Mellors, Bob Foster, S. 'Ginger' Wood, Karl Gall and others. Headed for many years by Norman Downs, New Imperial produced some interesting racing machines during the years. Among them 248cc and 348cc singles with Le Vack-designed experimental ohc JAP engines which proved fast, but not very reliable. The 497cc V-twins of 1934–1935 with 60-degree ohv engines, some supercharged, designed by Len Horton and mainly ridden by 'Ginger' Wood, proved to be very fast, but difficult to ride in road races, according to the famous Stanley Woods, who was also due to ride this machine in international events.

246cc New Imperial (ohv) 1926

246cc New Imperial (ohv) 1928

246cc New Imperial (ohv Racing-model) 1931

496cc New Imperial (ohv) 1936

246cc New Imperial (ohv) 1938

NEW KNIGHT / *England 1923–1931*
Small assembler of motorcycles with 147cc to 344cc Villiers two-stroke and 293cc JAP sv engines.

NEW MAP / *France 1920–late 1950s*
Built during the years a wide range of assembled machines with engines from 98cc to 998cc and engines made by Zurcher, JAP, Chaise, Blackburne, MAG, Ydral, AMC, Aubier Dunne, Sachs and Opti. New Map built also Mistral-engined 48cc mopeds and even small minicars with 123cc two-stroke engines. That was in the early 1950s, when motorcycle production concentrated around Ydral and AMC-engined models from 98cc to 248cc with two-stroke and ohv power units. Scooters and fully enclosed motorcycles were other products of this very versatile French factory.

NEW MOTORCYCLE / *France 1925–1930*
The Georges Roy-designed New Motorcycle had 246cc two-stroke and also 346cc ohv and ohc engines made by Chaise and MAG. Other power units made by these factories were also fitted.

NEWMOUNT / *England 1929–1933*
These machines — put together at Coventry — were really German Zündapp products with tubular frames. Engines fitted were 198cc, 248cc and 298cc Zündapp three-port deflector-type two-strokes and 348cc and 498cc Python four-valve ohv single-cylinders.

NEW PARAGON / *England 1919–1923*
Produced a range of single-cylinder two-stroke

machines with 235cc, 347cc and 478cc engines of own manufacture and with half-elliptic leaf-springs.

NEW RAPID / *The Netherlands 1933–1936*
Made by the Amsterdam factory of P. J. Meyer, New Rapid supplied Villiers-engined two-strokes of 98cc, 148cc, 196cc, 248cc and 346cc and four-strokes with ohv engines. These included 248cc, 348cc and 498cc four-valve Python engines and also 346cc and 498cc two-valve JAP ohv versions.

NEW RYDER / *England 1913–1922*
Assembled machines with single-cylinder and V-twin Precision engines in early years, but concentrated after 1918 on Villiers-engined 269cc models.

NEW SCALE / *England 1909–1925*
Harry Scale first built his Scale motorcycles in very small numbers, but when he reorganised his production in 1919, he called them New Scale. They were assembled machines with 348cc Precision two-stroke and 499cc Blackburne sv engines. They had two-speed gears and chain-cum-belt drive. Later the range of models increased by 346cc versions with Bradshaw ohv engines and mainly with sv and ohv Blackburne engines of similar size. An interesting model which was built by order had the 347cc ohc Dart engine, designed by Sidney. When New Scale came into difficulties, the factory was taken over by Dot.

NEWTON / *England 1921–1922*
Villiers-engined 269cc two-strokes of cheap design.

NICHOLAS / *England pre-WWI*
This small and now completely forgotten producer of motorcycles produced machines equipped with 1·5 hp engines which were probably made by MMC.

NICKSON / *England 1920–1924*
Assembled a variety of models with proprietary engines. These included the 247cc and 269cc Villiers two-strokes, the oilcooled 348cc ohv Bradshaw and Blackburne's 346cc, 499cc to 546cc sv singles.

NIESNER / *Austria 1905–1911*
Designed by Josef Niesner, the Vienna-built 3 hp, 3·5 hp and 5 hp Minerva- and Fafnir-engined motorcycles were among the first made in the old Austro-Hungarian Empire. They were of sound and strong design. Niesner was after-

wards Austrian importer for Norton, Royal Enfield and other makes.

NIMBUS / *Denmark 1920–1957*
Denmark's largest motorcycle factory ever, Fisker & Nielsen Ltd. at Copenhagen, concentrated all those years on only one model. This was a 746cc aircooled four-in-line with ioe and later ohv unit-design engines. With frames made from pressed steel, early models already had a rear suspension by means of open coil springs and a tank consisting of a wide-diameter tube. The trailing arm front suspension was superseded by a telefork and a triangular tank superseded the earlier one. Common to all Nimbus models was shaft drive and a very limited export.

746cc Nimbus (ioe four-cylinder spring-frame) 1924

746cc Nimbus (ohc four-cylinder) 1955

NINON / *France 1931–1935*
Small producer of 499cc JAP-engined ohv.

NIS / *Germany 1925–1926*
Another small factory which fitted 269cc two-stroke and mainly 293cc JAP sv engines into orthodox frames of own manufacture.

NISSAN / *Japan 1951–1956*
A range of 60cc machines with own ohv single-cylinder engines, made by a famous car firm.

NKF / *Germany 1924–1925*
Lightweight motorcycles with 132cc Bekamo-licence engines, which used a pumping piston in the crankcase.

NLG / *England 1905–1912*
This maker achieved fame when a NLG racing

machine with a large, 2913cc ohv V-twin JAP engine ridden by Cook reached 90 mph in 1909. Production versions housed 499cc single and 770cc V-twin JAP engines.

NMC / *Japan early 1950s–early 1960s*
Small 123cc and 173cc two-stroke machines, built by a small factory.

NOBLE / *England 1901–c1906*
The Noble was one of the first makes using the new central Werner position of engine location. The 2·25 to 4·5 bhp engines came from De Dion, Minerva, MMC, Coronet and also from their own production.

NORBRECK / *England 1921–1924*
D. H. Valentine's Norbreck machines housed 269cc Villiers and Arden (70mm bore × 70mm stroke) two-stroke engines. Models with 346cc and 496cc sv Blackburne engines were built on request.

NORDSTERN / *Germany 1922–1924*
Produced 2·5 hp two-strokes with own deflector-type engines. SFW took over this design when the original producer went bankrupt.

NORICUM / *Austria (Czechoslovakia) 1903–1906*
Built actually by Cless & Plessing at Graz in Austria, then the Austro-Hungarian Empire, the 2·75 hp and 3·5 hp singles and 5 hp V-twins supplied to the Czechoslovakian part of the Empire were renamed Noricum.

NORMAN / *England 1937–1961*
Entered the market with 98cc Autocycles, took over the design and production equipment for the 98cc Rudge Autocycle and also built motorcycles with 98cc to 247cc Villiers two-stroke engines. In some countries they were renamed Rambler. In the late 1950s they bought the remains of the German Achilles factory. In the early 1960s the Norman brothers sold out to the big Raleigh group of companies, and manufacture of Norman motorcycles came to an end.

246cc Norman (TS Villiers 'Trials') 1962

NORTON / *England 1901–*
One of the great names in the British motorcycle industry, founded by James Lansdowne Norton. The first machines had Swiss Moto-Rêve engines, built in England under licence, and French Peugeot engines, which drove the larger Norton models. With such a V-twin machine H. Rem Fowler won in 1907 the twin-cylinder class in the first Tourist Trophy at the Isle of Man. The Big Four, a 633cc sv single came on the market in 1908, the 3·5 hp model with a 490cc engine in 1911. The first ohv single was built in 1922 and the first ohc model was built for the 1927 TT. A year later, the first 348cc Norton came into being. J. L. Norton was only 56 when he died in 1925. A year earlier, his machines had their greatest triumph so far, when they won the Senior TT with Alec Bennett and the sidecar TT with George Tucker in the saddle. Tucker's passenger was a technician, who in 1923 had joined Norton, coming from the Douglas factory at Bristol: Walter William Moore. It was he who in 1927 designed the first ohc Norton. He left in 1930 to join NSU in Germany, while Arthur Carrol became his successor at Norton's Birmingham Bracebridge Street works. Joe

Craig, an Irishman who had retired from racing, was now in charge of the racing department. Typical for all Norton machines was their own single-cylinder engine with separate gearbox. The 633cc sv machine had 82mm bore and 120mm stroke, the 490cc sv and ohv models 79mm bore and 100mm stroke. This was also the case with the CS1, the first 490cc ohc production model in 1928. A 588cc ohv single added in the mid-1920s had a bore of 79mm and a 120mm stroke, the 348cc engines 71mm bore and 88mm stroke. The factory kept for many years to these specifications, and the very popular model 16H, a 490cc sv model used in large numbers during WWII, had the traditional 79mm bore and 100mm stroke. Even the last pre-war Norton range had only 348cc, 490cc, 596cc and 633cc sv, ohv and ohc singles. The greatest racing men in Europe rode and won during the years on Norton machines and Norton was the most successful English make in road racing. Among the riders were Stanley Woods, Freddy Frith, Jimmy Guthrie, Walter Rusk, Percy Hunt, Graham Walker, Pietro Ghersi, Tazio Nuvolari, Jimmy Simpson, 'Crasher' White, Harold Daniell, Karl Rührschneck, Otto Ley, Sepp Klein, Oskar Steinbach, Werner Mellmann, Jimmy Shaw, Piet van Wijngaarden, Walter Handley, Tom Simister, Eric Oliver and many others. Norton machines excelled also in trials; Harold Flook and Dennis Mansell—son of Norton's Managing Director Bill Mansell—were among the leading competitors in such

490cc Norton (sv) 1921

490cc Norton (ohv) 1924

490cc Norton (ohv) 1926

events. Others were Vic Brittain, Jack Williams and Graham Goodmann.

After Arthur Carroll's death in a road accident, Joe Craig became Norton's technical boss and head of the racing department. His works racing machines, already in heavy competition against German and Italian multi-cylinder supercharged racing machines (BMW and Gilera) had double-ohc engines in 1937. Unfortunately Norton retired officially from racing in 1938; Joe Craig joined BSA and soon afterwards AJS-Matchless in London. When the supercharged 498cc AJS racers competed in 1939 in the Ulster GP, Joe Craig was in charge. Norton produced over 100,000 machines during the war for the forces and when the war ended, C. Gilbert Smith became the new managing director in succession to Bill Mansell. C. A. Vandervell, who raced Nortons in the early 1920s and whose father founded the CAV company, became a member of the board of Norton. Joe Craig rejoined the factory in 1946, when production motorcycles for civilians was resumed.

The first models were old friends in the shape of the H16 and similar pre-war versions, now with telescopic forks. The demand was big especially for 348cc and 490cc ohc racing machines, as the bigger versions of ohc power units were also in demand for F-3 racing cars. There was a big export to the USA too, where riders such as Don Evans, Bill Mathews, Dick Klamforth and Bobby Hill won numerous races for Norton. In addition, there was a shortage of new machines in England and many were sold to racing men. The works team, again headed by Joe Craig, consisted now of Harold Daniell, Artie Bell, Johnny Lockett, Geoff Duke, Jack Brett, Reg. Armstrong, Ray Amm, Ken Kavanagh, Bob Keeler, Dickie Dale, John Hartle, Bill Doran, Bob Anderson, Reg. Tanner, Mike Hailwood, John Surtees, Derek Minter, Phil Read, Tom Phillis, Bob McIntyre, Bob Brown, David Chadwick, Alistair King, Terry Shepherd and others, who gained many successes with works and also privately entered Nortons. Famous also were leading tuners of these

machines: Francis Baert, Steve Lancefield, Bill Lacey, Bill Stuart, Joe Potts. A four-cylinder racing ohc model was due to supersede the famous Manx racing singles, but Joe Craig had no chance to finish this design. The commercial situation in the mid-1950s was not as it might have been, and such a new design was — including development and actual racing — quite expensive. Also a new single-cylinder with a horizontal ohc motor never reached production stage.

Herbert Hopwood, who had joined Norton with Joe Craig in 1946, now designed new production models; 497cc ohv vertical twins with 66mm bore and 72mm stroke. New also were 490cc ohv singles for trials, while steady development made the ohc racing Manx models faster and better. A big step forward was the McCandless-designed Featherbed frame, used on racing machines from 1950 onwards. The McCandless brothers of Belfast, Rex and Crommie, were excellent riders and technicians. Equipped with these Featherbed frames the 1951 production 30M 499cc and 40M 348cc Manx double-ohc racing machines became bestsellers. The 499cc had now 79·62mm bore and 100mm stroke, the 348cc version 71mm bore and 88mm stroke. They were, of course, developed during the years and in 1952 they got nearly square engines with 85·9mm bore and 86mm stroke for the 499cc and with 75·9mm bore and 77mm stroke for the 348cc version. From 1953 onwards, all Norton models had swinging-fork rear suspensions instead of the plunger-type and more models now had the excellent Featherbed frame. In the same year, Norton was bought by Associated Motor Cycles in London, manufacturer of AJS and Matchless motorcycles, who then also owned James and Francis Barnett. And another change in the 499cc Manx racer led to the 88mm × 82mm engine. A Streamliner built for racing was ridden by Ray Amm, but proved to be unsuitable. The once more redesigned

490cc Norton (ohc Model CS 1) 1927

490cc Norton (ohc Model CS 1) 1930

490cc Norton (ohv Model 18) 1927

490cc Norton (sv) 1931

490cc Norton (ohv 'Trials') 1935

490cc Norton (ohc 'International') 1933

496cc Norton (ohc 'International') 1935

works-engines were a success in 1954: 90mm × 78·4mm for the 499cc and 78mm × 73mm for the 348cc racer. These were short-stroke power plants, which were different from the production versions, which had 86mm × 85·6mm for the 30M and 76mm × 76·7mm for the 40M. For 1955 all sv models were dropped. The vertical ohv twins were now available with 597cc engines too.

Joe Craig left Nortons in 1955, to go into semi-retirement, but was killed two years later in a car accident in Austria. Bert Hopwood, who was for some years with BSA, returned to Norton as technical boss. Another leading technician was Doug Hele. Many production versions were built in the following years, but the racing Manx

models slowly faded out. When Norton was 60 years old in 1958, they built a 249cc parallel-twin with forward-sloping cylinders. A 648cc vertical-twin and also a 745cc version reached the market, after Norton moved from Birmingham to the London-based AMC factory in 1963. Norton machines became in the following years more and more a mixture of Norton, AJS and Matchless parts. In August 1966, AMC Ltd. ceased to exist and Dennis Poore of Manganese Bronze Holdings bought the remains. Production continued only of 647cc and 746cc ohv twins, mainly for the USA market. John Tickle, a former racing man, bought all remaining Manx parts and production rights and continued supplying them. He also produced improved

new machines on a limited scale. In 1968 Poore transferred engine production to the Wolverhampton works where he had bought earlier the Villiers engine factory. In 1970 he became managing director of this new set-up, Norton-Villiers Ltd. A new plant was erected in Andover, Hampshire, near the Thruxton race track. Poore, knowing the value of racing successes, re-entered road-racing officially with a team led by Peter Williams, son of former racing man and AMC Ltd. racing-department chief C. J. Williams. He also founded additional companies for the distribution, service, etc. of Norton machines. John Player & Sons sponsored the racing team, but for various reasons, things never worked as they should have. There were

828cc Norton (ohv twin 'Commando Roadster') 1974

498cc Norton (ohc 'Manx') 1947

498cc Norton (dohc 'Manx') 1962

348cc Norton (ohc 'Manx') 1938

828cc Norton (ohv twin 'Commando Interpol') 1974

fast 745cc and 828cc ohv twin-cylinder production racers ridden by Peter Williams and Paul Smart for a racing department headed by former racer Frank Perris. The basis for these were Norton Commando models with 73mm bore and 89mm stroke and bigger versions with 77mm bore and 89mm stroke, superb vertical ohv twins which had gained much popularity in the USA and other countries. Difficulties arose when Poore took BSA and Triumph into his group of companies and when even Wolverhampton had to stop engine manufacture. BSA had closed down earlier, Triumph production in Coventry (Allesley-Meriden) became detached from NVT (Norton-Villiers-Triumph Motorcycles International Ltd.) which now has its H.Q. at Shenstone, Staffs.

NORVED / *Germany 1924–1925*
Assembled on a limited scale 348cc and 498cc motorcycles with ohv and sv Kühne proprietary engines. By order, Blackburne single-cylinder engines could be fitted instead.

NOVA / *Hungary 1925–1928*
Produced sporting machines with engines from 248cc to 498cc. The single-cylinder engines came from the JAP and Blackburne factories. Also most other parts such as Amal carburettors, Best & Lloyd oil pumps, Sturmey-Archer gearboxes, Druid forks etc. came from England. Among successful Nova riders in races were both Stefan and Nikolaus von Horthy, the sons of Hungary's Reichsverweser (head of state), Stephan Kiss and Karoly von Hild.

NOVY / *Belgium early 1930s to early 1960s*
Produced two-strokes from 48cc to 244cc with mainly Ilo engines. Among the models also was a vertical twin.

NSH / *Germany 1923–1928*
This make should not be confused with the better known NSU. The NSH was an assembled machine of sound design with 173cc to 346cc Villiers to 490cc JAP engines. The Villiers-engined versions included the vertical 344cc twin of 1927–1928.

344cc NSH (TS Villiers twin) 1927

NSU/*Germany 1901–1958*

Prominent factory, which built during the years superb motorcycles which won big races and broke many international records. Great designers, including Walter William Moore, Otto Reitz, Schmidt and Roder produced many interesting designs and such leading riders as Wilhelm Herz, Heiner Fleischmann, Hermann Böhm, Werner Haas, Rupert Hollaus, H. P. Müller, Hans Baltisberger, Otto Daiker, Bill Lomas, Reg. Armstrong, Roberto Colombo, Kurt Nitschky, Karl and Otto Rührschneck, Karl Bodmer, Oskar Steinbach, Werner Mellmann, Tom Bullus, Hans Soenius, Paul Rüttchen, Guglielmo Sandri, Ted Mellors, Rudolf Runtsch, Max Reheis, Hans Kaufmann, Hans Stärkle, Ernst and Franz Islinger, Karl Scherer, Werner Huth, Fergus Anderson, Leonard Fassl and others showed again and again the excellence of NSU designs.

The first machines had the name Neckarsulm —where NSU machines were made—as trade mark. Swiss 1·5 hp Zedel engines powered them. Soon afterwards, their own single-cylinder

1¾ hp NSU (sv Zedel-engine) 1903

4 hp NSU (sv watercooled engine) 1905

6 hp NSU (ohv V-twin racing machine) 1909

326cc NSU (sv spring-frame) 1914

497cc NSU (sv) 1927

and V-twin engines with ioe valves were built. Already in pre-1914 days a rear suspension by means of a coil spring behind the saddle was available. Many models were built during the 1920s, including 498cc, 746cc and 996cc V-twins and unit-design singles from 248cc with sv, ioe and ohv engines. Among them were also 498cc unit-design sv singles. Factory riders even had 996cc ohv V-twins and raced reliable 248cc ohv machines from 1927 to 1929. When business was bad around 1930, they engaged the English designer Walter William Moore, formerly with Norton, who produced new models. Among them fast Norton-like 497cc ohc singles, which —then ridden by his compatriot, Yorkshireman Tom Bullus, by Paul Rüttchen, Toni Ulmen and Sepp Giggenbach—gained much popularity for the new NSU designs. The factory also built new two and four-strokes from 98cc to 598cc with a special eye on 98cc, 198cc and 248cc models, which became very popular. NSU became in the 1930s one of the biggest motorcycle producers in the world. In addition to the 498cc NSU ohc racing machine, a similar 348cc model also won races. Afterwards they had double-ohc heads and in 1937 Moore together with Roder created new NSU racing machines: supercharged sloping vertical twins with double-ohc and 348cc, later also 498cc. Teething troubles prevented successes in pre-war days,

but when Wilhelm Herz worked soon after the war on a 348cc twin, it soon became one of the best machines in its class. A 498cc four-cylinder in-line racing machine with the engine mounted transversely was built in 1950, but was not successful. Much better were 123cc double-ohc singles and 248cc double-ohc twins, designed in 1951 by Albert Roder and developed by Ewald Praxl and Walter Froede. These won German and World Championships. Wilhelm Herz broke many world records on supercharged 348cc and 498cc twins while H. P. Müller was doing the same with smaller engines in smaller classes on G. A. Baumm-designed versions.

NSU built during the years large numbers of 49cc mopeds, but also 98cc two-stroke and ohv machines. Their Quick, Quickly, Fox and Max models became good sellers in many parts of the

world. The Sportmax with its single-cylinder ohc engine had become a very popular racing machine when at the end of 1954 the factory closed the works racing department. H. P. Müller won with it the world championship in 1955 in the 250cc class. NSU built the Lambretta scooter during the 1950s under licence, and afterwards its own Prima scooter. After a long interruption—since 1929—NSU returned to the manufacture of cars. The end of motorcycle production came in 1957, when the works sold everything to the Yugoslavian Pretis works at Sarajevo. Interesting facts: during the last war an NSU chain-driven car with an Opel engine was built for the army; among the many superb works riders during the years were also two men who became famous F-1 racing-car drivers: Bernd Rosemeyer and Hermann-Paul Müller.

498cc NSU (dohc twin-cylinder supercharged works-racer) 1950

174cc NSU (ohc model 'Maxi') 1957

592cc NSU (sv) 1935

494cc NSU (ohv Model 'Sport') 1935

124cc NSU (TS 'Fox') 1951

248cc NSU (ohc model 'Supermax') 1957

NUT/*England 1912–1933*
Although founded only in 1912, NUT was already in 1913 a TT winner, when Hugh Mason won on a V-twin the Junior TT in the Isle of Man. The name was always closely connected with V-twins, with machines of 498, 678, 698 and 746cc capacity. Engines came from JAP as well as from their own production. There were

698cc NUT (sv V-twin) 1923

498cc NUT (ohv V-twin four-port) 1927

four-port 498cc and 698cc ohv models, and there were also 172cc Villiers-engined two-strokes and 248cc and 348cc ohv singles with JAP power units.

NUX/*Germany 1924–1925*
Small producer of 170cc machines with own three-port deflector-type two-stroke engines.

NV/*Sweden 1926–*
Now part of the big MCB-Monark group of companies, NV became known for fast 246cc ohv single-cylinder unit-design engines in excellent frames. There were afterwards two-strokes up to 123cc in production which had proprietary engines made by DKW, Royal Enfield, Sachs and others.

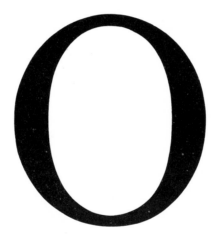

OASA/*Italy 1930–1932*
Designed and produced by the Aliprandi brothers, the Oasa had Ladetto's 173cc ohv engines and also 246cc and 346cc JAP single-cylinder ohv engines.

OB/*Austria 1904–1907*
Made at Vienna by Messrs. Opel & Beyschlag who imported Opel cars into the Austro-Hungarian Empire, the OB motorcycles had their own 2hp single-cylinder and 3·5hp V-twin power units and shaft drive.

OBERLE/*Germany 1927–1929*
Villiers-engined 147cc and 172cc two-stroke machines, designed by the racing motorcyclist Eugen Oberle.

OCMA (DEVIL)/*Italy 1953–1957*
These are the 123cc to 244cc two and four-

stroke machines which have already been mentioned under Devil.

OCRA/*Germany 1923–1925*
Ottomar Cramer, who built Lloyd motorcycles, was also designer/manufacturer of the 137cc Ocra bicycle attachment engines and of 293cc and 346cc sv and ohv motorcycles.

OD/*Germany 1927–1935*
The blue-grey machines produced by the Willy Ostner factory at Dresden were of good and sturdy design. Most models had 347, 497, 597 and 996cc ioe and ohv MAG engines; only some special racing versions including the 996cc 55hp V-twin ohv sidecar racer ridden by works rider Arno Zaspel had JAP power units. The big production 996cc MAG-engined version was the only German machine of the late 1920s and early 1930s with a reverse gear. Among the machines made were also 497cc racing models

with the MAG ohv racing D50 engine and from 1931 onwards a MAG-engined 846cc V-twin with the Le Vack-designed sv engine. There were also 198cc and 246cc models with Bark two-stroke engines and frames made from cast alloy. After the mid-1930s OD concentrated on three-wheelers, which were also made after 1945, when Ostner lived in West Germany. OD racing men besides Zaspel included Franz Heck, Ernst Bocktenk and Willi Zwolle.

996cc OD (ioe MAG V-twin) 1930

498cc OD (ioe MAG) 1931

498cc OD (ohv MAG production racer) 1932

498cc OD (ohv MAG Model 'Sport') 1934

ODA/*Germany 1925–1926*
Simple and cheaply built 293cc motorcycles with the JAP sv engine.

OEC/*England 1901–1954*
The name came from Osborn Engineering Company. Frederick Osborn built his first machines with Minerva and MMC engines. After an interruption of some years, his son John Osborn resumed manufacture in 1920, after the Blackburne factory decided to concentrate on producing proprietary engines only. That was the birth of the OEC-Blackburne, which later became just OEC. Fred Wood was also connected with the factory; he was a clever technician and invented among other things the duplex steering on OEC machines. There were 348cc and 547cc singles and 998cc V-twins with sv engines in the range of models in 1922–1923, among them a big 998cc sidecar version with a steering wheel instead of handlebars, which was also available with a 1096cc V-twin Blackburne engine. Very sporting was a 348cc ohv single. OEC also built many frames for record-breaking V-twins, among them the frame for Claude Temple's 996cc Hubert Hagens-designed British-Anzani ohc power unit. This was a double-loop frame with Harley-Davidson-type bottom-link forks.

Another OEC design was the duplex steering frame, used in 1930 by Joe Wright with a supercharged 85 bhp 996cc V-twin ohv JAP engine, when he reached a speed of 137·3 mph. This machine was fitted with a Powerplus supercharger. Another interesting frame was built in 1928, when the factory was on the verge of building the unorthodox Tinkler design in quantities. The Tinkler, first seen in the 1927 TT practice, had a fully enclosed 497cc flat single-cylinder engine with watercooling. The OEC production range included after 1925 347cc and 497cc Atlanta single-cylinder ohc engines with the camshafts driven by two pairs of bevel gears and a vertical shaft. Other models had Villiers two-stroke engines from 147cc to 342cc and JAP as well as Blackburne engines from 173cc to 998cc, including 678cc, 746cc and 998cc V-twins with sv and ohv engines. Villiers-engined machines and 498cc special Speedway versions which had been made from 1929 onwards again came into production after 1945. Among the models built in the second half of the 1930s were 248cc and 498cc, afterwards also 347cc singles and 998cc V-twins with JAP and Matchless ohv engines. Only the big version had an sv engine. The range included also the unorthodox Atlanta-Duo model with a 498cc ohv JAP and 746cc V-twin sv JAP engine. A 498cc ohv Speedway JAP engine was fitted to post-war speedway models. Road-going OEC machines had besides Villiers engines also the Brookhouse-built Indian 246cc sv unit-design single-cylinder engine.

346cc OEC (ohv Blackburne racing model) 1924

496cc OEC (ohv Matchless engine, Duplex steering) 1937

347cc OEC (ohv Matchless engine) 1938

986cc OEC (sv V-twin Blackburne 'Taxi') 1923

OFRAN / *Germany 1923–1925*
Concentrated on the production of a single model with its own 425cc two-stroke three-port engine.

OGAR / *Czechoslovakia 1934–1950*
Closely connected with a big accessory firm, Ogar was building superb 246cc two-stroke machines of very sporting appearance. Concentrating on this one model, they developed it from year to year. They built also a few water-cooled versions for the works riders, who competed successfully in races and in trials. There were also a few Ogar-built 498cc speedway machines with ohv JAP and also their own ohv power units. The black-green machines designed by František Bartuška were very popular among younger riders, and some leading racing men including Jan Lucak, František Fiala, Lada Steiner, Vašek Liška, Jiři Plichta and Anton Mikl rode them too. The speedway machines were ridden by Lucak and Hugo Rosák; afterwards by Šimek, Špinka and Němeček. After 1945 and nationalisation, Ogar designer Vincenz Sklenář created a new and modern 348cc ohc single with unit-design engine, telefork and plunger-type rear suspension. It never went into quantity production. The new Ogar was really a 346cc twin-cylinder two-stroke, designed on lines of the 246cc Jawa by Jawa designers. It had for some time the Ogar tank transfer, but became eventually the forerunner of all today's twins made by the big Czechoslovakian factory.

OGE / *Germany 1921–1924*
This was a 118cc two-stroke bicycle engine, designed by Oskar Giebel.

OGSTON / *England 1911–1913*
Name used during a short period for Wilkinson-TMC motorcycles.

OHB / *Germany 1927–1928*
Designed by Otto Hoffmann, this was an English-looking 490cc single with the JAP sv engine. Small scale production.

OK (OK-SUPREME) / *England 1899–1939*
Early OK motorcycles had De Dion, Minerva, Precision and Green engines. After WWI, the range used the company's own 292cc (70mm × 76mm bore/stroke) two-stroke and Blackburne 247cc and 347cc sv and ohv engines. There were also 348cc machines with the oilcooled Bradshaw engine and also JAP-engined versions from 246cc to 496cc. The 248cc racing models were famous; the young Walter Handley rode Blackburne-engined racers in 1922. From the mid-1920s onwards, JAP engines powered the 248cc racing models. Ridden by Frank Longmann, Alec Bennett, C. T. Ashby, Joe Sarkis, Rudolf Runtsch, Vic Anstice and others, they won many races. New Jones-designed 248cc long-stroke engines replaced the proprietary racing engines in the early 1930s, and 348cc ohc engines were added to the range of machines, which still relied on JAP engines up to 498cc. There was also a special grass-track version with a 348cc JAP ohv engine, still available in limited numbers after the war until the death of John Humphries, the son of one of the founders of OK, the late Ernest Humphries. Among the last OK-Supreme models were ohv JAP-engined high-camshaft versions with 248cc, 348cc and 498cc single-cylinder engines.

293cc OK (sv JAP) 1926

346cc OK (ohv Bradshaw oilcooled) 1926

248cc OK-Supreme (ohv JAP) 1928

346cc OK-Supreme (ohv JAP) 1929

346cc Ogar (TS twin) 1948

248cc OK-Supreme (ohc) 1936

OLIVA / *Italy 1920–1925*
The Oliva brothers built 120cc bicycle engines, afterwards a 173cc two-stroke motorcycle with the French Train engine.

OLIVERIO / *Italy 1929–1932*
Assembled motorcycles with 346cc and 496cc Sturmey-Archer ohv engines.

OLIVOS / *England 1920–1921*
Blackburne-engined 496cc sv singles in spring frames of the company's own design and limited manufacture.

OLLEARO / *Italy 1923–1952*
With the exception of early 131cc two-strokes, Ollearo became known as a producer of heavy motorcycles with unit-design 173cc to 499cc single-cylinder ohv engines and with shaft drive to the rear wheel. The 173cc models had two-stroke engines as well as ohv versions. They were probably the first shaft-driven, four-speed, unit-design 173cc models built commercially. After 1945, a 45cc bicycle engine with 1·25 bhp at 4500 rpm was made, followed by slightly modernised pre-war 173cc, 246cc, 346cc and 496cc singles. Neftali Ollearo, the founder of the factory, never showed interest in racing; his machines were destined to serve exclusively as good touring motorcycles.

OLMO / *Italy 1951–1961*
Produced lightweights, including mopeds, with 38cc Mosquito and 48cc two-strokes of various makes.

OLYMPIC / *England 1903–1923*
MMC engines with 2·75 hp powered the first Olympic motorcycles. After a long interruption,

new 1919 models had 269cc Verus and afterwards 261cc Orbit two-stroke engines. Frank H. Parkyn's factory supplied frames to other companies, also fitted Villiers, JAP and Blackburne engines and produced under the New Courier trade mark cheap versions of Olympic machines.

OLYMPIQUE / *France 1922–1958*
For many years Zurcher proprietary engines (two and four-stroke) and also JAP engines powered these Courbevoie-built machines. Most models had 98cc, 173cc and 346cc. After 1945 the range consisted of two-strokes from 98cc to 173cc and also of a Zurcher-engined 230cc model. There were also AMC-engined 123cc, 173cc and 248cc ohv and partly ohc singles and a 123cc scooter with a two-stroke engine. Like Thomann, Armor, La Francaise and other companies, Olympique was part of the Alcyon group.

OLYMPUS-KING / *Japan 1956–1960*
Built on English lines, most models had 123cc two-stroke and 346cc ohv single-cylinder engines.

OM / *Germany 1923–1925*
These machines had 173cc ohv, 346cc and 490cc JAP sv and ohv engines. The total production was small.

OMA / *Italy 1952–1955*
Built 173cc unit-design ohv and ohc singles with three-speed gearboxes.

OMB / *Italy 1933–1934*
Modern Angelo Blatto-designed 174cc ohv single-cylinder machines. Blatto was also connected with the machines produced by the Ladetto & Blatto concern.

OMC / *Italy 1933–1935*
This Giovanni Ladetto-designed 174cc machine was built by the Officine Meccaniche Calabresi. The engine was an ohv single.

OMC / *England 1930*
C. G. Vale's 172cc machine had a Villiers engine and was destined for trials riding.

OMEA / *Italy 1950–1953*
Interesting machine with a cast alloy frame designed by Carlo Bottari. There was a leading link fork and swinging arm rear suspension. The engine was a 124cc two-stroke with 5·4 bhp at 5400 rpm.

OMEGA / *England 1909*
Designed by A. J. Dorsett of Diamond fame, the old Omega had a horizontal 1·5 hp engine.

170cc Omega (TS Model 'Junior') 1923

346cc Omega (ohv JAP) 1926

OMEGA / *England 1919–1927*
When Premier in Coventry closed down, factory manager W. J. Green founded the Omega works. The first models had 269cc Villiers and 499cc Blackburne engines. Other models included Omega's own 170cc and 348cc two-stroke engines as well as JAP, Blackburne, Bradshaw and Barr & Stroud engines up to 678cc.

OMEGA / *Japan 1960s*
These were Kawasaki machines renamed for the American market.

OMER / *Italy 1968–*
Sporting lightweights with 49cc FB-Minarelli two-stroke engines.

348cc Ollearo (ohv shaft-drive) 1935

OMN / *Italy 1924–1925*
Villiers-engined 147cc and 172cc two-strokes, built in limited numbers.

OMNIA / *Germany 1931–1933*
Cheap two-strokes with 98cc and 147cc Villiers and 198cc Bark engines, built by the Imperia motorcycle works at Bad Godesberg.

OMT / *Italy 1949–1953*
Identical machines—248cc ohc vertical twins — to the MT.

ONAWAY / *England 1904–1908*
Unconventional design with low triangular frames, bucket seats and Kelecom 5 hp V-twins or the Berkley vertical-twin power unit.

OPEL / *Germany 1901–1930*
There were different periods when the big Opel car factory at Rüsselsheim, now owned by General Motors, built motorcycles too. The earliest models had 1·75 hp–2 hp and bigger versions 2·25 hp–2·75 hp single cylinder engines in open as well as in closed tubular frames. Production seems to have stopped around 1907 and was resumed soon after WWI. Leading link forks were used in 1906–1907. The next motorcycle engine, designed in 1914 but built after 1918, was a four-stroke sv bicycle attachment engine of about 123cc, which was fitted on the left side of the rear wheel. Opel, then a leading bicycle manufacturer, also supplied complete machines with strengthened frames and tanks which looked like fire extinguishers. There were also complete motorcycles with 148cc ioe engines and two-speed gearboxes from 1922 to 1925.

From 1926–1927 there was a 498cc single with an 84mm bore and 90mm stroke sv engine. 1928 saw the production of designer Ernst Neumann's Opel frames made from pressed steel, identical to the original Neander products. Opel built

2¾ hp Opel (sv) 1905

204cc Opel (ohv watercooled track-racing machine) 1922

140cc Opel (sv rear-engine) 1921

148cc Opel (sv) 1924

498cc Opel (ohv 'Motoclub') 1928   **498cc Opel (sv 'Motoclub') 1928**

them under licence at the former Elite-Diamant car factory, after they stopped building Diamant motorcycles and Elite cars. The new models, known as Motoclub, had 499cc sv and ohv engines with 16 bhp and 22 bhp respectively. These models were the last motorcycles made by this famous car factory. There were two interesting non-production Opel machines, ridden from 1922 to 1924 by Fritz von Opel and Philipp Karrer. One was a watercooled track-racing machine with a 204cc ohv engine, rearward facing exhaust port and a big outside flywheel. And a 1928 Motoclub with a 499cc ohv engine was tested — also by Fritz von Opel — with six rockets, three on each side of the rear wheel. The experiment was soon dropped.

OPRA / *Italy 1927–1929*
Designed by two famous designers, Pietro Remor and Carlo Gianini, the OPRA was an aircooled 490cc four-cylinder in-line ohc racing machine with the power unit mounted transversely. In later years it formed the basic design for the famous Rondine 4, which in 1937 became the first watercooled and supercharged 498cc Gilera Four and the forerunner of the latest aircooled Gilera and MV Agusta four-cylinder works racing models.

OR / *Italy 1928–1931*
Produced bicycle engines and 173cc motorcycles which were equipped with their own sv and ohv engines.

ORBIT / *England 1913–1924*
The versatile Dorsett also designed Orbit motorcycles, first with 346cc sv engines, and after 1919 261cc two-strokes. Although there was only a small output from the works, models with various Barr & Stroud, Bradshaw and Blackburne engines were added.

OREOL / *France 1903–WWI*
Pioneer motorcycle producer, whose rider Cissac broke many records on a 333cc single-cylinder model. Oreol also built V-twins with Zedel, Moto-Rêve and other engines.

ORI / *Germany 1923–1925*
Lightweight machines with 145cc two-stroke engines.

ORIAL / *France 1919–1926*
Was closely connected with the French MAG branch factory at Lyon and fitted MAG 346cc and 496cc ioe and ohv single-cylinder and V-twin engines into their own frames.

2½ hp Orient (sv Aster engine) 1901

ORIAL / *Germany 1929–1931*
This name came into being when the marriage between Triumph (TEC) in Coventry and Triumph (TWN) in Nuremberg was dissolved. The Germans had until then used mainly Coventry-made engines and parts. Now they fitted Swiss MAG engines and renamed the machines Orial for export into certain countries.

Afterwards they changed to TWN, which stood for Triumph Werke Nürnberg.

ORIENT / *America 1900–c1906*
Excellent design by Harry Metz, who fitted 2·25 hp and 2·5 hp engines into strong modified bicycle frames.

ORIGAN / *France 1933–early 1950s*
Lightweights with two-stroke engines (mainly Aubier-Dunne) from 98cc to 174cc.

ORIGINAL-KRIEGER / *Germany 1925–1926*
After the original KG design was sold to Cito and via Cito to Allright, the Krieger brothers left and founded a new company, producing first their 498cc models. After Allright intervention, they had to stop and used 346cc Blackburne sv engines in the slightly modified KG frames.

ORION / *Czechoslovakia 1902–1933*
Vilém Michl, the designer-manufacturer, built in the early years superb singles and V-twins with his own engines. He was assisted in the works by his sons, especially Zdeněk Michl who created many interesting designs after WWI. There was

348cc Orial (ohv MAG) 1929 (German)

746cc Orial (ioe MAG) 1929 (German)

241

a good 346cc two-stroke single as well as a 594cc double-piston two-stroke single. From 1927 onwards they made 496cc and 598cc sv singles and also a 496cc ohv machine. With Z. Michl, Václav Liška, Jarda Melzer etc. Orion machines gained many successes in sporting events.

ORIONE/*Italy 1923–1928*

Guido Carpi produced very fast 123cc and 173cc two-strokes with three-port deflector-type engines. Nello Pagani, Raffaele Alberti and Martino Soffientini were among the successful racing riders.

497cc Orion (ohv) 1929

347cc Orion (TS) 1923

4½ hp Orion (sv V-twin Model 'W') 1908

ORIONETTE/*Germany 1921–1925*
Built a range of good 129cc, 137cc, 148cc and 346cc two-stroke machines with mainly unit-design engines and two or three-speed gearboxes. The design department, headed by Engelbert Zaschka, also produced some interesting unorthodox designs. Among them was a 'combined' two and four-stroke with a valve in the crankcase. Only few of these 'overhead two-strokes' were actually made.

ORIX/*Italy 1949–1954*
Designed by Amedeo Prina, Orix built Ilo-engined 173cc two-strokes as well as a variety of 123cc and 173cc two-stroke scooters.

ORMONDE/*England 1900–c1906*
Once a well-known make. Fitted 2·25 hp and 2·75 hp Kelecom as well as 3·5 hp Antoine engines.

ORTLOFF/*Germany 1924–1926*
Lightweights with 185cc and 198cc Gruhn sv engines.

ORTONA/*England 1904–1906*
A 3·5 hp single-cylinder machine was the only model built by this factory.

ORUK/*Germany 1922–1924*
Interesting design. Oruk means without belt and chain (ohne Riemen und Kette). The engine was —not unlike the Opel of that period—a 189cc sv single, mounted outside the rear wheel with a direct shaft drive. It was not a great commercial success and Oruk was taken over by the Schüttoff works.

OSA/*Poland 1958–*
Made by WFM (Warszawska Fabrica Motocyklowa), a leading motorcycle factory, the OSA was a scooter with 123cc to 173cc two-stroke engines and a nice appearance.

OSA-LIBERTY/*France 1926–1932*
Assembled good motorcycles with JAP licence-built 346cc and 490cc sv and ohv engines. Manufacturer of the power units was the French Staub factory. Small 173cc and 246cc two-stroke engines were the company's own design and manufacture.

OSCAR/*England 1953–1955*
The only product of this short-lived English make was a scooter with 122cc and 197cc Villiers two-stroke engines.

346cc Orionette (TS) 1925

246cc Orionette (TS Prototype with ohv) 1925

189cc Oruk (ohv rear-engine) 1923

OSCAR / *Italy 1965–*
Franco-Morini-engined 49cc and 84cc lightweights of sporting appearance.

OSCHA / *Germany 1924–1925*
Watercooled 496cc flat twins with opposing cylinders. The sv engine was designed by Otto Schaaf. Only a small number were actually built.

OSMOND / *England 1911–1924*
A company belonging to James in Birmingham. Built machines with 485cc Precision single-cylinder engines, and after 1918 small 102cc and 110cc machines resembling mopeds with Simplex two-stroke motors. The last model had a 239cc two-stroke engine of Osmond's design and manufacture.

OSSA / *Spain 1951–*
The first models had two-stroke and ohv engines up to 174cc, but Ossa later concentrated entirely on two-strokes, including 49cc mopeds and mofas. Among the excellent models were the 246cc Wildfire and trials and moto-cross versions. The latest models are the 244cc trials version with 32 bhp, the similar 302cc and also 243cc and 345cc moto-cross machines. Others include Sixdays Replicas and there are also 123cc models in the range of the Barcelona factory.

244cc Ossa (TS 'Sixdays') 1973

230cc Ossa (TS 'Sport') 1966

250cc Ossa Explorer 1976

OTTO / *Germany 1921–1937*
These were really Flottweg machines with the Otto trade mark. The Otto works produced

246cc Ossa (TS 'Enduro America') 1973

Flottweg machines; the Otto name was used mainly in the late 1920s, when the factory built machines with 293cc and 198cc sv JAP engines.

OTTOLENGHI / *Italy 1928–1932*
Concentrated on the production of well-made sporting 174cc ohv machines with a variety of engines, including Piazza, Ladetto & Blatto and JAP. The JAP-powered versions had 246cc and 346cc ohv engines.

OVERDALE / *England 1921–1922*
The word England is not exact in this case, because the Overdale was offered by a Glasgow company, but the factory was in the Midlands, where the simple frame was fitted with a 269cc Villiers engine.

OVERSEAS / *England 1909–1915*
Built exclusively motorcycles for British Colonies. They had very strong and heavy frames. The engines were sv V-twins with 842cc.

P

PA / *Belgium 1921–1929*
For many years a leading make in Belgian races, the Praillet-designed machines were of typical English design. Equipped with 174cc, 247cc and 347cc sv and ohv Blackburne engines, they were occasionally ridden by Blackburne's British works riders, which included Paddy Johnston and Ernie Remington. From 1925 onwards, PA built their own 245cc two-stroke and 345cc ohv engines and also fitted after 1927 348cc and 490cc JAP and MAG sv and ohv engines.

PACER / *England 1914*
This short-lived motorcycle was built on the Island of Guernsey. The engine used was a 116cc single, made by JES.

PAFFRATH / *Germany 1923–1926*
Very interesting and unusual machines, designed by Paul Paffrath. For a description see MW. In 1949 Paffrath designed and built the Eilenriede bicycle attachment power units.

PAGLIANTI / *Italy 1958–1966*
Built 49cc mopeds and 75cc miniscooters with two-stroke engines.

PALLION / *England 1905–1914*
Assembled machines with various engines made by Minerva, Fafnir, JAP and Villiers.

PALOMA / *France early 1950s to late 1960s*
A fully enclosed three-speed scooter with a 70cc engine was among the first products. Other models included 74cc and 123cc scooters, lightweights and also 49cc and 58cc mopeds etc. with Lavalette and René Gillet two-strokes.

PAMAG / *Germany 1952–1953*
When Anker stopped production of motorcycles, Pamag took over and built 123cc, 174cc and 197cc two-strokes with Sachs and Ilo engines.

PAN / *Germany 1924–1925*
Equipped with an unusual leaf-sprung fork, these motorcycles were driven by 346cc ohv Kühne engines.

PANDRA / *Japan early 1950s to early 1960s*
Small, 147cc scooters built in large quantities.

PANNI / *Hungary 1959–1962*
Miniscooters with 48cc two-stroke power-units built by the state-owned Czepel works.

246cc Pannonia (TS twin) 1974

PANNONIA / *Hungary 1951–early 1960s*
Also made by the Czepel works, the Pannonia motorcycles had a certain similarity with Jawa products. The 247cc two-stroke was built with one and two cylinders and was also exported.

PANTHER (P&M) / *England 1900–1965*
Originally known as the P&M — for the founders Jonah Phelon and Richard Moore — the Yorkshire factory fitted the first Phelon-designed engines to frames made by the Beeston Humber Company. Humber afterwards built these machines under licence. All P&M machines had chain drive and already in 1904 a two-speed gear with countershaft. They also pioneered sloping engines. There were prototypes of a 90° V-twin in 1915 and of a 496cc vertical-twin in

1938, but typical for all models were single-cylinder sv and ohv machines. An exception was the 1926 Granville Bradshaw design called the Panthette, which had a 244cc V-twin unit-design engine transverse mounted. Never fully developed, the engine was superseded in 1928 by a 247cc two-stroke model. Most models made by P&M-Panther had 498cc and 598cc, but there were also 248cc and 348cc ohv singles built after

499cc Panther P&M (ohv Model TT) 1925

246cc Panther P&M (ohv transverse V-twin Model 'Panthette') 1928

the war with vertically mounted cylinders. Other versions had 646cc single-cylinder ohv engines of typical design and there were also 197cc and

245

Royal Automobile Club patrolman on a P&M, 1920s

645cc Panther ohv with Viceroy sidecar 1964

324cc Villiers-engined two-strokes. Special versions were built for a London dealer during the 1930s. These Red Panther models were of good quality at a reasonable price: in 1936 the 248cc ohv model was priced at £29.17s.6d., the 348cc ohv model at £35.15s. Panther also built trials models, while big 598cc and 648cc singles gained popularity as sidecar machines. Racing models with 498cc ohv engines were built in the mid-1920s and ridden by such famous men as Tom Bullus, Count Ashby, H. M. Walters, W. S. Braidwood and others. In the mid-1950s the Company went into receivership, but carried on in a small way for another ten years. Peter Marians was the last head of this once famous company, which supplied thousands of machines to the forces during WWI, especially the RAF. Bradshaw, who designed the unlucky Panthette, was also responsible in 1939 for a vertical twin which never reached the production stage. Frank Leach designed most models, including racing machines, between the wars.

PANTHER / *Germany 1903–1907*
Fafnir-engined 2·5 hp and 3·5 hp singles with strengthened bicycle frames.

PANTHER / *Germany 1933–mid-1970s*
Built in pre-war days mofas with 73cc and 98cc Sachs and Ilo two-strokes, after the war a wide range of 32cc and 48cc mopeds as well as motorcycles from 98cc to 174cc with Sachs engines. When Panther offered motorcycles in England during the 1950s, they had to be renamed Leopard, as there was already a Panther motorcycle factory in the UK.

PAQUÉ / *Germany 1921–1925*
The first product was a 140cc bicycle engine. Motorcycles had 147cc and 197cc ohv engines, which were also built as proprietary engines for Busse, Zürtz, Ammon and other factories. The last Paqué models had their own 497cc sv single-cylinder engines and there were also a few 198cc ohc engines built.

PARAGON / *England 1919–1923*
Produced a single model, a 348cc three-port deflector-type, only. The engine had 76mm bore and 79mm stroke and an Albion two-speed gearbox.

PARAMOUNT-DUO / *England 1926–1927*
Unusual design without top tube, with two bucket seats, a fully enclosed engine and rear wheel half enclosed by panels. This design was offered with 490cc and 990cc sv JAP or Blackburne engine, neither model succeeded in gaining many customers.

PARILLA / *Italy 1946–1967*

Giovanni Parilla's first design, a 248cc single-cylinder ohc machine, created quite a sensation, a 1947 racing version of it even a greater one. It was a beautiful design; unfortunately never as fast as Guzzi's production racer, the Albatross. Luigi Ciai and others rode the Parilla, but the best racing model was in Germany, where it was developed by Roland Schnell and its rider Hermann Gablenz. Schnell also built a 348cc version and developed improved frames for both models. The normal model had 17 bhp at 7250 rpm, racing versions around 30 bhp. These had two overhead camshafts and Electron crankcases. The first production model was a 247cc two-stroke of unit design, followed by 98cc and 123cc two-stroke versions. There was also a 123cc two-stroke scooter with a three-speed gearbox and fully enclosed. The following models had 248cc and 348cc vertical-twin ohv engines. Two very fast 123cc models had a two-stroke engine and a double-ohc engine with a telescopic fork and a swinging-arm rear suspension. The last one, a racing machine, developed 13·5 bhp at 10,000 rpm. Less hot machines were 148cc and 158cc two-strokes; a range of 173cc double-ohc sports machines with engines which were also supplied to the German Victoria works; an improved 347cc vertical-twin and a 98cc version; and the Slughi, with an enclosure which was nearly complete but also sporting. Engines fitted were a 98cc two-stroke with 50mm bore and 50mm stroke and a similar ohv version of 97·7cc with 52mm bore and 46mm stroke. Other Parillas included the Oscar scooter with a 158cc flat two-cylinder, two-stroke engine and a range of 48cc mopeds and sporting motorcycles up to 247cc. These included the 99cc Olympia, a Slughi design with an open engine which was either a 99cc ohv or a 123cc two-stroke unit. A special version called Impala, was made exclusively for the US.

98cc Parilla (ohv 'Slughi') 1958

PARVUS / *Italy 1921–1926*

Was among the first Italian producers of bicycle engines. In this case they were 104cc two-strokes. Motorcycles, made from 1923, had 123cc two-stroke engines.

PASCO / *Australia 1919–1922*

Built partly on American lines, these motorcycles had English 548cc single-cylinder and 746cc V-twin sv engines made by JAP.

PASQUET / *France 1932–WWII*

Aubier-Dunne 98cc and 123cc engines in motorcycles made in limited quantities.

PASSONI / *Italy 1902–1904*

Pioneer of the motorcycle trade. Used own 2 hp engines in strengthened bicycle frames.

PATRIA / *Germany 1925–1950*

The first models had 248cc and 348cc Roconova single-cylinder ohc engines, designed by Johannes Rössig, but from 1927 to 1949 only

173cc Patria (TS Ilo) 1950

mopeds were made. 98cc and 123cc Sachs and 98cc Imme engines powered post-war Patria motorcycles, which were of good design. Hans A. May, the owner of the Patria works, died suddenly in 1950 and the factory closed down.

PATRIARCA / *Italy 1925–1933*

Well-designed 124cc, 174cc and eventually 248cc singles, designed by Gustav Patriarca, who was one of Italy's better designers. Most models had ohv heads and the two or three-speed gearboxes in unit with the engine.

173cc Patriarca (ohv) 1927

PAUVERT / *France 1933–WWII*

Assembler of two-stroke machines with 98cc to 198cc. Limited production.

PAWA / *Germany 1922–1923*

Very unorthodox motorcycle designed by Kurt Passow. They had an unusually long wheelbase, a complete fairing from steering head to the centre of the rear wheel, partly enclosed front wheel, a bucket seat but a completely open chain to the rear wheel. The 226cc two-stroke engine had 60mm bore and 80mm stroke; a valve regulated the incoming mixture, but neither the engine or the frame parts were properly developed. The whole machine was more a designer's dream than a good commercial proposition and production ceased in 1923.

PAWI / *Germany 1922–1924*

Made by a small car factory at Berlin, Pawi motorcycles were built in small numbers only. They were powered by the well-known 493cc sv flat-twin proprietary BMW engine with 68mm bore stroke.

PAX / *England 1920–1922*

Orthodox motorcycles with 348cc and 499cc Blackburne single-cylinder sv engines. The bigger model had a 3-speed Sturmey-Archer gearbox and a Senspray carburettor. It cost £120.

PDC / *England 1903–1906*

Made by the old Imperial Company, these machines had Coronet 2hp, 2·75 hp and 3·5 hp proprietary engines.

PE / *Germany 1923–1924*

Lightweights with own 132cc three-port, deflector-type, two-stroke engines.

PEARSON / *England 1903–1904*

Equipped with 3 hp Aster engines, the Pearson is now a forgotten make.

PEARSON & SOPWITH/*England 1919–1921*
Sopwith, an aircraft pioneer and an enthusiastic motorcyclist, produced motorcycles with 318cc Dalm, 293cc JAP and 497cc Blackburne engines. With the exception of the two-stroke Dalm, the engines were sv models.

PEBOK/*England 1903–1909*
Was among leading English motorcycle producers. The 2·25 hp, 2·75 hp and 3·5 hp engines were of their own design and manufacture.

PECO/*England 1913–1915*
Supplied 349cc proprietary two-stroke engines and also complete motorcycles, when Calthorpe bought the Peco works at Birmingham.

PEERLESS/*England 1902–c1908*
These machines were identical with Bradburys built at Oldham. They had 2 hp and 2·5 hp engines, built like the frames under Birch patents.

PEERLESS/*England 1913–1914*
Small assembler, who fitted 292cc and 499cc Veloce (later Velocette) engines. The producer — International Mfg. Co. Ltd. — may have been a branch of Veloce Ltd.

PEERLESS/*America 1913–1916*
Strong 4 hp, 5 hp and 8 hp motorcycles with own ioe single-cylinder and V-twin engines, double-loop frames, telescopic fork and shaft drive. The factory was also connected with the four-cylinder Champion machines, made at the St. Louis works. The Peerless was built at Boston.

5 hp Peerless 1912 advertisement

PEGASO/*Italy 1956–1964*
Lightweight with 48cc ohv engines, built in large numbers. Producer was the SIM (Societá Italiana Motori), a company with many ex-Motom employees.

PEM/*America 1910–1915*
This motorcycle manufacturer was well known in the United States in the period before the First World War. It produced a single-cylinder 4 hp motorcycle with its own ohv engine.

PENNINGTON/*England 1897*
Regarded in some circles as a pioneer, the American 'inventor' E. J. Pennington was really a businessman who made promises to keep shareholders happy. His design had two horizontal and totally uncooled cylinders arranged behind the rear wheel spindle and driving directly on the cranks of that wheel. The machine had a kind of flywheel built into the wheel. By invitation of Harry John Lawson, Pennington arrived in England in 1896 and built two of his machines at the Coventry-based Humber Company, which was controlled by Lawson and his associates. Pennington reportedly took £100,000 for his design, which proved to be a complete failure. Only the two machines were actually built when Pennington bought a return ticket to America, instead of keeping his promise to motorise good old England.

PER/*Germany 1924–1926*
Kurt Passow, who created the unlucky Pawa, also built the 308cc Per. Compared with the Pawa, the Per was a much improved design. He again put the power unit behind a steel cover and used additional steel plates for covering most other parts. Again a bucket seat was used and everything done to make riding comfortable. The original 308cc engine was superseded by a more powerful 342cc unit with 12 bhp, but it was no use. The whole design was not really de-

344cc Per (TS) 1925

veloped as it should have been. According to the designer, the two-stroke engine could run on anything, including crude oil, benzol, spirit etc. The smaller model had a two-speed gearbox and belt drive; the bigger version two or three-speed gearboxes and — if required — chain drive to the rear wheel.

PERFECTA/*Switzerland 1946–1950*
Fitted French AMC ohv engines of 123cc, 148cc and 173cc into modern frames.

PERIPOLI/*Italy 1957–*
Producer of the Giulietta who also has a big output of 47cc and 49cc mofas, mopeds and similar lightweight models. Engines used included the German Zündapp.

PERLEX/*Germany 1924–1926*
One of the many small producers of the mid-1920s. Fitted 197cc sv Gruhn engines into simple frames.

PERKS & BIRCH/*England 1899–1901*
This was a 222cc sv single-cylinder engine, built into a driving wheel as a complete unit. These wheels were fitted to two and three-wheeled vehicles. The design was eventually taken over by the Singer factory.

PERMO/*Germany 1952–1954*
Post-war mopeds with 32cc Victoria two-stroke engines.

PERNOD/*France c1900*
Very much like the Birch design, the 1 hp Pernod engine was fitted to a separate wheel which could be bought and attached as a 'pusher' to existing bicycles.

PERPEDES/*Austria 1922–1926*
Yet another bicycle attachment engine. In this case the 110cc two-stroke had to be fitted above the rear wheel directly to the bicycle. Drive was by belt.

PERSCH/*Austria 1922–1925*
Built 110cc bicycle engines at a factory near the Puch works at Graz. Frames for Persch engines (strengthened bicycles with special attachments) were built by Krammer of Vienna.

PERUGINA/*Italy 1953–1962*
Menicucci built very nice 158cc and 173cc two-stroked and ohv machines and after 1956 248cc versions. He was also the man behind BMP motorcycles. The range also included 123cc versions and a fast 173cc ohc single.

PERUN/*Czechoslovakia 1904–1924*
Built 3·5 hp single-cylinder and 4·5 hp V-twin motorcycles probably with Fafnir engines. After 1918 manufacture concentrated on 1·4 hp bicycle engines.

PETA/*Czechoslovakia 1921–1924*
Lightweight motorcycles and scooters with 170cc two-stroke engines, built in small numbers.

PETERS/*Germany 1924*
Lightweights equipped with 143cc DKW two-stroke engines. These machines were only built in small numbers.

PETERS/ _England 1919–1925_
This was one of two motorcycle producers which built machines in the Isle of Man, but while the Aurora stayed there, designer-manufacturer J. A. Peters moved his production to London. The machine was of unorthodox design with the engine forming the support between the crank bracket and the underside of the large-diameter pressed steel tank, which formed part of the frame. The steering head was enclosed within the fore-part of the tank. The machine had a sprung frame and a variable pulley gear with a comparatively long belt to the rear wheel. Peters built his own 347cc 76mm bore/stroke engines, two-strokes with a big outside flywheel and Cox-Atmos carburettors.

PEUGEOT/ _France 1899–_
Famous pioneer of the motorcycle and car industries. Built singles and V-twin engines for other factories, including Norton, Dot etc. Used as far back as 1904 the Truffault swinging arm forks and won races with Cissac, Giuppon and other riders. A Peugeot V-twin engine in a Norton, ridden by H. Rem Fowler, won the first TT race (1907) in the twin-cylinder class. The most famous Peugeot racing machines, 494cc vertical-twins with double ohc engines, were first built in 1913. Designer was Jean Antoinescu. This machine had gear-driven ohc; versions built during the 1920s had the gears superseded by bevels and there were also single ohc models ridden exclusively—like all these machines—by works riders, who included Péan, Gillard and Richard. After 1927, Peugeot retired these very successful and technically very modern racing machines. The first production model which gained fame for Peugeot was a 334cc single with 2·5 hp, although the very first machine was a motorised bicycle with 1·5 bhp. After WWI, Peugeot's V-twins had 295cc,

Pierre Péan on his works Peugot, double ohc, 1924

173cc Peuget (TS) 1927

344cc, 738cc and 746cc engines. In 1921 there was also a new 269cc two-stroke single. A 173cc two-stroke and a new, modern 346cc ohv single were added in 1926. In the same year Peugeot built 110cc bicycle engines too. New 173cc, 246cc, 346cc and 496cc sv singles came into production during the late 1920s and a 198cc model was added afterwards, while the 346cc ohv single was developed as a sporting machine. All models had unit-design engines. One of the leading French factories, Peugeot concentrated after the war on lightweights, including a large number of 48cc mopeds, mofas etc. In addition there were 98cc to 248cc two-stroke motorcycles; the last one a vertical twin two-stroke. Peugeot was also building the 48cc Bima miniscooter with a horizontal power unit. A 124cc scooter and a 346cc two-stroke twin motorcycle were added in 1955–1956. During the next years, Peugeot concentrated more and more on 48cc models, which they still produce in large numbers.

PG/ _Italy 1927–1931_
Produced 123cc and 173cc ohv machines, gave up the smaller versions in 1929 and concentrated on different models of the bigger PG, designed by Giuseppe Parena.

PHÄNOMEN/ _Germany 1903–1940_
Produced in early years Fafnir-engined singles and V-twins, afterwards three-wheelers called

Champoneau on a racing Peugeot V-twin, 1904

Phänomobil, and cars. Motorcycle manufacture was resumed in 1930 with motorised bicycles which had 74cc Sachs engines and afterwards with 98cc and 123cc Sachs-engined lightweights, designed by Rudi Albert. These Ahoj models used rubber suspension both for the fork and for the saddle.

PHÄNOMEN / *Germany 1950–1956*
Identical model range to the Meister and Mammut. Engines fitted were from 98cc to 197cc, made by Sachs and Ilo.

PHANTOM / *Germany 1921–1928*
A manufacturer of touring motorcycles, Phantom built own 148cc, 198cc and 246cc sv engines and also fitted from 1926 onward JAP sv engines from 173cc to 490cc.

246cc Phantom (sv) 1923

PHILLIPS / *England 1954–1964*
Built mofas and mopeds with 48cc two-stroke engines. Part of the big Raleigh group of companies.

PHOENIX / *England 1900–1908*
A factory founded by former racing cyclist and motorcyclist, J. V. Hooydonk. Excellent design with 211cc and 345cc Minerva engines. Built also engines of the company's own design.

2½ hp Phoenix (sv) 1903

PHOENIX / *England 1955–1964*
The Eric Barrett-designed scooters had Villiers-engines from 147cc to 323cc. Barrett built also a range of mainly JAP-engined ohv racing machines from 248cc to 498cc, which he rode in many races, including the TT.

PHOENIX / *Germany 1933–1939*
Made by RMW of Neheim-Ruhr, the Phoenix range was identical to that range of models. It included Bark-engined 198cc and 246cc two-strokes and sv, ohv and even ohc models from 346cc to 498cc with Sturmey-Archer, Moser, Bark, Küchen and MAG engines. The company tried to re-enter motorcycle manufacture with its own 246cc two-strokes after 1945, but few were made.

PIAGGIO / *Italy 1946–*
World-famous producer of Vespa scooters, which are still in production with 121cc, 145cc and 198cc two-stroke engines. Also a wide range of 49cc mofas, mopeds etc. is in production. Piaggio at Genoa also owns the Gilera motorcycle works at Arcore near Milan.

PIANA / *Italy 1923–1931*
The first machines designed by Gualtiero Piana had 147cc Villiers engines, afterwards models with 247cc Villiers and 346cc and 490cc JAP sv and ohv engines followed. 248cc JAP-engined models were superseded from 1927 onward by Piana's own 248cc ohv motors in complete and very sporting machines.

PIATTI / *Belgium 1955–1958*
Designed by an Italian, the 123cc scooter was actually built in England and sold by a Belgian company. Piatti designed afterwards 248cc two-stroke engines for Associated Motor Cycles Ltd. in London. They failed to find many customers for this product.

PIAZZA / *Italy 1924–1934*
Small 124cc two-stroke bicycle engines were Antonio Piazza's first creations. Complete 174cc sv and ohv motorcycles followed and a 496cc ohv JAP-engined machine was added during the 1930s. While they were made in limited numbers only, 173cc Piazza ohv engines were popular and were also used by other Italian motorcycle producers.

PIERCE (ARROW) / *America 1909–1913*

Interesting design, in which a wide-diameter tube formed the tank. There were single-cylinder and 4 hp four-cylinder models with air-cooling and the cylinders in line. This model was offered for $400 and had, like the single cylinder version, shaft drive to the rear wheel. Pierce-Arrow was also a manufacturer of expensive motor cars.

PIERTON / *France 1922–1925*
Assembler, whose motorcycles had Aubier Dunne, Train, Villiers, Blackburne and JAP engines from 98cc to 498cc.

PILOT / *England 1903–1915*
Well-known factory. Produced 318cc two-strokes and fitted also Precision and JAP engines from 174cc to 598cc.

PIMPH / *Germany 1924–1926*
Assembled motorcycles with 490cc sv and ohv JAP engines and V-twin MAG power units as well.

490cc Pimph (sv JAP) 1926

PIOLA / *Italy 1919–1921*
Flat twins with opposing cylinders. The 620cc sv machines were made in small numbers only.

PIRATE / *America 1911–1915*
Ambitious factory which built ioe singles and V-twins with 3 hp, 6 hp and 8 hp. Most models had pedalling gears.

948cc Pirate (ioe V-twin) 1911

PIROTTA / *Italy 1949–1955*
Built 49cc bicycle engines designed by Gianfranco Viviani, afterwards also two-stroke and ohv motorcycles up to 158cc.

PITTY / *East Germany 1955–late 1960s*
Scooter with 147cc MZ two-stroke engines, built in large numbers.

PLANET / *England 1919–1920*
Fitted 269cc Villiers engines and 293cc to 546cc Union and Blackburne engines into open frames.

PLASSON / *France 1921–1924*
Lightweight machines of primitive design. Plasson fitted two-stroke and also 197cc sv engines of its own manufacture.

PMC / *England 1908–1915*
The name stood for Premier Motorcycle Company, but was not the Coventry based Premier. PMC of Birmingham was somehow connected with Wall (Roc) and Rex and produced motorcycles and three-wheelers under names like Warwick, Rex-JAP etc. with JAP engines from 393cc to 996cc.

PMZ / *Russia 1931–WWII*
One of the oldest motorcycle factories in Russia. The company originally produced bicycle engines, and subsequently progressed to 746cc and 996cc motorcycles with BMW-like flat twin sv engines, and V-twin engines reminiscent of the Harley-Davidson design. These were used by the Russian Army.

PO / *Italy 1921–1923*
Built a variety of 346cc single-cylinder two-strokes, designed by Pagni.

POINARD / *France 1951–1956*
Built motorcycles and scooters with 123cc to 248cc Aubier-Dunne, Ydral and four-stroke AMC ohv engines.

POINTER / *Japan 1946–1962*
Two-strokes from 123cc to 247cc with own engines. Was a big factory.

POLENGHI / *Italy 1950–1955*
Mopeds, mofas and similar 48cc vehicles.

POLET / *Italy 1923–1924*
Concentrated on 481cc singles with own ioe engines.

PONNY / *Germany 1924–1926*
Lightweights with mainly 142cc and 172cc DKW two-stroke engines.

PONY / *Germany 1924–1926*
German Pony with one 'n', but with 185cc sv engines.

PONY / *Spain 1952–1954*
Assembled machines with Hispano-Villiers 123cc two-stroke engines.

PONY-MONARK / *Japan 1951–early 1960s*
Produced 147cc ohv and 123cc to 247cc two-stroke motorcycles.

POPE / *America 1911–1918*
Made by a branch of famous car factory, the 499cc 3·5 hp singles and 998cc 7 to 8 hp V-twins were excellent ohv machines with plunger-type rear suspension.

499cc Pope (ohv) 1913

998cc Pope (ohv V-twin) 1914

POPET / *Japan 1957–early 1960s*
Miniscooter with 47cc two-stroke engines.

POPMANLEE / *Japan late 1950s to late 1960s*
Motorcycles with 124cc to 174cc and scooters with 49cc and 79cc two-stroke engines.

PORTLAND / *England 1910–1911*
This was the make of a big dealer in London, Maudes Motor Mart. Engines fitted were 498cc JAP and Peugeot.

POSDAM / *Italy 1926–1929*
The Alberto Da Milano-designed machines had 123cc, 147cc and 173cc ioe single-cylinder engines and with the exception of the 173cc machine, belt drive to the rear wheel. The biggest model had chain drive.

POSTLER / *Germany 1920–1924*
Designed by Walter Postler, who was a well-known racing-car driver, the first products were scooters with own 252cc ioe engines. After 1923 he built also a 246cc ohv machine with his own single-cylinder engine.

POTTHOFF / *Germany 1924–1926*
Built in limited quantities 185cc ohv machines with English Norman proprietary engines.

POUNCY / *England 1930–1938*
Built a range of Villiers-engined two-strokes, which included 147cc, 247cc and 346cc single-cylinder versions. The quarter-litre machine was also supplied with flat-top piston engines. From 1935 onwards, OEC rear suspension was available on all Pouncy models.

POUSTKA / *Czechoslovakia 1924–1934*
Made from English components, the Poustka had 147cc, 247cc and 346cc Villiers two-stroke engines. Like the Pouncy, it was a hand-made machine built in limited quantities.

POWELL / *England 1921–1926*
The first Powell with its 547cc Blackburne sv engine was a design which did not attract many customers. The factory also built 168cc, 198cc and 245cc two-strokes with their own engines.

POWERFUL / *England 1903–c1906*
French 2·25 hp Buchet and English MMC engines powered these machines.

2¼ hp Powerful (sv Buchet engine) 1903

251

P&P / *England 1922–1930*

Ealing Poppe, whose father owned the White & Poppe engine factory, designed these well-made sporting motorcycles. He made the first serious attempt to reduce engine noise and at the same time to keep the machine and the rider clean by introducing the superbly silenced and fully enclosed Silent Three, with a Barr & Stroud sleeve-valve power unit. Other models had JAP engines from 248cc to 996cc, which were actually made by the Montgomery works for P&P, which stood for Packmann & Poppe of Coventry. When a fire destroyed Montgomery's in 1925 P&P machines were not available for some time.

PRAGA / *Czechoslovakia 1929–1935*

Well-known car factory which merged with the Breitfeld-Daněk machine works and also took over the J. F. Koch-designed 499cc BD motorcycle. This single-cylinder ohc machine had 84mm bore and 90mm stroke. A 346cc ohc Praga was built in 1932 with 70mm bore and 90mm stroke. This time the fork and frame were made from pressed steel and the unit-design engine had shaft drive to the rear wheel.

PRECISION / *England 1912–1919*

For years connected with the American motorcycle industry, F. E. Baker returned to England before WWI and produced a wide range of proprietary engines and motorcycles exclusively destined for the Australian market. The situation changed after the war when he built motorcycles with 342cc two-stroke engines. After a short time, this factory was taken over by the Beardmore group of companies. This led to Beardmore-Precision motorcycles, still headed by Baker.

PRECISION / *England 1902–1906*

No connection with F. E. Baker's Precision works. Produced motorcycles with mainly 211cc Minerva engines.

PREMIER / *England 1908–1920*

Once a great name in the British motorcycle industry, Premier in Coventry built big V-twins with outside flywheels, afterwards mainly singles with 348cc, 445cc and 490cc engines of Premier's own manufacture. After a reorganisation in November 1914, the name was changed to Coventry-Premier. The last design was a 322cc two-stroke vertical twin arranged lengthwise in the frame. It never went into quantity production, and there were no Premier motorcycles built in England after 1915. The factory, founded by Messrs. Hillmann, Herbert and Cooper, was really controlled by the Rotherham family, which in 1910 founded a branch in Germany. It was headed by Basil Jones, who raced Premiers

348cc Praga (dohc shaft-drive) 1932

in the TT races and who eventually became a brother-in-law of Geoffrey Rotherham, who controlled in the 1920s and early 1930s yet another Premier factory. Coventry-Premier produced three-wheeled and even four-wheeled light cars when it was absorbed in the early 1920s by Singer.

PREMIER / *Germany 1910–1913*

This was the Nuremberg-based branch of Premier in Coventry. Real owner was the machine factory J. C. Braun, but Basil Jones controlled production which consisted of a 346cc single-cylinder sv machine, and also bicycles and prams. Bad economic situation forced a transfer of the factory over the border into the Austro-Hungarian Empire, to Eger which in 1918 became part of Czechoslovakia.

PREMIER / *Czechoslovakia 1913–1933*

This was the most active period of Premier, although real motorcycle production did not start until 1923. Earlier they had only the 346cc sv single and the manufacture of a few experimental light cars, as in England. Production at Eger commenced with a 269cc two-stroke, based on the English Triumph Baby. It had a round tank at first and was built for nearly ten years. Other models included JAP-engined 348cc and 498cc sv and ohv singles. From 1927 onwards, Premier's own engines of the same size were fitted, a 746cc V-twin sv engine added. New in 1929 was a 498cc longstroke ohv sloping engine. The factory, at that time the leading motorcycle producer in the country, was headed by Geoffrey Rotherham. Chief designer was Hans Baumann, but the longstroke was created by Otto Lausmann. The factory had a racing department,

348cc Premier (sv) 1913 (German)

498cc Premier (sv) 1930 (Czechoslovakia)

where they used JAP engines, until the long-stroke came into service. The JAP racing motors were of 348cc, 490cc, 746cc and 998cc; the leading riders Alois Kraus, Václav Lischka, Karl Tauber, Mila Stipek, Ernst Haubner etc.

498cc Premier (ohv Model 'Longstroke') 1930 (Czechoslovakia)

PREMO / *England 1908–1915*
One of the names under which Premier (PMC) of Birmingham traded their motorcycles.

PREMOLI / *Italy 1935–WWII*
Racing motorcyclist Guido Premoli built 498cc motorcycles of sporting appearance with four-valve Python (Rudge) and OMB engines. In addition, he created 174cc singles with his own ohc engines which he raced himself.

PRESTER (JONGHI) / *France 1926–late 1950s*
Produced a wide range of models from 98cc to 496cc with Aubier-Dunne and Chaise engines. A merger with Jonghi in 1936 led to new models which included the famous Remondini-designed 174cc, 248cc and 348cc double-ohc racing machines. After the war, production concentrated on models from 98cc to 248cc and included beautiful 123cc ohv machines, 248cc two-strokes and also a nice 123cc scooter.

PRESTO / *Germany 1901–1940*
Was a well-known car factory, but little known as producer of motorcycles. In early years they had Zedel, Minerva and Fafnir engines; after WWI the 197cc Alba sv engine was fitted, but production of Presto motorcycles was never large. During the 1930s Presto produced mopeds with 74cc and 98cc Sachs two-stroke engines.

PRIDE & CLARKE / *England 1938–1940*
Lightweight, offered by a famous London-based motorcycle dealer. It had a 63cc two-stroke engine.

PRIM / *England 1906–1907*
Money's Prim machines had a wide diameter petrol tank which formed the top part of the frame. The engine was a Belgian 5 hp V-twin, made by Sarolea of Liège.

PRINA / *Italy 1949–1954*
Offered under the Orix trade mark, Prina's motorcycles and scooters had 123cc, 147cc and 173cc two-stroke engines made by Ilo of Germany.

PRINCEPS / *England 1903–1907*
Once a well-known producer of singles and V-twins with the factory's own engines.

PRINETTI & STUCCHI / *Italy 1898–1911*
Famous pioneer who built bicycles, three and four-wheeled vehicles and afterwards motorcycles with engines designed by Carlo Leidi. Ettore Bugatti, whose Bugatti cars are still regarded as masterpieces, spent his first years in the trade with Prinetti & Stucchi. The first motorcycles had 2 hp engines, but there were also bigger models built.

PRIOR / *Germany 1904*
A German make unknown in Germany. Prior motorcycles were Hercules products renamed for sale in Britain, where there was already a Hercules factory owned by a British company.

PRIORY / *England 1919–1926*
Assembler of two-stroke motorcycles with 269cc Arden, 292cc Union and 147cc to 247cc Villiers engines.

PROGRESS / *Germany 1901–1914*
One of the leading makes in the early years of motorcycle production in Germany. Fitted Zedel and Fafnir proprietary singles and V-twins. Afterwards models with their own 532cc single-cylinder and 698cc V-twin engines came onto the market.

PROGRESS / *England 1902–1908*
The English Progress was a well-known motorcycle. Minerva, MMC, Antoine and other engines were fitted into strong frames.

PROGRESS / *Germany 1951–1957*
Another Progress, but this was a Sachs-engined 98cc, 147cc, 173cc and 198cc scooter.

3½ hp Progress (sv) 1905 (German)

PROMOT / *Poland late 1960s–*
Trials and moto-cross machines with 123cc Puch two-stroke engines.

PROPUL / *France 1923–1926*
Limited assembly of motorcycles with 246cc, 346cc and 498cc single-cylinder sv and ohv engines made by JAP, MAG and Blackburne. Built also a 98cc two-stroke.

PSW / *Germany 1924–1929*
Produced interesting 247cc two-strokes with inlet and exhaust ports in front of the cylinder, built a range of JAP and Blackburne-engined racing machines from 248cc to 490cc with single-cylinder ohv engines, and even minicars with 98cc engines for children.

PUCH / *Austria 1903–*

Austria's oldest motorcycle factory. During the early years, the company manufactured motorcycles with their own 2·75 hp, 3·5 hp and 4 hp single-cylinder and 4 hp and 6 hp V-twin engines. There was also a 6 hp flat-twin, built during WWI in limited numbers. Double-piston two-strokes dominated the production programme for some years after 1923; designed by Giovanni Marcellino, they appeared with 122cc, 173cc, 198cc, 248cc, 348cc and 496cc capacity. The 348cc single was built only in 1938, mainly for the army. The only four-strokes made by Puch between the wars were 490cc JAP-engined sv singles in 1928 and in 1936–1938 the 792cc transverse-mounted sv flat-fours, also mainly built for the army. Smooth-running 496cc vertical twins with the four-piston two-stroke engines were made since 1931 in various shapes, among them the models Z, N, V and VL. In this case, the second cylinder was standing behind the first. In 1938 a 60cc bicycle engine called Styriette came into production. Most famous of all Puch two-strokes at that period were the 248cc singles, especially the very sporting model

2¾ hp Puch (sv Model A) 1904

398cc Puch (sv) 1914

9 hp Puch (sv V-twin works racing-machine) 1907

496cc Puch (TS twin-cylinder, double-piston) 1932

246cc Puch (TS double-piston) 1932

792cc Puch (sv transverse flat-four) 1936

348cc Puch (TS double piston GS Trials) 1938

S4, built from 1934 to 1938 with a 14·5 bhp engine. Puch built during the years racing two-strokes, including in 1924 the Monza works machines with two 122cc cylinders on a common crankcase, and from 1929 onwards watercooled 248cc double-piston singles with a charging cylinder in the crankcase. These very fast machines won the German Grand Prix in 1931 as well as many other big events. Among leading Puch riders were Nikodem, Obruba, Wetzka, Medinger, Höbel, Cmyral, Toricelli, Hunger, Nowak, Sandler, Novotny, Suchanek, Runtsch, Karner, Kiss, Lukawetz, Puch Jun., Zick, Lehmann, Schlüpbach, Faraglia and others.

After 1945, the range of models included 123cc two-strokes with single-piston engines and pressed steel frames, but many 248cc double-piston models were kept in production and now got pressed steel frames too. Improved versions were still in production in the early 1970s, such as the SGS with 2mm × 45mm bore, 78mm

246cc Puch (TS double-piston Model 'SGS') 1966

49cc Puch (TS Model M50 Racing) 1974

49cc Puch (TS Model Monza 45 L) 1977

247cc Puch (TS Model MC Replica) 1977

stroke and 16·5 bhp at 5800 rpm. Still, main production concentrated now around 49cc mopeds, mofas, motorcycles and 123cc and 173cc machines with new, modern, single-cylinder and single-piston power units. Among them are various trials and moto-cross machines which gained success with riders such as Harry Everts, Walter Luft, Walter Leitgeb, Hans Sommerauer and others. Among present Puch motorcycles are the M50 Jet and M50 Monza GSL with 6·25 bhp 49cc engines, the MC50 Super with 49cc and 11·2 bhp at 11,000 rpm (moto-cross model), 123cc and 173cc versions with 23 bhp and 28 bhp and also a 246cc moto-cross Replica with 43·5 bhp at 8500 rpm.

PUMA / *Argentine 1954–early 1960s*
Mopeds and lightweights with 98cc two-stroke engines.

P&S / *England 1919–1921*
Identical with Pearson models, but the last versions built had the name changed to P&S (Pearson & Sopwith). They were actually made by Excelsior of Birmingham, owned by the Walker family.

PV / *England 1910–1925*
This London-based make fitted a variety of proprietary engines into sturdy spring-frames of their own design. JAP supplied mainly sv engines from 293cc to 996cc, Villiers two-strokes from 247cc to 347cc, while Barr & Stroud supplied 346cc sleeve-valve and Bradshaw 348cc oilcooled ohv engines.

PZI / *Poland 1936–1937*
Small producer of motorcycles with own 598cc single-cylinder and 1196cc V-twin engines. Most were supplied to the Polish army.

976cc PV (sv V-twin JAP) 1923

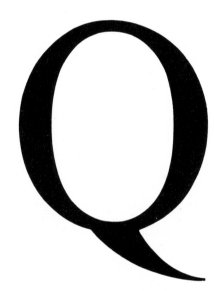

QUADRANT / *England 1901–1929*
Superbly made W. L. Lloyd-designed motorcycles. The first models had 211cc Minerva engines, but from 1903 onwards, the Birmingham works also produced engines of their own design. They included 374cc two-strokes; 498cc, 554cc, 654cc and even 780cc singles and 1130cc V-twins with sv engines as well as a 498cc ohv version. There was also a 654cc version with ioe valves, while other models had splash lubrication. Tom Silver, one of the great English pioneers, rode these machines successfully in sporting events for many years.

2 hp Quadrant with spring fork 1905

QUAGLIOTTI / *Italy 1902–1907*
Producer of 2 hp and 3 hp single-cylinder and of 5 hp V-twin machines. Carlo Quagliotti was regarded as one of the leading designer-manufacturer pioneers in the country.

654cc Quadrant (sv) 1926

R

RABBIT / *Japan 1946–1968*
A very popular scooter with own 90cc, 123cc and 199cc two-stroke engines.

RABENEICK / *Germany 1933–1958*
Produced in pre-war days mopeds with 74cc Sachs engines, after 1945 38cc and 48cc mofas and mopeds and a range of motorcycles with 98, 123, 147, 173, 244 and 247cc Ilo and Sachs engines. The machines were of excellent design and good finish. The works were bought by Fichtel & Sachs and now recondition car clutches.

248cc Rabeneick (ohv shaft-drive Prototype) 1955

RACER / *France 1953–1956*
Small factory which produced bicycle engines and lightweight motorcycles with own 49cc and 74cc two-stroke engines.

246cc Radco (TS) 1923

269cc Radco (TS) 1915

490cc Radco (ohv JAP) 1928

RADCO / *England 1913–1932*
Excellent 211cc and 247cc two-strokes with outside flywheels, afterwards 247cc ohv models with Radco's own engines and Villiers-engined 145cc and 198cc two-strokes. JAP-engined versions had 293cc and 490cc sv and 248cc and 490cc ohv motors. All had one cylinder, but the 490cc ohv machine was built in three versions: Touring, Sport and Super-Sport.

RADEX / *Germany 1951–late 1950s*
This name was used for some post-war machines built by the Express motorcycle factory. *See also* Express.

RADIOLA / *France 1933–1939*
These were bicycle attachments with a capacity of 98cc.

RADIOR / *France 1904–1960*

Old established factory. Fitted Peugeot and Antoine engines and during the 1920s their own 98cc to 247cc two-strokes as well as JAP and Chaise engines from 247cc to 498cc. Most Chaise-engined models were of unit design, some had ohv, others ohc. After 1945, most engines were supplied by the associated Nervor works, by AMC and NSU. The German factory also supplied 48cc and 98cc two-strokes for mopeds, lightweights etc. while Radior production included ohv models up to 248cc and also some interesting two-stroke vertical twins of the same capacity.

490cc Radior (ohv JAP) 1929

175cc Radior (ohv AMC engine) 1952

RADMILL / *England 1912–1914*

Assembled motorcycles with 269cc Villiers and 346cc Precision two-stroke engines. If required other Precision engines could also be supplied.

RADVAN / *Czechoslovakia 1909–1926*

See also Meteor. After 1924 Radvan supplied under his own name 145cc and 174cc DKW-engined two-strokes.

RAGLAN / *England 1909–1913*

Built motorcycles with 292cc, 347cc and 496cc Precision sv engines, watercooled 490cc Green-Precision singles and also with their own power units.

RALEIGH / *England 1899–1933*

Leading bicycle works and now part of Tube Investments Ltd.; a group which during the years absorbed most leading English bicycle works, including BSA, Rudge, Triumph, Sun, Carlton and others. Motorcycles were built up to 1906 and after 1919. Sturmey-Archer, producer of gearboxes and for some time also

3 hp Raleigh No. 2 aircooled 1905

698cc Raleigh (sv flat-twin) 1921

346cc Raleigh (ohv) 1928

motorcycle proprietary engines, is part of the Raleigh group. They supplied engines to Dunelt, Coventry Eagle, the German Mars, Nestoria, Allegro, Cotton, Soyer, Victoria and others. The Raleigh heyday during the 1920s saw 698cc flat sv twins and singles with 174cc, 248cc, 348cc and 498cc sv engines. In addition, there were 348cc and 498cc ohv models which in racing trim proved very fast. Also a 798cc sv V-twin was built at the Nottingham-based works. Chief designer during the late 1920s and early 1930s was the famous D. R. O'Donavan, who later built Carlton motorcycles. He designed some very fast ohv racing engines for Sturmey-Archer, ie the Raleighs and other users of Sturmey-Archer engines. Among leading Raleigh racing men were Tom Bullus, C. J. Williams, Bob McGregor, Jock Duncan and Arthur Tyler. The machines did well in trials with Hugh Gibson, Marjorie Cottle and other leading riders of that period. After Raleigh stopped manufacture of motor cycles, they built three wheelers for five years.

RAMBLER / *America 1903–WWI*

Producer of 4 hp single-cylinder and 6 hp V-twin motorcycles.

RAMBLER / *England 1937–1961*

This was the trade mark for some Norman models—especially the Villiers-engined 197cc two-stroke—in certain foreign countries.

3½ hp Raleigh watercooled 'Raleighette' 1905

173cc Raleigh (sv) 1924

RANZANI / *Italy 1923–1931*

Interesting make, because the Ranzani had not only 175cc sv engines from the German Heros factory, but also 170cc ohv engines from Norman in England, a proprietary engine factory which was not connected with Norman motorcycles. The last Ranzani motorcycles had their own unit-design ohv 173cc engines.

RAS / *Italy 1932–1936*

Made by Fusi, for many years FN Importer to Italy, the RAS had mainly JAP ohv engines from 173cc to 490cc, and some frame parts made by the FN works. A nice 248cc ohc single of their own design and manufacture was built in 1935. It was the last RAS model; after 1936, all machines used the Fusi tank transfer.

RASSER / *France 1922–1923*

Unusual design with rivetted pressed steel frame and 98cc two-stroke engine.

RATIER / *France 1955–1962*

Produced in the late 1920s small cars and was successor to the CMR and CEMEC works, which after 1945 built BMW-like motorcycles

496cc Ratier (ohv transverse flat-twin) 1958

with parts which were partly made in France by BMW for the German army during the war, and partly after the war in French factories. The first models were 746cc sv flat twins. Ratier built mainly 494cc and 597cc ohv models of pure French design and manufacture.

RATINGIA / *Germany 1923–1925*
Lightweights with 170cc and 195cc sv engines.

RAVAT / *France 1898–late 1950s*
An old established factory, which produced a range of models to 498cc. Among them were two-strokes of 98cc and 173cc.

RAY / *England 1919–1920*
Limited production of motorcycles with own 331cc two-stroke engines.

RAY / *England 1922–1925*
W. H. Raven designed the beautiful 193cc sv monobloc Ray, which weighed only 130 lb with a saddle height of 24 in. Another model with a Cohen-designed 172cc Villiers-Jardine engine was added in 1924, after the factory moved from Nottingham to Leicester.

RAYNAL / *England 1914–1953*
Early models had the 269cc Villiers two-stroke engine; during the mid-1930s and after 1945 the machines had 98cc Villiers engines.

READING-STANDARD / *America 1903–1922*
A leading make of the period and together with Indian, Harley-Davidson, Super-X, Henderson, ACE and Cleveland a very popular one. The production included 499cc singles and V-twins

990cc Reading-Standard (sv V-twin) 1917

990cc Reading-Standard (ohc V-twin works-racer) 1921

with 990cc and 1170cc. Most had sv engines, some racing versions ohv and even ohc power units, but the ohc engines were used by works riders only and were not for sale.

READY / *England 1920–1922*
Assembled machines of simple design. Engines used were JAP 293cc and 346cc sv units. Built later the 147cc Villiers-engined Rebro.

READY / *Belgium 1924–1939*
Originally known as Ready-Courtrai, the Ready motorcycles were of typical English design. Most engines came from England: Villiers, JAP, Blackburne and Python. The exception was the Swiss MAG. Models built had 173cc to 498cc.

REBRO / *England 1922–1928*
Of simple design, the Rebro, priced at £37, had a 147cc Villiers engine. After Rebro closed, Ready took over production of this model, but only very few such machines actually appeared.

RECORD / *Germany 1922–1924*
Equipped machines of simple design with their own 147cc two-stroke engines.

REDDIS / *Spain 1957–1960*
Small producer of 124cc two-stroke machines with Hispano-Villiers engines.

REDRUP / *England 1919–1922*
Created by a former aircraft-engine designer Charles Redrup, these machines had a 304cc radial three-cylinder sv engine of simple and practical appearance. Although offered also by two other makes — Beaumont and British Radial — the actual production of the engine was limited. Redrup also built a six-cylinder proto-type by putting two such engines together. It was a smooth machine, but not a good commercial proposition.

RED STAR / *Belgium 1902*
Built at Antwerp and fitted with a 211cc Minerva engine.

REFORM / *Austria 1903–1905*
Monarch in Birmingham, better known as the Excelsior works, supplied 2·25 hp sv engines for the Vienna-based Austrian manufacturer.

REGAL / *England 1909–1915*
Excellent machines of sound design. The range included 349cc two-strokes with Peco engines,

346cc and 492cc sv and ohv singles with air-cooled Precision and watercooled Green-Precision engines, while a 602cc twin was also made by Precision.

REGENT / *England 1920–1921*
Small manufacturer, who fitted 688cc Coventry-Victor flat twin sv engines into heavy frames of own design and manufacture.

REGINA / *England 1903–1915*
Early models had Minerva, MMC and Fafnir engines. Production stopped in 1907, but was resumed just before WWI, when the factory fitted its own 292cc two-stroke engines into orthodox frames. This machine was made at Ilford in Essex; at the same time identical machines were offered from an address in Derby.

REGINA / *France 1905–WWI*
Early French machines with Zurcher, Buchet and Peugeot proprietary engines.

REH / *Germany 1948–1953*
The Richard Engelbrecht-designed Reh was made in small numbers and was of good design and quality. The engines fitted were of Ilo manu-facture and had 173cc, 198cc, 244cc and 248cc.

REITER / *Italy 1927–1929*
Despite the German name, the Reiter was a sporting Italian machine, made mainly from English components by Timone and Fresia at Turin. The engines used were the 247cc sv and ohv Blackburne and the oilcooled 348cc ohv Bradshaw, the so-called 'oilboiler'.

RELIANCE / *America 1912–1915*
One of the smaller US works, Reliance built 4·5 hp single cylinder machines with ioe engines.

RENÉ-GILLET / *France 1898–1957*
Excellent heavy machines used by the French armed forces and the police. This concerned mainly the 748cc and 996cc V-twins with sv engines, which were run with sidecars attached. Another popular model was the 346cc single-

346cc René-Gillet (sv) 1928

248cc René-Gillet (TS) 1952

cylinder sv model. Improved versions of the big V-twins were built after the war, while main production switched to two-strokes of 48cc, 123cc and 246cc. All engines were of own design and manufacture. Never regarded as a very sporting make, René-Gillet machines were known as 'unbreakable' touring machines.

RENNER-ORIGINAL/*Germany 1924–1932*
Designed by Carl Ostner, brother of the manufacturer of OD motorcycles, Renner-Original concentrated on 346cc single-cylinder and 678cc V-twin machines with sv JAP engines. On request, they supplied also other JAP power units and also German Kühne and Küchen engines.

346cc Renner-Original (sv JAP) 1927

RENNSTEIG/*Germany 1925–1930*
Arms factory which took over the production of Original-Krieger machines and fitted 198cc to 497cc Blackburne engines into typical KG (Krieger-Gnädig) double-loop frames.

REPUBLIC/*Czechoslovakia 1899–1908*
Made by the Laurin & Klement factory (now Skoda) in the old Austro-Hungarian Empire, these machines were identical to Laurin & Klement products.

REVERE/*England 1915–1922*
Small two-strokes with 269cc Villiers engines with frames, built by Sparkbrook for Whitehouse & Co., the Revere manufacturer.

REVOLUTION/*England 1904–1906*
This was a conventional 2·75 hp single with power units made by NRCC.

346cc Rex (sv Blackburne) 1922

3¼ hp Rex (sv) 1905

REX (REX ACME)/*England 1900–1933*
This was once one of the greatest names in the British motorcycle industry. From 1903 onwards, Rex used the Werner engine position for their own power units, which included singles and V-twins. They used Blackburne engines after they dropped their own. Early ones had 532cc and 896cc with Roc patent gear-hubs and still earlier — around 1904 — there was a 372cc model which had the silencer cast in one piece with the cylinder. A 349cc two-stroke came in 1914 and there were then also big 940cc V-twins. A 550cc sv single, the first Rex after WWI, was dropped in favour of the new Blackburne-engined machines which were — if used with sidecars attached — supplied with longer wheelbases than solo models. The singles now had 499cc, the V-twins 998cc. In 1922 Rex amalgamated with Acme, another Coventry-based factory. The Rex Acme machines soon became famous in races with Walter Handley in the saddle. He eventually became a director of the company, but left in 1928 to ride for other makes. With his departure the name began to fade away. In 1932 the factory was taken over by the sidecar producer Mills-Fullford, which in 1933 gave

346cc Rex-Acme (ohv MAG) 1928

up manufacture of Rex Acme motorcycles. During their heyday in the 1920s, Rex Acme fitted a variety of engines from 173cc to 746cc. There were sv and ohv Blackburnes, sv JAP engines and also the 348cc sleeve-valve Barr & Stroud. Typical was the 1929 range: 346cc ohv models with two JAP versions, with 74mm × 80mm bore/stroke and with 70mm × 90mm bore/stroke; same machines with double-port engines; 746cc JAP-engined V-twin; 496cc sv singles with JAP or Blackburne engines; 300cc sv singles with cheaper frames and JAP or Blackburne engines and also similar 346cc versions; the Speed King with 346cc Blackburne ohv engines in two versions; and also two versions of a 496cc Blackburne-engined ohv single. In addition there was a 172cc Villiers-engined super-sports model. In the following years, Rex Acme also fitted MAG and Sturmey-Archer engines. Among Blackburne-engined works racing machines ridden by Handley, were 173cc singles and in 1926 even 498cc V-twins with ohv engines. Other Rex Acme riders included H. G. Tyrell Smith, Arthur Taylor, Charles Needham, Hans Hasenauer, Felice Bonetto, Karl Machu, and Otto Cecconi.

REX / *Germany 1923–1925*
Produced 283cc two-stroke machines in a small factory near Nuremberg.

REX / *Germany 1948–1964*
Built bicycle attachment engines with 31cc, 34cc and 40cc, afterwards a large number of mofas, mopeds and lightweights with 48cc two-stroke power units.

REX / *Sweden 1908–*
The first machines had Swiss Motosacoche engines. In 1908 Rex built their own 2·5 hp V-twin engines. Later there were Villiers and JAP-engined models from 147cc to 746cc. After WWI Sachs, Ilo, Husqvarna and other two-stroke engines from 48cc to 248cc were fitted.

REX-JAP / *England 1908–1915*
These machines officially had not much in common with Rex of Coventry, but the frames may have been made by that manufacturer. The Rex-Jap, built by the Premier Motor Company of Birmingham, was available with JAP engines from 293cc to 996cc.

REYNOLDS-RUNABOUT / *England 1919–1922*
Fully enclosed scooter-like machines with small wheels and a very low centre of gravity. Engines used were the 269cc Liberty two-stroke and the 346cc sv JAP.

269cc Reynolds-Runabout (TS Liberty-engine) 1921

REYNOLDS-SPECIAL / *England 1930–1933*
Made by Albert Reynolds, who founded in 1938 the AER motorcycle works and who for many years was closely connected with Scott, the Reynolds-Specials were actually modified and improved 498cc and 598cc two-stroke, twin-cylinder watercooled Scotts.

R&F / *Germany 1924–1926*
Another German 348cc ohv machine, but in this case the engine was R&F's own design and manufacture.

RHONSON / *France 1952–1958*
Built the 49cc Rhonsonette mopeds and other small machines and also 123cc two-stroke motorcycles.

RHONY-X / *France 1924–1932*
Built during the years a wide range of models. These included 185cc and 246cc two-strokes, in the late 1920s and 1930s also 98cc versions as well as JAP and Chaise-engined sv and ohv models up to 498cc. Some of the Chaise engines were ohc unit-design models.

RIBI / *Germany 1923–1925*
A Berlin-based manufacturer of 196cc and 248cc ohv single-cylinder machines with their own engines.

RICHARD / *France 1901–1904*
Car and motorcycle manufacturer, whose motorcycles had engines made by Peugeot and other proprietary engine manufacturers.

RICKMANN / *England 1959–*
See also Metisse. Rickmann's superb frames are used with many modern engines. These include the 736cc four-cylinder Honda, 646cc and 746cc Triumph twins, and the 903cc four-cylinder Kawasaki. Many Rickmann frames are exported to the USA and the Continent.

903cc Rickman (ohc four-cylinder Kawasaki engine) 1977

RIEJU / *Spain 1952–*
Built two and four-stroke ohv models up to 174cc. Among them 124cc and 174cc versions with the French AMC engines; also scooters.

RIGAT / *Italy 1912–1914*
Produced motorcycles with 487cc single-cylinder Fafnir engines.

RIKUO / *Japan 1953–1962*
Took a good look at other designs before they built a new model. The results were 996cc and 1198cc V-twins with a Harley-Davidson look

and 248cc and 348cc ohv singles with a BMW appearance.

RILEY / *England 1901–c1908*
Well-known carmaker. Built first De Dion-engined three-wheelers, then motorcycles with Minerva, MMC and also their own engines. Most models had 2, 2·5 and 2·75 hp engines. Just before WWII Riley became part of what is now Leyland.

RINNE / *Germany 1924–1932*
Concentrated on 124cc, 174cc and 248cc two-stroke engines. Complete machines were made in limited numbers with a horizontal cylinder. Racing versions were ridden by Max Hucke, Lücke and Rannacher and it was Hucke who built Rinne frames.

RIP / *England 1905–1908*
Peugeot, Stevens and White & Poppe engines drove these early machines, which had spring frames.

RIVIERRE / *France c1903*
Had a Megola-like engine, ie a 1·75 hp radial engine built into the rear wheel, but designer Gaston Rivierre offered also stronger engines up to 20 hp, built on similar lines. They were really two-strokes with the opposite cylinder working as a kind of scavenging pump for the intake of the mixture.

RIWINA / *Germany 1924–1925*
Assembler who built his machines at Bielefeld, then a centre of the German bicycle industry. The engine was a 142cc two-stroke, made by DKW. Other power units were also fitted.

RIXE / *Germany 1934–*
Produced in pre-war days 75cc and 98cc mopeds with Sachs engines as well as bicycles. After 1945 Rixe range included motorcycles up to 248cc; now production concentrates on 49cc mopeds, mokicks and other small machines with Sachs motors.

RIZZATO / *Italy 1972–*
Younger factory which uses 123cc Minarelli engines in sports machines, mostly trials models.

R&K / *Czechoslovakia 1924–1926*
Equipped lightweight motorcycles with 147cc and 172cc Villiers two-stroke engines. Kroboth later designed and built cars and — in Germany after the war — scooters.

RMW / *Germany 1925–1955*
The first machines built had their own 132cc and 148cc two-stroke engines. Later ones also had 198cc versions with 62mm bore and 66mm stroke. Four-stroke models used a variety of proprietary engines up to 498cc. Among them were Sturmey-Archer, MAG, JAP, Küchen, Moser and Bark products. RMW took over the Phoenix motorcycle works, used for some time screwed-together frames and had after 1945 a comparatively small production.

ROA / *Spain 1952–early 1960s*
Built motorcycles and three-wheeled transport vehicles with Hispano-Villiers engines with capacities up to 325cc.

ROBAKO / *Germany 1924–1926*
One of the many Berlin-based motorcycle assemblers of the 1920s. Fitted 129cc Bekamo and 132cc MGF two-stroke engines.

ROC / *England 1904–1915*
Designed by one of the great pioneers, A. W. Wall. The works, based at Guildford and afterwards at Birmingham, were financed by the famous author Conan-Doyle. Roc motorcycles had unusually long wheelbases with Precision and Roc engines of 2 hp, 2·5 hp and 3·5 hp; most of them were V-twins. The versatile A. W. Wall designed during the years many different and often unorthodox vehicles and other products. They included different kinds of gearboxes, three-wheelers with motorcycle engines and car-like bodies, bicycle attachment engines etc.

ROCHESTER / *France 1923–1929*
Concentrated on lightweight machines with engines up to 174cc.

ROCHET / *France 1902–c1908*
Was among the first producers of motorcycles with two-speed gears. The single-cylinder 1·75 hp ioe engine was of their own manufacture.

ROCKET / *Italy 1953–1958*
For its period an ultra-modern flat-twin ohv machine of 198cc only. The opposing cylinders were transverse-mounted and in unit with the engine. Drive to the rear wheel was by shaft. Made by IMN of Naples, the Rocket was an expensive, probably over ambitious design.

ROCKSON / *England 1930–1932*
Assembler who used 269cc Villiers two-strokes and 346cc Blackburne sv engines.

ROCO / *Germany 1922–1925*
Beautiful lightweight machines with 110cc, afterwards also 147cc two-stroke engines. Unconfirmed sources claim the engines were supplied by Cockerell. Among the owners of the Roco works were the famous designer and racing motorist Johannes Rössig and the Rosner brothers, also well-known racing men. The Roco had a triangular double-loop frame and a very low saddle position.

ROCONOVA / *Germany 1924–1926*
Designed by Johannes Rössig, who raced Douglas and Victoria machines, the Roconovas were the first 248cc and 348cc ohc singles built commercially in Germany. Racing versions of the quarter-litre machine won many races. Among the riders were Rössig, Thevis, Zadek, Count Bismarck, Perl, Nakonzer, Elsner, Pohle and others. Roconova also supplied engines to other factories including TX and Patria.

248cc Roconova (ohc) 1925

ROÉS / *France 1932–1934*
Lightweight machines with 98cc and 123cc two-stroke engines.

ROESSLER & JAUERNIGG / *Czechoslovakia 1902–1907*
Another make born in the old Austro-Hungarian Empire, in a town called Aussig. The Fehers-designed singles and V-twins were of excellent quality. Some models had rear suspension. The engines were of 2, 2·75 and 4 hp.

RÖHR / *Germany 1952–1958*
Scooters made by an agricultural-machine factory with 197cc Ilo engines.

ROLAND / *Germany 1904–1907*
Roland, Allright, Tiger, Vindec-Special etc. were all trade marks used by the Köln-Lindenthaler Motorenwerke AG at Cologne. Like the others, early Roland machines had Kelecom, FN and other engines built under licence. These engines were singles of 2·25 and 2·75 hp and V-twins of 5 hp. Roland motorcycles were also made available equipped with Truffault swinging-arm forks.

2¾ hp Roland (sv Truffault fork) 1905

ROLAND / *Germany 1923–1924*
Small producer of two-strokes with !32cc Bekamo and 145cc DKW engines.

ROLEO / *France 1924–1939*
See CP Roleo.

ROLFE / *England 1911–1914*
Ambitious factory which built good motorcycles with 498cc single-cylinder and 746cc V-twin sv JAP engines.

ROMEO / *Italy 1969–*
A make of the younger Italian generation. Romeo concentrates on 49cc two-stroke machines with Minarelli engines.

ROMP / *England 1913–1914*
Short-lived 499cc sv single with Precision engine.

RONDINE / *Italy 1923–1928*
Prinelli's two-stroke Rondine lightweights with 98cc Train engines had no connection with Rondine racing Fours.

RONDINE / *Italy 1934–1935*
Designed by Carlo Gianini and Piero Remor, the Rondine was a supercharged, watercooled 499cc four-cylinder racing machine. Its production by the Compagnia Nazionale Aeronautica at Rome was financed by Count Bonmartini. He also entered a team in races. His top riders: Piero Taruffi and Amilcare Rosetti. The design was bought by Gilera in 1936 and raced until after the war under that trade mark.

RONDINE / *Italy 1951–1954*
These Rondines, designed by Martino Siccomario, had 124cc and 147cc Sachs two-stroke engines.

RONDINE/*Italy 1968–early 1970s*
Yet another Rondine, designed by former MV-Agusta racing-team member Alfredo Copeta. His moto-cross and racing version had 48cc two-stroke engines.

ROND-SACHS/*The Netherlands 1971–1975*
Concentrated on the production of 49cc and 123cc moto-cross machines with Sachs two-stroke engines. The bigger had 22 bhp at 9300 rpm.

ROSENGART/*France 1922–1923*
Rosengart, where they built the old Austin 7 under licence like Dixi-BMW in Germany, was earlier connected with a lightweight motorcycle. It had a 98cc Train two-stroke engine, and did not become a world-beater.

ROSELLI/*Italy 1899–1910*
Probably the most famous pioneer of the Italian motorcycle industry, Emanuel di A. Rosselli produced first his 1 hp Lilliput, a bicycle with the engine in front of the pedalling gear. His next models included a 1·75 hp lady's motorcycle and a 258cc (2·5 hp) machine. Rosselli also produced cars.

ROSSI/*Italy 1950–1955*
The Parma-built machines had 123cc Sachs engines and proved the excellent design with successes in trials.

ROSSI/*Italy 1929*
With its frame made from aluminium alloy the 348cc 90 degree V-twin was a technically interesting but commercially not very successful design. Paolo Rossi, the designer, had insufficient resources to market this motorcycle on a bigger scale.

ROTARY/*Japan early 1950s–1961*
Modern two-strokes with 124cc, built by one of Japan's bigger factories.

ROTER TEUFEL/*Germany 1923–1925*
Berlin had many producers of two-strokes, but only few factories which built four-stroke motorcycles. This was one of them. The machines had 170cc sv engines.

ROTTER/*Germany 1924–1925*
Before the First World War, the Rotter factory had been used to build the Weltrad. For a time in the mid 1920s they fitted DKW engines into simple frames.

ROULETTE/*England 1918–1919*
Assembled machines with 269cc Villiers two-stroke, three-port, deflector-type engines.

ROUSSEY/*France 1948–1956*
Concentrated on lightweights, including 48cc bicycle engines as well as motorcycles and scooters with 123cc and 174cc power units.

ROVA-KENT/*Australia 1913–1914*
Unit-design 496cc single-cylinder machine with its own four-valve ohv engine.

ROVER/*England 1902–1925*
Equipped with orthodox diamond frames, Rover motorcycles were known for their sound design and excellent workmanship. In pre-1914 days they had an excellent 496cc sv single, which was also built after 1918. The engine had 85mm bore and 88mm stroke. There were also JAP-engined models, including 676cc V-twins. The last Rover models built had 248cc and 348cc ohv single-cylinder engines of own design and manufacture.

496cc Rover (sv) 1921

246cc Rover (ohv) 1923

ROVETTA/*Italy 1900–1906*
Once a well-known factory, Rovetta already produced in 1904 watercooled machines with their own 2·55 hp engines.

ROVIN/*France 1920–1934*
Roaul de Rovin was a very versatile man. He built motorcycles from 98cc to 499cc with two-stroke engines and also JAP and MAG sv and ohv engines. He built three-wheelers and very fast small sports and racing cars with JAP racing engines, which he successfully drove in races. He raced also Delage GP cars, bought in 1929 the San-Sou-Pap motorcycle factory and built after 1945 very neat small cars.

ROVLANTE/*France 1929–1935*
Built 98cc and 124cc two-stroke machines.

ROYAL/*America 1901–c1908*
Typical American design with the 445cc cylinder sloping rearward and the petrol tank above the rear wheel of a strengthened bicycle frame.

ROYAL/*Switzerland 1900–1908*
Was one of the first motorcycle producers in the country. The 1·5 hp and 2 hp engines were of Zedel manufacture.

ROYAL/*Italy 1923–1928*
Built by the Santogastino brothers at Milan, the little machine had their own 132cc two-stroke engine. In addition, they built a limited number of JAP-engined 346cc and 490cc sv and ohv machines.

ROYAL-AJAX/*England 1901–c1908*
Single-cylinder machines with 2·5 hp—probably MMC—engines.

ROYAL-EAGLE/*England 1901–1939*
This name on the tank of Coventry-Eagle machines was available until 1910.

ROYAL-ENFIELD/*India late 1950s*
Was originally a branch of Royal-Enfield (England) and concentrated on 173cc and other small machines with Villiers engines. When Royal-Enfield stopped motorcycle production in England, the Madras branch—Enfield India Ltd.—took over some designs and production equipment. This included the 346cc Bullet, which since 1976 is also exported to Europe, although the basic design is outdated.

346cc Enfield India

ROYAL-ENFIELD / *England 1898–1971*
Originally a branch of Eadie, Royal-Enfield built three-wheelers with De Dion engines, then motorcycles with 211cc Minerva engines mounted above the front wheel. The 346cc ioe V-twins with engines made by MAG especially for the Redditch works were famous before WWI. After the war, production included their own 225cc two-strokes and 976cc V-twins, soon followed by JAP-engined models from 246cc

348cc Royal Enfield (ohv Model Bullet) 1938

223cc Royal Enfield (TS) 1923

346cc Royal Enfield (ohv Model 352) 1926

to 996cc and —from 1925 onwards—more machines with their own power units. Among them were 346cc, 488cc and 976cc sv and 346cc ohv models. A 225cc sv machine and 498cc ohv singles followed. The factory also competed officially in races and had such good riders as Charly Barrow, Georges Reynard, Gordon Burney and Jack Booker. A 996cc V-twin with ohv JAP racing engine, ridden by E. Magner of

692cc Royal Enfield (ohv twin Model Super Meteor) 1959

496cc Royal Enfield (sv Model 501) 1929

496cc Royal Enfield (ohv Model GL 31) 1931

692cc Royal Enfield (ohv twin Model Airflow Meteor) 1960

Sweden, broke the world speed record for side-car outfits over one mile. During the 1930s the range included 148cc two-strokes and ohv models, 225cc two-stroke versions, very reliable 346cc, 570cc and 976cc sv machines and the famous Bullet range, with 248cc, 346cc and 499cc ohv — partly four-valve ohv — single-cylinder engines, designed by Tony Wilson-Jones, the RE chief designer. Other models, including a big 1140cc V-twin with RE's own

496cc Royal Enfield (ohv Model Bullet) 1936

996cc Royal Enfield (sv V-twin) 1936

power unit, followed during the late 1930s. All these models with exception of the two-strokes had sump lubrication. The factory also built successful trials machines and during the war supplied the forces with 346cc sv and ohv models in large numbers. After 1945 improved pre-war models were built, as well as a 123cc two-stroke, which had been developed during the war. A new 496cc vertical ohv twin appeared in 1948, and then a new 248cc ohv single. During the 1950s the 692cc Meteor — also a vertical ohv twin — made its appearance, to be followed by the 100 mph Super Meteor. Other models were the Prince, a 148cc two-stroke, a 496cc Meteor Minor version, a 248cc model with a sporting Villiers two-stroke engine and also a new five-speed 248cc Crusader ohv machine. The big 112 mph Interceptor and its even faster successors with 736cc vertical-twin ohv engines were among the most powerful motorcycles ever built by the British industry. Unfortunately this industry is now on the decline. At this point the RE works moved from Redditch to Bradford-on-Avon. The superb Interceptor, which was also delivered with the Rickman frame, and a 248cc ohv single called the Continental were the last models made by Royal-Enfield in England, where such riders as Johnny Brittain, Charley Rogers, Jack Stocker, Tom Ellis and others proved the high quality of these machines in many sporting events, especially trials.

ROYAL-MOTO / *France 1923–1933*
Built a wide range of lightweight machines with 98cc, 174cc and 244cc Massardin two-strokes and also four-strokes with 246cc to 498cc sv and ohv engines.

ROYAL NORD / *Belgium 1950–early 1960s*
Produced 48cc mofas, mopeds etc. and also motorcycles to 248cc with Villiers, Maico, Sachs and other engines.

ROYAL-RUBY / *England 1909–1933*
Excellent machines which before WWI already had fully enclosed rear wheel chains. Most models had the company's own sv engines, including 349cc and 375cc single-cylinder versions. The JAP-engined 976cc V-twin had leaf springs on both sides. Double-loop frames and saddle tanks were introduced in 1927, when the factory fitted 172cc to 346cc Villiers engines and 248cc and 348cc JAP ohv engines. The factory also built three-wheelers with motorcycle engines.

ROYAL SCOT / *Scotland 1922–1924*
The tank transfer was probably the only thing really made at the Glasgow Royal Scot works. The frame was built at the Glasgow Victoria motorcycle works for Royal Scot and the 348cc sleeve-valve engine was made in the nearby Barr & Stroud factory; most other parts and accessories were bought in England from specialised factories.

ROYAL SOVEREIGN / *England c1902*
Unorthodox machines with 211cc Minerva engines.

2¼ hp Royal-Sovereign (sv) 1903

ROYAL STANDARD / *Switzerland 1928–1932*
Pauchand's design was a vertical 398cc twin-cylinder unit-design machine, with a Zurcher engine built exclusively for this make. The design was ahead of its time.

ROYAL SUPER / *Italy 1923–1928*
Identical with the 132cc Royal two-stroke models.

ROYAL WELLINGTON / *England c1901*
Strengthened bicycle frames with 211cc Minerva engines.

R&P / *England 1902–c1906*
Was among the first commercially-built motor-cycles in England. Most machines had 346cc single-cylinder engines with their own engine fitted in what is now the standard centre position, developed by the Werner brothers in France.

RS / *Germany 1924–1925*
Unusual two-stroke, whose 380cc vertical-twin unit-design engine had a crank-pin rotary valve. The design was probably not fully developed when it was sold to another firm, and never appeared on the market.

RS / *Germany 1925–1928*
This was the successor to the above RS, but with an orthodox engine, the old 493cc BMW flat-twin. Still a mystery, because BMW stopped producing that engine in 1922. Such engines were probably still in stock with some dealers.

RUBINELLI / *Italy 1921–1927*
Built 122cc and 172cc two-strokes and also supplied these engines to other small motorcycle assemblers.

RUCHE / *France 1952–1954*
A short-lived producer of 123cc and 173cc two-stroke machines.

RUD / *Germany 1927–1930*
Assembled motorcycles in small numbers with Kühne, MAG and JAP engines from 348cc to 748cc.

398cc Royal Standard (ohc twin) 1932

RUDGE-WHITWORTH (RUDGE) | *England*
1911–1940

Was an old-established bicycle factory and entered motorcycle production with 85mm bore and 88mm stroke 499cc ioe singles. After WWI, they added an 85mm bore × 132mm stroke single, which had no less than 749cc. There was also a 998cc ioe V-twin. Rudge also built a variable gear with a possibility of up to 21 gear positions, the famous Multi-gear. The first all-chain Rudges were made in 1920, but the singles still had belt drive to the rear wheel. New models appeared in 1923, when the big twin got a four-speed gearbox, and 1924, when a new range of 348cc and 498cc singles with four-valve engines and four-speed gearboxes was introduced. The cylinder heads had flathead inlet and tulip exhaust valves. Saddle tanks were introduced in 1927 and the exhaust ports were now disposed radially instead of parallel. The 348cc models, not made since 1925, returned in 1929 and 248cc singles with sv and ohv JAP engines appeared. There was a 498cc Ulster racing model in the catalogue, and also from 1930 onwards a positive stop foot gear-change. A new 348cc racing version got hemispherical cylinder heads, and the valves on this model were now disposed radially. Based on experience in many races, new production TT Replica racers came into production in 1931; these were 348cc and 498cc models, followed by a 248cc version, which had four-valve cylinder heads. The factory, then headed by John Vernon Pugh with Fred Anstey as chief designer and George Hack in charge of the racing team, entered racing in 1927 and formed with Graham Walker, H. G. Tyrell Smith and Ernie Nott a very successful works team, which in the following years won many TT, Grand Prix and other races. The number of active racing men on Rudge machines was very big in all countries, as the racing models — Ulster and TT Replicas — were supplied ready to race and at comparatively cheap prices. Among English riders were Wal Handley, Jimmy Simpson, Charley Manders, Les Higgins and many others. Erich Tennigkeit, Hans Richnow, Bernhard Petruschke, Hans Marschall, Kurt Riese, Richard Schindel, the Port brothers, Von Bachmayer and others rode them in Germany; Martin Schneeweiss, Prince Windischgrätz, Otto

499cc Rudge-Whitworth (ioe Multi-gear) 1914

499cc Rudge-Whitworth (ohv four-valve Model Standard) 1926

499cc Rudge-Whitworth (ohv four-valve Model Sport) 1926

499cc Rudge-Whitworth (ohv Ulster) 1929

Steinfellner, Josef Illichmann, Franz Zederbauer
and Franz Kofler in Austria, Terzo Bandini,
Aldo Pigorini, Mario Ghersi etc. in Italy;
Aranda and Faura in Spain; Rzehak, Dvořak,
Henych, Siška, Boxhorn, Krystlik, Scheufler etc.
in Czechoslovakia; Zamecznik and Deli in
Hungary, etc. There were also many Speedway
riders, using Rudge Speedway machines built
since 1929. 248cc JAP engines were superseded
in 1932 by Rudge's own. From 1934 onward,
two-valve 248cc machines superseded the four-
valve ones. Rudge in Coventry also produced
from 1930 to 1935 the Python four-valve proprietary engines with 248cc, 348cc and 498cc
plus a 173cc version, specially built for Miller-
Balsamo in Italy. Among other users of Python
four-valve engines were Zündapp, Grindlay-
Peerless, AJW, Eysink, Lady, Imperial, Itala,
Premier and James. With riders including
Graham Walker — who was sales manager at
the factory — as well as Bob McGregor, Jimmy
Edwards and Percy Blamaire, Rudge was very
successful in trials. Official racing stopped

499cc Rudge-Whitworth (ohv four-valve Model Special) 1931

in the early 1930s; racing machine production
was stopped too. Production concentrated
around 248cc and 498cc models, when a 98cc
two-stroke Autocycle came into production in
1938. At about the same time, the Coventry
factory was sold and Rudge production moved
to Hayes. Soon afterwards, manufacture of
motorcycles was stopped, and production of
Autocycles sold to Norman at Ashford. Rudges
were sporting and popular motorcycles; internal
changes after J. V. Pugh's death in the mid-
1930s led to the end of a fine machine.

499cc Rudge-Whitworth (ohv four-valve Model Ulster) 1935

499cc Rudge-Whitworth (ohv four-valve Model Ulster) 1938

RUEDER / *Germany late 1910s to early 1920s*
Assembler who used 348cc Kühne ohv engines
in orthodox frames.

RULLIERS / *Czechoslovakia 1924–1929*
Two-stroke motorcycles with 147cc, 172cc and
346cc Villiers engines.

RUMI / *Italy 1949–late 1950s*
Designed by Dr. Rumi at Bergamo, these were
excellent 124cc twin-cylinder two-stroke machines with forward-facing horizontal cylinders
and sporting appearance. The cylinders each had
42mm bore and 45mm stroke. The production
sport model had a top speed of 80 mph, racing
versions were even faster. Rumi also built
scooters and introduced a range of very unorthodox V-twin ohc machines with 98cc, 124cc and
174cc, which never came into quantity production. There was in the mid-1950s also a Salmaggi-
designed 248cc twin-cylinder double ohc racing
machine, which was never fully developed and
never ran in a big race. Rumi's heyday was
around 1952 with the small Bees.

123cc Rumi (TS flat-twin) 1952

173cc Rumi (ohv v-twin) 1960

RUNGE / *Germany 1923–1926*
A small company which built 197cc sv machines
on a limited scale.

RUPP / *Germany 1928–1932*
Produced two models. One was a 198cc ohv
machine with its own engine, the other with a
498cc ohc single-cylinder three-valve Küchen
power plant.

267

RUSH / *Belgium 1922–1934*
Became well-known when the manufacturer-rider Van Geert won the 250cc class at the 1924 Monza GP. His machine had a 248cc Blackburne ohv engine. He also built 348cc single-cylinder ohv models. He built his own engines after 1927, when the range included 397cc, 497cc and 597cc sv and ohv models.

RUSPA / *Italy 1926–1929*
Built 124cc two-strokes and 174cc two-stroke and ohv machines. A 347cc single with chain-driven ohc was built in very small numbers only.

RUSSELL / *England 1913*
Limited production of 172cc and 492cc ohv machines.

RUT / *Germany 1923–1924*
Two-strokes of simple design with 124cc and an outside flywheel.

RUTER / *Spain 1957–1960*
Assembled machines with 95cc and 124cc two-stroke engines, supplied to the factory by Hispano-Villiers.

RUWISCH / *Germany 1948–1949*
Miniscooter with 38cc Victoria bicycle engines.

RWC / *Austria 1949–late 1950s*
Lightweight motorcycles made by a bicycle factory. The engine was a 98cc Rotax-Sachs.

RW SCOUT / *England 1920–1922*
Made by R. Wheaterell of London, was an assembled machine with 269cc Villiers and 318cc Dalm two-stroke engines, but Blackburne 346cc sv and ohv engines could also be fitted.

S

SACI / *Brazil 1959–late 1960s*
Scooter made with 174cc two-stroke engines.

SADEM / *France 1951–1954*
Lightweight machines with engines up to 98cc.

SADRIAN / *Spain 1956–1963*
Producer of three-wheelers, who also built Hispano-Villiers-engined 123cc to 198cc two-stroke motorcycles.

SAGITTA / *Czechoslovakia 1928–1930*
Limited assembly of machines with 247cc Villiers engines.

SALIRA / *Belgium 1955–early 1960s*
Assembler who used 98cc to 197cc Villiers engines, among others.

SALTLEY / *England 1919–1924*
Also an assembler, whose machines had 269cc Villiers, 347cc Vulcanus and 497cc sv Blackburne engines.

SALVE / *Italy 1925–1926*
The only model had a 496cc unit-design sv engine.

SANCHOC / *France 1922–1924*
Built two-strokes from 98cc to 246cc and sv machines up to 346cc.

SAN CHRISTOPHORO / *Italy 1951–1954*
One of the small Italian producers of 124cc two-stroke machines. The Simonetta had 54mm bore/stroke and 6 bhp at 4800 rpm.

SANGLAS / *Spain 1949–*
Producer of first-class single-cylinder ohv machines with their own 496cc engines with 89·5mm bore and 79mm stroke. These power units develop 27 bhp at 6000 rpm, are equipped with Electrostarters, have a 90 mph top speed and are mainly used by the Spanish Police, although available also for private and foreign customers. Earlier models, also four-stroke singles with ohv engines, had capacities from 248cc to 423cc. Sanglas is the only factory in the world which builds only ohv singles. They are developing a 747cc four-valve double-ohc single which should be on the market in 1978. The ohc drive is by toothed belt.

SAN-SOU-PAP / *France 1923–1936*
The name stands for 'without any valves', but this was correct only until the factory built Train-engined 98cc to 248cc two-strokes, and commenced manufacture of 248cc to 498cc sv and ohv singles with JAP and MAG power-units. San-Sou-Pap became part of the Rovin works in 1929.

SANTAMARIA / *Italy 1951–1963*
Mofas, mopeds, etc. with 49, 69, 98, 123 and 147cc Zündapp, Sachs and Ilo-engines.

SAN YANG / *Taiwan 1962–*
Assembled and built partly under licence various Honda models in Taiwan.

SANYO / *Japan 1958–1962*
Sporting machines, singles with Sanyo's own 248cc ohv engines.

SAR / *Italy 1920–1925*
Based on the design of the Elect, the 498cc SAR was a nice flat-twin sv and ohv machine. Another model had the oilcooled 346cc Bradshaw ohv engine, which had 68mm bore and 96mm stroke with automatic lubrication.

348cc SAR (ohv Bradshaw engine) 1924

SAR / *Germany 1923–1930*
The Raetsch-designed SAR engines were three-port two-strokes with 122cc, 147cc and 198cc.

SARACEN / *England 1967–1973*
Concentrated on the manufacture of Sachs-engined 123cc, 188cc and trials machines, and on 244cc Mickmar-engined moto-cross versions.

SARCO (SARCO-RELIANCE) / *England 1920–1923*
Concentrated on a 261cc two-stroke single with 68mm bore × 72mm stroke and a Burman two-speed gearbox.

SARENKA / *Poland 1961–*
A 123cc two-stroke, built by the well-known Polish WSK factory.

SARKANA-SWAIGSNE / *Latvia 1958–*
Supplies 49cc mofas, mopeds and similar means of transport.

SAROLEA / *Belgium 1898–1957*
Was among the first producers of motorcycles and of proprietary single-cylinder and V-twin engines. Became famous during the 1920s with with English-looking 346cc and 496cc sv and ohv singles. They built in the 1930s 124cc, 147cc and 174cc two-strokes and 596cc ohv models. The works rider 'Grizzly' (Gilbert de Ridder) rode after 1935 348cc and 498cc machines with their own ohc racing engines. Other well-known Sarolea riders were Gregoire, Claessens, Tom, Vidal, Stobart; Poncin of Luxembourg; Stěpan of Czechoslovakia; Dirtl, Gayer, Runtsch, Benesch and Trella of Austria; Arcangeli and Colombo of Italy and others. After the war, there was a production co-operative created with other Belgian factories, and Sarolea's production concentrated on two-strokes from 49cc to 248cc.

SARTORIUS / *Germany 1924–1926*
Limited production of 195cc sv and 348cc Kühne ohv engined singles.

SATAN / *Czechoslovakia 1929*
This was a machine with its own sloping 548cc sv engine. Small production.

SATURN / *Germany 1921–1927*
Made by the Steudel car and boat-engine works, Saturn motorcycles had 246cc two-stroke, 348cc ohv and 497cc V-twin sv engines. There was also a 149cc bicycle sv engine and a prototype of a shaft-driven version of the 497cc V-twin, built at a Steudel branch factory at Leipzig.

SATURN / *England 1925–1926*
Produced a small number of 346cc singles with own two-stroke engines.

SAUND / *India 1970–*
Originally a 98cc two-stroke DKW (Zweirad Union) design, the Sound—built with many parts made in India—is still influenced by the German design. The 98cc engine has 9·7 bhp at 6800 rpm.

SBD / *Germany 1923–1924*
Munich-built motorcycles with the 293cc Bosch-Douglas flat-twin engine with opposing sv cylinders.

SCARAB / *Italy 1967–*
These are Ancilotti's 49cc, 123cc and 245cc trials and moto-cross models with Sachs, Hiro and Franco-Morini two-stroke engines. The

49cc versions have 11 bhp at 10,500 rpm, the 123cc 24 bhp at 9500 rpm and the 245cc 32 bhp at 8000 rpm. Good design, excellent finish.

SCARABEO / *Italy 1968–*
Made by Aprilia at Noale, these excellent trials and moto-cross machines are two-strokes with 123cc Sachs or Hiro engines with six and seven-speed gearboxes. The factory also produces a wide range of models with 49cc engines.

SCHEIBERT / *Austria 1911–1913*
Motorcycles with strengthened frames and a 197cc sv engine mounted above the front wheel.

SCHICKEL / *America 1912–1915*
Interesting design with a cast light-alloy frame which included the petrol tank. Its engine was a 648cc two-stroke single.

198cc Schliha (TS with ohv) 1930

SCHLIHA / *Germany 1924–1933*
Was one of the many unorthodox two-stroke designs built during the 1920s and early 1930s in Berlin. Designed by Heinrich Schlüpmann, Schliha motorcycles were ohv singles from 129cc to 596cc.

496cc Sarolea (ohv) 1927

347cc Sarolea (ohv sport model) 1931

496cc Sarolea (ohv racing model) 1930

596cc Sarolea (ohv) 1932

SCHLIMME / *Germany 1924–1925*
Assembled machines with 142cc and 173cc DKW two-stroke engines.

SCHMIDT / *Germany 1921–1924*
Produced bicycle engines and 196cc lightweight motorcycles. The sv engines were of Schmidt's own design and manufacture.

SCHNEIDER / *Germany 1924–1926*
Another assembler, who fitted 142cc, 173cc and 206cc DKW engines.

SCHNELL-HOREX / *Germany 1952–1954*
Designed by racing motorcyclist Roland Schnell, who built these racing machines with 248cc, 348cc and 498cc single-cylinder gear-driven ohc engines in conjunction with the Horex works, the Schnell-Horex was made in limited numbers only and proved especially formidable in the 350cc size. Among the riders besides Schnell were Hermann Gablenz, H. P. Müller, Robert Zeller, Georg Braun, Erwin Aldinger, Fritz Kläger and others.

SCHROFF-RECORD / *Germany 1923–1925*
Simple 148cc three-port two-strokes with sloping engines.

SCHÜRHOFF / *Germany 1949–1953*
Producer of mofas, mopeds etc. with 49cc Sachs, Ilo and Zündapp engines and of lightweights with screwed triangular frames and 123cc to 173cc Ilo two-stroke engines.

124cc Schürhoff (TS Ilo engine) 1953

SCHÜTT / *Germany 1933–1934*
Equipped with frames made from Duralumin, the Paul Schütt-designed 196cc two-strokes had a transverse-mounted engine of his design.

SCHÜTTOFF / *Germany 1924–1933*
Made by a machine factory, Schüttoff motorcycles had 246cc sv, afterwards 346cc sv and ohv as well as 496cc sv and ohv single-cylinder engines. From 1930 onwards, they also fitted

347cc Schottoff (ohv Model Sport) 1927

198cc and 298cc DKW two-stroke power units. In 1932 Schüttoff became part of the DKW works. The 348cc ohv models were very successful from 1925 to 1929. With a works team consisting of the riders Ihle, Lohse, A. Müller, E. Hirth etc. they won many races, while Josef Mittenzwei gained success in trials with a 498cc sidecar outfit.

SCHWALBE / *Germany 1922–1924*
Lightweight motorcycles with 124cc and 198cc flat-twin engines. The smaller version was also delivered as a bicycle attachment engine. Producer of these machines, the Spiegler brothers, afterwards built Spiegler motorcycles at their Aalen factory.

SCHWALBE / *Switzerland 1901–1905*
The Rugg-designed Schwalbe had a strengthened bicycle frame and a 2·75 hp Zedel engine.

SCHWEPPE / *Germany 1949–1950*
A scooter with swinging arms on both sides and 143cc to 184cc Ilo engines, which eventually became the Pirol scooter.

SCK / *Germany 1924–1925*
Assembler, who fitted 348cc and 498cc sv and ohv JAP and MAG engines into own frames. Production was on a small scale.

SCOOTAVIA / *France 1951–1956*
Luxurious scooters with 173cc ohv AMC single-cylinder engines.

SCORPION / *England 1951–1956*
Motorcycles with pressed steel frames and 197cc and 246cc Villiers two-stroke engines.

SCOTO / *France 1949–early 1950s*
Miniscooter with 39cc Mosquito engines.

SCOTT / *England 1909–*
A. A. Scott, a two-stroke pioneer, built 333cc to 534cc machines which won many races, including the 1912 and 1913 TT. They were mostly watercooled, but on some models the heads were aircooled. The 1911 TT 534cc machine had a chain-driven rotary valve to improve breathing. During the 1920s and 1930s Scott supplied mainly two engine sizes: 496cc twins with 68·25mm bore/stroke and 596cc with 68·25mm bore and 74·6mm stroke. In 1929 there were aircooled 298cc and 348cc singles which failed to do well; in 1930 there were TT machines entered with watercooled vertical twins, and a 648cc model was offered to the public in 1931, but was never produced in large numbers. After 1927 the racing machines never recovered their former glory, when they were ridden by H. S. Meyers, Frank Phillip, Frank Applebee and others, although T. L. Hatch came in third in the 1928 TT, which was run under appalling rainy conditions. Other successful riders included Speedway star Frank Varey, Harry Langmann, Tim Wood, Eric and Oliver Langton, Germany's Ernst Zündorf, the Czech Stan Chaloupka and the Swiss riders Felber and Schwab. The last really new Scott was built in 1934: a 746cc three-

486cc Scott (TS watercooled twin) 1914

498cc Scott (TS watercooled twin) 1925

595cc Scott (TS watercooled twin 'Flying Squirrel) 1926

**498cc Scott (TS watercooled twin 'TT')
1929**

498cc Scott (TS watercooled twin 'TT Prototype') 1930

**996cc Scott (TS watercooled three-cylinder)
1935**

596cc Scott (TS watercooled twin) 1948

cylinder watercooled two-stroke. Production machines had the engine increased to 996cc, but few were actually built. Scott's first machines had been built for him by Jowett's of Bradford; then he built his own at the Shipley works. He himself left the company after WWI and produced unorthodox three-wheelers with two rear wheels and a right-hand front wheel. He died of pneumonia in 1923. In 1950 the company was still producing improved 496cc and 596cc watercooled two-stroke twins, but went into voluntary liquidation and were bought by Matt Holder of Birmingham, where they theoretically still are, but there is now no production. Scott-like machines are made by Silk.

SCOTTA/*France 1952–1955*
Unorthodox motorcycle with scooter wheels and 123cc Ilo engines.

SCOTT-CYC-AUTO/*England 1934–1950*
Early and typical English moped with Scott-built 98cc two-stroke engine.

SCOUT/*England 1912–1913*
Produced motorcycles with 498cc Precision single-cylinder sv engines.

SCYLLA/*France 1931–1937*
Lightweight machines with 98cc and 123cc Aubier-Dunne two-stroke engines.

SEAL/*England 1914–1921*
Very unorthodox motorcycle with a 996cc V-twin JAP sv engine, without handlebar and without saddle. It had a steering wheel in the attached sidecar.

SEARS/*America 1912–1916*
Made for Sears, Roebuck & Co. at Chicago, these machines had 9 to 10 hp V-twin engines produced by Spake. *See also* Allstate.

SEEGARD/*Germany 1924–1925*
Built singles with their own sv 146cc and 197cc engines.

SEELEY/*England 1966–*
Colin Seeley, formerly a successful sidecar racer, continued with the production of 348cc AJS and 498cc Matchless ohc racing singles and spare parts after AMC in London discontinued their manufacture. Afterwards he produced excellent frames for a variety of racing and sports machines. Now he supplies frame-kits, especially for 736cc four-cylinder Honda engines.

SEILING / *Italy 1938–1939*
After MAS motorcycle manufacturer Alberico Seilig left that make, he produced 247cc and 347cc sv singles with his own unit-design engines and rear suspension.

346cc Seiling (sv) 1938

SEITH / *Germany 1949–1950*
Mini-vehicles for children with 38cc Victoria two-stroke engines.

SENIOR / *Italy 1913–1914*
Sporting machines with 296cc and 330cc single-cylinder and 499cc V-twin engines supplied by Moser of Switzerland.

SERTUM / *Italy 1931–1951*
Precision instruments were the first products made by Fausto Alberti's Milan factory. The first motorcycle was a 174cc sv machine, which was followed by a 120cc two-stroke. Other models were 174cc ioe and ohv and 246cc sv and ohv versions. A 498cc unit-design sv vertical-twin with a four-speed gearbox was built in the mid-1930s. There were also 248cc ohv machines and the 174cc models were replaced by 198cc machines. 120cc, 248cc and 498cc models were also built after the war, when the 498cc vertical twin was dropped and a 498cc sv single took its place. Until 1950, when a new 125cc two-stroke single appeared on the market, all Sertum machines were of strong and heavy design. They competed in many trials with such riders as Grieco, Fornasari, Ventura and several others, but never in bigger races. In 1949–1950 the factory moved to new, modern and much bigger buildings, but two years later Sertum — despite a first class reputation for quality and finish — had to close down.

496cc Sertum (sv twin) 1938

SERVETA / *Spain 1973–*
Lightweight machines with 48cc two-stroke engines.

SERVICE / *England c1900–1912*
A sales organisation which sold under their own name motorcycles actually built by Connaught and Wartnaby & Draper.

SESSA / *Italy 1950–1956*
Small assembler of motorcycles with 147cc Ilo engines.

SETTER / *Spain 1954–1956*
Lightweight machines with their own 60cc engines.

SEWÜT / *Germany 1924–1926*
DWK-engined 142cc, 173cc and 206cc two-strokes, built in limited numbers.

SFM / *Poland 1956–1964*
While most motorcycles built in eastern countries are two-strokes, the machine built by SFM at Szeczin was a modern ohv design with 248cc and 348cc single-cylinder engines. It was called Junak.

S-FORTIS / *Czechoslovakia 1929–1931*
Produced a single model only, a 598cc ohv single with engine supplied by Sarolea. Few were actually made.

SFW / *Germany 1924–1926*
After Nordstern went bankrupt, SFW took over the manufacture of the 2·5 hp two-stroke machine.

S&G / *Germany 1926–1932*
A Nuremberg machine factory which produced 346cc ohv single-cylinder engines for the Hecker factory. They had much in common with similar AJS motors of that period. When S&G (Scharrer & Gross) built complete motorcycles, the range consisted of 346cc, 496cc and 596cc sv and 496cc ohv single-cylinder models. The factory also built three-wheeled delivery vehicles with motorcycle engines. The last motorcycles made had 172cc and 198cc two-stroke engines.

SGS / *England 1926–1933*
The name stood for Syd Gleave Special, after the well-known racing motorcyclist who won the 1933 Lightweight TT on a four-valve 248cc ohv Excelsior Mechanical Marvel. His motorcycles

had Villiers engines from 147cc and JAP ohv motors from 248cc to 490cc.

SH / *Germany 1925–1928*
Identical to the RS motorcycles.

SHARRATT / *England 1920–1930*
Assembler of good machines with JAP engines from 293cc to 996cc V-twins. After 1924 a reduced production only. Also fitted Villiers and MAG engines, but the last Sharratt motorcycles had 346cc sv and ohv JAP engines.

SHAW / *America 1909–1923*
Produced two single-cylinder 2·5 hp and 3·5 hp models, which had clutchless sv engines of own manufacture.

SHAW / *England 1904–1922*
Early machines had Kelecom and Minerva engines. After a long interruption, this company supplied American 115cc bicycle attachment engines made by Shaw Mfg. Co. at Galesburg, Kansas.

346cc Sheffield-Henderson (ohv Blackburne racer) 1922

SHEFFIELD-HENDERSON / *England 1919–1923*
A sidecar factory which produced 348cc ohv and 498cc sv machines with single-cylinder Blackburne engines.

SHIN MEIWA / *Japan early 1950s to early 1960s*
Scooter-like machines with pressed steel frames and flat 89cc, 123cc and 153cc two-stroke engines.

496cc S&G (sv) 1930

SHL / *Poland 1935–*
Probably the oldest Polish motorcycle factory. Produced in the 1930s Villiers-engined 123cc machines and after 1945 a range of 123cc, 147cc and 174cc two-stroke machines.

SHOWA / *Japan early 1950s to 1960*
Manufacturer of 49cc mopeds and of motorcycles from 123cc to 247cc with their own two-stroke engines. In addition there was also a 173cc ohv machine.

SIAMT / *Italy 1907–1914*
Designed by Luigi Semeria, the Siamt was an excellent machine and very successful in races. The range included 260cc, 262cc and 344cc singles and 494cc, 688cc and 731cc V-twins.

SIAT / *Italy 1924–1926*
Once a popular bicycle engine with 75cc capacity. The Turin-built Siat was a lightweight with two-stroke and ohv engines from 98cc to 198cc.

SIC / *France 1921–1925*
Assembler who fitted 98cc to 346cc proprietary engines made by Aubier-Dunne, Zurcher and Train.

SICRAF / *France 1947–1953*
Paul Vallée not only produced motorcycles, mofas, scooters, three-wheelers etc. with 49cc to 246cc Ydral and AMC engines, but was also the owner of F-1 racing cars.

SIEG / *Germany 1922–1930*
Designed by H. Jüngst, the Sieg was supplied with a wide range of engines from 110cc to 598cc. These engines were made by DKW, Cockerell, Ilo, Bober, Alba, Hansa, Villiers, JAP, MAG and especially Blackburne.

SIEGFRIED / *Germany 1925*
Lightweights with 142cc DKW engines.

SIGNORELLI / *Italy 1928–1930*
One of the many Italian producers of 173cc two-strokes in the late 1920s.

SILK / *England 1974–*
Designed by George Silk and David Midgelow, the 653cc Silk is really a successor to the Scott motorcycles. Built so far in very limited numbers only, the watercooled twin-cylinder two-stroke engine has 76mm bore and 72mm stroke and looks like an improved and developed Scott.

SILVA / *England 1919–1920*
One of the first scooters built in England. The ohv engine had 117cc.

SILVER PIDGEON / *Japan early 1950s to 1965*
Made by the Mitsubishi group, the Silver Pidgeon was a mass-produced scooter with 87cc two-stroke and 192cc ohv engines.

SILVER PRINCE / *England 1919–1924*
Was one of the many small motorcycle assemblers of the early 1920s. Engines used were the 148cc, 248cc and 269cc Villiers and the 346cc Blackburne.

SILVER STAR / *Japan 1953–1958*
Lightweights with own 123cc and 147cc ohv engines.

SIM / *Italy 1953–1955*
Produced unconventional scooters with 123cc and 147cc Puch engines. Also 147cc two-stroke machines with shaft drive to the rear wheel.

SIMARD / *France 1951–1954*
Lambretta-like scooters with 174cc Ydral engines.

SIMONCELLI / *Italy 1927–1935*
Concentrated on the production of 174cc machines, first with Train two-stroke and then with sv and ohv JAP engines. In 1934 the Simoncelli company had already introduced a good rear suspension.

SIMONETTA / *Italy 1951–1954*
This was a 124cc two-stroke machine, built at the San Christoforo works.

SIMONINI / *Italy 1973–*
Upcoming young producer of 49cc and 123cc moto-cross and trials two-strokes with engines made by Sachs and other factories. There is now also a 248cc version with a 33 bhp engine. Most models have six or seven-speed gearboxes. Since early 1975 Simonini — named after the designer Enzo Simonini — has been closely connected with Fornetti Impianti in Maranello.

SIMPLEX / *Holland 1902–1968*
Was for many years Holland's leading motorcycle factory. Fitted Minerva, Fafnir and MAG engines from 2 hp to 6 hp; from the mid-1920s also 346cc ohv Blackburne, 498cc sv Blackburne and 348cc ohv Bradshaw engines with oilcooling into strong frames. Other engines fitted were the 98cc and 148cc Villiers and the 98cc Sachs; during the late 1930s also the 60cc Sachs and the 124cc Villiers. In the years after the war, there was a close connection with Juncker and Gazelle. Leading-link forks and duplex frames were used in 1911, 9 hp V-twins with ioe Motosacoche engines were built in 1921, triangular frames were used in the mid-1920s and a 246cc single built in 1935 which had a watercooled Villiers two-stroke power unit.

SIMPLEX / *England 1919–1922*
Producer of 105cc 1 hp two-stroke bicycle attachment engines.

SIMPLEX / *Italy 1921–1950*
Luigi Pellini built beautiful little 124cc auxiliary engines and from 1927 onwards 149cc ohv machines with their own unit-design engines, followed by 174cc models. Improved 'Ala d'Oro' versions with engines which had fully enclosed valve gears and other modern design features were built in 1930. The range included also a 210cc and from 1934 a 496cc ohv with four-speed gearboxes. After 1945 models from 148cc to

498cc Sieg (ohv V-twin MAG engine) 1928

173cc Simplex (ohv) 1929 (I)

248cc based on pre-war designs were built in limited numbers.

SIMPLEX / *America late 1930s to late 1960s*
Lightweight machines for short distances, fitted with American 198cc industrial four-stroke sv engines.

198cc Simplex (TS Clinton Industrial engine) 1966 (USA)

SIMSON / *East Germany 1949–*
Was an arms factory which built sports cars and after 1949 the 246cc AWO ohv machines with shaft drive. They were eventually renamed Simson and built until the early 1960s. From then on, the works at Suhl in Thuringia concentrated on the mass-production of 49cc and 74cc mopeds, mofas and lightweights. Trials versions of Simson two-strokes are doing well in sporting events, including the Sixdays.

74cc Simson (TS Model Trials) 1972

SINGER / *England 1900–1915*
The first products were three-wheelers, followed by Perks & Birch-licenced motorwheels, which with their 208cc engines were fitted into bicycles. In later years a wide range of Singer motorcycles of sturdy conventional design appeared on the market. Included were watercooled singles and 346cc two-strokes, but the best sellers were sv models of 299cc, 499cc and 535cc. They had some monobloc engines and a variety of gearboxes. Everything was of Singer's own design and manufacture. Singer bought Premier of Coventry in the early 1920s, but was by then a car manufacturer only.

SIPHAX / *France 1951–1956*
Small factory which produced 98cc two-strokes with a horizontal cylinder. The engines were of AMC manufacture.

SIROCCO / *Czechoslovakia 1925–1928*
Designed by Gustav Heinz, the Sirocco was built on English lines and also had English Villiers engines from 147cc to 346cc.

SIRRAH / *England 1922–1925*
The Sirrah, designed by Harris, was available with a wide range of engines. These included the 211cc Wisemann and 292cc Union two-strokes and 248cc, 348cc and 490cc sv and ohv Blackburne and JAP engines. Wisemann at Birmingham — manufacturer of the Sirrah — produced also the Verus motorcycles. The Sirrah (Harris in reverse) was a cheaper version of the Verus. There was also a 996cc Sirrah model with the V-twin sv JAP engine.

SIS / *Portugal 1950–*
Bicycle producer J. Simones Costa became the Portuguese importer of Sachs two-stroke engines and founded his own motorcycle factory. His machines are fitted with 49cc and 98cc Sachs power units.

SISSY / *Austria 1957–*
Unorthodox miniscooter with 98cc and 123cc Rotax two-stroke engines. Produced by the old-established Lohner works.

SITTA / *Germany 1950–1955*
Scooters with 119cc and 123cc Ilo engines, 49cc mopeds and also Ilo-engined motorcycles from 123cc to 247cc.

SJK / *Japan 1956–early 1960s*
Built a variety of mopeds and motorcycles from 49cc to 249cc with their own two-stroke engines, but like several other manufacturers failed during the slump in the Japanese motorcycle industry.

SKF / *Russia 1961–1965*
Russian Jawa-like 348cc double-ohc racing twins, destined for official works riders only.

SKO / *Czechoslovakia 1924–1926*
Designed by František Skopec, the SKO had a 498cc single-cylinder two-stroke deflector-type three-port engine.

SKOOTAMOTA / *England 1919–1922*
Scooter with an open frame and an ABC 123cc ohv engine.

SL / *England 1924–1925*
Produced in limited numbers a 345cc single-cylinder machine with two inlet valves and one exhaust valve.

SLADE-JAP / *England 1920–1923*
A machine with a 346cc sv JAP engine. Small production.

SLANEY / *England 1921–1922*
Only one model was made by H. H. Timbrell's factory. It had a 688cc flat-twin Coventry-Victor sv engine.

SLAVIA / *Czechoslovakia 1899–1908*
The Slavia was built in the Austro-Hungarian Empire by the Czech Laurin & Klement factory. The name Slavia was also used by the Laurin & Klement machines built under licence in Germany.

173cc Sitta (TS Ilo engine) 1953

SLINGER / *England 1900–1901*
Extremely unorthodox motorcycle with three wheels in line. The two small front wheels, one of which was directly driven by chain from the watercooled 3·5 hp single-cylinder De Dion Bouton engine, had a common frame; the rear part was more or less an orthodox bicycle frame.

SM / *Poland 1935*
Had a 346cc single-cylinder ohv unit-design engine with shaft drive to the rear wheel. Was built in small numbers only.

SMART / *Austria 1925–1932*
Assembled motorcycles with sv and ohv JAP engines of 346cc, 498cc and 596cc.

SMART / *France 1922–1927*
Lightweight motorcycles with 198cc sv engines of own manufacture.

346cc Smart (sv JAP engine) 1928

SMS / *England 1913–1914*
Unorthodox 211cc two-stroke with a patented inlet port arrangement.

SMW / *Germany 1923–1933*
Built two types of motorcycles with flat-twin engines. One had the 293cc Bosch Douglas, built under licence, the other the 493cc BMW, as found in the Victoria and other makes. New models appeared in 1928, when chief designer Karl Rühmer designed 198cc two-strokes with Villiers engines and 198cc as well as 498cc singles with sv and ohv Blackburne and Sturmey-Archer engines.

S&N / *Germany 1901–1908*
Big machine factory which also built Erika typewriters. The motorcycles were called Germania, and for a short period Slavia. They were made under Laurin & Klement licence, and were partly directly imported from the then famous L&K factory at Jungbunzlau (now Mladá Boleslav). The models were identical to the L&K products.

SNOB / *Germany 1921–1925*
Was the leading four-stroke lightweight machine in Germany during the early 1920s. Production versions had 154cc ioe single-cylinder engines, while works racing models had ohv engines. Designed by Karl Döpfner, the leading works riders were Pongs and Mischke, who fought many hard battles in sporting events against DKW and Bekamo two-strokes.

SOCOVEL / *Belgium 1947–1955*
The first 123cc Socovel was a quite orthodox two-stroke lightweight. Less orthodox were the following Villiers-engined 123cc and 197cc machines with completely enclosed engines and pressed steel frames. They had a triangular shape, plunger-type rear suspension and teleforks. The next model was a 98cc Autocycle, followed by entirely new 246cc two-strokes with Jawa engines and Jawa-like frames. There was also a 346cc Jawa-engined twin. Other versions had Ilo, Sachs and also Coventry-Victor 296cc flat-twin engines; the last ones with opposing cylinders and transverse-mounted. These twins had very small wheels.

SOK / *Sweden 1925–1928*
Concentrated on a 346cc ohv machine with mainly JAP engines.

SOKOL / *Poland 1936–1939*
The Sokol was a 598cc sloper—not unlike earlier BSA models—with its own sv engine. The production of this motorcycle was destined for the army.

SOLO / *Germany 1949–*
Produces a variety of mofas and mopeds with their own 49cc two-stroke engines. There are also watercooled versions and an Electro-mofa as well.

SOS / *England 1927–1939*
Villiers engines always played an important part in the production of these machines. A few 490cc JAP-engined machines were made in earlier years but most models had 147cc to 347cc Villiers two-strokes. Among the models was a 172cc road-racing and a 172cc speedway machine. Earlier versions had three-port, deflector-type motors, later ones the flat-top Villiers. There were also watercooled 249cc versions and models with the 346cc Villiers Longstroke.

SOUPLEX / *Belgium 1947–1953*
Produced 123cc two-strokes with Villiers engines and afterwards 296cc sv twin-cylinder machines with transverse-mounted horizontal Coventry-Victor engines.

SOUTHEY / *England 1905–1925*
This was a small company which built its own motorcycles as well as frames for other motorcycle assemblers. The company's own machines had 246cc, 249cc and 346cc engines. The first ones were made by Villiers and the last one was a side-valve Blackburne.

SOYER / *France 1920–1935*
The first models had 247cc engines, and a lady's version had a frame without a top tube. Afterwards 98cc and 174cc two-strokes and sv as well as ohv models from 248cc to 498cc with Chaise, Sturmey-Archer and JAP engines were made. The two-stroke engines were of their own manufacture. A Soyer with C. J. Williams in the saddle won the 1930 French Grand Prix. The engine used was a 498cc Sturmey-Archer ohv single.

SPA-JAP / *England 1921–1923*
Small assembler, whose machines had 246cc and 293cc sv JAP engines.

SPAKE / *America 1911–1914*
Produced strong and heavy 550cc single-cylinder and 980cc V-twin models with own ioe engines. The engines also sold to other manufacturers.

SPARK / *England 1921–1923*
Made by Sparkbrook, the Spark was a utility model with the 269cc Villiers engine.

SPARK / *England 1903–1904*
This much older Spark had a 2 hp engine and a patented surface carburettor.

SPARKBROOK / *England 1912–1925*
A well-known manufacturer who fitted in the early years 746cc and 980cc V-twin JAP engines and after WWI a 269cc two-stroke Villiers. There were also 247cc and 346cc models with the two-strokes from Wolverhampton as well as 346cc singles with the JAP sv engine, the sleeve-valve Barr & Stroud and the oilcooled Bradshaw.

SPARTA / *The Netherlands 1931–*
Bicycle factory, which produced 49cc machines with attachment engines, and afterwards models with 98cc Sachs and Villiers engines. There were

244cc Sparta (TS twin Ilo engine) 1954

also 74cc Sachs-engined and eventually 198cc Villiers-engined motorcycles. During the late 1930s, 120cc and 123cc two-strokes with Ilo and

Sachs engines were added. Improved versions with 123cc to 198cc Villiers engines came after 1945; a 246cc two-stroke with a Victoria double-port engine was added in 1951. The Dutch factory also built a machine with the 244cc Ilo vertical two-stroke twin, but concentrated since the early 1960s on 49cc mopeds.

SPARTAN / *England 1920–1922*
Small production of 349cc single-cylinder two-stroke motorcycles with Brooler three-port deflector-type engines.

SPARTON/*Wales 1976–*
Barry Hart has designed two-stroke racing machines with watercooled 498 and 748cc four-cylinder square Phoenix engines. Other models have 498cc and 525cc engines; these two are watercooled two-strokes. The factory is at Caenarfon, Gwynedd, North Wales.

SPAVIERO / *Italy 1954–1955*
This was a short-lived factory which produced 98cc twin-cylinder motorcycles equipped with ohv engines.

SPECIAL-MONNERET / *France 1952–1958*
Georges Monneret, famous French racing motorcyclist, produced in Paris his own lightweight motorcycles of sporting appearance. The engines were 49cc VAP and Sachs.

SPEED / *France 1951–1956*
This was a scooter with 60cc, 115cc and 124cc engines, manufactured by a branch of the former Mors car works.

SPEED-KING-JAP / *England 1913–1914*
These motorcycles were made to a low price for a chain store. They were equipped with 293cc JAP sv engines.

SPHINX / *Belgium 1923–1926*
Made from mainly English components, the Sphinx had 346cc and 490cc sv and ohv engines made by JAP in London.

SPIEGLER / *Germany 1923–1932*
This make was the successor to the Schwalbe machines, also built by the Spiegler works at Aalen. The unusual frames, made from pressed steel and tubes with the tank forming the backbone of the frame, housed 346cc, 498cc and 598cc single-cylinder sv and ohv engines, made by JAP, MAG and at the works. A 198cc JAP-engined ohv single was introduced in 1929.

SPIESS / *Germany 1903–1905*
Assembler who bought his 2 to 2·75 hp engines from the Minerva, Zedel and Fafnir factories.

SPINDLER / *Germany 1922–1925*
Bekamo-engined 149cc two-strokes, built in limited numbers.

SPIRIDITIS / *Latvia early 1950s–*
These machines, built by the Sarkana-Swaigsne motorcycle works, had 123cc and 246cc two-stroke engines. According to unconfirmed information, the Riga factory now produces 49cc machines, mainly mopeds.

SPRING / *Belgium 1910–1940*
The first model was a four-cylinder with a frame which was sprung both front and back. New models which appeared after 1920 had transverse-mounted V-twin engines with 496cc, 746cc and 996cc. The last one was equipped with a reverse gear.

498cc Spiegler (ohv) 1929

SPRITE / *England 1965–*
This factory supplies moto-cross and trials machines in kit form. The range of these two-strokes includes engines of 123cc, 244cc and 405cc.

STABIL / *Belgium 1931–1933*
Limited production of 98cc and 123cc machines with Villiers engines.

STADION / *Czechoslovakia 1958–1966*
Moped factory, which used 49cc engines supplied by Jawa.

STAFFETT / *Norway 1953–early 1960s*
Another moped producer fitting 49cc engines.

STAG / *England 1912–1914*
The factory was at Sherwood Forest, Nottingham. Used Precision engines from 4·5 to 6 hp.

STAHL / *America 1910–1914*
Built at Philadelphia, the Stahl motorcycles had 4·5 hp single-cylinder and 7 hp V-twin engines.

STANDARD / *Germany 1922–1924*
One of the many workshops which built motorcycles in the early 1920s. These had simple frames and simple 132cc and 148cc three-port two-stroke engines.

498cc Spiegler (sv) 1928

497cc Standard (ioe MAG engine) 1927

STANDARD/*Germany*/*Switzerland 1925– early 1950s*
This was a very successful make. Wilhelm Gutbrod, who founded the factory, had been with the Klotz works until 1925. The first models had 248cc and 348cc ohv JAP engines, but he soon switched to Swiss MAG proprietary engines from 347cc to 998cc with ioe and partly ohv engines. Works racing models in 1929 had 347cc and 497cc Marchant-designed MAG ohc engines. A few 998cc racing V-twins with ohv JAP racing engines were also built. 1930 saw the introduction of 198cc and 248cc ohv singles with their own engines; 1931 the 498cc production racer with the then new ohv MAG racing engine. Brough-licence forks were used from 1929 onwards on many models, including the Rex models of the mid-1930s with Standard's own 348cc engine. Standard built Josef Ganz-designed small cars and mainly 198cc and 248cc two-strokes during the late 1930s. In the 1920s

497cc Standard (ohv MAG engine) 1931

198cc Standard (ohv JAP-Licence engine) 1932

846cc Standard (sv V-twin MAG engine) 1935

Wilhelm Gutbrod had bought the Swiss Zehnder factory and continued manufacture of these good lightweight machines; he also owned another Swiss factory where he built bigger machines, among them a beautiful 846cc V-twin with the MAG sv engine. There were Swiss versions of the popular 497cc MAG-engined ohv singles. There were attempts after 1945 to re-enter motorcycle production with modern two-strokes up to 248cc and there were also prototypes of various ohv models; unfortunately, few Standard machines were built in the early post-war period. Wilhelm Gutbrod died soon after the war and his sons concentrated on the production of Gutbrod cars and on agricultural machinery. Now they produce lawn mowers among other things. Connected with Standard motorcycles were such famous racing men as A. F. Dom (who was also an excellent designer), Karl Gall, Paul Rüttchen, Hermann Lang, Franz Ecker, Konrad Dürr. With first class design, quality workmanship and excellent finish, Standard motorcycles were among the best built between the wars.

STANGER / *England 1921–1923*
Interesting design, as the 538cc Stanger had a 70mm bore × 70mm stroke V-twin two-stroke engine and was probably the very first half-litre motorcycle with such an engine conception. It also had a spring frame and was offered for £95 in 1923. The engine with its big outside flywheel had a tendency to overheat, and the plugs to become fouled with oil.

STANLEY / *England c1902*
Made by a well-known bicycle factory, Stanley motorcycles had 2·5 hp power-units and friction drive to the rear wheel. The production was taken over by Singer.

STAR / *England 1898–1914*
Big factory with wide interests. Produced first three-wheelers and then motorcycles with De Dion engines. There was also a co-operation with Griffon of France. The last motorcycles built by Star were JAP-engined 625cc singles and 770cc V-twins. Star was also a well-known manufacturer of cars.

STAR / *Germany 1895–c1900*
According to unconfirmed information, Star built motorcycles under Werner licence with the 1·5 hp engines above the front wheel. This may have been around 1898 or possibly 1895, but this is doubtful.

STAR / *Germany 1920–1922*
Flat-twins designed by H. F. Günther which

eventually became the first D-Rad motorcycles. The 393cc engines with opposing cylinders were of the company's own design and manufacture. The first D-Rad versions were identical to the Star machines.

STAR / *England 1919–1921*
This was a small assembly plant for motorcycles with 269cc Villiers engines.

STAR-GEM / *Belgium 1930–1933*
Built small machines of 98cc and 123cc with their own and also Sachs two-stroke engines.

STEFFEY / *America c1902–1910*
Supplied 1·25 and 3 hp single-cylinder machines with aircooled and watercooled engines of their own manufacturer.

STEIDINGER / *Germany 1925–1927*
Lightweight machines with triangular frames. The two-stroke engines had 199cc.

STELLA / *Belgium 1921–1936*
The Stella range included frames made from tubes as well as from pressed steel. Engines were 98cc two-strokes and 346cc and 490cc sv and ohv singles made in France by Staub under JAP licence.

STELLAR / *England 1912–1914*
Interesting design of a vertical-twin two-stroke machine with its own watercooled 784cc engine and shaft drive to the rear wheel.

STERLING / *France 1952–1954*
Scooter with a fully enclosed 123cc Ydral two-stroke engine.

614cc Sterna (sv watercooled flat-twin; Designer J. Pässler) 1922

STERNA / *Germany 1922–1924*
This watercooled 614cc sv flat-twin with opposing cylinders was nearly identical to Aristos and Menos motorcycles.

STERVA / *France 1953–1956*
Another French scooter of the early 1950s. Engines used were the 98cc and 123cc Sabb.

STERZI / *Italy 1948–early 1960s*
Well-designed lightweight machines from the 47cc ohv Pony to 174cc ohv models. Among them were 123cc and 158cc two-stroke versions in a variety of models.

STEVENS / *England 1934–1937*
The Stevens brothers, founders of AJS, who lost that factory in 1931 to the Colliers brothers in London, re-entered the motorcycle market with 248cc, 348cc and 498cc single-cylinder ohv models. They also supplied AJW with 498cc proprietary engines. Stevens motorcycles were of typical English design and were supplied for use in trials with upswept exhaust pipes.

496cc Stevens (ohv 'Sport') 1937

STICHERLING / *Germany 1923–1926*
DKW-engined 145cc, 173cc and 206cc two-strokes, built by a small factory.

STIMULA / *France 1902–WWI*
Built motorcycles with Minerva, Buchet, Peugeot and also 346cc and 492cc sv and ohv engines of their own.

STOCK / *Germany 1924–1933*
The first Stock, a 119cc two-stroke, was made under Evans licence. Entirely new Heuss-designed 173cc, 198cc, 246cc and 298cc models appeared in 1929. Of advanced design with own unit-design three-port two-stroke engines, shaft drive to the rear wheel and double-loop frames.

119cc Stock (TS Evans-Licence) 1925

STOEWER / *Germany 1904–1905*
Was a well-known car factory which built three-wheelers first and then for a short period Fafnir-engined 2·75 hp motorcycles.

STOLCO / *Germany 1922–1924*
Lightweight machines with Grade-built 144cc two-stroke motors.

STROLCH / *Germany 1950–1958*
Gassmann-designed scooters with 98cc, 147cc, 173cc and 198cc Sachs engines. After a short period they were renamed Progress.

STRUCO / *Germany 1922–1925*
Built 147cc two-strokes and also 198cc models with their own sv engines.

748cc Stuart (TS watercooled twin, shaft-drive) 1912

STUART / *England 1911–1912*
This factory also built Stellar motorcycles. The Stuart was a single-cylinder 298cc two-stroke.

STUCCHI / *Italy 1901–1927*
Ettore Bugatti, Carlo Leidi and Adalberto Garelli were among famous technicians which were working for this once-famous firm, which built three-wheelers, motorcycles and four-wheeled vehicles. See also Prinetti & Stucchi.

STURM / *Germany 1923–1925*
These were assembled motorcycles equipped with 147cc Alba engines.

STYLSON / *France 1919–WWII*
Assembled motorcycles with JAP and STAUB (JAP licence) engines up to 996cc. Some Staub engines were modified to unit-design with shaft drive to the rear wheel. Other versions had the V-engine transverse-mounted. The company competed officially in races and Pierre Amort won many sidecar events with a 996cc JAP-engined racing machine.

STYRIA / *Austria 1905–1908*
The machines produced by this early Austrian factory had 2 hp single-cylinder and 5 hp V-twin Fafnir proprietary engines.

SUDBRACK / *Germany 1949–1951*
Bicycle factory with 98cc and 123cc motorcycles. The machines were equipped with two-stroke engines of Ilo manufacture.

SUDBROOK / *England 1919–1920*
This short-lived company assembled machines which were equipped with 269cc two-stroke Villiers engines.

SUECIA / *Sweden 1928–1940*
Built 248cc, 348cc and 490cc machines with JAP engines. There were also Suecia two-stroke models up to 248cc, actually made by Sparta of The Netherlands.

SULKY / *France 1954–1957*
Built by Motobloc, the Sulky miniscooter had AMC two-stroke engines of 98cc, 117cc and 124cc.

246cc Stock (TS shaft-drive) 1932

SUMITA / *Japan 1951–1955*
Producer of 123cc and 148cc motorcycles with their own ohv engines.

SUN / *England 1911–1961*
Belonging to the Parkes family and now to the Raleigh group, Sun produced bicycles and accessories before they entered motorcycle production with 346cc singles, which had Villiers ioe engines. After 1918 the range included 269cc and eventually 247cc models with Vitesse rotary-valve two-stroke engines as well as Villiers-engined models from 147cc to 247cc. Others had 346cc Blackburne and 246cc to 746cc sv and ohv JAP engines. There was no motorcycle manufacture during the second half of the 1930s. After 1945 production was resumed; now all models had Villiers two-stroke engines, including a scooter called Sunwasp. Engines used were from 98cc to 225cc.

SUNBEAM / *England 1912–1957*
Machines which were regarded as having the best workmanship and finish of all singles built in England, especially the original Marston versions, built until the late 1920s. Afterwards the factory at Wolverhampton was bought by ICI and sold in 1937 to Associated Motorcycles in London, who sold it again after two years, this time to the Birmingham-based BSA group. The first machines had 346cc and 996cc sv engines made by JAP, but soon afterwards their own engines of 347cc, 497cc and 597cc and eventually 347cc and 497cc ohv models. The Longstroke sports versions of the mid-1920s were famous and the 'big single' models with

492cc Sunbeam (sv Model 'Longstroke') 1924

497cc Sunbeam (ohc works racing Model) 1925

493cc Sunbeam (ohv Model TT 90) 1927

493cc Sunbeam (ohv Model TT 90) 1929

497cc Sunbeam (hc Model Sports) 1939

leaf spring forks were used mainly for sidecar work. Typical for all Sunbeams were the black enamelling with golden lines and fully enclosed rear chains on all touring models. The fast 492cc Longstroke model had 77mm bore and 105mm stroke. The ohv models were introduced in 1924, and in 1925 there were a few 498cc ohc racing models for the works riders only. The 347cc ohv models 8 and 80 and the 493cc versions 9 and 90 were famous and successful racers which had

saddle tanks after 1929. A 493cc speedway model was introduced in the same year. Most models got cradle frames in the 1930s and ohv models a fully enclosed valve year. There were also new 492cc and 598cc sv and ohv models, while a 246cc ohv model was made in the mid-1930s only. After 1945 production concentrated around entirely different vertical-twin ohc machines with 487cc unit-design engines and shaft drive to the comparatively small rear

wheel. These touring machines had 25 bhp at 5800 rpm and were designed by Earling Poppe, formerly co-owner of P&P and son of a famous motoring pioneer. They were the last Sunbeam models ever built; the S8 a more sporting version of the S7, but at 405 lb a heavy machine. Sunbeam's great days were during the 1920s with the J. E. Greenwood-designed singles, which won the 1920 and 1922 Senior TT races (sv models) and the 1928 and 1929 Senior TT events

746cc Super-X (ioe V-twin) 1927

(ohv machines). Leading riders: Graham Walker, Tommy de la Hay, Alec Bennett, Charlie Dodson, Luigi Arcangeli, Mario Colombo, Rupert Karner, George Dance, Laszlo Balasz, Erich Pätzold, D'Eternod etc.

497cc Sunbeam (ohc twin Model 8) 1950

SUPERBA / *Italy 1928–1935*
Sporting machines with 173cc Piazza and JAP sv and ohv engines.

SUPERB-FOUR / *England 1920–1921*
A really superb W. F. Hooper-designed 998cc four-cylinder in-line unit-design machine with an ohc engine and a three-speed gearbox. Only a few were actually built.

SUPERIA / *Germany 1925–1928*
Designed and ridden in races by Adolf Kornmann, Superia motorcycles had 348cc and 498cc Küchen ohc engines. A few models had the 496cc sv single made by ECE. Together with Erich Stolz, Kornmann also broke long-distance records.

SUPERIA / *Belgium early 1950s*
Concentrated on mopeds, mofas and other 49cc two-strokes with a variety of engines, including Sachs, Ilo, Victoria, Pluvier etc.

746cc Super-X (ioe V-twin) 1930

SUPER-X / *America 1924–1930*
Made by the Schwinn company of Chicago, the 746cc and 996cc Super-X machines were really successors to the American-X. All models had V-twin ioe engines and were of excellent design.

SUPPLEXA / *France 1922–1932*
Became well known with a JAP-engined 996cc V-twin machine with an extremely long wheelbase. The range included also 346cc and 490cc machines with various JAP engines.

SUPREMOCO / *England 1921–1923*
This factory assembled Defy-All motorcycles as well as Supremoco. Among the 247cc to 346cc engines fitted were the Villiers, Peco and Blackburne.

SUQUET / *France 1929–1934*
Lightweights with 98cc and 124cc Aubier-Dunne engines.

SUT / *Germany 1921–1927*
Built a variety of models with own sv and also ioe engines of own manufacture. They had 148cc, 172cc, 197cc and 247cc.

247cc Suzuki (TS Model Moto Cross) 1975

SUZUKI / *Japan 1936–*
The Suzuki Motor Co. Ltd at Takatsuka, Hamamatsu, is one of the leading motorcycle factories in the world. Famous for excellent two-strokes, they produce also 738cc double-ohc machines with transverse-mounted four-cylinder engines of 63 bhp at 8800 rpm, and also a 398cc double-ohc vertical with 36 bhp. The range of two-strokes goes from 49cc mokicks to the watercooled 738cc three-cylinder with 63 bhp at 6500 rpm. And there is also the Wankel-engined 497cc machine with 62·8 bhp at 6500 rpm. The Suzuki programme includes 88cc Freetime bikes with four-speed Aphon gearboxes, 123cc and 246cc trials machines, 246cc and 376cc moto-cross versions and road going 124cc twins, 184cc twins, 247cc twins, 371cc three-cylinder and 492cc two-cylinder versions. There are also aircooled 543cc three-cylinder machines and 738cc three-cylinder watercooled power units. Despite the Japanese trend towards four-stroke models, Suzuki is permanently improving and also increasing the two-stroke range, which also changes from country to country. From the early 1960s onwards, Suzuki two-strokes won many big races in Europe and other places. They won TT races with 49cc and 124cc models and were also doing well with 248cc versions, especially in production races. The 49cc machines were watercooled twins. The very flexible factory built for years special racing two-strokes; when in the mid-1970s they once more showed great interest in international road-racing, they built 499cc four-cylinder machines which gained the 1976 World Cham-

497cc Suzuki (rotary engine Model RX 5) 1975

124cc Suzuki (TS twin Model GT 125) 1975

539cc Suzuki (TS three-cylinder Model GT 550) 1977

738cc Suzuki (TS three-cylinder GT 750) 1977

pionship in the 500cc class with Sheene in the saddle. In addition, they created 700cc to 748cc fours with around 140 bhp. The number of riders who won on Suzuki machines is large and besides Sheene includes John Williams, John Newbold, Paul Smart, Stan Woods, Pat Hennen, Marco Lucchinelli and others. Moto-cross is another sport which brought Suzuki great success and of three world championships in 1976, Suzuki won the 125cc with Gaston Rahier and the 500 with Roger De Coster, who rode a 370cc single-cylinder two-stroke works machine with 43 bhp at 7000 rpm. Rahier's 124cc two-stroke had 26 bhp at 10,000 rpm.

SUZY / *France 1932–1933*
Made by a small factory, the Suzy had a fully enclosed 498cc ohc Chaise unit-design engine.

SWAN / *England 1911–1913*
This unorthodox design had a Ner-a-car-like open frame, which was bolted and rivetted of light alloy sheets and reinforced with steel. It had a leaf-spring rear suspension and the bottom part of the 499cc single-cylinder Precision sv engine was covered with plates which formed part of the frame.

SWIFT / *England 1898–1915*
Famous pioneer who built De Dion-engined three-wheelers and motorcycles with shaft drive for Starley. The Coventry-based factory also built cars. The Swift motorcycles had White & Poppe as well as their own 492cc and 768cc V-twin engines. Commercially and technically Swift was closely connected with the Ariel works at Birmingham, then headed by Charles Sangster.

SWM / *Italy 1971–*
The name of the young but very successful factory comes from Speedy Working Motors. Owned by Sironi, SMW concentrates on a wide range of trials and moto-cross machines with 49cc, 94cc, 123cc, 173cc and 248cc two-stroke engines. Among them are models for Juniors and also Sachs-engined seven-speed moto-cross 248cc models with 36 bhp at 7700 rpm. The Vergani-designed machines have gained an excellent reputation in a short time.

123cc SWM (TS Sachs moto-cross engine) 1974

SYMPLEX / *England 1913–1922*
Simple machines with 311cc Dalm two-stroke engines. Designer was J. J. Allen.

SYPHAX / *France early 1950s*
Built nice lightweights with flat 98cc single-cylinder AMC two-stroke engines and bigger two-stroke models with vertical Aubier-Dunne engines. These had 123cc and 174cc. Other versions housed ohv AMC engines with 123cc and 174cc.

T

TANDON / *England 1948–1957*
Built a variety of Villiers-engined models with 123cc, 147cc, 197cc, 224cc, 242cc and 322cc. The last two were vertical twins.

TAPELLA-FUCHS / *Italy c1957*
Concentrated on mopeds and used 49cc Fuchs two-stroke engines exclusively.

TAS / *Germany 1924–1931*
A bicycle factory which was closely connected with the French Gnome & Rhône works. The result was the use of 173cc and 248cc two-stroke and of 346cc and 498cc four-stroke sv and ohv engines made by the G&R works in TAS frames. When they broke that connection the German factory used Swiss MAG 347cc and 497cc ioe and ohv single-cylinder engines.

TAURA / *Italy 1927–1930*
Giulio Doglioli's motorcycles relied on English JAP and Blackburne engines. The range included first 173cc sv versions only, but in the next years models up to 490cc were built. Most of them had the 490cc ohv double-port JAP engine. A three-wheeler for invalids was also built.

TAURUS / *Italy 1933–1966*
The first models were 173cc two-strokes and a 173cc ohv version. Modern 346cc and 496cc ohc singles with unit-design four-speed gearboxes were built in 1934. New pre-war models were also 246cc and 498cc ohv singles, which had rear suspension, but the top design was without doubt the 1938 498cc double-ohc single. Unfortunately Taurus could not afford competing officially in races, but it was a superb design which needed only more development to become a first-class racing machine. The production version had 34 bhp at 6000 rpm and a top speed of 108 mph.

A 248cc single-ohc model built after 1945 had 14 bhp at 7000 rpm. After the war, production included 49cc engines, 158cc two-stroke machines and a beautiful 199cc ohv unit-design machine, while the older 248cc ohc single was superseded by a quite tame 248cc ohv version. New also was a 173cc ohv model.

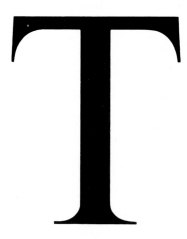

119cc Tautz (TS) 1922

TAUTZ / *Germany 1921–1923*
One of the first German scooters built. It had a 118cc DKW two-stroke engine but failed to gain much popularity.

TAVERNIER / *France 1921–1923*
Assembler, who built a range of machines with Zurcher, JAP and Blackburne engines.

TECNOMOTO / *Italy 1968–*
Concentrates on moto-cross and trials machines with 48cc Franco-Morini and 125cc Zündapp two-stroke engines.

TECO / *Germany 1920–1926*
Built mainly 198cc machines with sv, ioe and ohv engines of Alba manufacture although the crankcase bore the name Teco. The last model, built in small numbers, had a 346cc Kühne ohv engine.

TEDDY / *France 1922–1924*
Lightweight machines with 203cc sv engines.

TEE-BEE / *England 1908–1911*
Assembled machines with their own and also 293cc JAP sv engines.

TEHUELCHE / *Argentina 1958–1962*
75cc ohv machine of Italian design, built with many parts imported from Italy.

TEMPLE / *England 1924–1928*
The Temple was part of the OEC range of models. Claude Temple was a well-known rider and breaker of records as well as a technician. He broke many records on 996cc V-twins, which had Hubert Hagens-designed ohc Anzani engines. This 1923 machine developed 58 hp. Production versions had 496cc four-valve ohv Vulpine and 347cc and 497cc ohc Atlanta engines. From 1927 onwards the OEC also had duplex steering.

TEMPO / *Norway 1949–*
Built a range of lightweights with 49cc and 123cc two-stroke engines. Among the engines used were the Villiers, Ilo, CZ and Sachs.

TERRA / *Germany 1922–1924*
Simple two-strokes of own design and manufacture. They had 127cc, 143cc and 172cc.

TERROT / *France 1901–early 1960s*
This was for many years the factory with the largest motorcycle production in France. Terrot in Dijon was also a well-known make in races during the 1920s. Late in that decade they bought Magnat-Debon, but in the 1950s came under the influence of Automoto, ie the Peugeot group.

346cc Terrot (sv) 1929

348cc Terrot (ohv) 1930

498cc Terrot (ohv) 1952

In the meantime they built motorcycles on English lines, including 98cc, 174cc and 246cc two-strokes and sv and ohv models from 246cc to 746cc. The last ones were V-twins. Used Blackburne, JAP and mainly their own engines, of which in pre-war days the 246cc ohv singles were extremely popular. There was also in the late 1920s a Blackburne-engined 174cc ohv racing model. A 498cc works racing model, built in 1937, had a transverse-mounted ohv V-twin engine. After 1945, Terrot built a range of modern ohv singles up to 498cc and also two-strokes, including scooters of advanced design. Famous Terrot riders in the period between the wars: Rolland, Perrotin, Coulon, Fraichard, Durant, Boetsch, Simo, Riha, J. and H. Tichy, Zukal, Raab and others.

TERROT / *Czechoslovakia 1933–1935*
A branch factory of Terrot-Dijon built a 346cc sv model in Czechoslovakia.

TESTI / *Italy 1951–*
Built first machines with 49cc Sachs, later with Demm engines. Other models of identical size got FB-Minarelli power units, but there were also Sachs-engined versions with 147cc. The present Testi range includes mopeds, mofas and lightweights with 49cc engines. Competition

90cc Testi (TS) 1965

versions are built by the Bologna factory, which also builds miniscooters and similar lightweights.

TETGE / *Germany 1923–1926*
Produced on a limited scale 148cc and 172cc sv singles and also machines with MAG 597cc V-twins.

TGM / *Italy 1974–*
A young factory which concentrates on sporting machines for moto-cross and similar events. Engines used are the 123cc Hiro and the 248cc Villa. There is also a 49cc model.

THIEM / *America 1903–1914*
Built like other American factories of that period 550cc ioe single-cylinder and 890cc as well as 996cc V-twin machines of advanced design. Some had two-speed gearboxes.

THOMANN / *France 1912–1939*
Built two-strokes from 98cc to 248cc and was another factory which belonged to the Alcyon group from the mid-1920s onward.

THOMAS / *England 1904*
Assembler who built a limited number of motor-cycles with various engines including Minerva and Sarolea engines.

THOMAS / *America 1907–1908*
Made in a branch of the Thomas car works, the motorcycles had 3 hp single-cylinder engines with a sloping cylinder and belt drive to the rear wheel. The price: $175.

THOR / *America 1903–1916*
Produced proprietary engines for various factories, including Indian at Springfield. The Aurora Automatic Machinery Co. later built

6 hp Thor (ioe V-twin) 1915

complete V-twin motorcycles with 6 hp and 9 hp ioe engines, which had an excellent reputation among riders.

THOROUGH / *England 1903*
Another small assembler of motorcycles. These had MMC and Coronet engines.

THREE-SPIRES / *England 1931–1932*
Made by Coventry Bicycles Ltd, these little 147cc two-stroke machines were offered for £18.18s.

THUMANN / *Germany 1925–1926*
Although a comparatively small factory, Thumann built their own 246cc and 346cc sv engines.

THUNDER / *Italy 1952–1954*
Very up-to-date but expensive design of a 127cc vertical twin unit-design ohv machine with tele-fork, swinging-arm rear suspension, the dynamo incorporated in the crankcase, four-speed gear-box etc. The price was 285.000 lire, ie approxi-mately 100.000 lire higher than normal 124cc two-strokes.

TICKLE / *England 1967–1973*
Producer of 348cc and 499cc 'Manx' Norton single-cylinder double-ohc racing machines, after the Norton works decided to drop the manufacture of this model. Tickle also produced the necessary spares and parts when the original parts were no longer available.

TIGER / *America 1915–1916*
Attempted to produce a lightweight machine in the USA. The Fredricksen-designed Tiger had a 241cc two-stroke engine.

TIKA / *Germany 1921–1924*
Assembled machines with 145cc and 197cc Herko sv engines.

TILBROOK / *Australia 1950–1953*
Designed by Rex Tilbrook, these Villiers-engined 123cc and 198cc two-strokes were of advanced design, but failed to stay in the trade. A 123cc racing model was successful in Australian road events.

TILSTON / *England 1919*
Short-lived producer, whose machines had 225cc Precision two-stroke engines.

TITAN / *Austria 1927–1933*
The first product of this factory was the 144cc two-stroke, two-cylinder Austro-Motorette; the second design by Karl Schüber was the 346cc two-stroke Titan. This was probably the first commercially built two-stroke engine with the incoming mixture controlled by membranes. The aircooled engine had 75mm bore and 77mm stroke and 10 hp. Another model had first the 490cc sv JAP and later a Blackburne sv engine.

346cc Titan (TS Model Touring) 1928

TITAN / *San Marino 1975–*
Moto-cross machines with 49cc two-stroke engines built in the smallest European republic by a small factory.

TIZ-AM / *Russia 1931–1940*
Heavy 596cc single-cylinder sv machines built at the Taganrog factory.

TM / *Italy 1968–*
Another younger factory, which concentrated on sporting 48cc and 123cc machines with Franco-Morini and Zündapp engines, including the 49cc watercooled Zündapp.

TOHATSU / *Japan 1935–1966*
Was one of the leading Japanese motorcycle factories. Built two-strokes from 48cc to 248cc with rotary valves, including very fast 124cc two-cylinder racing versions.

TOMASELLI / *Italy 1931–1939*
Assembled sporting motorcycles with 173cc to 490cc sv and ohv JAP engines. The production was small.

TOMMASI / *Italy 1926–1927*
Produced 123cc and 246cc two-stroke machines with engines supplied by Della Ferrera. The bigger model had two 123cc power units coupled.

TOMOS / *Yugoslavia 1956–*
Leading motorcycle factory in Yugoslavia, which concentrated for many years on a variety of 49cc machines including mofas, mopeds and other lightweights. There were also racing machines. Bigger machines were added more recently, among them modern 87cc and 174cc single-cylinder versions with 18 bhp at 7000 rpm and sports models with 22 bhp at 8200 rpm. There is now also a branch factory at Epe in The Netherlands.

TOREADOR / *England 1924–1926*
Closely connected with Granville Bradshaw, designer of the oilcooled Bradshaw engines, Bert Houlding's factory produced not only 348cc ohv models, but also the rare 348cc Bradshaw ohc version, of which only very few were actually built. The Toreador range included models with 346cc and 490cc JAP and 496cc MAG ohv engines.

346cc Toreador (ohv oilcooled Bradshaw engine) 1926

TORNAX / *Germany 1926–1955*
Superbly built motorcycles with a variety of proprietary engines. These included JAP sv and ohv engines from 346cc to 996cc, Columbus vertical twin-cylinder 598cc and 798cc ohc engines and also 496cc and 596cc single-cylinder ohv versions made by the same factory. After 1945, Tornax production concentrated on two-stroke machines up to 248cc with mainly Ilo engines. A few 247cc models with the Küchen-designed Opti vertical twin-cylinder ohc engine were built as well. Tornax produced in the mid-1930s a nice sports car with the DKW two-stroke engine and built also many racing machines; the last one was a 124cc ohc single in 1952 which had a Küchen-designed engine. Most JAP-engined ohv racing machines had

746cc and 998cc V-twin engines. They were ridden by Kürten, Gosse, Theisen, Hobelmann, Ehrlenbruch and others.

548cc Tornax (sv JAP engine) 1927

596cc Tornax ohv Columbus engine Model Superior) 1934

244cc Tornax (TS Ilo twin-cylinder engine) 1953

TORPADO / *Italy 1950–*
Lightweight machines with 38cc Mosquito and 48cc and 74cc Minarelli two-stroke engines.

TORPEDO / *Czechoslovakia 1903–1912*
When Czechoslovakia was still part of the Austro-Hungarian Empire, the Torpedo was one of the best machines. Designed by František Trojan, it was built entirely at the Kolin factory. Not only the ioe engines but even carburettors were made there. Single-cylinder Torpedo engines had 3·5 hp and 4 hp, V-twin versions 6 hp and 8 hp.

TORPEDO / *Germany 1901–1907*
Assembled motorcycles with single-cylinder and V-twin Zedel and Fafnir engines.

TORPEDO / *England 1910–1920*
Another Torpedo bicycle factory which built strong frames with 294cc, 346cc and 499cc single-cylinder and V-twin Precision engines.

TORPEDO / *Germany 1928–1956*
Well-known bicycle factory which concentrated on 198cc machines with Blackburne sv engines and later with mainly Sachs and Ilo two-stroke engines.

TORROT / *Spain 1960–*
Once a branch factory of Terrot in Dijon, the Spanish changed the name slightly to Torrot and became independent producers of 49cc mopeds, mofas and lightweight motorcycles.

TOWNEND / *England 1901–1904*
Pioneer who fitted 2 hp and 2·5 hp engines into heavy bicycle frames.

TOYOMOTOR / *Japan 1957–early 1960s*
Built 246cc two-stroke twins, which had much in common with German Adler motorcycles of the same period.

TRAFALGAR / *England 1902–1905*
Pioneer motorcycle producer, who used MMC and Minerva engines and was also involved in the manufacture of wicker sidecars.

TRAFFORD / *England 1919–1922*
Assembled on a small scale motorcycles with 269cc Villiers engines.

TRAGATSCH / *Czechoslovakia 1946–1949*
This racing shop, owned by the author of this book, built track-racing machines with 348cc and 498cc JAP ohv engines. Long-track versions had a rear suspension which could be regulated to give various degrees of movement. Top rider: Hugo Rosak.

TRAIN / *France 1913–1939*
Was for many years a supplier of engines to other factories, many of which found their way to Italy, where the 173cc two-stroke versions became especially popular. Complete Train machines had two-strokes from 98cc to 346cc and sv and ohv engines from 246cc to 995cc.

346cc Train (ohv) 1931

Among them were 746cc and 995cc V-twins. Also a 124cc racing two-stroke was built and most versions were available with watercooling. The twin-carburettor racing engine had 6 hp at 5000 rpm and a top speed of 63 mph. 1930 saw the introduction of a 496cc four-in-line ohc engine which had shaft drive and—like most Train models at that period—a unit design. Another new model was a 1933 173cc sv single.

TREBLOC / *England 1922–1925*
Lightweight machines with their own 63cc engines.

TREMO / *Germany 1925–1928*
Singles with their own 308cc sv and ohv unit-design engines. Production on a limited scale.

TRENT / *England 1902–c1906*
Produced strengthened bicycles with 207cc power units.

TRESPEDI / *Italy 1926–1930*
Built good 173cc and 246cc two-stroke machines with their own engines, which were of the three-port deflector-type.

TRIANON / *Germany 1922–1926*
Bicycle producer who built only one motorcycle model, with their own 232cc two-stroke engines.

TRIBUNE / *America 1903–WWI*
As far as we know these machines had Aster and later Thor engines.

TRIPLE-H / *England 1921–1923*
The name came from the three founders of this make: Hobbis, Hobbis and Horrell. The machine was a simple 246cc two-stroke with a John Morris engine.

TRIPLETTE / *England 1923–1925*
Made at a low price, the Triplette was a simple machine with a 147cc Villiers motor.

TRIPOL / *Czechoslovakia 1925–1926*
Bicycle factory which built 246cc two-stroke Villiers-engined machines in limited numbers.

TRIUMPH / *America 1912*
There was a small branch Triumph factory at Detroit, where they built machines with parts from the 548cc sv single. After WWII, Triumph had HQs at Baltimore and Pasadena.

TRIUMPH (TEC) / *England 1903–*
For many years a leading English make, the Coventry Triumph works was founded by two Germans, Siegfried Bettmann and Maurice Schulte, in 1897. Triumph produced bicycles and in 1902 a 220cc motorcycle with a Minerva engine. Two more proprietary engines—JAP and the 3 hp Fafnir—were used, until Schulte designed their first single-cylinder sv engine of 3·5 hp, which in developed form powered many Triumph models in the following years. There was this basic version with 499cc (85mm × 88mm bore/stroke) and a slightly larger 547cc model (85mm × 97mm bore/stroke). Both became popular, especially after successes in the TT races. Jack Marshall won the 1908 single-cylinder TT class. Another successful model was the two-stroke Baby, with a 225cc engine, a machine which also inspired other designs such as the American Excelsior two-stroke. New

499cc Triumph (ohv four-valve Model Ricardo) 1923

498cc Triumph (ohv Model ST) 1929

148cc Triumph (ohv) 1935

246cc Triumph (ohv Model Tiger 70) 1938

497cc Triumph (ohv twin, Model 'Grand Prix') 1947

497cc Triumph (ohv twin, Model 'Tiger Daytona Sports') 1964

in the early 1920s were a unit-design 346cc sv single, a 249cc two-stroke and the famous 499cc Ricardo-designed Riccy, with a four-valve ohv engine, which was built until 1926 and then superseded by the Horsmann 498cc two-valve ohv model. There was a close co-operation with the German Triumph factory until 1929. Most Nuremberg-built Triumph motorcycles had engines and other parts supplied by the Coventry Triumph works. When they separated German Triumph got the names Orial and TWN, while the English Triumph was known — especially in Germany — as a TEC, which stood for Triumph Engineering Co., Ltd. The range of models varied considerably. There were 174cc two-strokes and 248cc ohv models and there were versions with vertical and also sloping sv and ohv engines. And there was — already in 1913! — a prototype of a 496cc sv vertical twin. The first production model, designed by Val Page, did not appear until 1933. This 649cc vertical ohv twin was priced at £70, when the price for a 493cc ohv single was between £58 and £80. It was built until 1936, when a reorganisation parted the Triumph car production from the motorcycle side and when Jack Sangster, the Ariel boss in Birmingham, bought Triumph and put his leading technician Edward Turner in charge of the Coventry Triumph motorcycle factory. Turner's first creation for Triumph was the fabulous 498cc vertical Speed Twin with an ohv engine, in 1937. It was the forerunner of many famous vertical-twin ohv models, including the Bonnevilles, Tiger 100s, Thunderbirds etc. from 348cc to 649cc. Not until the early 1970s did Triumph develop an entirely new model, the Trident, with the transverse-mounted aircooled 741cc three-cylinder ohv engine. The factory at Coventry, which supplied during WWI thousands of 547cc sv machines to the forces, was doing the same with 346cc sv and ohv versions during WWII when it was completely destroyed in the bombing of that city. In 1944, a new factory outside of Coventry between Allesley and Meriden resumed production. In 1947 the Grand Prix ohv models, as well as other twin-cylinder versions, gained world-wide recognition.

In the 1970s the British motorcycle industry underwent a period of severe concentration, which ultimately placed all mass production in the hands of one group, which comprised BSA, Norton Villiers and Triumph. This group produced two famous suviving marques: Norton in Wolverhampton; and Triumph at the Meriden factory. BSA at Small Heath, Birmingham, produced Triumph Trident engines. In the 'rationalisation' that followed in September 1973, it was decided that the Meriden plant should close, and production of the new Bonneville should stop. Resentment at this decision, belief in the potential of the new machine, and concern about unemployment provoked the workers at Meriden to 'sit-in'. At

**646cc Triumph (ohv twin, Model 'Trophy TR6')
1964**

**740cc Triumph (ohv transverse three, Model
'Trophy') 1974**

198cc Triumph (TS Model Cornet) 1954

a time when several of Britain's traditional industries were under strain, workers in a number of places had used the sit-in technique in order to try and avoid the closure of their factories. Some of these sits-in had been successful and this was the case with Triumph.

After eighteen months of negotiations between the British Government, Norton Villiers Triumph and the workers' representatives, the government made a grant of £¾ million and a repayable loan of £4·2 million to finance the operations of a workers' co-operative. The co-operative continued to produce the Bonneville, but the Triumph trademark and marketing rights were still owned by Norton Villiers Triumph. In May 1977, after a further £¼ million loan by the government, the co-operative bought these rights together with the rights for the Triumph Trident.

The greatest attraction of the machines produced by the new Triumph co-operative is their pedigree. The marque has found new life as the property of the Triumph co-operative though this hopeful development can hardly guarantee its long-term future. Famous Triumph riders:

Ernie Lyons, David Whitworth, H. B. Halford, Walter and Dennis Brandish, Crommie and Rex McCandless, Freddy Edmonds, Tom Simister, Freddy Clarke, Alan and Nick Jefferies and others.

TRIUMPH/*Germany 1903–1957*
(ORIAL–TWN)
Built for a long period nearly identical machines to English Triumph, including a 269cc, afterwards 248cc Baby-type two-stroke, called 'Knirps'. After the break with Triumph in Coventry, the German factory used their own 198cc and 294cc two-strokes and fitted Swiss MAG engines from 347cc to 742cc with ioe and ohv. The big model was a V-twin with ioe. There was also a 493cc model with the MAG ohv racing engine, while some versions of the MAG engines were made at Nuremberg under licence, especially the new 347cc and 497cc sv MAG engines. There was also an 846cc sv V-twin, while German Triumph works riders like Otto Ley and Toni Fleischmann rode 348cc ohc singles with MAG works engines. Chief designer Otto Reitz, who joined Triumph in 1931, designed in the mid-1930s a 198cc two-stroke with shaft drive, a unit-design engine and pressed steel frame. The two-strokes were built with capacities from 98cc to 344 cc. Among them was a 246cc double-piston model with rotary valve. New 49cc two-strokes were introduced in 1953 and there were also 198cc scooters, machines with electric starters and other good designs. After 1945 no four-strokes were built and when the last German Triumph range was made it included only two-strokes of 123cc, 197cc, and 247cc and the vertical twin 344cc model, which then had 16 bhp at 3800 rpm. The factory was sold to the Grundig group.

246cc Triumph (TS) 1926 (German)

TROPFEN/*Germany 1923–1924*
An airship firm which built very unorthodox 248cc and 308cc two-stroke motorcycles. Everything—engine, frame, wheels and all—was enclosed in an airship-shaped shell. The whole thing was so unusual that nobody bought it.

TRUMP (TRUMP-JAP)/*England 1906–1923*
Two leading racing men, F. A. McNab and Colonel Stewart, were among the owners of this ambitious factory, which built a couple of very fast racing machines. Together with Mrs. Stewart —who eventually became the famous Gwenda Hawkes of racing car fame—they broke many records. Trump motorcycles were not only built with 248cc to 996cc JAP engines, but also with 269cc Peco two-strokes and the big 996cc V-twin ohv engine made by British Anzani.

TSUBASA/*Japan 1950s*
Built a range of 246cc machines with their own ohv engines.

TÜRKHEIMER/*Italy 1902–1905*
The designer, a leading Milan-based motorcycle importer who imported the first Hildebrand & Wolfmüller motorcycles into Italy in 1896, fitted 1·25 hp engines into his own machines.

TX/*Germany 1924–1926*
One of the most unorthodox machines ever built, the TX had a tube of wide diameter which acted as a tank and replaced the steering head too. The tank cap was in front of the steering and the front fork, which had a leaf spring, was made from pressed steel. The 132cc and 174cc two-stroke Bekamo-licence engines had forced induction by using a second piston as a pump in the bottom of the crankcase. A few 248cc ohc racing machines with Roconova engines were also built. Designer was Kurt Pohle.

173cc TX (TS Bekamo engine) 1925

TYLER/*England 1913–1923*
Built lightweight motorcycles with 198cc Precision, 269cc Villiers and also with own 269cc two-stroke engines.

TYPHOON/*Sweden 1949–1951*
Designed by the famous Folke Mannerstedt, this machine was a 198cc two-stroke of advanced design.

TYPHOON/*The Netherlands 1955–early 1960s*
Well-known manufacturer of mofas, mopeds etc. with 49cc two-stroke engines.

U

UDE/*Germany 1924–1925*
A small producer of a 249cc two-stroke machine with a deflector-type three-port engine.

ULTIMA/*France 1908–1958*
Built a range of machines with Zurcher, Aubier-Dunne, JAP and other engines. Among them were 248cc and 348cc single-cylinder and 498cc V-twin sv machines. After WWII, the factory concentrated on two-strokes up to 198cc, among which was a very successful 124cc model with a horizontal cylinder. Ultima built new 498cc twin-cylinder double-ohc racing machines with horizontally-mounted cylinders in 1951, but the promising design was never fully developed.

UNIBUS/*England 1920–1922*
The Boultbee-designed Unibus was one of the best scooters made after WWI. It had a 269cc two-stroke engine and 16 inch × 2·5 inch tyres. With the exception of the handlebar, everything was fully enclosed. The pressed steel chassis was made on car lines and leaf suspension was used.

UNION/*Sweden 1943–1952*
Sporting single-cylinder machines with 348cc and 498cc JAP ohv engines.

UNIVERSAL/*Switzerland 1928–1964*
Famous factory which produced Helvetia motorcycles with 170cc PA engines before they built Universal machines. These had a variety of proprietary engines including JAP, Python, Anzani, Ilo and others with capacities up to 998cc. Among them were racing versions with big V-twin JAP ohv engines of 55 bhp and Python-engined 248cc racing machines. V-twins with their own 676cc and 990cc sv engines were made for the Swiss Army. The outstanding model after the war was a 578cc flat-twin with the ohv engine transverse-mounted and with shaft drive to the rear wheel. The engine was of Universal's own design and manufacture. The

same was true of a 248cc ohv single, which came on the market in 1956. Like the bigger twin, it too had a unit-design engine and shaft drive. A licence was sold to the German Rabeneick factory, but this factory never went into quantity production. Famous riders such as Kirsch, Franconi, Alfter, Bianchi, and H. Taveri raced the machines between the wars.

UNIVERSELLE (UNIVERSAL)/*Germany 1925–1929*
Designed by Erich Landgrebe and made by a cigarette machine factory, the little ioe four-stroke machines originally had 183cc unit-design engines with big outside flywheels. Improved versions with 197cc and 247cc followed. Universelle built also delivery three-wheelers.

678cc Universal (ohv transverse flat-twin, shaft-drive) 1955

183cc Universelle (ioe) 1926

244cc Universal (TS twin-Ilo engine) 1952

996cc Universal (ohv V-twin JAP) 1937

URANIA/*Germany 1934–1939*
Assembled 98cc and 123cc two-stroke machines with Sachs and Ilo engines.

UT/*Germany 1922–1959*
Built on English lines, UT motorcycles were assembled machines with Bekamo, Blackburne, JAP, Küchen and Bark engines in pre-war days, while Sachs and Ilo engines played the

most important part after 1945. The first 247cc two-strokes built in the mid-1920s had flat single-cylinder engines and triangular frames; the biggest models had 598cc single-cylinder JAP and Blackburne ohv engines. The two-strokes which were built after the war had 122cc, 173cc, 197cc and 244cc engines. The last one was a vertical twin with an Ilo engine. Some 246cc twins with the Küchen-designed Opti ohc engine were also built. The factory had a successful

racing department in the 1920s with Frenzen, Kohfink, Blind and other good riders.

UTILIA/*France 1929–1936*
Was a well-known producer of two-strokes from 98cc to 498cc and of sv and ohv machines with JAP, LMP and Chaise engines. The two-stroke engines came from the Sachs, Duten and Train factories; some were also built by Utilia.

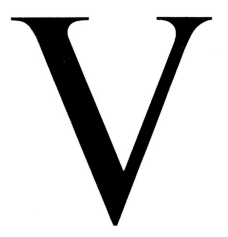

VAGA/*Italy 1925–1935*
Produced 124cc two-strokes, afterwards 174cc machines with JAP and Blackburne sv and ohv as well as CF ohc engines. The last models, 348cc ohv versions, had Sturmey-Archer engines.

VAL/*England 1913–1914*
This was a sidecar producer who also built JAP-engined 488cc single-cylinder sv machines in limited quantities.

VALIANT/*America late 1960s*
Produced Simplex lightweight machines with modified 124cc Clinton lawn-mower engines.

VAP/*France early 1950s to early 1960s*
VAP was a mass-producer of 49cc mopeds, mofas etc. and was closely connected with Alcyon, Rhonson, Lucer and other factories.

VAREL/*Germany 1952–1953*
Mopeds and miniscooters with own 43cc engines and scooters with 99cc Mota two-stroke engines.

VASCO/*England 1921–1923*
Only a single model was made by this small

factory. It had 261cc Orbit engines; when Orbit went out of business, Vasco switched over to 349cc Broler engines. Both were single-cylinder two-strokes.

VASSENA/*Italy 1926–1929*
Designed by Pietro Vassena, these machines had 124cc two-stroke engines with a horizontal cylinder.

VATERLAND/*Germany 1933–1939*
A bicycle factory which built lightweight machines with 98cc and 120cc Sachs engines.

VECCHIETTI/*Italy 1954–1957*
Moped producer who used 49cc two-stroke engines made by Victoria in Germany.

VELAMOS/*Czechoslovakia 1927–1930*
Like the Sirocco, the Velamos was made by Gustav Heinz. While the Sirocco had Villiers engines, the Velamos had its own two-stroke engines with 246cc, 346cc and 496cc. All were singles with three ports and deflector-type pistons. In races they were ridden by Kliwar, Zwesper and Heinz. Velamos still exists as a nationalised bicycle factory.

Velocette advertisement from 1930s brochure

VELOCETTE/*England 1904–1968*
This once world-famous make was the successor to Ormonde, VMC and Veloce. Headed by Percy and Eugene Goodmann, the company first built a 496cc sv single, followed in 1912 by a 276cc single with ioe valves and two speeds. A 344cc two-stroke came into production in 1913,

followed by a 217cc version and one of 247cc which was of modern design, reliable and very fast. The first ohc model, with 348cc and 74mm bore × 81mm stroke, was built in 1925. It was designed by Percy Goodmann, and was the forerunner of all the famous ohc Velocettes, up to the successful KTT Mk VIII racing models. A prototype spring frame built under Draper patents appeared in 1928, and a positive foot change soon afterwards. Headed by Harold Willis, who raced and developed Velocettes, the KTT and other ohc models won in the Isle of Man TT, broke records at Brooklands and gained on the Continent a reputation for reliability and speed. Among the models built in the early 1930s were 249cc two-strokes and different versions of the 348cc ohc model, followed by 248cc, 349cc and 495cc ohv versions, with high-camshaft engines of their own manufacture. The KTT as the racing version of the 348cc ohc machine continued to be built in developed

348cc Velocette (ohc Model 'KTT' racer) 1929

249cc Velocette (TS) 1924

348cc Velocette (ohc Model 'K') 1929

349cc Velocette (hc Model 'MAC') 1935

348cc Velocette (ohc Model 'KTS') 1936

forms until the 1950s. The last version was the Mk VIII in 1939, although there was development work going on after 1945. There were also in the 1930s 498cc single-cylinder ohc and double-ohc works racing machines and, at the time Harold Willis died in 1939, even a 498cc vertical-twin racing model with supercharger, the Roarer, which as a result of his death and the war was never fully developed. New 249cc ohc singles for works riders were built in 1951, almost the last Velocette racing machines. Main production in post-war years concentrated around 149cc and later 192cc LE models with watercooled and transverse-mounted flat-twin sv engines, which also had the gearbox in unit, shaft drive and spring frames. This was a very good and unorthodox design which was also used by police forces. The horizontally opposed twin developed 8 bhp at 5000 rpm and was very quiet. A luxurious version of the LE, the Vogue, never gained as much fame; this was also the case with

the more sporting Valiant, in which the horizontally opposed 192cc ohv engine was aircooled and had 12 bhp at 7000 rpm. All the other models were ohv singles with high-camshaft motors. Among them were the 499cc MSS, the sporting 36 bhp and 38 bhp Venoms and the scramblers and endurance models, which had half-litre engines. In the 350cc class, Velocette built the Viper models and also a scrambler. It was a sad day when this factory had to close down, as it had always been a family business belonging to the Goodmanns and the Denlys. Mrs. Denly was a sister of the Goodmann brothers. Their sons, Bertie and Peter, not only played an important part in the works, but also raced successfully. Phil Irving and Charles Udall should be remembered as technicians. The great Velocette riders included Stanley Woods, Freddy Frith, Alec Bennett, Bob Foster, Walter Rusk, David Whitworth, Les Archer, Fergus Anderson, Tommy Wood and Freddy Hicks.

198cc Velocette (sv transverse watercooled flat-twin) 1948

VELOX/*Czechoslovakia 1923–1926*
Designed by racing motorcyclist Hynek Vohanka, Velox lightweights had 147cc Villiers and afterwards 123cc and 174cc Bekamo two-stroke engines.

VELOSOLEX/*France 1945–*
Leading producer of bicycle engines and 48cc lightweights. Since 1975 united with Motobecane.

VENUS/*England 1920–1922*
Was one of the many machines built during the early 1920s in England. Only a single model with the 318cc Dalm engine was in production.

VENUS/*Germany 1920–1922*
Scooter with 98cc, 147cc and 174cc Sachs engines, made by a small factory.

VERGA/*Italy 1951–1954*
Small two-strokes with 73cc and frames with swinging-arm rear suspension.

VERLOR/*France 1930–1938*
Aubier-Dunne and Stainless-engined 98cc and 124cc two-stroke machines.

VEROS/*Italy 1922–1924*
Blackburne-engined 346cc sv and ohv machines built by Verus in England were renamed Veros when exported to racing motorcyclist Oreste Garanzini, who represented this make in Italy. One of the design differences was the fully enclosed rear chain on the Veros sv models.

346cc Veros (sv Blackburne engine) 1925

VERUS/*England 1919–1925*
Made by Wisemann in Birmingham, Verus motorcycles had their own 211cc and 269cc two-stroke engines and also 246cc to 996cc four-strokes made by Blackburne and JAP. Wisemann built also Sirrah and Weaver motorcycles.

VESPA/*Italy 1946–*
Piaggio, producer of the famous Vespa scooters, still supplies 121cc, 145cc and 198cc versions and also produced earlier models with other power units. The factory, which took over the Gilera works at Arcore in 1970, produces also a variety of 49cc mopeds and similar lightweights.

VESUV/*Germany 1924–1926*
A small make. Had an open frame and its own 246cc two-stroke engine.

VIATKA/*Russia 1958–*
Leading scooter in the USSR. The engine is a 148cc two-stroke.

VIBERTI/*Italy 1955–late 1960s*
Built Victoria-engined 47cc mofas, mopeds and similar machines. Motorcycles made by this factory had 123cc ohv engines.

VICTA/*England 1912–1913*
Built 499cc single-cylinder motorcycles with Precision proprietary engines.

VICTORIA/*Scotland 1902–1926*
The Victoria motorcycle for many years was Scotland's leading make, being built at Glasgow (Dennistoun) and never in England. Typically English was the whole design and most of the components. Villiers, JAP, Blackburne and Coventry-Victor engines from 127cc to 688cc were mounted in Scottish frames, which were of excellent quality. There was never a connection between this factory and the German-built motorcycles of the same name.

VICTORIA/*Germany 1899–1966*
Founded in 1886 by Max Frankenburger and Max Ottenstein as a bicycle factory, Victoria built their first motorcycles 13 years later and fitted Zedel and Fafnir engines into their frames. After WWI, production concentrated on 493cc machines with two horizontally opposed cylinders in the popular sv proprietary engine built by BMW. When the Munich factory decided to produce complete motorcycles, Victoria of Nuremberg engaged the former BMW designer Martin Stolle, who designed new ohv engines which were built for Victoria at the Sedlbauer factory at Munich. After a while Victoria bought the engine factory and continued building ohv 498cc and afterwards 598cc ohv flat-twins. Successor to Stolle after 1924 was Gustav Steinlein, who designed in 1925 the first supercharged racing machines with 498cc flat-twin engines in Germany, which in 1926 broke the German speed record with nearly 104 mph. New single-cylinder models were introduced in 1928. The engines were of Sturmey-Archer manufacture and had from 198cc to 499cc; a 348cc ohv version was built by Horex (Columbus) under Sturmey-Archer licence for Victoria. Racing versions of this and 499cc machines as well as 598cc flat-twins were officially raced by the

346cc Victoria (ohv transverse V-twin, shaft-drive) 1955 (D)

works, where they had excellent riders with Kurt Füglein, Othmar Mühlbacher, Josef Möritz, Adolf Brudes, Hans Escoffier, Albert Richter, Josef Alt, H. P. Müller, Karl Bodmer, Eugen Grohmann, Georg Dotterweich and others. Among models built during the 1930s were two-strokes from 98cc to 198cc and new Stolle-designed 497cc vertical ioe and ohv twins with triangular pressed steel frames and completely enclosed unit-design engines. Richard Küchen and Albert Roder were Victoria designers in the 1930s. After 1945 production concentrated first on two-strokes from 38cc—a bicycle attachment—to 248cc. The first new four-stroke came into production in 1953. Also designed by Küchen, it had a transverse-mounted 348cc ohv V-twin unit-design engine with shaft drive to the rear wheel, telescopic fork and plunger-type rear suspension. New also were scooters, 38cc and 48cc mopeds, and the 198cc Swing, a very modern motorcycle with the engine and rear wheel on a swinging arm. Designed by Norbert Riedel, it was costly to produce. The last new model had a 173cc ohv engine, made by Parilla in Italy. Victoria supplied to the Italians in exchange small 49cc two-stroke moped motors. Soon afterwards the Zweirad-Union was founded and Victoria became part of it. While motorcycle manufacture stopped immediately, production of mopeds etc. under the Victoria trade mark continued for some time.

VICTORY / *Italy 1950–1955*
Produced lightweight machines with 98cc and 123cc Villiers engines.

VILLA / *Italy 1968–*
Like other Italian factories, Villa builds a wide range of 49cc two-strokes but his fame was won with excellent moto-cross and trials machines of 123cc, 246cc, 308cc, 354cc, 376cc and 442cc. The last one has 42 bhp at 7000 rpm. These machines are designed by former racing motorcyclist Francesco Villa, brother of World Champion Walter Villa. Franco-Morini engines are used, but mainly engines of Villa's own design and manufacture.

VILLOF / *Spain 1951–early 1960s*
Produced motorcycles with Hispano Villiers two-strokes and own engines from 75cc to 123cc.

496cc Victoria (ohv flat-twin engine) 1923 (D)

4½ hp Victoria (ioe Fafnir engine) 1904 (D)

493cc Victoria (sv flat-twin BMW engine) 1920 (D)

496cc Victoria (ohv twin-cylinder Model 'KR 9') 1937 (D)

VINCENT (VINCENT-HRD) / *England 1928–1956*
Philip Vincent bought in 1928 the manufacturing rights of HRD, the make founded in 1924 by Howard R. Davies, the well-known racing motorcyclist. He continued using 346cc, 498cc and 598cc sv and ohv JAP engines, but equipped the new models with a rear suspension of his own design. Entirely new 497cc high-camshaft ohv engines of his own design and manufacture came into production in 1935 and machines with this engine were priced from £79.10s. to £98 for the TT Replica racing model. Late in 1936 appeared

the first 998cc Vincent with its V-twin high-camshaft engine, rear-wheel springing and twin brakes in each wheel. The cylinders were set at 47 degrees and were nearly identical to those used on the 497cc Meteor single. After the war, Vincent concentrated on improved versions of this big twin such as the Black Knight, the Black Prince and the very fast Black Lightning, a racing version of the 84mm bore × 90mm stroke 100 bhp engine, which broke many speed records in the hands of George Brown, Roland Free, René Milhoux and others. Free reached 156·71 mph with his special machine, running on alcohol fuel. In 1950 Vincent also brought back

996cc Vincent (hc V-twin Model 'Rapide') 1954

996cc Vincent (hc V-twin Model 'Black Knight') 1955

499cc singles, which were almost the twins without the rear cylinder. A racing version, the Grey Flash, was built but did not win many road races. John Surtees rode them successfully. The 998cc twins won many races, including the Clubmans TT and among the riders were Phil Heath, Dennis Lashmar, Cliff Horn, Jock Daniels, Joe Davis and others. The last works riders competed in 1937 races. Phil Vincent's big twins had gained a world-wide reputation and there were times when demand was much bigger than supply. But they were expensive in production and when motorcycle sales went down in the late 1950s the situation became very difficult. The manufacture of the Firefly bicycle engine and co-operation with NSU of Germany could not put off the end of the Vincent.

VINCO / *England 1903–1905*
Small firm which built motorcycles with 211cc Minerva engines.

VINDEC / *England 1902–1929*
These machines were made by Brown Bros. Ltd., the famous supplier of parts and accessories. The range included 172cc and 224cc two-strokes and 490cc JAP-engined sv machines; the last model built had the 293cc JAP sv engine.

VINDEC-SPECIAL (VS) / *England 1903–1914*
Was really a machine built for the English market by Allright at Cologne in Germany and identical to Allright models in those far-off days. The South British Trading Co. in London was the importer. Most versions had V-twin engines, made by FN, Minerva, Fafnir etc. There were Truffault-designed swinging-arm front forks from 1905 onwards. After 1909 the machines were renamed VS to avoid confusion with the Brown brothers' Vindec motorcycles.

1000cc Vincent 'Black Lightning' 1960

VIPER / *England 1919–1922*
Limited production of machines with 293cc sv JAP engines in open frames.

VIRATELLE / *France 1907–1924*
Built many models with proprietary engines, some of them unusual. The last one was a 686cc V-twin sv machine with a very long wheelbase.

VIS / *Germany 1923–1925*
Very interesting design. There was the comparatively orthodox 249cc two-stroke Vis-Simplex single with a forward inclined engine, but there was also the Vis-Duplex with a 496cc opposed twin-cylinder two-stroke engine, built in line with the duplex cradle frame. This engine suffered from overheating of the rear cylinder and was built in limited numbers only.

VITTORIA / *Italy 1931–*
Carnielli's machines had 98cc Sachs, 173cc and 248cc JAP, 346cc and 496cc Küchen and 499cc four-valve Python ohv engines. Most models

built since the war — including delivery three-wheelers — had two-stroke engines up to 98cc.

VOLLBLUT / *Germany 1925–1927*
Assembler of sporting motorcycles with 248cc and 348cc ohv Blackburne engines.

VOMO / *Germany 1922–1931*
Moped-like machines with 1 hp and 1·75 hp two-stroke engines.

VORAN / *Germany 1921–1924*
Yet another small motorcycle, a typical light-weight with a 143cc two-stroke deflector-type three-port motor.

VOSKHOD / *Russia late 1940s–*
These are the mass-produced Russian 174cc two-strokes. Now with 10·5 bhp at 5500 rpm, they are of quite modern conception, having originally been very similar to DKW and Jawa designs.

VULCAAN / *The Netherlands 1911–1927*
Was closely connected with Zedel, the proprietary engine factory. Built 264cc and 299cc sv singles and also a range of sv V-twins, of which some were Vulcaan's own power units, probably built with some Zedel parts.

VULCAN / *Czechoslovakia 1904–1924*
See also Perun motorcycles, built by Zdarsky. The successor Ružička concentrated on the manufacture of spare parts in the period after WWI.

VULCAN / *England 1922–1924*
Like other English firms, this one concentrated on 248cc two-strokes and on 293cc sv machines with JAP engines.

2¾ hp Vindec-Special (sv FN engine) 1903

W

WACKWITZ/*Germany 1920–1922*
These 108cc engines were supplied as bicycle attachments or complete with strengthened bicycle frames.

WADDINGTON/*England 1902–1906*
Single-cylinder motorcycles with a variety of engines which included Minerva, MMC and other products.

WAG/*England 1924–1925*
One of the very few makes which produced 496cc V-twin machines with two-stroke engines. The actual production was limited.

WAGNER/*Czechoslovakia 1930–1935*
Offered motorcycles from 98cc to 499cc with two-stroke as well as sv, ohv and even ohc engines. The only evidence for the existence of these machines is documentary.

WAGNER/*America 1901–1914*
One of the pioneers of the American motorcycle industry. This firm built 1·5, 2 and 2·5 hp machines equipped with their own as well as with Thor engines.

WAKEFIELD/*England c1902*
One of the first factories fitting Minerva and MMC engines above the pedalling gear of bicycles.

WALBA/*Germany 1949–1952*
Ilo-engined scooters from 98cc to 173cc, designed by W. Baibaschewski.

WALLIS/*England 1925–1926*
Technically interesting 348cc and 498cc machines with hub-steering, not dissimilar to the Ner-a-car. The engines used were mainly JAP ohv engines. Wallis, a superb technician, was also the designer of Comerford-Wallis speedway frames.

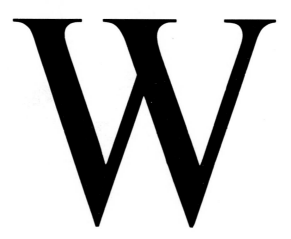

346cc Wallis (ohv Blackburne engine) 1926

WALMET/*Germany 1924–1926*
Limited production of 246cc two-strokes with own engines and 346cc models with Kühne ohv power units.

WALTER/*Germany 1903–1942*
Assembler whose first machines had Fafnir engines. From the 1920s to the mid-1930s Villiers two-strokes from 172cc to 347cc were fitted into excellent frames of modern design. After 1935 production concentrated on mopeds with 98cc Sachs and Ilo engines.

172cc Walter (TS Villiers Model 'Sport') 1923 (D)

WALTER/*Czechoslovakia 1923–1926*
The factory, still headed by Josef Walter, designed in 1917 a 746cc flat-twin machine. It never went into production when Josef Zubatý, the designer, left. The Itar factory took over manufacture after the war in 1922, when Walter director Plocek had a new 746cc on the drawing board. This was a transverse-mounted ohv V-twin machine and was built—like the Itar—mainly for the Czech army. The factory, now also building cars and aircraft engines, also produced a few enlarged 998cc racing machines, which proved very fast. Demand for cars and aircraft engines increased, and that was the end of the motorcycle manufacture at the Jinonice Walter factory. Successful Walter riders: Vašek Liška, Bohumil Turek, Stanislav Chaloupka, Jaroslav Knapp.

746cc Walter (ohv transverse V-twin) 1923 (CS)

WALTER/*Czechoslovakia 1900–1949*
Josef Walter built first-class single-cylinder and V-twin motorcycles with his own engines, afterwards also three-wheelers with modified motorcycle power units. In 1922 he left the Walter works and founded a new Walter factory for the manufacture of gears, sprockets etc. There he designed—in conjunction with his sons Jaroslav and Jan—new 496cc sv singles in 1926. In 1938 Jaroslav Walter created superb 248cc ohv racing engines and soon afterwards an even better ohc version, which after the war gained many racing successes on road and track. In 1947 a new 348cc ohc racing single was added which —together with the 248cc ohc engine—was taken over in 1949 by the big CZ factory, when Jaroslav Walter joined the Strakonice works. Successful Walter riders: Václav Hovorka, Jan

Lucak, Vojta Diviš, Jan Horak, Václav Stanislav, Eman Hajek, Jarda Kost, Peter Kopal, Lada Steiner and others.

4½ hp Walter (sv V-twin Model 'B') 1906 (CS)

WANDERER / *Germany 1902–1929*
Was a well-known manufacturer of high-class motorcycles. Built 327cc and 387cc singles and 408cc and 616cc V-twins with own sv engines. Many of them were used by the Germans during WWI. After the war, Wanderer built a nice 184cc ohv single with a horizontal cylinder and a range of 708cc and 749cc ohv V-twins with unit-design engines, some with 8 valves. A new 498cc ohv single with unit-design engine, shaft drive and pressed steel frame, designed by Alexander Novikoff, was built in 1927. In 1929 this design, complete with all drawings and production equipment, was sold to Jawa at Prague, then a new company. That was practically the end of Wanderer motorcycle production, although they signed an agreement with NSU and produced during the 1930s motorised bicycles. Wanderer was a successful make in races during the 1920s. The top riders were Schuster, Urban, Kohlrausch, Ebert.

4½ hp Wanderer (sv V-twin) 1923

WARD / *England 1915–1916*
Two-strokes with 298cc engines. The war prevented production on a bigger scale.

WARDILL / *England 1924–1926*
Unorthodox two-stroke machines with a patented 346cc engine, which was not fully developed when it was put on the market.

WARRIOR / *England 1921–1923*
Concentrated on one model with the 247cc Villiers engine.

WASSELL / *England 1970–1975*
Built excellent 123cc trials and moto-cross machines with German Sachs two-stroke engines; the untimely death of W. E. Wassell led to the demise of motorcycle production by this well-known accessories factory.

WATNEY / *England 1922–1923*
Assembler who fitted 269cc Villiers, 293cc sv JAP and 346cc sv Blackburne engines.

WAVERLEY / *England 1921–1923*
Another assembler whose Harry Cox-designed motorcycles had 269cc Peco two-strokes and 346cc and 496cc Blackburne sv engines.

WD / *England 1911–1913*
Modern 496cc single-cylinder machines with own ioe power units.

WEARWELL / *England 1901–c1906*
One of the first factories producing motorcycles in England. The company also built Wolfruna and Wolf machines as well as frames for other factories and assemblers. The first engines used for Wearwell machines had 2·5 and 3·25 hp and were a product of the Stevens brothers who afterwards founded the AJS factory.

WEATHERELL / *England 1922–1923*
Concentrated on sporting Blackburne-engined 349cc ohv machines, but also supplied 248cc versions and a machine with an ohv 676cc V-twin Blackburne engine.

WEAVER / *England 1922–1925*
The original model had a 142cc ohv single-cylinder engine, other versions used 147cc Villiers and AZA two-stroke engines.

WEBER-MAG / *Germany 1926–1927*
Assembled motorcycles with MAG engines of 346cc, 498cc and 746cc. All had ioe engines. The production was small.

WEBER & REICHMANN / *Czechoslovakia 1923–1926*
Produced 142cc and 172cc machines with pressed steel frames under DKW licence. The engines were supplied directly by DKW.

WECOOB / *Germany 1925–1930*
Built a variety of motorcycles. With 142cc Rinne two-stroke engines, 172cc to 347cc Villiers motors and also 348cc to 996cc JAP power units. Despite the large number of models, actual production was small.

WEE McGREGOR / *England 1922–1925*
Made at Coventry Bicycles Ltd. by former Hobart employees, this was a 170cc two-stroke machine, with the engine capacity later increased to 202cc.

WEGRO / *Germany 1922–1923*
Very unorthodox — and not very good — Passow-designed 452cc vertical two-stroke twin with a very long wheelbase and disc wheels.

WELA / *Germany 1925–1927*
Assembled 348cc single with the Gnädig-designed Kühne ohv engine.

WELLER / *England 1902–1905*
Pioneer factory, which also produced cars. The motorcycles had their own 1·75 and 2·25 hp single-cylinder power units.

WELS / *Germany 1925–1926*
These machines had a BMW-like frame with 348cc Kühne ohv and 490cc JAP ohv engines fitted.

346cc Wels (ohv Kühne engine) 1925

WELT-RAD / *Germany 1901–1907*
A bicycle factory and motorcycle pioneer which fitted its own 3·5 hp single-cylinder and 6 hp V-twin engines into strong frames.

WERNER / *France 1897–1908*
The Werner brothers, Russians living in Paris, were probably the greatest pioneers in motorcycling. The first machines had the Labitte-designed engine still above the front wheel, but in 1901 the Werners put it just in front of the pedalling gear behind the front down-tube. The 2 hp 230cc Werner was a good seller; other models had 2·75 and 3·25 hp. Already in 1904 they built vertical twins. Lawson, the English pioneer,

217cc Werner (sv) 1901

founded in 1899 a Werner branch factory at Coventry and many other factories bought Werner patents for engines and Werner-type machines.

WERNER-MAG / *Austria 1928–1930*
Designed by Konstantin Leschan, Werner-MAG motorcycles used 498cc double-port single-cylinder ohv engines from the Swiss engine factory. Other models of 746cc and 996cc capacity had MAG ioe V-twin power units.

WERNO / *Germany 1921–1924*
The Werner Noel-designed ohv singles had their own 154cc and 197cc engines.

WESPE / *Austria 1937–1938*
Designed by Thos. G. Harbourn, who for many years imported English Triumph motorcycles into Austria, the 123cc Wespe had an unlucky life. Just when it entered quantity production, Hitler entered Austria, Nazi industrial dictatorship meant the end of a nice lightweight.

WESTFALIA / *Germany 1901–1906*
Zedel, De Dion and Fafnir supplied most of the 1·75 and 2·5 hp engines fitted to these early motorcycles.

WESTFIELD / *England c1903*
Assembler who fitted 2·75 hp MMC power-units.

WESTOVIAN / *England 1914–1916*
Had a big model range with TDC, Villiers, Precision and JAP engines from 197cc to 498cc.

WFM / *Poland 1947–*
Well-known make which concentrated on the production of well-designed 123cc, 147cc and 173cc two-strokes.

W&G / *England 1927–1928*
A transverse-mounted 490cc two-stroke twin with the cylinders facing slightly forward, not unlike the big DKW twin of that period. But while the DKW was a success, the W&G soon disappeared.

WHEATCROFT / *England 1924*
Was the successor to the New Era and had 318cc Dalm two-stroke and 546cc Blackburne sv engines.

WHIPPET / *England 1903–c1906*
This factory had many patents for engines and motorcycles and produced 1·75, 2·25, 2·5 and 3 hp machines. Early models used Aster and FN engines.

WHIPPET / *England 1920–1921*
Scooter of advanced design with 180cc ohv engines and 16-inch wheels.

WHIPPET / *England 1957–1959*
Unusual lightweight, which really was a combination scooter and moped. It had ohv engines of 49cc, 61cc and 64cc.

WHIRLWIND / *England 1901–1903*
Made by the Dorman Engineering Co., the factory which in 1925–1927 built Granville Bradshaw's 348cc oilboilers, ie oilcooled ohv proprietary engines. Among earlier products was a 1·5 hp bicycle engine and complete motorcycles with 2 and 2·5 hp.

WHITE & POPPE / *England 1902–1922*
Built V-twin motorcycles and in 1906 a 489cc

996cc Werner-MAG (ioe V-twin MAG) 1928

vertical twin, which was available with water-cooling too. The factory produced also proprietary engines for motorcycles and cars, which included at that time the 493cc Ariel engines and after 1918 a 347cc two-stroke.

WHITLEY / *England 1902–c1906*
Another manufacturer of proprietary engines, whose own motorcycles had 2·75 and 3·5 hp single-cylinder engines.

2¾ hp Whitley (ioe) 1903

WHITWOOD / *England 1934–1936*
Offered with 248cc, 348cc and 490cc ohv JAP engines, the OEC-built Whitwood-Monocar was a motorcycle with a car-like body; not unlike the Mauser Einspurauto of ten years earlier. It was an unusual vehicle which did not find many customers.

WHIZZER / *America 1947–1954*
Moped-like means of transport, of quite unusual appearance. The engine was a 199cc sv unit.

WIGA / *Germany 1928–1932*
Made by a small factory, the Wiga was of good design and while production stopped in the early 1930s, there was a prototype of a new JAP-engined model with rear suspension made in 1938. The range included Küchen and JAP-engined models of 198cc, 93cc, 348cc and 498cc. The ohc Küchen engines had three valves.

WIGAN-BARLOW / *England 1921*
Small production of motorcycles with 293cc sv JAP and 346cc Barr & Stroud sleeve-valve engines.

WIKRO / *Germany 1924–1926*
The first machines had 346cc Precision engines while newer versions were powered by 347cc and 497cc Blackburne sv engines.

WILBEE / *England 1902–c1906*
Advanced design with 2 hp Minerva engines and good frames made from BSA parts.

WILHELMINA / *The Netherlands 1903–1915*
A motorcycle importer, who built a range of machines in earlier years, but had the biggest output just before WWI with a 2·5 hp single-cylinder Precision-engined model.

WILIER / *Italy 1962–c1970*
Concentrated on 49cc mopeds and lightweight machines.

WILKIN / *England 1919–1923*
Was using 499cc sv Blackburne engines in spring frames, but had a small output only. A 346cc model with an identical frame was also built.

WILKINSON-ANTOINE / *England 1903–1906*
Built in England 2·25 and 2·75 hp machines with Belgian Antoine single-cylinder power-units.

WILKINSON-TAC (WILKINSON-TMC) / *England 1909–1916*
Made by the famous sword (now razor-blade) company, the Wilkinson was a very unusual machine with a 676cc, afterwards 844cc four-cylinder engine with aircooling. It had a long wheelbase, front and rear suspension, a bucket seat, and even a steering wheel until it was superseded by a handlebar. That was when the TAC (Touring Auto Cycle) became a TMC (Touring Motor Cycle).

844cc Wilkinson-TMC (ioe aircooled four-cylinder) 1911

WILLIAMS / *America 1912–1920*
Unusual design with a rotating single-cylinder engine built into the rear wheel.

WILLIAMSON / *England 1912–1920*
Excellent air and watercooled 996cc flat twins with opposing cylinders. The engines were made by Douglas exclusively for Williamson. Machines built after 1919 had 770cc V-twin sv JAP engines.

WILLOW / *England 1920*
Another early scooter which was not a success. The engine used was the 269cc Villiers two-stroke.

WIMMER / *Germany 1921–1939*
A still existing factory. Built during the years 134cc bicycle engines, then 137cc and 172cc single-cylinder ohv unit-design motorcycles with watercooling. The last ones proved very successful in races with such riders as Kolm, Kolmsperger, Gmelch and others. From 1928 onwards aircooled 198cc and 247cc models, afterwards also 299cc and 497cc versions were made. During the 1930s there was also a 346cc ohv trials version and a 198cc two-stroke, both with Bark engines. No Wimmer motorcycles were made after the war.

173cc Wimmer (ohv watercooled) 1925

247cc Wimmer (ohv) 1931

346cc Wimmer (ohv Model GS) 1936

WIN / *England 1908–1914*
Built a two-model range with 499cc and 599cc Precision single-cylinder sv engines.

WINCO / *England 1920–1922*
Assembled motorcycles with 261cc Orbit two-stroke engines.

WINDHOFF / *Germany 1924–1933*
Built radiators before entering motorcycle production with superb watercooled 122cc and 173cc two-strokes. These had Bekamo-type horizontal-cylinder engines with a second

297

scavenging) piston at the bottom of the crankcase. They were very successful in races. A sensational Windhoff appeared on the market in 1927: an oilcooled 746cc four-cylinder unit-design ohc engine as the centre of the whole machine. There was no real frame; everything was bolted onto the power unit. Shaft drive was another feature. A 996cc model built on similar lines was in prototype stage, but never built in quantities. Instead, a BMW-like 996cc Windhoff was built. It had a twin-cylinder sv engine transverse-mounted, shaft-drive and was, like the smaller Four, without a real frame. The last Windhoffs were the most conventional, using 198cc and 298cc Villiers-licence two-stroke engines. The Berlin-based factory also supplied these power units to other motorcycle manufacturers. Successful Windhoff riders: Erich Tennigkeit, Walter Ebstein, Karl Wittig, Richard Scholz.

173cc Windhoff (TS watercooled Bekamo-Licence engine) 1926

746cc Windhoff (ohc oilcooled four-cylinder engine) 1928

996cc Windhoff (sv transverse flat-twin, shaft-drive) 1929

WITTALL / *England 1919–1923*
Assembled machines with 269cc Villiers engines.

WITTEKIND / *Germany 1952–1954*
Moped producer who fitted 40cc Komet engines.

WITTLER / *Germany 1924–1953*
Produced during the 1920s a 249cc two-stroke machine with its own engine. After 1949 production of 49cc mopeds with Sachs and Zündapp engines was resumed and there was also a 124cc lightweight with the Sachs engine.

248cc Wittler (TS) 1925

WIZARD / *Wales 1920–1922*
Build in Wales, this machine had the Wall-designed 269cc Liberty two-stroke power-unit.

WK / *Germany 1920–1922*
This was a 249cc sv engine built into a wheel which could be attached to any bicycle.

WKB / *Austria 1923–1924*
Another bicycle engine. Designed by Hermann Medinger, it had 183cc and was a two-stroke three-port engine.

WMB / *Germany 1924–1926*
Lightweight machines with own 1·8 hp sv engines. Small production.

WOLF / *England 1901–1939*
Besides Wolf motorcycles also built the Wearwell and Wolfruna at the Wolverhampton works. In the early years Moto-Rêve engines were used; all Wolf machines had proprietary power units, among them Blackburne and JAP engines up to 678cc. From 1928, Villiers two-strokes up to 248cc were used including deflectorless flat-top versions of 123cc and 248cc.

247cc Wolf (TS Villiers engine) 1936

WOTAN / *Germany 1923–1925*
Like many others of that period, the Wotan was a simple 170cc two-stroke with a three-port engine.

WOOLER / *England 1911–1955*
John Wooler was a designer with many brilliant ideas and all his creations were very unconventional. His first 344cc two-stroke had a flat single cylinder and a double-ended piston, using the bottom part for pre-compression inside the crankcase. The machine had both wheels sprung by plunger suspension and was of advanced design throughout. Similar frames were used for 346cc and 496cc twins with horizontally opposed cylinders or over-head-valves on the *side* of the cylinder heads. A 611cc single, the only vertical engine known to be made by John Wooler, was built in 1926 as a prototype, but never in quantities. After WWII he built a variety of 498cc four-cylinder machines with opposing cylinders transverse-mounted, shaft drive, spring frames etc. These beautiful ohv machines were actually built in very small numbers for sale; the last one was priced at £292.4s1d.

346cc Wooler (sv flat-twin) 1921

499cc Wooler (semi-ohv flat-twin) 1924

WSE / *Germany 1924–1925*
Small producer of 249cc sv machines, who also supplied the engines to other assemblers.

WSK / *Poland 1946–*
Leading Polish motorcycle factory. Produces modern 123cc and 173cc two-strokes of sporting appearance. A 240cc version was also built in the Swidnik works.

WSM / *Germany 1919–1923*
Built 496cc Stolle-designed flat twins with

opposing cylinders and with ohv for Victoria until that company bought the whole WSM (Sedlbauer) factory at Munich. Earlier machines had 493cc BMW-made flat twin sv engines, but the manufacture of complete Sedlbauer motor-cycles was never on a large scale.

WUCO / *Germany 1925*
Lightweights with own 174cc sv engines. JAP-engined 248cc, 348cc and 490cc models were also made.

WURRING / *Germany 1921–*
Known for their excellent frames, Wurring motorcycles had a variety of proprietary engines. Among them were DKW, Villiers, Küchen, Kühne, Columbus, Bark, Sachs, Ilo and other makes with capacities from 142cc to 596cc. The last ones were 244cc Ilo vertical two-stroke twins. *See also* AWD.

WÜRTTEMBERGIA / *Germany 1925–1933*
Made by a big agricultural machine factory, these machines always had 198cc to 596cc sv and ohv engines made by Blackburne. Good design and workmanship.

W&W / *Austria 1925–1927*
The Josef Wild-designed machines had 498cc single-cylinder MAG ioe engines while 746cc and 996cc V-twins — also MAGs — could be supplied on order.

XY

XL / *England 1921–1923*
Strong machines with double loop frames and 490cc JAP and 538cc Blackburne single-cylinder sv engines.

XL-ALL / *England 1902–c1906*
Built 2 and 4 hp V-twins with their own engines which — according to the producer could run on one cylinder if for any reason the second one fell out. Early models were lightweights and had the cylinders set at 90 degrees. The frames were of the loop bicycle type and had a long wheelbase.

X-TRA / *England 1920–1922*
This was really a three-wheeler with a 346cc single-cylinder Villiers engine. It had two front wheels and a body which was not unsimilar to a sidecar of the early 1920s.

YALE / *America 1902–1915*
Was a well-known machine in the USA; especially the big 950cc V-twin with two-speed gear-box and chain drive to the rear wheel. The price in 1915: $260.

YAMAGUCHI / *Japan 1941–1964*
Once a leading factory, Yamaguchi concentrated on a variety of 49cc models including mofas, mopeds etc. and also built 123cc two-strokes with vertical twin-cylinder engines. The range in-cluded trials machines. When the factory closed, Hodaka took over the works.

247cc Yamaha (TS Model DT) 1974

YAMAHA / *Japan 1954–*
Motorcycles from 48cc to 748cc, two and four-strokes, touring and sports as well as racing machines are built by one of the largest factories in the world. Taking the many variations of each model into account, Yamaha has probably the widest range of motorcycles. They are also com-paratively good value for money. World-wide sales are supported by up-to-date designs and by success in races over the last twenty years. Great riders, including Phil Read, Giacomo Agostini, Rod Gould, Charles Mortimer, Tony Rutter, Dieter Braun, Takazumi Katayama, Johnny Cecotto, Victor Palomo and many others have proved many times the worth of Yamaha two-strokes. Yamaha is also one of the few factories which sells first-class racing machines, which dominate especially races in the 250cc and 350cc class, where the new TZ models with 46bhp at 10,000 rpm and 56 bhp at 9500 rpm are in front for privateers. Yamaha supplies in addition to these watercooled twins also the big TZ750, a watercooled 747cc racer with four cylinders, 90 bhp at 10,000 rpm and a top speed of over 165 mph. On the other end of the scale we have 49cc lightweights, 49cc and 72cc City Bikes, 97cc singles, 195cc and 247cc as well as 398cc two-stroke twins, and there are enduro, trials and

moto-cross versions in nearly all sizes too. Yamaha now has many four-stroke models. Among them are 356cc twins, 498cc double-ohc eight-valve twins, 653cc single-ohc twins and a 748cc double-ohc three-cylinder model. For enduro there is a single-cylinder, single ohc 499cc slope in the Yamaha range. Despite the success achieved by the two-strokes, a trend towards four-strokes is evident. The latest one is the XS1000, due to be introduced in 1977, first in the USA and then in Europe. The engine is a 998cc double-ohc in-line four-cylinder model which is transverse-mounted. Like the XS750, the machine will have shaftdrive and a five-speed gearbox.

743cc Yamaha (ohc two-cylinder) 1974

498cc Yamaha (dohc four-valve twin Model XS 500) 1977

124cc Yamaha (TS twin Model RD) 1974

247cc Yamaha (TS twin RD 250 DX) 1977

YANKEE/*America 1922–1923*
Built cheap 269cc two-strokes, but disappeared quickly from the motorcycle industry.

YANKEE/*America 1970–1974*
This machine was made in co-operation with the Ossa factory by the American Ossa Importer. It was a 488cc vertical twin two-stroke, based on 244cc Ossa engines. It had 40 bhp at 6500 rpm.

YORK / *Austria (Germany) 1927–1930*
These machines were actually made by Omega in England according to a design by Robert Sturm, who left Vienna in 1929 and continued production in Germany. All models had sv JAP engines of 346cc, 490cc and 746cc, but the 490cc version was also built with ohv. The 746cc was a V-twin. Before 1927 Sturm imported Omega motorcycles into Austria.

YOUNG / *England 1919–1923*
Made by the producers of Mohawk motorcycles, the Young was a 269cc bicycle engine, which could be mounted above the rear wheel. A new 130cc two-stroke version was introduced in 1923, but production of it went to the Waltham Engineering Co. Ltd.

YVEL / *France 1921–1924*
Lightweight machines of 174cc and 233cc with their own sv engines.

490cc York (sv JAP engine) 1929

Z

ZANELLA/ *Argentina 1958–late 1960s*
Built on Italian lines, the Zanella was a sporting two-stroke design, which used partly Italian components. The machines were of 49cc, 98cc and 123cc.

123cc Zanella (TS) 1963

ZEDEL/ *France 1902–1915*
While the Swiss parent company Zürcher & Lüthi concentrated on the manufacture of proprietary engines, the French branch supplied complete machines with 2, 2·25, 2·5, 2·75, and 3·5 hp single-cylinder and V-twin engines.

ZEGEMO/ *Germany 1924–1925*
When some partners of the Zetge factory left, they founded the Zegemo works. Designed by Hans Knipp, the Zegemo was a 248cc two-stroke with the rare Baumi engine.

ZEHNDER/ *Switzerland 1923–1939*
The 110 Zehnder called Zehnderli, was a very popular lightweight. It had a two-stroke engine with a horizontal cylinder, not unlike the German Cockerell. Zehnder's racing versions had 123cc engines with watercooling. There were 148cc models and from 1929 onwards a 248cc two-stroke single with a vertical cylinder, which was also built as a sports model. In the early 1930s the factory was bought by Wilhelm Gutbrod,

owner of the German Standard motorcycle works, who continued the production of Zehnder machines in Switzerland. Otto Zehnder won many races in the 125cc and 250cc class. The quarter-litre racing models also had watercooled engines. Other leading riders were Graf, Wiedmer, and Liechti. After 1945 there were to be new Zehnder motorcycles; a design was ready for production when the designer, Robert Zehnder, died suddenly. Price for the complete 110cc 2·2 hp Zehnder in 1929: Fr. 885, in 1937: Fr. 700.

110cc Zehnder (TS flat-single) 1926

ZEHNER/ *Germany 1924–1926*
The Zehner was a 197cc sv machine, designed by Otto Dehne. Made by a small manufacturer, comparatively few machines reached the market.

ZENIT/ *Italy 1954–1956*
Assembled machines with French 123cc and 174cc AMC ohv engines.

ZENITH/ *England 1904–1950*
The first products were 'Bi-cars' with Fafnir engines. The first Zenith motorcycles built had Fafnir engines. Other engines fitted were the Green, the watercooled Green-Precision, Bradshaw, JAP and the Villiers. Equipped with Gradua gearboxes, Zenith machines gained many successes in pre-1914 days, and also during the 1920s, when George Himing won races on JAP-engined 248cc and 348cc singles. When Freddy Barnes designed 980cc and 996cc V-twin racing machines with ohv JAP engines, they

348cc Zenith (ohv JAP engine) 1929

496cc Zenith (ohv oilcooled Bradshaw flat-twin) 1922

broke many records. Riders on these machines were Joe Wright, Ivan Riddoch, Bert Le Vack, Jack Knight, Pat Brewster, Jack Emerson, Count Ashby and Tom Allchin. Actually Emerson's Zenith had a 994cc V-twin Blackburne engine. Production versions commenced with Villiers-engined 172cc two-strokes. In the early 1920s the oilcooled 498cc horizontal twins with opposed cylinders and Bradshaw engines were famous, afterwards the 678cc V-twins with sv JAP engines. The Gradua gear, a variable pulley, was used until 1923 on a JAP-engined 654cc version. JAP engines powered all Zenith machines in the mid-1930s, when the range commenced with a 248cc ohv single and finished with an 1100cc sv V-twin. The small model was then priced at £43, the biggest at £88.10s. Production after 1945 concentrated on a 748cc V-twin with the sv JAP engine.

676cc Zenith (sv V-twin JAP engine) 1929

ZEPHYR / *England 1922–1923*
Bicycle engines which were also available as complete lightweight machines. The two-stroke engine had 131cc and was of the deflector-type three-port variety.

ZETA / *Italy 1948–1954*
Very ordinary and primitive scooter-like vehicles with 48cc and 60cc proprietary engines, built by Cucciolo, Ducati and other producers of similar small power units. The Zeta had very small wheels.

ZETGE / *Germany 1922–1925*
Built well-designed two-strokes with 142cc and 173cc DKW engines as well as with 147cc to 173cc engines of Zetge (Gehlich) design and manufacture.

ZEUGNER / *Germany 1903–1906*
Pioneer assembler, who fitted Fafnir, Zedel, Minerva, FN, Peugeot and other proprietary engines.

ZEUS / *Czechoslovakia 1902–1912*
The Christian Linser-designed Zeus machines, actually made when Czechoslovakia was still part of the Austro-Hungarian Empire, were among the leading singles and V-twins built. The range included 3 and 3·5 hp singles and 4 and 4·5 hp V-twins. Zeus machines were also sold under the Linser trade mark.

ZEUS / *Germany 1925–1927*
Equipped with double-loop frames, German Zeus motorcycles had 348cc and 498cc Küchen three-valve ohc engines.

ZIEJANÜ / *Germany 1924–1926*
Built 211cc and 246cc two-strokes, while a 449cc single-cylinder two-stroke never went into production. Instead the factory assembled motorcycles with 348cc and 498cc sv and ohv JAP engines.

ZIRO / *Germany 1919–1924*
Designed by Albert Roder, who eventually became chief designer at the NSU works, the 148cc and 346cc Ziro were excellent two-strokes with a rotary valve in the crankcase. After Ziro closed down, Roder was with Ermag, Zündapp and Victoria before he eventually joined the firm of NSU.

ZÜNDAPP / *Germany 1917–*
The first models built by this famous factory had 211cc and 246cc deflector-type three-port two-stroke engines; these motorcycles soon gained a reputation for reliability. From 1928 onwards, 198cc and 298cc two-strokes came into production and in 1930 also a 498cc four-valve ohv single which had an English Rudge Python proprietary engine. By 1933, 100,000 Zündapp motorcycles were made. The same year saw the introduction of a new Richard and Xaver Küchen-designed range of models with pressed steel frames and 198cc to 798cc engines. The biggest one was a transverse-mounted sv flat four with 22 bhp, others included 498cc sv and ohv flat twins built on identical lines as the four, and there were also 198cc and 348cc vertical two-stroke singles which—like the other new models—had pressed steel frames and unit-design engines with shaft drive to the rear wheel. 1938 saw the introduction of a 348cc ohv single with a more orthodox frame and when in 1942 the 250,000th Zündapp was built, it was a big 746cc flat twin with four speeds, a reverse gear and a drive to the sidecar wheel. This model was built exclusively for the army. From 1929 to 1933 Zündapp motorcycles were handled in England under the Newmount trade mark. After 1945 Zündapp production concentrated on a sporting 596cc flat twin

211cc Zündapp (TS Model Z22) 1921

249cc Zündapp (TS Model K 249) 1927

298cc Zündapp (TS Model Z 300) 1929

which again had the ohv engine transverse-mounted, but which had again a tubular frame. In 1950 the Nuremberg-based factory built new works at Munich and commenced in 1952 the mass-production of 49cc two-strokes for mofas, mopeds, lightweight motorcycles etc. In addition, Zündapp still builds a variety of two-stroke motorcycles up to 248cc as well as the excellent Bella scooter. There are also 74cc and 98cc

598cc Zündapp (ohv transverse flat-twin Model KS 601) 1950

machines, and with 49cc machines Zündapp breaks records at Monza in Italy. Still, the strength of the machines lies in their reliability, and these two-strokes represent Germany in the Sixdays and many other trials and moto-cross events. Famous riders including Hieronymus, Kittner, Rohde, Von Krohn, Stork, Weiss, Schmider, Brandl, Witthöft, Hau, Neumann and others won again and again. The present range includes mofas, mokicks, mopeds, 49cc lightweights, watercooled 49cc and 173cc versions, 124cc machines including trials versions and also 49cc scooters. A new 348cc model with a watercooled engine will soon enrich the Zündapp range.

123cc Zündapp (TS Model KS 125 Sport) 1971

49cc Zündapp (TS watercooled KS 50) 1977

797cc Zündapp (sv transverse flat-four) 1936

746cc Zündapp (ohv transverse flat-twin army Model KS 750) 1941

ZÜRTZ-REKORD / *Germany 1922–1926*
Interesting design with a wide top tube, which served also as tank. The Zürtz brothers used a variety of engines including 142cc and 173cc DKW two-strokes, the rare 198cc ohv Paqué and also the 249cc Columbus with ohv, as used by the first Horex. A small number had 346cc and 490cc sv and ohv JAP engines.

ZWEIRAD-UNION / *Germany 1958–*
Originally a combination of the DKW, Express and Victoria works with the HQ at the Nuremberg Victoria factory. Hercules was added in 1966 and eventually taken over by the big Fichtel & Sachs group of companies.

ZWERG / *Germany 1924–1925*
Lightweights with own 147cc and 187cc two-stroke deflector-type engines.

ZWI / *Israel 1952–1955*
Only motorcycle factory in Israel. Founded by former Hungarian racing rider Stefan Ausländer, it built exclusively 123cc two-stroke machines with JAP and Villiers engines.

ZZR / *Poland 1960–*
Concentrates on the manufacture of 49cc two-stroke machines, which are being sold under the Komar trade mark.

THE SPEED RECORDS

THE FIRST official world speed record for motorcycles was established on April 14, 1920, at Daytona, by Ernie Walker, riding a 994cc Indian V-twin. The motorcycle was by then sufficiently reliable to achieve such feats, and new records were set regularly in the period up to the outbreak of the Second World War. The 1930s were great years. Bert le Vack set a speed record in 1929 on a Brough-Superior. But less than a month later, Ernst Henne of Germany set a new record on a 733cc BMW. This happened near Munich, and a fight began for the record, with Henne taking on all comers. Claude Temple had retired from competition, but continued designing. Joe Wright set a new record riding a Temple-OEC with a supercharged 996cc JAP V-twin in 1930 at Arpajon. Again, in less than a month, Henne and his BMW took the record back.

Next, Joe Wright's intention was to get the record back to England before the Olympia motorcycle show opened in November, 1930. He went to Cork, in Ireland, with the Temple-OEC and a Zenith with a nearly identical engine. His first run was so fast that the only photographer present left the scene in a hurry to dispatch the picture to his agency, but technical trouble prevented the return run, and another try on the Zenith was successful.

When the Olympia show opened, there on the OEC stand was a machine labelled 'the fastest motorcycle in the world'. There had been no photograph of the Zenith; OEC must have known that it had not been their machine which broke the record, but J. A. Prestwich (JAP) reasoned that the engines were almost identical anyway, and they had sponsored the attempt. OEC gave them better sales publicity, as the Zenith factory was having financial difficulties. It was a while before the controversy died down.

In 1932, 1934, 1935 and 1936 Henne broke his own records. Then Eric Fernihough, a lone Englishman who bought and tuned his own machines, broke the record in Hungary using a Brough-Superior frame and a 996cc supercharged JAP. Piero Taruffi held the record next, with a supercharged and watercooled Gilera four.

Eric Fernihough was killed in a 1938 attempt, when his machine went into a wobble at about 180 mph. There were no new record holders until 1951, when William Hertz reached 180 mph near

THE FASTEST MEN ON TWO WHEELS

Date:	Course:	Driver:	Motorcycle:	ccm:	(km/h)	mph)
1920	Daytona (USA)	Ernie Walker	Indian	994	167.670	104.12
1923	Brooklands (GB)	Claude Temple	British-Anzani	996	174.580	108.41
1924	Arpajon (F)	Bert Le Vack	Brough-Superior	998	191.590	118.98
1926	Arpajon (F)	Claude Temple	OEC-Temple	996	195.330	121.30
1928	Arpajon (F)	O. M. Baldwin	Zenith-JAP	996	200.560	124.55
1929	Arpajon (F)	Bert Le Vack	Brough-Superior	998	207.330	128.75
1930	Arpajon (F)	Joe Wright	OEC-Temple	994	220.990	137.23
1930	Ingolstadt (D)	Ernst Henne	BMW	735	221.540	137.58
1930	Cork (Irl)	Joe Wright	Zenith-JAP	998	242.590	150.65
1932	Tat (H)	Ernst Henne	BMW	735	244.400	151.77
1934	Gyon (H)	Ernst Henne	BMW	735	246.069	152.81
1935	Frankfurt-Ab. (D)	Ernst Henne	BMW	735	256.046	159.01
1936	Frankfurt-Ab. (D)	Ernst Henne	BMW	495	272.006	168.92
1937	Gyon (H)	Eric Fernihough	Brough-Superior-JAP	995	273.244	169.68
1937	Brescia (I)	Piero Tarffi	Gilera	492	274.181	170.27
1937	Frankfurt-Ab. (D)	Ernst Henne	BMW	495	279.503	173.57
1951	Ingolstadt (D)	Wilhelm Herz	NSU	499	290.322	180.29
1955	Christchurch (NZ)	Russell Wright	Vincent-HRD	998	297.640	184.83
1956	Bonneville (USA)	Wilhelm Herz	NSU	499	338.092	211.40
1962	Bonneville (USA)	Bill Johnson	Triumph	649	361.410	224.57
1966	Bonneville (USA)	Bob Leppan	Triumph Spec.	1298	395.280	245.60
1970	Bonneville (USA)	Don Vesco	Yamaha	700	405.25	251.66
1970	Bonneville (USA)	Cal Rayborn	Harley-Davidson	1480	410.37	254.84
1970	Bonneville (USA)	Cal Rayborn	Harley-Davidson	1480	426.40	265.49
1975	Bonneville (USA)	Don Vesco	Yamaha	1496	487.515	302.92

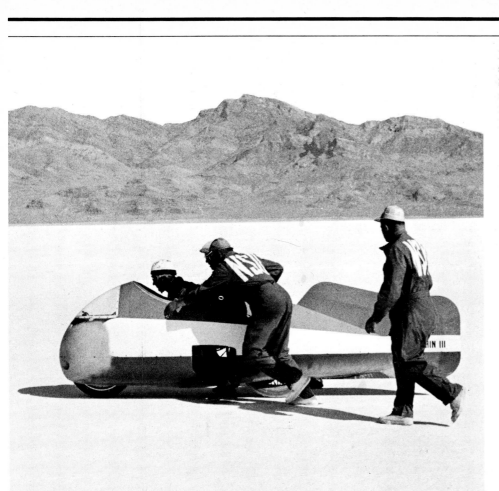

Bonneville Salt Flats in Utah has been the scene of many record-breaking attempts. Successful machines have included the supercharged NSU ridden by Wilhelm Herz in 1956 (left), and Bob Leppan's Triumph-powered Gyronaut of 1967.

Munich. Next, Russel Wright set a new record near Christchurch, New Zealand, riding a tuned 998cc Vincent-HRD.

In 1956, the German NSU factory sent Herz to the USA. The new venue was Bonneville, where the salt flats permitted higher speeds than anywhere in Europe. Herz had two record machines, one of which was a 499cc super-charged dohc twin in a streamlined shell. At Bonneville, he reached 211·4 mph, with Johnny Allen slightly in front at 214·5 mph. Allen's machine was powered by a 650cc Triumph twin engine. However, his American record was not ratified. In 1962, Bill Johnson, riding yet another Triumph-engined record breaker of 649cc, reached a new record of 224·57 mph. Two similar engines powered Robert Leppan's 'projectile' when he reached 245·6 mph at Bonneville in 1966. Just four years later he was beaten by Cal Rayborn whose 1480cc Harley-Davidson reached 265·5 mph. This record stood until September 1975 when Don Vesco reached 302·92 mph on his improved 1496cc Yamaha Streamliner.

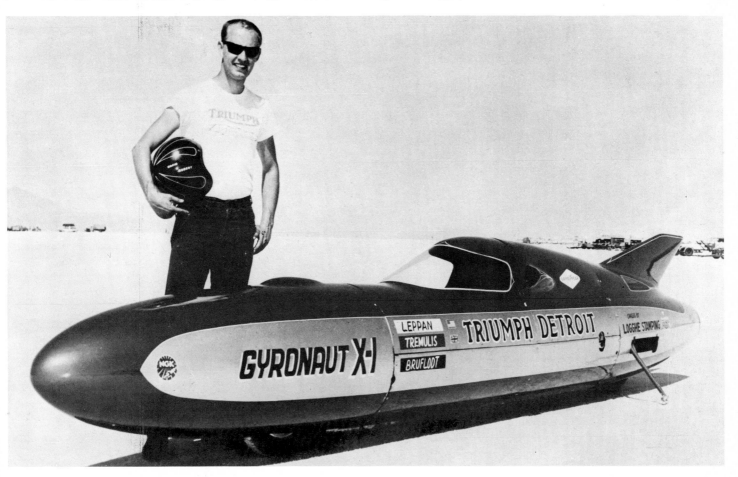

The Leading Models.... From the Golden Age to the Present

The 1920's

Marque:	Country:	Cyl:	Bore:	Stroke:	CCM:	HP:	2 or 4 Stroke:	Engine:
A.J.S.	GB	1	74	81	349	2¾	sv	Own
		2 V	74	93	799	4–7	sv	
Albertus	D	1	60	75	212	3	2	Löwy
Alecto	GB	1	76	76	344	3½	2	Own
Allon	GB	1	70	76	292	2½	2	Own
Ardie	D	1	72	75	305	3	2	Own
Ariel	GB	1	60	88	249	2½	sv	Blackburne
		1	92	100	662	4½	sv	Own
		2 V	73	95	796	6–7	ioe	MAG
		2 V	82	94	994	8	ioe	MAG
BAT	GB	1	70	90	347	2¾	sv	JAP
		2 V	70	88	676	5	sv	JAP
		2 V	85.5	85	986	8	sv	JAP
Beardmore	GB	1	70	90	347	2¾	sv	Precision
		1	81	96	494	3½	sv	Precision
		1	89	96	598	4½	sv	Precision
Bekamo	D	1	50	66	129	2½	2	Own
BMW	D	1	68	68	249	2½	ohv	Own
		2	68	68	493	6.5	sv	Own
		2	68	68	493	16	ohv	Own
Bianchi	I	2 V	70	78	600	—	sv	Own
Bradbury	GB	1	74.5	80	349	2¾	sv	Own
		1	89	89	554	4	sv	Own
		2 V	74.5	86	749	6	sv	Own
Brough	GB	2 F	70	64.5	496	3½	ohv	Own
		2 F	70	90	692	5–6	sv	Own
Brough-Superior	GB	2 V	72	91	742	6	ioe	MAG
		2 V	85.5	86	976	8	sv	JAP
		2 V	90	77.5	984	8	ohv	JAP
B.S.A.	GB	1	72	85.5	349	2¾	sv	Own
		1	80	98	493	3½	sv	Own
		1	85	98	557	4¼	sv	Own
		2 V	76	85	770	6	sv	Own
		2 V	80	98	985	8	sv	Own
Burney	GB	1	81	96	495	3½	sv	Own
Calthorpe	GB	1	67	69	247	2½	2	Peco
Campion	GB	1	70	76	293	2¼	sv	JAP
		1	71	88	347	2¾	sv	JAP
		2 V	85.5	85	976	8	sv	JAP
Cedos	GB	1	62	70	211	2¼	2	Own
		1	67	70	247	2¾	2	Own
Chater Lea	GB	1	70	70	269	2½	2	Own
		1	71	88	349	2¾	sv	Blackburne
		1	85	96	545	4¼	sv	Own
		2 V	85.5	85	976	8	sv	Own
Clément	F	2 V	54	75	345	3	sv	Own
		2 V	64	77	496	3½	sv	Own
Cleveland	USA	1	70	70	269	3½	2	Own
Clyno	GB	1	70	70	269	2½	2	Own
		2 V	76	102	925	8	sv	Own
Connaught	GB	1	73	70	293	2½	2	Own
		1	76	77	348	2¾	2	Own
Cotton	GB	1	70	70	269	2½	2	Villiers
		1	60	88	248	2½	sv	Blackburne
		1	71	88	348	2¾	sv	Blackburne
		1	71	88	348	2¾	ohv	Blackburne
Coventry-Eagle	GB	1	55	60	147	1¾	2	Villiers
		1	71	88	348	2¾	sv	Blackburne
		2 V	85	85	998	8	sv	JAP
Coventry-Mascot	GB	1	70	90.6	349	2¾	sleeve	Barr & Stroud
Coventry-Victor	GB	2 F	75	78	688	6	sv	Own
D-Rad	D	1	82	94	496	10	sv	Own
Diamond	GB	1	55	62	147	1¾	2	Villiers
		1	70	90.6	349	2¾	sleeve	Barr & Stroud
Dolf	D	1	62	66	199	3	2	
Dot	GB	1	60	70	198	2¼	2	
		1	70	70	269	2¾	2	Villiers
		1	70	76	293	2¾	sv	JAP
		2 V	85	85	986	8	sv	JAP

Marque:	Country:	Cyl:	Bore:	Stroke:	CCM:	HP:	2 or 4 Stroke:	Engine
Douglas	GB	2 F	60.8	60	348	$2\frac{3}{4}$	sv	Own
		2 F	68	68	496	$3\frac{1}{2}$	sv	Own
		2 F	74.5	68	595	4	sv	Own
		2 F	83	68	733	6	ohv	Own
Dunelt	GB	1	85	88	499	$3\frac{1}{2}$	2	Own
Duzmo	GB	1	89	79	497	$3\frac{1}{2}$	ohv	Own
Economic	GB	2 F	52.5	38.5	163	$1\frac{3}{4}$	2	Own
Excelsior	GB	1	55	62	147	$1\frac{1}{4}$	2	Villiers
		1	67	70	247	$2\frac{1}{2}$	2	Villiers
		1	71	88	348	$2\frac{3}{4}$	sv	Blackburne
		2 V	76	85	770	6	sv	JAP
		2 V	85.5	85	976	8	sv	JAP
F.N.	B	1	65	86	285	$2\frac{3}{4}$	sv	Own
		1	74	80.5	348	$2\frac{3}{4}$	sv	Own
		4	52	88	749	8	sv	Own
Francis-Barnett	GB	1	70	76	293	$2\frac{3}{4}$	sv	JAP
		1	70	90	346	$2\frac{3}{4}$	sv	JAP
Garelli	I	1	50	89	348	$2\frac{3}{4}$	2	Own 2-Piston
Gnome & Rhone	F	1	85	88	499	$3\frac{1}{2}$	sv	Own
		1	85	88	499	$3\frac{1}{2}$	ohv	Own
Hanfland	D	1	55	65	149	3	2	Own
Harley-Davidson	USA	2 F	69	76	584	5	sv	Own
		2 V	84	88.9	989	9	ioe	Own
		2 V	87	101	1208	12	ioe	Own
H.E.C.	GB	1	67	70	247	$2\frac{1}{2}$	2	Villiers
Henderson	USA	4	68.3	88.9	1303	$11\frac{1}{2}$	sv	Own
Henley	GB	1	68	96	348	$2\frac{3}{4}$	ohv	Bradshaw
Hobart	GB	1	60	88	248	$2\frac{1}{4}$	sv	Blackburne
		1	71	88	348	$2\frac{3}{4}$	sv	Blackburne
Humber	GB	1	75	79	348	$2\frac{3}{4}$	sv	Own
		2 F	75	68	600	$4\frac{1}{2}$	sv	Own
Indian	USA	2 V	70	78	596	4	sv	Own
		2 V	79	100	998	7–8	sv	Own
		2 V	82	112	1204	10	sv	Own
Invicta	GB	1	70	90	346	$2\frac{3}{4}$	sv	JAP
Ivy	GB	1	75	79	348	$2\frac{3}{4}$	2	Own
James	GB	1	73	83.5	349	$2\frac{3}{4}$	sv	Own
		2 V	64	77	499	$3\frac{1}{2}$	sv	Own
		2 V	73	89.5	749	7	sv	Own
J.E.S.	GB	1	60	60	169	$1\frac{1}{2}$	2	Own
J.N.U.	GB	1	73	76	318	$2\frac{3}{4}$	2	Dalm
K.G.	D	1	80	99	497	4	ohv	Own
Lea Francis	GB	2 V	64	77	497	$3\frac{1}{2}$	ioe	MAG
		2 V	64	92	592	5	ioe	MAG
Levis	GB	1	62	70	211	2.1	2	Own
Lutéce	F	2	75	113	997	7	sv	Own
Mabeco	D	2 V	70	78	600	11	sv	Simens & Halske
Mars	D	2 F	80	95	956	7.3	sv	Maybach
Martinsyde	GB	1	70	90	437	$2\frac{3}{4}$	eoi	Own
		2 V	70	88	678	6	eoi	Own
Massey	GB	1	71	88	348	$2\frac{3}{4}$	sv	Blackburne
Matchless	GB	1	71	88	348	$2\frac{3}{4}$	sv	Blackburne
		2 V	85	85	980	8	sv	JAP
		2 V	82	94	993	8	ioe	MAG
McKenzie	GB	1	60	60	170	$1\frac{1}{4}$	2	Own
Metro-Tyler	GB	1	70	70	269	$2\frac{1}{2}$	2	Own
Megola	D	5	52	60	640	6.5–14	sv	Own Radial
M.F.Z.	D	1	64	77	249	3	2	Own
Mohawk	GB	1	70	70	269	$2\frac{1}{2}$	2	Villiers
Moto-Rêve	CH	1	61	85	248	$2\frac{1}{2}$	ohv	Own
Motosacoche	CH	2 V	54	75	345	3	ioe	MAG
		2 V	64	77	496	4	ioe	MAG
		2 V	72	91	750	6	ioe	MAG
New Comet	GB	1	70	76	293	$2\frac{1}{2}$	2	Climax
New Gerrard	GB	1	70	90.5	384	$2\frac{3}{4}$	Sleeve	Barr & Stroud
New Hudson	GB	1	62	70	211	$1\frac{3}{4}$	2	Own
		1	70	90	346	$2\frac{3}{4}$	sv	Own
		1	79.5	100	498	$3\frac{1}{2}$	sv	Own
		1	87	100	596	4	sv	Own
New Imperial	GB	1	70	76	293	$2\frac{1}{2}$	sv	JAP
		1	70	90	348	$2\frac{3}{4}$	sv	JAP
		2 V	85.5	85	976	8	sv	JAP
Nimbus	DK	4	60	66	746	7	ioe	Own
Norton	GB	1	79	100	490	$3\frac{1}{2}$	sv	Own
		1	79	100	490	$3\frac{1}{2}$	ohv	Own
		1	82	120	633	4	sv	Own
N.S.U.	D	1	58	72	190	$1\frac{1}{2}$	ioe	Own
		1	73	78	326	$2\frac{1}{2}$	ioe	Own
		1	85	88	499	$3\frac{1}{2}$	ioe	Own
		2 V	58	75	396	3	ioe	Own
		2 V	63	80	499	$3\frac{1}{2}$	ioe	Own
		2 V	72.5	90	749	6–14	ioe	Own
		2 V	75	94	931	$6\frac{1}{2}$	ioe	Own
		2 V	80	99	998	8–17	ioe	Own
N.U.T.	GB	2 V	64.5	76	499	$3\frac{1}{2}$	sv	Own
		2 V	64.5	76	499	$3\frac{1}{2}$	ohv	Own
		2 V	70	88	676	$4\frac{1}{2}$	sv	Own
O.E.C.	GB	1	71	88	348	$2\frac{3}{4}$	sv	Blackburne
		1	85	96.8	549	4	sv	Blackburne
		2 V	85	88	998	8	sv	Blackburne
O.K.	GB	1	70	70	269	$2\frac{1}{2}$	2	Villiers
		1	60	88	248	$2\frac{1}{4}$		Blackburne
Olympic	GB	1	68	72	261	$2\frac{1}{2}$	2	Orbit
Omega	GB	1	60	60	170	$1\frac{1}{2}$	2	Own
		1	71	88	348	$2\frac{3}{4}$	2	Own
Paragon	GB	1	76	79	349	$2\frac{3}{4}$	2	Own
Peugeot	F	1	52	52	110	1	2	Own
Puch	A	1	36×2	60	123	1	2	Own

Marque:	Country:	Cyl:	Bore:	Stroke:	CCM:	HP:	2 or 4 Stroke:	Engine:
P. & M. (Panther)	GB	1	84.1	100	555	5	sv	Own
P. & P.	GB	1	70	90.5	349	2¾	Sleeve	Barr & Stroud
Quadrant	GB	1	79	100	490	3½	sv	Own
		1	87	110	654	4½	ioe	Own
Radco	GB	1	67	70	247	2½	2	Own
Raleigh	GB	1	71	88	348	2¾	sv	Own
		2 F	77	75	698	5–6	sv	Own
Ray	GB	1	60	70	198	1½	sv	Own
Reading-Standard	USA	2 V	85.7	101.6	1170	10	sv	Own
Ready	GB	1	70	76	293	2¾	sv	JAP
Rex-Acme	GB	1	70	90.5	349	2¾	Sleeve	Barr & Stroud
		1	85	95	550	4	sv	JAP
		1	60	88	248	2½	ohv	Blackburne
Rover	GB	1	63	80	249	2½	ohv	Own
		2 V	70	88	678	5	sv	JAP
Royal Enfield	GB	1	64	70	225	2.5	sv	Own
		2 V	85.5	85	976	8	sv	JAP
Rudge	GB	1	85	88	499	3½	ioe	Own
		2 V	85	88	998	7–9	ioe	Own
R. & H.	GB	1	55	62	147	1¼	2	Villiers
Sarolea	B	1	85	97	553	4	sv	Own
Scott	GB	2	70	63.5	487	3.5	2	Own
		2	73	63.5	532	3¾	2	Own
Sparkbrook	GB	1	67	70	247	2½	2	Villiers
Sun	GB	1	70	70	269	2½	2	Vitesse
		1	71	88	348	2¾	sv	Blackburne
Sunbeam	GB	1	70	90	347	2¾	sv	Own
		1	77	105.5	492	3½	sv	Own
		1	85	88	499	3½	sv	Own
		1	85	105.5	599	4½	sv	Own
		2 V	85.5	85	976	6–8	sv	JAP
Stanger	GB	2 V	70	70	538	4	2	Own
Triumph	D	1	70	72	277	2½	2	Own
Triumph	GB	1	67.2	70	249	2¼	2	Own
		1	80.9	97	499	3½	ohv	Own
		1	85	97	550	4	sv	Own
Trump	GB	1	70	90	348	2¾	sv	JAP
		2 V	76	85	748	6	sv	JAP
Velocette	GB	1	62	73	220	1¾	2	Own
		1	63	80	247	2¼	2	Own
Victoria	GB	1	79	70	347	2¾	2	Villiers
Victoria	D	2 F	70.5	64	499	6.5	ohv	Own
Vindec	GB	1	70	76	293	2½	sv	JAP
		2 V	85.5	85	976	8	sv	JAP
Vis-Duplex	D	2 F	63	80	498	3½	2	Own
Wanderer	D	1	65	76	251	2	sv	Own
		2 V	65	76	502	4	sv	Own
		2 V	70	80	615	4	sv	Own
		2 V	71	94	749	6	ohv	Own
Weaver	GB	1	56	61	149	1¼	ohv	Own
Wee McGregor	GB	1	60	60	170	1¼	2	Own
Wolf	GB	1	71	88	348	2¾	sv	Blackburne
Wooler	GB	2 F	60	60.5	345	2¾	ioe	Own
Zenith	GB	1	70	76	293	2¾	sv	JAP
		1	70	90	348	2¾	sv	JAP
		2 F	68	68	496	3½	ohv	Bradshaw
		2 V	70	88	678	5	sv	JAP
		2 V	85.5	85	976	8	sv	JAP
Zündapp	D	1	62	70	211	2¼	2	Own

The 1930's

Marque:	Model:	Country:	Cyl:	Bore:	Stroke:	CCM:	2 or 4 Stroke:	Engine:
A.J.S.	S 4	GB	1	74	93	399	sv	Own
	S 5		1	74	81	349	sv	Own
	S 6		1	74	81	349	ohv	Own
	S 8		1	84	90	498	ohv	Own
	S 2		2 V	84	90	996	sv	Own
A.J.W.	B. Fox	GB	1	57.1	67	172	2	Villiers
	Flying Fox		1	70	90.5	348	ohv	Python
	Flying Foy		1	85	88	499	ohv	Python
	680		2 V	70	88	675	ohv	JAP
	8–55		2 V	80	90	996	ohv	JAP
A.K.D.	70 Merkur	GB	1	60	61	172	ohv	Own
	40 Polar		1	76	77	348	sv	Own
Allegro	Supersp.	CH	1	57	67	172	2	Villiers
	Grand Sport		1	79	101	498	ohv	Sturmey-Archer
Ardie	Jubilee	D	1	85.7	85	490	sv	JAP
	Silberpfeil		1	85.7	85	490	ohv	JAP
	750		2 V	70	97	743	sv	JAP
Ariel	L 1 F	GB	1	65	75	248	ohv	Own
	V F		1	81.8	95	497	ohv	Own
	S B		1	86.4	95	557	sv	Own
	4 F		4 Sq	51	61	497	ohc	Own
Austria		A	1	70	90	346	2	Villiers
Bianchi		I	1	59.5	62.5	174	ohv	Own
BMW	R 2	D	1	63	64	198	ohv	Own
	R 52		2 F	63	78	486	sv	Own
	R 57		2 F	68	68	494	ohv	Own
	R 62		2 F	78	78	745	sv	Own
	R 63		2 F	83	68	735	ohv	Own
Brough-Superior	500	GB	2 V	62.5	80	492	ohv	JAP
	680		2 V	70	88	676	ohv	JAP
	SS 80		2 V	85	85.7	998	sv	JAP
	SS 100		2 V	80	99	998	ohv	JAP
BSA	B 1	GB	1	63	80	249	sv	Own

Marque:	Model:	Country:	Cyl:	Bore:	Stroke:	CCM:	2 or 4 Stroke:	Engine
	B 3		1	63	80	249	ohv	Own
	L 5		1	72	85.5	349	sv	Own
	L 6		1	72	85.5	349	ohv	Own
	S 7		1	80	98	493	sv	Own
	S 9		1	80	98	493	ohv	Own
	E 11		2 V	76	85	770	sv	Own
	G 12		2 V	80	98	986	sv	Own
Condor	312	CH	1	72	85	348	ioe	MAG
	322		1	82	94	498	ioe	MAG
	GP 572		1	82	94	498	ohv	MAG
Calthorpe	Ivory	GB	1	74	81	348	ohv	Own
Coventry-Eagle	G 22	GB	1	67	67	196	2	Villiers
	G 45		1	70	90	348	sv	Sturmey-Archer
	G 44		1	71	88	348	ohv	Sturmey-Archer
	G 54		1	79	101	496	ohv	Sturmey-Archer
	G 55		1	85.7	85	490	ohv	JAP
	F 130		2 V	85.5	85	996	sv	JAP
Diamond		GB	1	67	70	247	2	Villiers
Delta-Gnom		A	1	71	88	348	ohv	Sturmey-Archer
			1	82	94	496	ohv	Own
			2 V	85.5	85	996	sv	JAP
DKW	VR	D	1	63	64	198	2	Own
	300		1	74	68	296	2	Own
	500		2	68	68	494	2	Own
Dollar		F	1	66	70	239	ohv	Chaise
			1	75	79	349	ohv	Chaise
			1	89	79	492	ohv	Chaise
Douglas	B	GB	2 F	60.8	60	347	sv	Own
	D		2 F	68	82	595	sv	Own
	G		2 F	68	82	595	ohv	Own
D-Rad	R9	D	1	82	94	496	sv	Own
	R10		1	82	94	496	ohv	Own
Dresch	E	F	1	76	77	348	sv	Own
	C		2	64	77	495	sv	Own
Dunelt	J2	GB	1	65.5	88	298	sv	Sturmey-Archer
	J4		1	71	88	348	ohv	Sturmey-Archer
	J5		1	79	101	496	ohv	Sturmey-Archer
	J7		1	86.8	101	598	sv	Sturmey-Archer
Elfa	T200	D	1	63	64	198	2	Windhoff
	LS300		1	68	64	294	2	Kühne
	LS350		1	70	90	346	ohv	Küchen
	LS500		1	79	100	492	sv	Küchen
Elite (E.O.)	Sport	D	1	86	86	496	ohv	Küchen
Excelsior	A 4	GB	1	61	67	196	2	Villiers
	A 9		1	62.5	90	248	ohv	JAP
	A 12		1	85.7	85	490	ohv	JAP
FN		B	1	74	80.5	348	sv	Own
			1	85	87	495	sv	Own
			1	85	87	495	ohv	Own
Francis-Barnett	Hawk	GB	1	61	67	196	2	Villiers
	18 Falcon		1	61	67	196	2	Villiers-DP
Frera	Sport	I	1	53	79	174	sv	Own
	Sport		1	63	79	247	sv	Own
	Sport		1	71	88	347	sv	Own
	Spinta		1	84.5	88	497	ohv	Own
Garelli	314	I	1	50	82	348	2	Own 2 Piston
	315		1	50	89	349	2	Own 2 Piston
Gilera	Sixdays	I	1	84	90	498	sv	Own
Gillet Herstal	Welttur	B	1	79.5	70	348	2	Own
	SS		1	70	90	348	ohv	Own
	T		1	84	90	498	sv	Own
	Rekord		1	84	90	498	ohv	Own
Gnome Rhone	Touring	F	1	69	82	306	sv	Own
	CM 1 GS		1	73	82	344	ohv	Own
	GS 500		1	85	88	497	sv	Own
	V2		2 F	68	68	495	sv	Own
Harley-Davidson	C	USA	1	70.6	101.6	493	sv	Own
	D		2 V	69.8	96.8	743	sv	Own
	V		2 V	86.9	101.6	1208	ioe	Own
Henderson	De Luxe	USA	4	58.8	89	1301	ioe	Own
Horex	S 200	D	1	57	78	198	ohv	Columbus
	T 500		1	80	99	496	sv	Columbus
	S 500		1	79	101	496	ohv	Columbus-S.A.
	T 600		1	80	118	596	sv	Columbus
Hulla	Bremen	D	1	60	68	196	2	DKW
Husqvarna		S	1	64.5	76	248	sv	Own
			1	62.5	80	248	ohv	JAP
			1	79	101	496	ohv	Sturmey-Archer
Imperia	Ulster	D	1	70	88	346	ohv	Python
	Grand Sport		1	85	88	498	ohv	Python
	Sport		1	80	94	498	ohv	MAG
	Berggeist		1	90	94	598	ioe	MAG
	Rheingold		1	70	88	676	ohv	JAP
James	C 10	GB	1	57.5	67	172	2	Villiers
	C 4		1	73.5	83.5	348	ohv	Own
	C3		1	85	88	498	ohv	Python
	C 2		2 V	64	77.5	497	ohv	Own
Jawa		CS	1	58	65	173	2	Lic. Villiers
			1	63	80	246	2	Lic. DKW
			1	84	90	499	ohv	Lic. Wanderer
Keller	O 1	CH	1	79	81	397	sv	Own
Koehler-Escoffier	KG 35	F	1	72	85	347	ohv	MAG
	K 50		1	80	99	498	ohc	Own
Levis	Z	GB	1	67	70	247	2	Own
	A 2		1	70	90	346	ohv	Own
Magnat-Debon	LMP	F	1	57	68	174	2	Own
	MOSSE		1	59	90	246	ohv	Own
	CSS		1	85.5	85	490	ohv	JAP

Marque:	Model:	Country:	Cyl:	Bore:	Stroke:	CCM:	2 or 4 Stroke:	Engine:
Mammut	2 T	D	1	61	67	196	2	Villiers
	4 T		1	56.3	79	198	sv	Blackburne
MAS	119 L	I	1	60	61.5	173.8	ohv	Own
	125/3		1	85	61.5	348	ohv	Own
Matchless	R 7	GB	1	62.5	80	246	sv	Own
	D		1	69	93	347	sv	Own
	C/S		1	85.5	85.5	495	ohv	Own
	X/3		2 V	85.5	85.5	990	sv	Own
	S. Arrow		2 V	54	86	398	sv	Own
	S. Hawk		4 V	50.8	73	593	ohc	Own
Miller-Balsamo	Erretre	I	1	57	67	172	ohv	Own
	TT-Replica		1	85	88	498	ohv	Python
La Mondiale	LT	B	1	75	68	308	2	Own
	ZS		1	75	79	349	2	Own
	GS		1	70	90	346	ohv	JAP
	GSSS		1	85.7	85	490	ohv	JAP
Monet-Goyon	AT	F	1	67	70	247	2	Villiers
			1	72	85	348	ioe	MAG
			1	82	94	498	ohv	MAG
Montgomery		GB	1	62.5	80	248	ohv	JAP
			1	70	90	348	ohv	JAP
			1	85.7	85	490	sv	JAP
			2 V	70	88	676	sv	JAP
Moser	STD	CH	1	60	61	174	ohv	Own
			1	74	81	348	ohv	Own
			1	79	100	498	ohv	Own
			1	85	106	598	ohv	Own
Motobécane (Motoconfort)	B1	F	1	46	60	99.6	2	Own
	B2		1	56	70	172	2	Own
	B4		1	70	90	346	ohv	Own
	B7		4	54	81.7	749	ohc	Own
	B 75		4	54	54.5	499	ohc	Own
Moto Guzzi		I	1	68	68	248	ohc	Own
			1	88	82	499	ioe	Own
			1	88	82	499	ohc	Own
Motosacoche	316	CH	1	72	85	347	ioe	Own (MAG)
	317		1	72	85	347	ohv	Own (MAG)
	417		1	82	94	498	sv	Own (MAG)
	714		2 V	72	91	746	ioe	Own (MAG)
MT	H 29	A	1	79	70	342	2	Villiers
	N.O.		1	85.7	85	490	sv	JAP
	TSP 4		1	79	101	496	ohv	Sturmey-Archer
	2 29 B		2 V	70	97	746	sv	JAP
New Hudson	31	GB	1	70	90	346	sv	Own
	33		1	70	90	346	ohv	Own
	3		1	79.5	100	496	ohv	Own
	1		1	83.5	100	547	sv	Own
New Imperial	Leinster	GB	1	62.5	80	248	ohv	Own
	10 Prince		1	70	90	348	ohv	Own
	11 Prince		1	86	86	499	ohv	Own
Norton	JE	GB	1	71	88	348	ohv	Own
	CJ		1	71	88	348	ohc	Own
	16H		1	79	100	490	sv	Own
	18		1	79	100	490	ohv	Own
	CS		1	79	100	490	ohc	Own
	19		1	79	120	588	ohv	Own
	Big Four		1	82	120	633	sv	Own
NSU	Pony	D	1	45	40	63	2	Own
	175Z		1	59	64	174	2	Own
	201 Z		1	63	64	198	2	Own
	251 TS		1	63	80	247	ioe	Own
	351 TS		1	71	88	346	ohv	Own
	501 TS		1	80	99	494	sv	Own
	500 SS		1	80	99	494	ohc	Own
OEC		GB	1	70	90	346	sv	JAP
			1	85.7	85	490	ohv	JAP
	Flying Squad		2 V	80	90	994	ohv	JAP
OK-Supreme	N	GB	1	85.7	85	490	sv	JAP
	A		1	70	64.5	248	ohc	Own
	M		2 V	70	97	749	sv	JAP
Peugeot	P 109	F	1	54	76	174	sv	Own
	P 107		1	72	85	348	sv	Own
	P 105		1	72	85	348	ohv	Own
P. & M.-Panther	50	GB	1	84	90	498	ohv	Own
	90 Redwing		1	79	100	490	ohv	Own
	25		1	65	70	247	2	Villiers
Praga	350	CS	1	70	90	346	ohc	Own
	500		1	84	90	499	ohc	Own
Premier	A 1	CS	1	70	70	269	2	Own
	S2		1	71	88	346	sv	Own
	S3		1	85	88	499	sv	Own
	SL		1	75.5	110	494	ohv	Own
	S6		2 V	76	82	744	sv	Own
Puch	250	A	1	45×2	78	248	2	Own
	500Z		2	45×2	78	496	2	Own
Radco	L	GB	1	55	62	147	2	Villiers
	P		1	67	70	247	2	Own
Raleigh	MO	GB	1	65.6	88	298	sv	Own–S.A.
	MT		1	71	88	348	ohv	Own–S.A.
	MH		1	79	101	496	ohv	Own–S.A.
Ready		B	1	70	90	346	sv	JAP
			1	85.7	85	490	ohv	JAP
René-Gillet	H	F	1	70	90	346	sv	Own
	G		2 V	70	97.7	749	sv	Own
	J		2 V	80	97.7	981	sv	Own
Rhony'X	VM	F	1	46	60	100	2	Own
	H3		1	70	90	346	sv	Own

The 1930's
continued

Marque:	Model:	Country:	Cyl:	Bore:	Stroke:	CCM:	2 or 4 Stroke:	Engine:
	H5		1	83	90	490	sv	Own
RMW	200	D	1	62	66	198	2	Own
			1	71	88	348	sv	Sturmey-Archer
			1	82	96	498	ioe	MAG
			1	82	96	496	ohv	MAG
Royal-Enfield	C	GB	1	70	90	346	sv	Own
	CO		1	70	90	346	ohv	Own
	HA		1	85.5	85	498	sv	Own
	JA		1	85.5	85	498	ohv	Own
	H		1	80.5	99.25	570	sv	Own
	K		2 V	85.5	85	976	sv	Own
Rudge-Whitworth	250	GB	1	62.5	81	249	ohv	Own
	350		1	70	90.5	349	ohv	Own
	500 Spec.		1	85	88	499	ohv	Own
Sarolea	A	B	1	75	79	347	sv	Own
	S		1	80.5	97	494	ohv	Own
Schliha		D	1	69.3	70	193	2	Own
			1	82.4	86	349	2	Own
			1	102.5	86	498	2	Own
Schüttoff	200	D	1	60	68	192	2	DKW
			1	74	68	296	2	DKW
			1	72	85	346	ohv	Own
			1	80	99	494	sv	Own
			1	80	99	494	ohv	Own
Scott	Squirrel	GB	1	73	71.4	298	2	Own
	Fl. Squirell		2	68.25	68.25	498	2	Own
	Fl. Squirell		2	74.6	68.25	596	2	Own
	TT Replica		2	66.6	71.4	498	2	Own
	TT Replica		2	73	71.4	596	2	Own
SMW	S IV		1	61	67	196	2	Villiers
	S III		1	81	96.8	498	ohv	Blackburne
Soyer	500 Block F		1	80	91	498	ohc	Own
	500 S Sport		1	80	91	498	ohc	Own
Standard	DS 250	D	1	62.5	80	249	ohv	Own
	CT 350		1	72	84	342	ioe	MAG
	CS 500		1	82	94	498	ohv	MAG
	Rennsport		1	82	94	498	ohv	MAG
	BT 1000		2 V	82	94	997	ioe	MAG
Stock	Extra		1	55	50	119	2	Own
	Kardan 200		1	66	58	197	2	Own
	GR 300		1	74	68	292	2	Own
Sunbeam	10	GB	1	74	80	344	ohv	Own
	Lion Longstroke		1	77	105.5	492	sv	Own
	9 (90) TT		1	80	98	493	ohv	Own
Super-X	Touring	USA	2 V	76	83	752	ioe	Own
Terrot	LPP	F	1	57	68	174	2	Own
	FST		1	67	70	247	2	Own
	OSSE		1	59	90	246	ohv	Own
	NSSL		1	85.5	85	490	ohv	JAP
	V		2 V	70	88	676	sv	JAP
Titan	Spezial	A	1	75	77	340	2	Own
	500		1	81	96.8	498	sv	Blackburne
Train	M-5	F	1	64	54	173	2	Own
			1	76	76	344	2	Own
			1	76	76	344	ohv	Own
Triumph	X	GB	1	59.5	62.5	74	2	Own
	WO		1	63	80	249	ohv	Own
	WL		1	72	85.5	348	sv	Own
	NT		1	84	89	493	ohv	Own
	ND		1	84	99	548	sv	Own
Triumph (TWN)	SK 200	D	1	59	72	197	2	Own
	T 350		1	72	85	346	ioe	MAG
	SST 500		1	82	94	498	ohv	MAG
	RR		V 2	72	91	741	ioe	MAG
Universal		CH	1	70	90	348	sv	JAP
			1	85.7	85	490	ohv	JAP
U.T.		D	1	60	68	193	2	Bark
			1	70	90	348	ohv	JAP
			1	85.7	104	599	ohv	JAP
Velocette	GTP	GB	1	63	80	249	2	Own
	KTP		1	74	81	348	ohc	Own
	KTT		1	74	81	348	ohc	Own
Victoria	KR 20	D	1	60	88	248	sv	Sturmey-Archer
	KR 35		1	71	87	348	ohv	Sturmey-Archer
	KR 50		1	79	101	492	ohv	Sturmey-Archer
	KR 6		2 F	77	64	596	ohv	Own
Wimmer	GG 25	D	1	67	71	247	ohv	Own
	GG 50		1	84	90	499	sv	Bark
Wolf	Utility	GB	1	61	67	196	2	Villiers
Württembergia	BL 200	D	1	56.3	79	196	sv	Blackburne
	SS 350		1	71	88	348	ohv	Blackburne
	RL 600		1	85	105	596	sv	Blackburne
Zündapp	S 200		1	60	70	198	2	Own
	S 300		1	68	82.5	298	2	Own
	S 500		1	85	88	499	ohv	Python

The post-war period

Marque:	Model:	Country:	Cyl:	Bore:	Stroke:	CCM:	2 or 4 Stroke:	Engine:	Bhp:
Adler	M 100	D	1	50	50	98	2	Own	3.8
	M 150		1	54	59	147	2	Own	8.4
	M 250		2	54	54	247	2	Own	16
Aermacchi	125	I	1 F	52	58	123	2	Own	5
Aero-Caproni	Capriolo	I	1	47	43	75	ohv	Own	3.5
A.J.S.	16 M	GB	1	69	93	347	ohv	Own	15.2
	18		1	82.5	93	498	ohv	Own	21.1

Marque:	Model:	Country:	Cyl:	Bore:	Stroke	CCM:	2 or 4 Stroke:	Engine:	Bhp:
	7R Boys Racer		1	75.5	78	349	ohc	Own	30
Alpino	Sport	I	1	53.5	55	123	2	Own	6.5
Ardie	BD 175	D	1	60	61	172	2	Own	9
	B 252		1	66	72	244	2	Own	13
Aeriel	NG	GB	1	72	85	347	ohc	Own	14.2
	VG		1	81.8	95	497	ohv	Own	22
	VH Red Hunter		1	81.8	95	497	ohv	Own	24.6
	VB		1	86.4	102	598	sv	Own	15.5
	4G Square Four		4 Sq.	65×4	75	997	ohv	Own	34.5
Astoria	Sport	I	1	56	60	148	2	Own	6.3
B (Motobi)	115	I	1	52	54	115	2	Own	5.2
	200	I	2 F	48	54	196	2	Own	9
Bauer		D	1	68	68	246	ohv	Own	16
Benelli	Sport Leoncino	I	1	54	54	123	2	Own	6.5
	Leonessa		2	53	56	247	ohv	Own	16
Beta	Sport	I	1	57	62	158	2	Own	7.5
Bianchi	Freccia Celeste	I	1	52	58	123	2	Own	7.5
BMW	R 25/2	D	1	68	68	245	ohv	Own	12
	R 51/3		2	68	68	494	ohv..	Own	24
	R 67/2		2	72	73	590	ohv	Own	28
	R 68		2	72	73	590	ohv	Own	35
Bonvicini	BM 160	I	1	58	66	174	2	Ilo	6.5
Borghi	Olympia	I	1	52	58	123	2	BSA	5.5
BSA	C 10	GB	1	63	80	249	sv	Own	8
	C 11		1	63	80	249	ohv	Own	11
	B 31		1	71	88	348	ohv	Own	17
	B 33		Z	85	88	499	ohv	Own	23
	M 20		1	82	94	496	sv	Own	13
	M 21		1	82	112	591	sv	Own	15
	M 33		1	95	88	499	ohv	Own	23
	A 7		2	66	72.6	498	ohv	Own	27.4
	A 10 GF		2	70	84	646	ohv	Own	35.5
Bücker	TZ 200	D	1	62	66	198	2	Ilo	11
	Ilona II		2	52	58	246	2	Ilo	15.1
Carnielli	75	I	1	46	44	73	2	Vittoria	3
Ceccato		I	1	54	54	123	2	Own	5.5
Cimatti	SS	I	1	57	62	158	2	Own	7
C.M.		I	1	52	58	123	2	Own	4.5
			2	52	58	246	2	Own	8.5
Condor	25 De Luxe	CH	1	63	72	225	2	Villiers	10
	Racer		2	58	66	348	2	Own	14
	580 Ralye		2 F	70	75.2	577	sv	Own	20
	750 Touriste		2 F	78	78	748	sv	Own	25
Cotton	Vulcan	GB	1	79	72	197	2	Villiers	7.6
	Herald		2	50	63.5	249	2	Villiers	8.5
	Messenger		2	57	63.5	324	2	Villiers	—
CZ		CS	1	52	58	124	2	Own	5.6
			1	57	58	148	2	Own	6.5
			1	60	61	173	2	Own	6.5
			1	65	75	247	2	Own	9
Delta Gnom	Luxus	A	1	52	58	123	2	Rotax	5.8
DKW	RT 125	D	1	52	58	123	2	Own	4.75
	RT 200		1	62	64	192	2	Own	8.5
	RT 250		1	70	64	244	2	Own	11.5
	RT 350		2	62	58	348	2	Own	18
Douglas	Standard Mk. III	GB	2 F	60.8	60	348	ohv	Own	20
Dot	200 SCH	GB	1	59	72	197	2	Villiers	7.6
	250 SCH		1	66	72	246	2	Villiers	8.5
Dürkopp	MD 150	D	1	53	60	150	2	Own	7.5
	MD 200		1	61	64	198	2	Own	10.2
Ducati	48	I	1	39	40	48	ohv	Own	1.5
EMW	R 35/3	DDR	1	72	84	340	ohv	Own	14
Excelsior	Autobyk	GB	1	50	50	98	2	Brockhouse	2.2
	Consort	1	47	57	98	98	2	Villiers	2.8
	Condor		1	50	62	123	2	Villiers	5
	Courier		1	55	62	148	2	Villiers	6.5
	Roadsmaster		1	59	72	197	2	Villiers	8.5
	Talisman		2	50	62	244	2	Villiers	12.8
Express	SL 107	D	1	48	54	98	2	Sachs	3.1
	Radex 200		1	62	66	197	2	Ilo	11.2
	Radex 252		2	52	58	244	2	Ilo	15.1
F.B.M.	Gabbiano	I	1 F	52	58	122	2	Own	4.75
F.B.-Mondial	200	I	1	62	66	198	ohc	Own	12
Farrari	Tourismo	I	1	54	54	124	2	Own	6
FN	22	B	1	45×2	55	173	2	BP	8.3
	13250		1	63	80	249	ohv	Own	11
	13350		1	74	80	344	sv	Own	10
	13350		1	74	80	344	ohv	Own	13
	13450		1	84.5	80	444	ohv	Own	18
	20		2	63	80	498	ohc	Own	22
Franchi		I	1	57	58	147	2	Sachs	6.5
Francis-Barnett	66	GB	1	50	62	122	2	Villiers	5
	62		1	59	72	197	2	Villiers	8.4
	68		1	63	72	225	2	Villiers	9.7
	80		1	66	73	249	2	Villiers	12.8
Fusi	250	I	1	68	68	248	ohc	Own	13
Galbusera	Lusso	I	1	57	58	147	2	Sachs	6
Ganna	Sport	I	1	40×2	59.6	148	2	Puch	6.5
Gilera	150 S	I	1	60	54	152	ohv	Own	6.5
	Nettuno S		1	68	68	248	ohv	Own	14
	B 300		2	60	54	306	ohv	Own	13
	Saturno		1	84	90	498	ohv	Own	22
Gillet (Herstal)	150 S	B	1	55	60	143	2	Own	6.5
	175 S		1	57	68	172	2	Own	8
	200 Belgica		1	61	68	194	2	Own	9
	250 S		1	65	72	248	2	Own	9
	250 Milan		1	65	72	248	ohv	Own	11
	300 S		1	70	76	292	ohv	Own	13

Marque:	Model:	Country:	Cyl:	Bore:	Stroke:	CCM:	2 or 4 Stroke:	Engine:	Bhp:
	500 S		1	77	105	488	ohv	Own	17
Gitan	Turbine	I	1	52	58	158	ohv	Own	7.5
Göricke	200 S	D	1	62	66	198	2	Ilo	11
Greeves	20 DB	GB	1	59	72	197	2	Villiers	9
	25 DC		2	50	63.5	249	2	Villiers	13.2
Guazzoni	150 SS	I	1	56	62	148	2	Own	8
	250 T		1	68	68	246	2	Own	9
Harley-Davidson	XLH	USA	2 V	76	97	833	ohv	Own	
	FLF		2 V	87.3	100.8	1213	ohv	Own	
Hecker	K 175	D	1	58	66	173	2	Ilo	8.5
	K 250 Z		2	52	58	246	2	Ilo	15.1
Hercules	313	D	1	57	58	147	2	Sachs	6.5
	315		1	65	75	248	2	Ilo	11.2
Hoffman	250	D	1	65	75	248	2	Ilo	12.8
	Gouverneur		2 F	47	58	248	ohv	Own	13.4
Horex	Regina	D	1	69	91.5	342	ohv	Columbus	19
	Regina		1	74.5	91.5	399	ohv	Columbus	21.2
Honda	Benly C 92	JAP	1	44	41	124	ohc	Own	11.5
	Dream C72		2	54	54	247	ohc	Own	20
Husqvarna	30	S	1	55	50	120	2	Own	6
	281		1	60	61.5	174	2	Own	7
Iso	200	I	1	44×2	64	199	2	Own	10.5
Itom	Alba MT 34	I	1	39	40	48	2	Own	0.7
Ifa	BK 350	DDR	2 F	58	65	343	2	Own	15
James	Captain	GB	1	59	72.8	199	2	Villiers	9
	Commando		1	66	72.8	249	2	Villiers	12.8
Jawa	250	CS	1	65	75	248	2	Own	9
	350		2	58	65	348	2	Own	12
	500		2	65	73.6	498	ohc	Own	26
Kreidler	K 50	D	1	38	44	50	2	Own	2.2
KTM	R 100	A	1	48	54	98	2	Rotax	3
	125 T		1	54	54	123	2	Rotax	6.1
Laverda	75 Sport	I	1	46	45	75	ohv	Own	3.2
Leprotto	Tourismo	I	1	46×2	60	198	2	Own	10.5
Maico	Fanal	D	1	61	59.5	174	2	Own	9.2
	M 200 T		1	65	59.5	197	2	Own	11
	M 250 S		1	67	70	246	2	Own	13.2
	Taifun		2	61	59.5	348	2	Own	18.2
	Taifun		2	65	59.5	394	2	Own	21.2
Mammut	257 S	D	1	57	58	147	2	Own	6.5
Mars	Stella	D	1	58	62	174	2	Sachs	9.5
MAS	Zenith	I	1	62	57.5	174	ohv	Own	7.5
Matchless	G3L	GB	1	69	93	347	ohv	Own	16.6
	G80		1	82.5	93	498	ohv	Own	23.5
	G9		2	66	72.8	498	ohv	Own	30
Miller Balsamo	175 Sport	I	1	58	66	174	2	Own	6.5
	250 Jupiter		1	62.5	81	249	ohv	Own	16
Mival	125S	I	1	52	58	123	2	Own	6
M.M.	AS	I	1	64	77	247	ohc	Own	
	CT		1	76	77	349	ohc	Own	
Monark	M88B	S	1	57	58	148	2	Sachs	6.5
	M550		2	52	58	244	2	Ilo	15.1
Morini	125 Sport	I	1	52	58	123	2	Own	7.5
Motobécane	D45S	F	1	51	60	122	sv	Own	4.3
	Z54C		1	52	58	124	ohv	Own	5.4
	Z2C		1	56	71	174	ohv	Own	8.5
	L4C		2 V	56	71	348	ohv	Own	
Moto-Guzzi	65	I	1	42	46	65	2	Own	2
	Galetto		1	62	53	158	ohv	Own	5
	Airone Tour.		1 F	70	64	249	ohv	Own	9.5
	Falcone		1 F	88	82	498	ohv	Own	23
Motom	Delfino	I	1	62	54	158	ohv	Own	7.5
M.V.-Agusta	125 T	I	1	53	56	123	2	Own	6
	150 S		1	56	60	149	2	Own	8
	500 Sport		4	54	54	497	ohc	Own	45
Norton	16H	GB	1	79	100	490	sv	Own	12
	18		1	79	100	490	ohv	Own	20
	Intern. 40		1	71	88	348	ohc	Own	24
	Intern. 30		1	79	100	490	ohc	Own	29.5
	Manx 40		1	71	88	348	ohc	Own	27
	Manx 30		1	79.6	100	499	ohc	Own	33
NSU	Fox	D	1	50	50	98	ohv	Own	5.2
	2 T Fox		1	52	58	123	2	Own	5.4
	2 T Lux		1	62	66	197	2	Own	8.6
	Max		1	69	66	247	ohc	Own	17
	Consul		1	80	99	497	ohv	Own	22
Omea	125 C	I	1	56.5	50	124	2	Own	5.4
Orix	175 GS	I	1	66	58	173	2	Ilo	8.6
Panther (P. & M.)	60	GB	1	60	88	248	ohv	Own	11
	70		1	71	88	348	ohv	Own	18
	100		1	87	100	499	ohv	Own	26
Panther	KS 175	D	1	58	62	173	2	Sachs	9
Parilla	125 Sport	I	1	54	54	124	2	Own	7
	250 Boxer		1	65	75	249	2	Own	9
	Fox		1	59.8	62	174	ohv	Own	9
	Fox SS		1	59.8	62	174	ohc	Own	12
	Veltro Twin		2	62	58	349	ohv	Own	16
Peugeot	55 TA	F	1	51	60	124	2	Own	4.5
	176 GS		1	60	60	174	2	Own	10
	256 TC4		2	51	60	248	2	Own	13
Puch	125 SVS	A	1	38 × 2	55	124	2	Own	8
	175 SVS		1	42 × 2	62	172	2	Own	12.3
	250 SGS		1	45 × 2	78	248	2	Own	16.5
Rabeneick	F 250/1	D	1	65	75	247	2	Ilo	12.8
Rondine	SS	I	1	53	56	124	2	Own	5.8
Royal Enfield	Re 2	GB	1	53.8	55	123	2	Own	4.5
	Ensign		1	56	60	148	2	Own	8
	Clipper		1	64	77	248	ohv	Own	11.2

Marque:	Model:	Country:	Cyl:	Bore:	Stroke:	CCM:	2 or 4 Stroke:	Engine:	Bhp:
	Bullet		1	70	90	348	ohv	Own	18.3
	Bullet		1	84	90	498	ohv	Own	25.4
	500 Twin		2	64	77	496	ohv	Own	25.4
	Meteor		2	70	90	692	ohv	Own	36.5
Rumi	Sport	I	2 F	42	45	124	2	Own	8.5
RWC	T 98	A	1	48	54	98	2	Rotax	2.3
Sarolea	Carena	B	1	60	70	198	2	Own	7.5
	Vedette		1	75	79	349	ohv	Own	15
	Continental		1	75	90	398	sv	Own	10.5
	Atlantic		2	63	80	498	ohv	Own	26
	Atlantic Major		2	70	78	599	ohc	Own	30
Sitta	250	D	2	52	58	244	2	Ilo	15
Sparta	125	NL	1	50	60	122	2	Villiers	5
	250		1	67	70	247	2	Villiers	10.3
Sunbeam	S7 & S8	GB	2	70	63.5	487	ohc	Own	25.4
Taurus	B8	I	1	65	60	199	ohv	Own	13.8
Terrot	ETD	F	1	52	58	123	ohv	Own	5.5
	OSSD		1	68	68	247	ohv	Own	11
	RGST		1	84	90	499	ohv	Own	22
Thunder	Twin	I	2	43	44	127	ohv	Own	5.5
Tornax	K 125 H	D	1	52	58	123	2	Ilo	5.9
	KTV 200		1	62	66	197	2	Ilo	11
	Z 250		2	52	58	244	2	Ilo	15.1
Triumph (TWN)	BDG 125	D	1	35.5 × 2	62	123	2	Own	6.5
	BDG 250		1	45 × 2	78	246	2	Own	11
	Boss		1	53 × 2	78	344	2	Own	16
Triumph	T 15 Terrier	GB	1	51	58.5	149	ohv	Own	8
	T 20 Tiger Cub		1	63	64	199	ohv	Own	10
	T 5 Speed Twin		2	63	80	498	ohv	Own	27
	T 100 Tiger		2	63	80	498	ohv	Own	34
	T 6 Thunderbird		2	71	82	649	ohv	Own	34
	T 110 Tiger		2	71	82	649	ohv	Own	42
Universal	Junior	CH	1	67	70	247	ohv	Own	14
	Meteor		2 F	72	71	578	ohv	Own	30
U.T.	KTN 125	D	1	52	58	123	2	Ilo	5.9
	TS 250		1	65	75	248	2	Ilo	12.8
Velocette	Le II	GB	2 F	50	49	198	sv	Own	8
	MAC		1	68	96	349	ohv	Own	14.3
	KSS Mk II		1	74	81	348	ohc	Own	
	MSS		1	86	86	499	ohv	Own	39
Victoria	Bifix	D	1	51	60	123	2	Own	5
	KR 25		1	67	70	247	2	Own	10.5
	KR 26 Aero		1	67	70	247	2	Own	14
	Bergmeister-Sport		2 V	64	54	345	hc	Own	21
Vincent HRD	Comet	GB	1	84	90	499	hc	Own	28.4
	Rapide		2 V	84	90	998	hc	Own	45
	Black Shadow		2 V	84	90	998	hc	Own	55
	Black Lightning		2 V	84	90	998	hc	Own	70
Zündapp	Norma Luxus	D	1	60	70	198	2	Own	8.3
	Elastic 200		1	60	70	198	2	Own	9.5
	Elastic 250		1	67	70	236	2	Own	13
	KS 601 Sport		2 F	75	85	597	ohv	Own	32

The present day

Marque:	Model:	Country:	Cyl:	Bore:	Stroke:	Ccm:	2 or 4 Stroke:	Engine:	Bhp:
Ancillotti	Cross	I	1	40	39.5	49	2	Sachs	11
	Cross		1	54	54	123	2	,,	24
	Cross		1	71.5	61	245	2	,,	32
Aspes	Cross	I	1	54	54	123	2	Own	24
	Hopi		1	54	54	123	2	Own	21
Avello	Nebraska	E	1	38	43	49	2	Puch	5
	Cobra		1	48	39.7	72	2	Puch	10
Benelli	125	I	1	56	49	120	2	Own	15.4
	125 Enduro		1	56	49	120	2	Own	15.4
	125 2C		2	52.5	44	124	2	Own	16
	250 2C		2	56	47	232	2	Own	30
	250 Quattro		4	44	38	231	4 ohc	Own	26.6
	500 Quattro		4	56	50.6	498	4 ohc	Own	55
	750 Sei		6	56	50.6	748	4 ohc	Own	75
Beta	125 SG	I	1	54	54	124	2	Own	20
	250 GS		1	70	64.5	249	2	Own	34
	250 CR		1	70	64.5	249	2	Own	36
BMW	R 60/7		2	73.5	70.6	599	4 ohv	Own	40
	R 75/7		2	82	70.6	745	4 ohv	Own	50
	R 100/7		2	94	70.6	980	4 ohv	Own	60
	R 100 S		2	94	70.6	980	4 ohv	Own	65
Bultaco	Mercurio GT 175	E	1	61.15	60	176.2	2	Own	12.5
	Metralla GT 250		1	72	60	244	2	Own	22.7
	Alpina 250		1	71	60	237.6	2	Own	14.1
	Alpina 350		1	83.2	60	326	2	Own	21.6
	Sherpa Trials		1	54.2	51.5	119	2	Own	9.12
	Sherpa Trials		1	71	60	237	2	Own	14.1
	Sherpa Trials		1	83.2	60	326	2	Own	18.5
	Pursang MC		1	51.5	60	124	2	Own	24.5
	Pursang MC		1	72	60	244	2	Own	34.3
	Pursang MC		1	85	64	363	2	Own	40.2
CCM	MC 500	GB	1	84	90	498	4 ohv	Own	45
CZ	125	CS	1	52	58	123	2	Own	11
	175		1	58	65	172	2	Own	15
	175 Enduro		1	62	57	172	2	Own	16
	250 Enduro		1	70	64	246	2	Own	20
	250 Twin		2	52	58	246	2	Own	17
	350 Twin		2	58	64	343	2	Own	21
	Moto Cross 125		1	55	52	123	2	Own	21
	Moto Cross 250		1	70	64	246	2	Own	34

Marque:	Model:	Country:	Cyl:	Bore:	Stroke:	CCM:	2 or 4 Stroke:	Engine:	Bhp:
	Moto Cross 400		1	82	72	381	2	Own	42
DKW	MC 125	D	1	54	54	122	2	Sachs	24
	GS 250		1	71.5	61	245	2		32
Dnéiper	M 10	USSR	2	78	68	649	4 ohv	Own	34
Ducati	125 ISDT	I	1	54	54	123.7	2	Own	22
	350 GTL		2	71.8	43.2	349.6	4 ohc	Own	27
	500 GTL		2	78	52	496	4 ohc	Own	40
	500 S. Desmo		2	78	52	496	4 ohc	Own	50
	750 Super Sport		2 V	80	74.4	748	4 ohc	Own	68
	GT 860		2 V	86	74.4	864	4 ohc	Own	65
	900 Super Sport		2 V	86	74.4	864	4 ohc	Own	72
Fantic	Caballero Reg.	I	1	55	52	123.5	2	Own	21.5
	Caballero Cross		1	55	52	123.5	2	Own	26
Garelli	50 RSL Electr.	I	1	40	39.5	49.6	2	Own	6.3
Gilera	150 Strada	I	1	60	54	152.6	4 ohv	Own	14.2
Gori	Codice 50	I	1	40	39.5	49	2	Sachs	6.5
	Moto Cross		1	54	54	123	2	,,	22
	Competizione		1	71.5	61	245	2	,,	33
Greeves	250 MX	GB	1	70	64	246	2	Own	28.5
	380 MX		1	82	72	380	2	Own	44
Harley-Davidson	SX 125	USA	1	56	50	123	2	Own	12
	SX 175		1	61	59.6	174	2	Own	17
	SX 250		1	71.8	59.6	243	2	Own	20
	SS 250		1	71.8	59.6	243	2	Own	19
	XLH (XLCH)		2 V	80	97	975	4 ohv	Own	65
	FX (FXE)		2 V	87.3	100.8	1207	4 ohv	Own	66
	Electra Glide		2 V	87.3	100.8	1207	4 ohv	Own	66
Hercules	K 50 Sprint	D	1	38	44	49	2	Sachs	6.25
	K 50 Ultra		1	38	44	49	2	,,	6.25
	K 125 S		1	54	54	122	2	,,	17
	125 GS		1	54	54	122	2	,,	22
	175 GS		1	60	61	173	2	,,	26
	250 GS		1	71.5	61	245	2	,,	32
	Wankel 3 Chamber					294			27
Honda	ST 70 (Dax)	J	1	47	41.4	72	4 ohc	Own	5.2
	CB 125 S		1	56.5	49.5	124	4 ohc	Own	14
	CB 125 disc		2	44	41	124	4 ohc	Own	15
	CB 200 disc		2	55.5	41	198	4 ohc	Own	17
	CJ 250 T		2	56	50.6	249	4 ohc	Own	27
	CJ 360 T		2	67	50.6	356	4 ohc	Own	34
	CB 500 T		2	70	64.8	498	4 2×ohc	Own	42
	CB 400		4	51	50	408	4 ohc	Own	37
	CB 500		4	56	50.6	499	4 ohc	Own	48
	CB 550		4	58.5	50.6	539	4 ohc	Own	50
	CB 750		4	61	63	736	4 ohc	Own	63
	GL Gold Wing		4 F	72	61.4	999	4 2×ohc	Own	82
	TL 125 S		1	56.5	49.5	124	4 ohc	Own	9
	CR 125 Elsinore		1	56	50	123	2	Own	24
Indian	ME 125	USA	1	55	52	123.5	2	Own	19
Jawa	23	CS	1	38	44	49.9	2	Own	4
	634		2	58	65	343	2	Own	26
	GS 175		1	62	57.5	174	2	Own	22.5
	GS 250		1	70	64	246	2	Own	28.5
	GS 350		1	78	72	344	2	Own	35
	GS 370		1	80	72	362	2	Own	36
Kawasaki	KH 125	J	1	56	50.6	124	2	Own	
	KX 125 M/C		1	56	50.6	124	2	Own	22
	KX 250 M/C		1	40	64.9	249	2	Own	34
	KX 400 M/C		1	82	76	401	2	Own	42
	KE 125		1	56	50.6	124	2	Own	13
	KT 250 Trials		1	69.5	64.9	246	2	Own	16
	KH 250		3	45	52.3	249	2	Own	28
	KH 400		3	57	52.3	400	2	Own	40
	KH 500		3	60	58.8	498	2	Sachs	52
	City Bike		1	46	44	73	2	Own	4.2
	Z 200		1			198	4 ohc	Own	
	Z 400		2	64	62	398	4 ohc	Own	36
	Z 750		2	78	78	745	4 ohc	Own	51
	Z 650		4	62	54	652	4 2×ohc	Own	64
	Z 1000		4	70	66	1015	4 2×ohc	Own	85
Kreidler	Florett RSL	D	1	40	39.7	49.8	2	Own	6.25
KTM	GP 50 RS Comet	A	1	38	44	49	2	Sachs	6.25
	GP 125 RS Comet		1	54	54	122	2	,,	17
	MC 125		1	54	54	124	2	,,	26
	MC 250+GS 250		1	71	62	246	2	Own	34
	MC 400+GS 400		1	81	69	356	2	Own	42
	GS 125		1	54	54	124	2	Own	24
	GS 175		1	63.5	54	172	2	Own	27
Laverda	H 125 TR	I	1	55	52	124	2	Own	24
	H 250 Tr		1	68	68	247	2	Own	27
	500 Twin		2	72	61	497	4 2×ohc	Own	46
	750 SF 3		2	80	74	744	4 ohc	Own	50
	1000		3	75	74	980	4 2×ohc	Own	78
Maico	MD 50	D	1	38	44	49	2	Own	6.3
	MD 125		1	54	54	124	2	Own	16
	MD 250		1	76	54	245	2	Own	27
	GS 125		1	54	54	124	2	Own	21
	GS 250		1	67	70	247	2	Own	36
	GS 400		1	77	83	386	2	Own	43
	GS 450		1	82	83	438	2	Own	47
Malanca	125 E2C	I	2	43	43	124	2	Own	15
	125 E2C Sport		2	43	43	124	2	Own	18
	150 GT		2	46	46	149	2	Own	20
Mondial	Touring	I	1	55	52	123	2	Own	9
	Regolaritá		1	54	54	124	2	Own	12
Montesa	Enduro 250	E	1	70	64	246.3	2	Own	27
	Cota 123		1	54	54	123	2	Own	13
	Cota 247		1	72.5	60	247	2	Own	20

Marque:	Model:	Country:	Cyl:	Bore:	Stroke:	CCM:	2 or 4 Stroke:	Engine:	Bhp:
	Cappra 125 Reg.		1	54	54	123	2	Own	24
	Cappra 250 VB		1	70	64	246	2	Own	36
Morbidelli	Competizione	I	2	44	41	124.6	2	Own	35
Morini	Corsarino ZZ50	I	1	41	37	49	4 ohv	Own	4.5
	125 T		1	59	45	123	4 ohv	Own	14
	3 1/2 V		2 V	62	57	344	4 ohv	Own	35
	3 1/2 Sport VS		2 V	62	57	344	4 ohv	Own	39
Motobécane	125 LT	F	2	43	43	125	2	Own	16
	350		3	53	52.8	349.5	2	Own	38
Moto Guzzi	250 TS	I	2	56	47	231	2		25
	350 GTS		4	50	44	345	4 ohc	Own	38
	400 GTS		4	50	51	397	4 ohc	Own	40
	Falcone Sahara		1	88	82	499	4 ohc	Own	27
	750 T		2 V	82	70	748	4 ohv	Own	70
	850 T 3		2 V	73	78	844	4 ohv	Own	68
	850 T 3 California		2 V	73	78	844	4 ohv	Own	68
	V 1000-Convert		2 V	88	78	949	4 ohv	Own	71
	850 Le Mans		2 V	73	78	844	4 ohv	Own	81
Mototrans-Ducati	350 Road	E	1	76	75	340	4 ohc	Own	28
Münch-4	1200 TSS-E	D	4	78.5	66.5	1278	4 ohc	NSU	104
MV Agusta	125 Sport	I	1	53	56	123.5	4 ohv	Own	12
	350 Sport		2	63	56	349	4 ohv	Own	35
	800 S		4	67	56	790	4 2×ohc	Own	82
	900 S		4	70	58	893	4 2×ohc	Own	95
MZ	150 TS	DDR	1	56	58	143	2	Own	11.5
	250 TS		1	69	65	249	2	Own	19
Norton	Commando	GB	2	77	89	828	4 ohv	Own	51
Ossa	250 S.Pion.	E	1	72	60	244	2	Own	27
	350 S.Pion.		1	77	65	302	2	Own	30
	GS 250 Desert		1	72	60	244	2	Own	32
	350 MAR Trial		1	77	65	302	2	Own	18
Planeta (Jupiter)	Sport	SU	1	76	75	355	2	Own	32
Puch	M 50 Jet	A	1	40	39.7	49	2	Own	6.25
	M 125 GS		1	54	54	124	2	Rotax	23
	M 175 GS		1	62	57.5	174	2	Rotax	28
	M 250 GS		1	74	57.5	247	2	Rotax	32
	MC 250 Replica		1	70	64	246	2	Puch	43.5
	MC 50 Super		1	40	39.7	49	2	Puch	11.2
Rickmann	Kawasaki CR	GB	4	66	66	903	4 ohc	Kawa	82
Sanglas	400 F	E	1	82	79	422	4 ohv	Own	24
	500 S		1	89.5	79	496	4 ohv	Own	27
Seeley	Honda-750	GB	4	61	63	736	4 ohc	Honda	67
Simonini	Long Range R	I	1	54	54	123	2	Sachs	21
	H.R.Cross		1	54	54	123	2	Sachs	24
Suzuki	TS 125	J	1	56	50	123	2	Own	13
	TS 250		1	70	64	246	2	Own	18.7
	RM 125		1	56	50	123	2	Own	25
	RM 250		1	67	70	247	2	Own	36
	RM 350		1	77	80	372	2	Own	42
	GT 125		2	43	43	124	2	Own	14.2
	GT 185		2	49	49	184	2	Own	15
	GT 250		2	54	54	247	2	Own	26
	GT 380		3	54	54	371	2	Own	33
	GT 500		2	70	64	429	2	Own	38
	GT 550		3	61	62	539	2	Own	48
	GT 750		3	70	64	738	2	Own	63
	RE 5-Rotary					497	Ro.	Wankel	63
	GS 400		2	65	60	398	4 2×ohc	Own	36
	GS 750		4	65	56.4	738	4 2×ohc	Own	63
SWM	Silver Vase	I	1	40	39.7	49	2	Sachs	10
	Cross		1	40	39.7	49	2	,,	11
	Silver Vase		1	48	54	97	2	,,	19.5
	,,		1	54	54	123	2	,,	24
	,,		1	60	61	173	2	,,	28
	,,		1	72	61	248	2	,,	34
	,,		1	73	61	255	2	,,	35
Testi	Easy Raider	I	1	52	55	123	2	Minarelli	9
	Corsa 2000		1	52	55	123	2	,,	16
Triumph	Bonneville	GB	2	76	82	744	4 ohv	Own	53
	Trident		3	67	70	741	4 ohv	Own	64
Villa	Enduro 125 F	I	1	54	54	123	2	Morini	16
	Reg. + Cross		1	54	54	123	2	,,	22
	Reg. + Cross		1	85	78	442	2	Own	42
Voskhod	175	SU	1	62	58	174	2	Own	10.5
WSK	M 06 B3	Pl	1	52	58	123	2	Own	7.3
	M 21 W2		1	61	59.5	174	2	Own	14
Yamaha	RD 50 DX	J	1	40	39.7	49	2	Own	6.26
	RS 100 DX		1	52	45.6	97	2	Own	10.5
	RD 200		2	52	46	195	2	Own	22
	RD 250		2	52	54	247	2	Own	27
	RD 400		2	64	62	398	2	Own	43
	YZ 125		1	56	50	123	2	Own	24
	YZ 250 Moto-Cross		1	70	64	246	2	Own	34
	YZ 400 ,, ,,		1	85	70	397	2	Own	41
	TZ 250 Racer		2	54	54	247	2	Own	46
	TZ 350 ,,		2	64	54	347	2	Own	54
	XT 500		1	87	84	499	4 ohc	Own	27
	XS 500		2	73	59.6	498	4 2×ohc	Own	48.5
	XS 650		2	75	74	653	4 ohc	Own	51
	XS 750		3	68	68.6	748	4 2×ohc	Own	60
	TZ 750 Racer		4	66.4	54	747	2	Own	90
Zündapp	KS 50 Sport	D	1	39	41.8	49.9	2	Own	6.25
	KS 50 Super–Sport		1	39	41.8	49.9	2	Own	6.25
	KS 50 W/c		1	39	41.8	49.9	2	Own	6.25
	KS 125 Sport		1	54	54	123	2	Own	17
	KS 175		1	62	54	163	2	Own	17
	KS 350		2	62	57	344	2	Own	27
	GS 125		1	54	54	123	2	Own	18

GLOSSARY

Acceleration
The time in which the motorcycle attains a given speed from the state of rest.

Advanced ignition
Term used to describe the setting of the ignition-timing of the engine so that the spark occurs at the plug points before the piston reaches the top of its stroke.

Air cooling
Term referring to the method of dispersing the heat produced in the cylinder (cylinders) of the engine.

Air intake
The port through which the air-supply to the carburettor is drawn.

Automatic inlet valves
Inlet valves which open atmospherically, without any mechanical control. Used on early engines.

Ball joint
A joint in which a ball on the end of a rod or lever moves in a socket provided in another member, thus providing for movement in different directions.

Balloon tyres
Tyres of large cross-section, containing air of relatively low-pressure. Used in the late twenties mainly.

Beaded-edge tyres
Outer cover of pneumatic tyre which has a hard edge or beading to fit into a channel at each side of the wheel rim. Had its heyday in pre-war years.

Belt-drive
Made from leather or some other flexible material, belts were used for the power transmission from engine or gearbox to the rearwheel of motorcycles. Lightweight machines had such drive until the early thirties. Bicycle-engines often had belt-drive to the frontwheel also.

Benzole
Motor fuel, derived from the distillation of coal-tar. Was used together with petrol in road-racing, after the use of alcohol-fuel was disallowed by the FIM.

Bevel drive
Usually, gear which actuates overhead camshaft. Sometimes used in shaft-drive systems, or to actuate magnetos.

Bhp
Brake horsepower (the brake horsepower available at the engine flywheel).

Bialbero
Two overhead camshafts (double-ohc).

Big end
Name given to the lower part of the connecting-rod at its point of attachment to the crank-pin.

Blower
Better known as supercharger; means of forced induction.

Bore
Visually, the diameter of the cylinder, measured in millimetres (mm).

Bottom dead centre
Description of the position of the piston when it reaches the lowest point in its travel within the cylinder and is about to begin its upward journey.

Camshaft
The shaft or spindle, with or upon which the cam rotates. The cams are sometimes formed in one piece with the camshaft.

Capacity
Cylinder capacities of engines are expressed in cubic centimetres (cc). A thousand cubic centimetres equals one litre. A 500cc machine is therefore a half-litre motorcycle.

Carburettor
A device for converting the engine fuel into a vapour and mixing it with the necessary amount of air to form an explosive mixture.

Cardan shaft
Replaces on many machines the chain as a drive from the gearbox to the rear wheel.

Chain drive
Term used generally to denote the transmission of power from one sprocket-wheel to another by means of a chain. Chain drive is used mainly for driving the rear wheel; also used for transmitting the power from engine to the gearbox to the magneto or the overhead-camshaft.

Charge
The volume of fuel vapour and air which is sucked into the cylinder of an engine by the induction stroke of the piston.

Combustion chamber
Space above the piston in the cylinder in which the explosive charge is compressed and ignited.

Compression
The reduction in volume of a mass of material due to externally-applied pressure. The term is used to denote the compression of the explosive mixture in the cylinder by the action of the piston. This compression is usually defined in terms of lbs per square inch.

Connecting rod
A light metal bar connecting the underside of the piston to the crankshaft. It is provided with bearings on each side.

Contact breaker
A mechanical device which constantly breaks and restores a low-tension circuit in order to create ignition from the spark plug.

Crankcase
The metal casing which surrounds and encloses the crankshaft and its assembly.

Crankpin
The shorter part of the crankshaft which receives the downward thrust from the piston.

Crankshaft
The main revolving shaft of the engine which converts the up and down movements of the pistons into rotary motion.

Cubic centimetre
A metric system measure of the volume or capacity of an engine.

Cylinder
The cylindrical metal chamber in which combustion of fuel takes place. This explosion converts the fuel into power.

Diesel engine
A type of engine first devised in 1892 by Dr Rudolf Diesel. In such engines, a charge of air is drawn into the cylinder by the piston and then highly compressed. The compression effected is so high, that the air becomes hot enough to ignite a charge of fuel which is injected into the cylinder-head just at the end of the compression stroke. Ignition follows, and the piston is driven downwards again by the expansion of the burning mixture.

Dry-sump lubrication
A system of engine lubrication in which two oil-pumps are used. One of the pumps feeds oil from a reservoir around the engine bearings under pressure, the other pump removes surplus oil from the sump and returns it to the oil reservoir.

Duralumin
Name given to a class of aluminium alloys containing aluminium, copper magnesium and manganese in varying proportions.

Dynamometer
An instrument which measures the brake horse power of an engine.

Exhaust
The conduit through which the exhaust gases from the cylinder are expelled into the air.

Exhaust gases
The products of the combustion taking place within the cylinders. Exhaust gases are normally composed of carbon dioxide, carbon monoxide, steam, nitrogen, together with varying amounts of oil-vapour, and traces of unburnt fuel and hydrocarbon gases.

Exhaust stroke
The upward stroke of the piston which pushes out through the raised exhaust valve the burnt charge within the cylinder.

Exhaust valve
The cylinder valve of the engine which is made to open once for every two revolutions of the flywheel in order to permit the escape of the combusted mixture.

Expansion
The increase in volume of a material which occurs when it is heated. The power developed by the ignition of the fuel mixture within the cylinder is mainly due to the heat generated during the rapid chemical combination of the constituents of the vapour.

Fins
Metal ribs which are formed on the exterior of air-cooled cylinders and in adjacent positions. Their object is to present as great a surface as possible to the cooling action of the air.

Float
The light hollow metal box which, forming part of the carburettor, regulates the supply of petrol to the float chamber.

Float chamber
The metal case or cylinder in which the carburettor float is housed and which serves as a reservoir for the supply of petrol to the jet or other vapourising device of the carburettor.

Flywheel
A heavy steel or cast-iron wheel mounted on the main shaft of the engine, the purpose of which is to balance the intermittent power impulses given to the crankshaft by the pistons. The flywheel gives the character of steady-running to the engine.

Four-stroke cycle
This is the engine cycle which has four successive piston movements, for induction, compression, power and exhaust.

Friction drive
A form of friction gear, once used on some motorcycles. This form of gear dispenses with the ordinary type of gearbox-clutch assembly and substitutes for it an arrangement of friction discs making variable contact with the flywheel from which the drive is taken.

Gasket
The gasket is a washer made up of various packing materials such as thick paper, thin rubber, asbestos, oiled fabric etc. which is placed between two metal faces in order to produce a gas-tight joint.

Gate change
Term referring to the method of changing gears by a hand lever on old motorcycles, the gear-lever being moved into various positions in the gate.

Gearbox
Train of pinion wheels arranged in a metal casing. Various combinations of the wheels can be engaged, thereby enabling engine power to be transmitted from the crankshaft to the road-wheels in varying ratios.

Gear ratio
The ratio between the input and the output speeds of a train of gear wheels. Applied to motorcycle practice, the term denotes the ratio of engine revolutions to the number of road-wheel revolutions.

Gudgeon pin
A steel rod which passes horizontally through the piston on its underside and which serves to connect the small end of the connecting rod to the piston, thus enabling power to be transmitted to the crankshaft.

Horizontal engine
Engine which has its cylinders placed horizontally.

Horsepower
The conventional unit of motive power. One horsepower represents the power required to raise 33,000 lb by 1 foot in 1 minute. Many other local systems have been used in the past.

Indicated horsepower
The power expended by the burning fuel mixture in driving the piston downwards. So-called because an instrument termed an 'Indicator' can be used to measure or indicate the downward pressure on the piston. Indicated horsepower does not account for the power lost by friction within the engine. Hence it does not represent the external power-output of the engine.

Induction pipe
The metal pipe or conduit which conveys the explosive mixture from the carburettor to the cylinders of the engine.

Inlet valve
The valve which admits the mixture of fuel vapour and air into the cylinder at regular intervals, the valve being operated by means of a cam.

Kilometre
A metric measure of length originating in Europe. One kilometre equals a thousand metres.

Leaf springs
Name given to springs which consist of a number of thin leaves or strips of spring steel clamped together. Such springs were used up to the thirties on some front forks and also on some rear-suspensions.

Litre
The metric unit of volume, which is used to indicate the cylinder capacities of engines. One litre equals 1000cc.

Little end
The upper end and bearing of the connecting-rod at its point of connection to the gudgeon-pin of the piston.

Magneto
A special form of dynamo comprising an armature which revolves between the poles of one or more permanent magnets. It is employed in many machines as a generator of high-tension current for ignition purposes.

Manifold
A term which denotes a short passage or chamber through which gases may flow, as for instance the exhaust manifold of a motorcycle engine, through which the gases flow from the exhaust ports of the cylinders. The term manifold is also used for the mixture-inlet, or induction pipe assembly.

Mechanical efficiency
The ratio of the brake horsepower of an engine to the actual horsepower obtained from it under running conditions. The mechanical efficiency of an engine is governed by varying factors, including the speed at which it runs.

Metre
The fundamental unit of length in the metric system of measurements. Equals 39·3707 inches.

Mile
The unit of road measurements which originated in Britain. One mile equals 1760 yards or 1·6 kilometres.

Near-side
The left-hand side of a motorcycle as seen from the driving position.

Otto cycle
The four-stroke cycle of operations which produces the power within the cylinder of an internal combustion engine. It is called after Dr Nicolas Otto (1833–1891) who introduced it in his 'silent' gas-engine in 1876.

Overall length
Applied to a motorcycle, this is the total length, ie the distance between the foremost projection and the farthest point at the rear.

Over-heating
Refers to the point at which the internal temperature of the cylinder produces inadequate lubrication between piston and cylinder, together with other unwanted effects. Overheating often occurs in modern two-stroke racing machines.

Petrol
Highly-inflammable, colourless liquid, obtained by the distillation and refinement of crude petroleum. It is a mixture of a large number of hydrocarbon liquids.

Petroleum
The naturally-occurring mineral oil from which commercial petrol is distilled.

Pinking
Characteristic light tapping sound which is generally in evidence when the engine is under heavy load or when it is accelerating. Occurs mainly when the ignition is too far advanced or the petrol used is of low octane.

Planetary gear
A form of gearing, common in change-speed mechanisms in which small pinion-wheels revolve sun-and-planet-wise, around a larger central wheel. Used on some old designs.

Plunger
This term usually denotes a small piston provided with a hand-operating stem and knob, which is used as a forcer of liquids in small pumps, including suspension units.

Poppet valve
Ordinary type of valve employed in four-stroke motorcycle engines.

Port
A passage or opening leading to the interior of the cylinder through which gases are drawn or expelled. Thus the terms inlet port, transfer port and exhaust port of a cylinder.

Power
Term which should be distinguished from force, as the two are not synonymous. Power is best described as the rate at which work is performed. This power is divided by time.

Push rods
Steel rods which operate overhead valves, being themselves actuated by revolving cams below.

Retarded ignition
Term used to denote the setting of the ignition-timing of the engine, so that the spark occurs at the plug points after the piston has reached the top of its stroke and has begun again its downward journey.

Revolution indicator
Instrument for registering the number of revolutions per minute of a wheel or shaft. They work on principles similar to those of an ordinary speedometer.

Rocker
Pivoted lever having a rocking motion by means of which it conveys movement from one point to another. Used mainly in valve mechanisms.

Rotary valve
A special form of valve which is driven off the camshaft by means of a spiral screw. It is usually mounted in the normal side-valve position and by its operation it establishes communication successively between the cylinder and the exhaust pipe. The rotary valve is silent in operation.

rpm
Recognised abbreviation for 'revolution per minute'.

Scavenging
Term used to describe the clearing out of the products of combustion from the cylinder during the exhaust stroke of the piston. In some engines special devices are fitted to effect the maximum degree of scavenging.

Seizing
The act of two rubbing surfaces binding together owing to the frictional heat generated having locally melted the parts and causing them to become welded together. Seizures occur mainly between cylinders and pistons in highly stressed two-stroke racing machines.

Side-valve
Any type of valve set in the side of the engine. Seldom used in modern motor-cycle engines.

Silencer
Device fitted to the exhaust system of an engine whereby the pressure of the exhaust gases is considerably reduced before they reach the outer air. By this means, the noise of the escaping gases is considerably reduced. Silencers generally utilise expansion chambers in which the exhaust gases can dissipate a good deal of their energy before gaining access to the external air. The design of expansion chambers is of particular importance to the efficiency of two-stroke engines.

Slide valve
A type of engine valve, in which the entry and exit of the cylinder gases is controlled by two concentric sliding sleeves placed between the piston and the cylinder.

Spray lubrication
Simplest and oldest system of engine lubrication, in which oil contained in the crank-chamber is, by the rotation of the

crankshaft, thrown up and distributed in the form of a spray over the lower parts of the engine. Known also as splash lubrication.

Stroke
Distance which the piston travels during its upward or downward movement in the cylinder. The stroke is always measured in millimetres.

Suction stroke
Downward stroke of the piston which sucks or draws the mixture of fuel vapour and air into the cylinder through the inlet valve.

Supercharger
A device which forces more fuel vapour and air into the cylinder than could be taken into it normally by the induction stroke of the piston. The use of any engines with superchargers or any other kind of forced induction is now not permitted in road races.

Tappet
A steel rod which transmits the lifting motion of the valve cams to the valves, so that they are regularly opened.

Tappet clearance
Minute space provided between the end of the valve stem and its tappet in order to allow for the expansion of the valve stem when heated.

Thermal efficiency
Ratio of heat converted into work to the total amount of heat produced by the engine.

Throttle
Valve which controls the entry of the gaseous mixture into the cylinder or cylinders.

Titanium
Hard, light metal with a high melting-point. Comparatively costly.

Top dead centre
Position of the piston when it reaches the top of its travels within the cylinder and is about to begin its downward journey.

Torque
A twisting effect. The turning tendency of a shaft. Torque is supplied to the crankshaft by the downward movement of the piston.

Transmission shaft
Shaft which transmits power from the gearbox to the rear-wheel.

Tube ignition
Early system of firing the explosive mixture by means of a small platinum tube which was heated to redness. Now obsolete.

Two-stroke
Engine cycle in which the power impulse on the piston occurs at every alternate stroke, the engine combining compression of the mixture with an explosion at every revolution of the crankshaft. The two-stroke engine eliminates the use of valves and timing gears.

Universal joint
Joint between two rotating shafts which permits the side-to-side movement of one shaft without severing the power connection between them.

V-engine
Engine whose cylinders are set opposite one another in the shape of a letter V.

Wheelbase
Term used to denote the distance between the centres of the front and rear wheels.

Worm gear
A form of gearing comprising a gear-wheel whose teeth mesh with a worm of endless screw.

Yard
Measure of distance, originating from Britain. One yard equals 3 feet (36 inches) or 0·91 of a metre.

This book was designed and produced by Quarto Publishing Limited, 13 New Burlington Street, London W1.

Phototypeset in Britain by Filmtype Services Limited, Scarborough, Yorkshire. Printed by G. A. Pindar & Son Ltd., Scarborough, England.

Edited and written by Erwin Tragatsch. *Additional text by* David Minton and Graeme Ewens. *Text Editor* Donald Clarke. *Original photography by* Jasper Spencer Smith. *Library photography from* the collection of Erwin Tragatsch. *Jacket illustration by* Roy Coombs. *Art Editor* Moira Clinch. *Art Director* Robert Morley.